CRITIQUE OF VIOLENCE

Beatrice Hanssen has conducted a fascinating exploration of social and political theory, from Hegel to Fanon, by way of Benjamin and Arendt, and into our post-structural present, through the prism of the question of violence. Cosmopolitan in its range and subtle in its readings, this is a book from which I learned a great deal.

K. Anthony Appiah, Professor of Afro-American Studies and Philosophy, Harvard University

...an excellent book ... clear, innovative, suggestive. The question of violence is a very topical one.

Chantal Mouffe, University of Westminster, London

Displaying a sovereign mastery of contemporary critical theory in all its motley variety, Beatrice Hanssen strives to rescue the most compelling arguments from each tradition to lessen the darkness that surrounds the intractable problem of violence.

Martin Jay, University of California, Berkeley

Beatrice Hanssen is one of the most sophisticated theorists of her generation. ... her rich notion of inter-cultures (rather than contenders) in contemporary ideological battles lowers the heat, casts much light and enables us to force new forms of solidarity.

Cornel West, Alphonse Fletcher Jr. University Professor, Harvard University

Critique of Violence is a highly original and lucid investigation of the heated controversy between poststructuralism and critical theory. Leading theorist Beatrice Hanssen uses Walter Benjamin's essay "Critique of Violence" as a guide to analyze the contentious debate, shifting the emphasis from struggle to dialogue between the two parties. Regarding the questions of critique and violence to be the major meeting points between both traditions, Hanssen positions herself *between* the two in an effort to investigate what critical theory and poststructuralism have to offer each other. In the course of doing so, she assembles imaginative new readings of Benjamin, Arendt, Fanon, and Foucault, and incisively explores the politics of recognition, the violence of language, and the future of feminist theory.

This groundbreaking book will be essential reading for all students of continental philosophy, political theory, social studies, and comparative literature.

Beatrice Hanssen was trained in Comparative Literature at Johns Hopkins University and is Associate Professor of German at Harvard University. She is the author of *Walter Benjamin's Other History: Of Stones, Animals, Human Beings, and Angels* (1998) and an editor of *The Turn to Ethics* (Routledge, 2000).

WARWICK STUDIES IN EUROPEAN PHILOSOPHY

Edited by Andrew Benjamin

Professor of Philosophy, University of Warwick

This series presents the best and most original work being done within the European philosophical tradition. The books included in the series seek not merely to reflect what is taking place within European philosophy but also to contribute to the growth and development of that plural tradition. Works written in the English language as well as translations into English are included, engaging the tradition at all levels – whether by introductions that show the contemporary philosophical force of certain works, collections that explore an important thinker or topic, or signifcant contributions that call for their own critical evaluations.

Also available:

BATAILLE
Writing the Sacred
Edited by Carolyn Bailey Gill

BLANCHOT
Extreme Contemporary
Leslie Hill

RETREATING THE POLITICAL
Philippe Lacoue-Labarthe and Jean-Luc Nancy

HEGEL AFTER DERRIDA
Edited by Stuart Barnett

EMMANUEL LEVINAS
The Genealogy of Ethics
John Llewelyn

TEXTURES OF LIGHT
Vision and Touch in Irigaray, Levinas and Merleau-Ponty
Cathryn Vasseleu

ON JEAN-LUC NANCY
The Sense of Philosophy
Edited by Darren Sheppard, Simon Sparks and Colin Thomas

THE HYPOCRITICAL IMAGINATION
Between Kant and Levinas
John Llewelyn

MAURICE BLANCHOT
The Demand of Writing
Edited by Carolyn Bailey Gill

ESSAYS ON OTHERNESS
Jean Laplanche

PHILOSOPHY AND TRAGEDY
Edited by Miguel de Beistegui and Simon Sparks

DELEUZE AND PHILOSOPHY
The Difference Engineer
Edited by Keith Ansell Pearson

RELATING NARRATIVES:
Storytelling and Selfhood
Adrianna Cavarero

BODY- AND IMAGE-SPACE
Re-reading Walter Benjamin
Sigrid Weigel

KANT TROUBLE
Obscurities of the Enlightened
Diane Morgan

VERY LITTLE ... ALMOST NOTHING
Death, Philosophy, Literature
Simon Critchley

INTERRUPTING DERRIDA
Geoffrey Bennington

PASSION IN THEORY
Conceptions of Freud and Lacan
Robyn Ferrell

CRITIQUE OF VIOLENCE

Between Poststructuralism and Critical Theory

Beatrice Hanssen

London and New York

First published 2000
by Routledge
11 New Fetter Lane, London EC4P 4EE

Simultaneously published in the USA and Canada
by Routledge
29 West 35th Street, New York, NY 10001

Routledge is an imprint of the Taylor & Francis Group

Typeset in Perpetua by Taylor & Francis Books Ltd
Printed and bound in Great Britain by The University Press, Cambridge

British Library Cataloguing in Publication Data
A catalogue record for this book is available from the British Library.

Library of Congress Cataloging-in-Publication Data
Hanssen, Beatrice.
Critique of violence: between poststructuralism and critical theory / Beatrice Hanssen.
p. cm.–(Warwick studies in European philosophy)
Includes bibliographical references and index.
1. Violence. 2. Violence–Philosophy. 3. Critical theory. 4. Poststructuralism.
I. Title. II. Series.
HM886 .H35 2000
303.6'01–dc21   99–045123

ISBN 0–415–22339–3 (hbk)
ISBN 0–415–22340–7 (pbk)

CONTENTS

ACKNOWLEDGMENTS

The essays collected in this book reflect several years of intense debate, discussion, and intellectual exchange. They are the product of encounters with students, friends, and colleagues, at home and abroad – encounters punctuated by vigorous exchange, moments of agreement, give-and-take, more deliberation, some disagreement, sometimes resistances, but always full of productive tensions. Among interlocutors whose interactions proved especially fruitful or generated further thought and reflection, I wish to acknowledge K. Anthony Appiah, Andrew Benjamin, Seyla Benhabib, Stanley Cavell, Dorrit Cohn, Marjorie Garber, Sander Gilman, John Guillory, Werner Hamacher, Peter Hohendahl, Martin Jay, Barbara Johnson, Isaac Julien, Ernesto Laclau, Richard Macksey, Jane Mansbridge, Mark Nash, Chantal Mouffe, Naomi Schor, Werner Sollors, Doris Sommer, Susan Suleiman, Sarolta Takács, Maria Tatar, Samuel Weber, Sigrid Weigel, and Cornel West. I am grateful for the Harvard Faculty Research grants and leaves I was awarded in support of this project and for the generous help I received over the years from my graduate research assistants, William Nathan Alexander, Christian Schlesinger, Carol Forney, and Melissa Feuerstein. Portions of this study were completed while I was on leave as a 1995–96 Andrew W. Mellon Faculty Fellow at Stanford University and as a 1997–98 Fellow at Harvard's Bunting Institute.

Writing these essays proved in many ways an intellectual adventure, and engaging with the provocations of the texts under scrutiny often led me to revisit older positions – all in an attempt to live up to the challenge of critical *ēthos*. My appreciation now, as before, goes to my graduate and undergraduate students in my literature and theory seminars – students from Harvard's Departments of German and Comparative Literature, Philosophy, the Literature Program and Social Studies, the Harvard Divinity School, and Harvard's Graduate School of Design. Entering into dialogue with them in the classroom always proved an exhilarating and invigorating experience. Finally, I dedicate this book, as always, to Hildegard and Karin Rieder-Hanssen.

INTRODUCTION

When do debate and discussion become a fight, a *querelle*, and when does a *disputatio* become a dispute? At what point do argument and argumentation transform into entrenched antagonisms? When we enter the current critical field or arena, do we adopt the guise of the adversary or interlocutor? In negotiating between our different positions, do we give in, capitulate to a supposed antagonist, or are we instead persuaded by the rational force of the argument that our fellow interlocutor presents? For some, the political field, including the expansive terrain of cultural politics, is an intersubjective arena, structured according to the noncoercive rules of debate or discussion, which may yield consent or, at the very minimum, gesture towards the interlocutors' concerted attempt to reach agreement and, if need be, compromise. For others, every discursive exchange is not so much a dualistic antagonism as an encounter that of necessity and from the very start is structured by struggle and "agonism."[1] *Agon* here refers not to violent combat but to the inherent, not necessarily forceful, interplay between the multiple differences that inflect the structural positions of speaking partners. According to this agonistic script, to demand "consent" or "consensus," either as the zero-point condition for starting any conversation or as the projected outcome and horizon of discussion, would amount to effacing difference at every possible level of identity formation.

The terms of encounter and verbal communication, sketched here in broad strokes, are familiar through debates in political theory that in past decades have taken place among communitarians, deliberation-oriented political thinkers, and so-called agonistic theorists. But what would happen if one were to appropriate these models, originally meant to adjudicate or negotiate between different conceptions of either liberal or radical democracy, to look at the discursive, sometimes contentious, encounters that continue to inflect the current critical field? What if one were to reconsider the critical arena not only in static terms as a set of competing methodologies but also as an active field of vigorous debate and spirited discursive exchange?

In the wake of the far-reaching disciplinary changes that have occurred in past decades, the cultural critic now has at her disposal a seemingly inexhaustible array of analytical tools, all minted to solve newly defined tasks. But amidst the diversity of perspectives available, two intellectual traditions in particular seem to command unique attention for the tenacity with which they have been locked in an unwavering, prolonged exchange over their reciprocal epistemological and political merits: post-structuralism and critical theory.[2] Have these two critical traditions come to represent the ossified, adversarial poles of a potentially wide critical spectrum, or might there be grounds for a possible negotiation between the two?

A watershed date in the annals of the long-standing dispute between critical theory and poststructuralism is the year 1985, when Habermas's *The Philosophical Discourse of Modernity* first appeared in German, soon to be translated into English. His strong indictment of the alleged anti-Enlightenment stance occupied by postmodernism, and with it poststructuralism, unleashed a furor paralleled perhaps only by the debates over antihumanism that took place in the 1970s and 1980s. Over the years it seems that positions, if anything, have become more entrenched and have led to collateral charges – charges not so much that the other side is driven by antidemocratic intent, but rather that it remains impervious or blind to the ineluctable antidemocratic outcome that would evolve from the premises underlying its standpoint, were they to be taken to their logical *limit*. According to this ethico-political script, good intentions don't count, only political effects. In the most extreme case, poststructuralism (it hardly bears repeating) has been accused of indirectly fueling an antidemocratic, anti-Enlightenment irrationalism – its Nietzschean error – whose dangers, for one, were borne out by the revelations about Paul de Man's collaborationist past. In a weaker version of such criticism, poststructuralism is accused of canceling out all normativity so that it fails to provide ineradicable blueprints on the basis of which the ethical or political justification of situated actions can be assessed. On the level of agency, post-structuralism lacks a model of intersubjectivity and thus is believed to lead to an ethico-political determinism or quietism, as when antihumanistic discursive practices are said not just to rule but to form subjects to the point where it becomes impossible to legitimize or justify autonomous, free, individual actions. Critical theory, in its second-generation variant, represented by Habermas's discourse ethics, for its part has been charged with an old-time humanism, with the fallacy of a Kantian universalism that blots out cultural difference and particularisms, thus inadvertently tapping into conservative politics. In sum, while most observers, bystanders, and some participants seem to agree that the goals of both critical factions are indisputably democratic, the conceptual means for reaching these ends are markedly at odds with one another.[3]

Are we left, then, with quibbles and spats that take place on the fringes of real poli-tics? Or are we operating with "false antitheses" between compatible viewpoints, as Nancy Fraser has suggested?[4] Must we negotiate between factions and camps, or do these positions in truth remain nonnegotiable, wedged apart by an unbridgeable either/or? Must we remain forever poised between these two seemingly reified poles, or is it possible to negotiate a middle ground, which nonetheless manages to hold at bay the political conservatism currently associated with the "third way" in politics?

In order to formulate answers to these complex issues, it seems fitting that we first reconsider some of these traditions' pronounced ideological differences. Diverse and multifaceted as these debates are (no less than the questions they have sparked in their wake), the present book singles out two clusters for particular focus: the fate of critique, including ideology critique, and the disagreement over the conceptual borders of such political "key words" as power, force, and violence. As this book will suggest, critique and violence are two axes of a major juncture at which critical theory and poststructuralism meet. For it is over the viability and "essence" of what constitutes critique, as well as the borders that rift power from violence, that both intellectual traditions are still tied in dispute.

Critique

It can count as more than sheer philosophical providence that in 1921 Walter Benjamin authored an essay called "Critique of Violence" ("Zur Kritik der Gewalt"). With his usual uncanny gift for intellectual foresight and scholarly divination, he grasped the inordinate significance the pair "critique of violence" and "violence of critique" would gain in years to come. In its double attempt to practice critique and to understand power/violence (both rendered by the German word *Gewalt*), Benjamin's essay already set the tone for debates that decades later, if in altered guise, are still with us.

As far as the substance of Benjamin's intervention is concerned, the essay squarely fits in an antiliberal tradition that does not shun force to achieve its transformative sociopolitical agenda. Conceived at a time when the crisis of parliamentary democracy in the Weimar Republic had already made itself felt, the essay probed the legitimacy of the use of force against the foil of Max Weber's theory that the modern liberal state owns a monopoly over violence. In his eulogy of Georges Sorel's *Reflections on Violence*, which presented an all-out defense of the violent proletarian strike, Benjamin resolutely sympathized with left-wing, antiliberal appropriations of revolutionary force as he advocated the use of an insurrectionary counterviolence (*Gegengewalt*). Eventually, however, as the essay progressed, the theological realm showed clear signs of winning out over the secular-political arena, for, in typical Benjaminian fashion, the tract ended with a bow to the sublime "violence" of the divine name.

Yet this utopian Judeo-Marxist-messianic manifesto might never have had the impact it did were it not that, by default, it already exposed the fatedness of the critical tradition. Virtually unnoticed by Benjamin's contemporaries (except for a handful of close friends and intellectual allies), this relatively short essay in recent years has generated a number of noteworthy responses, most prominently Jacques Derrida's "Force of Law,"[5] which masterfully unraveled its implications for legal discourse and for the practice of critique. Thus, as Derrida noted, Benjamin's essay sought to offer not just an exercise in mere criticism, but also a genuine *critique* of violence. On purely formal grounds the text seemingly adhered to, or at least played with, the technical conventions of Kantianism and neo-Kantianism anchored in the philosopher's revolutionizing conception of *Kritik*. This explains why (in an initial phase of the analysis, at least) Benjamin meant to establish a typology of different manifestations of violence that discriminated the secular from the theological, the legal from the illegal, law-preserving from law-positing force. Taking literally the term critique, from the Greek *krinein* [6] (to cut, rift, separate, discriminate, but also to decide), he sought to separate categories of legitimate power from sheer force. In the end, however, the critical project, in its most rigorous assumptions, proved untenable, as he was moved to acknowledge the persistence of force in liberal institutions. Did Benjamin's essay testify to the crisis of the critical project a few years before its author would embrace the Marxist tradition of ideology critique? Did he simply revert to a theological dogmatism as he paid tribute to the sovereign power of the divine name, or, quite to the contrary, might the undoing of the critical project eventually lead not to an irreversible crisis but to hopeful regeneration? Such are the difficult questions with which Benjamin's all too brief, condensed tract seems to leave us.

Appropriating Benjamin's title, "Critique of Violence," this book takes his timely essay – a situated response to the dangers and conflicts of the Weimar period – as a guiding line for the "crisis of critique" that in many ways has become representative of our "post-Marxist condition." But is it sure what we mean when we use the term "critique" nowadays? As a practice whose inception coincides with the arrival of the modern epoch, the term critique has had a history marked by as many vicissitudes as the genealogy of modernity. Its intellectual span runs from Kant's inaugural, monumental project to overcome philosophical dogmatism and skepticism, Hegel's turn to intersubjectivity and immanent critique, and Marx's ideology critique, to the critical theory of the Frankfurt School. [7] In its perhaps most banal, etymological signification, as indicated above, the word derives from the Greek root *krinein* and, related to this term, *diakrisis*, and thus unmistakably refers to the acts of separation and distinction. In addition to signaling the act of incisive cutting, it also has acquired the meaning of "passing judgment." Taken in a historical (not Kantian, universalist) sense of the sort popularized by critical theory, "critique" has come to mean passing judgment on the present, [8] with an eye towards the realization of a (utopian) future as a way of undoing the errors of the past. Both Habermas and Foucault, as we shall see, have maintained that the critical project as such remains inextricably tied to the inception of the modern period in which the interrogation of the historical conditions that define the questioning "we" gains center stage. Whatever the inflections lent to the term or however much the borders of critique may have shifted over the decades, critique invariably involves rigorous legislation of the field over which it holds court, the setting up of a tribunal but also vigilant border patrol. Whether thought of in ahistorical, universalist, or, quite to the contrary, historicist terms, critique most often relies upon a firm bedrock of generalizable norms or, alternatively, on an axiology of values that, for all practical purposes, are passed off as consensual norms.

For Kant, critique was meant to secure the conclusive demarcation of the transhistorical conditions of possibility that underlie knowledge, moral deliberation, and aesthetic judgment. As such, critique transpired within the limits defined by experience on this side of another register of knowledge that, while inherently metaphysical, nonetheless proved valid and worthy of consideration. Not just for metaphorical or figurative reasons, Kant's tract on pure reason started off defining "critique" as the tribunal of reason. By deploying this prohibitive term, Kant did not simply enthrone a secular power or, better yet, establish the legislature of eternal, universal reason in place of divine law. In combating the tyranny of dogmatism, he meant to set an end, a limit, so to speak, to political despotism as well, to which his "What Is Enlightenment?" would further testify. In effect, Kant saw his critique as setting limits to speculative reason, much as the police's chief task is preventive, meant to avert the eruption of violence among the citizenry. But unlike Benjamin's essay, which condemned the ways in which the police routinely overstep their purely law-preserving function, Kant's model of reason required the patrolling of strict police lines that could not be crossed. That is why, as he explained in the preface to his *Critique of Pure Reason*, the critique of reason simultaneously has a negative, limiting effect as well as a positive result: "To deny that [the] service of criticism [critique, *Kritik*] is of any *positive* utility would be as much as to say that the police are of no positive utility because their chief business is to put a stop to the violence that citizens have to fear from other citizens, so that each can carry on his own affairs in peace and safety."[9] Critique in this sense safeguards against reason running amok, against the idle swerving of pure speculation, which in idling trespasses on blocked-off property. Critique draws limits, both in the sense of prohibitive limits (*Schranken*) and enabling bounds (*Grenzen*).[10]

Kant's critical undertaking merely initiated a tradition whose subsequent genealogy proved long and eventful. The German sociologist Reinhart Koselleck has demonstrated how, from the start, critique and crisis were linked not only etymologically but also conceptually in that, initially, critique designated the Enlightenment bourgeois and private practice of subjective judgment, while crisis referred to an objective, historical process.[11] Not until the coming of the crisis defined by the French Revolution would the privatizing tendencies of critique be shattered, as it now developed into an indictment of absolutism, to which Kant's own text, "What Is Enlightenment?," defining the historico-ontological status of the Enlightenment, paid testimony. But there can be no doubt that it was through Hegel's dialectical model (subsequently transformed under Marx's hands) that the critical project took on world-historical, as well as intersubjective dimensions, forever leaving the precinct of the solitary, monological Kantian subject behind. As Seyla Benhabib reminds us in her comprehensive *Critique, Norm, and Utopia*, it was Marx who first introduced a decisive rift between what constituted mere "criticism" and genuine critique, the latter defined as ideology critique. Informed by Hegel's dialectical method, Marx and Engels's *Holy Family* practiced *immanent critique* and, in a derogatory tone, painted predecessors and contemporaries – especially the Young Hegelians – as mere practitioners of criticism, who considered their object of analysis to be extraneous to their interpretive practice. Real critique, by contrast, "refuses to stand outside its object," i.e., society, "and instead juxtaposes the immanent, normative self-understanding of its object to the material actuality of this object."[12] Marx's lessons would not go unappreciated. In an effort to consolidate the principles of the movement that only after the Second World War would be called the Frankfurt School, Horkheimer, in his programmatic 1937 essay, "Traditional and Critical Theory," proposed a similar account of immanent, in his words, dialectical critique. Writing from the position of exile, he emphasized that "in a historical period like the present true theory is more critical than affirmative."[13] Such a critical activity, or perhaps "theoretical activism"[14] (as one is inclined to understand Horkheimer's analysis, not yet affected by the ban on theory that characterizes our own critical present), has "society itself for its object," which it investigates via the dialectical critique of political economy. Decrying the institutional hegemony of neo-Kantianism, Horkheimer followed Marx when he stated that for critical theory there is no outside, no factors that remain external to the production of knowledge, for to believe so is to be ensnared in ideology. Assuming the epistemological implication of the knowing subject in its object of critical analysis, he circumscribed the always elusive boundaries of ideology as follows:

> The thinking subject is not the place where knowledge and object coincide, or consequently the starting-point for attaining absolute knowledge. Such an illusion about the thinking subject, under which idealism lived since Descartes, is ideology in the strict sense, for in it the limited freedom of the bourgeois individual puts on the illusory form of perfect freedom and autonomy.[15]

It would be erroneous, however, to assume that the Marxist elimination of a pure, idealistic "outside" to theory or knowledge production also results in the obliteration of normative distinctions or demarcations, least of all those rifting the fettering socio-economic conditions of the present from the utopian prospect of a violence-free future. Rather, such an erasure of normative differentiations is the legacy of the revolution Nietzsche single-handedly forged as he exchanged the interests of the classical philologist for the toolkit of the iconoclastic genealogist. In his early writings on language, especially "On Truth and Lies in an Extramoral Sense," Nietzsche advanced a rhetorical critique of epistemology, demolishing the last idol of the tradition, the knowing subject, in a sweeping gesture that would find its concluding moment in French poststructuralism and antihumanism. In the second *Untimely Meditation*, Nietzsche literalized the cutting sharpness of critique, calling for a new historical understanding that would sever the roots of a dilapidated, atrophied historicism. Decades later, Foucault still echoed the Nietzschean style, when he asserted that "knowledge is not made for understanding; it is made for cutting."[16] Yet no other text more so than the *Genealogy of Morals* set an end to the stronghold of the normative presuppositions that underwrote Kantian critique. With its call to leave behind Kant's transhistorical, a priori conditions of understanding and its plea to procure "a knowledge of the conditions and circumstances"[17] out of which values grew, Nietzsche's genealogical "critique of moral values" testified to the *Wertstreit* that dominated nineteenth-century philosophy as it shifted away from its adherence to universally valid norms.[18]

Obviously, whether it is a matter of "critique" or "ideology critique," these are terms poststructuralism might not want much to do with, insofar as critique assumes a normative yardstick on the basis of which it passes judgment. Poststructuralism's epistemological antifoundationalism, or heightened awareness of contingent foundations, forces it to regard the undivided adherence to universalist and universalizing norms as anathema. The erasure of a binary conception of "difference" through the labor of *différance* and iterability has become associated with deconstruction, which replaces the divisionism of "either/or"[19] with "neither/nor," that is to say, with the necessary, constitutive undecidability that guides every ethico-political act or decision. But though it might brush aside universalizing moral philosophies or generalized theories of (distributive) justice, poststructuralism does not remain averse to, say, a deconstructive ethics or the future arrival of a justice-yet-to-come.[20] Ethico-political decisions based on normative "values" have been supplanted by either situated, historicist genealogies or quasi-transcendental scripts profiling an undecidability that nevertheless is said to remain enabling and generative. That less favorable responses have detected in this model a suspect decisionism, a political sin most often associated with the authoritarian thought of the legal theorist Carl Schmitt, is well known. Normative critique is said to have been demolished by the violence of deconstruction, echoing Nietzsche's forceful hammer blows.

Setting aside for the moment this bleak assessment of poststructuralism, I would like to turn briefly to the field of feminist theory, in which the contentious encounter between poststructuralism and critical theory has emerged prominently. That such mutual challenges, as documented in *Feminist Contentions* (1995), are of relatively recent date is borne out by the fact that several of the collection's contributors appeared together in the 1987 *Feminism as Critique*.[21] While in the early project the term "critique" functioned as an inviting label under which an eclectic group of feminist theorists could come together, the more recent *Feminist Contentions* shows the signs of a firm sedimentation between, on the one side, normative critique, inspired by the founders of a Frankfurt-style critical theory, and poststructuralist, performative "re-signification," on the other. Thus, Judith Butler distanced herself from a Frankfurt-style normative "critique" as championed by Nancy Fraser, charging that " 'critique,' to use Fraser's term, always takes place *immanent* to the regime of discourse/power whose claims it seeks to adjudicate, which is to say that the practice of 'critique' is implicated in the very power-relations it seeks to adjudicate."[22] But in thus distancing herself from the Frankfurt School critical tradition, she also suggested what a transfigured understanding of "immanent critique" might mean, insofar as the object of analysis from which the subject can no longer extract itself is "power." Furthermore, in order for this statement to gain the full force of all its deconstructive implications, one must read power as more or less identical with violence or force. Force here is not so much wielded by a will-ing individual agent, as it is implemented by the "subject-ing" regime of disciplinary discursive practices. Recasting the rudiments of the debate in this way, Butler also seemed to rescript the terms and conditions laid out by Foucault's critique of power. For, as we shall see, it was this French philosopher (also one of the leading historians of violence) who consolidated the epistemological grounds on which poststructuralism's narrowing of the difference between power/force would come to pass. To do so, he needed to leave behind the theory of a legitimate, consensual power to which political liberalism had lent wide circulation.

Power/Violence

The signs of the conceptual erasure to which the conventional borders between violence and power would be subjected in poststructuralist theory are already visible in Benjamin's "Critique of Violence." The now historic 1989 Cardozo Law School conference dedicated to Derrida's "Force of Law" pulled the essay out of relative obscurity, granting it the exemplary position it deserved. Reading Benjamin's antiliberal tract as a precursor of deconstruction, Derrida showed how its critique ended up with the entanglement of power/violence, terms rendered in German by the word *Gewalt*. That Benjamin's and Derrida's works were discussed together at a prominent law school did not simply attest to the discipline's concern with a violence spun out of control but also gave evidence of the discipline's increasing willingness to consider the persistence of violence in the law. In addition to Robert Cover's relatively early essay "Violence and the Word,"[23] it was above all the groundbreaking, revolutionizing work of critical legal studies that demonstrated how renewed probes into the law's authority could do much to expand our understanding of the exclusionary gestures that result from allegedly universal legal assumptions. Many of the rejoinders written in response to Derrida's Benjamin exegesis, originally published in a special issue of the *Cardozo Law Review*, considered the potential challenges it presented to a jurisprudence traditionally held to be free of violence.[24] Given the enormously fruitful perspectives these assessments have yielded, both for the practice no less than for the theoretical understanding of the law, the present study shifts the center of analysis slightly in that it seeks to situate the conflation of power/violence thematized in Benjamin's essay in a wider philosophico-political context. The focus on how critique *and* violence appear entangled in the contemporary critical arena allows one to call attention to a discursive side of the debate that has tended to go less noticed.

Though some of the essays collected in this study broach legal issues, the volume's main concern is neither with the law nor jurisprudence; nor does it claim to provide a sociological or anthropological key to understanding the anatomy of violence. Surely, a book dedicated to violence *as such* would have to be broad. It would be the largest possible global encyclopedia of human atrocities, systems of domination, oppression, and exploitation, without regard for national borders or cultural particularisms. Its final chapter would return to the tradition of nonviolence and pacifism, holding out the future of hope, which some, without a doubt, would greet with the same kind of whimsical irony they reserve for Kant's proverbial innkeeper, beckoning his guests with "Eternal Peace." Though beginnings are being made for such a much-needed encyclopedia of violence,[25] the present project, however, does not purport to lay claim to such global scope. Instead, it remains self-consciously local in that it targets the critical discourse over power/violence that holds poststructuralism and critical theory locked in an uneasy embrace. To abstract from this specific angle in order to tender generalizations about a universal economy of violence would mean to lapse into a position that loses sight of the partiality of its vision. The result would be a theoretical form of violence that simultaneously exerts undue interpretive force over its object/field of analysis while damaging the practice and viability of theory in the larger critical arena.[26]

Though primarily cultural-historical rather than sociological or anthropological in tenet and methodology, the essays that follow nonetheless fill out a historical episode in the conceptual vicissitudes of violence, whose typology in modernity has expanded considerably. Stretched beyond its former clearly demarcated boundaries, meaning "the use of physical force" (a characterization still to be found in standard dictionary definitions), violence now includes such phenomenologically elusive categories as psychological, symbolic, structural, epistemic, hermeneutical, and aesthetic violence. In a survey of the shifting conceptual demarcations to which the terms power/violence have been subjected, the one philosopher's name that returns without fail is Nietzsche, who seems to have laid claim to the dubious distinction of being modernity's first true philosophical advocate of violence. More than any other of his works, the *Genealogy of Morals* presents itself as a primer that compactly lays out the diverse fields to which the founding principle of force/violence can be applied. Thus, his philosophy allowed for the slippage away from a justification of morals (moral evil) and theology (the origin of evil) to a quasi-Darwinian struggle of the fittest, a genealogy in which moral values were exchanged for the forceful battle of wills.[27] His genealogical model unmasked the *agon* of wills and the resulting hermeneutical violence that accompanied the imposition of contingent signifying regimes. His description of the punitive festival of suffering, executed in the name of Kant's categorical imperative, reveled in the kind of unsavory detail that would define the transgressive aesthetics of violence and avant-garde representational practices of the century to come. His perspectivism called for a reconsideration of the moral law in terms of a proto-Freudian model of psychological interiorization.[28] Finally, his relentless insistence on the rule of force in law set back the modern tradition of contractarianism. Thus, Nietzsche straddled the categories of modern political theory that, on the basis of a liberal theory of the state, strictly demarcate legitimate, justifiable manifestations of violence from illegitimate ones, the first being state-sanctioned, the second not. In casting doubt on the main theses of Hobbes's *Leviathan*, which had hailed the suppression of the *status naturalis* through the social compact, Nietzsche explicitly deconstructed the contract as fraught by violence. Undoubtedly, it is also to

Nietzsche that Benjamin paid tribute when in "Critique of Violence" he uncovered the mythical, fate-like origin of modern law.

Appearing on the scene in this post-Nietzschean epoch, Foucault transformed Nietzsche's genealogy of hermeneutical force into a large-scale investigation of the insipid channels through which institutions perpetrate epistemic or discursive violence. If in his earlier work he unmasked the will to knowledge of the human sciences, then his writings of the middle period seemed intent on fusing Nietzsche's insights with a social theory that radically rethought the premises of poststructuralist Marxism. Althusser's famous essay on ideological state apparatuses described a category of symbolic violence not only exerted by the liberal state's police or military but also enacted through the institutions of church and family. To some degree, Foucault similarly focused on state-sponsored and state-sanctioned institutional forms of violence, such as systems of surveillance, regimes of disciplining, and the advent of the modern penal system. But he also did decidedly more by shifting to the surreptitious manifestations of violence that riddle civic space. By analyzing the rise to prominence of "governmentality" in the modern period, he pushed beyond the hegemonic, monolithic theory of the autonomous state, still present in Althusser's tract; for to believe in "statism," as orthodox Marxism did, was to preserve the monarchical, sovereign enthronement of power and to remain impervious to the myriad, capillary, strategic force fields of power that run through the political and civic realm.

Though Foucault first and foremost remained a historian, he also intervened in debates that more properly belong to political theory. For at the center of his project stands a radical rethinking of traditional liberal conceptions of power, according to which power is politically enabling and an end in itself. Indeed, no liberal thinker perhaps more so than Hannah Arendt defined the strict parameters of power, as she sought to avert the reversal between enabling power and abject force in a post-Holocaust and postnuclear age. In her foundational *The Human Condition*, but also her lesser-treated *On Violence*, to which several of the following chapters will turn, she rigorously demarcated violence/force from power, using the time-honored parameters of means and ends.[29] If violence was in essence strategic, manipulative, or instrumental in character, consensual power was to be thought of as an absolute end in itself. Taking issue with this liberal tradition early on, Foucault's extensive body of work demonstrated the multiple ways in which the boundaries between violence and power proved untenable, even permeable. Not until his very last writings, as we shall see, did he seek to redress the conceptual erasure of the two terms, under whose aegis he produced most of his major writings.

The concerns that second-generation Frankfurt School theorists have addressed at poststructuralist critics such as Foucault mainly involve the purported onslaught on the legacy and principles of the Enlightenment. This is not surprising, given the impact that Habermas's position, featured in his *Philosophical Discourse of Modernity*, has had on the discussion: by adhering to the totalizing critique of reason that Adorno and Horkheimer advanced in their jointly authored *Dialectic of Enlightenment*, postmodernism and poststructuralism (Foucault's historicist variant not excluded) inveighed against the Enlightenment principles of modernity – the universality of reason, the ends of history, the autonomous subject[30] – while simultaneously proving unable to shed the premises of subject philosophy, whose foundational principles they simply reversed. In annulling the vital, political difference between force and power, Foucault merely prolonged the philosophico-political mistakes already committed by Adorno and Horkheimer, or so at least Habermas did not fail to point out. In their anatomy of instrumental reason, whose reifying economy they detected in the epistemological, aesthetic, and moral realms, the founders of the Frankfurt School proved too Nietzschean, upsetting the solid edifice of reason. To hollow out the base of a self-governing, secular reason meant to give way either to unreason or to an authoritarian-bound decisionism. But what has perhaps been less emphasized is that Habermas indicted poststructuralism's relativistic position also on methodological grounds, for putting at risk the viability of the (ideology) critical project *tout court*. To be sure, Habermas's point, and that of other like-minded critics, could not be to advocate anachronistically a rigorous adherence to Kant's transcendental critique. In the trail of Hegel's turn to intersubjectivity and Marxist ideology critique, Kant's emphasis on subjectivity and the ahistorical conditions of possibility that rule knowledge, moral deliberation, or aesthetic judgment have indisputably been proven to be untenable. That much acknowledged, it is of the essence, however, to ask once again whether Foucault's position truly endangers the critical project *as such*? Perhaps the dispute around how Foucault precipitated the end of critique, while seemingly settled, needs to be considered yet again. Indeed, it comes as somewhat of a welcome surprise that, towards the end of the 1970s, Foucault sought to overcome the gap between both intellectual schools by throwing a bridge to critical theory. Seeking a *rapprochement* of sorts with the critical tradition, he no longer purely turned to the overly charismatic, precarious figure of Friedrich Nietzsche, but rather to the sober historical writings of Immanuel Kant. Using the lens of the latter's "What Is Enlightenment?," he sought to regain the liberatory, insurgent potential of Kantian critique, forging a new critique that would breach (*franchir*) the dilapidated frontiers of the old *epistēmē*. Has there emerged a new "rapport," perhaps, between both sides, whose terms and conditions Foucault laid out in his later writings when he reclaimed the legacy of Kantian philosophy and the Frankfurt School?

Critical Tools

Questioning the distinctions between power/violence, Benjamin still wielded the "sharp axe of critique," Nietzsche the merciless knife and shattering hammer of genealogy, Foucault the "blunt knife" of a newly fashioned "effective history." All still played with the privileged trope of instrumental reason while also practicing a destructiveness that expressed the iconoclastic violence with which old idols, allegorical figures from ancient times, are thrown to pieces. The demand to mint new conceptual or epistemological implements remained persistent in Foucault's work and perhaps is not unaffiliated to structuralism's famous call for a new science that would proceed via *bricolage*, a tinkering with critical tools.[31] Similarly, in its attempt to retool the critical field, poststructuralism followed Nietzsche when he sought to go beyond the hegemony of the *ratio* by turning reason against itself. For didn't the *Genealogy of Morals* end with the prediction that nihilism would eventually overcome itself by turning against itself? In his Nietzsche lectures (from which Foucault learned most, as he admitted in his last interview), Heidegger described how Nietzsche meant to overcome (*überwinden*) metaphysics by pushing it to its limits, hoping to overturn it from within. Common to poststructuralism's bid for a new utopian realm, altering the confines of the paradigm that needs to be shed, demolished, destroyed, or overcome is the Nietzschean belief that, as Foucault put it, philosophy must be turned against itself (*la retourner contre elle-même*).[32] Clearly, this desire also informs the way poststructuralism recasts critique as re-signification: in turning the model of convention against itself, social customs and rites are to be parodically reenacted in an effort to release their revolutionizing potential.

In his *Contingency, Irony, and Solidarity*, Richard Rorty lends a pragmatist perspective on the well-known trope of the toolkit. Indirectly invoking Wittgenstein's famous ladder as the instrument that can be discarded after it has proven its use, he describes the tools of pragmatism as instruments for which the blueprint has gone missing. Pragmatism not only unsentimentally lets go of the ladder or other tools it no longer needs, but it also doesn't draw preparatory diagrams, since there are no longer any edifices it seeks to construct. Or, to put it in terms of the logic of choice and decisions we have tangentially pursued thus far: instead of *either/or* or *neither/nor* now comes *and/and*. It seems that references to pragmatism have steadily accrued over the last few years, indicating that this philosophical school has perhaps become a viable, alternative route, one that could lead out of the rut poststructuralism and critical theory have found themselves in.[33] At the same time, the term "critique" keeps returning, even though its deficit has been announced by certain pragmatists, while the term "ideology critique," for its part, has not fared much better. If conservatives, encouraged by the fall of communism, have declared the end of ideology critique, then poststructuralists, foremost among them Foucault, have done so from a post-Nietzschean epistemological antifoundationalism, noting that the very concept, however left-leaning, is still the offshoot of a questionable "will to truth." In the wake of such a débâcle, must we agree with the position Rorty has recently put forth: that poststructuralism (and presumably critical theory, which cannot fare any better) must concede defeat to pragmatism because, on *philosophical* grounds, it cannot advance watertight justificatory narratives without lapsing into a *petitio principii*? That, on *political grounds*, poststructuralism (together with the "cultural left," as it has come to be called disparagingly) must give way to a new pragmatism? Are poststructuralism and critical theory reduced to the level of useful analytical tools that have run their course when it comes to offering utopian or not so utopian phantasmagoria of the future? We must ask whether the critical field, nowadays, is divided between those who hold fast to older paradigms (whether a norm-infused critical theory or the antifoundationalism of postmodernism and poststructuralism), and those who, believing all foundationalist metanarratives to be false, have opted for a neopragmatic solution, the revamped, ameliorated version of an older pragmatism that proved blind to regimes of power. Indeed, critical theorists such as Nancy Fraser have seen in neopragmatism a way of avoiding the false dualisms of these two schools.[34] I am inclined to agree with her position but only if we take pragmatism here to mean nothing more than a heuristic device, call it a tool. For while a "weak" form of pragmatism seems advisable enough – the revamped version, as it were, of the earlier structuralist, Levi-Straussian image of the *bricoleur* – one must wonder whether a "strong" pragmatism that champions utilitarianism or is the mouthpiece of a difference-obliterating liberalism is recommendable for a radical democratic, pluralistic project that averts the dangers of the past. By adding the term "weak," I wish to demarcate this approach from a "strong" pragmatism, which – qua philosophical movement – uncritically advocates an *unreflective* political liberalism, whose principles it no longer needs to justify in the wake of its globally realized triumph. As this book *inter alia* hopes to demonstrate, much of the stalemate between critical theory and poststructuralism can be reversed once poststructuralism brings its cryptonormativity, utopianism, and belief in a justice-yet-to-come, to the surface, and once critical theorists are willing to abandon their reluctance to engage poststructuralism's premises on equal terms. Perhaps then the new critical *attitude*, or *ēthos*, Foucault upheld in his Kant texts may be realized: the critical interrogation of the present, in light of the future, which actualizes the "unmined" historical potential of the past.

If we return now, in closing, to the questions laid out at the beginning of this introduction, it will be evident that this project can hardly favor an adversarial model in which friends and foes compete. To set up a dualism, a Schmittean "friend–enemy" division, between poststructuralism and critical theory would mean to reify positions, to pin interlocutors down, to congeal fluid positions. For intrinsic to the antagonistic model that underpins most conceptions of social struggle, there remains an adversarial component according to which the "other" is my potential enemy rather than contesting interlocutor. In one of his late texts, "The Subject and Power," Foucault seemed to gesture – if only fleetingly, as we shall see – to an "agonism" at the heart of his conception of freedom,[35] one that does not amount to antagonism; the latter implies mere opposition and dualism, whereas agonism refers to the "permanent provocation" that takes place between reciprocal partners, that is, the "reciprocal incitation and struggle" inhabiting the multiple force fields of power. While this book takes exception to the sometimes bellicose undertone that marked the model of struggle Foucault championed until the very last, it wants to retain the element of *provocation* that his statement evoked. To provoke then no longer means "to anger" or "to enrage" but "to stimulate" or "be stimulated," to be drawn out of one's ritualized borders and entrenched limits or confining horizon. Placing more emphasis on dialogue than on struggle, the essays collected in this book, as its subtitle indicates, position themselves *between* poststructuralism and critical theory. That is, they draw on both traditions, not in an effort to side conclusively with the one or the other, or to remain suspended in indecision, but to expose their fundamental differences as well as the terms on which they might agree. The preposition "between," therefore, is not to be taken in the sense of a hesitant undecidability, on the cusp of a decision that cannot be made. Rather, it signals the creation of a space of possibility, an interval, a moment of respite, the possibility of reaching altogether innovative decisions or choices, without getting rid of the contesting differences that must inflect democratic critical discussions. Though the project may prove risky as factions are so entrenched that not siding with one or the other may mean being faulted for a lack of loyalty, principles, or a confounding of foundational premises, still such a risk seems worth taking in the interest of renewed dialogue.

In a final moment, it also seems necessary to affirm that *Critique of Violence* tries not to fall into the trap of "presentism," the adulation of the present, or the "now," an empty moment lacking the utopian potential that still infused Benjamin's now-time (*Jetztzeit*). Instead, the study seeks to bring to the surface some of the assumptions or premises that structure the encounters, sometimes conflicts, of these critical inter-locutors, premises that are not always pronounced in so many words but that nonetheless stake out the parameters of what is debatable or not. Quite simply, the essays that follow seek to take stock of several dominant critical lines of argumenta-tion that return with some consistency. Indeed, one "figure" of violence, whose persistence and recurrent circulation in contemporary poststructuralist thought the book pursues is that of a counterforce or counterviolence (*Gegengewalt*) that takes the form of what Foucault and Derrida respectively have called "antidogmatic" or "antimetaphysical" violence. Thus, the use of a symbolic, figurative, discursive force, wielded as a counterprinciple, is meant to undo metaphysical, institutional sedimenta-tions of force, especially the violence exercised by instrumental reason, with its logic *and* practices of exclusion. As they revisit the canonical texts of the Western philosoph-ical tradition — above all, Hobbes's *Leviathan*, Hegel's *Phenomenology of Spirit*, and Nietzsche's *Genealogy of Morals* — many of the counterdiscourses operate with a reversal of Clausewitz's dictum that war is the continuation of politics by "other means," yielding the view of modernity as perpetual war or violence. Are such claims about the historical past and present merely descriptive rather than prescriptive, as some would argue? Can such counterdiscourses be shown to operate with a limited, inadequate technique of (Nietzschean) reversal? Do such subversive technologies stifle or instead enable the possibility of transformative change, violence-free communica-tive exchange or ethico-political action? Such seem to be the challenges and stakes of the debates involved.

Chapter 1, "On the Politics of Pure Means: Benjamin, Arendt, Foucault," begins with a reading of Benjamin's "Critique of Violence" against the backdrop of Arendt's *On Violence* and Foucault's understanding of strategic force. The Foucauldian strand of argumentation is further pursued in Chapters 2 and 3 respectively, "Between Kant and Nietzsche: Foucault's Critique" and "Power/Force/War: On Foucault's 'Society Must Be Defended'," which expose the relatively unknown, "critical" side of his later thought. Chapter 4, "The Violence of Language," focuses on how liberalism in general works with the presupposition that (political) speech can and must be freed of violence, while poststructuralism contends with the agonistic potential of discursive practices. Chapter 5, "Violence and Interpretation: Enzensberger's Civil Wars," queries the attempt by a new wave of neoconservative thinkers, including Fukuyama, to pronounce the death or end of ideology critique. In turning to contemporary conceptions of multiculturalism in terms of recognition, the discussion here already sets the tone for the next chapter, "Ethics of the Other," which further probes what "recognition" might entail, whether it can inflect a new ethical attitude and to what extent this novel modality ought to be rethought through Fanon's category of "ethical transitivism." Chapter 7, "Limits of Feminist Representation," takes the work of well-known Austrian writer Elfriede Jelinek as a starting point for an analysis not only of how poststructuralist feminism has assumed discursive violence as a critical principle but also how this project, despite its apparent fatedness, remains tied to a pronounced ethico-political commitment to social change – in the case of Jelinek, the fight against the lingering presence of fascism in post-Holocaust Austria. Finally, a concluding chapter, "Whatever Happened to Feminist Theory?," takes the controversial collection Feminist Contentions as its point of departure to examine the triangulation that has divided poststructuralist, Frankfurt-style, and neopragmatist feminists. Once again, the apparent contentious, antagonistic state of discussion, I argue, should not necessarily lead one to adopt a skeptical outlook as to the future of the critical field or the state of feminisms. Rather, when seen within the history of the critical endeavor, it becomes possible to read these and other equally intense debates as part of an ongoing conversation and dialogue, with much agreement and also, fortunately, plenty of productive dissent and disagreement.

1

ON THE POLITICS OF PURE
MEANS

Benjamin, Arendt, Foucault

When Walter Benjamin's "Critique of Violence" first appeared in the journal *Archiv für Sozialwissenschaft*, it looked "quite out of place," as Gershom Scholem recalls in his *Story of a Friendship*.[1] It had originally been commissioned for the journal *Weiße Blätter*, whose editor, Emil Lederer, deemed Benjamin's treatise on violence far too long and too difficult. In it, as Benjamin noted in a letter to Scholem, he aspired to have captured the element of violence: "There are still questions concerning violence that I do not touch on in this essay, but I nevertheless hope that it has something essential to say."[2] Written in 1921, "Critique of Violence" to no small degree reflects Benjamin's contacts with Hugo Ball and Ernst Bloch, with whom he repeatedly met in 1919 during his studies at the University of Bern. Not only did they confront him with the "question of political activity"[3] in the wake of the Bolshevik Revolution, the collapse of the German empire, and the short-lived 1919 Munich Soviet republic, but they also introduced him to the work of Georges Sorel. Representative spokesperson of French Syndicalism and author of *Réflexions sur la violence*, Sorel was to be foundational for Benjamin's political thought well beyond the 1921 violence essay.

As the only completed piece in a series of projected texts that were to become part of Benjamin's broadly conceived *Politik*,[4] "Critique of Violence" survives as an isolated, yet seminal fragment of his politics of violence. But apart from the dubious praise the violence essay would earn him from jurist and later theorist of the National Socialist state Carl Schmitt, the text's political effects on the whole remained rather minimal. Precisely because of its embarrassing affinities to conservative theorists such as Sorel and Schmitt, it seemed all too clearly to participate in the tradition of violence that has marked twentieth-century German history. Not until the 1960s, at a time when the normative foundations and legitimacy of German liberal democracy were radically shaken by the upsurge of left-wing violence, would "Critique of Violence" become the subject of much debate, notably in the writings of Oskar Negt, Jürgen Habermas, and Herbert Marcuse — with the notable exception of Hannah Arendt, from whose 1969 polemical treatise *On Violence* Benjamin remained conspicuously absent. But even then the fronts were divided. Writing in response to the assassination attempt on Rudi

Dutschke, the ensuing *Springer* blockades, and student revolts, the sociologist Oskar Negt interpreted Benjamin's essay as an early reflection on the nature of structural violence. Advocating the legitimate use of counterviolence (*Gegengewalt*), the essay, Negt suggested, could serve to unmask the dissimulation of liberal-democratic systems, which, while holding that violence ought not to be used as a means in politics, in reality sustained structural or institutional violence.[5]

If Negt and Marcuse interpreted Benjamin's revolutionary violence in materialistic-political terms, Habermas, by contrast, cautioned against seeing Benjamin as the theologian of the revolution. In his 1972 essay "Walter Benjamin: Consciousness-Raising or Rescuing Critique," he pointed to the covert connection between Benjamin's theory of violence and the fated politics of Surrealism, placing him squarely in the camp of conservative revolutionaries.[6] More recently, Habermas's 1987 review of Schmitt in translation warned that Benjamin's violence essay was indebted to Schmitt's theory of sovereignty and aesthetics of violence in that both authors championed "the violent destruction of the normative as such."[7] Thus, if Habermas's analysis from the 1970s maintained that Benjamin's "politics of pure means" set an end to all purposive rationality and therefore was counter to political praxis, the later essay went even further, charging that he in fact had crossed over to the side of Schmitt's conservative antiliberalism. This shift in interpretation should not be surprising. Benjamin's intellectual debts to the contested jurist have been no secret, ever since the 1977 publication of a formerly suppressed letter to Schmitt, in which he avowed his indebtedness to the *Political Theology* for his analysis of the German mourning play (*Trauerspiel*). And, if, furthermore, the language of decisionism (*Entscheidung*, *Ausnahmezustand*) can be said to traverse Benjamin's writings – from the *Origin of the German Mourning Play* to the theses on history – this only seemed to confirm Benjamin's perilous affinities to Schmitt's conservatism.

That a theory of violence could bring him dangerously close to the battlefront of fascism is a threat Benjamin addressed on only a few occasions, one being an encounter with the French fascist Georges Valois. In 1927, his interview with this former student of Sorel appeared in *Die literarische Welt* in the form of a short article on dictatorship, titled "Für die Diktatur" ("For Dictatorship").[8] Here, on the eve of National Socialism's ascent to power, Benjamin seemed forced to reflect on how precarious, indeed, perhaps nonexistent, the difference between left- and right-wing violence really might be. Praising Sorel for being the "greatest and most truthful theoretician of syndicalism," he also scoffed him for providing the "best nursery" for fascist leaders, as was apparent from recent European events – an allusion, no doubt, to Mussolini, who, as a young socialist, had found inspiration in Sorel's school of thought.[9] Valois's appropriation of unbloody, bloodless revolutions, as well as the workers' insurrection for the fascist cause, provided further evidence of how fluid the demarcation line between the two political factions could be. At the same time, Benjamin was quick to dispel the myth of the fraternal feud propagated by the new fascism, which liked "to confront its movement with Bolshevism, as whose hostile twin brother it sees itself."[10] How persistent the myth of a fraternal conflict between fascism and Marxism could be is apparent from Schmitt's 1923 *Crisis of Parliamentary Democracy*, which proclaimed that Proudhon's anarcho-syndicalism converged with the Catholic, counterrevolutionary conservatism of Donoso-Cortès in that both ideologies celebrated the "great battle," or "great struggle," that was to set an end to all forms of parliamentarism. Resolutely rejecting the image of two feuding brothers, Benjamin's short essay nonetheless still begged the question of how the violent tactics of the left were to be justified in light of right-wing violence.

Benjamin's silence on the issue is especially noteworthy in view of "Critique of Violence," which clearly announced itself as a philosophico-political attempt to furnish a classification or taxonomy of different modes of violence insofar as it differentiated divine from inauthentic, human manifestations of force. Following the Kantian philosophical tradition, the term "critique" in the essay's title signaled not only the attempt to lay bare the transcendental conditions of possibility of the phenomenon but also, as Derrida argued in "Force of Law," critical separation and demarcation.[11] The decisive cutting force expressed by the word *Kritik* derives etymologically from *krinein* ("to separate") and is echoed in the essay's preoccupation with the language of *Entscheidung*.

Thus, the following analysis takes up the methodological task Benjamin's text assigned itself, namely, that of providing a transcendental critique (*Kritik*) of violence, as well as a *diacritical* model on the basis of which just manifestations of force were to be distinguished from their inauthentic counterparts.[12] Benjamin's essay emphatically did not celebrate a monolithic, "substantialist" force or violence that could serve as a dynamic, energic *archē* or foundation, but rather proposed an apology for a *pure*, unalloyed mode of revolutionary violence, which was to set an end to all mythic force. In so doing, he introduced a critical praxis of violence that would mark his future writings. For, against Ernst Jünger's cultist celebration of eternal war as "the highest expression of the German nation" or against fascism's "aestheticization of violence," Benjamin would hold the predatory Angelus Novus, the anarchistic force of the destructive character, the *schlagende Gewalt* of language, the citational violence of Kraus's aphorisms, or, again, the disruptive, revolutionary force of *Jetztzeit* (now-time), which shattered the false continuum of history conceived as mere progress.

To be sure, these figures of thought by now have become part and parcel of Benjamin scholarship. All the more urgent, therefore, is the task of reexamining them in light of the program for a "politics of pure means" and revolutionary force that "Critique of Violence" mobilized – a force that, Benjamin believed, would radically rupture the eternal cycle of violence and counterviolence constituting human history. Benjamin hoped once and for all to break the vicious circle of violence by radically rethinking a long-standing philosophico-political tradition according to which violence was to be conceived as *instrumental* in nature, that is, as a means or implement to be ıt to the service of (political) ends. This tradition runs from Aristotle's syllogistic ˙nition of the means–ends relation to Kant's qualification of *Gewalt* as a disposition external objects or means, to the theory of war that the German military strate-

18

gist Carl von Clausewitz laid down in his well-known dictum that "war is the continuation of politics by other means."[13] Furthermore, such a conception of instrumental violence surfaced in Engels's *Anti-Dühring*, which maintained that the "triumph of violence" depended on the implements it uses, or the production of armaments. Finally, instrumental violence further constituted the target of Arendt's *On Violence*, to receive perhaps its most radical response in Foucault's analysis of the myriad technologies that mediate power.

As a political theory, liberalism abjures all forms of violence that surpass the boundaries of individual self-defense or the legitimate monopoly of violence that the liberal-democratic state exercises. Already in her treatise on revolutions, Arendt suggested that violence makes up the limit of the political, so that "a theory of war or a theory of revolution … can only deal with the justification of violence because this justification constitutes its political limitation."[14] Mindful of this liberal tradition, my reading of Benjamin's violence essay nonetheless will ask to what degree the phenomenon of violence, for example, in the form of violent anticolonial struggle, also shows up the blind spots of political liberalism.[15] In many ways, this essay thus elaborates further on the theses about the antiliberal embrace of force that Stephen Holmes put forth in his *Anatomy of Antiliberalism*. That is to say, if the tradition of antiliberalism – whether in its left-wing or right-wing forms – approves of the use of violence, then to what extent does (political) violence – under certain circumstances – also constitute a limit to liberalism's model of political analysis? In order to pursue this inquiry, my analysis locates Benjamin's essay at three crucial historical junctures: first, the Weimar Republic and Schmitt's concept of the political; second, Arendt's response to the counterviolence of the 1960s, and, in conclusion, Foucault's variant of poststructuralism, which spells the end, perhaps, of all (transcendental) critiques of violence.

Benjamin's Politics of Noninstrumental Means

Placed within its historical context, Benjamin's "Critique of Violence" appears to be a timely response to the violence of the First World War, the ensuing debates about pacifism and militarism, and the peace settlement achieved by the Treaty of Versailles. To no small degree it furthermore contributed to the discussions about state theory and the malaise of the Weimar Republic, already apparent in 1921, whose crisis of parliamentarism was to find its most notorious detractor in Schmitt. But in its critique of the mythic violence that was said to inhabit the legal order (*Rechtsgewalt*), the essay also reacted to the crisis that afflicted the value-free discipline of positivistic law. No longer able to guarantee the legitimacy of the legal order, legal positivism instead attested to the discrepancy between legality and legitimacy that was to become typical of modernity.[16]

By underscoring the mythic, fate-like nature of profane law – a thought already developed in his 1919 essay "Fate and Character" – Benjamin opposed his former teacher, the neo-Kantian Hermann Cohen, whose transcendental project to establish an ethics of the pure will defined the science of law as a "theoretical factum," that is, as the mathematics of the human sciences, analogous to the role mathematics fulfilled for the natural sciences. Proposing a "historico-philosophical view of law" instead,[17] "Critique of Violence" charted the genealogy of a profane form of violence, which it traced from earliest primitive, mythic times, through its institutionalization in jusnaturalism and statutory law, to nineteenth- and twentieth-century variants of vitalism apparent in Darwinism and Kurt Hiller's activism. Thus, while the essay argued that the critique of violence should find its starting point in the realm of law, or right, Benjamin ultimately formulated a pure, bloodless and – crucially – just violence, which radically escaped all legal norms. To accomplish this, Benjamin – in stark contrast to Arendt, as we shall see – first needed to show the mutual contamination and duplicity (*Zweideutigkeit*) of two political traditions, those of power and of violence, a contamination indicated by his refusal to separate the meaning of *Gewalt*, used to render the Latin *potestas*, or power – evident in such expressions as *Rechtsgewalt* or *Staatsgewalt*, *Macht* – from *violentia* and *vis*, or force.[18]

Though Benjamin's ultimate goal was to devise a transcendental critique of violence understood as a principle (*Prinzip*), it is noteworthy that in an initial, heuristic stage of his analysis he adopted the historical vantage point of positive law. Unlike transcendental philosophy, positive law historicized the phenomenon, insofar as it offered an implicit typology of different forms of violence, based on whether or not they had been historically sanctioned. In this initial moment of differentiation (*Unterscheidung*, *Entscheidung*), Benjamin took on what he regarded to be the "substantialism" of natural law, for which the use of force signaled the expenditure of natural, vital energy. Yet he relinquished this preliminary point of departure in positive law when he established that in place of the demonic duplicity and indecisiveness that inhabited *Rechtsgewalt* was to come absolute decisiveness (*Entscheidung*) and justice, anchored in the divine and thetic name of God. In a radical repudiation of the executive, legislative, and juridic division of powers upheld by the liberal constitution – what in German is called *Gewaltenteilung*, as the critic Horst Folkers has noted[19] – Benjamin ultimately established that "Divine violence, which is the sign and seal but never the means of sacred execution, may be called sovereign violence."[20]

The decidedly antimodern gesture with which the essay located sovereignty not in the *dēmos* but in divine violence – a gesture that one could perhaps call a de-secularization of sorts if modernity is the product of a radical secularization – has played no minor role in discussions about Benjamin's political theology or decisionism. However, less attention has been paid to the radicality of his attempt to rupture the syllogistic bond that since Aristotle has informed the means–ends relationship,[21] to posit, on the one hand, what he called pure, unalloyed means, that is, language and the revolutionary, proletarian strike (in the Sorelian sense), and, on the other, pure ends: divine justice, or divine violence/power.

While Benjamin's critique appeared to be informed by Kant's fundamental distinction between morality and legality in that he too sought to define the morality of an action by disengaging it from the judicial system, he purported to surpass the correlation between justified means and just ends that still informed Kant's moral philosophy. To be sure, the second formulation of the categorical imperative offered in Kant's *Foundations of the Metaphysics of Morals* was meant to overcome the arbitrariness of the hypothetical imperative, which qualified violence (as Horst Folkers has argued convincingly) as the real and potential disposition over means (expressed in German as *in seiner Gewalt sein* or *etwas in seiner Gewalt haben*). Yet even this formulation of the categorical imperative, Benjamin contended, did not definitively exclude potentially using the other as a means. The injunction formulated in the *Foundations* ("Act in such a way that at all times you use humanity both in your person and in the person of all others as an end, and never merely as a means") still raised the question, Benjamin wrote, "whether this famous demand does not contain too little, that is, whether it is permissible to use, or allow to be used, oneself or another in any respect as a means."[22] Whereas Kant's *Metaphysics of Morals* established the system of ethics as a "system of the ends of pure practical reason," which comprised the doctrines of virtue and of law (*Tugend-* and *Rechtslehre*),[23] Benjamin, by contrast, not only problematized the very notion of just ends but also announced the deficiency of the legal realm as such. Finally, though Benjamin, following Kant's *Perpetual Peace*, argued that every individual, singular peace treaty, or *pactum pacies*, reiterated the belligerent potential of war, he could hardly have had on mind Kant's call for a federation of nation-states when he invoked the Idea of eternal peace. Seemingly afflicted and even corroded by an insidious form of violence (in the sense of *violentia*), *Rechtsgewalt* could no longer set a halt to the belligerence inherent to the state of nature, or *status naturalis*.

By seeking to advocate a radical destruction of the legal order, Benjamin aimed to overcome the fundamental doctrine that upheld natural law no less than positive law, namely, that the means justify the end. Both legal traditions remained locked in an antinomic relation in that for the one just ends were to be attained by justified means, whereas for the other justified means were to be used for just ends – a vicious circle Benjamin sought to break by positing his paradoxical notion of noninstrumental pure means, which were neither lawmaking nor law-preserving. "All violence as a means," Benjamin maintained, "is either lawmaking or law-preserving. If it lays claim to neither of these predicates, it forfeits all validity. It follows, however, that all violence as a means, even in the most favorable case, is implicated in the problematic nature of law itself."[24] One could add, moreover, that it also followed from Benjamin's argument that pure, unalloyed means, insofar as they were no longer "contaminated" by the sphere of profane law, were neither lawmaking nor law-preserving.

The consequences of Benjamin's ingenious formulation of what I will call his "politics of noninstrumental means" are far-reaching. Located neither in the party politics of the compromise nor in the Weimar parliament (which, afflicted by a form of amnesia, no longer recalled its roots in the revolutionary violence of 1918), these means were to be found, first, in the realm of private persons who, following the "culture of the heart," engaged in unalloyed, uncontaminated speech or nonviolent conference (*Unterredung*), and, second – in rare instances – in the public realm, among diplomats who, through nonviolent agreement, aimed to overcome conflicts peacefully, thus fulfilling "a delicate task that ... is beyond all legal systems, and therefore beyond violence."[25] Crucially, the same abolition of lawmaking and law-preserving violence distinguished the proletarian revolutionary strike in that its anarchistic force targeted the repeal of law and, in the final analysis, the annihilation of all state power, or *Staatsgewalt*. Such, furthermore, was the logic of pure means that "the violence of an action can be assessed no more from its effects than from its ends, but only from the laws of its means,"[26] so that even if it were to produce bloody or catastrophic effects, the proletarian strike remained at core pure. No longer bound to the thetic force of the legal order, revolutionary violence found its very condition of possibility in divine justice, as it gestured towards the coming of a new historic era, on the other side of all mythic violence.

If the first paradox Benjamin sought to think was that of noninstrumental means, the second paradox related to the fact that he tried to retain an unalloyed technique of discussion while simultaneously advocating revolutionary force. Put differently, Benjamin seemingly retained the legacy of liberalism in *Unterredung* while also opting for the violence of an antiliberal proletarian strike. To do so, he needed to modify Sorel's revolutionary model and reject Schmitt's variant of antiliberalism. Thus, Benjamin did not adopt Bergson's theory of *élan vital*, which centrally informed Sorel's revolutionary spontaneism, nor did he take over the latter's concept of myth as the condition of class identity.[27] The critique of Kurt Hiller's activism at the end of the violence essay exemplarily targeted all manifestations of biologism and vitalism, which were to be dispelled by divine justice – a justice, as Derrida has maintained, that took on a decidedly Judaic form. Furthermore, Benjamin needed to divest the proletarian strike of its bellicose roots in war and military strategy that so clearly still underpinned Sorel's *Réflexions sur la violence*, indebted as it was to Proudhon's "radical anarcho-syndicalism." Just as Proudhon's monumental *La guerre et la paix* conceived the workers' uprising on the model of the "Napoleonic battle," celebrated for its total annihilation of the enemy,[28] so Sorel compared the strike to military warfare, commending the total elimination of the class adversary.

At the same time that Benjamin implicitly took issue with Sorel, he also diverged from Schmitt's counterrevolutionary political stance, which would be expressed most clearly in his later *The Concept of the Political* (1927). By arguing that the total, sovereign state found its condition of possibility in the antithesis of friend and enemy,[29] Schmitt first of all established as the common enemy liberalism, whose theory of economic competition and of debating adversaries radically de-politicized and dissipated this fundamental, belligerent duality.[30] But he also took on French syndicalism, which after 1906 and 1907 – in the figures of Sorel, Berth, Duguit, and others – proclaimed that the strike provided the economic means par excellence for incurring the death of the state and spelling the end of its sovereignty. Thus, if Benjamin, despite his admiration for Schmitt, managed to keep the jurist's protofascist program at bay, it was only because he did not share his political anthropology, which glorified a primordially belligerent human nature. Warfare for Schmitt was more than just the strategic brandishing of violent implements. It was eminently an existential mode, a mode of being, as well as the "revelation" (*Offenbarung*) of the originary binary opposition between friend and *hostis*, which founded the political.

It is no coincidence that, in defining the political, Schmitt relied upon the military theorist von Clausewitz, whose unfinished *On War*, published in 1832, drew on the terminology of means and ends to advance a quasi-Kantian critique of war. Defining war as a "duel (*Zweikampf*) on a larger scale," Clausewitz argued that if the "maximum use of physical force" constituted the means of war, and war in turn aimed at the total destruction of the enemy, then war itself could never amount to "a complete, untrammeled, absolute manifestation of power." Never to be considered in isolation, war instead remained a "political instrument" and thus eminently "a continuation of political activity by other means."[31] Going against the interpretive tradition in Clausewitz scholarship, Schmitt emphasized not the instrumentality of warfare, but its role as the extreme instance of the decision (*Entscheidung*) about who counts as a friend, who as a public enemy.

> The military battle itself is not the "continuation of politics by other means" as the famous term of Clausewitz is generally incorrectly cited .... War, for Clausewitz, is not merely one of many instruments, but the *ultima ratio* of the friend–enemy grouping .... As the most extreme political *means* it discloses the possibility which underlies every political idea, namely the distinction of friend and enemy.[32]

Clearly, counter to Schmitt's decisionism, Benjamin's "Critique of Violence" opposed founding the political in belligerent violence, for to do so would risk installing violence as an absolute end in itself. All the same, a number of lingering questions remain. One must ask what the critical, even *dia-critical*, force of the "pure" violence Benjamin advocated might be. Did it truly succeed in disengaging pure means from (political) ends and thus accomplish his ambitious, indeed, utopian, program of rupturing the vicious cycle of violence? Didn't the essay rather reintroduce a theological foundationalism, that is, a decisive, authoritative ground, which was to sustain secular forms of violence?

Benjamin's ill-fated "politics of pure means" remained indebted to the Blochian Judeo-Marxist messianism, expressed in his "Theologico-Political Fragment," which defined the Kingdom of God not as the goal (*telos*) but the end (*finis*) of history.[33] Seeking to think through the paradoxical politics not of a legal but a *legitimate* mode of violence, he speculated that pure violence escaped being trapped in the circularity of means and ends. Needless to say, in the course of doing so his essay fell short of providing an incisive differentiation between just and unjust uses of violence, and therefore, in the final analysis, of offering a credible critique of violence.[34]

How important this thought pattern was to remain in his later work is evident from the fact that the early politics of pure means re-emerged in the 1930s, notably in his celebrated "The Work of Art in the Age of Mechanical Reproduction," a text that, I would suggest, can also be read as an extended reflection on the relations between means, the mediality of the (film) medium, and political ends.[35] In this Marxist attempt to reappropriate the means of (re)production, Benjamin hoped to separate the pure, unalloyed use of technological means, that is, film as revolutionary medium, from its exploitation in fascist propaganda. War itself, in the final analysis, testified to the abuse of technological means, enacting the slave rebellion of technology. Much as in "Critique of Violence," the essay's afterword again tried to demarcate left- from right-wing politics. The extent to which this project proved fated, even duplicitous, is evident in Benjamin's oft-cited and chiastic phrase that in place of the aestheticization of politics is to come the politicization of aesthetics. Read against "Critique of Violence," this statement now can be interpreted not only as a call for the politicization of a *pure* film medium but also as an injunction to revolutionize pure violence.

Arendt's Theory of Instrumental Violence

Clausewitz's dictum about means and ends to no small degree also served as a foil against which Hannah Arendt formulated her theory of violence as mere instrumentality and power as an end in itself. When her polemical pamphlet *On Violence* first appeared in 1969, it sought to characterize a post-Holocaust and postnuclear world in which all differences between violence and power had been erased. The destructive potential of the century belied the ostensibly marginal position to which the phenomenon of violence had been relegated in nineteenth-century social and political theory. Thus, she argued:

> Whether it is Clausewitz calling war "the continuation of politics by other means," or Engels defining violence as the accelerator of economic development, the emphasis is on political or economic continuity, on the continuity of a process that remains determined by what preceded violent action.... Today all these old verities about the relation between war and politics or about violence and power have become inapplicable.[36]

Coming at the height of the Cold War, the nuclear arms race, the violence of decolonization, and the student revolts of the 1960s, Arendt's treatise diagnosed what she regarded to be a global, all-pervasive state of violence. Against the backdrop of these spectacular scenes of violence, it seemed as if Clausewitz's and Engels's "nineteenth-century formulas" or "old verities" had been inverted to the point where peace itself now appeared to be the continuation of war by other means.[37] The nuclear arms race in particular confirmed the arbitrariness and "all-pervading unpredictability" inherent in all violence.[38] As the disturbing sign of an aberrant instrumentality gone awry, it announced the end of *all conventional, strategic* warfare, thus rendering the old dictum of war as the *ultima ratio* obsolete. The relapse into a state of pure, absolute war or nature seemed imminent, for "where violence is no longer backed and restrained by power, the well-known reversal in reckoning with means and ends has taken place. The means, the means of destruction, now determine the end – with the consequence that the end will be the destruction of all power."[39]

Crucially, Arendt's diagnosis did not merely call for the undoing of this reversal. Instead, the postwar malaise provided her an occasion to analyze the liberal-democratic conception of power. Contemporary political thought seemed to be fraught by a confusion of power with violence, of *potestas* with *violentia*, she contended, because it equated power with coercion, thus implicitly adhering to Clausewitz's definition of war as "an act of violence to compel the opponent to do as we wish."[40] Arendt's argument was, above all, with social scientists, particularly Max Weber, who regarded "the body politic and its laws and institutions" as "merely coercive superstructures, secondary manifestations of some underlying forces." At issue was his influential definition of the state in *Politics as a Vocation* as "the rule of men over men based on the means of legitimate, that is allegedly legitimate, violence," which according to Arendt limited the concept of power to "the power of man over man."[41] As such, Weber's theory of power was a relic of the age of absolutism, as it "accompanied the rise of the sovereign European nation-state."[42]

Seeking to overcome these terminological inadequacies, Arendt radically separated power from violence, arguing that they stood to one another in a nondialectical, asymmetrical relationship.[43] Thus she adopted the (Aristotelian/Kantian) means–ends model to define violence (always in need of implements) as instrumental:[44] "Phenomenologically, it is close to strength, since the implements of violence, like all other tools, are designed and used for the purpose of multiplying natural strength until, in the last stage of their development, they can substitute for it."[45] To the extent, further, that violence was "effective in reaching the end that must justify it,"[46] it was fundamentally rational in nature – a statement directed against psychological and anthropological theories of violence, particularly those advanced by Konrad Lorenz, which qualified violence as natural, irrational aggression. By contrast, power was the very condition of possibility of all political action, "the very condition enabling a group of people to think and act in terms of the means–ends category."[47] Invoking, in turn, Kant's *Perpetual Peace*,[48] which qualified eternal peace as an end in itself, Arendt defined power as an absolute or pure *Ziel* (end):

> The end of war – end taken in its twofold meaning – is peace or victory; but to the question And what is the end of peace? there is no answer. Peace is an absolute, even though in recorded history periods of warfare have nearly always outlasted periods of peace. Power is in the same category; it is, as they say, "an end in itself."[49]

Arendt's revision of the means–ends model, evident in her account of violence, is in fact part and parcel of her theory of communicative action. Thus, in her 1963 study *On Revolution* she wrote that "violence itself is incapable of speech," for "where violence rules absolutely, as for instance in the concentration camps of totalitarian regimes, not only the laws ... but everything and everybody must fall silent."[50] Anchored in Aristotle's double definition of man as a "political animal" and a "being endowed with speech," the assertion is indicative of Arendt's conviction that violence was to be located outside the political no less than outside political speech. In line with her *Human Condition* (1958), which sought to replace Gehlen's anthropology of purposive action with an anthropology of linguistic action,[51] Arendt – as Habermas put it in his 1976 Arendt essay – dissociated power from the teleological model, to project the "consensus-building force of communication"[52] as a "coercion-free force" or end in itself. Language was to be used in an illocutionary way, "i.e., to establish intersubjective relationships free from violence."[53] At the same time, however, as Habermas emphasized, Arendt narrowed "the political to the practical" on the basis of an outmoded Aristotelian notion of praxis, thus reducing politics to a pristine, violence-free realm. "For this," Habermas continued, "Arendt pays the price of screening all *strategic elements* out of politics as '*violence*,' severing politics from its ties to the economic and social environment in which it is embedded via the administrative system, and being incapable of coming to grips with appearances of *structural violence*,"[54] for "structural violence is not manifest as violence; instead [as ideology] it blocks in an unnoticed fashion those communications in which are shaped and propagated the convictions effective for legitimation." Not only did her political theory not recognize the presence of structural violence in the political arena, but since strategic action, which, like the warfare of the ancient Greeks, was located outside the walls of the *polis*, must appear as a manifestation of violence, one could argue that within Arendt's framework all *strategic violence* amounted to nothing more than a tautology.[55]

Arendt's blindness to structural violence, of the sort Oskar Negt found thematized in Benjamin's critique of *Rechtsgewalt*, as well as her assertion that violence occurred "outside the political realm,"[56] have as their flip side a rejection of all forms of "counterviolence" (*Gegengewalt*), which are seen as the glorification of violence, its anti- or even nonpolitical justification. At stake in Arendt's analysis were not only Sorel's and Pareto's politics of violence but also, as mentioned earlier, the representatives of the New Left, that is, Sartre, Fanon, and the leaders of the student movement, whose use of force found its philosophical justification in Marcuse's *Critique of Pure Tolerance*.[57] As the heirs to a left-wing revolutionary tradition, these insurrections, Arendt maintained, found their dubious theoretical foundation in a Hegelian and Marxist "trust in the dialectical 'power of negation'"[58] and an accompanying, erroneous concept of history, the offshoot of nineteenth-century conceptions of progress. As she added:

> If we look on history in terms of a continuous chronological process, whose progress moreover, is inevitable, violence in the shape of war and revolution

may appear to constitute the only possible interruption. If this were true, if only the practice of violence would make it possible to interrupt automatic processes in the realm of human affairs, the preachers of violence would have won an important point.... It is the function, however, of all action, as distinguished from mere behavior, to interrupt what otherwise would have proceeded automatically and therefore predictably.[59]

The student revolts amounted simply to de-politicized "behavior," not to be confounded with true political "action," through which humans distinguished themselves from animals. At issue in these lines was nothing less than the politics of mimesis or the return of an aberrant, natural mimicry. Inasmuch as the German student leaders aimed to unmask the hypocritical practice of state violence, Arendt found them to be the heirs of Robespierre's despotic "war on hypocrisy," which led to the Reign of Terror as the revolution began to devour its own children.[60]

In Arendt's reading of Fanon's *Wretched of the Earth*, the limitations of her liberal model of instrumental violence become apparent. Tellingly, in taking position against the antiliberal program of the New Left and anticolonial violence, her political tract did not incorporate a moment of reflection of the sort that seemed to characterize Sartre's contemporaneous reception of Fanon.[61] True, Sartre's model equally remained caught in a problematic dialectic, when he maintained that the European (colonial) "masters" were to learn from the violence thrown back to them by their former slaves. Nonetheless, Sartre's endorsement of Fanon's liberating "mad fury" can be read differently, that is, as an awareness that the violence of decolonization spelled an end to Western humanism's monopoly of violence.

Foucault's Radical Instrumentality

In conclusion, let me briefly turn to Foucault, whose historicizing analysis of force relations not only announces the end of all transcendental critiques of power but also, by implication, of a (Benjaminian) "critique of violence." His notion of a proliferation of technologies (*technē*), set forth in *The History of Sexuality*, I would argue, served radically to destroy an old, humanist understanding of instrumentality, at the cost, however, of seemingly conflating war and politics. Indeed, not only has Arendt's conception of instrumental violence, insofar as it remained tethered to action theory, been taken to task by Habermas, who queried it from the perspective of systems theory; it has also been criticized by Foucault, whose theory of force relations likewise sought to provide a corrective to Arendt's model, already apparent when he addressed epistemic and discursive manifestations of violence.[62] Whereas Arendt presented legitimacy rather than justification as the diacritical moment in her definition of power and dissociated *communicative* power from purposive instrumentality, or means and ends, Foucault aimed to explode the means–ends relation altogether. Thus, his antihumanistic rejection of enabling, consensual power ended up presenting both war and politics as radicalized instances of instrumentality. In the first volume of his history of sexuality, Foucault, like Benjamin, rejected the conventional Western juridico-political model, which located legitimate power in the state apparatus. Unmasking such power as the problematic legacy of monarchical notions of sovereignty, he instead turned to those power mechanisms and operations that surpassed *Staatsgewalt*, thus demonstrating the inability of the judicial mode to codify power absolutely. Discarding all monolithic codifications of power, whether institutional power, or, in Weber's version, a legalized mode of subjugation and system of domination, Foucault instead thematized what he called a multiplicity of force relations.

Not surprisingly, in the course of his analysis Foucault likewise glossed Clausewitz's famous statement on war, when in *The History of Sexuality*, he posed the following question:

> Should we turn the expression around, then, and say that politics is war pursued by other means? If we still wish to maintain a separation between war and politics, perhaps we should postulate rather that this multiplicity of force relations can be coded – in part but never totally – either in the form of "war," or in the form of "politics"; this would imply two different strategies (but the one always liable to switch into the other) for integrating these unbalanced, heterogeneous, unstable, and tense force relations.[63]

That is to say, the relation between war and politics was no longer one of possible reversal or ascendancy, as Arendt still held, but war and politics now appeared as the very encodings of force relations, strategies, or micro powers.

Pace Arendt, Foucault here appeared to push politics to the point where it became mere strategy, or the "strategic codification of these points of resistance."[64] War, violence, and politics were different noninclusive encodings, ways of coding points of resistance in the strategic field of power relations, which could "circulate without changing their form from one strategy to another, opposing strategy."[65] While such strategies remained rational technologies, they were divorced from a liberal, humanistic subject, which used certain means to achieve determinate ends. Dismissing the notion of a generative principle, implicit in Clausewitz's emphasis on war as the continuation of politics, Foucault instead assumed a relativistic, nominalistic perspective by reducing power to "the name one attributes to a complex strategical situation in a particular society." Adopting a radically historicist point of view, he refused to take the inherently Kantian step from the analysis of historical force fields of power to a regulatory principle, a "general analytics of every possible power relation." Ultimately, Foucault's *History of Sexuality* thus replaced a theory, or critique, of power with a radically *historical* "analytics of power."[66]

Despite the limits that mark the Foucauldian model when it comes to discriminating politics from warfare or strategic violence, it might be valuable to retain his insight that power ought not be seen as a regulatory principle and that violence, too, in its many, even intractable manifestations, ought to be analyzed locally. Indeed, along the same lines, Clifford Geertz recently has argued against the pervasive use of a globalizing or universalizing definition of nationalistic violence, at the expense of the particularity or specificity of ethnic violence. As a typical occidental concept – indicative of how epistemic violence eliminates ethnic and multicultural differences – the term remains the offshoot of nineteenth-century nationalism, dependent on the liberal nation-state, so that it is worthy of replacement by more anthropologically refined concepts such as "primordial loyalties." Without wanting to conflate conceptual differences in turn, it seems to me that his position corroborates what I conceive to be a lasting insight that can be gleaned from Benjamin's otherwise flawed "Critique of Violence": that even if the critique of violence must fall short of reaching its goal or end, one would do well to discard all monolithic analyses of violence. It is perhaps this insight, more than anything else, that Benjamin aspired to have communicated when he wrote to Scholem that he hoped to have said the essential about violence.

2

BETWEEN KANT AND NIETZSCHE
Foucault's Critique

When, in 1969, Hannah Arendt published her treatise *On Violence*, she might just as well have called it *On Power*. Writing during the upheavals of the 1960s, marked by riots, rebellions, insurrections, and revolutions, her principal aim seemed to be to restore the clear lines, borders of terminological delineation that threatened to be erased, violence masquerading as power, power as violence. At the roots of this terminological obfuscation lay an imprecise understanding of the concept of power, the history of an error that went back to Max Weber's *Politics as a Vocation*, which translated consensual power into the coercive domination of "men over men" – or humans over humans. For Arendt, all violence was intrinsically instrumental and strategic in nature; power, by contrast, was, much like Kant's eternal peace, an end in itself. Yet this end was not utopian or messianic, belonging to an altogether different, transcendent order, but defined a horizon of expectation, a guiding principle or norm for every future empowering mode of political action. Where power was generative – or "productive," to use Foucauldian nomenclature – violence was but destructive, for out of the barrel of a gun power could never arise, she emphatically maintained, quoting Mao against himself. The only politically acceptable limit case of violence were democratic revolutions – her grand exemplar being the American Revolution – which consisted of nation-founding acts of violence, animated by a revolutionary spirit that unfailingly espoused the ideals of "public freedom, public happiness, public spirit."[1] In addition to calling for a rigorous discrimination of force from power, Arendt's critical project meant to neutralize a second widespread misconception, namely, that violence was fundamentally *irrational* at core. Two intellectual factions were equally misguided in this regard: the so-called *polemologists* (at the forefront of whom was psychiatrist Konrad Lorenz), who in their concerted Darwinian return to the animal world denied violence's instrumental rationality; and political activists and philosophers, such as Sorel, Pareto, Fanon, and Sartre, who, in advocating the innately creative, plastic capacity of violence, revealed themselves to be the descendants of a Nietzschean or Bergsonian vitalism. Suspect glorifiers of violence, they plainly testified to the atrophy of modern man's political "faculty of action." For, as Arendt underscored: "Neither violence nor power is a natural phenomenon, that is, a manifestation of the life process; they belong to the political realm of human affairs whose essentially human quality is guaranteed by man's faculty of action, the ability to begin something new."[2]

Against the background of Arendt's normative paradigm, Foucault's work may easily appear to offer up incontrovertible proof that the erasure of normative distinctions between violence and power – or, what Habermas described as its "affirmative de-differentiation"[3] – has taken firm hold over poststructuralist political theory. In the period of genealogy (especially *Discipline and Punish* and *The History of Sexuality*), Foucault not only redefined power as struggle, perpetual war, force, or domination, but also as the arena of multiple force fields in which social agents interacted by means of strategic instrumentality. Underneath the veil or mask of sophisticated liberal ideas, such as contract theory or rights discourse, merely lay concealed the brute, even bloody, facts of history as relentless struggle and war. Insofar as power appeared to reside solely in a realm of strategic means and short-term ends, the horizon of peace as the ultimate end in itself had entirely been lost. We reside then wholly in an order of pure, immanent mediality – or so, at least, would seem to be the assessment of the outside onlooker who, wielding the perhaps somewhat outmoded optical tools of conventional analysis, surveys the Foucauldian conceptual field. The logical conclusion that hence might seem to issue from this state of affairs is that under Foucault's all too agile hands the critical edifice comes tumbling down, ushering in the end of critique. For not only did Foucault's historiography dissolve the premises of Kant's critical program but, with one and the same blunt stroke, he also swept aside all forms of ideology critique, thus bringing to a halt the long process of critical self-reflection endemic to the Enlightenment and political modernity.

Commentators and critics alike have pointed out that Foucault's thought moves from an almost exclusive concern with epistemology, or theories of knowledge, laid out in *The Order of Things* and *The Archeology of Knowledge*, to a broadly conceived account of power – a transition from the structuralist history of *epistēmēs* to social theory. Frankfurt School critics Jürgen Habermas and Axel Honneth in particular have seen in this switch from an archeology of the human sciences to a genealogy of social power Foucault's drifting away from the position of the intellectual historian to that of the social theorist. As a consequence, Foucault's later work – fairly or unfairly – has not infrequently been evaluated against the standards of social theory. Apart from being attacked for its impudent erasure of normative validity claims in the moral-practical realm, his work has been measured with the yardstick of action theory (Talcott Parsons) or thought to resemble functionalist systems theory (Niklas Luhmann).[4] In other words, Foucault becomes the historian, or even theorist, of violence not so much for such exacting tracts as *Discipline and Punish*, which chronicled the rise of the modern penitentiary, but, really, because his operative conception of power merely rehabilitated the already suspect parity between power and domination that Weber set up. To be sure, the capital shift Foucault introduced into this constellation led from "repressive" to "productive" dominating power – but dominating nonetheless.

At the nucleus of the long-standing disputes that second-generation Frankfurt

School critics have conducted over Foucault's philosophico-political legacy, there lie two clusters of charges that tend to surface with a certain regularity, one (located at the epistemic and methodological level) claiming logical inconsistency, or, worse, mere confusion, the other (targeting his politics) alleging political naivety, or, worse still, neoconservatism. Above all, Foucault is said to operate with a "catchall" concept of power (to quote from Nancy Fraser's influential appraisal), which is weak on epistemological and ethico-political grounds. "Foucault writes," observes Fraser, going against Arendt's and Habermas's less affirmative assessment of Weber,

> as though he were oblivious to the existence of the whole body of Weberian social theory with its careful distinctions between such notions as authority, force, violence, domination, and legitimation. Phenomena that are capable of being distinguished through such concepts are simply lumped together under his catchall concept of power. As a consequence, the potential for a broad range of normative nuances is surrendered, and the result is a certain normative one-dimensionality.[5]

To be sure, having turned from the archeology of the human sciences to the genealogy of power, Foucault made it his lifelong project to rescript power, seeing it no longer exclusively in function of statism – including the state's purported monopoly on violence – but redirecting his analytical gaze to the operations of capillary micropowers or situated power strategies. To maintain, then, that Foucault operates with a "catchall" category of power is to posit that he does not escape the globalizing tendencies of conventional power paradigms – a charge easily made on the basis of Foucault's oft-cited assertion from *The History of Sexuality* that "power is everywhere." Either his account of power is still transcendental, in which case it would (ironically) still have truck with Kant's project of uncovering the sempiternal laws of knowledge and moral action, power being the a priori form – if not "substance," as some Foucault critics might add – that underlies all historical permutations and the plurality of history's "evenementality." Or, his account does not unequivocally avoid the grandiose claims to global interpretive hegemony that he himself ascribed to Marxism and psychoanalysis, which he reproved for endorsing the so-called repressive, or Reichean, hypothesis.

Taking aim at these persistent reproaches, in their measured study *Michel Foucault: Beyond Structuralism and Hermeneutics* Rabinow and Dreyfus counter that his understanding of power was hardly meant to "apply as a generalization to all of history."[6] But their firm claim that his is an analytics, not a theory of power, may not necessarily suffice to allay the allegations proffered by less sympathetic Frankfurt School critics. Initially, Rabinow and Dreyfus's insistence on such a restrictive clause seems to provide an easy escape route for Foucault – by profession a historian – inasmuch as the discipline of history characteristically is thought to be descriptive rather than prescriptive. Having shed the illusions of Enlightenment history, with its emphasis on universal historical laws and teleologies, the discipline truly came into its own with the arrival of post-Hegelian historicism. Nonetheless, to put one's stakes on the divide between description and prescription might mean to open Foucault up to the suspicion (however undeserved) that he still harbored Ranke's oft-quoted naive historicist illusion following which the historian simply reproduces history's pure factuality, *wie es eigentlich gewesen* – a tendency that, surely, must be resisted. Though right about the antiprescriptive intentions that attended Foucault's radical reconfiguration of historiography, such a critical counterstrategy may, in the end, fail to take the sting out of the cutting charges that critics like Habermas have heaped on Foucault's entire project, angled at the historian's "happy positivism," presentism, empiricism, and crypto-normativity. Since Habermas's assessment of Foucault has acquired considerable resonance in the critical arena – especially the charge that he was the harbinger of an irrationalist, dark counter-Enlightenment tradition – it seems worthwhile briefly to review his main objections and tenets.

Within the wide-spanning account of modern philosophy that Habermas drew in *The Philosophical Discourse of Modernity*, Foucault's project appeared as but one alternative in a growing repertoire of like-minded philosophical solutions that exacerbated, rather than redressed, the impoverished life-world increasingly defining cultural modernity. Habermas unmistakably followed Weber when he understood the condition of disenchanted modernity in terms of the vicissitudes of reason. Opening his lectures with a discussion of the rationalization that governed the administered world, he went on to map modernity's predicament against the background of Kantian and Hegelian philosophy. The division among the critical faculties, exemplified by Kant's three *Critiques*, was reflected in the creation of autonomous spheres of validity, comprising science, morality, and art, as well as in the rise to prominence of insular expert cultures. Having sundered itself from tradition and the firm grounding provided by metaphysics and theology, modernity now faced the quintessential problem of how it was to "*create its normativity out of itself.*"[7] In his philosophy of unification, Hegel first demonstrated that the rift, lost harmony, or diremption of substantive reason[8] needed to be overcome through a radically revised understanding of reason, which meant that the dialectical potential dwelling in rationality needed to be set free, or released. Following the ruin of normative ground that attended the demise of theology and metaphysics, Hegel crafted a reconciliatory philosophy, initiating the dialectic of Enlightenment as the dialectic of reason, but faltering as he eventually opted for a philosophy of the absolute. Seeking to amend the ills of Hegelian and post-Hegelian philosophies of the subject, no less than Marx's equally fated labor paradigm, Habermas aimed to retrieve a communicative rationality whose standards were radically distinct from the socio-economic rationalization that had encroached upon values and norms and whose tenets were no longer purely to be subsumed under rational instrumentalization or purposive activity.[9] Against Adorno and Horkheimer's exclusive concern with an instrumental reason that fettered inner and outer nature, Habermas upheld communicative reason, whose emancipatory potential and achievements rested upon the "universalistic foundations of law and morality" and were incorporated "into

the institutions of constitutional government, into the forms of democratic will formation, and into individualistic patterns of identity formation."[10]

Unmistakably ideology-critical in nature, Habermas's lectures sought to discriminate a negative aesthetic, avant-garde modernism from true political modernity, with
an eye on soldering the "internal relationship between modernity and rationality."[11]
The extent to which the two poles were disaffiliated was evident, he asserted, in the
sociological postmodernism of Arnold Gehlen, which subscribed to a functionalist
conception of a self-propelled, automatized modernity, no less than in the cultural
postmodernism of the so-called Young Conservatives, bearing the mark of Nietzschean
aestheticism. At the root of the problem lay a cultural modernity that had gone awry,
having subjected its political, emancipatory Enlightenment potential, lodged in the
self-reflective capacity of reason, to a far-going process of aestheticization, triggered
by Nietzsche. Where Hegel and the Young and Right Hegelians tried hard to secure a
"renewed revision of the concept of reason," proposing ways of overcoming modernity's diremption, Nietzsche was the first to abandon the project of an *immanent*
critique of reason altogether. Hailing the irrational, the "other of reason," and the
violence of myth, he proclaimed that "knowledge" — and, by implication, reason —
"*must* turn its sting against itself."[12] Reducing all norms indiscriminately to normalized, cultural sedimentations of force, Nietzsche's theory of power contended that
"behind apparently universal normative claims [lay] hidden the subjective power
claims of value appraisals."[13] To aestheticize politics in effect meant to relinquish the
discriminatory capacity of reason and to enthrone the faculty of taste as the supreme
critical instance. In Nietzsche's "genealogical critique," Habermas observed, the negative force of philosophy was replaced with affirmation, and consensual rational norms
with aesthetic acts of self-positing, while history was reduced to the endless power
play among active and reactive forces.

Also on methodological grounds, Nietzsche's philosophy proved flawed and, in
fact, self-refuting, for, ensnared in a dogged paradox, it proceeded via an "unmasking
critique of reason that sets itself outside the horizon of reason."[14] In effect, it is this
very contradiction of how a critique of reason is still tenable if reason itself has been
totally disabled that Habermas again and again would isolate in post-Nietzschean
thought (hard-hitting criticism, which, as we shall see, Foucault summarily dismissed
as the "blackmail of the Enlightenment"). Inasmuch as they were the heirs of the "dark"
philosopher, poststructuralists not only adopted an antihumanistic, decentered subjectivity but they also embraced the "other" of reason (as Foucault himself had done in
Madness and Civilization), thus failing to espouse the positive, emancipatory potential,
and universalizing effects of reason, realized in democratic laws or human rights.
Equally heedlessly, they construed a totalizing, self-enclosed critique of reason, which,
in reducing all rationality to instrumental reason, exerting violent force over inner
and outer nature, got them entrapped in a *petitio principii*: with the assault on reason
the foundational premises of their own critique were irrevocably eliminated.

Since Habermas's diagnosis of the cloaked yet pernicious irrationalist counter-

Enlightenment streak in poststructuralism has tended to obscure his less spectacular criticisms directed at its methodological and epistemo-critical shortcomings, his commentary deserves further elucidation. For in charging that Foucault, together with like-minded post-Nietzschean poststructuralists, exited the legacy of the Enlightenment and left the project of political modernity unrealized, Habermas also accused him of setting an end to the Enlightenment tradition of ideology critique. For all its flaws, Marxist ideology critique at least tried to unmask "an inadmissible *mixture of power and validity*" in supposedly value-free, neutral theories, through which it unmistakably participated in the project of self-enlightenment. Through this mode of immanent critique, Habermas continued, "enlightenment becomes reflective for the first time; it is performed with respect to its own products—theories."[15] Yet this first level of reflection deplorably was followed by the excesses of hyperreflection, whose telltale document was Adorno and Horkheimer's *Dialectic of Enlightenment*. "The drama of enlightenment," Habermas maintained, "first arrives at its climax when ideology critique *itself* comes under suspicion of not producing (any more) truths – and the enlightenment attains second-order reflectiveness."[16] Adopting a quasi-Hegelian stance, Habermas defined the aberrations or false doubles of ideology critique as reflections to the second degree, that is, solipsistic, Romantic arabesques, which emulated the movements of Hegel's unhappy consciousness. On this second level of reflection, doubt poisoned reason, which is what Adorno and Horkheimer did when they created a free-floating critique that drifted loose from the foundations in which it was supposed to be moored. The result was the "self-destruction of the critical capacity," manifested in Adorno and Horkheimer's penchant for "performative contradiction inherent in totalized critique."[17] In the end Foucault, too, was saddled with a "genealogical historiography" operating "no longer as critique, but as a tactic and a tool for waging a battle against a normatively unassailable formation of power."[18] Claiming that poststructuralism's antihumanism, wedded to a decentered subject, merely reversed subject philosophy, Habermas again and again accused its proponents of adhering to a romanticized philosophy of reflexivity, which shot far beyond the beneficial dose of self-reflection that enabled the process of rational self-enlightenment. Leaving behind the precinct of ideology critique, they either engaged in "aestheticism" (Nietzsche), "ad hoc determinate negation" (Adorno and Horkheimer), "performative contradiction" (Adorno), or mere warfare (Foucault's genealogy). Relying on the standards of his normative, critical theory, Habermas in particular took on Foucault's assertion that genealogy would result in a "felicitous positivism," now chiding him for his empiricism, then for his hidden transcendentalizing impetus, but always with an eye on what he considered to be Foucault's ill-conceived, anarchistic revolt against normative, normalizing validity claims.[19] But in attacking the vicious circle that imbued Foucault's conflation of power/force, Habermas did more than simply accuse him of logically flawed arguments. Condemning his "totalizing critique of reason," he presented the historian with a double charge: first, that in denying reason's emancipatory potential, he turned reason's "sting against itself," and, second, that in so doing he produced the ancillary effect of an ideology critique that had "turned against itself." As such, Foucault merely drew the fatal consequences of "the critique of ideology's totalizing self-overcoming" that Nietzsche had inaugurated[20] – an assessment certainly corroborated by Foucault's repeated rejection of the representational category of ideology.

If this epistemologically oriented critique was already devastating, then no less so were the appraisals of the political platform that critical theorists (in the wake, often, of Habermas's Frankfurt lectures) have extracted from the voluminous, hardly unified, body of Foucault's writings. In particular, such critical evaluations have concentrated on revealing the contradictions between his avowed allegiance to emancipatory politics – including sexual politics – and the suspect political presuppositions that, for the most part, remain hidden, unspoken, undertheorized. Either Foucault's historiography and account of power are taken on for rejecting an explicit normative value system that scaffolds and decisively directs ethico-political action, or it is said to adhere covertly to a cryptonormative edifice that remains unaccounted for. By reducing power to strategic action, by rejecting contract theory, and by neglecting the politics of democratic consent, Foucault is said to fall back behind the insights of contractarianism, serving up the unpalatable spectacle of the struggle of "all against all" that Hobbes described in his *Leviathan*. Consider, for instance, Axel Honneth's *Critique of Power*, which is careful to observe that Foucault's economy of power must be situated within the context of action theory. In this respect, Foucault's mature philosophy fundamentally differed from Nietzsche's, whose "will to power" suffered from mere naturalism and vitalism. However, in the absence of intersubjective consent or agreement, social agents were locked in an asymmetric power battle, in which momentary stabilization of one pole's victory could only be accomplished through coerced inculcation – hardly peaceful agreement or compromise. Failing such an adherence to a politics of consent, Foucault's account of power became politically naive, if not seditious and suspect, for, taken to its logical conclusion, it unquestionably led to a condoning of the worst. Thus, where some American political theorists have reproached Foucault for embracing an "infantile leftism" or anarchism,[21] critical theorists see hiding under his left-leaning radical agenda the premises of a conservative, authoritarian antiliberalism, which tacitly sanction a Hobbesian bloody war of all against all, a Schmittean decisionism, or a Nietzschean eulogy of eternal war. By perpetuating the submerged Nietzschean irrationalism with which Lukács's *The Destruction of Reason* impugned the conservative German philosophical tradition, the historian's project was said to pare back the undeniable emancipatory advancements of the Enlightenment. Clearly, when Habermas went so far as to assert that in Foucault's later work strategic struggle took the guise of a fierce adversarial battle between opponents, then the specter of Carl Schmitt is looking on from the wings. For it was Schmitt who reduced the political to the ever-present possibility of an existential, mortal combat between foes, a model Ernst Jünger fantasized about in his wartime diaries and Klaus Theweleit uncovered as the imaginary of the *Freikorps*. Phrased succinctly, rather than pointing to the Kantian humanistic ideal of perpetual peace, Foucault's thought is held to gesture towards perpetual war.

In one form or another, the sundry charges I have summarized thus far have circulated frequently in the critical field, adding considerably to the virtual stalemate between opposing ideological factions. Focus has been principally on what is commonly regarded to be the second phase of Foucault's work, starting from *Discipline and Punish* onward, when he left behind a more narrowly defined interpretive model, the archeology of disciplinary knowledge, for a more politically oriented account, or analytics, of power. Less discussed, until quite recently, because of their purported status as late anomalies in his corpus, the last completed volumes of his projected history of sexuality, *The Use of Pleasure* and *The Care of the Self*, only seem further to have compounded an already murky political picture. Together with the interviews "On the Genealogy of Ethics" and "Politics and Ethics," to some commentators they prove beyond doubt that Foucault deplorably lapsed into a self-contained individualism that, if nothing else, curiously jarred with the critique of humanism set forth in such early works as *The Order of Things*, especially the chapter "Man and His Doubles." Worse still, in endorsing what he termed – following the nineteenth-century German historian and friend of Nietzsche, Jacob Burckhardt – the "aesthetics of existence," Foucault appeared to act out the baneful symptoms of a Nietzschean aestheticism, diagnosed by Habermas. The earlier concern that Foucault merely provided a functionalist theory of power now seems to have receded into the background to make way for an indictment of his self-enclosed aestheticism, as if the French historian retroactively simply lived out the labels that critics earlier had affixed to him.

The more these critical, negative evaluative coins have been passed around, the more the debates themselves have become insolvent, leaving no room for dissenting views. Is it still possible, in the wake of either the prolific affirmative applications Foucault's thought has found in a wide range of areas or else the mostly negative appraisals dispensed by certain Frankfurt School members, to say anything fundamentally new about Foucault's historicist paradigm? The answer, I believe, must be positive. For one, we must heed the *caveat* pronounced by two of Foucault's editors, Mauro Bertani and Alessandro Fontana, that until all of Foucault's writings – especially the lecture courses delivered at the Collège de France – are published, our understanding of his theory of power will necessarily remain fragmentary. Thus, as I intend to show in the present and subsequent chapters, the recent publication of his 1976 lecture course on war, *"Il faut défendre la société"* (*"Society Must Be Defended"*), allows us to shed additional light on what Foucault labeled the Nietzschean hypothesis, which informed most of his thought. But it also might be timely to delve more deeply into the other philosophical heritage that defined his critical apparatus, over and beyond the overpowering shadow cast by Nietzsche: that of Kant. Too little treated (with a few notable exceptions[22]), Foucault's various reflections on the subject of Kant's critique and the Enlightenment may demonstrate that the historian, rather than determined to end the lasting legacy of Kantian critique, redefined or relocated its borders (*Grenzen*).

Rather than seeking to halt the heritage of the Enlightenment, he too, much like Habermas, in fact wondered whether the project of the *Aufklärung*, defined by Kant as reaching autonomy and maturity (*Mündigkeit*), had truly been fulfilled, brought to completion in our present. Nor did he hesitate to align his research with that of the Frankfurt School, inserting his critique of power in the trajectory started by Weber's critique of rationalization and instrumental reason, all the while aware of deeper-lying differences. Taking off from Weber, he sought to invent "another way of investigating the links between rationalization and power," as he put it in "The Subject and Power."[23] In light of these realities, it is hard to explain the curious fact that in a short 1984 essay, conceived on the occasion of Foucault's untimely death, Habermas expressed genuine surprise at the French historian's avowal that his own thought merely stood in the trail of Kant, whose original project of supplying a "historical ontology of the present" was carried on by Hegel, Nietzsche, Weber, and the Frankfurt School.[24] Must not the critical theorist's astonishment at these elective affinities be cause for wonder, given that in his own Foucault lectures Habermas ideologically knotted the French historian's "dark" *oeuvre* to Adorno and Horkheimer's somber assessment of the Enlightenment? As the ensuing analysis will argue, Foucault's self-professed affinities to the German philosophical tradition, above all the Frankfurt School, are less than astonishing in view of a series of Kant lectures he composed between 1978 and 1983, dedicated explicitly to the status of philosophical critique and the undiminished relevance of the Enlightenment.

On the basis of a reading of these lesser-discussed Foucault texts, the present and following chapters will advance two alternative angles of vision on what only deceptively seems well-traversed terrain. First, I will maintain that we will need to ask, quite simply, what Foucault means when he deploys the term "critique," as he repeatedly does, both in its Nietzschean and Kantian sense. Second, I will suggest that most commentaries of his work often give preference to the constellation *pouvoir/savoir* or else look for the drawbacks that might result from Foucault's stretching of the category "power." Less has been said, it seems to me, about the constellation *pouvoir/guerre* (power/war),[25] though there is no doubt that Foucault paid more than casual attention to struggle, war, and battle, which according to him constituted defining "grids of intelligibility" for modernity. This is why in the 1976 "war" lecture course, delivered at the Collège de France, he admitted that all of his work, until that year, was written under the rubric of *war-repression*, or what he designated as the Nietzschean/Clausewitzian matrix. Somewhat hastily, perhaps, this frank acknowledgment was accompanied by the halfhearted vow that now it was of the essence to leave that matrix behind.

To sum up, my analysis will propose the following theses:

1 *Critique* On the face of it, one can chart a progress in Foucault's intellectual trajectory, as he moved from a pronounced preoccupation with a Nietzschean genealogical critique, expressed in the quintessential 1971 "Nietzsche, Genealogy,

History," to aligning himself with Kantian critique. Though he would never relinquish his allegiance to Nietzsche, in shifting to a more explicit concern with Kant and the Frankfurt School, he adopted a "historical ontology of the present," which investigated the changing historical constellations between power/knowledge, truth, and the subject. While never fully renouncing his earlier *The Order of Things*, which had drawn the progressive demise of (Kantian) *transcendentals* (*transcendentaux*) in post-Kantian modernity, the later Foucault adopted a radically *historicized* Kantianism, refracting critique through historical reflection. Pointing to a historico-philosophical attitude, or *ēthos*, which he regarded to be emblematic of the Enlightenment and modern period, Foucault advocated a drastic reconceptualization of modernity, whose plight could no longer be qualified exclusively in terms of the vicissitudes of reason, at least as codified by Habermas. While Foucault's thought, on the whole, remained engaged with the "history of reason," he rejected its universalist variant, studying instead its *contingent history* through the multiple techniques, technologies, or types of rationality whose ascendancy to power demanded to be analyzed in all their overwhelming, messy detail. Sizing up the foundational differences between the two approaches, he characterized himself as "far more historicist and Nietzschean" than Habermas, for whom it was a matter of making a "transcendental mode of thought spring forth against any historicism."[26]

2 *Force* Having supplied an archeology/genealogy of institutional violence in *Madness and Civilization*, *The Birth of the Clinic*, and *Discipline and Punish*, Foucault advanced his most extended discussion of "power as force" in the inaugural volume of *The History of Sexuality*. Much as in *Discipline and Punish*, power was said to function both as negative, prohibitive, *and* as productive force. Following the methodology and nomenclature of *The Order of Things*, which had called for a focus on "grids of intelligibility," by the mid-1970s Foucault would be studying violence/war as one such ruling grid of modernity. Fastening on hermeneutical and epistemological practices, *"Il faut défendre la société"* demonstrated how "war," starting roughly in the seventeenth century, functioned in at least a double way: first, war signaled the welcome emergence of the historical *récit*, or narrative, which launched an offensive against the hegemony of political theory for covering up the contingencies, passions, brute, bloody facts of effective history as "evenementality"; second, war became Foucault's own preferred grid of analysis for the salutary arrival of what he hailed as *political historicism*. Contrary to appearances, it is not only the Hobbesian/Clausewitzian moment that rules Foucault's work of the mid-1970s but also, as the lecture course would have it, the shadow of the nobiliary historian Boulainvilliers, surprisingly for him the father of modern French historiography.

3 *Counterforce* Though holding fast to a regulative utopian idea of human freedom (a tendency especially evident in later texts, such as "The Subject and Power" (1982)), Foucault remained situated squarely in the tradition of counterviolence

(*Gegengewalt*). Aligning this "counter-"strategy at times with the mechanisms of dialectical "reversal," he did not reduce it purely to the well-known figure of turning what is false upside down, much as Marx, notoriously, sought to set Hegel, and history, back on his/its feet. Rather, Foucault devised a subversive strategy that sought to breach – not transcend – present conditions by pressing at the limits from within. As such, this method of inversion must be assessed in light of Heidegger's 1930 Nietzsche lectures, which interpreted the philosopher's "reversal" of metaphysics as the inauguration of a new beginning for philosophy. But Foucault's counterstrategy should also be considered in view of the analysis Marx and Engels advanced of the trope. For, in their jointly authored *German Ideology*, they diagnosed the belief in reversal as outright mistaken, indeed, as symptomatic of the Young Hegelians' entrapment in ideology, whose inadequate "materialistic" critique of Hegel failed to topple the dominance of spirit (*Geist*). At the very least, Foucault's critical counterstrategies raise the question of what the place of "anti-dogmatic violence"[27] might be in the context of his reconceptualized Kantian critique.

4   *Differentiating power from violence*   In the final stages of his scholarly development, Foucault seemed willing to admit that his concept of power remained all too elusive. As we shall see in the chapter that follows, in "The Subject and Power," a text appended to Rabinow and Dreyfus's Foucault study, he seemed to have made a last-ditch effort to return to Arendt's diacritical typology, seeking to divorce power from force/violence while remaining faithful to an agonistic conception of social action and freedom.

Before we address the vicissitudes of the "grid" *pouvoir/guerre/force* in more detail in the next chapter, it seems propitious first to circumscribe Foucault's understanding of *critique*, as it materializes in his work of the 1970s, to find its final definition as "self-critique" in the late work, *The Use of Pleasure* and *The Care of the Self*. To do so, it is necessary to heed the transformations that Foucault's thought incessantly underwent, most notably the shifts in emphasis as he moved from a general study of the alienating effects of "governmentality" to more narrowly conceived, individuating forms of resistance, the technologies of self and self-government. Thus, as Foucault readjusted the focal point of his research, the transsubjective "will to knowledge" seemed to take second place to a more articulated concern with the individual will, autonomy, and *self-critique*. Furthermore, in operating these transitions, Foucault slid away from a proto-Nietzschean rejection of "asceticism," in accordance with the letter of the *Genealogy of Morals*, to a remarkable reconceptualization, even celebration, of *askēsis* as ethical attitude.

Intending to engage Foucault's work on its own terms, the analysis that follows seeks to release alternative models of interpretation and understanding, beyond some of the more conventional charges that have been imposed on his thought. To do so, one must be willing to go along with this thinker of, and at, the limits, so as to gauge to what extent he relocated the frontiers of critique.

What Is Critique? (Foucault between Nietzsche and Kant)

In genealogies of his own thought, autobiographical statements, and interviews, Foucault has traced the bulk of his work back to his earliest interest, which remained consistent: epistemology, or theories of knowledge, whose study was spurred on and renewed by Nietzsche's writings on the history of reason and the will to truth.[28] Though sworn early on to the philosophical triumvirate Marx/Nietzsche/Freud, he was pushed by Nietzsche's logic to renounce the principles of Marxist ideology critique, which, tethered to a firm demarcation between truth and falsehood, simply remained the progeny of a suspect occidental will to knowledge. But if in the early 1970s Foucault proved indebted to Nietzsche's genealogical transvaluation of Kant's critical project, then towards the end of that decade he sought a closer alliance to the Enlightenment philosopher, no less than to the first-generation representatives of the Frankfurt School.

How is one to understand Foucault's seemingly equivocal position, balanced between Nietzsche and Kant? With what kind of ease does he migrate from the flamboyant philologist-philosopher to the sober, ascetic Enlightener, whose critical project remained vested in recovering the transhistorical a priori that was to be reclaimed from historical contingency? How is Nietzsche to be conjoined to Kant if one recalls that the *Genealogy of Morals* was presented as a grandiose demolition of Kant's critical edifice? For didn't Nietzsche, driven by a historical, rather than transcendental impulse, put forward a historicist critique of all moral values, consisting in the relentless interrogation of the transcendental "value" that underpinned these various value registers? Hadn't he proclaimed that "we need a *critique* of moral values," meaning that *"the value of these values themselves must first be called in question"*?[29]

But if one looks, first of all, at the history of Foucault's textual production, one notices that from the very start Nietzsche stood to Kant as a reflection stands to its original. Early on, the figures of these philosophers fused, interlocked, becoming inseparable, though Kant for quite some years ostensibly retreated again into the background. Together with Deleuze, Foucault early on edited the French edition of Nietzsche's collected works, for which they co-authored a general introduction in 1967,[30] while Foucault himself translated Nietzsche's *Gay Science* and posthumous fragments. Indeed, as Foucault would later point out in the important overview interview with Gérard Raulet, "Critical Theory/Intellectual History," his interest in Nietzsche lay in the history of knowledge and rationality, as a way mainly of breaking out of the confines of phenomenology, especially its theory of the transhistorical subject, which conceived the history of reason in terms of the primordial, founding act of the subject.[31] Unlike these *arche*-typological theories, he added, Nietzsche opened up the perspective of a history of truth as necessary error. But as early as

1961, Kant rivaled Nietzsche in importance, as is evident from the fact that Foucault had already rendered Kant's *Anthropologie in pragmatischer Hinsicht abgefasst* (*Anthropology from a Pragmatic Point of View*) into French. Together with a long, as yet unpublished, introduction, he submitted this annotated Kant translation to the Sorbonne as a "complementary thesis," in addition to his *Madness and Civilization* (1961), so as to obtain his doctorate *"en lettres"* (procured under the direction of Jean Hyppolite).[32] Yet there can exist no question that traces of the early work on Kant's anthropology surface in *The Order of Things* (1966), which, in reading Kant as more or less suspended at the juncture of the Classical and modern *epistēmēs*, already summoned Nietzsche upon the scene, for being the one who ruthlessly set an end to modernity's self-imposed "anthropological slumber." By virtue of that proto-Nietzschean gesture, Kant himself now seemingly was relegated to the folds of history, for not until the late 1970s would Foucault explicitly dedicate several lectures to the Enlightenment philosopher. However incompatible Nietzsche's genealogy and Kant's critical philosophy were – insofar as Nietzsche moved from a Schopenhauerian embrace of Kant's thing-in-itself in *The Birth of Tragedy* to the later destructive genealogy of Kantian conscience and the categorical imperative – the incongruity did not stop Foucault from being fascinated by both, but rather helps to explain his later quasi-Dilthean attempt to historicize Kant.[33] No longer was this eighteenth-century philosopher simply the antiquarian thinker whose critiques aspired to reach suprahistorical transcendental foundations, but he now emerged as the modernist who in answering the question "What Is Enlightenment?" for the first time captured the historical consciousness of the "now" as an "ontology of the present" and of "ourselves," thus designing a new philosophical *ēthos* that revealed a *historicized* understanding of the present. For, as Foucault time and again asserted, history, with all its incongruities, discontinuities, singularities, invariably served as a welcome corrective in the face of grandiose, prescriptive claims to universality, pronounced in the name of reason.

Nietzsche's Historicist Critique

Contrary to appearances, Foucault's *The Order of Things* proved to have been conceived under the aegis of an epistemological antifoundationalism, inspired by Nietzsche's early essay "On Truth and Lies in an Extramoral Sense" and the later *The Gay Science*. Foucault's archeological excavations were aimed at the sedimentary strata of occidental knowledge, meaning to lay bare its topography, architecture, or spatial regimes of ordering systems. In a first tempo, *The Order of Things* drew the history of the respective "archeological mutations" through which Classical epistemic grids or "ordering codes" had been replaced by modern ones. Thus, with the coming of the modern age, natural history was eclipsed by the study of life, or biology; general grammar, or the order of discourse premised on an inextricable link between words–representations–things, was supplanted by the objectifying mode of a scientific philology, while the tabulation of wealth and production would be substituted by the science of economics. But in the eclipse of one ontological ordering system by another, Kant's philosophy held out the uneasy, tension-filled intersection between two conflicting *epistēmēs*. Each of his *Critiques* still sought to circumscribe the perimeters that defined human knowledge of nature, thus continuing the Classical *epistēmē*, whereas his prescient *Logic*, by dint of raising the question, "What is Man?," already portended the rise to prominence of anthropology that was to enchant the century to come. Though Kant had established the fissure between the empirical and the transcendental, this chasm was to be overcome in the nineteenth-century quest for a vitalistic unity of experience, culminating in the ascendance of anthropology, according to which humans served as the foundations to their own finitude.[34] Moreover, while Kantian critique signaled the crisis of representation, setting an end to classical metaphysics no less than the representational doctrines of the contemporaneous French "Ideologists," it spawned two philosophical responses that mirrored each other: either a vulgar positivism, which shied away from all fields that surpassed empirical experience, or a new metaphysics, which set its hopes on Life, the Will, and the Word.

In a second tempo, Foucault's study also examined the pitfalls that followed from this paradigm switch. For though the modern *epistēmē* inaugurated the "end of metaphysics," it at once instated the stronghold of a suspect humanism, no less than an overly optimistic historicism that went hand in hand with it. Crucially, towards the end of the pivotal chapter "Man and his Doubles," whose title alluded to Nietzsche's *Zarathustra*, Foucault staged a primal scene in which Nietzsche put an end to the sins of his philosophical forbears, clearing away the obstacles of an enervating anthropology, thus rudely awakening modernity out of its harmful slumber. Appropriately, Foucault assigned Nietzsche, the incorrigible iconoclast, a double role. First of all, his stubbornly nominalistic philologism accelerated the dispersal of a naturalized discourse, according to which words naively coincided with things. Second, by thus facilitating the turn to historical analysis and historicism, he simultaneously uncovered the recidivist metaphysical baggage that clandestinely came along with modernity's new analytic of finitude: the invention of man and the emergence of modern humanism. But Nietzsche's unraveling labor, Foucault continued, did not stop there. Uncovering this truth, he also spelled out an unwanted "Promise–Threat" – as Foucault termed it, coming all too close to Nietzsche's ominous rhetoric – namely, that the modern paradigm eventually would exhaust itself, bringing about the very "end of man." Couched almost entirely in quasi-Nietzschean, quasi-Heideggerian language, the chapter in no uncertain terms greeted the void left by Nietzsche's iconoclastic thought. Clearing away the rubble of older philosophical edifices amounted to reclaiming the freedom of philosophical thought, as it allowed for "the unfolding of a space in which it is once more possible to think."[35] In prophesying the end of man and the humanistic philosophy that went along with it, Nietzsche opened the way for a fresh beginning of philosophy, as Foucault gnomically observed. Signing off on the chapter with the phrase that to the contorted manifestations of humanism one could "answer only with a philosophical laugh"[36] – preferably a silent one – he went so far as to impersonate Zarathustra, imitating the excesses of that unlikely prophet's disdainful gaiety.

In unequivocal terms, *The Order of Things* established that Nietzsche was the first philosopher-philologist to entrust the "philosophical task with a radical reflection upon language."[37] Setting adrift the vocabulary of metaphysics, Nietzsche's philosophy uncovered the "double movement proper to the modern *cogito*," the interplay between reason and its uncanny double or unthought, its so-called Other, which, unlike what metaphysical convention said, proved to be co-original with the Same. Thus, Nietzsche's "general critique of reason," with its unwavering interrogation of the "limits of thought,"[38] might help thwart modernity's deleterious course as it advanced "towards that region where man's Other must become the Same as himself."[39] Still, both *The Order of Things* (1966) and Foucault's subsequent book, *The Archeology of Knowledge* (1969), placed themselves mainly under the aegis of an archeological methodology,[40] not yet grasping the full, radical force later work would attribute to Nietzschean "genealogy." Divested of all nostalgia for a primordial origin, or *archē*, the antiscience of "archeology" set out to unseat the transcendentalizing tendencies of Kantian philosophy and Husserlian phenomenology. Offering a postmetaphysical "discourse about discourses," archeology aimed to operate the "dispersion," "scattering," "decentering" of the Western archives of knowledge, as it diagnosed the rules of formation and procedures proper to discursive practices, or verbal performances. Though laying bare the deep structures and performative rules of discourse, archeology promised to resist the "ontology of structure," proscribed by a "totalizing" structuralism, whose formalism failed to deal with the dynamics of history, let alone institutional power.[41] How to come up, then, with a "theory of discontinuous systematization," which, in analyzing discursive events, would "accept chance as a category" in their production,[42] such was the paradoxical task on which Foucault labored, as he put it in the programmatic "Discourse on Language," which he appended to *The Archeology of Knowledge*. To draw out the implications of this mission, Foucault's inaugural speech, delivered at the Collège de France in 1970, relied extensively on Nietzsche's critique of epistemology. For the project of future work, he informed his audience, consisted in the disassembly of "the prodigious machinery of the will to truth," with "its vocation of exclusion"[43] and with its assortment of dividing practices: those that regulated politics and sexuality (power and desire), demarcated reason from folly and truth from falsehood or error. Thus, underneath the lecture's tightly scripted systematicity, whose proximity to structuralism Foucault did not always successfully fend off,[44] lay a firm commitment to Nietzsche's antiphilosophy, as was evident in the two methodologies – critique and genealogy – that he selected for the task. Hardly affiliated to Kant's philosophy, the variant of "critique" Foucault had in mind would assume the interruptive, interventionist force of Nietzschean "counterknowledge." For, as it insinuated itself in a corpus of normative, discursive practices, it would bring to the surface the immanent rules that helped rarefy discourse or project a false "ethics of knowledge" and truth. Using the figure of reversal, critique unmasked the legitimizing codes of "truth discourses" as falsehood. But it needed to be aided by a complementary methodology, attentive to diachronic power alignments and to the "external conditions of existence" that enabled the seemingly smooth functioning of a given discourse. Genealogy, therefore, concentrated on the historical formation of discursive performances, operating with the principles of discontinuity, specificity, and exteriority, in order to pry discursive events loose from the enveloping, legitimizing narratives in which they had been embedded. As such, this new historiography followed the signs of the time. For, in keeping with the post-Heideggerian campaign against metaphysics that held poststructuralist philosophy in its sway, so Foucault, the representative of historiography, contributed to this deconstructive project from the side of history.[45]

Inasmuch as the "Discourse on Language" targeted the "will to knowledge" and "will to truth," it placed itself in the trail of Nietzsche's epistemological relativism and rhetorical analysis of discursive power, consecrated in "On Truth and Lies in an Extramoral Sense."[46] However, the lecture left much unexplained when it came to accounting for the links between power and genealogy featured in Nietzsche's mature work. This was the assignment Foucault hoped to complete in his 1971 essay, "Nietzsche, Genealogy, History," even as he left behind the polished, highly systematized, academic style of the "Discourse on Language" to set loose the parodic powers of language. Weaving together a confoundingly great number of textual strands culled from Nietzsche's vast corpus (from the early Basel period to *Genealogy of Morals* and *Zarathustra*), the essay returned to the two Nietzschean strategies of "critique" and "genealogy," the warp and woof of the "Discourse on Language." Indeed, in sections 1 through 6, Foucault chiefly followed *On the Genealogy of Morals* (1887), which in anti-Kantian fashion exposed not the transhistorical edifice of normative moral values but the historical sedimentation of relations of force in moral norms and nomenclature, which turned out to be the petrified code words for what originally proved to be techniques of coercive imposition. Using postmetaphysical expressions such as *Herkunft* (descent) and *Entstehung* (emergence), Nietzsche conceived a new genre of historiography called genealogy, or effective (actual) history (*wirkliche Historie, l'histoire effective*), definitively setting an end to philosophies of origin (*Ursprung, archē*), whose undiminished hold over modernity had already formed the target of Foucault's *The Order of Things*.[47] By contrast, the essay's final part, section 7, explicitly reverted to Nietzsche's earlier Basel phase, to the second *Untimely Meditation*, or *On the Uses and Disadvantages of History for Life* (1874), which advanced a devastating, if vitalistic, critique of nineteenth-century historicism in its antiquarian, monumental, and critical modalities. Parodying these diverse anti-Platonic modes, Foucault appropriated them for his own insurrectionary program, albeit in novel garb, as he hoped to shed the untenable race politics that underpinned the Nietzschean text.

In combating metaphysical quests for origin, essence, identity, ends (teleology) or continuity, Foucault's genealogy would attend to the rediscovery of nontotalizable "events," laying bare a history of cruelty and violence rife with discontinuities, accidents, errors, atavisms, unusual heredities, new and false beginnings. Importantly, Foucault's larger claim was that Nietzsche's philosophy of force had made a revolutionary, materialistic practice of history-writing possible, a new "history of the event," one that not only focused on the hermeneutical, interpretive violence inscribed on "subjected bodies," but could also view the historical arena afresh, as it relinquished "the anticipatory power of meaning" (in the strong, hermeneutical sense of *Sinn*) for "the hazardous play of dominations."[48] Indeed, it is this two-pronged project of renewal that Foucault saw reflected in the Nietzschean terms "descent" and "emergence." As an analysis of descent, or "stock" (*Herkunft, Erbschaft*), Foucault explained, genealogy probed the interacting articulations of body and history to uncover a "body totally imprinted by history and the process of history's destruction of the body."[49] Steeped deeply in Nietzsche's rhetoric, he aimed to neutralize the vitalistic, even racist, undertones and resonances of terms like "stock," as is evident from the unusual energy with which he harped on Nietzsche's so-called deconstruction of the German "national character" in *Beyond Good and Evil*.[50] Far from subscribing to racist, monocausal narratives of a species' evolution or homogeneity, he maintained, the genealogical investigation of descent precisely unraveled such organicistic scenarios of nation and self to reveal not a natural origin but myriad dispersed beginnings, events, mutations, and accidents.

Where the pursuit of "descent" gave preference to the effects of force on bodies, "the inscribed surface of events," "traced by language and dissolved by ideas,"[51] the study of "emergence" (*Entstehung*) tried to pinpoint the historical "moment of arising," "apparition," or "eruption," of various regimes of subjection. If history presented a potentially infinite, agonistic playing field of contending forces, then the specific historical junctures and various impositions of interpretive rituals to which it had been submitted needed to be located. Here, too, Foucault tried to divest Nietzsche's "pathos of distance" of its racist and vitalistic baggage, insofar as the phrase now would capture the dynamics of differential force fields. Though "emergence" as a study of the "entry of forces" presupposed a "place of confrontation," the latter had little to do with a "closed field offering the spectacle of a struggle among equals."[52] Rather, emergence pointed to an agonistic, differential, interstitial "'non-place,' a pure distance, which indicates that the adversaries do not belong to a common space."[53] In other words, emergence designated an inaccessible, impalpable, yet enabling nonspace – an ungrounded ground of sorts – by virtue of which history's antagonistic drama of domination was incessantly repeated, fixed in endless series of normative conventions and rituals.

The regime of force Foucault meant to expose was that of "hermeneutical" or "interpretive violence," the coercive imposition of systems of thought that had become ossified in historical practices of interpretation, such as laws and normative rules. It will be recalled that in his *Genealogy of Morals*, Nietzsche aligned genealogy with the discipline of true history, or historiography, for only the history-bent genealogist could get the better of the oneiric metaphysician, who stubbornly mistook, say, the purpose or utility of a law for an index about its genesis/origin. Foucault followed suit when he maintained that such hermeneutical violence inhered in the realm of the law, or the legal system. The origins of legal rituals were not so much to be sought in ancient purification rites – to allude to René Girard's anthropologico-philosophical study, *Violence and the Sacred* – as in regimes of force and domination, witness the "festival of violence" behind the discourse of the law, whose horrors Nietzsche conjured up when he sneered that "the categorical imperative smells of cruelty."[54] Indeed, it was Nietzsche who first comprehended the underlying truth of Hobbes's *status civilis*, when he discerned in reason a rational tool with which affective goals, the satisfaction of the passions, were to be reached. Seen this way, moral principles were the outgrowths of an ascetic ideal, which, in order to gain strength, had turned against the body.[55] In effect, despite Foucault's hesitations towards the psychoanalytic paradigm, the same cultural pessimism commonly imputed to Freud, author of *Totem and Taboo* and *The Future of an Illusion*, returned in the Nietzsche essay in altered guise. For, in referring to moral and political conventions as social "rituals" (at once a distinctly Althusserian moment),[56] Foucault revealed the sublimated persistence of animistic, quasi-theological behavioral patterns in secular, post-Enlightenment history. In fact, it is fair to say that all of Foucault's early genealogical derivations, in a Nietzschean vein, demonstrate the same principle, namely, that high moral-political values as well as Enlightenment ideals, such as universal freedom, and presumably other natural or human rights, amounted to ascetic "sublimations" of instincts, drives, passions. There scarcely can exist any doubt that, at this stage, the implications to be drawn from Foucault's rhetoric were decidedly anti-Kantian: Kant's "kingdom of common ends," "universal reciprocity," and perpetual peace were demystified as mere shams, in reality the incessant infliction of violence upon violence.

According to Nietzsche's contra-hermeneutics, the pregiven meaning (*Sinn*) of tradition and cultural heritage was to make way for an analysis of the "use of force" that invariably attended the imparting of meaning, the founding and hierarchizing of values. Following this cynical world view, the success of adversarial agents and actors was measured by their capacity to seize (cathect) new rules, to invert them, in other words, by how well they managed to bend existing interpretations to their wills. More than anything else, genealogy as the analysis of "emergence" laid bare the history of "the development of humanity" as a "series of interpretations."[57] The altered perspective therefore also called for a recoining of the object under analysis – the event – which could no longer be reduced to "a decision, a treaty, a reign, or a battle [*une bataille*]," the proverbial historic event paraded in traditional history books. Within the new transvaluation of historical values, the event now designated "the reversal of a relationship of forces, the usurpation of power, the appropriation of a vocabulary turned against those who had once used it, a feeble domination that poisons itself as it grows lax, the entry of a masked 'other.' The forces at play in history neither obey a destiny nor a mechanism, but rather submit to the chance character of struggle [*le hasard de la lutte*]."[58] By casting the "history of the event" in terms of struggle, Foucault evoked the entire baggage of connotations these words had collected in the political realm, supplying a translation of the German word *Kampf* – a category at the center not only of the master–slave antagonism with which Nietzsche's *Genealogy of Morals* started off, but, crucially, of Hegel's *Phenomenology of Spirit* and Marx's class struggle. For, as Deleuze observed in his *Nietzsche* study, the master–slave divide of the *Genealogy of Morals* itself provided a transliteration of the Hegelian master–bondsman struggle, which, one might add, counted as a displaced response to Hobbes's state of nature.[59] Thus, Foucault indisputably laid the groundwork for what the 1976 war lecture course "*Society Must Be Defended*" would label the Nietzschean hypothesis, or power/force/war. Moreover, implicitly, the 1971 essay discarded the Marxist grid of an antagonistic class struggle – no doubt for being still too humanistic – in favor of an agonistic conception of history, molded on Nietzsche's understanding of the origin as the differential dynamic of active and reactive forces.

Having laid out the benefits of "descent" and "emergence," Foucault affirmed that Nietzsche's *wirkliche Historie* was the only "disciplinary" front his new genealogy possibly could assume as it took on the absolutes of "traditional history" in the hopes of reactivating the true "historical sense." Initiating a transition from metaphysics to a history of the event, his genealogy operated a shift away from essence to "accident and succession," and from a rationalist foundationalism to a recovery of the bodily passions, an agonistic fermenting ground of epistemic disputes in which personal conflicts "slowly forged the weapons of reason."[60] By resolutely leaving the province of metahistory behind, genealogy was to "record the singularity of events outside of any monotonous finality."[61] For, with unswerving dedication, traditional historiography leveled the singularity of historical events by inserting them into an idealized teleology, a teleology whose existence Kant, in prototypical fashion, had sought to validate when he demanded empirical or phenomenological signs for the (transcendental) assumption that human history was progressively propelled forward. However, in history's arena of ever-competing forces, genealogy operated as a "counterforce," a "counterhistory" powerful enough to upset, reverse the balance, or status quo, held in place by the "suprahistorical perspective," the oppressive grip of metaphysics' "will to power."[62] Much as did the "Discourse on Language," so the 1971 Nietzsche essay hoped to come to terms with "chance" as it undid the hackneyed values of traditional history. That is, history's course no longer abided by the laws of Christian or Greek world views – all gossamer spun by Nietzsche's proverbial spider – but resembled an entangled web of events, an intractable arena in which the "iron hand of necessity" shook "the dice-box of chance."[63] The result was an intricate game of mastery, subjugation, and insurgence, in which the "will to power's" attempt to master history's unruliness merely generated "the risk of an ever greater chance."[64] Disavowing the metaphysical (Platonic) "drive to truth," coveted by traditional history, effective history reversed the set relations between proximity and distance, body and soul/mind, to privilege the depreciated, subordinated value. Furthermore, as a "curative science," effective history refused to emulate the so-called value-free, or objective, stance of traditional history. Informed by Nietzsche's theory of perspectivism, the new genealogy did not deny its own immersion in history's volatile force field or its cognitive entanglements in its objects of analysis.[65] In fact, rather than ending in epistemological pessimism, genealogy's awareness of its own limits made possible a new economy of gain in which the loss of "truth" threw open a new field of knowledge, one whose subject remained conscious of its own contingency and errors. Fully embracing Nietzsche's "affirmation of knowledge as perspective," the historian would not hesitate to trace the genealogy of his own acts of cognition.

Where the "Discourse on Language" had still set up critique and genealogy as two separate methodologies, Foucault's Nietzschean manifesto essentially collapsed the terms. Cutting through smooth, homogeneous surface – the histories of truth and reason as "error" (laid down in Nietzsche's "How the 'Real World' at last Became a Fable") – the new genealogy reclaimed the incisive, dissecting strength of critique's original power. Indeed, it is in this sense that one must understand the numerous allusions to the "cutting knife" of critical history, which especially accrued as the Nietzsche essay drew to a close. Taking a detour via Nietzsche's second *Untimely Meditation*, Foucault returned to the etymological roots ("descent") of the term "critique" (*krinein*). Just as Nietzsche in the end defended a critical historiography that would recklessly cut the roots of traditional history's organic tree, so Foucault ended up honing knowledge (*savoir*), turning it into history's newly sharpened cutting device. Declaring that effective history would piece up the continuities of traditional history, he explained: "This is because knowledge is not made for understanding; it is made for cutting."[66] In other words, knowledge was not designed for grasping with the hand – the French "com-prendre" plays on the German *be-greifen* (*greifen* meaning "to grasp"), as conceptual and physical grasping – but for cutting with the knife.[67] Surrendering himself to the hazardous chance play of *aleatory* history, the genealogist evidently was not concerned with the critical acts of separation performed by the law in normative decisions (*Entscheidung*), just as little as he was preoccupied, one must assume, with the moral repertoire of acts involving existential decision making.

As he summed up the benefits of his new program, Foucault listed the three new uses to which history, or better, counterhistory, were to be put, all three of which "[opposed] and [corresponded] to the three Platonic modalities of history," whose hegemony over Western tradition they hoped to crush: first, parody, which debunked history as reminiscence and recollective recognition (*anamnēsis*); second, dispersal, which shattered the identity of "the same," stored in the "continuity" of tradition; and, third, the most destructive modality, which, in "sacrificing" the historical subject, took on traditional history as the knowledge of truth. All in all, the production of this new history as "countermemory" (*contre-mémoire*) demanded an utterly different deployment of temporality, a new attitude that was untimely and revolutionizing at the same time, as it contested history's so-called teleological progress and retrieved altogether unheard-of annals and records.[68] In fact, Foucault's threefold counterstrategy proved to be modeled on the counterhistorical remedies that Nietzsche had proscribed in his second *Untimely Meditation*. For, first, in adopting the parodic mask, the genealogist poked fun at the monumentalizing tendencies of Western history, centered on great individuals and deeds; second, the standard historical narratives about monolithic, national(istic) or native identities he dissected were those furnished by antiquarian history; lastly, critical history needed to be disengaged from the old fable of truth, so that its trenchant, cutting force could be used for different ends, to lay bare "the endless deployment of the will to knowledge."[69] Not averse to Nietzsche's violent rhetoric, Foucault declared that such a genealogy of power would even sacrifice – if need be – the conventional category of the "subject of knowledge."[70] At once mimicry and displacement, parody was to be pushed to the limit so that it could surrender its dialectical force, so that the potentially venomous antidote (*pharmakon*)[71] could release its benign potency.

As suggested at the outset, Foucault's invocation of these critical tools requires closer scrutiny, even though solving the riddle of the various guises, or masks, under which he appropriated Nietzschean strategies, especially the figures of reversal (*Umkehrung, Umdrehung*) and "countermovement," is not an easy task. Already in *The Order of Things*, Foucault described the disappearance of the classical "metaphysics of infinity," eclipsed by modernity's mundane analytic of finitude, as an inversion, or reversal, of "the entire field of Western thought."[72] In his "Discourse on Language," the principle of "reversal" was elevated to the status of a veritable *terminus technicus* or methodological tool with which the historian might unseat rarefying discursive procedures, for example, the author function, expressive of modernity's "will to truth."[73] Both a method and a dynamic operative in the discursive course of history, the term "reversal" resurfaced prominently in *"Society Must Be Defended,"* the 1976 lecture course on war, which aimed to lay bare the "origins of totalitarianism" by rendering National Socialism and Stalinism as inversions of an older discourse about interracial warfare.[74] The matter of what status one is to ascribe to this Nietzsche-inspired trope of reversal is not inconsequential, since Foucault repeatedly couched his newly forged strategic discipline in the language of *contre-*, speaking, as we saw, of genealogical inquiry as countermemory. Waging a battle against traditional history meant that the genealogist would "over-power" universalist philosophies of history (*Geschichtsphilosophie*) no less than a post-Kantian ascetic historicism, to make genealogical use of it, to turn its weapons against itself.[75] In order to grasp the full implications of these movements, we must consider more closely one specific passage in the 1971 essay, notably, the one in which Foucault, mimicking Nietzsche's mocking tone against nineteenth-century historicism, derided the base nature of a hypertrophied "historical sense," no less than the posturing of the conventional historiographer, the Socratic demagogue, better known as Nietzsche's "theoretical man."[76] Having engaged in a lengthy tirade against positivistic historiography, with its "plebeian" origins, he asked how the new genealogy had managed to emerge out of such lowly origins and beginnings. The answer was by doing what Plato "could have done," but failed to do, to Socrates, in order to countervail the latter's consolidation of Western metaphysics, whose principles were consecrated in the doctrine of immortality. What Plato could have done but neglected to do was turn philosophy against itself. Calling, centuries later, for an analogous destruction of traditional historiography, Foucault amended the injunction, demanding now that history be turned against itself:

> The locus of emergence of metaphysics was surely Athenian demagoguery, the vulgar spite of Socrates and his belief in immortality. But Plato could have seized this Socratic philosophy, he could have turned it against itself [*il aurait pu la retourner contre elle-même*], and, undoubtedly, he was often tempted to do so. But his defeat was that he managed to found it instead. The problem in the nineteenth century was not to do for the popular asceticism of historians, what Plato did for Socrates's asceticism. One should not found this popular asceticism in a philosophy of history, but dismantle it, beginning with what it has produced: one must become master of history [*se rendre maître de l'histoire*] in order to turn it to genealogical use, that is to say, a rigorously anti-Platonic usage. Only then will the historical sense free itself from suprahistorical history.[77]

Thus, Foucault implied, the errors of reason were to be rectified, however not by discarding reason altogether in favor of an abject, suspect irrationalism. Rather, by spinning reason against itself, pointing the *tools* – a word Foucault did not cease using, as if he were the tinkerer, or *bricoleur* – against their original intent, the historian was to unlock unfathomed historical horizons and novel vistas of possibility from *within*, through a radically reconfigured immanent critique that drew upon Nietzsche's perspectivism.[78]

More than just standing for the negating force of *anti* – also featured in Deleuze and Guattari's contemporaneous *Anti-Oedipus* – Foucault's *contre* appeared to be modeled on Heidegger's understanding of Nietzschean thought as a fundamental "counterposition" or "countermovement" (*Gegenbewegung*),[79] that is, as a way of thinking that insinuated itself into the folds of metaphysics so as to unsettle it from within. Not insignificant in this context is that Foucault repeatedly paid tribute to Heidegger's Freiburg Nietzsche lectures in interviews, underscoring how he hardly knew *Being and Time* at all in the early stages of his intellectual development.[80] For in the Nietzsche lectures Heidegger had sought to come to terms with the formative principle of reversal upon which Nietzsche's entire philosophy rested, expressed as early as 1870–71 in a famous note: "My philosophy an *inverted Platonism*: the farther removed from true being, the purer, the finer, the better it is. Living in semblance as goal."[81] Throughout his philosophical career, Nietzsche banked on the technique of reversal, with which he hoped to undo the deleterious, idealistic reversals of reason and the ascetic ideal, as it turned against itself. It was precisely to get out of these abstractions or the false, reflective inversions of an ascetic reason that Nietzsche proposed his radical perspectivism, which relied on a theory of affects as will. In his *Genealogy of Morals*, for example, he explicitly set up his perspectivism as an escape route out of the value-free objectivism of philosophy and science. "There is *only* a perspective seeing, *only* a perspective 'knowing'; and the *more* affects we allow to speak about one thing, the *more* eyes, different eyes, we can use to observe one thing, the more complete will our 'concept' of this thing, our 'objectivity,' be."[82] In much the same way, Foucault's historicist genealogy, fastening on the historical vicissitudes of reason, sought to step outside of the imprisoning periphery decreed by a normatively conceived faculty of reason.

But if Foucault's critical counterstrategy emulated Nietzsche's favorite tropes, it wasn't always clear whether he just followed in the philosopher's footsteps or also took in the standard criticism of Nietzsche's technique of inversion, namely, that, in the end, it failed to undo what it turned upside down.[83] Might Foucault's forceful method, in reworking the philosophical tradition it hoped to upset, also take along some of its flawed premises and methodological errors? There is no question that critical pressure needs to be applied to Foucault's celebration of inversion and "counterwielding," whose beneficial effects he all too uncritically took for granted. To be sure, as it replicated Nietzsche's odious diction, the 1971 essay took over a genealogical method that, through destructive, forceful interventions, hoped to inaugurate a new historical beginning.[84] But in advocating that traditional history's tools be wielded against themselves, Foucault also espoused the forceful rhetoric of revolutionary counterviolence (*Gegengewalt*). When he demanded that genealogy do away with historical asceticism and overpower history by revolving it against itself, he still appeared informed by the logic of "dialectical moments" that burdened idealistic philosophy. Indeed, despite Foucault's outspoken, often strident critique of Hegel, one must be prepared to ask whether there doesn't emerge a dialectical residue in his thought, inherited from German idealistic philosophy, according to which – pushed to the limit, at the brink – the negative may turn into a positive. Dispensed in sufficient quantities, counterviolence will redeem itself. In that sense, the critical violence Foucault advocated – however figurative or metaphorical – still operated as a dialectical tool, activating the force of negation, which, he conjectured, might bear productive or generative effects. In fact, it is this very dialectical violence that Arendt thematized in her *On Violence*, when she observed, "Hegel's and Marx's great trust in the dialectical 'power of negation,' by virtue of which opposites do not destroy but smoothly develop into each other because contradictions promote and do not paralyze development, rests on a much older philosophical prejudice: that evil is no more than a privative *modus* of the good, that good can come out of evil; that, in short, evil is but a temporary manifestation of a still-hidden good."[85] Taking on the entire philosophical arsenal of dialectical weapons, Arendt resolutely countered that "violence can destroy power; it is utterly incapable of creating it." To be sure, it is debatable whether the Manichean theological origin, mentioned in Arendt's analysis, played as much of a role in the secularized dialectical script under review as she surmised, or that it had any relevance for Foucault's work. What seems certain, nonetheless, is that Foucault early on – if for radically different reasons, and though opposed to dialectical tricks – clandestinely operated with a modicum of dialectical violence that often took the form of a transgressive force, intended not to gain access to transcendence but to alter matters from within. Which is why one may agree with Alexander Nehamas that Nietzsche and Foucault remained "adversarial thinkers,"[86] especially if we take the description to mean that they were also dialectical thinkers.

Critique, Foucault seemed to say, becomes productive crisis when the critical knife of reason is wielded against itself, releasing change through destruction.

Kant's Critical Ethos

In the previous section I argued that Foucault's programmatic Nietzsche text defined critique as effective history (*wirkliche Historie*) primarily in the third mode, that of critical historiography. Appropriating Foucault's own frequent method of differentiating negative definitions from their positive ones, let me advance the following thesis: this outspoken Nietzschean period in Foucault's scholarly work constitutes the negative phase of critique, while the positive one stands under the sign of Kant. In these later quasi-Kantian writings, he pressed towards an extended reflection upon the historical boundaries of the present, yet still in order to redraw the old frontiers, to undo the policing of borders that had bound the epistemological, ethico-political, and aesthetic planes, and – in the final analysis – to outline a new ethico-political attitude that might open up an unfettered, unconstrained field of freedom. To understand this position better, we must now have a closer look at Kant's legacy in Foucault's later work and especially in a sequence of three lectures:

1 "Qu'est-ce que la critique? (Critique et *Aufklärung*)," the earliest piece, an until recently lesser-known Sorbonne lecture that Foucault presented to the French Society of Philosophy on May 27, 1978;[87]

2 "The Art of Telling the Truth," an excerpt from the January 5, 1983 lecture of his penultimate Collège de France course, called "Le gouvernement de soi et des autres" ("The Government of Self and Others");[88]

3 "Qu'est-ce que les *Lumières*?" (1983), a contemporaneous lecture that was published in English as "What Is Enlightenment?" in Rabinow's *The Foucault Reader* (1984).[89]

By way of providing the reader with some anticipatory signposts for the analysis to follow, a few preliminary suggestions seem to be in place. At the heart of all these texts – some fragmentary or unfinished, but all more ascetic and austere in tone than the slightly ecstatic 1971 Nietzsche essay – lies Foucault's desire to reinvigorate Kantian critique and the legacy of the Enlightenment for the present, no less than the attempt to reconnect his own philosophico-historicist project, as he now called it, to Kant and the first-generation Frankfurt School. Above all, he sought to reverse what he perceived, in no unwavering terms, to be Habermas's prejudiced, hence strictly speaking, counter-Enlightenment use of the historical label *Aufklärung* for "blackmailing purposes." By all accounts, Foucault was well familiar with Habermas's criticisms by the beginning of the 1980s — no doubt even before, as evidenced by the various veiled or explicit references to the social philosopher that speck his later writings and interviews. Soon after its delivery, Habermas's 1980 Adorno prize speech, "Modernity — An Unfinished Project," which featured Foucault briefly as an antimodern "young conservative," appeared in English.[90] Not unimportant — as Habermas observes in his preface to *The Philosophical Discourse of Modernity* — is the fact that the success of the Adorno prize speech and the subsequent publication of Lyotard's *The Postmodern Condition* made the subject ever more topical, leading him to dedicate an entire lecture course to the issue in the 1983 summer and 1983–4 winter semesters. What is more, Habermas delivered the first four lectures at the Collège de France in March 1983 and had several meetings with Foucault during that period.[91] As he reports, Foucault suggested that they convene, together with Hubert Dreyfus, Richard Rorty, and Charles Taylor, in November of 1984 for a private conference to discuss Kant's "What Is Enlightenment?"[92] Tragically, the dialogue that was to have resulted in such a transatlantic conference on the Enlightenment was aborted by Foucault's untimely death. His "The Art of Telling the Truth" now commonly is thought to contain the précis of the contribution he might have presented at the conference, while Habermas's "Taking Aim at the Heart of the Present" is the no doubt abridged response to his Kant work, delivered in the form of a "eulogy" on the occasion of the historian's untimely death.

Whether covertly or outspokenly, all of Foucault's Kant lectures engage in a debate with the Frankfurt School theorist, though it would surely be cynical, if not counterfactual, to assume that he merely construed a revisionist account of his own earlier phase, affirming his commitment to the Enlightenment for the sole purpose of countervailing Habermas's aspersions about his insidious irrationalism. For one, Foucault's earliest 1978 Kant lecture was held well in advance of Habermas's Adorno prize speech. Perhaps more to the point is the fact that, much as was the case with other key concepts, Foucault's account of the Enlightenment underwent a profound sea change and reappraisal, as he sought to take stock of what he called the always "revolving door of rationality."[93] Already his *Discipline and Punish* had acknowledged the "dialectic of Enlightenment," insofar as it did not necessarily dispute the advances and developments inaugurated by the Enlightenment but rather criticized the cost at which these were implemented. As Foucault put it pithily: "The 'Enlightenment,' which discovered the liberties, also invented the disciplines."[94] Bent over the parchment of the Enlightenment's foundational documents, he was more prone to weigh its "effects of despotism," including the inhuman exploitation of colonialism, than to celebrate its declarations of human rights. Indicating as much in his laudation for the historian of science, Georges Canguilhem, in whose path he placed his own research, he observed that in this work, "two centuries later, the Enlightenment returns: but not at all as a way for the West to take cognizance of its present possibilities and of the liberties to which it can have access, but as a way of interrogating it on its limits and on the powers which it abused. Reason as despotic Enlightenment."[95] In other words, at the crux of Foucault's assessment lay the glaring discrepancies between the Kantian hope of Enlightenment and the cruel realities, including the disciplinary regimes of exclusion that this dream had spawned.

However, by the time Foucault started crafting his new Kant exegesis in 1978, the critical weight of his argument swung back in favor of a decidedly positive valorization of the Enlightenment and the rationalist philosopher whose work towered above that of his contemporaries. The new interpretation seemed far removed from his earlier *The Order of Things*, in which he had assessed Kant's critical philosophy primarily in light of the resurgence of metaphysics that, despite appearances, reigned over the post-Kantian epoch. In studying Kant's anthropological writings, Foucault contested the humanistic level of interrogation that, regrettably, would rule the modern *epistēmē* to come. And, in diagnosing how the Kantian legislation of critical limits had mercilessly inaugurated the crisis of representation, thus marking "the threshold of our modernity," he showed how such legislation in reality had opened the space for a new post-Kantian wave of metaphysical doctrines. For, if Kantian critique had sanctioned "the withdrawal of knowledge and thought outside the space of representation," then subsequently "the unlimited field of representation, which Classical thought had established, which Ideology had attempted to scan in accordance with a step-by-step, discursive, scientific method, now appears as a metaphysics."[96] Indeed, the space opened by the representational crisis subsequently was occupied by the emerging philosophies of life and of the will, no less than by an equally deleterious reduction of the *epistēmē* to positivism.[97]

Only after he attenuated his Nietzschean assessment of the fallacies of humanism, anthropology, and epistemological foundationalism (also the butt of *The Order of Things* and *The Archeology of Knowledge*) would Foucault be able to profoundly reconsider Kant's relevance for the present. Speaking of the Enlightenment not so much as a historically delimited epoch, harboring under the false illusions of a universalist philosophy, but as an *attitude* that needed to live on, he proposed a thorough revalorization of Kantian critique, which could help to rescript the dogmatic boundaries that, even in the very present, still constricted experience and freedom. In fact, the arduous task that awaited Foucault was how to reclaim a positive concept of the Enlightenment that shed the fallacies of a universalist, monolithic understanding of reason in favor of a particularistic, historical account that pursued the twin ascendancy of power and reason.

Not entirely surprisingly, in order to do so, Foucault privileged Kant's peripheral historical essays, which he considered in conjunction with the larger project of the three *Critiques*. Though hardly a devotee of a German-style, idealistic philosophy of history, in this last period Foucault would not let go of Kant's *opuscules*, or small writings on history, which he studied using the Aubier edition of 1947.[98] Significantly, his interest in these works, which at the time were being rediscovered by a generation of philosophers, uncannily paralleled Arendt's late phase, during which she pronounced her acclaimed lectures on Kant's political philosophy. But, once again, there emerged a vital difference between the two thinkers. Charging that Kant relinquished political theory for a lamentable interest in the philosophy of history, Arendt maintained that the *opuscules*, when probed in conjunction with the third *Critique*, revealed the ungerminated seeds of Kant's unwritten critique of political reason. Analyzing Kant from the perspective of her theory of communicative action, she singled out the faculty of judgment, showing how the focal task of enlightenment as *Selbstdenken* (to think for oneself) also came with the demand to use one's imagination, that is, to "enlarge one's mind," through which the Kantian subject, or "world citizen," emphatically adopted the position of the other.[99] Foucault, quite to the contrary, was out to design a redemptive reading of Kant's philosophy of history that extracted a *historicist* moment from writings that ordinarily were interpreted as blueprints for a dusty Prussian republicanism or an improbable universal history. Almost in quasi-Dilthean fashion (though one must be careful not to push the analogy too far), his primary goal was to retrieve the *historicist* relevance from Kant's otherwise universalist critical project. With unparalleled urgency, he proposed to read the historical present in function of the epochal definition of modernity Kant advanced in the *Critique of Pure Reason*, when he observed that "Our age is the genuine age of critique [*Kritik*], to which everything must submit."[100]

In his earliest contribution, the 1978 Sorbonne presentation, Foucault mainly returned to the Enlightenment philosopher as if wanting to validate his own historico-philosophical method of genealogy by setting it on sound Kantian footing. Anchoring his Kant analysis in contemporaneous research he had done on "governmentality," Foucault determined Kantian critique as an act of epistemo-political insubordination, or the will "not to be governed thus." The later 1983 Kant texts, however, pushed much further. Quite unlike Habermas's *Philosophical Discourse of Modernity*, Foucault unflinchingly declared that it was Kant, not Hegel, who emerged as the first philosopher of modernity for having asked about the *now*, or the radical historicity that defined modernity's self-grounding, as it disengaged itself from a dogmatic past, delivering itself from prejudice. Seeing this sometimes vertiginous quest for ground no longer as a (Habermasian) crisis of self-legitimation but as a challenge to the period's bid for self-realization, Foucault conjectured, in his distinctively provocative tone, that Kant's prognosis found its most suitable answer in Baudelaire's dandyism. As the culmination of the modern practices through which the subject fashioned itself, Baudelaire's aestheticism truly initiated what Foucault termed a new "historical ontology" of "ourselves." In the final analysis, Kantian critique no longer was to be interpreted purely negatively, as, for example, *The Critique of Judgment* ordained when it described the activity of (self-)enlightenment as "that merely negative attitude."[101]

Critique no longer principally required that one attend to the strictly legislated, circumspect limits of experience, but, more so, invited one to clear a previously uncharted plane of freedom. Thus, in the course of the Kant exegesis, Foucault's understanding of the reciprocal relations between critique and Enlightenment almost imperceptibly changed. Moving away from framing critique by the politics of governmentality, he steadily became more interested in the ethics of self-government – work he was pursuing in *The Use of Pleasure* and *The Care of the Self*. In addition, he increasingly became concerned with the temporal logic of "the present" that infused Kant's Enlightenment essay and the ramifications it had, precisely, for the art of self-government, realized in the "permanent critique of ourselves." Either way, he proposed a startlingly innovative version of the process of *Aufklärung*, which, though quite dissimilar from Habermas's account of how the fates of reason and modernity were enmeshed, did not wholly relinquish the Weberian point of departure. In order to finetune this initial assessment, we must now engage in a more detailed reading of the three available Kant lectures, together with a number of closely associated peripheral texts and interviews.[102]

What Is Critique?

The territorial recovery of liberty *within* the (prohibitive) boundaries (*Grenze*) of what is given to experience constituted one of the major themes of Foucault's 1978 lecture, "What Is Critique?" Tellingly, as he took up the anatomy of Kant's philosophy, Foucault felt called upon to apologize to the philosophers gathered that day at the Sorbonne for trespassing onto their terrain. As a first indication of how far he would venture beyond conventional Kant commentaries, Foucault recast Kant's method of "critique" in the language of practical philosophy, holding it to denote an "attitude" – a term that, no doubt, already at this point translated the Greek word *ēthos*, which would claim center stage in the late ethical work. To be sure, as he initially confirmed to the assembly, critique was to be defined negatively, much as Kant had done in *The Critique of Pure Reason* when he delegated to it a policing role whose task it was to guard the limits of experience, preventing reason from committing errors. But more fundamental than the injunction not to err at the epistemological level was another ethico-political imperative, one prescribing that one ought not simply to be governed "thus" or "so much." Signaling that he intended to foreground this ethico-political dimension of critique, Foucault placed great stress on the critical attitude as general virtue.[103]

As he inscribed Kant into his own critique of power, Foucault characterized the critical attitude in terms highly dependent upon parallel research he had conducted into power–domination as "governmentalization." In a 1978 Collège de France lecture course, "Security, Territory, and Population," as well as the 1979 Tanner lectures, "*Omnes et Singulatim*,"[104] Foucault studied the origin ("emergence") of modern political discourse about "the art of government," pursuing its permutations from Christian pastoral power and Machiavelli's infamous glorification of the prince's sovereignty to the arrival of a rationalized process of governmentalization – an intentionally cumbersome term largely meant to evoke the rationalization of state, economy, and science that came to a head in the nineteenth century. If Machiavelli or later sixteenth- and seventeenth-century theorists sought to derive the art of governing others from the principle of sovereignty, then this model was altered radically, Foucault maintained, starting in the eighteenth century, with the arrival of political science and political economy, accompanied by the rise of population control and statistics. Though the 1978 Kant lecture failed to delve into such detail, it is clear that the process of governmentality formed the template against which Foucault demarcated critique, investing the term with a rupturing, incisive, rebellious force. For, as he explained, the critical attitude was locked into a "truth game" with the process of governmentalization, of which it was at once the "partner" and "adversary." Having a transformative, interventionist, limiting function, critique comprised acts of insubordination, or the "art of not being governed so much" ("l'art de n'être pas tellement gouverné").[105] Clearly, in pressing to the limit Kant's understanding of critique as antidogmatic thought, Foucault darted well beyond the letter of the philosopher's political views, lending to them a revolutionary fervor entirely at odds with the Enlightener's less than lenient attitude to collective insubordination and disobedience.[106] Moreover, he located the origin of this critical attitude not in the Enlightenment – as Kant had done when he hailed his own epoch as "the age of critique"[107] – but regressed further into time, back to the Renaissance. For, as the period in which the modern process of governmentalization first took shape, the Renaissance was rife with counteracting forces and antidogmatic resistances in three notable areas: religion (Reformation), the law (natural law/right), and science. As a matter of fact, in the discussion that followed the lecture, Foucault even reverted to the Middle Ages, isolating mysticism as one of the earliest authentic examples of how institutionalized and individualized struggles joined forces against a common adversary. In mysticism's resistance to pastoral power and the law of scriptures, "the historical practice of revolt, the non-acceptance of real government" met "the individual experience of the refusal of governmentality."[108] Critique, as Foucault summarized in the lecture's opening section, quintessentially amounted to the interrogation of the multiple games played between power and truth. Projecting Kant onto his Nietzschean-style epistemological antifoundationalism, he classified critique as the intervention in a historically determined power–truth wager, yielding strategic acts of "desubjectification [désassujetissement]," which defied the dominant regime of subordinating, or subjecting, power.[109]

As the art of "voluntary inservitude" and "reflective indocility,"[110] critique primarily called for resolute historical interventions that transpired in an ethico-political register. But more so than in the three Critiques, Foucault continued, this definition of critical insubordination lay crystallized in Kant's 1784 journal article in the Berlinische Monatsschrift, "An Answer to the Question: 'What Is Enlightenment?'"

Obviously, it is readily apparent why Foucault made this transition from the *Critiques* to the Enlightenment essay, at whose center lay a probe into the art of government no less than autonomous self-government. For, in his appeal to the courage and will of the public to throw off the yoke of dogmatism and servile obedience, Kant admonished the people to realize their autonomy, to seize the "freedom to make *public use* of one's reason in all matters."[111] Warning against unwarranted tutelage and too much oppressive government (capsulated in the German *leiten*, a word Foucault italicized), Kant's essay called for the harmonious order of republicanism, which held the balance between individual autonomy, tolerance, and the requisite stifling of dissent in one's private exercise of reason. Interested more in the philosophical than historical relevance of Kant's tract, Foucault – quite unlike Arendt – sidestepped the ramifications that followed from the Enlightener's conservative political views. Instead, for Foucault, "What Is Enlightenment?" principally unlocked the panorama of an altogether novel period, which, in vying against prejudice and self-incurred tutelage, invited unheard-of acts of courage in religion, right, and knowledge, as behooved a period not afraid to interrogate epistemological limits, including "the knowledge of knowledge." Concluding the first part of the lecture, he admitted that there existed conceptual distinctions between Kantian critique and the Enlightenment. Similarly, he conceded that Kant had placed more stress on how to gain liberty through acknowledging the limits of our knowledge than through brazen acts of courage. Nonetheless, in ascribing to critique the task of "knowing knowledge," Foucault accentuated, Kant had ensured that critique meant adopting a de-subjecting role with regard to the game of power–truth. As such, critique henceforth would function as a prolegomenon to all possible forms of *Aufklärung*, in the immediate present no less than in the distant future.

To fathom the full complexity of Foucault's lecture, it is necessary to see that its second section discussed the negative consequences that resulted from the historical fact that the two poles of the constellation critique-*Aufklärung* – comprising knowledge and the will "not to be governed thus" – had drifted apart. For, if the lecture's introduction established that critique, together with the *ēthos* of Enlightenment, constituted the two inseparable sides of the same historico-critical attitude, then much of what followed recounted the loss of this organic unity, chronicling their gradual split in the post-Kantian era. Now, Foucault seemed to go so far as to imply that Kant himself had inadvertently created the dangerous possibility that critique might be situated "in retreat with regard to the Enlightenment," holding him accountable for the resulting chasm (*décalage*) between critique and Enlightenment.[112] What he drew here, in bold strokes, was nothing less than the crisis Kantian critique underwent in post-Kantian philosophy, resulting in a functionalist, self-perpetuating critical apparatus that had lost touch with the historico-political duty of progressive enlightenment. Criticizing the resulting positivism, the rise to prominence of statism and the rationalization that took hold of economy and society in the post-Enlightenment age, Foucault clearly embarked on a Weberian analysis of bureaucratic,

administered modernity. In Weber's sociological analysis of the process of rationalization, Kant's inquiry into the connections between Enlightenment and critique
returned as the suspicion that reason was responsible for the excesses of power,
evinced in modernity's rush towards an ever-accelerating governmentalization. In fact,
in asking the question of how reason and power intertwined, Weber and the first-
generation founders of the Frankfurt School launched into a critical inquiry of "the art
of government," engaging in critical resistance and acts of insubordination along lines
mandated by Kantian critique. But distinct national differences existed, Foucault
noted, between France and Germany as to how this tenuous relation between critique
and Enlightenment was played out. In France, the fallacious reduction of Kantian
critique to a narrowly defined epistemology manifested itself as an overbearing
concern with the history of the sciences, all the way from Auguste Comte up to the
disciplinary revolution that, at long last, shook up the European academy in the 1960s.
Quite the opposite proved to be the case in neighboring Germany, observed Foucault,
privileging the left-leaning tradition in German-Jewish philosophy while ignoring the
culture's conservative mandarins. To be sure, in early twentieth-century French philosophy, reason and rationalization were avidly criticized, but by the political right (for
the wrong set of reasons) so that the questions raised by the Frankfurt School did not
emerge until the arrival of phenomenology, which, in interrogating the constitution of
meaning, would at least begin to focus on language's coercive force. Overall, Foucault
thus readily admitted to the strong, if somewhat submerged, links that bound him to
the German tradition – from the Young Hegelians to the Frankfurt School – with its
critique of positivism, objectivism, rationalization, *technē*, and technicization at the
center, also, as he meticulously added, of Husserl's *The Crisis of European Sciences and
Transcendental Phenomenology*. Averse historical circumstances notwithstanding, it was
now of the essence, he avowed, to recapture this submerged "fraternal bond" and to
forge a new alliance between the French philosophical tradition and the Frankfurt
School. To do so implied pledging allegiance to a new historico-philosophical practice
that committed itself to the cardinal "problem of modern philosophy," that of the
Enlightenment.

By all accounts, Foucault thus paid tribute to his intellectual pedigree, seeking to
recapture the elective affinities between his own critique of power, Weber, and
Frankfurt School social theory. Indeed, such intellectual advances towards the school's
original members very much became a staple of his writings during the late 1970s.
Whether in interviews with Raulet, Trombadori, or others,[113] Foucault repeatedly
acknowledged the significance of critical theory, adding that an earlier encounter with
its thought might have prevented him from taking some digressive by-roads. Still, it
would be wrong to assume that he agreed with all of the school's methodological or
philosophical premises, especially with its understanding of the "dialectic of reason." In
his "*Omnes et Singulatim*: Towards a [Critique] of 'Political Reason'" and the closely
connected "The Subject and Power," both of which were composed under the aegis of
Kant's Enlightenment essay, Foucault insisted that he could not readily adopt the

Frankfurt School's globalizing critique of reason – one of the few points about which he seemed to be in tacit agreement with Habermas. "*Omnes et Singulatim*," delivered at Stanford University in 1979, especially is of note here as it meant to advance a "critique of political reason"; a somewhat "pretentious" title, as Foucault admitted in the lecture's introduction – no doubt, one speculates, because of the reference to Kant's unwritten fourth *Critique*, to whose omission Arendt had drawn attention in her 1970 Kant lectures. At the core of Foucault's analysis lay the question of political reason, of reason and politics, no less than their interconnections, whose mandatory analysis Kant had first prescribed. Since Kant, Foucault averred, "the role of philosophy has been to prevent reason going beyond the limits of what is given in experience; but from the same moment – that is, from the development of modern states and political management of society – the role of philosophy has also been to keep watch over the excessive powers of rationality ...."[114] In the trail of Kant's philosophical decree, scholars from the nineteenth century onward had begun to register the fated intermeshing of "rationalization and the excesses of political power," though, in the end, they ventured too far in their singular determination to detect the ills of reason. So as to stave off possible misunderstanding of his position, Foucault immediately added that he refused to occupy the position of the irrationalist – mindful, no doubt, of the criticism that Habermas but also Derrida had launched early on against the untenable bifurcation between reason and unreason that upheld such texts as *Madness and Civilization*. As Foucault explained, in seeking to correct the insights of the Frankfurt School, he targeted above all its *totalizing* critique of reason, while recognizing the necessity of conducting research into the multiple rationalizing technologies of power, no less than into the manifold existing varieties of "rationalities." This crucial correction at the address of the school's "critique of reason" returned in "The Subject and Power," which urged critics to relinquish the conventional bifurcation between reason and unreason so as to render visible the multifarious resistances that transpired within truth/power games.

From the viewpoint of these texts, as reread through the 1978 Kant lecture, one begins to gauge the full span of what Foucault understood by "critique": the critical function of techniques of resistance as they revolted against the dominant "art of being governed so much," coupled to the project of critical historiography, which consistently assailed normative bifurcations and conventional critical "dividing practices," including the divide that pitted reason against unreason.[115] The point is particularly cogently made in the notable interview Foucault conducted with Gérard Raulet, an interview dedicated to the insights of critical theory. Agreeing with Raulet that the Frankfurt School's struggle for emancipation pertained to " the dialectical continuity of reason, and of a perversion that completely transformed it at a certain stage – which it now becomes a question of rectifying,"[116] Foucault defined his own project as concerned with discursive systems of exclusion and the inordinate consequences that followed from the discursive self-enactment of the subject as it spoke the truth about itself. But the interview also provided him with an occasion to amend Habermas's assessment of his work in an earlier French interview with Raulet, in which the social scientist briefly praised Foucault's "masterly description of the bifurcation of reason" in the eighteenth century.[117] For Foucault, this misconceived appreciation of *The Order of Things* exposed Habermas's allegiance to a monolithic conception of reason, which aimed to recover a true form of rationality – even if it was no longer substantive – thus operating with only one possible mode of bifurcation. Instead, "it was a question of isolating the form of rationality presented as dominant, and endowed with the status of the one-and-only reason, in order to show that it is *one* possible form among others," as Weber, the Frankfurt School representatives, and Canguilhem had done.[118] The fallacious conception of one possible bifurcation between reason and its other needed to be dispelled for "an endless, multiple bifurcation – a kind of abundant ramification," for an "abundance of branchings, ramifications, breaks and ruptures," for the "different modifications in which rationalities engender one another, oppose and pursue one another." In the end, this meant that it was impossible "to assign a point at which reason would have lost sight of its fundamental project, or even a point at which the rational becomes the irrational." As he exchanged a universal history of reason for a genealogy of its contingencies, he also disputed the so-called trap of a *petitio principii* his position allegedly entailed, quite obviously in riposte to Habermas. For "the blackmail which has very often been at work in every critique of reason or every critical inquiry into the history of rationality (either you accept rationality or you fall prey to the irrational)," he observed, "operates as though a rational critique of rationality were impossible, or as though a rational history of all the ramifications and all the bifurcations, *a contingent history of reason*, were impossible."[119] As a matter of fact, at the risk of overly schematizing distinctions, one might say that the Habermas–Foucault dispute in many ways revolved around claims to the universality of reason. If Habermas saw so-called particularist "neopopulist" movements like feminism as unable to realize that universality, then for Foucault requiring such a universalist program amounted to buying into the despotism and colonialism of the Enlightenment.[120]

The foregoing assemblage of texts shows, then, that despite the reservations Foucault expressed at the address of the Frankfurt School, he continued to consider himself the heir to the Frankfurt School, acknowledging that he pursued their genealogy of reason, albeit in a distinctly altered form. Testifying to this intellectual heritage, he assuredly contested more conventional readings of the *Dialectic of Enlightenment*, which foregrounded its latent nihilism. For, rather than setting an end to reason and therewith to the unfinished project of Enlightenment (as Habermas would not stop warning in the Frankfurt lectures), Adorno and Horkheimer, Foucault indicated, quite to the contrary complied with the mandate lodged in Kant's critical philosophy as they sought to rejoin critique and *Aufklärung*.

While such were the explosive political insights that lay compressed in the 1978 Kant analysis, it is equally true that the lecture for the most part remained attuned to the solemn occasion taking place at the Sorbonne, namely, that of opening the dialogue between French historians and philosophers. To facilitate such an exchange in the spirit of Kantian critique required, Foucault advised, that both parties commit themselves to a new historico-philosophical practice. Caution was in order, though, as this new "attitude" should subscribe neither to the philosophy of history nor to the history of philosophy. Thus, on the level of disciplinary learning, Foucault's address to his philosophical audience at once appealed to an unprecedented practice of interdisciplinarity, inviting it to cross the threshold that habitually divided philosophers in search of knowledge's deep structures from tabulating historians, ordinarily wedded to empirical history. Now, Foucault exhorted his public, it was time to craft one's proper history, to dare "fabricate history as if by fiction" — history henceforth being the terrain in which structures of rationality and mechanisms of subjection intersected. Critique meant breaching the tightly restricted operating fields of empiricist historians and philosophers alike, requiring the expert help of altogether different tools and manuals to scrutinize the multiple constellations between relations of *power, truth, and the subject*.

Applied to the discipline of historiography, this meant that an alternative critical methodology needed to be crafted, which would take on the self-indulgence of an epistemological apparatus that had acquired a life of its own, producing a surplus of rationalization, whose effects, he added, were noticeable in an entire generation of philosophers, from Dilthey to Habermas. As proof that they posed the question of the Enlightenment inadequately, that is to say, by invoking the constrictive standard of knowledge (*connaissance*) divorced from power, Foucault cited their "inquiry into the legitimacy of the historical modes of knowing."[121] In criticizing this practice of scientific legitimation, he obviously returned to his roots in a Nietzschean antifoundationalist epistemology. For the quest to demarcate truth from illusion, symptomatic of a metaphysical will to knowledge, was to make way for an investigation into how coercive processes managed to get wrapped in the mechanisms of rationality and efficacy. In studying the nexus *power/knowledge*, the critical historian scrutinized the interconnections between mechanisms of coercion and contents of knowledge, probing how they had become justified as rational, calculated, and efficacious techniques. By the same token, the historian relinquished the work of ideology critique, bracketing the search for ultimate legitimacy that discriminated science from ideology, error, and illusion, while he also steered clear of the search for universal transcendentals. Relying no longer on conventional procedures of knowledge and legitimacy, the genealogist would map the history of the event, or eventialization (*événementialisation*).[122] Rather than isolating transhistorical universals, the historian intrepidly confronted history's inchoate fray, the immanence of pure singularities.

Overhauling Kantian nomenclature, Foucault did not call for a probe into the transhistorical, a priori conditions of possibility that underpinned knowledge structures. Instead, the constellation *savoir/pouvoir* required an examination of the "conditions of acceptability" that produced power/knowledge "events." To master the task, he prescribed three interacting sets of methodological tools, the familiar archeology and genealogy, to which he added the analysis of strategies. On the procedural level, "archeology" directed the focus of analysis away from procedures to an inquiry into the system of acceptability, while "genealogy" jettisoned the conventional monocausal model of derivation in favor of multiple "descendants" to investigate "conditions of apparition" that allowed multiply determined historical singularities to congeal. Finally, he added yet another dynamic principle to the constellation power/knowledge, reflected in the third tool, the analysis of strategy, which surveyed the plurality of effects that transpired in these perpetually mobile, competing games. As such, these procedures permitted the historian to expose a contentious agonistic field of struggles, in which, to emulate Foucault's exegesis of Kant's Enlightenment essay, dogmatic impositions of knowledge/power merely *obeyed* certain "conditions of acceptability," while rebelling counterstrategies *contested* the rules of "being governed so much." Retooled this way, Foucault's new historiography would reveal "a field of possibilities, of openings, of indecisions, of reversals, and of eventual dislocations that make them fragile, that make them impermanent, that make of these effects events – nothing more, nothing less than events." Or, as he rephrased it, using the language of unprecedented possibilities, "in what way can the effects of the coercion proper to these positivities not be dissipated by a return to the legitimate destination of knowledge and by a reflection on the transcendental or the quasi-transcendental that fixes it, but rather be inverted or undone inside a concrete strategic field [*champ*], this concrete strategic field that induced them, and from the decision precisely to not be governed."[123]

With the Sorbonne lecture, Foucault far exceeded the task of providing an anatomy of the historical present. Designing a prescriptive text, he also specified the assignment awaiting the philosopher-historian as he sought an exit out of historiography's deadlock. In unyielding terms, he devised that history's path was to be traveled in inverse direction, curving back from a self-perpetuating, near-functionalist aberrant mode of "critique" to a recovery of the Enlightenment's lost bequest. Equally deserving of further attention, however, is the language of volition in which this injunction was clad. For, in the text's concluding lines, the word "will," *volonté*, almost surreptitiously reemerged: "the decisive will not to be governed, this decisive will, an attitude at once individual and collective, to leave, as Kant said, one's immaturity. A question of attitude."[124] Evoking the loaded words of political decision and will, Foucault obviously returned to the opening paragraph of Kant's "What Is Enlightenment?," which had explained the activity (or verb) of "enlightenment" in terms of the will or resolution to use one's reason (understanding) autonomously, without relying on the external guidance of others. For Foucault, Kant's injunction disclosed ramifications that shot far beyond the field of historiography, or the study of epistemology in its connections with a genealogy of power. For, so he pondered during the discussion that followed the presentation, might not the critical attitude on the one hand signify "the historical practice of revolt, the non-acceptance of a real government" and, on the other hand, "the individual experience of the refusal of governmentality"?[125] In many ways, the passage drew consequences that flew in the face of the earlier Nietzsche work; now, the ominous "will to truth" needed to be resisted, countered by a "will to revolution," avowing to one's desire "not to be governed so much" in *all* possible domains, whether epistemological, ethico-political, or even aesthetic.

Revolutionizing the Present

The rather minimal reference to the will at the end of the Sorbonne address, it turned out, anticipated a motif that would emerge more prominently in the 1983 lecture course, "The Government of the Self and of Others," to which we must now turn. Taken together, the lecture "The Art of Telling the Truth" and the contemporaneous "What Is Enlightenment?" (both related to the 1983 Paris course) give us some indication of the way in which Foucault hoped to interlace the various strands of his Kant analysis with the focus on ethics as self-government that dominated his late phase. Meant to rehabilitate philosophical *ēthos* as the "permanent critique of ourselves," the two Kant lectures no longer harped so much on the need to overcome the historical breach wedged between critique and Enlightenment as the Sorbonne address had done, but started off from the vantage point of their original *rapprochement*. If again both pieces took their impulse from Kant's "What Is Enlightenment?," what appeared substantially new was the way in which they indirectly engaged debates about modernity that were topical at the time, more specifically, the temporality, or temporal logic, of modernity. But where "The Art of Telling the Truth" contextualized Kant's Enlightenment piece by reading it in tandem with the philosopher's response to another contemporary event – the French Revolution – the longer lecture, "What Is Enlightenment?" pursued the full span of the philosophical trajectory to which Kant had given rise – from Baudelaire's theory of modernity to the most recent present: Foucault's own "philosophical historicism."

Much as the Sorbonne address had tied the practice of critique to the project of the Enlightenment, so the 1983 "The Art of Telling the Truth" added yet another constellation, that of the Revolution, thus developing further the reference to the "revolutionary will" faintly audible at the end of the 1978 lecture. What proved truly unprecedented within the history of philosophy, Foucault now accented, was that Kant's Enlightenment essay was the first to have explicitly reflected on the status of the "present" and "actuality," thus initiating modernity's contemplation of itself. In asking "what is happening now?," in interrogating the status of the Enlightenment, Kant did not simply subordinate actuality to the exigencies of a transhistorical philosophy but turned the present into an event, a "philosophical event to which the philosopher who speaks of it belongs."[126] Preeminently, it was Kant who first fathomed that the status of historical "actuality" confronted the historical subject as a veritable philosophical question. More so, raising this awareness to the level of philosophical deliberation he implicated his "own discursive contemporaneity"[127] in the project of collective interrogation, thus exchanging the position of mere distanced observer for that of active agent-actor. In so doing, the Kant essay in fact designated philosophy the role of the "discourse of modernity on modernity." Peeled loose from a confining academic discipline, philosophy now amounted more to "a way of being" or style that "problematized" the present and cajoled the philosopher to question the present to which he belonged and "in relation to which he has to situate himself."[128] Belying his reputation as the philosopher of universalisms and universality, Kant did not so much foreground the position of a universal "us" – "how one belongs to a human community in general" – but rather a radically historicized locus of identity, "how one belongs to a certain 'us,' to an us that concerns a cultural totality characteristic of one's own time."[129] In adding this nuance, Foucault seemed all too aware of how his reinterpretation of the Kantian corpus played into the embattled universalism debates that at the time were already dividing proponents of poststructuralism and critical theory.

As another such response to the contemporary adherents of critical theory, one may also read the alternative "genealogy of modernity" the lecture advanced, which directly involved modernity's temporal logic and rested upon two interrelated theses. First, like Habermas, Foucault comprehended modernity not just as a past historical period, epoch, or even style – say, the battle between *les anciens et les modernes*, to be studied by the history of ideas or cultural history – but as an unfinished politico-philosophical project. Certainly, that project no longer was wedded to the exigencies of a universalizing rationality, yet Foucault shared with Habermas the conception of modernity as potentiality or process that needed to be realized, actualized, though, to be sure, no longer as history's inner teleology. Second, in labeling modernity not just as process but as a *permanent* process to boot, Foucault ventured further afield, describing the double temporal logic that was said to inflect the *Aufklärung*, insofar as it was simultaneously a "singular event" that inaugurated European modernity and a complex historical operation that needed to be renewed in every singular historical "now." Skillfully, he thus already here neutralized the charge of mere "presentism" that Habermas repeatedly supplicated against him, rejecting the cult of the present, which adulated the fad, fashion, immediacy, and whose contours, as we shall see, he would draw in his analysis of Baudelaire.

To elucidate the politico-historical consequences that issued from his Kant exegesis, Foucault turned to another Kant text, this time structured around another seminal "event," namely, the comments about the Revolution that lay lodged in his 1798 *The Contest of Faculties*, whose second part sought to adjudicate the disciplinary disputes between the faculties of law and philosophy. There, Kant proffered an answer to the query at the crux of both disciplines: whether the human race was continually improving, and, if so, whether the causality of such constant progress could be exemplified by an event in the present. Because it was impossible, Kant noted, to take up an absolute point of view when it came to predicting humankind's free action, prophetic history needed a sign, or historical event, that could corroborate humanity's teleology towards its own betterment. To gain further validity and efficaciousness, the sign was to merge three temporal axes, being at once rememorative, demonstrative, and prognostic.[130] It was precisely such a sign of humanity's "moral disposition" and hence of the cause of its historic progress that Kant believed to have recognized in the French Revolution. Yet not so much the deeds enacted under the French Revolution garnered the Enlightener's attention as the dynamics between the revolutionary spectacle and its spectators. Steering his lens away from the revolutionary agents to the onlookers, Kant gleaned in their "sympathy of aspiration bordering on enthusiasm"[131] a "moral disposition within the human race."[132] Indeed, for Kant enthusiasm was nothing less than an *Affekt*, through which humans "[embraced] the cause of goodness."[133]

Once again, it is fascinating to see how Foucault actualized Kant's political views, much as he had sought to modernize the Enlightenment essay. In setting Kant up as a participating actor rather than a mere bystander when it came to confronting the political question of modernity, Foucault seemingly went against Arendt's Kant interpretation, which had linked the economy of spectatorship traversing his thought to the melancholic, passive disposition dominating his philosophy of history. However the case may be, in stressing Kant's agency and co-implication in the process of philosophical self-interrogation, Foucault doubtlessly alluded to the theatrical spectator–actor dualism that underpinned the philosopher's reflections on the French Revolution. But, where Arendt discerned in this philosophical spectacle the high point of Kant's conservative republicanism, Foucault gleaned a commitment to a "will to revolution." To be sure, the observation was somewhat perplexing considering the turn Kant's *The Contest of Faculties* soon thereafter would take. For soon enough, Kant moved from discussing "revolution" to celebrating "evolution," shying away from the potential violence that inevitably accompanied revolutionary wars. Instead, it was the evolution of a republican constitution ruled by natural right that he now detected as the public rejoiced, "with universal and disinterested sympathy," in the presence of the French revolutionaries.[134] Thus, in the final analysis, the realization of the Platonic noumenal ideal of republicanism in the phenomenal world of experience constituted the moral duty of mankind. Even though this ideal might have to be procured through bellicose violence, it nonetheless constituted the eternal norm for all civil constitutions and the "means of ending all wars."[135] In this sense, *The Contest of Faculties* returned to *Perpetual Peace*, which similarly had looked to build a universal republic, or league of nations.

To draw the full consequences of this Kantian "will to revolution" meant to practice voluntary resistance – one of the tasks that awaited philosophical modernity. It meant to reinvent the philosophical practice of questioning, not to procure an "ontology of being" – not even Heidegger's historicized ontology advanced in *Being and Time* – but an "ontology of the present, an ontology of ourselves."[136] Indeed, the weighty legacy of the Enlightenment persisted in the present in at least three different ways at once: as singular event, permanent process, and philosophical question. In asking about the present, Kant launched two congruent modes of critical interrogation in particular: "What is the *Aufklärung*?" and "What is the Revolution?," or, phrased differently, "What is to be done with the will to revolution?" Ever as much as during Kant's lifetime, the Enlightenment endured in the form of a *philosophical question* indelibly impressed into modern thought – a "permanent process manifested in the history of reason, in the development and establishment of forms of rationality and technology, the autonomy and authority of knowledge."[137] In the face of this question, one would err if one were animated by a dangerous form of piety for the past that strove to preserve the *Aufklärung* "living and intact," stowing away the remnants of what was left of it. Quite to the contrary, the requisite courage was needed to understand the legacy of the Enlightenment as the question it truly was, that is, as a question whose challenge needed to be perpetually renewed, whose "unthought" demanded to be thought through. What needed to be preserved was "the very question of that event and its meaning (the question of the historicity of thinking about the universal)."[138] As he thus described the persistence of an inquiry that defied definitive, doctrinal answers, Foucault again came uncannily close to describing the Enlightenment as the "unfinished project of modernity" – much as Habermas had done in his Adorno prize speech. Not disputing Kant's concern with the universal as he quested after a sign of humanity's moral disposition, Foucault instead foregrounded the historicity of that thinking. Similarly, he stressed that the "question of the *Aufklärung*, or of reason" was "a historical problem" that had ruled the history of post-Kantian philosophy. Significantly, it is here that he reinvented Kant's notion of enthusiasm as *the will to revolution*,[139] a gesture by which he revised Kantian nomenclature no less than his own discourse of will. For this non-Kantian phrase did not only go against the latter's discourse of the will, located in the *Critique of Practical Reason* – a text that, as Arendt reminds us, defined the individual qua individual – but it also violated the letter of Kant's text, which rejected revolutions in favor of the evolution to autocracy and republicanism.[140] What mattered, however, was that Kant's text called for a merger of the individual and collective wills, attesting to a communal willingness to leave one's self-imposed historical immaturity behind.

If, in the end, Kant's philosophy kindled two defining strands of philosophical analysis, then, regrettably, one had neglected to pay heed to his prescient historicism. Branching off from Kant's work, one school of thought restricted itself to the "analytics of truth," committed as it was to an ahistorical universalism and the assessment of the "conditions of possibility" that underwrote knowledge, while the other engaged with an "ontology of the present" or "of ourselves." Spanning the gamut of modern philosophy, from "Hegel, through Nietzsche and Max Weber, to the Frankfurt school," this historicizing school of philosophy had in fact laid the very foundations for the kind of tradition within which Foucault himself had tried to work.[141] But as he thus inscribed himself into the long line of historical modernity, Foucault once again adjusted the bifurcation between universalism and particularism under which some of his own earliest work had harbored. For, far from renouncing philosophy's concern with universal truths, his preferred historical school of analysis repudiated a doctrinal essentialism, executed under the banner *truth/connaissance*, to address "the question of the historicity of thinking about the universal" along the axis *pouvoir/savoir*.[142]

Critique as Limit-Attitude

Perhaps more so than any other text of the period, Foucault's longest Kant lecture, expressly titled "What Is Enlightenment?," reads like a programmatic document, laying down the goals, expectations, stakes, and consequences that informed his refashioned historico-philosophical practice. Rich in interpretive observations and *aperçus*, the lecture audaciously appropriated the title of Kant's essay in a conscious effort to echo it. Hardly playful, Foucault pondered what it might be like to consider his own lecture as a response to an imaginary contest, modeled on the prize competition of the *Berlinische Monatsschrift*, but asking this time around, "What is modern philosophy?" Faced with such a query, he would feel compelled to answer: "the philosophy that is attempting to answer the question raised so impudently two centuries ago: *Was ist Aufklärung?*"[143] Adding his own reflections to the generations of philosophers preoccupied with the challenge of the Enlightenment – from "Hegel through Nietzsche or Max Weber to Horkheimer or Habermas"[144] – the lecture (at least on the face of it) at first appeared more generous to Habermas. But this impression soon was belied as Foucault contentiously entered into discussion with the theorist, even if he did not polemicize against him *expressis verbi*. Rather than accept doctrinal renditions of rationality, the lecture suggested, the adherents of Foucault's newly conceived modernity were to assume another, more felicitous attitude, or *ēthos* – a term that, as he explained, reverberated with a host of meanings: it defined "a mode of relating to contemporary reality; a voluntary choice made by certain people; in the end, a way of thinking and feeling; a way, too, of acting and behaving that at one and the same time marks a relation of belonging and presents itself as a task. No doubt, a bit like what the Greeks called an *ēthos*."[145]

Taken as a whole, the lecture proposed a sustained reflection on the nature of limits, on the *ēthos* of Enlightenment, and on modernity as a *limit-attitude*. How to breach the old frontiers as a way of rethinking "who we are," how to provide our own "historical ontology," how to regain and achieve our autonomy to the fullest – such were the questions that Foucault's philosophical essay (or exercise) handled. Heeding Kant's warning against the twin threats of dogmatism and skepticism, he pursued alternate tracks of actualizing the philosopher's injunction to secure the autonomy of freedom in the historical present. Engaged in a formalized "essay" that thought through the Kantian "limit" in view of its ramifications for the present, Foucault directed his undivided attention at the *enabling*, freedom-imparting power that issued from Kant's negatively defined critique. But if now, as before, it was of the essence to test one's limits, then it was always with an eye on how it might be ethically viable to breach uncharted ground. What better way to revitalize the critical project than by returning to Kant's "What Is Enlightenment?," which delineated the *Aufklärung* negatively as an "exit," or "way out," of self-inflicted immaturity and tutelage? To signal this exit, Kant had resorted to ethico-political language, interpreting the period's motto, or adage – *Sapere aude!* (Dare to know!) – as a matter of the will, autonomy, and the use of reason, an injunction in which lay encapsulated the resolution to exercise one's reason rather than servilely to obey dogmatic authority. Resisting heteronomy and doctrinal prescriptions, the enlightened subject was to adjudicate "the conditions under which the use of reason is legitimate in order to determine what can be known [connaître], what must be done, and what may be hoped."[146] Refusing simply to identify the temporal perimeters of a circumscribed epoch or period, Kant laid out a practical attitude whose rudiments could best be gauged by setting it in relation to a constellation of related, consonant attitudes: those of critique, history, and modernity. Designating individual acts as well as a collective process that exacted the free, universal, and public usage of reason, Kant's description of Enlightenment *ēthos* privileged the work of critique, which prescribed the "conditions of possibility" enabling the exercise of reason but also staked off its prohibitive limits. In the spirit of his Sorbonne lecture, Foucault here too ignored the transcendental function of critique, seeking to vindicate instead Kant's philosophy of history. Willing to apply pressure to the Kantian text to the point of radically (some would undoubtedly say, unrecognizably) modernizing it, Foucault distilled a startlingly different modernity from the philosopher's *oeuvre*, which defied the quest for the internal historical logic or universal teleology one unmistakably can discern in Kant's shorter writings on history. For, crucially, the lecture formulated the provocative hypothesis that Kant's Berlin essay – this "little text," as Foucault called it – was situated "at the crossroads of critical reflection and reflection on history."[147] By establishing critique in unprecedented manner as the "new attitude of modernity," Foucault counseled, Kant dislodged his critical project from conventional historical hermeneutics, vested in tradition, no less than from the search for the historical totality of mankind, giving it an uncommon relevance for our own present (*le présent, l'actualité*). Stated differently, Kant's critical project combined an analysis of knowledge with an understanding of history, for, in reflecting on the *difference* today makes with respect to yesterday, it devised that such temporal reflection was to permeate all philosophical thinking, granting it the luster of the most pressing historical task (*Aufgabe*).[148]

More than simply a period bounded by a pre- and postmodernity, the Enlightenment designated an altogether different temporality in that it called for its permanent, unwavering (quasi-Kierkegaardian) repetition – never simply a Nietzschean "return of the same" – through the perpetual reactivation of the philosophical *ēthos*. Kant's political imperative ordained the "permanent critique of our historical era"[149] through "a type of philosophical interrogation – one that simultaneously problematizes man's relation to the present, man's historical mode of being, and the constitution of the self as an autonomous subject."[150] To subscribe to this *ēthos* implied to reject the attitudes of countermodernity with which it seemed trapped in battle (*lutte*). Doubtlessly, Foucault's observations unabashedly envisaged Habermas's aspersions about postmodernism and poststructuralism's irrational undertone, when he regretted the "blackmailing" tactics of a rationalist discourse that expected interlocutors to endorse its premises. In the same vein of adding tort to retort, one must also understand Foucault's remarks about what he considered to be "the always too facile confusions between humanism and Enlightenment."[151] Existing in tension with conventional forms of "humanism," the Enlightenment attitude instead exacted a "principle of a critique and a permanent creation of ourselves in our autonomy."[152]

Having advanced what he still considered to be a *negative* delimitation of the philosophical *ēthos* – what it was not – Foucault proceeded to a positive account, consisting in a critique of the present that would generate the desired "historical ontology of ourselves."[153] This philosophical *ēthos*, he advised – bringing to a head preceding allusions to or ruminations about the Kantian limit – was to be interpreted as a *limit-attitude*. For if Kant commanded that critique exposed what ought to remain off limits to calibrating knowledge, then this negative injunction also came with a positively oriented practical directive of border-passing (*franchissement*). To practice critique meant to reject the alternative of inside/outside, choosing instead the danger of *situating* oneself at the frontiers:

> [Critique] indeed consists of analyzing and reflecting upon limits. But if the Kantian question was that of knowing [*savoir*] what limits knowledge [*connaissance*] must renounce exceeding, it seems to me that the critical question today must be turned back into a positive one: In what is given to us as universal, necessary, obligatory, what place is occupied by whatever is singular, contingent, and the product of arbitrary constraints? The point, in brief, is to transform the critique conducted in the form of necessary limitation into a practical critique that takes the form of a possible crossing-over [*franchissement*].[154]

To translate Foucault's *franchissement* here as "transgression" would mean to suggest that his philosophy of the limit approximated Bataille's "heterological idea of delimitation."[155] But, though such a Bataillean economy of transgression and expenditure might have animated the younger Foucault, such intentions were far removed from the program that determined his late Kantian phase. Where Kant qualified critique *ex negativo* in terms of the threshold that knowledge should not cross, Foucault transformed this negative, limit-bound, restrictive definition into a positive prescription, asking us to invent a new *limit*-attitude. To be sure, in the margins one might note that Kant to no small degree thematized the difference between positive and negative limits in the three *Critiques*, and in the *Prolegomena*, where it was a matter of securing the ground that would permit the philosopher and theologian to continue to ask questions about the noumenal. Thanks to what lay beyond the positive boundary of reason, Kant explained, we continued to be able to raise philosophical and theological questions. So as to make this point, Kant in fact distinguished between positive bounds (*Grenzen*) and negative limits (*Schranken*). Describing the positive boundary as that which belonged to the object, he stipulated that the bound referred to what lay within it, as well as to the space that resided without its periphery. Though the limitation of reason was that it could not say anything certain, except about objects of possible experience, this limitation did "not prevent reason from leading us to the objective boundary of experience, viz., to the reference to something which is not itself an object of experience but must be the highest ground of all experience."[156] Even if Foucault failed to draw these critical demarcations, using the French term "limite" indiscriminately for both *Grenze* and *Schranke*, it is evident that he operated within the Kantian parameters of the "enabling boundary." However, he replaced the Kantian conception of the boundary (*Grenze*), permitting metaphysics and theology to carry on with their quest for the noumenal, the thing-in-itself, with a refashioned understanding of the term that instead allowed one to fathom the possible renewal of the historical present beyond the fixity of the now. Rather than resulting in the infraction of the law, such critical border-crossing (*franchissement*) of older well-traveled terrain, Foucault suggested, constituted morally correct behavior, the kind of ethical attitude that lived up to the high standards of Kant's moral philosophy, or practical critique. Certainly, the new historicist critique no longer was to subscribe to the formalized laws of the universal but needed to address the singularity of "evenementality," marked by an esteem for the contingent – a formulation in fact quite close to the anti-Platonic injunction that Adorno formulated in *Negative Dialectics* when he stipulated that philosophy ought to reclaim what had been cast out by its orthodoxy. As such, critique involved methodological innovations of the kind inaugurated by Foucauldian archeology and genealogy, which said farewell to the old laws that regulated what we can and cannot do:

> [Critique] is no longer going to be practiced in the search for formal structures with universal value, but rather as a historical investigation into the events that have led us to constitute ourselves and to recognize ourselves as subjects of what we are doing, thinking, saying. In that sense, this [critique] is not transcendental, and its goal is not that of making a metaphysics possible: it is genealogical in its design and archeological in its method. Archeological – and not transcendental – in the sense that it will not seek to identify the universal structures of all knowledge [*connaissance*] or of all possible moral action, but will seek to treat the instances of discourse that articulate what we think, say, and do as so many historical events. And this critique will be genealogical in the sense that it will not deduce from the form of what we are what it is impossible for us to do and to know; but it will separate out, from the contingency that has made us what we are, the possibility of no longer being [*la possibilité de ne plus être*], doing, or thinking what we are, do, or think.[157]

In laying out the anatomy of a *historico-critical attitude* that knotted the three *Critiques* to Kant's essays on history, Foucault's lecture opposed standard Kant interpretations that routinely privilege his ahistorical transcendentalism. The point of critique,

Foucault repeated, was not to enable metaphysics to acquire the status of a science – a clear reference to Kant's *Prolegomena*, as was indeed the entire discussion of limits. Rather, the cooperation between archeology and genealogy shifted the weight from universal conditions to historical singularities, and from the legislation of the limits of tradition, with its politics, or "dividing practices," of exclusion, to historical "evene-mentality." The end goal was to set free the "indefinite work of freedom,"[158] as Foucault adamantly underscored, using a phrase that recaptured a notion of the infinite quite distinct from the emptiness associated with mathematical infinitude, thus lending full force to Kant's revolutionizing understanding of freedom. Critique required a radically experimental attitude, meaning the essaying of oneself through reinvention. In inventing a historical ontology of ourselves, we might then, it seemed, be able to reclaim the other enabling, no longer simply determining, meaning of power, tele-scoped in the French term *pouvoir*, which literally meant ability and *potentiality*.[159] What, indeed, were the limits by which we were bound, were these limits still valid, or might we need to breach them in order to grasp our freedom as potentiality? How to realize "the critical ontology of ourselves as a historico-practical test of the limits we may go beyond, and thus as work carried out by ourselves upon ourselves as free beings?"[160] Such were the questions that Foucault gleaned from Kant's text, whose movement he purported to trace in all its pertinence or relevance for the present.

What then, finally, were the practical consequences that issued from this reconfig-ured definition of the critical task? If all critical research was to be historically localized, eschewing grand universalizing schemes, then how might a general critical economy that abstained from mere "vulgar" positivism and empiricism be workable? To these methodological conundrums Foucault responded by stressing that the preoccupation with partial and local inquiries, rather than universal or global projects, would by no means result in "disorder and contingency." To the contrary, the resulting research was guided by well-determined stakes and possessed a gener-ality, systematicity, and homogeneity, respectively. Defining the general stakes of his revamped Enlightenment project as "the paradox of the relations of capacity and power," Foucault reconnected directly to the Frankfurt School's critical legacy. Eschewing, like Benjamin or Adorno, the Enlightenment's language of progress, he explained that it was a matter of investigating whether the "growth of capabilities" – "growth" being a code word of sorts for "progress" – could be "disconnected from the intensification of power relations."[161] Under the caption "homogeneity," he mapped out the terrain of investigation, referring to the collectivities of "practical ensembles" (*ensemble* rather than *system*, as the English translation proposes), or, put differently, human practices, which were to be analyzed from two angles: their tech-nical side, which stressed the modes of rationality that directed these practices, and the strategic side, which accented the freedom on the basis of which subjects inter-acted in the social field of struggle. In fact, these practices comprised three systematic fields, ruled by the axes of knowledge, power, and ethics – fields, in truth, that seemed to be modifications of the Kantian tripartite division between the epistemological, practical, and aesthetic realms. Finally, by the examination of generalities, Foucault understood the study of common "patterns" of regularities and recurrences – not necessarily "structures," since he had long abnegated his so-called links to structuralism – that were to be detected across centuries. Here, it was a matter of focusing not on metahistorical continuities but on "problematizations," including certain normalized bifurcations or dividing practices, which needed to be examined in light of their historical singularity.

Overall, Foucault seemed to want to ensure that he did more than take over the ethical *substance* of Kant's practical philosophy. For the Kantian demarcation of the Enlightenment was to be seen as a *permanent* task, only to be achieved, paradoxically enough, through its continuous *historical* transformation. To profess the Kantian task meant to live, to exist, according to an ethical attitude, a historical ontology of ourselves, which translated into "the critique of what we are," which in turn was "at one and the same time the historical analysis of the limits imposed on us and an experiment with the possibility of going beyond them [*de leur franchissement possible*]."[162] That Foucault's arguments were meant to resonate with Habermas's conjecture about modernity's unfinished project is nowhere more explicit than in the lecture's concluding moment, where he seemed ready to admit that it was not sure whether we had attained maturity, thrown off our self-incurred tutelage. If the historical ontology of ourselves demanded the remodeling of three intersecting fields of inquiry at once – knowledge, power, and the self (in its relation to others) – then what remained to be done was to materialize this historico-critical, philosophical attitude into myriad historical inquiries of the present that joined archeology to genealogy and combined methodological or practical coherence with a profound faith in the Enlightenment. Only such steady, patient labor might accord with our deep-seated "impatience for liberty."[163] Only such ever-renewed, reinvented historical toil might preserve the endowment of the Enlightenment.

Baudelaire's Aestheticism

Aside from displaying these manifest overtures to Kant, Foucault's 1983 lecture "What Is Enlightenment?" exposed two seemingly incongruous tendencies that similarly ran through other, post-Kantian reflections, especially the studies on ethics: on the one hand, the explicit retreat into an analysis of technologies of the self – Foucault's clear-cut answer to Kant's call for autonomy – and, on the other, the reappearance of a conspicuously Nietzschean stamp in the midst of a Kantian setting, designated by the long tribute to Baudelaire, which formed the piece's unusual center. Complying with Kant's practical postulate to realize one's autonomy, as the lecture devised, meant engaging in an arduous exercise of rediscovery, which required the new "production," "elaboration," and "invention" of the self, nothing more or less than "a critique of what we say, think, or do." In this respect, the Kant lecture proved quite representative of Foucault's late phase, when he repeatedly and emphatically asserted that his entire life-work had been concerned not so much with power relations as with the reflexivity of the self upon the self – an avowal nowhere more outspoken than in "The Subject and Power." Elaborating further on the theme struck in the Kant lectures, this essay suggested that the completion of the unfinished project of modernity would open up the prospect of a newfound freedom, the "possibility of no longer being thus" – on condition, that is, that the subject draw upon the requisite measure of self-government to match the art of not "being governed so much." For Foucault, such technologies of the self made up the subversive, resisting tactics that were mobilized in a new lineage of identity politics, locked in an agonistic battle with the subjecting forces of statism and oppressive governmentality, whose pernicious strategies included the spurious category of a fabricated "individuality." In the course of modernity, he argued, statist political power had imbibed the techniques of pastoral power, manufacturing new, previously unknown "individualizing" tactics, which helped to govern the institutions of family, science, and pedagogy. In contrast, the agonistic struggles, fought in the name of dissident identity politics, strove to unmake these oppressive patterns of collective social alienation, thus revitalizing the Kantian question "What are we? in a very precise moment of history."[164]

However, when it came to clarifying further how these collective strategies of identity formation were to be implemented historically and politically speaking, Foucault abandoned Kantian terrain, resorting to what amounted to a Nietzschean conception of self-fashioning, mediated through Baudelaire's aestheticism. Curious though the reference to the French poet might seem, it can hardly be deemed a coincidence that Foucault drew upon his piece about Constantin Guys, "The Painter and Modern Life," given that the article also featured briefly in Habermas's *Philosophical Discourse of Modernity*. In point of fact, Foucault's lecture invites comparison with Habermas's disparaging assessment of aesthetic modernity, not in the least because of the virtually asymmetric solutions both offered to the question as to how a nondogmatic (normative) footing for ethico-political action was to be secured. Both, it is clear, defended incompatible views of modernity's "presentist" philosophy of time. Finally, a brief comparative analysis of their positions may help one better to assess why in his "Taking Aim at the Heart of the Present" Habermas harshly reproved Foucault's peculiar blend of Kantian philosophy and Nietzschean politics.

For Foucault, Baudelaire's intervention in modernity did not simply result in the indolent adulation of the "now" or the cheap promotion of fashion but in a profound transvaluation of the present.[165] Familiar with Walter Benjamin's Baudelaire interpretation, he established that the poet's characterization of Guys as the exemplary modern individual differed categorically from that of the *flâneur*, the latter being just an antiquarian collector, out to assemble a "storehouse of memories."[166] Rejecting the posturing of the *flâneur* for the authenticity of the modern artist, Foucault reinvented Baudelaire's dandyism, detecting in it a historico-philosophical attitude guided by a threefold sensibility: the "ironic heroization of the present," the "transfiguring play of freedom with reality" through the work of the imagination, and, crucially, an "ascetic elaboration of the self,"[167] all of which were to be realized through the pursuit of art. Essentially, Baudelaire's essayistic work thus confirmed, explained Foucault, that the modern no longer could be defined conventionally as a practice of discontinuity that radically broke with tradition. Not merely disruptive, even less so nostalgic, artistic virtuosity instead transfigured the real, as it at once respected and impinged upon existing reality in a bid weld the transient to the eternal — a figure that, if only obliquely, returned in Benjamin's theory of allegory.[168]

Foucault's appreciation of Baudelaire could not be farther removed from Habermas's more conventional, condemning appraisal of aestheticism. Following the Weberian theory of societal rationalization laid out in his *Theory of Communicative Action*, Habermas's Adorno prize speech, "Modernity — An Incomplete Project," cautioned that all attempts to recover the political dimension of an isolated aesthetic sphere merely hypostatized *aesthetic* modernity, confirming just how much it constituted but one split-off field of *cultural* modernity at large. As he indicated here, but really fleshed out in *The Philosophical Discourse of Modernity*, by following Nietzsche's lead, the dandyish trailblazers of aestheticized modernity, together with their neoconservative postmodern and poststructuralist heirs, misinterpreted the crisis of normativity that beleaguered the modern age, reading in it an appeal to engage in aesthetic self-creation, which might fill the existing void. Indulging in a latter-day fantasy of creation *ex nihilo*, they neglected the serious task of constituting an integrated, democratic collective, lacking the commitment to restore communicative action. At bottom, aestheticism, *l'art pour l'art*, and modernist art movements that idolized autonomous art were purely the symptoms of a deplorable diremption, testifying to the desperate quest for self-grounding that overshadowed an unhinged modernity. Aestheticism could never supply a political remedy, insofar as it really was a reaction-formation to societal modernization, which had penetrated the life-world to the point of "disturbing the communicative infrastructure of everyday life." In other words, as a manifestation of protest and revolt, aestheticism was simply an epiphenomenon of the encroachment of instrumental and strategic action upon communicative rationality.[169] How else could one read Baudelaire's poetic *oeuvre*, then, if not as a staple of aestheticism's precarious tradition, which tellingly displayed how the "problem of grounding modernity out of itself first comes to consciousness in the realm of aesthetic criticism."[170]

Aesthetic modernity's violent onslaught on "all that is normative," on the "normalizing functions of tradition," including the "standard of morality and utility," clearly lay congealed in its philosophy of time. Newness constituted its critical hallmark, tradition its enemy — a "spirit and discipline" to which Baudelaire first had lent "clear contours."[171] Advocating radical innovation, early aestheticist avant-garde movements coveted a "changed consciousness of time," whose arrival they aspired to bring about through the subversive, anarchistic explosion of a linear, progressivist continuum of time, that is, through the dangerous shock experience and the exaltation of the present. Yet no emancipatory effect was to be gained from shattering an autonomous cultural sphere, from "the false negation of culture," as "terroristic" art movements, such as Surrealism, had tried to do. For in taking on the culture industry and art's alleged autonomy, these vanguards, Habermas explained, artificially sought to force a reconciliation between art and life, yielding a "false *Aufhebung* of art," which envisioned the "liquidation of appearance as the medium of artistic representation."[172] Not only had this failed aesthetic modernity aged, he admonished, but it was now of the highest urgency to achieve "a correct mediation of art with the life-world."[173] To do so, one might have to bring to completion the however weak, but still emancipatory intentions of the Enlightenment philosophers as they aimed to release the "cognitive potentials" of the three cultural spheres — objective science, universal morality and law, and art — setting them in dialogue with one another for "the rational organization of everyday social life."[174]

It is precisely against the background of Habermas's investigation into this skewed philosophy of time, cherished by a misguided aesthetic tradition, that one must also read his appraisal of Foucault in "Taking Aim at the Heart of the Present."[175] Though this obituary piece almost exclusively dealt with Foucault's "The Art of Telling the Truth," without explicit indications as to whether he was familiar with the 1983 Kant lecture, the gist of his argument very much is in keeping with the critique of "presentism" that galvanized his understanding of aesthetic modernity. Furthermore, Habermas's eulogy questioned Foucault's self-avowed allegiance to the Frankfurt School and detected serious inconsistencies in his argumentation insofar as the historian departed from the logic that allegedly imbued his earlier thought, to wit, a denunciation of political modernity from the vantage point of postmodernity.[176] How was it possible, wondered Habermas, that the poststructuralist theoretician of power did not recoil in scorn in the face of Kant's *The Contest of Faculties*, with its commitment to universal teleological history, perpetual peace, and freedom? The answer might lie, Habermas suggested, in the lecture's unresolved, underlying aporias between a residual commitment to a postmodern *posthistoire* and an inexplicable desire for the kind of political enthusiasm that Kant anatomized as he strove to understand humanity's moral commitment to perfectability and progress.

Not persuaded by Foucault's overtures to Kant, Habermas dwelled on what he considered to be an underlying anti-Kantian penchant, whose symptoms he couched in unflattering figurative language drawn from his contemporaneous *Philosophical Discourse of Modernity*. Under the stoic gaze of Foucault the archeologist, as Habermas maintained, the flow of history in reality appeared "frozen into an *iceberg* ... covered with the crystalline forms of arbitrary discourse formations," while "under the cynical gaze of the genealogist" history transmogrified into a "senseless back-and-forth movement of anonymous processes of subjugation in which power and nothing but power keeps appearing in ever-changing guises."[177] At issue for the social theorist were again Foucault's methods of archeology and genealogy, the first out to detect synchronic discursive practices, the second committed to mapping a moving historical playing field, set adrift by the endless interplay of power/force games. Thus, on the level of genealogy, Habermas faulted Foucauldian history for following the perpetual motion of the "return of the same," propelled by an ever-revolving will to power, in keeping with Nietzsche's revival of Greek cyclical, historical motion. But to it Habermas now added the flaws of the archeological method, which subjected history to a process of "crystallization," a term normally associated with the neoconservative anthropology of Arnold Gehlen. Under the guise of querying Foucauldian history for its "presentism," Habermas implicitly likened it to Gehlen's nihilistic anthropology, which, in hailing in the epoch of *posthistoire*, had imputed such a temporal atomization to modern culture. A closer look at *The Philosophical Discourse of Modernity*, especially its opening lecture, allows one to gain a better sense of the stakes involved.

Providing a *Begriffsgeschichte* of the pair ancient/modern, the course's inaugural lecture commended Hegel's philosophy of history for the perspicacity with which it had first identified modernity as the period that needed to ground its own normativity.[178] Reviewing modernity's changing conceptions of historical time, Habermas argued that the untenable commodification of time in the fleetingness of fashion, championed by Baudelaire's modernism, eventually made way for a radical critical history, or "effective history" (*Wirkungsgeschichte*), a project that stretched "from the Young Hegelians via Nietzsche and York von Wartenburg right down to Heidegger."[179] But at the endpoint of this radical rethinking of history as effective history really stood the work of Benjamin, as Habermas added, further elaborating on a point made in the Adorno prize speech. There, he had already distinguished Benjamin's theory of "now-time" (*Jetztzeit*) from that of the Surrealists, insofar as Benjamin's "posthistoricist attitude" took on a "false normativity in history," propagated by an unwholesome, objectifying post-Hegelian historicism.[180] However, in view of Habermas's earlier Benjamin exegesis put forth in "Consciousness-Raising or Rescuing Critique," the new interpretation came as somewhat of a surprise, indicating how much he had revised his negative assessment of the critic.[181] No longer reducing his *Jetztzeit* merely to a mystical, messianic moment that interrupted the flow of history as progress, Habermas now understood *Jetztzeit* to denote a decisive intervention in modern conceptions of how the past, present, and future interacted. As the most radical transformation of "effective history," it turned from a shortsighted, narcissistic obsession with the future-orientation of history to fathoming the unrealized potential of the past. Indicative of an underlying "ethical universalism" and "universal historical solidarity," Benjamin's rewritten historiography ascribed "to all past epochs ... a horizon of unfulfilled expectations," while to "the future-oriented present" it delegated "the task of experiencing a corresponding past through remembering, in such a way that we can fulfill its expectations with our weak messianic power."[182] As he isolated the ethico-political duty of a collective historical solidarity in Benjamin's thought, Habermas downplayed the charges of recondite mysticism and harmful aestheticism tendered in other contexts.

Precisely because of Habermas's altered perspective, the question as to why the largess imparted to Benjamin was not due to Foucault's praxis of history remains all the more unanswerable. For it is possible to read Foucault's version of historiography as a secularized response to Benjamin's "effective history." Indeed, in expanding the horizon of present and future expectations to include the unmined potential of the past, Foucault hoped to release past possibilities, rescuing them from dogmatic truth games. Just as much as Benjamin's, Foucault's trajectory retreaded the paths of the past, aiming to uncover – hence genealogy – bygone violations, bringing to articulation lost prospects, stifled voices, in order, unmistakably, to transform the future. Yet rather than interpreting Foucault's branch of historiography from such an expanded standpoint, Habermas's eulogy isolated its freezing grip on the temporal potential of history and – indirectly – its presentism, much as his "Modernity – An Incomplete Project" had rejected modernity's adulation of the now, together with the concomitant revolt against all that was normative. As for the alleged commitment to a Kantian Enlightenment to which Foucault professed: Habermas only seemed prepared to acknowledge the repetition of supposed Kantian flaws in his argument, above all an idealistic adherence to a logic of aporias. For, pulled between his earlier vociferous rejection of modernity and the startlingly new affirmative gesture with which he endorsed Kant's Enlightenment bequest, the historian could not but produce an account riddled with unsolvable contradictions. Just as Kant had gotten ensnared in the contradictions between the phenomenal and noumenal as he looked for an empirical sign to match mankind's moral disposition in *The Contest of Faculties*, so Foucault sought to wed an antinormative "critique of power" to an undertheorized normative analytic of the true, thereby again lapsing into a self-refuting argument, which, deep down, drew its validation from Nietzsche's nihilistic, aesthetic creation of new values.

That Foucault declined to take the conventional route of repudiating aesthetic modernity for its voluntarism or decisionism plainly comes to the fore in the 1983 "What Is Enlightenment?" lecture. Using language from the contemporaneous *Care of the Self*, he instead hoped to rekindle the redemptive, political kernel lodged in Baudelaire's aestheticism as he looked beyond its narcissistic, solipsistic veneer. Calling for a new *ascetic elaboration of the self*, he exhorted the modern subject to invent, produce itself, yet, evidently, not quite along the guidelines of Nietzsche's ecstatic program of self-creation. Furthermore, inasmuch as Foucault's directives asked for a collective form of ethical self-recreation, they also seemed to formulate a direct response to modernity's challenge to ground itself. Still, it is all but transparent how exactly Foucault hoped to manufacture a synthesis between ethics and aesthetics, if one just goes by the 1983 Kant lecture. To cast light on the matter, we must now consider Foucault's ethical writings from his last period.

Foucault's Turn to Ethics

As we pursued the twin figures Nietzsche–Kant through the main texts of Foucault's *oeuvre*, it became evident that a Nietzschean strand of aestheticism reemerged in the midst of what seemed to be sober reflections on Kant. Discernible in the 1983 Kant lecture, this Nietzschean current had in fact already gained force in other work from Foucault's last phase, distinguished by a determined turn to ethics. For, as he moved from archeology to genealogy and, finally, to ethics,[183] Foucault's trajectory led to the somewhat untypical last volumes *The Use of Pleasure* and *The Care of the Self*, accompanied by a host of contemporaneous interviews and lectures, the last ones dedicated to truth-telling (*parrhēsia*) as virtue.[184] The final two installments of his history of sexuality at first met with wonder, short of encountering veritable disapproval, even from long-time sympathizers. By all accounts, these late works elicited much speculation, not just because of their sober, almost antiquarian philological style but also for their ostensible change in course. Could it be that Foucault, lifelong historian of countercultural, insurrectionary techniques and chronicler of sexual counterpractices, at the end of his life truly considered the study of sex "boring,"[185] withdrawing into a genealogy of ascetic self-mastery and an austere, Stoic individualism, following a movement that, to some at least, seemed to border on moralism? Reservations of the sort have been raised, compounded often by far graver allegations that strike at the core of Foucault's critical projects. Predictably, they concern two repeatedly heard accusations: first, the theoretical confusion, self-refuting contradictions or aporias that burdened his work, as it moved from what seemed an outspoken poststructuralist posthumanism – the death of the author, the immolation of the subject – to individualized practices of the self, culminating in what, on the face of it, amounted to a humanistic conception of personal autonomy and freedom; second, the political neoconservatism or elitism articulated in his unreserved advocacy of aestheticism. Always given to controversial statements, Foucault in this late phase repeatedly admitted that his main interest lay in recovering what he called an "aesthetics of existence." In a comprehensive overview interview held at Berkeley called "On the Genealogy of Ethics" (1983), he hazarded the only deceptively naive question: "Couldn't everyone's life become a work of art?"[186] Though Foucault modeled the phrase on Burckhardt's study of the Renaissance and on Baudelaire's poetic aestheticism, it might not be entirely justified to read in it a simple relapse into nineteenth-century dandyism – as, indeed, his friend, the classicist Pierre Hadot, feared – or even an embrace of a California-style aestheticized "body- and psycho-culture."[187] Rather, seen from our perspective, we must ask anew how Foucault managed to think together his quasi-Kantian project to rehabilitate the Enlightenment with an aestheticized ethics of self-cultivation that remained inspired by Nietzsche. Why did he return to the dust-covered dietary manuals, tracts, and personal diaries of early Greek, Hellenistic, and Greco-Roman antiquity, as well as early Christian traditions, roughly from the fourth century B.C. to the second century A.D., and, eventually, the fourth and fifth centuries of the late Roman Empire?[188] What did he mean when he defined ethics as the "care of the self" (*epimeleia heautou*)? And, to fasten on our main problem, how is one to understand the fact that his *turn to ethics* – not to be confused with a "return of morality"[189] – was overlaid by an undivided, unwavering commitment to aesthetics? Stated differently, to what extent did Foucault seek to think through the contradictions of an *ascetic aestheticism*? In order to gain a better grasp of these issues, we do well first to return briefly to his Kant interpretation.

In the 1983 Kant lecture, "What Is Enlightenment?," as we observed, Foucault specified that research conducted under the auspices of a "historical ontology of ourselves" branched off into three broad, interconnected areas or, alternatively, axes. The resulting conceptual map he drew advanced a dramatic yet still recognizable reconfiguration of the philosophical division of labor that Kant had distributed among the three *Critiques*: relations of control over things (the axis of knowledge / truth), relations of action upon others (the axis of power), and relations to oneself (the axis of ethics) – the latter, one might add, also being the province of aesthetics.[190] In "On the Genealogy of Ethics," Foucault filled in the contours of this map, which, as he now explained, established three interconnected "domains of genealogy." The first one referred to the "historical ontology of ourselves in relation to truth, through which we constitute ourselves as subjects of knowledge"; the second one concerned the "field of power, through which we constitute ourselves as subjects acting on others"; lastly, the historical ontology in relation to ethics was the one through which subjects established themselves as moral agents.[191] With the benefit of hindsight, Foucault now projected these axes back onto his lifelong *oeuvre*, stating that the three genealogies *grosso modo* coincided with the consecutive stages of his work. Where all three axes were present in his early *Madness and Civilization*, the truth axis, he observed, was the focus of *The Birth of the Clinic* and *The Order of Things*, while the power axis governed *Discipline and Punish*; ethics emerged in the final stage, in his history of sexuality, comprising *The History of Sexuality, Volume I: An Introduction*, *The Use of Pleasure*, *The Care of the Self*, and an unpublished tract on early Christianity, *Confessions of the Flesh* (*Les Aveux de la chair*).[192] Obviously, there existed more of an overlap between these axes than Foucault indicated, if only because all three together added up to the constellation *savoir / pouvoir / sujet*. Furthermore, if the late work filled out the third subfield of Foucault's quasi-Kantian call for a "historical ontology of ourselves," still his project on ethics in the final analysis remained but one installment of a far wider design, essentially concerned with a more general *history of truth*. In a sense, *The Use of Pleasure* and *The Care of the Self* continued the probe into the subject's mode of truth-telling announced in *The History of Sexuality*, which analyzed the contradictory, antinomic nature of confessional discourse, insofar as it simultaneously imparted the injunction to tell the truth while placing stark silencing prohibitions upon sexuality.[193] More in general, the break in "style" that marked the late work expressed Foucault's attempt to downplay the epistemological concern with truth and power, which earlier writings privileged at the expense of "individual conduct." Meant to amend this state of affairs, the research on ethics eventually would culminate in an investigation of Socratic veridiction, the technique of truth-telling, whose public and private virtues he honored in his very last course lectures.

Judged on the basis of Foucault's account in *The Use of Pleasure*, the turn to ethics seemed almost like a chance by-product of his history of sexuality, as if the question of ethics imposed itself on him with a force he could not ignore. In line with the trajectory of his broadly conceived crosscultural genealogy of sexuality, or "sex series," *The Use of Pleasure* treated "sexual ethics" – though, as always, Foucault's view was pulled beyond the periphery of sexuality and desire, a tendency even more pronounced in *The Care of the Self*. But in the intersections that he established between sexuality and ethics, one must see more than the mere outgrowth of a reductionist Nietzschean- or Freudian-inspired cultural pessimism for which all moral praxis could be reduced to an ascetic lifestyle, gained through the repression or sublimation of sexuality. To gauge the differences, we must delve deeper into the self-styled account this latter-day ethicist gave of his developing research.

As the introduction to *The Use of Pleasure* relates, Foucault's investigation into the nature of ethical conduct initially meant to take on ossified codes about "sexuality," such, for example, that it was a constant, or could only be examined historically by focusing on the mechanisms of repression and interdiction. How, he asked instead, had sexuality become an object of moral solicitation – a query that would start him on an ever-receding history, from early Christianity back to the Greeks,[194] as he sought to chronicle the singular, historical *experiences* of sexuality. Confirming that nothing would remain stable in the course of this inquiry, even the term "experience" had to be rethought as a complex constellation. For it brought into play the "correlation between fields of knowledge, types of normativity, and forms of subjectivity in a particular culture,"[195] that is, the interplay between *savoir*, *pouvoir*, and *sujet (assujettir)*. In advancing a genealogy of sexuality, Foucault fastened on the advent of the "sexual hermeneutics" that individuals practiced on themselves and others. As he studied this "hermeneutics of the self," he applied pressure to a phrase fashionable in the theoretical climate of the 1970s, that of "the desiring subject," principally because "desire" was anything but a transhistorical, constant value. Rather than simply accepting the locution as a given, Foucault launched a historical genealogy of "the subject of desire" – a double genitive that indicated how the subject was at once produced by but also the producer of desire, manufacturing itself into existence. Having stamped new tools to investigate (discursive) formations of sciences (*savoirs*) and systems of power – to wit, archeology and genealogy – he yet hoped to understand how individuals might relate to themselves as subjects of sexuality. And, having studied the constitution of discursive practices in the human sciences, together with the rational techniques through which power was exercised, he yet had to devise a toolkit for understanding the *jeux de verité* of the self, the very truth games through which the self put itself on display. Assuming, once again, the posture of the historian chronicling his own *oeuvre*, Foucault proffered the following record of the successive methodological stages that guided his work:

1   *archeology*, which focused on "the forms of discursive practices that articulated the human sciences" – "the games of truth (*jeux de verité*) in their interplay with one another";

2   *genealogy*, which traced "the manifold relations, the open strategies, and the rational techniques that articulate the exercise of power" – the games of truth in "their interaction with power relations, as exemplified by punitive practices";

3   the third stage – at this point called the *genealogy of the self* – which addressed "the games of truth in the relationship of self with self and the forming of oneself as a subject."[196]

Yet Foucault also introduced a notable shift in his disciplinary allegiance. If but a few years earlier – in 1978, in the presence of the Sorbonne gathering – he had breached the field of philosophy with a measure of hesitation, he now resolutely crossed over into that court. For, as *The Use of Pleasure* advised, the study on ethical action, including the broader history of sexuality, could not solely draw on the labor of the historian but presupposed rigorous philosophical exercise. In truth, *The Use of Pleasure* was to be considered a philosophical "essay" – a term through which Foucault meant to do more than acknowledge the philosophical tradition inaugurated by his forebear, Montaigne. Essay, Foucault now conjectured, was to be interpreted as "'ascesis,' *askēsis*, an exercise of oneself in the activity of thought."[197] Essay, he further specified, constituted the "living substance of philosophy." For, if philosophy was to avoid being the "simplistic appropriation of others for the purpose of communication," then it needed to become the "assay or test by which, in the game of truth, one undergoes changes."[198] Fundamentally, the refocusing of his angle also brought along a shift in the workings of critique, as becomes noticeable in Foucault's retooled, finetuned definition, showing that "critique" acquired different inflections as it migrated through his thought. Now, in keeping with the call for a "critical ontology of ourselves," he defined critique as *self-critique*, that is, as a "testing" or essay-ing of ourselves. Critique amounted to the labor "that thought brings to bear on itself. In what does it consist, if not in the endeavor to know how and to what extent it might be possible to think differently, instead of legitimating what is already known?"[199] By thinking through one's own history, thought would be released in freedom, allowing it to transform itself in the process.

Adopting the "persona" of the first philosopher, struck by Socratic *thaumazein* (wonder), Foucault approached the question of the desiring subject afresh, asking, "why is sexual conduct, why are the activities and pleasures that attach to it, an object of moral solicitude?" Why, he wondered, this "ethical concern" about sexual behavior, or its "moral problematization," deploying the two terms "ethical" and "moral" at this early stage of the analysis more or less interchangeably.[200] One of his most intriguing hypotheses was precisely that in the Greek and Roman world – roughly from Socrates to Seneca and Pliny[201] – ethical conduct translated into an "aesthetics of existence," in which moral "problematizations" intertwined with "arts of existence" (*ars* or *technē*, "know-how"), or, to use another term (not invoked here by Foucault), the practice of self-government. The antique Greek and Greco-Roman *ethico-aesthetic* manuals recorded a catalogue of technologies, arts of living, that is, the "intentional and voluntary actions by which [humans] not only set themselves rules of conduct, but also [sought] to transform themselves, to change themselves in their singular being, and to make their life into an *oeuvre* that carries certain aesthetic values and meets certain stylistic criteria."[202] Together, these primordial technologies for crafting an aesthetics of existence all added up to an artistic labor upon the self that Foucault, referring to Plutarch, called *etho-poetic*.[203] Not since Burckhardt's study of the Renaissance had a serious attempt been made in the modern period to study these technologies of the self in more detail,[204] meaning that through his "genealogy of ethics" Foucault sought to suture an interrupted tradition, harking back to the nineteenth-century Swiss historian and Nietzsche's precept of style, no less than to Benjamin's Baudelaire interpretation, which had described the poetic harness the French poet manufactured as he prepared to brace the exigencies of modernity.[205]

Fundamentally, Foucault's ethics redirected the focus from a passive subject, defined by the interdictions of a moral, prescriptive code, to the volitional activity of ethical choice and self-interrogation – activities he described by the verb "problematization," indicating their constructivist rather than timeless, constant nature. To be analyzed through a combination of genealogy and archeology, these problematizations constituted moments in the history of truth rather than "ideologies," a term he dispelled with typical consistency. For, as Foucault declared in *The Use of Pleasure*, his aim was to replace a "history of systems of morality based, hypothetically, on interdictions" with a "history of ethical problematizations based on practices of the self."[206] Crucially, this meant that the traditional concept of "morality" needed to be rethought. Only one shade of its meaning referred to a prescriptive code, to "a set of values and rules of action that are recommended to individuals through the intermediary of various prescriptive agencies such as the family (in one of its roles), educational institutions, churches, and so forth."[207] Stretching the term beyond its usual purview, Foucault asserted that the label also needed to embrace actions and conducts, or the "real behavior of individuals." Becoming even more specific, he distinguished between rules of conduct (codes), actual conduct (*askēsis*) and, third, ideal conduct, or "the manner in which one ought to form oneself as an ethical subject acting in reference to the prescriptive elements that make up the code."[208] Thus, his "genealogy of ethics," as he named it, rewriting Nietzschean convention, aimed to reclaim a primordial ethical sensibility or attitude, defined by the relation to the self, from under age-old, sedimented, petrified moral codes. Admittedly, in so doing, he traveled back to some of the ethical tradition's canonical texts – Plato's dialogues, no less than to Aristotle's *Nicomachean* and *Eudemian Ethics*. However, rather than simply focusing on virtues and moral categories such as *sōphrosynē* (moderation) or *phronēsis*, his genealogical gaze actually meant to unearth what lay at the foundation or limits of these rarefied principles, namely, the problematization of pleasures (*aphrodisia*) into a focal point of ethical deliberation.

Prior, then, to the installment of modernity's set normative codes, ethics took the form of an activity of and upon the self, a cultivation or government of the self, which he respectively captured by the terms *askēsis* in *The Use of Pleasure*, and *epimeleia heautou* (care of the self) in the third volume of the history of sexuality. But in analyzing this ethical self-cultivation, procured through distinctive modes of subjectivation, the genealogical ethicist should not consider the subject's compliance with the law, values, or rules as code-driven moral systems prescribed. To the contrary, at the core of this radically different examination were four conditions that together comprised the process through which selves acted upon themselves as ethical subjects and whose transformations were historically determined: first, the ethical substance – for example, the Greek "ethics of pleasure,"[209] with its stress on managing pleasures (*aphrodisia*), the Christian obsession with flesh, or concupiscence, Kant's emphasis on "intention," modernity's focus on feelings;[210] second, modes of subjection (*assujettir*), which signaled the systems through which agents recognized their moral obligations, the latter prescribed, for example, by natural law, divine law, or – in the case of Kant's practical philosophy – the rational, universal law; third, forms of elaboration of ethical work (on the self), or how subjects shaped themselves to become ethical subjects through the self-fashioning activity of asceticism; finally, the moral teleology, or telos, which projected the ideal that the subject aimed to become. Phrased still differently, these four vectors constituted the ontology, deontology, ascetics, and teleology of the moral experience of sexual pleasures.[211] Together, they enabled one to account for a gamut of cultural-historical differences among ethical modes of agency. Though (Western) forms of codification across the ages and cultures remained very similar, it was specifically in the technologies of self-subjectivation that the greatest historical variety was to be observed. For example, where the Greeks harbored prohibitions not any less so, or even always dissimilar, from Christians, the relation to self was conspicuously different. The Greek *telos* was the beautiful life, asceticism a matter of elitist personal choice, the aim being to avoid slavery to others and to one's passions through the control or regulation of sexuality, which considered the adoption of a sexually active role – that is, domination through, for example, penetration – more important than the love object's gender.[212] If code-oriented moralities, such as the Christian one, anchored in codifications of conduct in fact coexisted next to ethics-oriented moralities, as Foucault was careful to specify, then the latter were more prominent in Greek and Greco-Roman antiquity. Crucially, differences between Greek and Christian morality were the product of alterations not in the code but in the ethical relation to self, as signaled, for example, in the changing relation to the practice of homosexuality.

While not really part of the "sex series,"[213] *The Care of the Self* further drew the anatomy of the art of existence, described in *The Use of Pleasure*. Care, or *epimeleia*, was the task of philosophy, which also comprised love of virtue and truth-telling, and was enriched by care of the other as one came to understand who one is.[214] Thus, the "cultivation of the self" was one specific art of how to live – *technē tou biou* – ruled by the creed that one needed to take care of oneself; it was "a way to work on ourselves" in order "to invent" – not discover – "a way of being that is still improbable."[215]

Historically speaking, Socrates was the one who consecrated the "care of the self" in Plato's *Alcibiades* when he admonished his eponymous love object to attend to the personal self should he hope to fulfill his political ambition of statesmanship. If in this Platonic dialogue care at once referred to "an active political and erotic state,"[216] then, gradually, this Greek technique was disengaged from care of the *polis*, transforming into a veritable "technē of the self," or social practice, a matter of personal choice.[217] Finetuned by Epicurus, "care of the self" eventually underwent a change in the "*mode d'assujettissement*," insofar as with the Romans, Seneca and Pliny, it would become something "very general," no longer simply a personal choice but an obligation for all rational beings.[218] Treating the Stoic techniques of the self, Foucault considered the practice of *askēsis*, which, unlike its Christian variant, did not signal renunciation but "the progressive consideration of self, or mastery over oneself, obtained not through the renunciation of reality but through the acquisition and assimilation of truth."[219] Among the other spiritual exercises that Foucault singled out for special treatment was the "writing about the self" as a mode of self-exercise, exemplified by the many extant uplifting diaries, the so-called *hypomnēmata*, or "spiritual 'notebooks,'" where thoughts of others are written which could contribute to the edification of the writer."[220]

In the course of these historical peregrinations, as he set out to unseat conventional philosophical distinctions, Foucault radically recoined the meaning of the terms "morality" and "ethics." While morality, as we saw, could refer either to an individual's moral conduct or to normalized moral codes (whether in their Christian or pseudo-Kantian versions), "ethics," just as in the Kant lectures, indicated a more primordial sensibility or attitude, which gave rise to a specific social practice. Defining an originary "relation to the self," ethics no longer had anything to do with a Kantian-infused rational conception of an individual will that answered to a universal moral law. If asked to draw a comparison to an established philosopher, one might reply that Foucault's *ēthos* had most in common with Kierkegaard's account of self-willing, rendered, for example, in *The Sickness onto Death*, or even with the latter's fulminations against the universality of Hegelian ethics, formulated in *Fear and Trembling* – minus, of course, the Danish philosopher's negative valuation of the aesthetic sphere, which is where such analogies must end.[221] Further, as Foucault stressed in his long Berkeley interview, ethics was completely detached from religion or the law, for as a more primordial "structure of existence," it had not yet been consolidated in normative moral, religious, and legal codes ("the juridical *per se*"), that is, been subjected to an "authoritarian system" and "disciplinary structure."[222] Ethics, as recorded in these ancient Greek and Greco-Roman manuals, defined "the conscious practice of freedom," where freedom signaled "the ontological condition of ethics" and ethics, in turn, "the form that freedom takes when it is informed by reflection."[223] Aimed at a far more originary understanding of ethics, Foucault's travels back to the pre-Christian Greeks and Romans thus were a calculated attempt to retrieve a moment of freedom and choice in the form of individualized self-fashioning, well in advance of calcified social codes that were passed off as the universal, normative moral law.

Finally, if Foucault defended a "morality [better ethics, bh] with no claim to universality,"[224] then not one that was determined by the transcendence of the other. Rather than being other-directed, as in the Christian injunction to love one's neighbor, Kant's categorical imperative to see the other as an end in herself, or Levinas's being-towards-the-other, Foucault's ethics radically zeroed in on the self. The relation to the other remained dependent on self-labor, its starting point being the happiness or well-being of the self. That Foucault did not entirely give up the question of intersubjectivity comes to the fore in his concern with the Aristotelian *topos* of the "politics of friendship." *Ēthos*, in the Greek sense, he observed, also involved "a relationship with others, insofar as the care of the self enables one to occupy his rightful position in the city, the community or interpersonal relationships"[225] and hence to engage in *epimeleia ton allon* (care of the other). If it was true, he noted, that friendship was reciprocal while sexual relations were not, then it might also be necessary to ask about an ethics of pleasure in which the "pleasure of the other" was recognized.[226]

Recapitulating, then, one could say that, from the vantage point of his new genealogy, Foucault retroactively recast the long history of occidental ethics, originating with the Greeks, as an intricate network of changing activities of self-governing, whose various codifications were determined by the structural relations among the four different axes outlined above. If one is willing to go along with Foucault's self-definition, then, from this entirely new perspective, all of his work in retrospect reveals itself to be a series of philosophical essays or ascetic exercises, requiring the right dose of ethical exertion, expenditure, or *epimeleia*. But if such are the rudiments of Foucault's late phase, then the question still remains of how we are to assess the Nietzschean streak in his ethics. Ethics for the late Foucault was the crux of the matter, but it is not readily clear how he combined a supposedly Nietzsche-informed "genealogy of ethics" with the Kantian project of Enlightenment. To what extent was Foucault's ethical project not Nietzschean, to what extent was it less than Kantian?

The truth of the matter is that the unique angle Foucault offered was a history of ethics, like and unlike Nietzsche's. First, it was unlike Nietzsche's in that Foucault – at least, in this final stage – clearly lacked the impulse to reduce the course of history, with its moral codices, to a sublimation of affects or to the level of forceful interiorization via normalization, reminiscent of Nietzsche's genesis of moral conscience, a position adopted in the 1971 Nietzsche essay and *Discipline and Punish*. Nietzsche suspected that morality might constitute the "danger of dangers,"[227] which is why he called for a thorough critique of the value that upheld all moral values. In the philological note to the first essay of the *Genealogy of Morals*, he directly addressed the philosophical faculty, exhorting its members to embark, with the help of physiologists, on "*historical* studies of *morality*."[228] Prize essays were to answer the question of how linguistics or etymology could shed new light on "*the history of the evolution of moral concepts.*" The historical method that Nietzsche designed, informed by nominalism, sought to redress overdetermined (*überladen*) misinterpretations and (causal) projections of meaning through moral procedures and guidelines. Invoking a vitalistic economy of pain and pleasure that spoofed utilitarianism, his gripe was especially with asceticism. For, as the mere expression of a slave-like *ressentiment* that tried to overpower life itself, asceticism fundamentally signified the throes of self-contradiction, the paradox being that "we stand before a discord that *wants* to be discordant, that *enjoys* itself in this suffering and even grows more self-confident and triumphant the more its own presupposition, its physiological capacity for life, *decreases*."[229] If such an "incarnate will to contradiction and antinaturelness is induced to *philosophize*," the result would be the confusion of truth with error, of the kind that lay at the base of Kantian philosophy. Kant's concept of the noumenal, "intelligible character of things," Nietzsche now stressed, was nothing but an example of how "this lascivious ascetic discord ... loves to turn reason against reason."[230] Revising his earlier embrace of Kant in such texts as *The Birth of Tragedy*, Nietzsche now scolded that the thing-in-itself was merely the limit through which the intellect in the end comprehended that such noumenal objects of pursuit were incomprehensible – a biting quip in which he cast Kant's enabling boundary (*Grenze*) as mere error.

Unlike Nietzsche, Foucault's interest did not lie in the etymological unpacking of *concepts*, linguistic values, or the mustering of discursive coins so as to determine "the *order of rank among values*,"[231] though such works as *The History of Sexuality* were certainly by no means averse to nominalism.[232] Granted, Foucault did regress to the origin of Western moral discourse when he returned to the Greeks, but he did not seek to furnish a "moral genealogy" in the Nietzschean sense, which would mean showing how the origins of morals were sheer nominalist conventions enforced by the upper or master class's "pathos of distance." Nor was he out to uncage the reign of the incalculable or interested in digging beneath the layers of a "reactive" morality, with all the politically suspect connotations that came with that term. If he did enlist the tools of etymology to pierce beneath the surface of conventional, historically encrusted moral codes, it was really to hark back to the "conservative" Greek sense of terms such as *askēsis* or *ēthos*. Basically, rather than emulating Nietzsche's critique of morality, Foucault really historicized it, ascribing to it a set place in the philosophical canon.

Having considered arguments that suggest how Foucault's transvaluation of ethics intrinsically diverged from Nietzsche's antiphilosophy, we must now return to the charges that, in the end, his proposal for an antiuniversalist ethics backslided into an irredeemable, not to say opprobrious, Nietzschean-style aestheticism. Certainly, what is perhaps most remarkable is the unanimity with which critics and adherents of the most various ideological persuasions have joined hands in condemning Foucault's ethical project outright. Whether coming from critical theorists, poststructuralists, Marxists, or liberal pragmatists, the charges have ranged from neoconservatism (Habermas), "pan-aestheticism" (Wolin), a fascination with marginal lifestyles (Žižek), a perverse defense of "public school virtues" (Eagleton), and neo-Romanticism (Rorty), the larger implication being that Foucault's antiuniversalist ethics opened the door to decisionism, voluntarism, authoritarianism, particularism, individualism, or the Romantic quest for authenticity.[233] No less extraordinary is that, at times, Foucault appeared all too willing to accept the incrimination that his project ventured too close to Nietzsche's, and, moreover, that he seemed inclined to concede that not a few of the misunderstandings surrounding his work were the result of his unwavering "fundamental Nietzscheanism."[234] Must we assume, then, on the basis of these indictments, by no means the exception, that Foucault simply withdrew into an inward-turned aestheticism, ending his life as a faltering aesthete, not unlike Gustav Aschenbach, with the paint of too much self-fashioning running down his face (on the model of Visconti's filmic adaptation of Mann's *Death in Venice*)? To pose this question with such urgency is not to deny, to be sure, that Foucault's ethics might be fraught with the danger of aestheticism; nor can the point here be to submit to partisan politics. At the same time, it seems only fair to extend the benefit of doubt to Foucault's unfeigned attempt to recover a redemptive component in the aesthetic lifestyle as a way of enriching the contemporary life-world. Moreover, while some forms of criticism leveled at his ethical work contain valid warnings about the project's potentially detrimental implications, others, by contrast, seem to fly in the face of what Foucault aimed to achieve or miss the gist of his ethical program. No less striking is the fact that not a few of these criticisms are accompanied by the covert or outspoken reproach that his project regrettably slipped into the particularism of gay identity politics.

As a first segue into an examination of these critical responses, one might note that at least part of the provocation Foucault's ethics has exerted concerns the ambivalent category "style" that he deployed as he called for novel, unheard-of "ways of living." On the one hand, the term "style" was of antique provenance, for rather than signal "distinction," it captured an originary Greek notion of the subject as artisan and the self as work – work, precisely, on itself.[235] Foucault came to the term, as he repeatedly acknowledged, with the help of various classicist scholars, especially Pierre Hadot, Paul Veyne, and Peter Brown, whose research all pointed to a domain of conduct not yet submitted to normalizing codes and dominating truth.[236] Abstracting, often, from the universalist aim that, for one, accompanied Stoic practices of the self,[237] Foucault noted that ethical labor according to Greco-Roman tradition consisted in self-creation, meaning that ethically inclined subjects essentially were engaged in molding themselves into aesthetic works of art. Yet, in other settings, he seemed far more keen on hinting at the term's Nietzschean and neo-Nietzschean implications. In the Berkeley interview, for example, he admitted, in response to one of the interviewers' prodding questions, that the idea of aesthetic self-cultivation had much to do with Nietzsche's advocacy of style. For hadn't Nietzsche in *The Gay Science* advised "that one should create one's life by giving style to it through long practice and daily work."[238] In addition to such direct avowals of allegiance to the philosopher, one also encounters quasi-Nietzschean turns of phrase interspersed in his ethical work, evident, to give but one example, in the suspect form/matter dualism upon which he drew to gloss the Greek *technē tou biou* as a process in which "the *bios*" functioned as "material for an aesthetic piece of art."[239] Not a small portion of the critique Foucault faced, in fact, concerns precisely his movements back and forth between these two conceptions of "style," as he slid from a Greek notion of autonomy to a Nietzschean aestheticism. At its worst, the fear was that this sliding into Nietzsche's direction might give rise to the frightful prospect that violence and terror would force their entry into the realm of the ethical, as subjects sought to foist their fickle "will to power" upon others. To no small extent, these suspicions seemed further fueled by Foucault's pronouncements on the topic of the gay lifestyle in several of the interviews he gave during the last decade of his life, in which he often celebrated homosexuality as the freeing of polymorphous pleasures or rejoiced at the prospect that "gays will create as yet unforeseen kinds of relationships that many people can not tolerate."[240] Despite his assurances that S&M amounted to "a kind of creation, a creative enter-prise" and a nonviolent "desexualization of pleasure,"[241] when judged from the standpoint of normalized sexual codes, he seemed to trespass the brink that separated amoral violence from accepted mores.

To gain a better handle on the critical responses to Foucault's "intemperate" aestheticism, it seems worthwhile to consider two examples in more detail, examples, moreover, by no means the harshest of the lot, namely Nehamas's and Rorty's. Indeed, especially the chapter that Nehamas's *The Art of Living* dedicates to Foucault's Socrates interpretation can count as one of the most engaging, illuminating, and, surely, serious discussions of his "ethics as aesthetics." Drawing on Foucault's 1983 Berkeley course, "Discourse and the Truth," and his final lectures at the Collège de France, consecrated to Socrates and the Cynics, Nehamas situated Foucault's endorsement of "philosophy as a way of living" in its classical setting, pursuing the historian's examination of the term *epimeleia* in the Platonic dialogues.[242] Following Hadot, Foucault – so Nehamas noted – considered philosophy to be a practical, experiential way, or style, of life rather than a theoretical mode of contemplation.[243] But for all its philological and philosophical precision, Nehamas's analysis quickly reduced Foucault's excursion into ethics to a one-way street that abruptly came to a halt in the historian's personal biog-raphy. Certainly, Nehamas was right to note that Foucault's appreciation of Socratic verediction (*parrhēsia*) really was animated by a belief that "philosophers of his sort, self-fashioners who create new possibilities for life, are directly useful to the public." The Socratic prototype was "particularly useful to excluded, oppressed groups that have not been able to speak in their own voice so far," an insight significant for Foucault, as Nehamas added, insofar as "he, in particular, was primarily (though by no means exclusively) concerned with homosexuals."[244] Noting that Foucault should be deemed an intellectual who belonged "to the individualist strain of the tradition of philosophy as the art of living,"[245] Nehamas tendered some unusual theses about how the historian's personal and private "art of living" impacted his ethical, but also his broader epistemological, projects. Relying on James Miller's informative yet all too vitalistic monograph about the French historian, he posited that Foucault's turn to ethics in truth boiled down to a "personal, aestheticist turn" and, at core, to "an abandonment of politics."[246] Extrapolating further from Foucault's endorsement of an aesthetics of living, Nehamas drew the inference that he surrendered to a highly solipsistic, aesthetic position. The trend was not entirely out of character, Nehamas conjectured, for "it took Foucault a long time – most of his life – to come to think of himself as a philosopher who had always been concerned with the care of the self and whose project, despite its general applications, was essentially individual."[247] Advancing yet another psychologizing interpretation, he suggested that Foucault exchanged his early overindulgent, Parisian disposition, expressed in gloomy, systemic analyses of power, for a liberal optimistic view arduously secured in late life, thanks to his trips to California.

Rorty's essay, "Moral Identity and Private Autonomy," enables one further to understand the thrust of Nehamas's analysis as it best captures the contradiction between a commitment to social justice and a supposed Nietzschean fascination with force that has troubled the critics of his anti-universalist ethics. Using Descombes as a guide, Rorty offered a "physiognomic" reading of Foucault's two philosophical faces, the one showing a good-natured American liberal, the other a troubling French anarchist. Thus, the first Foucault endorsed a liberal concept of autonomy and hence entertained affinities to Dewey, whose political pragmatism called for social experimenting as it eschewed outmoded justificatory, rationalistic scripts; but the second one was a separatist, cut off from humanity, with a proclivity for a derelict French Nietzscheanism, reducing all consensual power, freedom, and progress to a conception of normalizing power that had the vacuity of Nietzsche's "will to power."[248] Torn between his anarchistic and liberal sides, Foucault experienced a peculiar tension that was "characteristic of a Romantic intellectual who is also a citizen of a democratic society."[249] For the strain concerned the split between his moral and ethical identities, the first referring to one's relation to others, the latter to the autonomy of the self (rapport à soi), a value most prized by the poetic mindset, from Blake to Baudelaire, but also, more troublingly, from Nietzsche to Heidegger. Apart from the perils of solipsism that might afflict the individual overemphasizing the relation to self, the real danger was that such a search for one's autonomy might turn Nietzschean, if one tried to act upon it no longer in the privacy of one's own home but in the public sphere.[250] In the end, Foucault privileged his anarchistic, rebellious side rather than avowing to be the true American liberal he at heart really was, sworn to the ideals of reducing pain and augmenting freedom. Parting company with Habermas's demand for a universalist, normative moral philosophy and his concomitant indictment of Foucault's relativism, Rorty exempted the historian from the task of having to secure a foundationalist normative position. Rather than demanding such a universalist script à la Habermas, Rorty presupposed a democratic community congregated by virtue of a contingently formed social contract and united through a shared, common vocabulary that all understood.[251] In other words, if relativism was a moot point, this did not release Foucault from the demand of having to commit to a common vocabulary, *in casu*, liberalism's, as this provided the best means to alleviate social suffering, expand human choice, and ensure consensual, communicative power. Deplorably, rather than explicitly adhering to the (social) *conventions* of a (historically delimited) liberalism, Foucault engaged in too much *invention*, abridging the rich lexicographic meanings of the word "power" to the negative force of "statism."[252]

Unquestionably, both Nehamas's and Rorty's readings present Foucault's ethics with an array of challenges that should not go unaddressed. Rorty, in particular, clearly identified the perplexing ambiguities that emanated from Foucault's work, with its commitment to social justice but concomitant ballast of a Nietzschean rhetoric that often seemed to muddle more than it clarified.[253] Because we will have occasion to consider the limitations of Foucault's theory of power more fully in the next chapter, in the conclusion of this analysis I will instead advance some possible alternative readings of Foucault's "aesthetic ethics" to suggest how it can also be put to use in different, positive ways and thus potentially help expand our experience and understanding of the political.

Notwithstanding his genuine endeavor to be fair to Foucault's overall project, Nehamas's interpretation drew a set of conclusions that are debatable. Thus, it seems important to stress, more so than did Nehamas, that Foucault's conception of artistic self-creation has little to do with "thoughts of genius, unlimited freedom, absolute spontaneity."[254] Foucault eschewed such concepts, precisely because they amounted to tacit endorsements of mere "lived experience," a condition that – certainly in view of his analysis of bio-power – was to be associated with the irrationalism of vitalism (*Lebensphilosophie*). More like Benjamin on this score, Foucault meant to dispel a Bergsonian–Diltheal subjectivistic *Erlebnis*, whose symptoms he discerned in existentialism with its quest for authenticity. Opposing such a vitalistic *Erlebnis*, he hoped to retrieve another historical *Erfahrung* in *ēthos*.[255] Moreover, just as much as the Frankfurt School, Foucault remained in the ban of the alienation model of modern subjecthood, aiming to rethink the impoverishment of "experience" through the reinvention of styles, or ways of living, and techniques of the self, yet stripped of all claims to pure immediacy and irrationalism. If anything, his provisos about these ethico-aesthetic ways of life envisaged subjects engaged in the personal management of their lives, through which they counteracted an administered bio-politics. Thus, his aim was to revalorize not just ethics but also aesthetics, to pry it loose from the commodified object as a way of reclaiming the beautiful life. Indeed, for Foucault, the history of truth as error entailed the loss of the aesthetic, which he sought to recover at all cost.

There exist, then, other styles of reading Foucault's ethics than those proposed by Nehamas and Rorty, interpretive glosses that attend to the utopian dimension of his aesthetics, with its pursuit of a lost "promesse de bonheur." It is not necessary to graft Foucault's ethics onto the threatening program of a Nietzschean aestheticism, if this means the antidemocratic, aggressive imposition of transvalued values upon one's unsuspecting neighbors, as laid out in Nietzsche's *Birth of Tragedy*, *Genealogy of Morals*,

or *Will to Power*. For all his explicit advances to Nietzsche, Foucault's endeavor to rean-
imate the aesthetic seemed to have more affinities with the Frankfurt School's project
to invent a post-Schillerian "aesthetics of reconciliation" (Habermas). That said, one
might still wonder whether this meant, then, that he sought to reintegrate an encum-
bered life-world through blowing up, magnifying the aesthetic, at the expense of the
other realms of cultural modernity, gestures indicative of a nostalgic desire to regress,
perhaps, to a premodern origin. It will be recalled that this was one of the charges
Habermas launched at the one-sided project of the European modernist avant-garde,
especially Surrealism, as it sought to aestheticize the life-world. If one considers
Foucault's 1983 Kant lecture, however, it appears that the aesthetic was but one of the
three cultural fields whose eventual remapping was part of the "historical ontology of
ourselves" on which he was at work. Seeking to reconnect ethics, aesthetics, and
knowledge (of the self), Foucault thought of their union as a more primordial phase,
which did not so much lie at the origin of Western history, as that it needed to be
recaptured in the "history of the present," through modes of self-fashioning that, in the
end, would critically redefine the limits of our being. Such a historical reinvention of
oneself, however, would not automatically usher in an aestheticization of politics, or
ethics, for that matter, but initiate a renewal of the original historico-philosophical
task that lay stashed away in Kant's writings. Much as did Habermas's analysis of
cultural modernity, so Foucault's ethico-aesthetic praxis disputed the separation
between marooned fields of human praxis, claiming that art and the aesthetic experience could have a significance for the life-world beyond the purview of expert
cultures. Though it is undoubtedly true that Foucault avoided Habermas's rationalist,
foundationalist nomenclature, his project did not necessarily contradict the latter's
avowal that as soon as aesthetic experience is deployed "to illuminate a life-historical
situation and is related to life-problems, it enters into a language game which is no
longer that of the aesthetic critic. The aesthetic experience then not only renews the
interpretation of our needs in whose light we perceive the world. It permeates as well
our cognitive significations and our normative expectations and changes the manner in
which all those moments refer to one another."[256]

Certainly, Foucault's movement back to the Greeks was nostalgic in that, in
Benjaminian fashion, he aspired to revitalize its ethico-political potential for the
future. As we saw, Foucault's main interest in an early Greek ethics of personal choice
stemmed from its prototypical opposition to all modes of "normalization," even
though this *telos* eventually was counteracted by the arrival of enforced modes of
subjection on the historical scene of action.[257] Yet mere reduplication of the Greek
ethical style, he advised, would only amount to imitation, at the expense of facing up
to the challenges of the present.[258] If he brought the present into a provocative
constellation with past tradition, it was because he claimed to perceive pressing similarities between then and now. Taking at times liberties with the philological materials
while overlooking the "religious and metaphysical dogmatism" that overshadowed
antiquity no less than the Renaissance,[259] Foucault maintained that the ostensible

absence of strict legislation and rigid normalization in early Greek culture found its echo in the diversity of values that marked the present. Today, he noted, "most of us no longer believe that ethics is founded in religion, nor do we want a legal system to intervene in our moral, personal, private life. Recent liberation movements suffer from the fact that they cannot find any principle on which to base the elaboration of a new ethics."[260] As these pronouncements make clear, Foucault's aim was not to foist a normative alternative upon the present but to reconstruct instead a genealogy of ethical problems or problematizations. For, the context-dependent, ethico-political decision that needed to be made every day was which choice was the least perilous, meaning that true critical reflection needed to detect the "moment of highest danger" in what looked habitual, ritual, or normative.[261] Such insights, he was sure, would not yield solipsistic apathy but concrete political action, even if it resulted in "a pessimistic hyper-activism, a hyper- and pessimistic activism."[262]

What I have tried to do, then, in the preceding analysis, is to show how these and other statements make it possible to mitigate the suspicion, voiced by Rorty and others, that the Foucauldian ethicist merely seeks to force his personal will upon society, or, equally problematic, that he gives others license to do so, in the absence of normatively negotiated directives (Habermas) or an unambiguous adherence to a common vocabulary (Rorty). For, read differently, Foucault's ethical project seems powered by the aim to increase the range of ethical choices, to broaden the spectrum of noncoercive identity positions that subjects can occupy beyond those listed in conventional, normative handbooks. Perhaps one might even venture so far as to ask whether Foucault's line of thought necessarily stands in contradiction to a situation-dependent, contextualizing ethics that relies on *phronēsis*, notwithstanding the fact that he refused to lay down what the "good life" might look like and notwithstanding the traces of "formalism" that infused his ethical styles. With Arnold Davidson one might agree that Foucault's ethics did not simplistically sanction an extremely particularistic aestheticism that simply meant to have done with all universal action-oriented norms. Following quite another tack of analysis, Davidson has urged Anglo-American philosophers in particular to fathom the sea change Foucault introduced in the field as he rotated the emphasis away from a sociological analysis of mores or a philosophical query that stayed within the periphery of moral codes to the complexity of ethical conduct, including the duties to ourselves, no less than those to others.[263]

However one assesses the consequences that follow from Foucault's ethics, it is sure that he could not just have had in mind either a self-enclosed individualism or even the mere propagation of a "sexual ethics" that would amount to a "hedonistic" liberation of oppressed collectivities, to invoke that intensely old-fashioned term. To appreciate this point, one might consider again Foucault's intent to connect his "ethics of the self" to a Kantian practice of communal enlightenment, enacted by a collective of historical subjects, as well as his observation that the "care of the self," in its "articulation with relations to others," was located at the crossroads of two other fields, subjectivity and governmentality.[264] As his Kant lectures advised, a collectivity of we's, constituting a group of (possibly) like-minded "I's," would question the borders of self-definition, animated by a fervor, enthusiasm, or will to revolution. That said, it is, of course, once again evident that pressure needs to be applied to the assumed category of the "collective," which remained to a large extent unaccounted for, so that it risked turning oppressive itself in turn. As one such negative repercussion resulting from Foucault's omission to consider the full range of positions that constitute collectivities of I's, we's, not to forget you's, one might read the phallogocentric and ethnocentric models of subjecthood that his ethical project unwittingly carried along. Clearly, in interviews given during his ethics period, it should be stressed, Foucault always plainly expressed his reservations towards Greek culture insofar as it fostered a "monosexual masculine society."[265] But even if his genealogy of ethics did not explicitly identify the male subject position as normative, it did little to diversify the history of women in ethics or to counteract the heritage of the most conventional ethics, premised on the exclusion of women and other minorities from the category of agency.[266]

At least one other set of remarks pertaining to the issue of collective historical change in its application to Foucault's ethics seems pertinent in this context. It bears emphasizing again how problematic it seems, to say the least, that, in taking issue with the supposed overdose of solipsism that anaesthetized the later Foucault, some critics prove animated by an underlying identarian logic, according to which his investment in gay politics, individualism, and the particularism of (sexual) identity politics are tacitly put on a par. In rebuking Foucault for receding from a universalist ethics into pure particularism, such responses fail to take seriously his attempt to rethink the dividing practices that have produced a noninclusive universal, that is to say, his project to historicize Western thought about universalism.[267] That matching counter-charges have been hurled at ethical programs endorsing transhistorical, normative claims and a potentially difference-blind universalism is well known. Indeed, Foucault himself did not leave the opportunity unused, for example, when he expressed his hesitations about Habermas's ideal speech act situation, or a communication free of coercion, stating that for him, by contrast, it was a matter of how not "to dissolve [power relations] in the utopia of completely transparent communication," or of how "to acquire the rules of law, the management techniques, and also the morality, the *ēthos*, the practice of the self, that will allow us to play these games with as little domination as possible."[268] To be sure, Foucault always was very explicit about how the labor on the self translated on a "disciplinary" level, which he himself practiced as the comprehensive retooling of the field of historiography. His pioneering work in sexual politics illustrated his limit-displacing labor on lifestyles, practices, discourses, and technologies, traditionally expelled from the territory of normative sexual codes. All the more necessary it is, therefore, to underscore that the range of ethico-political struggles he had in mind did not just pertain to culturally defined identity positions but also extended to those conducted in the name of economic redistribution and justice. At the same time, it remains true that more work needs to be done to help clarify what precise articulations such ethico-political labor might assume in social struggles that relate not exclusively to the need for equal cultural respect, proving that a commitment to the politics of recognition need not stand in opposition to fights for economic redistribution.[269]

Given the unfinished nature of Foucault's work, we have no indications of whether he might have wanted to amend or expand his analytical model on this score. However, what is certain is that in the course of his diverse historico-philosophical pursuits, Foucault relocated his focus of analysis from a broadly conceived, large-scale analysis of power, including disciplinary power, to the self-disciplining of subjects in *askēsis*,[270] and from "governmentality" to the more individualized practice of "self-government." Such, then, was the arc his *oeuvre* drew as it moved from its early indictment of ascetic historiography eventually to an embrace of the "ascetic" self, going beyond a Nietzschean genealogy of morals no less than a quasi-Kantian critique of morality. That Foucault's changing concept of critique often raised queries not always amenable to clear-cut answers has become abundantly clear. Added to this came the circumstance that terms such as the "aesthetic" brought along a wealth of political connotations not all of which Foucault mastered or controlled, though it seems that, most often, he intended the term to rouse the benign meaning he once invoked in an interview, when he noted that "aestheticism" really meant the transformation of oneself through knowledge.[271] But regardless of the limitations that beleaguer aspects of Foucault's philosophical thought, it is no less clear that his philosophy has opened up an immense span of potentially new vistas in the field of historical analysis. Herein, then, lies one of the challenges of Foucault's critical project, namely, that not only does it tender unheard-of recommendations about the many ways of history writing but also that it calls for labor on the practice of reading. Reworking convention, Foucault's boundary-displacing work on and at the frontiers of critical thought does not stop asking how we are to relate to ourselves as critical subjects.

3

POWER/FORCE/WAR

On Foucault's *"Society Must Be Defended"*

In his *Critique of Power*, Frankfurt School sociologist Axel Honneth charts the historical transitions in Foucault's thought from a narrowly circumscribed epistemic theory or a "semiologically oriented analysis of knowledge," to a social-theoretic conception of power, "the territory also inhabited by the tradition of the Frankfurt School."[1] Having realized that his immanently regulated model of "knowledge systems" failed to provide an adequate social-structural analysis, Foucault amended it, noted Honneth, by means of a dualistic framework, which he first laid out in his "Discourse on Language." There, power and desire operated as social "dispositions" that sustained knowledge and discourse, the latter to be conceived as a strategic force field of ever-contending discursive acts.[2] However, though the new dualistic model allowed for a more refined account of institutionalized "technologies of social control," still a vague naturalistic undercurrent animated Foucault's "will to knowledge," all too reminiscent of Nietzsche's instinct-driven *Lebensphilosophie*. Correcting the flaws of his earlier epistemological account of the drive to knowledge, with its residual vitalism, Foucault gradually opted for a new, monistic dynamic of power, which came to approximate a systems-theoretical perspective, meaning that, instead of mere cultural analysis, "a social-theoretic analysis can now emerge that investigates the external (i.e., functional or causal) relations between the empirical constituents of a social system, between knowledge formations and power relations."[3]

Honneth's study thus proposed a more nuanced interpretation of the bulk of Foucault's work than Habermas's more condemning *Philosophical Discourse of Modernity* could ever offer, insofar as the latter tended to reduce Foucault's entire historicist project to a Nietzschean vitalism. Indeed, Habermas went so far as to impose a Schmittean mold on Foucault, the paradigm of existential decisionism laid out in Carl Schmitt's *The Concept of the Political*, which defined the political in terms of the friend–enemy opposition, fraught by the potential danger of violent, existential combat. Thus, he charged that "in his later studies, Foucault will fill out [his] abstract concept of power in a more tangible way; he will comprehend power as the interaction of warring parties, as the decentered network of bodily, face-to-face confrontations, and ultimately as the productive penetration and subjectivizing subjugation of a bodily opponent."[4] Especially in view of Foucault's pronounced attempt to identify the dangers of an administratively exercised "bio-power" (a program at the center of *The History of Sexuality*, which subsequently supplied the theoretical footing for much AIDS politics and activism) such allegations of a persistent vitalism seemed, to say the least, counterintuitive. To be sure, Honneth, too, as we saw, still detected weak symptoms of naturalism in such early formulations as the will to knowledge but observed that "for the purposes of a theory of society an action-theoretic interpretation seems … more meaningful."[5] To this goal, he would "reconstruct Foucault's theory of power from a model of action built upon a concept of 'struggle' and not from a doctrine of dispositions, as would be suggested by Nietzsche's philosophy."[6]

In sliding the focus away from Nietzschean naturalism to action theory, the analysis that followed did much to complicate the Frankfurt School reception of Foucault, though it simultaneously still demanded more of the historian's work than the latter ever promised: a watertight, normative plan of sociopolitical action. Over and against Habermas's intersubjective theory of communicative action, which condemned manipulative, merely strategic behavior, Foucault, so Honneth maintained, ended up reducing social power to a "continuous struggle of social actors among themselves."[7] Transfixed in intersubjective battle rather than engaged in dialogue, social agents appeared not so much motivated by the collective goals of social struggle as by the egocentric "self-interest" of individuals, whose bellicose anatomy Hobbes laid bare in his *Leviathan*.[8] In marked distinction to the chapter that Talcott Parsons dedicated to Hobbes in *The Structure of Social Action*, confirming, in Durkheimian fashion, every society's need for "commonly recognized values,"[9] Foucault eliminated normativity from all political, legal contracts or pledges of consent for being riddled with the vestiges of a lingering violence. In rejecting the founding, but also generative, capacity of normative consent and agreement, his model ushered in, submitted Honneth – concurring here with Habermas – a political decisionism of the sort that, no doubt, accompanied a Schmittean authoritarianism.[10] By far the principal shortcoming was Foucault's failure to explicate clearly the "social stabilization" of positions of power, for which there existed only three solutions: either "normatively motivated agreement," "a pragmatically aimed compromise," or the "permanently emplaced use of force."[11] By diminishing societal norms to mere inculcated rituals of normalization, as his *Discipline and Punish* seemed to do, Foucault's theory of institutionalized power demonstrated that it rested entirely upon two modes of operation: "ideology" (despite his disclaimers to the contrary) and physical force – descendants of the cardinal virtues "Fraud" and "Force," which Hobbes regarded to be indispensable in the brutish state of nature.[12] As a result, Foucault's account of social power in the end failed to supply a two-sided, reciprocal power dynamics, favoring more often than not a one-sided sedimentation of force, inflicted upon subjects from the top down. Not given, furthermore, to the insights of psychoanalysis, he would leave open the question of how such inculcation was accomplished, neglecting what Honneth termed the process of the intrapsychic adoption of common objectives. Finally, though *The History of Sexuality* assumed the existence of a positive, productive power next to power's negative, dominating force, its author omitted to clarify the operations of such productivity adequately. Only once one centered upon the "regulated feedback system" he set up among norm, body, and knowledge, did it become apparent that production was to be understood, yet again, as normalization through subjugation, that is, as the compulsive instillment of power via three interacting structural domains: practical operations and procedures for the extraction of information; disciplining force; and an administered bio-politics that controlled behavior.[13] In the final analysis, Foucault's account of behavioristically produced subjects, so Honneth surmised, got the better of his original interest in an action-oriented understanding of the "field of social struggle." Falling behind the insights of action theory, he ended up with a functionalist analysis that privileged the maximization of coercive social power, providing but a "systems-theoretic solution" to Adorno and Horkheimer's no less bleak *Dialectic of Enlightenment*.[14]

There can be no doubt that Honneth's analysis is astute in showing up the blind spots that inevitably marred Foucault's vision when gauged from the standpoint of a normative social theory. Yet, in its quest for systematicity, his critique may seem to bend away, in turn, the complexity of the Foucauldian text. Must we assume, with Honneth, that Foucault's analytic of power, in overemphasizing the productive force of institutionalized, disciplinary violence and reducing all potentially normative agreement to procedures of normalization, became reductive, even deterministic, eliminating the playing field of social struggle and, with it, freedom? Is it true that he omitted to put forth a remedial program that would amount to more than a romanticized, insurrectionary "enthusiasm" or the manipulative operations of counter-strategies? Did Foucault's thought, in the end, do no more than redescribe the disciplinary boundaries of historiography, cultural studies, and other fields of study practiced within the intramural confines of university departments or the drawing room of the private ironist, to allude to Richard Rorty? Once again, the commonly heard charge that poststructuralism fails to proffer a normative blueprint for social change reappears in altered guise – witness, furthermore, the persistent demands made of theorists such as Judith Butler that she prescribe what makes one act merely conventional, another transformative insurrection.[15] To be sure, taking strong positions on the issue of normativity, poststructuralist thinkers other than just Foucault have been reticent to lay down the normative benchmarks that must guide social action. As a result, such theorists – again, Foucault not excluded – have often been faulted for harboring a cryptonormativity and covert transcendentalism, and for operating (notwithstanding assertions to the contrary) with undertheorized universal, even global, claims and presuppositions about social change. Inadequacies such as these have led philosophers like the pragmatist Rorty to write poststructuralism's politics off as "private irony," and other, similarly disposed cultural critics to adopt a "weak" brand of pragmatism that is more concerned with the immediate practices of oppression than with the long-term or distant scripts of airtight methodological or political justification. Such a "weak pragmatism" has the added advantage that it avoids the decision of having to choose between the one and the other, allowing for a creative *bricolage* in which straightforward results count more than lengthy justifications.

Leaving aside, for the time being, the consequences that follow from these various options for the wider critical field, in the present chapter I propose to return to the letter of Foucault's text, *in casu*, the 1976 Collège de France lecture course on power/war, *"Society Must Be Defended" ("Il faut défendre la société")*, in order to examine more closely one particular cluster of charges, that of the cryptoirrationalism, even threat of totalitarianism, that is said to seep from his agonistic model with its emphasis on force, struggle, strategy, battle, war. As it so happens, the matter of how to assess the political premises that uphold Foucault's analytics is singularly complicated. For one, the suspicion that Foucault's philosophy at times dallied with the politically suspect is not altogether unfounded. Thus, in the course of one of the opening lectures in *"Society Must Be Defended,"* written under the spell of what he called the "Nietzschean hypothesis," there occurs a startling moment when Foucault unexpectedly, unabashedly, asserts – seemingly in mock-Homeric fashion – that he will sing the eulogy of war. Besides conjuring up Nietzsche's myth of the "blond beast," the course also enlists the help of the conservative, even reactionary, French nobiliary historian Boulainvilliers – according to Arendt, one of the precursors of Nazi race thinking – to provide a lengthy defense of counterhistory, now called "political historicism."[16] Certainly, there can hardly exist doubt that Foucault's use of risky, insurrectionary rhetoric, far from seeking to promote adversarial combat or militarism, is animated by much more solemn, sober, deep-down pacifist intentions, despite his frequent overtures to subversive counterstrategies. But another important, less obvious point needs to be made. These extended dialogues with the oppositional, conservative "enemy" in the end often take the form of pedagogical *exercises* or essays that were meant to provide a quasi-dialectical reading of counterhistory. Despite assertions to the contrary (and I wish purposely to emphasize the disparity between stated appearance and underlying practice, against the view of some other Foucault interpreters), Foucault to no small degree remained a strategically minded, dialectical thinker, ever willing to grasp negative truths so as to turn them upside down in an effort to release their supposed positive kernel of political redemption. Inasmuch as a reappraisal of Foucault's *oeuvre* is in order, such a reassessment might start with a more studied consideration of the dialectical strategies he brought to bear upon the (historical) objects under his investigation. This means that attention needs to be paid not only to the content of his utterances, or *énoncés*, but also to the very "style" of his enunciation. Rather than merely probing the substance of Foucault's pronouncements for philological accuracy or political compliance, one might turn, then, to his methodology, or to what he called making use of genealogical knowledge *tactically*. For what tactical purposes, one might ponder therefore, did Foucault resort to privileging the strategy of "war?" Why is it that in the mid-1970s he will be riveted to the constellation power/force/war, not just in the lecture course, but also in *Discipline and Punish* and *The History of Sexuality*? Is it really plausible that the Nietzschean matrix power/war in the end stood for real physical, mortal combat, as some critics contended? Or, doesn't Foucault *a limine* reject an *antagonistic* conception of social struggle, including Marx's forceful class struggle, to unlock another *agonistic* playing field, one no longer tethered exclusively to the historical category of economic redistribution? Indeed, as various pronouncements from the period of the Collège de France war course corroborate, Foucault seemed intent on dismantling what he considered to be the worn-out category of the "class struggle," stripping the term of the component "class" in order to grant full consideration to the "struggle" as such. To pursue this itinerary in his thought it will be necessary to burrow deeper into the intricacies of Foucault's course materials on war, chiefly *"Society Must Be Defended,"* whose rendition of history needs to be counterbalanced to the model of agonism Foucault proposed in a relatively late text, "The Subject and Power" (1982). Conceived as a lecture course, rather than a completed study meant for publication, *"Society Must Be Defended"* is full of hiatuses, ruptures in argument, conjectures, indicating that Foucault, more than anything else, was setting up a vast canvas within which some of his propositions remained schematic, others overdrawn, no doubt also for didactic, pedagogical purposes. At the same time, such provisos about how to read the course should not detract from the fact that it reveals Foucault at work, trying out the limits of his conceptual model power/force, while remaining throughout all too aware of the danger that, in reconfiguring the category of "social struggle," he might end up with nothing but a "permanent war," invariably at work in the most diverse manifestations of social conflict.

Defending Society

From January 7 until March 17, 1976, Foucault conducted a series of public lectures at the Collège de France, which only recently have been made available in their integrality, thanks to the historian's course preparations and participant audio tapes. Previously, the two opening lectures appeared in English translation in the collections *Power/Knowledge* and *Critique and Power*, one separately in the *Oxford Literary Review*, while its final lecture, "Faire vivre et laisser mourir: La naissance du racisme," was published in article form in *Les temps modernes*.[17] As Alessandro Fontana and Mauro Bertani, the editors of *"Il faut défendre la société,"* explain, the course took place in the interval between two publications, *Discipline and Punish*, which appeared in February 1975, and *The Will to Knowledge* (*La Volonté de savoir*; better known in English as *The History of Sexuality, Volume I: An Introduction*), published in October 1976.[18] In the course of these scholarly activities, Foucault's already complex analytics of the historical vicissitudes that beset the constellation *power/knowledge* gained ever more precision. From a concern with *sovereign power* and *disciplinary power* – covered also in *Discipline and Punish* – he gradually moved to a more pronounced interest in *bio-power*,[19] a trajectory that *The History of Sexuality*'s final chapters, in highly condensed manner and, no doubt, with overhasty speed, likewise traversed. Foucault's determination to advance a historically diversified analytics of power relations very much becomes visible in the sequence of the 1976 lectures, which characteristically vacillated between, on the one hand, epistemological issues pertaining to the discipline of history (in the sense of historiography) and, on the other hand, difficult historico-political questions regarding such matters as the historical emergence of state-sponsored biological racism, which counted as one of the most disturbing transmutations of bio-power. The course thus paid witness to the modulations Foucault's vigorous thinking incessantly underwent, spurred on by the genealogical research and empirical material he would not cease to assemble.

Without doubt, the complexity of *"Society Must Be Defended"* only rivals the intricate multilayered analysis that structures the contemporaneous *History of Sexuality*. In many ways, the course's density at first seemed the result of the wealth of historical materials it compressed in just eleven lectures, spanning the high points of political modernity, roughly from the sixteenth century to the rise of National Socialism and Stalinism. However, the profusion of empirical evidence in truth was the product of Foucault's characteristic style of inquiry, which joined the analytical method to the historical one. Thus, in crafting his new analytics, or typology, of power/war, he projected its various manifestations linearly across history, thereby traversing what appeared to be the consecutive stages of modernity. Holding together these various levels of analysis was Foucault's main target: to provide a new analytics of power as war/strategy, which would dispel conventional liberal but also Marxist misconceptions, especially the theory of sovereign power, economic functionalism, statism, no less than the paradigms of ideology critique and class struggle. However irreducible these diverse levels of interpretation might seem, in the end Foucault hinged them all on an assumption that, in one aphoristic modality or another, without fail resurfaced in virtually every lecture: that modern civil society, in truth, merely proved to be the continuation of a perpetual war by other means. Whether intended or not, in charting the vicissitudes of power as war, rather than mapping the progressive advance of reason, Foucault along the way drew the genealogy of a war-ravaged modernity, whose deplorable endpoint was the totalitarian regimes of the twentieth century. At the base of his reconfiguration of power lay the historical hypothesis that war, during the course of modern history, had changed from being a strategic, military principle -- the fare of martial experts – to becoming part of the inmost fabric of civil society, where – to use the course's ornate language – it was wired into the filigree of peace. As it gradually left its position at the nation-state's outer periphery, where it served to subtend state boundaries, protecting the nation against external foes, war migrated inward, culminating in an "internal colonialism," enacted in the state-sponsored regimes of "bio-power," which aimed to control, eventually to eliminate, the inner social enemy, or other.

The synopsis that Foucault submitted for the course at the end of the academic year, part of his teaching requirements at the Collège de France, indicates succinctly what the course's overall scope and tenets were. Positing that power was to be assessed in terms of *force relations*, Foucault pressed further, wondering whether this meant that power had to be "deciphered ... according to the general form of war? Can war serve as an effective analyzer of power relations?"[20] In probing whether war operated as the principal "grid of intelligibility" for understanding power no less than the *history* of those power relations, the analysis was guided by a set of subsidiary, ancillary questions:

- Should war be considered as a primary and fundamental state of things in relation to which all the phenomena of social domination, differentiation, and hierarchization are considered as secondary?
- Do the processes of antagonism, confrontation, and struggle between individuals, groups, or classes belong, in the last instance, to the general processes of warfare?
- Can the set of notions derived from strategy or tactics constitute a valid and adequate instrument for analyzing power relations?
- Are military and war-related institutions and, in a general way, the methods utilized for waging war, immediately or remotely, directly or indirectly, the nucleus of political institutions?
- But perhaps the question that needs to be asked first of all is this one: How, since when and how [*sic*], did people begin to imagine that it is war that functions in power relations, that an uninterrupted combat undermines peace, and that the civil order is basically an order of battle?[21]

Scaled down to their essentials, these questions, it seems, reflected a sequence of underlying postulates or hypotheses, whose various presumptions the course did not always treat with all the depth and precision they were due. First of all, in its broadest sense, the homology "power/perpetual war" rested upon an assumption that was of the order of social theory. Reversing Clausewitz's statement that "war continued politics by other means," Foucault understood the social arena to be a dynamic, open-ended strategic field of social power relations between subject-antagonists and their discursive practices. That is, he did not just rely on the antagonistic model of discursive strife and contending *récits*, already laid out in *The Archeology of Knowledge*,[22] but now evoked a limitless, mobile field of social struggles and counterstruggles. Within this volatile arena, some practices or strategies coagulated through hegemonic, institutionalized sedimentation, others – "resisting counterstruggles" – were driven by the insurgent intent to topple them. Second, in a more limited sense, the thesis about an underlying "perpetual war" specifically envisioned the liberal, rational paradigm of sovereign power, pointing to the very real injustices that went hiding under liberal claims to justice. In keeping with his critique of sovereign power, prominent also in *Discipline and Punish* and *The History of Sexuality*, Foucault proclaimed that the span of occidental politics had been dominated by the supposedly pernicious, illusive discourse of political theory, covering up the memory of "real war" that in reality lay at the genesis of sovereignty. Whether it was a matter of the law, individual rights, the doctrine of free will, or contractarianism, all, in truth, were enforcers of violence, proving that a discrepancy existed between the liberal (normative) ideal and the everyday real. Closely related to this thesis was the course's third main objective, the pursuit of what it considered to be the contentious struggle between the specious discourse of political theory, represented mainly by Hobbes, and a more factual political historicism. In imposing its "game of truth," political theory, or the configuration truth/power/law, sought to obliterate one of the chief insights of its adversarial counterdiscourse, political historicism, according to which sovereign power invariably came at the expense of violent conquest, invasion, domination. Relying on the constellation *pouvoir/savoir*, Foucault examined the emergence on the scene of a new historical *récit* that radically reconfigured the discourse of historiography. Persuaded of the potentially insurgent mettle of this new historicist discourse, he aimed to pinpoint the exact moment of its historical emergence. Who, he asked, had first raised this insight into the belligerent nature of power as warfare to the level of historical self-consciousness? And, additionally, who, he queried, had first consciously transformed historiography into an instrument or tactic of political struggle, deploying it as an "operator," or *dispositif*, of power? Disentangling the historical strands and knots of knowledge production, Foucault thus traced at what particular junction the historiographical counternarrative had entered the competing field of discursive practices. But he also did more. In addition, he was again scripting the genealogy of his own counterdiscourse, seeking to identify his intellectual forebears, who, in the figure of Boulainvilliers, he situated well in advance of Nietzsche's heyday, despite unfading loyalty to the philosopher. No less so than in other projects of the period, in the final analysis he engaged in an impassioned inquiry into the use and abuse of the discipline of historiography for political life. Last but not least, this general probe into the material conditions of *power/domination* was accompanied by a more historically circumscribed investigation into the emergence of the first, truly subversive historico-political discourse, centered on an adversarial, binary battle between races, whose various historical transformations helped to clarify how, in modern societies, war had congealed into a permanent trait of social relations.[23] Though Foucault deplorably in the end would make his discussion of race subservient to the broader probe into the material nature, or "how," of power relations, he lent extraordinary gravity to the "race war" matrix for two tactical reasons in particular. First, the interracial warfare, raging in society, ravaged its alleged homogeneity and claims to ethnic unity, thereby also belying the representational nature of sovereign power, with its claims to consent, unity, and collective will. Second, arguing that this matrix was subsequently seized, invested, reinvested, colonized by other historico-political discourses, Foucault used it to explicate the ensuing logics to which the "evenementality" of history was subjected, notably the Marxist class struggle and biological racism. In so doing, the lectures outlined how the "*dispositifs*" of knowledge (*savoirs*) about war gradually developed and proliferated, but also how they were streamlined and, in the final analysis, subjected to a series of historical reversals.

Surely the most provocative, controversial hypothesis Foucault defended was that of a foundational myth about racial war, whose permutations he tracked across the centuries. Thus, he declared that the "grid" of interracial warfare first rose to discursive prominence in England at the end of the wars of religion, especially during the period of the English Civil War and Commonwealth, when, taking on the monarch's sovereign power, both moderate, "bourgeois" groups and radical, antiroyalist populist factions, such as the Puritans, the Diggers and the Levelers, rekindled the memory of the "Norman yoke."[24] Exposing the British monarchy, with its system of right, to be nothing but the progeny of William the Conqueror and his Norman invaders, the counterdiscourse, crafted by the likes of Sir Edward Coke and John Lilburne, cast British history in terms of a protracted, hostile battle between two competing races or "nations," Saxons and Normans. Similar politico-rhetorical figures resurfaced towards the end of the seventeenth century in France, yet played out this time on "the inverse side,"[25] namely, in the aristocracy's scathing criticism of both Ludovican absolutism and the Third Estate, whose full armor was displayed in the writings of the French nobiliary historian Boulainvilliers, charged with the political education of Louis XIV's heir apparent, his grandson, the Duke of Bourgogne.[26] In a gesture analogous to Coke's and Lilburne's strategic return to the Battle of Hastings, the nobleman's historical account of the French state privileged the fourth- and fifth-century Frankish invasions into Roman-occupied Gaul. Disconcerted by Louis XIV's strategic advances to the Third Estate, Boulainvilliers specked his account with critical reflections, meant to remind the king of the aristocracy's noble Frankish origin, even to reprove him for accommodating the lowly descendants of the servile Roman-ruled Gauls.

Having dedicated the proportionally speaking greater number of his lectures to Boulainvilliers, Foucault followed the recodifications of this biracial war matrix across the eighteenth and nineteenth centuries. With secure grip, he magisterially navigated from the juridico-political conception of power that found its footing in seventeenth-century theories about natural law and obedience to the sovereign (consolidated in Hobbes's *Leviathan*) to its historicist counterdiscourse, then on to the advent of the first nobiliary conception of *nation*, which came to stand in opposition to the sovereign state's self-declared unity and sufficiency. Effortlessly, he moved from the aristocracy's smoldering contempt for Ludovican absolutism to the unstoppable arrival of the Third Estate and the bourgeois revolution, with its demand for "constitutionalization," voiced in Sieyès's *What is the Third Estate?* Keeping up step, he maneuvered from inspecting militaristic techniques and tactics of domination, touted in the French aristocracy's martial account of history, to assessing the ranks of economically rationalized and administered modes of disciplinary power in the physiocratic eighteenth century, entrenched in such institutions as government bureaux, depots, and national libraries for the control of historical knowledge. He then tracked the gradual *embourgeoisement* of society, and, with it, the further "translation," "recodification,"[27] or rearticulation of the original war narrative, as it partially transformed into the class struggle. Finally, he surveyed how military warfare, ordinarily launched against the state's external, public

105

foe, receded behind friendly lines, evolving into an interiorized social struggle, which translated into the battle cry – alluded to in the course's title – that society's frail organism needed to be defended against internal enemies.

At the pinnacle of Foucault's trajectory lay the assertion that the dichotomous matrix of interracial war, codified in the Saxon–Norman and Frankish myths, had gradually evolved into two major directions: a monistic biological racism and the dualistic Marxist conception of class struggle. If the class struggle retained the revolutionary potential of the original discourse, albeit in dialectical form, then the eliminationist racism and science of eugenics that disfigured the nineteenth century testified to "the grand *reversal* of the historical into the biological, of the constituent into the medical that takes place in the thought about social war."[28] Privileging the historical articulations of biological racism, to the detriment of a detailed analysis of the class struggle, he ended the course with a brief analysis of its state-supported modulations, realized in National Socialism and Stalinism. In stating that both derived from the same matrix of interracial warfare, Foucault thus at once supplied their aetiology, contributing his own speculative version, as it were, of the "origins of totalitarianism." In the final analysis, he did not hesitate to argue that the dynamics of contemporary society, especially racism, still derived from an earlier polarized, antagonistic confrontation between friend and enemy. Paralleling Adorno and Horkheimer's flawed and, to say the least, controversial understanding of National Socialism as the outgrowth of liberalism and capitalism, Foucault proceeded under the assumption that the genealogy of power/war to be disinterred in liberal societies logically and historically found its ultimate manifestation in totalitarian regimes.[29] In other words, if bio-power, as the most recent transmutation of interracial warfare, sustained modern liberal-democratic societies, then its "extreme points of exercise,"[30] he concluded, were realized in political regimes of state-sanctioned racism.

In the long run, racist discourse was nothing but the deplorable reversal of the original, "indefinite" war of the races, which it replaced with a "biological, post-evolutionist battle for life."[31] In all too broad strokes, the lecture course thus outlined how the "decentering discourse" of biracial war was progressively "centralized," first under the hegemony of the universal state, propagated by the bourgeoisie, later through the centralization of state racism, and how these procedures of control invariably were negotiated through disciplinary power, notably the codification of historical knowledge by the state.[32]

With these challenging, not to say highly debatable, postulates, Foucault advanced his own variant of political historicism, launching an offensive (to render his insurgent rhetoric) against the hegemony of conventional theories about power. Lengthy advocacies of historiography as counterhistory and counterdiscourse, the lectures aimed to rescind the dominance of political philosophy and theory, singing the praise of the historicist's position *tout court*. Deploying a self-reflective gesture that would become defining for the entire course, Foucault doubled his observations about the historical matrix power/war, applying them to his own discursive interventions. Waging his struggles on several fronts simultaneously, he literally tried to unseat the unitary claims to power/knowledge, represented by sovereign and statist embodiments of power, giving free reign to polymorphous fields of warring micro-powers, in which *savoirs* functioned as discursive tactical devices. Whether the political theory crafted by the likes of Hobbes, Rousseau, and other contractarians; the philosophy of history (*Geschichtsphilosophie*), propagated by German idealists such as Kant and Hegel; or even the dialectical materialism designed by Marx and Engels, all were mercilessly brushed aside on the charge of imposing a totalizing, universalizing logic onto the disparity and discontinuity of history as "evenementality."

All in all, what proved remarkably stimulating about the course for the seasoned Foucault reader was that one believed at long last to have become witness – in real time – to the unraveling mechanisms or maneuvers that made up the brunt of his genealogical method. At the same time, however, one could not help but wonder how the course managed to intertwine these singularly complex strands of analysis, given the inordinate richness of argument and wealth of historical material these few lectures condensed. Whence, furthermore, the extraordinary verve and energy with which Foucault pitted the insights of his historicism against the reputed figments of political theory, exemplified primarily by Hobbes's *Leviathan*? And, more basically, how precisely did he reconfigure his analytics of power as he amended his historicist methodology?

Tactics and Strategies

At first glance, the Collège de France lectures seemed to sail the methodological course laid out in *The Order of Things*, insofar as Foucault once again set out to uncover the rise and fall of discursive patterns – "grids of intelligibility"[33] – that structured Western modes of knowledge production. To be sure, *The Archeology of Knowledge* and "Nietzsche, Genealogy, History" had further refined the historiographer's *instrumentarium*. Rotating the antiquated axis "truth/knowledge" (*connaissance*) out of the conceptual orbit, these works seized upon the axis "discourse/power" (*savoirs*), combining the search for epistemological answers with the staking out of political questions, premised on the assumption that the "will to knowledge" was animated by an ominous "will to (political) power." Though *Society Must Be Defended* still operated with some of the older terminology, it also explicitly announced the renunciation of earlier research procedures. For one, Foucault now rescripted his own techniques of archeology and genealogy, drawing on the rhetoric of war and struggle to define the practice of critique as battle. As if to prepare his audience for the overhaul of his methodology, he started the course by situating the new genealogy of war against the canvas of the countercultural intellectual and activist climate that had defined France during the last decades. Celebrating the highly prodigious "theoretical inventiveness" of past years, his opening lecture heaped praise on the "dispersed and discontinuous offensives" of antipsychiatry, prison reform, Deleuze and Guattari's *Anti-Oedipus* – all work attesting to the proliferation of the critical activity or, as he put it, the "criticizability [*criticabilité*] of things, institutions, practices, discourses."[34] But for all the revolutionizing labor of these diverse critiques, the danger of "totalitarian theories" (a designation with which he, remarkably, targeted Marxism *and* psychoanalysis) had not been subdued. As if realizing how politically explosive and overdetermined the phrase was, assuming as it did a covert homology between these interpretive matrixes and totalitarianism, he immediately qualified the statement, calling psychoanalysis and Marxism "enveloping and globalizing" instead. For, as he contended, though both traditions had provided locally usable analytical tools and instruments, they dogmatically insisted on the theoretical unity of their discourse, in stark contrast to the "autonomous, decentralized theoretical production" of local critique. In effect, local critique concretely had come about by throwing off such globalizing theoretical casts, allowing for the return, even "insurrection of subjected (*assujettis*) knowledges (*savoirs*)," which, critically, in turn relayed the awareness that power was war.

Throughout the course, Foucault would similarly join substantive claims about the operation of power relations, defined as struggle, conflict, war, to methodological contentions about genealogy as insurrectionary struggle. Here, in the opening lecture, these two levels, the one unabashedly substantive, the other arguably formal, tied together in several intricate ways. First, Foucault's localized genealogical research challenged the hegemony of globalizing, unitary interpretive theories about power, as he set out to retrieve, even liberate (*dégager*), the blocs of subjugated historical knowledges (*savoirs*) that went hiding in "functionalist or systematizing thought."[35] Second, these subjugated knowledges (comparable, he proposed, to Deleuze's "minor discourses"), comprised stretches of erudite, so-called disciplinary learning, vestiges of archival, even scholarly knowledge, no less than popular, mythical experience coming from down-up, from the people. In other words, in a doubling moment, these dissident counternarratives or antisciences were said to transmit the "historical knowledge of struggles," as far as their subject matter or content was concerned – knowledge that attested to an unsquelchable memory of brutal combat, invasion, unjust war. The resurgence of historical "contents," which formerly had lain buried under the stifling labor of systematizing functionalism, included material about asylums or prisons – examples Foucault obviously took from his own research. Such suppressed "blocs" of historical knowledge could lead the genealogist back to the "ruptural effects [*clivages*] of conflict and struggle,"[36] covered up by hegemonic master discourses. Reinterpreting his research of the past years in light of this new vantage point, he now recast genealogy as the utensil with which these two types of subjected knowledges could be conjoined and, in the end, set free, allowing for the reconstruction of the historical knowledge of struggles as well as the deployment of such knowledge in actual subversive tactics. If archeology, as Foucault observed, was the proper method for the analysis of local discursivities, then genealogy, qua incendiary critique, was to take up tactical arms, mount a struggle in order to retrieve the submerged, stifled memory of power as real struggle or war. But to do so meant to relinquish the principle of "discontinuity" that had structured *The Order Of Things* and

The Archeology of Knowledge. The latter study had defined the archive in terms of its alienating effects on the present, for as the display of that which was located "outside our language [*langage*]," it "[deprived] us of our continuities."[37] Tempting though it might seem to continue accumulating disparate fragments of knowledge, as Foucault conceded to his audience, now it was time to say farewell to such a methodological principle of "discontinuity." Burrowing himself ever deeper into the quagmire of bellicose rhetoric, he called for a regrouping not just of the fragments of earlier research but of collective forces, with the aim of launching an offensive against the prime adversary: the "tyranny of globalizing discourses"[38] about power. If genealogy made up Foucault's broader strategy, then only because it was premised on an understanding of power as contending force relations.

Having thus reconfigured the critical field in starkly adversarial terms, Foucault prescribed that genealogical research was to operate via local procedures of historicist critique, forging analytical tools that could topple totalizing critique, without lapsing into a naive empiricism or vulgar positivism. Though he sought to avoid an unsophisticated antitheory position, he relentlessly targeted the hegemony of "theory," embodied, it seemed, not just in Marxism and psychoanalysis but, crucially, political liberalism. To a large extent, these three unificatory discourses would function as ideological foes throughout subsequent lectures – though the commentary on psychoanalysis was principally relegated to *The History of Sexuality.* The uncommon measure of pathos with which Foucault went about his often overdrawn critique of these theories, especially psychoanalysis, only loses some of its perplexing effect if one recalls that the course was animated, in the end, by a critique of globalizing theories, which were often uncritically merged with the totalitarianism of National Socialism and Stalinism. In much the same vein, the opening lecture started out signaling towards the not so distant de-Stalinization of the Soviet bloc. In fact, in a way, aspects of what Foucault wrote in a later book review about Deleuze and Guattari's *Anti-Oedipus* also applied to the course, namely, that if the functionaries of theory and the bureaucratic establishment of psychoanalysis were the book's tactical enemies, then fascism, ultimately, was its strategic adversary. So, too, in *"Society Must Be Defended,"* fighting the totalitarianism of fascist power in all its insidious manifestations was Foucault's larger strategic aim.

Against this background, it becomes possible to read the first, better known lecture as a "propaedeutic," which aimed to teach by negative example how the anatomy of power could be approached differently, namely, on condition that the prejudicial lens with which power had been surveilled would be deactivated. Thus, in a first stage of his critique, Foucault took on the "economism" that burdened entrenched conceptions of power, setting up an unusual alliance between Marxism and liberalism, the latter represented mostly by contractarianism, or *contract power.* Both, he maintained, converged insofar as they crafted models of "functional subordination" and "formal isomorphism" to explicate the interaction between politics and the economy. Going back mostly to the seventeenth century, the modern juridico-legal discourse manufactured political power on the formal mold of commodities, rendering it as rights, or, in Foucault's wording, as objects that could be possessed, ceded, exchanged, insinuated into a circuit of legal or economic contractual transactions. No less sworn to the "economic functionality" of power, Marxism's critique of statism, together with its conception of the class struggle, narrowly subordinated power to contrivances of economic exchange, distribution, and class domination, from which political power was believed to derive its "historical raison d'être."[39]

Vowing to add alternatives to this prevailing functionalist mold, Foucault recognized but two contenders when it came to isolating a noneconomic analysis of power: the theory that defined power on the basis of its repressive actions and, alternatively, the theory of force. Interestingly, though he would do so later on in his career, at this point he refrained from directly engaging with Arendt's brand of action theory, which certainly might have figured in his list as yet another alternative to economic functionalism. Vying away from casting power as commodified "thing," Arendt emphasized time and again that power could not be stocked up in a storehouse. Rather, that spatial metaphor needed to be reserved for the arsenal of material means and implements of violence that could be housed in it instead. Power, for Arendt, was fundamentally a potentiality, albeit one that only existed when collectively actualized in (democratic) words and deeds; power was not an "unchangeable, measurable, and reliable entity like force or strength," but a dynamic that "springs up between [humans] when they act together and vanishes the moment they disperse."[40] In disregarding this consensual paradigm of power, Foucault's 1976 lecture course to a certain extent anticipated the logic of later pronouncements, when he increasingly was asked to comment directly on Arendt's political theory. As he would point out in several later interviews, he agreed that her type of "consensual politics" might "at a given moment serve either as regulatory principle, or better yet as critical principle with respect to other political forms."[41] But such a liberal political theory should not come at the cost of dissociating domination from power.

Not surprisingly, when it came to choosing between the two alternatives the opening lecture outlined, Foucault unflinchingly rejected the view that power amounted to the exercise of repression – the so-called *Reichean* hypothesis – opting instead for the second alternative, or the *Nietzschean hypothesis*, following which "the basis of the relationship of power lies in the hostile engagement of forces."[42] In the somewhat truncated justification that followed, he first set up an analogy between Marxism and psychoanalysis, much as earlier he had advocated the improbable thesis that liberalism and Marxism mirrored each other in their endorsement of an economic functionalism – reverting back, in fact, to a similar thesis propounded in *The Order of Things*. Now Marxism and psychoanalysis were said to meet each other halfway insofar as both interpreted power as repressive – a figure, Foucault added, that both traditions borrowed from Hegel. For all the wide-ranging differences that existed between both schools of thought, power in the paradigm they shared was an agency that forcefully repressed, regardless of whether it was "nature, the instincts, a class, individuals."[43] Always given to controversial statements, Foucault took on the twin figures of Marx and Freud, obviously seeking to depose one of the dominant paradigms that ruled the insurgent, countercultural climate of the Parisian sixties and seventies. In deploying the somewhat mocking label "Reichean hypothesis," he conceivably not only tackled the popularity of Marcuse, but also the powerful ideology-critical paradigm that, joining Marx to Freud, found its pinnacle in Althusser's influential theory according to which ideology produced subjects through repressive subjection. In fact, in seeking to rid himself of the repression notion, he applied considerable self-critique, since the concept had been the operative mechanism in his *Madness and Civilization*, generating a dualistic scheme for which Derrida had taken him to task.[44]

Thus, in keeping with the (intransigent) logic that structured many of Foucault's writings, the dominant strategic figure of operation that guided *"Society Must Be Defended"* was again the by now familiar Nietzschean figure of reversal, or the transvaluation of (normalized) values. Surprisingly, however, Foucault, in truth, dwelt less on Nietzsche than on the military views of the Prussian strategist Clausewitz, reversing the latter's dictum that war continued politics by other means.[45] From it, Foucault explained, followed at least three applications for the matrix power/force. Going against the foundations of Kantian political theory, he held that liberal politics, far from installing tranquil peace, sanctioned and sustained a "disequilibrium of forces," as it continued an unspoken, tacit warfare in the civic realm, a hold it exerted through economic inequality (*economically administered power*) and the institutionalized disciplining of bodies and subjects (*disciplinary power*). Second, and related to the first point, the successive alternations of struggles among political systems merely perpetuated war, as did the state of civil accord, so that Kant's ideal of *perpetual peace* deserved to be brushed aside as untruth. Finally, and most troublingly, according to the (conservative) adherents of this proto-Nietzschean transvaluation of history, the cyclical pattern of perpetual war could only find an end through the forceful intervention of an ultimate, apocalyptic decision, betokened by the final battle. In more interesting ways than was the case in *Discipline and Punish* and *The History of Sexuality*, Foucault now emphasized that it was not so much a matter of finding out who first turned Clausewitz's adage upside down. Spectacularly, it was in fact the Prussian strategist who had inverted and hence – as Foucault implied – covered up an unpleasant preexisting truth. Adding staggering reflection upon reflection, Foucault proclaimed that "the problem is not so much to know who has reversed Clausewitz's principle as to know which principle Clausewitz reversed or, rather, who formulated the principle that Clausewitz reversed when he said: 'But, after all, war is nothing but the continuation of politics.'"[46] In subsequent lectures, then, it would be up to Foucault to demonstrate that the undistorted truth about society's bellicose underside was fully developed in the historical writings of Boulainvilliers, who, well before Nietzsche, conceived of history as the play of conflictual, dominating forces, traversed by a cyclical conception of history that shaped the course of modernity.

Replacing the Reichean with the Nietzschean hypothesis, Foucault indicated, meant that power was to be conceived in terms of relations of force that were lent "concrete expression" in strategy, struggle, conflict, and war. But before we can broach Foucault's critique of the repression hypothesis, it seems appropriate that we inquire more deeply into the anatomy of the war/power matrix as it informed Foucault's thought, whose complexities we have only just started to comprehend. In other words, it is necessary that we embark in turn on a genealogy of the historian's shifting understanding of power/war.

Power in *Discipline and Punish* and *The History of Sexuality*

As a survey along the various stages of Foucault's genealogy of power indicates, the provenance of the Nietzsche hypothesis goes back to the 1971 essay "Nietzsche, Genealogy, History," which already described the field of history in terms of a struggle (*lutte*) among contingent forces. Granted, as he crafted his new method of genealogy, Foucault did not yet advance a comprehensive, let alone concrete, account of power relations, though it is evident, with the benefit of hindsight, that the entire exposé dealt with what the 1976 lecture course would designate as *power–domination*. The urgent task that confronted the genealogist, the Nietzsche essay prescribed, was to untangle history's aleatory play of force relations. Effective history, as the history of disparate, chance events, refused to lend itself to the recovery of mythical or metaphysical origins, as much as it resisted being subsumed under the epic fictions of progress and perfectibility that Kant and other Enlightenment philosophers ascribed to universal human history. Proceeding via the methods of descent (*Herkunft, Erbschaft*) and emergence (*Entstehung*), this new, revolutionizing historiography located its analysis at the multiple intersections where body and history visibly became entangled. If the vantage point of "descent" helped the genealogy-bent historian to decipher the forceful imprints that history left on material bodies, then "emergence" prompted him to center on regimes of subjection, to be understood as "the hazardous play of dominations," the struggle waged between adversarial forces, all striving for ascendancy. In characterizing genealogy as the assessment of differential force relations, Foucault in fact rescripted the odious master–slave dialectic with which Nietzsche's *Genealogy of Morals* opened, abstracting from its racist overtones and logic of *ressentiment*, determined as he was to expose a more general *agonistic* play of forceful differences, "the endlessly repeated play of dominations." Dismantling humanistic conceptions of historical progress, he unraveled the vicissitudes of a history of cumulative violence. In accordance with Nietzsche's contention that right was might, masquerading violence, he proclaimed that humanity did "not gradually progress from combat to combat until it arrives at universal reciprocity, where the rule of law finally replaces warfare; humanity installs each of its violences in a system of rules and thus proceeds from domination to domination."[47] But though Foucault advised that the articulations of history were to be studied in and through the body, his highly "theoretical" analysis lacked tangible instructions about how the methodology was to be implemented concretely, remaining in its manifesto style very similar to the inaugural 1970 "The Discourse on Language." For example, though he made occasional references to recognizable social categories, such as class, it wasn't entirely clear who was being dominated, who was doing the dominating. Nor did he yet demarcate economic struggle from "nonfunctionalist" social identity struggles, as he would in his later essay "The Subject and Power." In that sense, his concept of differential struggle seemed to occupy a position similar to Derrida's *différance*, capturing a quasi-transcendental negative logic, not unlike Adorno's negating force, even as it transpired as an immanent, transitive force *in* history.

With the epoch-making *Discipline and Punish*, Foucault provided a concrete, book-length example of the genealogical method, grounded in a fascinating historical trajectory across the changing institution of punishment, from spectacle to surveillance. True to the thrust of the Nietzsche essay, he studied the "political technology of the body," examining the economico-political mastery and knowledge of bodies, procured through punitive technologies. For this, it was necessary to appraise penal mechanisms as "complex social factors," and to attend not just to their manifestly repressive, or freedom-curbing, functions but also to their less straightforward generative, productive force. Importantly, the analysis allowed Foucault to present his first comprehensive typology of power relations, of which sovereign power, or the "power of the law," and disciplinary power, or the "power of the norm," were just two possible modulations. As his genealogical survey took him along various regimes of punishment, he moved from violent punitive spectacles – the privileged technique of sovereign power – via the speculative proposals of the French "ideologues," such as Destutt de Tracy, who hoped to quell moral evil by setting punitive examples, to the advent of disciplinary power; then he traced how disciplinary power changed as it left the cordoned-off precinct of prison compounds and penitentiaries to be coded as an elaborate surveillance system in Bentham's *Panopticon*, and finally, how it migrated into the innermost layers of what in essence turned out to be a carceral civil society.

Traditionally, *Discipline and Punish* has been lauded (or chided, as the case may be) for its arresting analytics of disciplinary power. Less commented upon, in general, are the statements the book advanced about how war formed the secret, underlying lattice of society, or even the peculiar "tug of war" in which Foucault himself got ensnared as he assailed the lasting bequest of liberal political theory – tactics very similar indeed though not wholly identical to those of the war lecture course. Like *"Society Must Be Defended,"* so *Discipline and Punish* pursued the inward migration, interiorization of sorts, of punitive right, ending with a brief, almost suppressed, yet significant reference to the "distant roar of battle"[48] that was dimly audible in the coercive disciplining of bodies in modern society. The curve the book thus described ran from preliberal, absolutist regimes in which the criminal was targeted as the sovereign's adversary, to modern disciplinary societies in which he was reduced to the internal enemy of society in need of being subdued. If this process paid witness to the transition from the sovereign's right over life and death to a more insidious disciplinary power, then *The*

History of Sexuality provided the sequel, so to speak, to this historical movement, postulating the emergence of a generalized bio-power.

In a manner quite representative of Foucault's mature writing style, the tract on punitive technologies spiraled back and forth between, on the one hand, empirical analysis, describing the steady infiltration of militaristic disciplining techniques into all layers of civil society, and, on the other hand, allusions to an underlying "perpetual war." But though ruled by the power/domination matrix, *Discipline and Punish* never ventured so far as to suggest that war should be "considered as a primary and fundamental state of things,"[49] as *"Society Must Be Defended"* did. Rather, on the empirical level, Foucault adduced textual material to prove that, since the advent of modernity, multiple disciplining practices as diverse as pastoral power, religious asceticism, militarism, pedagogy, but also objectifying machine-age labor, had been instrumental in producing disciplined, potentially docile subjects. On the theoretical level, he rebuked conventional codifications of power, whether advocated by liberalism, Marxism, or even Althusser's poststructuralist variety of ideology critique, which explored the "interpellation" of the subject by the law. Thus, his "micro-physics" of insidious, intractable power relations could no longer be contained by the dyad violence/ideology, nor could it be embodied exclusively in large state apparatuses (including Althusser's ideological state apparatuses) or dominant classes.[50] Absorbed in archival material about military discipline, Foucault reconceptualized the technologies of power in military terms, casting power as the interplay between strategies and tactics. Preoccupied as he was, here as elsewhere, with Clausewitz, he stated that "it may be that war as strategy is a continuation of politics," yet specified that "it must not be forgotten that 'politics' has been conceived as a continuation, if not exactly and directly of war, at least of the military model as a fundamental means of preventing civil disorder."[51] Far from suggesting that war was the exemplary model of the political, he qualified politics rather restrictively, as "a technique of internal peace and order," describing instead how the technical knowledge of militarism was executed, seeping deep into the pores of society. Though implementing a series of critical separations that distinguished power as strategy from ideology, contract, privilege, class domination, Foucault never went further than stating that "one should take as [power's] model a perpetual war rather than a contract regulating a transaction or the conquest of territory."[52]

While never admitting to it openly – quite unlike he did in *"Society Must Be Defended"* – Foucault drew upon Hobbes's *Leviathan*, the authoritative seventeenth-century tract about sovereign power, using it as a background against which he outlined his alternative anatomy of the body politic. Specifically, he alluded to Hobbes's differentiation of sovereign reigns acquired through obedience or conquest – to which he would return in the lecture course – and to a *perpetual war*, fashioned, presumably, after the *status naturalis*. Going against liberal conceptions of power as a possession that can be ceded to the sovereign, much as Hobbes had stipulated in *Leviathan*, Foucault already here established that power was not a substance or commodity but only existed immanently in the network of transitive, strategic relations, as the effects exerted upon those who were dominated. Immediately, he sought to forestall a possible misconception, warning against the potentially passive connotations that might emanate from the word "effect" – as if subjects were merely on the receiving end of a Moloch-like contraption. Faithful to his dynamic model of competing forces, he understood these force relations not as one-dimensional but as defining "innumerable points of confrontation, focuses of instability, each of which has its own risks of conflict, of struggles, and of an at least temporary inversion of the power relations."[53] Resistance, itself a form of power relations, transpired as the inversion, reversal or overthrow of specific, historically articulated micro-powers, and comprised various actions, including acts that need not be violent themselves – a point that deserves to be accentuated, against repeated interpretive misconceptions of Foucault's work. Clearly, Foucault here still pursued the earlier project of unmasking a transsubjective "will to knowledge," of which disciplinary power was one manifestation, rendering subjected bodies into objects of knowledge, except that such strategies were no longer solely in the hands of cunning sovereigns – even princes – and their military strategists.

Foucault's analytic stands out for the force with which it mounted a rebuke against the universal and universalizable claims of liberal theory, especially those grounded in Enlightenment ideals. Yet, upon closer inspection, one notices that he did not so much aim to dismiss the discourse of rights as to bare the hidden bequest of Enlightenment liberal discourse: the encroachment of new disciplinary power upon the scene. At the nucleus of *Discipline and Punish* lay a critique of the exclusive claims to dominance of juridico-political discourse and an account of the antagonistic struggle between two discursive practices in particular: *law* and *counterlaw*. In the book's seminal section, dedicated to the "power of the norm/normalization," Foucault pitted two historically differentiated punitive regimes against one another, "the traditional penalty of the law" and the "penalty of the norm," or the "value-giving" measures of "normalizing judgment," which began to emerge at the end of the Classical age.[54] Sure enough, the eighteenth century saw the rise of an "egalitarian judicial framework, made possible by the organization of a parliamentary, representative régime"; but it was equally true that the subsequent generalization of disciplinary techniques "constituted the other, dark side of these processes."[55] In the same vein, Foucault granted that seventeenth- and eighteenth-century political theorists had designed well-intended compact theories, and he hardly disputed that mercantile societies produced contracts to be closed off among liberal, free, individual subjects. But impeding these democratizing trends were the technologies of disciplining power, engaged in a quite different fabrication of the "individual," which functioned as the uncanny double of the agent addressed by mercantile, contractual associations. In stark competition with liberal narratives, then, Foucault declared, existed the dream of a disciplined society of automatized docility. As he battled the jurists and philosophers who busied themselves with pacts and contracts, his worry was more with soldiers dreaming up and belaboring "procedures for the individual and collective coercion of bodies."[56] For the juridical discourse that guaranteed what was, in principle, an egalitarian, symmetrical system of rights, was supported by "tiny, everyday, physical mechanisms, by all those systems of micro-power that are essentially nonegalitarian and asymmetrical that we call disciplines," meaning, in effect, that the "real, corporal disciplines constituted the foundation of the formal, juridical liberties." Though the contract might have formed "the ideal founda-tion of law and political power; panopticism constituted the technique, universally widespread, of coercion."[57] Thus, as if to rectify the fictionality of utopian law- and norm-bound discourses, Foucault reproved the traditions in political theory that harked back to eighteenth-century conceptions of the social compact or even to a pris-tine origin of nature. Appealing to the registers of the real rather than a utopian ideal, he seemed inclined to deny the human capacity to tender persuasive social promises, criticizing these for being so many flagrant lies in the face of reality – often with a deter-mination that seemed to approximate Paul de Man's deconstruction of the promise at the crux of Rousseau's contractarianism. Calling attention to the martial, tactical side of discipline/power, Foucault's analysis of these punitive codes and procedures clearly anticipated the materialistic technologies of the self and the analytic of "individualizing power" of later work, such as "Governmentality" or "The Subject and Power."

But it was really in the final chapters of *The History of Sexuality*, more so than in any other tract published during his lifetime, that Foucault ostensibly provided his most sustained treatment of power relations, though the chapters also spelled out proposi-tions folded away in *Discipline and Punish*, to which he added a new analysis of bio-power. Making for its somewhat unwieldy structure, this relatively slim book moved from examining the history of discursive misconceptions about sexuality to an in-depth inves-tigation of the codes of power that propped this flawed discourse, and, eventually, to a full-length anatomy of power relations. In devising an analytics, not a theory, of power, as Foucault underscored, he intended to set down its field of operation as well as to remold the methodological instruments with which it should be handled.

Best known from *The History of Sexuality* is, of course, Foucault's critique of the repressive hypothesis, which, when first voiced, proved revolutionizing, if not contro-versial, for the energy with which it attacked what it called the theoretical avant-garde's "ideology" of transgression. Not hiding his impatience for the popular, countercultural understanding of sexuality as a (substantivist) dose of submerged energy, he rejected the view of "a rebellious energy" that was checked by the law, together with the accom-panying transgressive economy of an untarnished desire, "beyond the reach of power."[58] Power–repression, he argued again and again in the book's analytical chapters, needed to be replaced by the study of disciplinary power, a constellation of strategies and accompanying tactics that could explain the production and subjugation of modern subjects no less than their resistance through counterdiscourses.

Within the context of a history of sexuality, debunking the repressive hypothesis, or *power–repression*, as embraced by psychoanalysis, seemed plausible enough. But this seemed less the case with the unfamiliar terrain Foucault additionally breached – the territory of political theory, which he took on in the guise of juridico-discursive representations of *power–law*. Only when read in conjunction with *Discipline and Punish* and *"Society Must Be Defended"* does Foucault's genealogical interest in the supersession of the codes of power espoused by political theory make sense, in a book that ostensibly proclaimed to be dedicated to the more restricted topic of sexuality. Yet, to raise such objections would mean to miss the point that sexuality was enmeshed in a complex network of power relations. Living on into the present, remnants of a monarchical *power–law* or *power–sovereignty* infused modern, post-Revolutionary codifications of power, maintained Foucault, which, in truth, had tragically failed to behead the king. Even psychoanalytic discourse about how desire was constituted through the law (a stab at Freudian and, no doubt, Lacanian psychoanalysis) labored under the overbearing collusive forces of power–law. In the future, to revolutionize historicist discourse would mean to set an end to sovereign-power with its cumbersome baggage of "right and violence, law and illegality, freedom and will, and especially the state and sovereignty." In its stead needed to come the study of *power–discipline*, which would research "the new methods of power whose operation [was] not ensured by right but by technique, not by law but by normalization, not by punishment but by control, methods that [were] employed on all levels and in forms that [went] beyond the state and its apparatus."[59] Yet, where *Discipline and Punish* left off with disciplinary power, *The History of Sexuality* drew the sequel, adding another epoch to the history and typology of power. Like its precursor, it drew on the forceful economy of subjection (*assujettir*) that powered the production of disciplined subjects, though it also went further as it examined the historical emergence (*Entstehung*) of bio-power. Putting the lie on Aristotle's belief in man as a *zōon politikon* (political being),[60] the political present proved rather one in which the vitalistic category of "life" had completely infiltrated the terrain of politics. Furthermore, if in early modernity the sovereign wielded the right over his subjects' life and death (Hobbes), now functionalist power was "exercised at the level of life."[61] Attesting to this intrusive administration of life-forces were strategic wars that, supposedly waged to guarantee the survival of populations, proved to be at the service of a vitalistic struggle for the race: "The principle underlying the tactics of battle – that one be capable of killing in order to go on living – has become the principle that defines the strategy of states."[62] For, where disciplinary power targeted the "anatomo-politics of the human body," the new regulatory controls of bio-power that erupted with full force in the nineteenth century meant to manage the masses, or more precisely, a calculable population.[63] The new technology of social engineering, dictated by the laws of a functionalist economics, could no longer be chalked up to what Weber had diagnosed as "the role of an ascetic morality in the first formation of capitalism." Signaling the "entry of life into history,"[64] bio-power subjected the living to the cold calculations of value and utility, replacing the power of the sword and the law with the imposition of regulating norms.[65] If one applied these insights to the field of sexuality, so Foucault went on to argue, it similarly became possible to uncover an elaborate "technology of sex," which embraced a motley catalog of tactics, some directed at disciplining the body, others at preventive population control. Yet, no doubt most challenging to ingrained representations of power was the interface between sexuality and race that Foucault exposed to be at the center of bio-power's operations. Thus, as nineteenth-century Western societies transitioned from sovereign and disciplinary power to the hegemony of bio-power, they went from being suffused with "a *symbolics of blood* to *an analytics of sexuality*."[66] In order to clinch this point, Foucault took on the cult around Sade, glorified in the countercultural, neo-Reichean climate of sexual politics. Sade's so-called transgressive politics, he advised, really belonged to a bygone era, permeated as his irreverent antics and escapades remained by an *ancien régime* conception of "sanguinity." More worthy of analysis, according to Foucault, was how Sade's old-regime, sovereign understanding of law and blood subsequently resurfaced in the modern period: first stealthily, in the control of sexuality, magisterially realized in psychoanalysis's attempt "to ground sexuality in the law";[67] then, not too much later, the same atavistic blood politics exploded full-blown in the biologizing, state-sponsored variants of racism (*étatisation*), which peaked in eugenics. In that sense, Nazism merely recovered the older "thematics of blood" from the era of sovereign power for its new eliminationist race politics. If Foucault was already here charting a troubling parallel course between psychoanalysis and race politics, then such analogizing was entirely in line with *"Society Must Be Defended,"* which similarly intended to unseat what it considered to be the covert entrapments of "totalizing power."

In chronicling the successive permutations of power, Foucault probed further below the surface, examining power's successive, sometimes overlapping codes or codifications. Preferring the materialistic encodings of power relations to the realm of spirit and speculation, he introduced the term "code" to replace the more loaded "representation" (*Darstellung*), whose crisis had figured prominently in *The Order of Things*.[68] Not only did "code," etymologically speaking, derive from the "code of laws" (*codex*), but it could also designate the military system of encoding messages, so that it seemed to telescope the desired trajectory that led from power/law to disciplinary power, and on to bio-power. Statism, the sovereign state's legal monopoly over violence, the rights discourse of law, and all other general systems of domination were simply *"terminal* forms," crystallizations, or embodiments of strategies that power could adopt.[69] In the long history of grappling with the question of how one was to "decode" power, errors arose whenever such singular, context-dependent codifications were identified as the very stuff or substance of power, at the expense of the potentially limitless, unconstrained constellations among force relations. Relying on the insights of nominalism, whose insurgent force Nietzsche had put to frequent use, Foucault operated with the rhetorical figure of metalepsis, charging that such conventional theories of power confused cause and effect. Laws, institutionalized state apparatuses, and various manifestations of social hegemony were but the endpoints, or effects of power, that congealed bundles of forces as networks of power strategies colluded at or between the boundaries of institutions. Foucault's oft-quoted definition of power deserves to be spelled out full-length once more, so that the gradations of his argument can gain better contour:

[Power] must be understood in the first instance as the multiplicity of force relations *immanent* in the sphere in which they operate and which constitute their own organization; as the process which, through ceaseless struggles and confrontations, transforms, strengthens, or *reverses* them; as the support which these force relations find in one another, thus forming a chain or a system, or on the contrary, the disjunctions and contradictions which isolate them from one another; and lastly, as the strategies in which they take effect, whose general design or institutional crystallization is embodied in the state apparatus, in the formulation of the law, in the various social hegemonies.[70]

As the passage indicated, Foucault's definition of power stretched across several segments of analysis. Power transpired as a process but also included the reciprocal support structures and the strategies through which these relations took effect. Such relations, Foucault implied, could be institutionalized in state apparatuses or social "hegemonies," a term that undoubtedly alluded to Gramsci's analysis of power relations according to their articulatory constellations. In that power was immanent, not transcendent, the model abjured a grounding edifice or substance that was external to the relational field. Indeed, it might therefore be slightly misguided to maintain, on the sole basis of this section, that Foucault came precariously close to assuming Kant's opposition between the phenomenal and the noumenal, though it was true that he demarcated power's various finalized manifestations from what he called – using unmistakable quasi-Kantian terminology – power's "condition of possibility." But, as he hastened to clarify, this "condition of possibility" ought not be confused with an a priori transcendent power that surpassed history – a force grounding power relations in turn – nor could it be confounded with the institution of a sovereign, autonomous source. Rather, these conditions referred to a "moving substrate of force relations which, by virtue of their inequality, constantly [engendered] states of power" – states of power, to be sure, that were not static but always capillary, local, unstable, mobile, transitory. On the face of it, therefore, the Kantian specter of transcendentalism was held at a distance by the fact that Foucault engaged in a micro-physics of power that presupposed the radically concrete materialist nature of strategies and technologies of power. Nor did he erect the scaffolding of an a priori transcendental structure, for force relations were transitive, immanent, always in flux, exercised from innumerable points.[71]

If power relations were nonsubjective, yet nonetheless intentional, the latter qualification specified that they were exercised with certain strategic objectives in mind, though never by just one person, group, caste, class, or state apparatus. Radically emptying out, it seemed, the category of agency and, with it, the figment of a controlling center in charge of steering power's rational course, Foucault embarked on what critics have often derided as his "functionalist" analysis of power. Yet, rather than underwrite an automatized, self-sufficient feedback system of power, Foucault held fast to the oppositional force of liberatory revolt, expressed through myriad points of resistance, whose operations were never exterior to the strategic field of power relations. Which is why it was high time, he stressed, that abstract, monolithic narratives about revolutionary struggle made way for a different political imaginary, one that operated with an infinitely expanded lattice of strategic power relations, in which various resisting tactics could be bundled, coordinated, or subsequently reconfigured in the interests of changing strategies. To handle this new task, the genealogist-historian needed to adapt his critical and analytical instruments, ready to tackle changing societies in which force relations, which "for a long time had found expression in war, in every form of warfare, gradually became invested in the order of political power."[72] Once again, the juridico-political standard of analysis needed to yield to a more attuned *strategic model*, able to inspect discursive practices "on the two levels of their tactical productivity (what reciprocal effects of power and knowledge they ensure) and their strategical integration (what conjunction and what force relationship make their utilization necessary in a given episode of the various confrontations that occur)."[73] More than anywhere else, this posthumanistic condition of power found best expression in Machiavelli's theory of strategic power, from which modernity's violent course took off, except that, henceforth, the genealogist would have to "do without the persona of the Prince, and decipher power mechanisms on the basis of a strategy that is immanent in force relationships."[74] Paradoxically, if Foucault's caustic rhetoric again smacked of force, this was only because he hoped to set his genealogical method all the more productively at the service of humanitarian causes, living up to the ethos of an altogether different Enlightenment tradition.

Capping this postmetaphysical examination of power, Foucault resorted to the tactic of nominalism, a technique he often used, together with a revitalized "positivism," to deactivate the suspect logic of the philosophy of history, as Balibar has pointed out. Both techniques served, Balibar explained, as a "supplement to materialism necessary to stop a particular form of materiality – economic, political, or discursive – from turning back into metaphysics," thus enabling Foucault to practice philosophy *in* history, rather than a philosophy *of* history.[75] The far-reaching consequences that followed from this radical, antifoundationalist nominalism emerge in the somewhat oblique reflections on the nature of war and revolution that Foucault advanced in the chapter "Method." Dismissing the possibility that the concept of power could ever be limited to a political institution, structure, let alone ideology, he clarified that power, in fact, was but a "name that one attributes to a complex strategical situation in a particular society,"[76] comprising a virtually limitless arsenal of mobile strategies and concrete tactics. Aware that such a radical nominalism jeopardized the categorical distinctions between war and politics, as indeed seemed to be the case in Clausewitz's famous maxim, Foucault hastened to explain that the two in effect were "two different strategies (but the one always liable to switch into the other) for integrating these unbalanced, heterogeneous, unstable, and tense force relations." Rather than reduce the one to the other, then, he put them on a par, though this balance was always threatened by the possibility that the one could readily reverse into the other.

Thus, though Foucault's un-grounding of epistemological convention aimed to show that the code words "war" and "politics" were to be rethought as historically articulated bundles of tactics and strategies, his analysis at times seemed to come remarkably close to Nietzsche's radical nominalism, according to which truth, even political discourses about the truth, amounted to nothing but a volatile, mobile army of tropes.[77]

Implementing the Nietzschean Hypothesis

Seen against the template of *Discipline and Punish* and *The History of Sexuality*, "*Society Must Be Defended*" clearly occupies a transitional, perhaps even experimental, place in Foucault's developing understanding of power–strategy, power–domination, and power–repression. Nowhere better do the signs of the course's transitional nature rise to the surface than in the set of ambiguities that beleaguered the war/power matrix, whose unruliness Foucault had not yet managed to contain fully. Granted, the Nietzschean hypothesis needed to supplant the Reichean one, but, to all appearances, the switch, initially, proved less than straightforward, a problem largely due to the equivocation that affected the term "repression," which seemed to cut across both hypotheses at once. For a moment, it even appeared that the opening lecture would collapse the two paradigms – repression and force – even as Foucault thrust the outdated mold of juridico-political sovereign power, or power–contract, aside, in favor of *war–repression*. For "repression" in the latter compound, as he was cautious to specify, did not signal the abuse of power under contract theory, rendered by the compound *contract-oppression*. Rather, it referred to "the mere effect and continuation of a relation of domination," so that it was "none other than the realization [*mise en oeuvre*], within the continual warfare of this pseudo-peace, of a perpetual relationship of force."[78] Following these directions, the genealogist eschewed the transhistorical, normative paradigm of sovereign legitimacy, fastening on the historical antagonisms between struggle and subordination, while remaining engaged with procedures of repression only insofar as they fell under the rubric power–domination.

To say the least, Foucault's initial attempt to retain a legitimate connotation of the embattled term "repression" proved confusing. Moreover, as a further indication of the complexities involved in implementing the power–war constellation, one must understand another revealing moment of hesitation that punctuated his opening lecture, not unlike some other pauses that were to follow during subsequent course meetings. Having acknowledged that all of his own work, up to that point, had been conducted under the aegis of *struggle–repression* (or *domination–force*), he now granted that he might be obliged to reconsider, even relinquish, the paradigm. As he conceded, not just perfunctorily, "these two notions of repression and war must themselves be considerably modified if not ultimately abandoned. In any case, I believe that they must be submitted to closer scrutiny."[79] Now, if one looks at the lecture course in its entirety, then surely Foucault managed to shed at least one of the two cumbersome terms, insofar as the lecture of January 14 debunked the notion "repression" once and for all. Clarifying what remained unsaid about the repressive hypothesis in *Discipline and Punish* and *The History of Sexuality*, Foucault explained that the ambivalent term "repression" merged several registers together, attesting to the overlap between *power–law* (or *sovereign-power*) and *power–discipline*, whose interface the course, along the way, tracked. As a polyvalent "politico-psychological" instrument of critical analysis,[80] the term either participated in the discourse of contract power, centered on the law and the sovereign rights of individuals, or, when used in a psychological sense, it proved the irritating descendent of the human sciences and hence – as Foucault asserted, without further elucidating the point – of disciplinary power. Concluding his excursion into the matter, he sanguinely proclaimed this "juridico-disciplinary" hybrid wholly unfit for further critical use. However, for all the attention Foucault's debunking of the repression hypothesis has received, it should not go unnoticed that, at bottom, he also seemed concerned about the intractability of the power/war matrix. Certainly, the above lines, voicing hesitation about his own work, can be interpreted as the simple expression of a wish for epistemological renewal and thus as an early sign of his later turn to the technologies of the self and ethics. But it is definitely conceivable that, in expressing his impatience with repression, he simultaneously targeted power–domination and the war grid as such. Yet, was it realistically possible to discard the one and retain the other? Even his relatively late overview essay, "The Subject and Power," as we shall see, cast doubt on the success of his determination to sail a course away from the seductive power/force matrix.

The moment of hesitation about his methodological presuppositions, audible at the end of the inaugural lecture, was echoed in subsequent meetings, indicative of a hovering, persistent ambivalence about the entire project. For much as repression remained a polysemous term, whose shades of meaning overlapped with those of power–domination, so the conceptual limits between the course's main analytical categories at times seemed permeable. To be sure, even as he subscribed to the Nietzschean hypothesis, Foucault was acutely aware of the fact that holding power/force/war apart would pose severe demands on the historian's critical acumen. Though using the course as a testing ground to try out a series of potential analogies between domination, force, and war, he remained all the while vigilant about their incongruity. His aim, he stressed, was not so much to conflate power, force, and war, as to peel them apart, epistemologically speaking, as they should neither on historical, even less on philosophical, grounds be confounded with one another. Rather, in line with the logic of extremities that guided his genealogical analysis, he therefore lent to war the status of *exemplarity*, seeing it as "an extreme [case], in the sense that war can pass as the maximum point of tension, the nakedness as such of force relations."[81]

That the decision to elevate "war" to such a prominent level – basically the defining grid of analysis for power – remained loaded, appears in the host of unresolved questions that Foucault raised, asking whether all relations of antagonism should necessarily be clad in the armor of war: "Can and must the fact of war be considered as primary with respect to other relations (relations of inequality, dissymmetry, divi-

sions of labor, relations of exploitation, etc.)? Can and must phenomena of antagonism, rivalry, confrontation, struggle between individuals or between groups and
classes, be regrouped in this general mechanism, in this general form that is war?"[82]
Dedicated to a genealogical investigation of historically specific epochs of Western
modernity, Foucault was reluctant to tender generalizations about power relations as
such and, hence, would hardly want to proclaim war "the master of all things." But
these questions about whether "war" genuinely was the matrix that *preceded* all other
conflictual modes of interaction also implied that the course, hypothetically speaking,
risked doing more than just advance the martial matrix as a contingent, historically
specific mold. Here, and elsewhere in the course, one sees Foucault waver about
whether "war" functioned as just one possible *historical* matrix for force relations, or
whether it operated as a more general, primary *arche*-principle of sorts, indispensable
to an analysis of political power.[83] At times, his focus seemed to be nothing less than
theoretical (despite the course's sustained criticism of theory, particularly political
theory), determined as he was to identify the economy of power in general, which
prompted him to peer beyond history's contingent, empirical playing field. At other
moments, however, he vowed to remain true to his historian's bearings, adhering to a
more narrow, localized historicist program, and to the strand of nominalism and
constructivism according to which "war" was but a grid, much as he did in *The History
of Sexuality*. As we shall have further opportunity to note, the duplicities resulting from
these two competing vantage points – the one theoretical, the other historicist –
would plague the entire course.

If *"Society Must Be Defended"* lent a slightly different stature to power/war than did
Discipline and Punish or *The History of Sexuality*, still, it formally and structurally very
much followed an analogous trajectory, as it advanced a historicized typology of
power, glossing the sequential codifications – fixations of sorts – to which a potentially infinite plurality of force relations had been reduced. Successive lectures
illustrated how a restrictive conception of political power, defined by the unificatory
mechanisms of monarchical or state sovereignty, steadily disintegrated, clearing the
way for a social conception of power that irreversibly exploded older authorizing
fictions of unity. As Foucault maneuvered away from the *juridico-sovereign* conception
of power to *power–domination*, he rejected once again the principles of liberal political
theory no less than "law-abiding" versions of left-wing thought, very much in the spirit
of his published studies on punitive and sexual techniques. Launching, first of all, a
critique of liberal contractarianism, he relinquished the foundational fictions upon
which it rested, foremost that of sovereign power. Now it was time, Foucault
declared, to depose of the artificial monster Leviathan, which adorned the frontispiece
of Hobbes's treatise, symbol of the communal, collective will, whose soul was constituted by the sovereign. For while it might be true that Hobbes, along with other
contractarians, sought to curb sovereign power, laying down its legal limits, Foucault
took the antipodal stance, interrogating what legal rules power abused to produce
accredited discourses, licensed by the truth. Not the constitution of the sovereign

garnered his interest, he announced, but rather the concomitant fabrication of subjects and the various *techniques* of domination that were instrumental in the process of subject formation. Seen from this vantage point, what thus appeared in full view were the three foundational fictions, set into operation by the discourse of sovereignty: first, the subjection of the subject; second, the alleged unity of power; and, finally, the so-called originary naturalness of the law. Revealing a fissure between law and legitimacy, sovereign power in reality only provided the shallow grounding to the edifice of law. Sustained by the vicious circle of self-legitimation, sovereignty in fact preceded the law, as it were, functioning as its antecedent foundation – *préalable*, as Foucault's French stressed time and again – which granted ultimate legitimacy to the discourse of right.[84] Wholly impervious to the potentially positive manifestations of sovereignty, Foucault rejected the entire term out of hand and, with it, its full potential spectrum, ranging from the medieval feudal monarchy up to and including parliamentary democracy, which, as defined by Rousseau, for example, was premised on a collective, democratized sovereignty and public right.

But to this denunciation of liberal political principles, Foucault added a vociferous critique of leftist political theory. Stating that global conceptions of ideology critique needed to be jettisoned, he urged that universalizing categories such as "class," but also the "bourgeoisie," be dispensed with. In place of ideology critique now came "localized critique," an analysis that, coming from down below, focused on material operations, forms of subjection, local systems and techniques of knowledge, all of which, acting in concert, made up power–domination. At long last liberated from both burdensome traditions, the genealogist investigated how subjects were constituted by means of "operators" or "*dispostifs*" of domination,[85] to be wrested from power relations.[86] Working again with his immanent model of power, Foucault now specified what he meant by strategic power relations, explaining that they comprised an arsenal of technologies, which could be usurped, colonized, redistributed. But the changed course of investigation did not bode that one would lose sight of the "global" as a result of the "local." As a *micro*-physics of power, Foucault's analysis also permitted the examination of power's *macro*-structures, to the extent that the interface between general structural, or institutional, power relations and micro-operators transpired as the interplay between strategies and tactics, meaning that the "global strategies" that "traversed and utilized the local tactics of domination"[87] needed to be mapped as well. As he thus closed off his preparatory observations about the new methodology, Foucault seemed sure that these materialistic strategic analyses would replace the defunct representationalist category of ideology once and for all.

Political Historicism

Foucault's own insurrectionary, performative historiography tried to set loose, release, not just from under the dust but from the shackles of antiquarian historiography the counterrevolutionary forces that, for too long, had been locked up. On a methodological level, he practiced genealogy as the retrieval of British and French antimonarchical historical tracts – mainly those by Coke, Selden, Lilburne, and Boulainvilliers – in whose annals he gleaned a critique of sovereign power, aroused by the irrepressible memory of real combat and the recollection of a historical, biracial warfare that left lasting rifts through the social body. At the vanguard of the counter-discourse stood British lawyers, such as Coke and Selden, and especially the Levelers, headed by Lilburne, who disputed the usurped rights of the king, understanding the monarchy and aristocracy as the spoils of the Norman conquest, which had left the original Saxon inhabitants ravaged, trammeled serfs.[88] In France, it was the nobleman Boulainvilliers who, as he assumed the political education of the king's heir, ingeniously inserted himself into the monarch's historical discourse, recovering the suppressed fable of Frankish courage to further his own aristocratic interests. Always willing to dispense polemical statements, Foucault maintained that this tradition of real, not "ideal" armed struggle inaugurated the first rigorous "historico-political discourse," ready to take on the contemporaneous philosophico-juridical paradigm, emblematized by Hobbes, who loomed large as the founding father of contractarianism and political theory. If in chapter 13 of his *Leviathan*, the British philosopher had defined the *status naturalis* as a "state of war," then, in truth, he had but advanced a highly contrived, idealized image of war, suppressing the factual violence of former conquest. Premised on the triple unities of law, subject, and sovereign, Hobbes's theory above all proved moored in the fiction of an originary, mythical battle of all against all – the *bellum omnium contra omnes* – which had been subdued by the political compact. Far, then, from unwittingly lapsing behind the position of Hobbes's contractarianism back into a brutish natural state, Foucault deliberately took on the British philosopher for having brushed over – or so he maintained – the multiple, intractable determinants of history. Certainly, Hobbes, Foucault agreed, was the first modern thinker to have introduced the discourse of war into the hub of political theory. Still, contractarianism announced the beginning of a modern master discourse of law and sovereignty, which, under its shining armor or panoply, hid the realities of war and all the messy facts of history, and which Foucault placed on a par with the "*history of the event*," defined in his earlier Nietzsche work.

Penetrating deep under the surface of Hobbes's treatise, Foucault's analysis intended to disclose how the description of the *status naturalis* placed "equality" above "difference," privileging a semiotic register of signs and a discourse of representation over the differential play of force. Thus, only against the setting of Foucault's philosophy of difference, which he shared with Deleuze, does it become evident – though not necessarily more convincing – why he reached the seemingly counterintuitive conclusion that Hobbes's imaginary war amounted to a "war of equality."[89] Reading Hobbes in neglect of interpretive tradition, Foucault maintained that it was in fact the "natural lack of differentiation" between warring contenders that generated "insecurities, risks, hazards, and, consequently, the will, on both sides, to confront each other," so that, in the end, it was "the aleatory [*l'aléatoire*] in the primitive relation of forces that creates this state of war."[90] Undoubtedly, Foucault's exegesis of chapter 13 of *Leviathan* could not have been further removed from what Hobbes's tract ostensibly asserted. For, seeing that they were moved by an identical desire for the same object, or the same ends, contending parties calculated the risks involved in the struggle, letting their desire for self-preservation gain the upper hand over their material interests. Ceding their own power to the sovereign, humans chose to live under a common power and common law, practicing restraint on their natural passions. But Foucault chose to ignore Hobbes's postulate of a collective desire for self-preservation, when he instead presumed an underlying common will for a battle on life and death, the net result being that his reading ended up having more in common with Hegel's account of violent strife, at the root of the master–slave dialectic.[91] Moreover, what further heightened the artificiality of Hobbes's imagined state of nature, Foucault added, was the calculated play of wills, the games of representations through which potential contenders, filled by fright, hoped to read the signs of imminent danger imparted by their adversaries, so as to assess the potential danger to their livelihood. In the final analysis, then, Foucault inferred, the Hobbesian contract proved to be the result of the "fearful will of the subjects."[92] Surely, it is interesting to note that, in the course of his analysis, Foucault never directly discussed Hobbes's royalism or the quasi-republican elements that some commentators have discerned in his understanding of the king as a representative of the people rather than as a divinely ordained monarch.[93] Nor was he interested in considering the counterdiscourse to war: that of pacifism or universal peace. Rather, on the basis of *Leviathan* he established that Hobbes stifled the national recollection of past and present atrocities and injustices, committed in the name of sovereignty, thus effectively setting up factual war as his sworn enemy. Perplexed, furthermore, by the fact that *Leviathan* recognized a sovereignty of conquest next to a sovereignty of institution, Foucault concluded that Hobbes covered up the din of a permanent civil war, which explained why he had been given "the senatorial title of father of political philosophy."[94]

Where a tyranny of equality and a construed egalitarianism determined Hobbes's consensual contract no less than the "state of war" that preceded it, political historicism gave free reign to difference, honoring history's differential play of force relations. Using language also to be found in *The History of Sexuality*, Foucault proclaimed that the new historicism was "a discourse, that, au fond, cuts off the head of the king, dispenses in any case with the king and denounces the king."[95] All too aware of the disrepute that historicism had slipped in, ever since its academic rise to prominence in the post-Hegelian era, Foucault nonetheless celebrated a *political historicism*, whose earliest harbingers – Coke, Lilburne, Boulainvilliers – upheld a "historicist historian's" point of view against the oppression of unifying, idealizing theoretical constructs. No longer deploying "historicism" as a term of opprobrium, as he had done in the 1971 Nietzsche essay, he now reclaimed the disparaged label from Nietzsche's ire to flesh out the mechanisms of *counterhistory*, whose outlines he had first sketched in that very same Nietzsche article. In that sense, it does not seem out of line that Foucault, here as elsewhere, shirked from embracing the promissory notes tendered by political theory, preferring the brute facts that constituted history's "evenementality."

With characteristic splendor, if not astounding interpretive versatility, Foucault deduced a catalog of explosive insights from these English and French antimonarchical archives, documents, and treatises. And, though he was not blind to the wealth of disparate political tactics for which these antiroyal invectives had been marshaled, in an initial phase, at least, he seemed ready to downplay historical distinctions in the interest of providing a generalized economy of political historicism. Among the principal strategies — all quasi-Nietzschean transvaluations of values — that he enumerated were the following:

1   Drawing on real, historical episodes of conquest, the historicist counterdiscourse put in perspective phantasmatic accounts of a primeval, originary state of nature, or *status naturalis* — a charge, as we saw, mainly leveled at the Hobbesian tradition.

2   Unlike what liberal theories asserted, political power did not commence where war ended, nor did law, for its part, originate in nature, imposed as it had been through the force of real battles.

3   Exploding the unitary claims of hegemonic right, entrenched in sovereign power, the historicist counterdiscourse replaced the figment of a unitary or universal subject by a partisan, particularized, combating subject, or adversary.

4   Showing the body politic to be fractured among real enemies, the discourse injected a binary, dualistic motor into the course of history, which only later, under the yoke of Hegelianism, would receive its dominant encoding in a "logic of contradictions," curbing the differential play of agonisms.

5   In arousing the forgotten memories of brute conquest, on which the monarchy in reality proved founded, the counterdiscourse short-circuited the abuse to which historiography had been put in the past, serving the greater glory or laudation of the sovereign. Rupturing a mnemic tradition that dated back to the Romans and was characteristic of Indo-European modes of history-telling, this counternarrative's divinatory texture had more in common with Judaic models of prophecy.

6   The fiction of the natural savage, idolized in the brand of Rousseauism that the bourgeoisie all too readily embraced, was supplanted by the prowess of the fierce barbarian, "the blond beast."

7   Foundational to the new historicist counterdiscourse was a cyclical conception of history, spurred on by the vicious cycle of revenge and the anticipation of a final, even apocalyptic battle — a conception of history that would come to stand in stark contrast to the bourgeois view of history, in which the state (Hegel) and the "now" of the present (Sieyès) would come to be the bearers of the universal.

8   Though revolutionary in nature and intent, the new historicist counterdiscourse was at once critical *and* mythical, for as a new political tool, it could be appropriated for democratic, left populist causes no less than for reactionary, right-wing purposes.

While it will not be possible to consider all of these assertions in full detail, clearly some deserve to be analyzed in more depth, including the perhaps far-reaching political consequences that Foucault inferred from the list, not only for his genealogy of history but also for his own methodology. We must start, first of all, with one of the overriding polarizations that structured his analysis, "universality–singularity," which proved very much related to the antagonism "global–local," with which, as we saw, the opening lecture had started off. Most unexpected, perhaps, but entirely in line with the twists to which Hobbes's treatise had been subjected, was the fact that in referencing the mythico-historical discourses about the Norman and Frankish invasions, Foucault derived nothing less than a critique of the universal subject from this account. Focusing not on the excluded, silent victims of real warfare or even disciplinary violence, as he had done in earlier work, surprisingly, he now drew the profile of an armored, adversarial, belligerent subject. And, rather than assuming a neutral stance, this subject emerged as the partisan enemy, not galvanized by humanitarian causes but radically particularized by the war into which he had been recruited. Localized, partisan, and singular, the new historical subject of the historicist *récit* sang not of peace or tranquil nature but rhapsodized about battle, vicious adversaries, and vengeful enemies.

In a thinly veiled stab at Kant's political philosophy, Foucault scorned the mediating figure of the philosopher-legislator, quickened by visions of eternal peace and global justice. He summarized his charges as follows:

> The role of the one who speaks is therefore not the role of the legislator or the philosopher, between camps, the figure of peace and of armistice, in that position of which already Solon had dreamt, and also Kant. To establish oneself between adversaries, at the center and above them, to impose a general law on each and to found an order that reconciles: this is not at all what is at issue. At issue, rather, is the positing of a right marked by dissymmetry, the founding of a truth linked to a relation of force, a weapon-truth [*une vérité-arme*] and a singular right. The subject that speaks is a warring – I won't even say, polemical – subject.[96]

No longer occupying the universalizing position of the philosopher or jurist, the subject that emanated from these forgotten narratives was *the warring subject*, stationed in the trenches, surrounded by adversaries, out to attain a highly particularized victory, and able only to command a highly perspectival view of the truth, *sui generis*.

It is not hard to see that dominant *leitmotifs* from the 1971 Nietzsche essay, which rearranged the conventional hierarchy between passions, affects, and reason, returned with full force in *"Society Must Be Defended."* Counterhistory, Foucault now commented, amounted to a *critical* discourse, a term to be taken in the strong, cutting sense Nietzsche ascribed to critical history in the second *Untimely Meditation*. Besides unleashing the infinite play of history and dissymmetry of conflicting forces, this counterhistory also attended to the battle cries of war, exposing from under the fugacity of history "the blood that has dried in the codes," not "the absolute of law/right."[97] What the new historicist war discourse dictated was nothing else than that juridical and political power did not stem the tide of belligerent violence. Much as Benjamin's "Critique of Violence" had declared that the imposition of the law did not amount to pacification or armistice, so Foucault's Nietzschean historian believed in a war that continued to rage under the cover of peace. And, just as much as Nietzsche's *Birth of Tragedy* took on the natural right tradition in the figure of Rousseau's and Homer's naive natural man,[98] so Foucault detected in Rousseauism an idle bourgeois fantasy of antihistoricism,[99] with its misguided conceptions of natural law and the nostalgic idyll of an untarnished, pristine nature, contaminated by culture. Reversing calcified values, traditional polarities, and equilibriums, this counterhistory consolidated a novel historical explication, rising from the bottom, the most obscure level, from a violent chaos made up of bodily passions, hatreds, contingencies. In this battlefield, bodies and passions and volatile chance events enmeshed, making up the permanent weft of history and society, conceived in physico-biological terms. Above this explosive arena, Foucault declared – now seemingly rendering passages from the Nietzsche essay almost verbatim – an ever-ascending rationality would build its edifice, full of calculations, strategies, aimed to maximize power but also, crucially, replete with illusions and fraudulent ruses. Riveted to the interplay between power/knowledge with its treacherous games of truth, Foucault once again celebrated how old Platonic truths were upset, much as Nietzsche had done. Inverting the commonly held relation between law and history, he posited that this counternarrative did not disclose history to be erected on the pillars of a permanent rationality, crowned by the ideals of the just or the good. In reality, history had metastasized into a violent hazardous, physico-biological series of brute facts, whose effects – as Foucault summed it up, intoning Nietzsche – proved to be the "inversion [*renversement*], therefore … of the explicative axis of the law and of history."[100]

As he thus turned to the anatomy of counterhistory as "evenementality," Foucault did not merely intend to dismiss the unificatory mold of political theory and right. His critique was equally directed against the philosophy of history, especially dialectics, which obeyed its own sets of laws, those legislating the relation between cause and effect in history. For the counternarrative of the never-ending eternal war, he conjectured, installed a novel, previously unknown *binarism* into the discourse about history, a sort of motor that came to replace the medieval pyramidal design, the tertiary model, as well as the organic body-politic metaphor that structured Hobbes's thought. Regrettably, with the passing of time, this powerful, explosive discourse gradually dissipated as it got absorbed into the rigid dualism of dialectical thinking, subjected to its "logic of contradiction." Passionately opposed to all "ideal schemas," be it those that heeded the natural-right tradition or believed in a divinely ordained course of history, Foucault saw the historical field as bounded by two equally treacherous philosophical counterpoles: the all-powerful Hobbes, the most influential spokesperson of politico-juridical sovereignty, and, at the far end of modern history, Hegel, whose dialectic – including its offshoots in Marxism – definitively tamed and colonized history's intractable, contingent facts. For nothing would be more erroneous, Foucault now maintained, than to believe that the dialectic, "as the discourse about the universal and historical movement of the contradiction and of war," presented the grand, philosophical validation of historicist discourse. Quite to the contrary, Hegelianism constituted "its resumption [*reprise*] and displacement in the old form of philosophico-juridical discourse."[101] What else did this mean than that Hegel's dialectic sublated volatile difference by subjecting it to the double process of totalization and rationality? Though, curiously, as we observed before, Foucault never engaged directly with the master–slave dialectic of the *Phenomenology*, often read as an interpretation of Hobbes's state of nature, he did allude to Hegel's philosophy of right, upon whose advocacy of the teleological rationality of the state he again placed strictures. For, as Foucault explained, winding up his Hegel critique, "the dialectic assures the constitution, across history, of a universal subject, a reconciled truth, a right in which all particulars would have their ordained place. The Hegelian dialectic, and all that have followed ... must be understood ... as the authoritarian colonization and pacification, by philosophy and right, of a historico-political discourse that is at the same time a report, proclamation, and practice of social warfare."[102]

Boulainvilliers's Improbable Historicism

Having considered the principles of Foucault's counterhistory in some detail, we must now address the vexed question as to why he chose to fasten on Boulainvilliers with the dedication that he did, in defiance, it seemed, of the historian's aristocratic conservatism. Applying what often seemed to be an undue dose of interpretive force to Boulainvilliers's multi-volume history of French government, Foucault ascribed to the nobiliary historian the strategies and procedures of his proper genealogical method, so that he eventually emerged as a stand-in for Nietzsche and, *a fortiori*, the Nietzschean hypothesis as such. Not only in French history but also within the discipline of historiography at large, Foucault generalized, Boulainvilliers was to be awarded a place of distinction for being the first to have fashioned a veritable "genealogy of war" and for the unique prescience with which he consolidated one of modernity's defining "grids of intelligibility," that of a permanent civil war festering in the fiber of the social body. Against the natural law of equality, Boulainvilliers counterpoised the differential law of history, with its reign of force and inequality, exposing right's corruption by conquest. Uncovering "the relational character of power,"[103] he understood history in its longitudinal sense as the mobile agonism of struggles and the ever-changing calculation of forces. As he tracked the fate of the original Franco-German noble caste across the centuries, he proved concerned with the mechanisms of reversal that befell the initial imposition of force, trying seriously to understand how the Franks' aristocratic ascendance had finally turned into its opposite. Honors were due to Boulainvilliers not just because he uncovered the matrix *power–domination*, but also because he proved a scholar of disciplinary power *avant la lettre*. As he further refined the mythical counter-discourse initiated by Coke and Lilburne, he studied the economic distribution of arms among the Germanic tribes, thus paying due attention to the institution of militarism. Furthermore, as one of the principal representatives of the nobiliary reaction against Louis XIV, he above all took aim at one distinct mechanism of *savoir/pouvoir*, namely, the ties that bound historiography to statism. Contesting how the state's absolutism depended on its administrative, bureaucratic apparatus, which consolidated "the discourse of the State about the State,"[104] he battled its administrative, juridical, and historical discourse, reanimating the memory of the usurpations and strategic manipulations that had left the nobility disempowered and impoverished. Angled at once at the ever more influential Third Estate, Boulainvilliers's rallying cry in support of his aristocratic kin touted its unlimited right of privilege, whose vindication he found in the Frankish invasion and the nobility's descent from the prowessed Germanic warrior class, the blond barbarian.[105] As if wanting to temper Boulainvilliers's truculent rhetoric, Foucault explained that the "warring subject" around which this counter-*récit* was emplotted really amounted to the "nation." For, in its original meaning, he clarified, the term "nation" designated a collective or "society," in this case, the society or circle of nobles, grouped around the body of the king. However aristocratic the category's provenance might be, it was nonetheless out of this early conception of the "nation," Foucault commented, that the later revolutionary meaning of the term, the nationalisms of the nineteenth century, and the harrowing problem of state-sponsored racism would arise.

All too aware of the controversial theses he espoused, Foucault paid extra care to justify the reversal that topped all, to wit, that it was the aristocracy – not the rising bourgeoisie or the pauperized proletariat – that turned out to be the genuine "subject of history."[106] The reason, he revealed, quite plainly lay in the French nobility's preoccupation with its own historic wars, which allowed it to turn armed struggle into its genealogical object, "war being at once the point of departure of the discourse, the condition of possibility for the emergence of a historical discourse and the point of reference, the object towards which the discourse turned, war being at once the basis of the discourse and that about which it speaks."[107] According to this vertiginous logic, war constituted simultaneously the object of the counterdiscourse, its strategic tool, *and*, even more fundamentally, its very enabling "ground" in the first place.

What one sees at work here, in this stunning exercise in genealogical commentary, is not so much a case of *petitio principii* as the reflexive mechanisms of what could best be called Foucault's "hermeneutical circle" of power/violence, which hinged on a subject "being thrown" into violence rather than meaning. For no matter how far the historian receded into the past, Foucault announced – clearly opposing conventional philosophies of origin – never would he stumble upon a founding bedrock, be it nature, the law, order, or peace. Moving backwards, the genealogist inevitably encountered the differential play of martial force, "the indefinite of war," which figured as the ungrounded ground (*fond*) of the force field of history and of politics as domination,[108] but also doubled as the strategic implement that historicist discourse deployed, "a tactical *dispositif* inside this war." In other words, as he brought to a close the figure of "ungrounded grounding," Foucault parodied hermeneutics, evoking a "circle" or "cycle" of force, whose fundament of meaning, the secure staple of humanism, had been demolished. In the end, the movement in which history and force were caught exposed an "indissociable circularity between historical knowledge (*savoir*) and the wars that are at once told by it and that, nonetheless, traverse it."[109] In one and the same stroke, Platonism with its hallowed union between truth and knowledge, was turned upside down, as its eternal values proved contaminated by violence and war.

As Foucault thus strategically felt his way through the vast chronicles of the French historian-aristocrat, he set up a binary system in which Boulainvilliers, thinker of particularism and difference, stood in opposition to the rising bourgeoisie, propagators of a suspect universalism. Championing highly different conceptions of constitutional power, reconciliatory history, and historical time, these respective factions conveniently constituted the antipodal ends of a political spectrum. If the bourgeoisie's ahistorical Rousseauism, social contract theory, and quest for a democratic constitution, thematized by Sieyès and Augustin Thierry, resisted the differential play of history, envisioning a democratic equilibrium or balancing of forces, then Boulainvilliers, in contrast, held fast to a theory of constitutional power premised on the sovereign imposition of force. The incipient bourgeoisie, Foucault remarked, resolutely averted its glance from the past, for, peering towards the future, it anticipated the arrival of the future universal state, demanding the transition from nation to statism, pining after "the contact of the universal and the real in the immanence of the present."[110] Much in contrast, Boulainvilliers coupled his understanding of constitution to the original meaning of the term "revolution," referring to a cyclical return of cosmological proportions, and thus refused to honor sovereign power as being anchored in a legitimate body of laws. Hoping that the unlawful constitution might be toppled by revolution, he introduced a rhythmic, repetitive understanding of history, powered by revenge and a bid for the eventual overturn of the injustice wreaked. Even before Nietzsche imagined his eternal return of the same, Foucault advised, a cyclical conception of history slowly but surely made its way into modernity, calling for the millenarian reconstitution of a primordial equilibrium of forces. Unmistakably in the thrall of his Nietzschean hypothesis, Foucault concluded – not altogether unexpectedly – that, after the French Revolution, Boulainvilliers's prophetic insight into power/war was recolonized, redistributed over myriads of small wars and struggles, subjected, at long last, to a moment of "auto-dialectization" by the bourgeoisie. For, quite independently of the reconciliatory logic that Hegel cemented in his phenomenology of world history and philosophy of right, the bourgeoisie succumbed to the ruse of a universalistic logic, which it saw realized in the sovereign state. If this convergence confirmed that bourgeois history and philosophy eventually joined hands in lauding the present as the carrier of "the universal," it also proved that the aristocrat's resourceful historicist matrix once and for all was brushed aside in the trail blazed by an ascending new historico-political discourse, in which the bourgeoisie's claim to universalism reigned supreme.[111]

Now what made Foucault's strategic exegesis of Boulainvilliers highly unusual, if not improbable, is that he refrained from castigating his odious discourse out of hand for being the precursor of the worse totalitarian violence to come. Much as it was curious that Foucault neglected to consider Arendt's aetiology of National Socialism and Stalinism, given that her *Origins of Totalitarianism* first set up the mirroring dualism between "race thinking" and "class thinking," so it was no less peculiar that he failed to take cognizance of how she classified the historian as the principal French instigator of racism before the advent of institutionalized "race thinking."[112] Indeed, Arendt's path-breaking study demonstrated how in counteracting Louis XIV's tactical overtures to the Third Estate, Boulainvilliers vindicated the French nobility's undisputed claim to historical privilege through its descent from the Franks, invoking the "eternal right of conquest" in which obedience was "always due to the strongest."[113] Though Boulainvilliers derived these ideas from seventeenth-century might-right doctrines, foremost among them Spinoza's, he supplanted might by conquest, grounding the distinction between classes and ethnic groups not in a people's physical race markers but in their forceful deeds. Besides being a precursor of the worst institutionalized French racist ideologies of the nineteenth century, especially de Gobineau, Boulainvilliers furthermore figured prominently in yet another strand of conservative cultural nationalism, the one that idolized the so-called Germanic roots, or *germanité*, of French culture.[114]

In all truth, one must acknowledge that in the course of his lectures Foucault several times went out of his way to condemn Boulainvilliers for being the reactionary he really was.[115] Furthermore, the lecture of February 18 seemed to take the nobiliary historian on for being one of the principal fomenters of the myth of "the blond beast." Worshiping the Franks, who put an end to the Roman Empire's tyranny and decadence, as the founders of his own caste, Boulainvilliers imputed virtue-like vices to these barbarous Germanic hordes, revering their ferocity above all else. Interpreted in light of the Latin word *ferox*, the Germanic adjective *frank* did not so much have the benign sense of "free,"[116] meaning liberty as equality or respect of the other, but rather bluntly expressed the ferocity of domination. Being antijuridical, Boulainvilliers was also antinature, for the "blond barbarian" no longer conjured up Rousseau's noble savage but instead the man of history, the propagator of "pillage" and "arson," in short, of supreme domination. Elaborating further on the earliest account of the so-called auspicious Germanic origins of the French, a discourse thought to have been initiated by François Hotman in the seventeenth century, Boulainvilliers's more vicious version of the fable would have a lasting impact on a number of French reactionary thinkers. Still, the most infamous propagator of this "noble barbarism" was Nietzsche, who solidified the myth of the blond beast, amongst others, in his *Genealogy of Morals*.[117] For Nietzsche, Foucault explicated, "freedom will be the equivalent of a ferocity that is the taste of power and determined avidity, the incapacity to serve but the always ready desire to submit [*assujettir*]."[118] For the German philosopher, "frank" meant "impolite and gross mores, hatred of Roman names, language, and lore. Amateurs of freedom, valiant, light, unfaithful, greedy for gain, impatient, restless."[119]

And, yet, despite these explicit denunciations of Boulainvilliers's theory of *germanité*, Foucault did not refrain from situating the French aristocrat's Frankish legend of brute force in the context of his own philosophy of "evenementality," nor did its atavism stop him from putting the logic of forceful imposition on a par with that of difference.[120] Abstracting, furthermore, from the essentialist presuppositions about race and pure bloodlines that Boulainvilliers blatantly embraced, Foucault did not analyze how "race" and "stock" operated as "biological" categories, assuming race instead to be a structural marker of difference. So intent was he on deconstructing sovereign power through the dynamics of rifting ethnic strife, as it cleaved its path through the feigned homogeneity of the body politic, that he also left the troubling cultural nationalism of Boulainvilliers underattended. As a result one sometimes sees Foucault mindlessly duplicating the disquieting rhetoric of a Franco-Germanic nationalism, as when he proposed that the counterlaw of history in Boulainvilliers's thought stood for a "*germanité*" towards nature.[121] Perhaps as an indication of how much in flux Foucault's thoughts on the topic possibly were, one can read his interventions in a now famous, heated round-table discussion, "The Game of Michel Foucault," which took place not too long after he had ended his course cycle *Society Must Be Defended"* at the Collège de France. Following a discussion of the theory of biopolitics set forth in *The History of Sexuality*, one of the interlocutors called attention to Boulainvilliers, noting how his work embraced a biological racism, anchored in hereditary blood laws, not just the cultural myth of noble superiority. In his retort, Foucault claimed to have said as much about Boulainvilliers in that study, all the while emphasizing how essential it remained to differentiate between the nineteenth-century scientific discourse of a racist biology and the earlier cultural racism of the aristocracy.[122] However, if the nobleman-historian made a cameo appearance in *The History of Sexuality*, it was only as a critic of sovereign power and only in the penultimate chapter, not in the study's last chapter, in which Sade figured as a stand-in for *ancien régime* blood laws.[123]

In order to shed further light on this state of affairs, one might recall that, early on in the lecture course, Foucault acknowledged the potential contradictions his interpretation might trap him in, ascribing this condition to what he considered to be the *ambiguity* of the new "antisovereign war" paradigm. Conducted, historically speaking, by widely diverse factions, this new grid would be favored both by the "proto-left" no less than by aristocrats, out to challenge the sovereign power of the absolute monarch. Amenable to both the left and the right, to democratic populists no less than aristocratic strategists, the discourse finally would emerge in its most atrocious variant in the writings of nineteenth-century biological racists and eugenicists.[124] In other words, next to the so-called subtle or popular insurrectionary knowledges that were mediated through this counterdiscourse now emerged the most retrograde,

dark mythologies, vitalized by the belief in eternal war, including the rise to prominence of the *Führer* myth.[125] In order to explain the discourse's malleability, Foucault
adduced a theory about the fluidity of historical discourse that perhaps left more
unexplained than it clarified. Thus he invoked a "stretched epistemic weft" (*une trame
épistémique très serrée*), which spanned across the course of French history and whose
various strands could be used, reused, knotted, even "colonized," by various political
factions. In this way, for instance, it became clear why the myth of the barbarian
could become a precursor of eliminationist racism, or, why, conversely, others could
hail the Gallo-Roman municipality as an early precursor of the Third Estate. For the
law of historiography that Foucault claimed to lay bare devised the following: the
more historical "knowledge" proved regular or homogeneous, the easier it became for
historical subjects as they insinuated themselves into the historical *récit* to locate
themselves on either side of the dividing line that separated (political) adversaries
from one another. In other words, "the tactical reversibility of the discourse is a direct
function of the homogeneity of the formation rules of this discourse. It is the regularity of the epistemic field, the homogeneity in the mode of formation of the
discourse, that will render it usable in extra-discursive struggles."[126]

Foucault's treatment of the matrix *power/war* in the end proved highly duplicitous,
mainly because he combined historicist statements with what, on the face of it,
seemed theoretical generalizations. Between the two sets of observations there often
existed no small degree of tension, even potential contradiction, insofar as the one
paid attention to and acknowledged Boulainvilliers's conservatism, while the other
simply sought to magnify his supposed revolutionizing potential for the purposes of
the new counterhistory. As a consequence, one catches Foucault rereading
Nietzschean philosophy and his Nietzschean hypothesis, mediated through the views
of the controversial French historian. Have we traveled, then, in the course of
analyzing *"Society Must Be Defended,"* from the materialistic category "power/force" to
the biologistic realm of brute, physical force? To the corporeal encounter of warring
opponents, as some of Foucault's critics have contended?

War, the Master of All?

Should one suspect that Foucault's highly speculative exegesis of Boulainvilliers propagated conservative political thought? Hardly. Rather, the uncomfortable proximity he
sought to the conservative thinker again stems from his desire to reverse the legacy of
traditional historical knowledge (*connaissance*) as well as his aim to expose the violence
of normative liberalism – thus, ironically, often duplicating the violence of liberalism's
counterdiscourse. Added to that comes the fact that – with one and the same auda-
cious gesture – he simultaneously attempted to invert the political conservatism
whose very thought figures he sometimes all too closely engaged. No wonder that the
result is often dizzying and certainly tenuous to all unwilling to leap bravely into the
fray of Foucauldian historiography. Surely, it would be misguided to call Foucault an

advocate of violence, even more so to see him as the glorifier of war. One does more justice to his discourse if one starts to think of it, for one, as participating in a long genealogy of philosophical thought about war. As a philosophical *topos*, the figure of war as the father of all goes as far back as Heraclitus, whose dictum that war was the master of all things Heidegger much cherished.[127] From Heraclitus via Hegel to Heidegger, Western philosophy has been weighed down by a being-towards-death, often to the point of elevating violence's so-called interruptive, disjunctive force to a philosophical counterprinciple. It is for this reason that Arendt took issue with the violent potential of dialectical negation, laid down in the tradition's privileged narrative – the master-slave dialectic. And it is for this reason, too, that Levinas opposed the thanatological legacy of Western philosophy, as when he observed at the beginning of *Totality and Infinity*, hardly concealing his contempt: "We do not need obscure fragments of Heraclitus to prove that being reveals itself as war to philosophical thought, that war does not only affect [philosophical thought] as the most patent fact, but as the very patency, or the truth, of the real."[128] As a way of countering this assumed homology between war and the real, Levinas designed his ethics of the other, striving to retrieve another beginning, which lay in advance of the mythical *status naturalis*. Obviously, Foucault had no such Levinasian intentions, not even in the antisystem of ethics he drafted towards the end of his life, going against the normativity of established, conventional moral codes. In presenting him, therefore, as the historian of violence one comes closer to respecting the letter of his text, though merely stating that his model is descriptive, rather than prescriptive – as some critics have wanted to do – may not necessarily get him off the proverbial political hook. We must therefore return to the questions raised at the outset, namely, whether Foucault merely remained mired in bellicose empiricity, bent myopically over the grayness of the historical parchment,[129] so that in the end he became, against best intentions, too antiquarian and monumental, unable to reclaim the critical force of historiography. More than just rhetorical questions, these queries certainly call for answers that are less straightforward than at first might seem to be the case.

In the opening lecture of *"Society Must Be Defended"*, Foucault announced that his aim was not to advance "a homogeneous and solid theoretical ground to all dispersed genealogies," specifying that he did not want to "superimpose on them a sort of theoretical crowning that would unify them."[130] Similarly, he gave great care to emphasize that "war" was not a transcendent law or ground, but quite to the contrary, the "historical principle of the functioning of power."[131] Despite his repeated insistence that every desire to transcendentalize "war" into a suprahistorical category would be thwarted, it appears that he did not fully succeed in keeping that specter at bay. "War," it seemed, started to operate as more than simply modernity's privileged grid of intelligibility or a codification of power – as he called it in *The History of Sexuality* – functioning at times as a grounding, foundationalist principle of sorts. As a result, a potential conflict arose between his antitheoretical design and the actual operations of the grid, which – allegedly extracted from the frazzle of history via inductive means –

came to predetermine and stratify the evenementality of history. Surely, it would be possible to abstract from the war model in Foucault's thought or to deconstruct it, that is, to see it as no more than an all too seductive trope or figure. Yet, it seems more important to pursue its logic in all its details, not in the interest of debunking Foucault's work but to estimate fully the burdensome freight that came along with the matrix power/war – a problem he seemed aware of when early on in the course he noted that it might be necessary to shed this interpretive mold. For this reason, we must now reconsider some of the underlying operative theses concerning the force of history that can be distilled from the course.

1. The Critical / Mythical Grid "War / Force"

It is fair to say that throughout *"Society Must Be Defended,"* "war" functioned as an overdetermined nodal point, a veritable crossing-point in which a great many analytical lines converged. As we saw, early on in the lecture course Foucault conceded that the historical discourse about power/war, essential to political historicism, was equivocal, as it could be enlisted by both left- and right-wing factions, resulting in a "discourse at once darkly critical and intensely mythical."[132] To all appearances, he did well to draw attention to the ambivalence of the grid "war," though one might add that the category wasn't just elusive because of the wide range of political stratagems for which it could be usurped, but also for the slippery nature it subsequently acquired in the lecture course. Fundamentally, the very status of the homology power/war lacked clarity, which was partly due to the deceptive term "force," whose elusive nature became more obvious in *"Society Must Be Defended"* than, say, in *The History of Sexuality*, evinced by the sometimes counterintuitive, even irreverent, interpretations to which Boulainvilliers's pronouncements were subjected. Granted, in Deleuzean style, Foucault adopted a nonphysical conception of force, which referred to a differential process of "evenementality" rather than advocating real, naturalistic combat, as Habermas charged. But the problem still remained that Foucault *did* glean the differential play of forces and politics of difference *from* the real, bloody tussle of armed struggle. Having applied multiple reversals to the history of Western discourse – from Coke and Lilburne, via Boulainvilliers, Sieyès, Thierry, and Nietzsche, to Hitler and Stalin – Foucault was left with a "weft" (*"reseau"*) that, on the one hand, stood for historicist antiscience and antihegemony but, on the other hand, eventually deteriorated into the precursor of the gravest totalitarian violence. If the counterdiscourse supposedly provided a critique of (totalitarian) violence, it remained no less vicious, which was the tricky, duplicitous logic Foucault never explicitly dealt with and whose dangers tended to slip out of his view. Laying out his quasi-hermeneutical circle of violence, he never fully escaped its doubling force. Thus, his methodological euphoria over having uncovered a new short-circuiting grid – eternal war at the heart of civil society – was tempered by the realities of what it would spawn on the plane of world history. Such, indeed, seemed to be the dialectic of Enlightenment that eventually the

137

myth, having served its critical, enlightening function, reemerged with full-blown, violent force. Further, though Foucault rejected the origin of pristine nature just as much as Hobbes's idealized *status naturalis*, he still operated with a notion of "force" – an ungrounded ground of sorts – which appeared to be at the root of history. "In the beginning was force" (Derrida) might well have been Foucault's transcription of Genesis.

2. *(Discursive) History as a Series of Reversals*

To subscribe to the Nietzschean hypothesis meant to adhere to several interconnected strategic operations at once. It implied that power was to be conceived in terms of relations of force, which were concretized or materialized in struggle, conflict, and war; further, that the genealogist be mindful of epistemological matters, intent on exposing the games of truth, power, and law, or the instrumentality of legal discourse in producing truth effects; finally, that the genealogist be riveted to the agonistic playing field of *power–domination*, more specifically, to the mechanisms of reversal that transpired among competing force relations, all contending for domination. But the term "reversal" cut across various levels of analysis simultaneously. First, it captured the myriad manifestations of subversive historical upheavals, part of history's contestatory force fields, which upset, then reconfigured, patterns of hegemony or prevailing force relations. Reversal was a (discursive) tactic through which historical agents – the nobility, the bourgeoisie, the "ideologues" of biological racism – seized a position of discursive domination or else blocked such hegemony, all the while operating within immanent force fields. As would follow naturally from this state of affairs, in its second meaning, reversal and inversion also signaled the genealogist's preferred strategic trope (a word itself derived from *trepein*, "to turn" or "reverse"). Inversion therefore was also a rhetorical figure that went against the hegemony of sedimented tropes such as metalepsis – to allude to de Man's rhetorical repertoire – on the basis of which (historical) cause and effect were confused, insofar as their real link could only be rhetorical or nominalistic.[133] Many are the instances of such reversals in Foucault's work, besides the by now familiar Clausewitzian one. Indulging in a posthumanist *boutade* or quip, in *Discipline and Punish* Foucault overturned Platonism, seeing the soul – for him merely the regime and regiment of metaphysical violence – as the prison of the body. Or, in *The History of Sexuality*, as we saw, Foucault (much like Heidegger, unlike Arendt) assailed the order of priority between politics and life, encapsulated in Aristotle's notion of *zōon politikon*.[134] But the figure, arguably, acquired greatest consequence in *"Society Must Be Defended."* By anchoring his analysis in Boulainvilliers, Foucault did not simply posit that the knowledge about the "continuation of war in peace" entered sociocritical consciousness long before Nietzsche's *Genealogy of Morals* or even Weber's social theory. Centrally, the significant stations of historical modernity, the course implied (if it did not always state it in so many words), proceeded through reversals of the original seventeenth-century counterdiscourse about the "struggle between the races." According to this highly speculative pattern of reasoning, not always backed up by the requisite empirical evidence, the state-sponsored racisms of National Socialism and Stalinism were in truth the final episodes in a series of discursive "revolutions." For they were the most excruciating examples of how the original root narrative (*racine*) of "inter-racial struggle"[135] had shed its explosive, historicist potential to receive, on the one hand, a new revolutionary, if dialectical, transcription in the "class struggle,"[136] and, on the other hand, a "biologistic transcription" in a monistic "biologico-social racism," invigorated by a (postevolutionist) "struggle for life."[137] In other words, the mechanism of discursive recodification and rearticulation proceeded via the device of "substitution,"[138] which meant, for one, that the dynamic, relational "struggle of races" was replaced by a pseudo-scientific "purity of race." Rather than consider biological racism to be a free-floating ideology that suddenly appeared on the scene of nineteenth-century Europe, Foucault tightly coupled it to the class struggle and – as if fleetingly alluding to Marx's figure of ideology as a *camera obscura* – concluded that racism was "literally the revolutionary discourse [of the class struggle], but upside down."[139] For sure, Foucault's imaginative genealogy of these reversals, returns, repetitions, or in more traditional parlance, ideological constructions, makes it possible to pursue the reemergence of racist thought patterns across vast segments of Western modernity, attesting to the agonizing persistence of violence in imperialism, colonialism, persecution, and contemporary manifestations of genocide.[140] Such benefits notwithstanding, one must still wonder whether Foucault – at the "theoretical" level at least – did not retain a highly schematic explication of modern history governed by the quasi-mechanical contraption of discursive reversals and substitutions. Furthermore, neo-Marxist philosopher Etienne Balibar has cautioned against the tendency to collapse the race and class struggles on the basis of the underlying dualism that imbues both, noting that "unlike a historiosophy of the racial or cultural struggle or the antagonism between the 'elite' and the 'masses,' a historical dialectic can never present itself as the mere elaboration of a Manichean theme."[141] That *Society Must Be Defended*" ended up promoting a homogenizing script of history is certainly curious given the circumstance that Foucault firmly rebuffed Hegel and Marx for imposing a "logic of contradiction" onto history, ascribing to both what Derrida has called "metaphysical violence." But no less so than these speculative "foes," in the final analysis, Foucault himself adduced a dialectical mold of sorts: for instance, when he considered the bourgeoisie as the agents of a universal state, involved in a complex process of "auto-dialecticizing" historical discourse; or when he presupposed that racist discourse was "at bottom but a particular and localized episode of this grand discourse of war of the struggle between races";[142] or, again, when he seemed to give the impression that anti-Semitism itself derived from the same original discursive source, thus contradicting the existence of premodern manifestations of anti-Semitic bigotry – a point he corrected in one of the lectures, in response to queries from the audience.[143]

3. The Hegelian "Skeleton"

Much as Deleuze did in *Difference and Repetition*, so Foucault endorsed the "philosophy of the event," taking on the hermeneutical tradition and all kindred idealistic schools of thought, for being premised on a presumed "history of meaning." To do so was not the same as saying that history was nonsensical but simply to specify that the hermeneutical category of sense/meaning, with its connotations of plenitude and essentialism, needed to make way for the category of "intelligibility." Such, indeed, were the stipulations Foucault laid out in one of the most compact accounts he ever gave of the "history of the event," an interview with Pasquale Pasquino, called "Truth and Power." In it, he clarified his refusal to go by structuralism's signifying, synchronic structures and symbolic formations, preferring instead "analyses conducted in terms of the genealogy of force relations, of strategic developments, and tactics." In seeking to graph history's playing field, the genealogist related not to "the grand model of language and signs, but [to] that of war and battle."[144] As these provisos indicated, the stand-off between political historicism and political theory itself was mapped on a binary model that thrust "force" against "*logos*."

> The history which bears and determines us has the form of a war rather than that of a language; relations of power, not relations of meaning. History has no "meaning," though this is not to say that it is absurd or incoherent. On the contrary, it is intelligible and should be susceptible to analysis down to the smallest detail — but this is in accordance with the intelligibility of struggles, of strategies and tactics. Neither the dialectic, as logic of contradictions, nor semiotics, as a structure of communication, can account for the intrinsic intelligibility of conflicts. "Dialectic" is a way of evading the always open and hazardous reality of conflict by reducing it to the Hegelian skeleton; and "semiology" is a way of avoiding its violent, bloody, and lethal character by reducing it to the calm Platonic form of language and dialogue.[145]

Now, it is precisely this "Hegelian skeleton" and its entire dialectical apparatus — the subsumption of the singular and particular under the hegemony of the universal, the tricks of sublation and reconciliation — that formed the butt of *Society Must Be Defended.* Yet, as has become abundantly clear in the course of our analysis, Foucault's critical focus came with a string of theoretico-political assumptions that not infrequently proved debatable. In the grip of an undertheorized value system that placed "difference" and "singularity" virtually automatically above the "universal," he even ventured so far as to privilege a nobiliary politics of force over the democratic accomplishments of the bourgeois revolution. Another binarist divide that had similar repercussions was the one that paired off "decentralization" with "centralization." For, if the original counterhistory of the "race war" was deployed as an instrument of struggle by "*decentered* camps,"[146] then in the course of history its "polyvalent mobility"[147] was "*recentered* to become precisely the discourse of power, of a power that is centered, centralized, and centralizing," resulting in state-sponsored racism.[148] Too much in the sway of a counterstrategy that purported to undo the grammar of the universal, the global, and the total, Foucault ended up identifying these various terms with what, in the final analysis, turned out to be an underdeveloped conception of totalitarianism. Using the implicit equation "totalizing = totalitarian," his genealogy put so-called totalizing discourses, including psychoanalysis, on a par with National Socialism or the horrors of colonialism. The extent to which Foucault's analysis was powered by such unexamined, implied analogies comes to the surface whenever he paratactically linked together such mutually irreducible terms as "recodification" and "recolonization," indicating not just that they were more or less interchangeable, but, more gravely, that the entire complex process of colonization risked being reduced to a discursive *dispostif* or tactic.[149]

To appreciate better Foucault's path of reasoning, one does well to recall why he concentrated on the grid of an internal "civil war," waged among multiethnic factions in nations such as England and France. For the assumption of such a biracial internal warfare, dividing nationals among friends and enemies, permitted him to put the lie on the claims to a homogeneous, national unity tendered in the name of sovereign power. Once one recognizes the ulterior aims that fueled Foucault's "strategic" interpretation, mainly his aspiration to salvage the diversity of what were intrinsically multiethnic, modern nation-states, then his counterintuitive glosses of Boulainvilliers's thought lose at least part of their illogical ring. Then, they very much start to resemble the kind of subversive reappropriations to which other political conservatives have been subjected in recent years, not the least of whom is Ernest Renan. Indeed, Renan's essay "What is a Nation?" in particular has experienced a rebirth, not so much as the egregious specimen of a dangerous cultural nationalism but as a critical model that, in propagating a "voluntaristic" conception of the nation-state, denied "any naturalistic determinism of the boundaries of nations."[150] Furthermore, Renan's insight that the constitution of nation-states was based on the suppression of the memory of conquest and its attendant violence has been invoked to assess the resurgence of neo- and ultra-nationalisms in the twentieth century, no less than the volatile birth and reconstitution of nation-states in the post-Cold War era. Yet it should not be forgotten that, much like Boulainvilliers, Renan remained one of the most diligent advocates of France's so-called auspicious *germanité*, or Frankish roots, who unabashedly eulogized the mythical triumphs of the invading Franks, and whose writings were not infrequently intermixed with no small dose of anti-Semitism.

Still, despite the potentially versatile readings Foucault supplied as he interpreted the West's political unconscious, filled with nightmarish fantasies about "politics as war," it remains a sign of grave omission that he only fleetingly touched upon the realities of colonialism, as if the latter amounted to scarcely more than a discursive process in which strongholds, outposts, territories of meaning and power were cathected, traded, exchanged, and usurped.[151] That he was not preoccupied with the cultural and political dynamics of racism or with "the history of racism in the general and traditional sense of the term" is, to be sure, a point he stated explicitly in the lecture of February 4.[152] But as a consequence of this disclaimer, he all too quickly assumed that "race," as used in Boulainvilliers's "counterhistory," operated simply as a grid for gauging the mechanisms of shifting power relations. Never really acquiring a "stable biological meaning," the term functioned as a structural marker of difference, indicating that the links between warring groups or nations were purely defined by a power differential established on the basis of the experiential "violence of real war."[153] Time and again, Foucault surrendered his analysis to the implacable genealogical logic of this interracial war paradigm, obsessively pursuing its discursive permutations, proving more interested in how this explosive economy fractured the myth of sovereignty or how the internal enemy was subjugated at home than in the real experiences of the colonized other. Nowhere is this more tangible than in a passage in which he considered the rhetoric of power that permeated sixteenth-century royalist discourse, in a tract by A. Blackwood, who sought to vindicate Charles V's conquest of North America and the West Indies by placing it in line with the Norman invasion of England. Rather than taking the passage as an occasion to dwell on the history of colonial imperialism, Foucault merely deduced from this and similar material that the practice of colonialism had a "return effect on the juridico-political structures of the West."[154] As a result, Foucault ended up reducing real colonial exploitation to an "idealized," internal colonialism that fractured the homeland. In fact, this move uncannily resembled the substitution of "ideal" for "real" warfare, whose practice he had taken to task in the progenitors of political theory. Finally, the same unrelenting pursuit of counterhistory's logic prevented him from drawing on the wide range of existing countercolonial discourses, for example, the writings of Frantz Fanon, which astutely diagnosed, in all their psychological horror, the colonial consequences that issued from the logic of dialectics. For if it is true that Hegel's dualistic dialectic served to "colonize" the disorderliness of real history, as Foucault cautioned, then it might still prove more productive to understand its workings differently, much as Fanon did, namely, as articulating the truth about the "rationality" with which European imperialism set out to colonize the non-Western other.[155]

4. Struggle as the "Motor" of History

Just as startling as the elision of colonialism was Foucault's failure to analyze the complexities of the Marxist class struggle or to address the prominence of Clausewitz in left-wing thought, let alone the defense of armed struggle in Sorel's *Reflections on Violence* and Engel's *Anti-Dühring*, to cite but two of the better-known instances.[156] To be sure, Foucault's reticence towards the Marxist paradigm as displayed in *"Society Must Be Defended"* was anything but new, since already in the 1960s, he had participated in the well-known stand-off between Marxism and structuralism.[157] However, as Balibar perspicaciously has observed, throughout Foucault's career, his attitude towards Marxism remained highly ambivalent. According to Balibar, his "strategic complexity follows a general format, which is repeated several times, in which a movement is made from a *break* to a tactical *alliance*, the first involving a global *critique* of Marxism as a 'theory'; the second a partial *usage* of Marxist tenets or affirmations compatible with Marxism."[158] Foucault's latent ambivalence towards Marxism may explain the contradictory gestures that motivate some of his writings on the subject. In *The Order of Things*, for instance, Marxism was presented as the offspring of liberalism and one of the main culprits in the rise of "totalizing thought" that came to define the nineteenth century. *Discipline and Punish*, in contrast, attested to a more diversified approach, insofar as Foucault sought a rapprochement to Marx's *Capital*, explaining how disciplinary power was not external to but mediated through the techniques of industrial capitalism. In keeping with Marx's analysis of the "productive power of social labor," following which the accumulation of capital was dependent on the technological control of humans, Foucault defined time and labor as surplus value extracted from disciplined, docile subjects.[159] But with *"Society Must Be Defended,"* this rapprochement again disappeared insofar as Marxism was said to be premised on a problematic "will to truth," evinced in its theory of ideology, no less than that it was in the thrall of an economic functionalism, which is why it limited the infinite playing field of power to economic exploitation, to the exclusion of other struggles.

5. The Post-Marxist Struggle

In many ways, Foucault's transition from class struggle to a post-Marxist category of "contention" seems very close to Laclau and Mouffe's *Hegemony and Socialist Strategy*, which appraised and sought to overcome the theoretical crisis of contemporary left-wing thought. Taking on the "ontological" categories of the working class and its anticipated revolution, they noted how an outmoded socialism failed to take cognizance of the "plurality of contemporary social struggles."[160] For the proliferation of points of antagonism and rise of new forms of social conflict demonstrated how subject positions "traverse a number of class sectors."[161] Proclaiming the end of normative epistemologies, universal discourses and closed logical paradigms, their neo-Marxist project steered away from historical necessity to contingency, away from the presumed, constrictive laws that commanded history. To do so, they proposed a deconstructive, nonessentialistic reading of Gramsci, whose notion of "hegemony," referring to a "unity existing in a concrete social formation,"[162] introduced a historically situated, relational category that shot beyond stale class alliances, cut across various groups, thus confounding the determinism of Marxism's economic scheme.

Balibar's comments on Foucault's Marx interpretation in fact offer supporting material for placing him in line with post-Marxism. According to Balibar, the main point of contention that split Foucault from Marx was "the concept of 'social relations,' or contradiction as a structure internal to power relations," the latter underpinning Marx's theory of historical materialism.[163] While Foucault's philosophy still worked within the broader parameters of a historical materialism, he replaced the materiality of social relations with those of bodies, the historicity of class contradictions with the historicity of the event. How to the point Balibar's observations are, is corroborated by the energy with which Foucault time and again censured the "discourse of dialectical contradiction" for the violence with which it thrust preset laws upon an open-ended, indeterminate field of antagonisms. Some of Foucault's most sustained comments on the issue are to be found in a 1978 interview with the Japanese philosopher Ryumei Yoshimoto.[164] Indeed, much of their encounter focused on what the interviewer considered to be the prime tensions between a Hegelian/Marxist theory of teleological history, on the one hand, and an aleatory, chance-like understanding of historical "evenementality," on the other, according to which all holistic metanarratives of oppression automatically capitulated to a metaphysical philosophy of history. This pivotal interview goes a long way towards elucidating Foucault's views, for it explains, first, how his own "politics of strategy" sought to refashion Western philosophies of "the will," and second, why he considered the switch from class struggle to "polymorphous" struggles, divested of an exclusive concern with class differences, absolutely necessary.

In reconfiguring leftist politics and historiography, so Foucault explained to Yoshimoto, his main aim was to ignite a "new political imaginary,"[165] to whose aridity Marxism to no small degree had contributed, with its coercive force, scientific claims, prophetic aura, philosophy of the state, and ideology of class. Casting aside the Japanese philosopher's appeal to Hegel's collective political will, and its transformations in Engels's and Lenin's thought, Foucault submitted a quite different typology of the will, shedding considerable light on his own volitional matrix, which seemed closer to Gramsci than he was ready to acknowledge (Gramsci remaining the unspoken and unnamed of this and many other exchanges). Western thought, he explicated, conventionally had conceived of the will according to two registers only: "nature/force" and "law/good and evil." In the first one, the model of natural philosophy (Leibniz), will was force, while in the second, that of the philosophy of right (Kant), will was a moral category, designating the individual conscience of good and evil. Reconceptualizing the category, Schopenhauer was the first to have forged an alliance with Eastern thought, whose innovative impetus subsequently was incorporated into Nietzsche's will to knowledge and power. Taking his cue once again from Nietzsche, Foucault now advanced a third alternative, which was the method of military strategy. Or, as Foucault maintained, by casting the question of will in terms of struggle it would henceforth be possible to analyze conflicts as manifold webs of antagonisms in which social agents moved as adversaries, trapped in a battle whose aim was to win. For too long, he emphasized, sociologists had only dealt with the class side of struggle as the "motor of history," at the expense of grasping the elemental nature of struggle, which functioned as "conflict" or "war." Pursuing his standard critique of economic functionalism, Foucault advised that the sociology of classes needed to yield to the strategic method of the struggle. For in turning his lens to the pluriformity of incidents, antagonisms, and conflicts, the genealogist would be able to address their complexity afresh, with altogether new questions, such as: "Who entered into the struggle, with whom and how? Why does the struggle exist and on what does it rest?" From such a nonnormative vantage point, "the innumerable voices of subjects were to be heard" for "the voices of the excluded were the ones in the struggle."[166]

Investigating the historically situated hegemony of discursive practices, their translation and rearticulation, Foucault no longer resorted to the category "class" but to assemblages of collective and singular wills that were constituted and unraveled, realigned, undone across a wide spectrum of identity and subject positions. Thus, aside from numerous references to collective agency, his writings abound with tributes to the revolutionary will power of resisting, dissident singularities. Universalizing collectivities, which might at any point congeal into hegemonic, stabilized enclaves of power, were to make way for rebellious singularities – a point of view Foucault also defended in some of the controversial remarks he tendered about contemporary world politics in his lifetime. Most extreme among Foucault's political interventions was, no doubt, his endorsement of Khomeini's Iranian revolution, as expressed in the *Le Monde* Op-Ed piece "Is It Useless to Revolt?"[167] Unable to see the Iranian revolution within the parameters of religious fundamentalism, he celebrated instead the Iranian people's willingness to risk death in order to interrupt the flow of history. Lauding this massive revolt as the entry of *subjectivity* onto the stage of history, he endorsed an "antistrategic theoretical morality," which would speak in defense of the singularities that rebelled against the rule of the universal. Thus, the philosophico-political presuppositions underlying Foucault's argument only gain clarity if one reads his response in relation to the Hegelian dialectic between particularism and universalism, whose enactments on the plane of history he sought to countervail.

6. Schmitt's Decisionism

Finally, we must consider the charges of a Schmittean authoritarianism that several critics see lurking behind Foucault's analytic of power, not in the least behind the constellation power/war. In this respect, it is helpful to weigh Charles Taylor's reservations expressed in "Foucault on Freedom and Truth," which takes on the historian's reversal of Clausewitz's aphorism for bracketing out all potential political countermodels, above all that of liberal humanitarianism.[168] Indeed, within the limits of Foucault's political argumentation, such a liberal countermodel remained inconceivable because he engaged in a relentless appraisal of the "totalizing" violence endemic to all variants of liberalism, whose outgrowths, the underlying assumption often was, led to totalitarianism. Because he propagated an understanding of power as strategy and struggle, his project might seem to have more in common with Schmitt's conservative critique of liberalism, thus seemingly confirming the unholy alliance between left- and right-wing thinkers, one of whose main historical points of convergence has been antiliberalism.[169] As he put forth his sometimes baffling transvaluations of political values, Foucault's theory of the warring subject risked coming remarkably close to

Schmitt's *The Concept of the Political* or even his later, postwar *Theory of the Partisan*, so that, in the end, it may prove surprising that explicit references to the German constitutional jurist are missing from Foucault's extensive *oeuvre*. Opposing the purported "neutralizations and depoliticizations"[170] circulated by liberalism, which threatened to negate the political and the state, Schmitt hinged his definition of the political on what he considered to be the root political distinction, namely the *antithesis* or *antagonism* between friend and enemy. Against the liberal-economic "competitor" and the intellectualized "debating adversary," he mounted the "friend and enemy concepts to be understood in their concrete and existential sense, not as metaphors or symbols, not mixed and weakened by economic, moral, and other conceptions, least of all in a private-individualistic sense as a psychological expression of private emotions and tendencies."[171] The enemy in the political sense, Schmitt italicized, was the public enemy, or collective *hostis*, not the personal adversary. Revealing, in this context, were Schmitt's numerous appeals to the category of the "real," that is, to a descriptive level of analysis that stood radically at a distance from any normative claims. Taking on Hobbes's *Leviathan*, Schmitt regarded all ideals to be abstractions, all normative prescriptions fictions. Thus, it was utterly irrelevant whether this originary friend–enemy antithesis was merely "an atavistic remnant of barbaric times" for his concern was "neither with abstractions nor with normative ideals, but with inherent reality and the real possibility of such a distinction."[172] Insofar as the existential term "combat," "the real possibility of physical killing,"[173] constituted an "ever present possibility,"[174] Clausewitz's dictum about war merely perpetuating politics needed to be rejected, if it was misinterpreted to mean that war was a means to a political end, rather than politics' *ultima ratio*.[175] As no one else better than Leo Strauss made clear in his notes on *The Concept of the Political*, at the bottom of Schmitt's politics as *polemos* lay an anthropological world view at odds with the pacifism of liberalism, insofar as humans were ultimately evil, motivated by force (*Macht*), presuppositions through which the legal theorist restored "the Hobbesian concept of the state of nature to a place of honor."[176]

Now, it is perhaps not inconceivable that Foucault's portrayal of the warring subject in *"Society Must Be Defended"* might have relied on Schmitt's *Theory of the Partisan*, which profiled the first so-called partisan warfare, namely, the Spanish resistance against Napoleon, as a critique of state-sponsored militarism, whose revolutionary seeds could also be detected in the writings of Napoleon's strategic foe, the Prussian general Clausewitz.[177] But should we conclude from this that Foucault anchored the political – or, more precisely, the play of history – in an adversarial antagonism between friend and enemy, on the model of Schmitt's *The Concept of the Political*? Such a conclusion, indeed, seems less advisable, not just because of the implicit libertarian goals that motivated his work, but because Foucault's philosophy of difference in the end aimed to operate with a multiplicity of force fields that were *agonistic*. Though real war was one of the topics of *"Society Must Be Defended,"* ultimately the principle upon which the course rested was a nonnaturalistic mode of struggle, different from the possibility of violent, antagonistic combat that underwrote Schmitt's understanding of the political. But, for all these differences, it is clear that the danger of potential confusion with Schmitt's inherently belligerent political theory seemed built into Foucault's historiographic model, at least the one he espoused in the 1976 war lecture course. For, while it would be implausible to assume that Foucault promoted the kind of conservative anthropology that validated Schmitt's antiliberal doctrine, following which humans were innately dangerous, if not evil, there is no doubt that *"Society Must Be Defended"* relied on the anthropological pessimism assumed by Machiavelli, Boulainvilliers, Nietzsche, and others. Regardless of whether such references merely served strategic purposes, such allusions, together with the strong, unmitigated invectives against political theory *tout court*, give rise to the suspicion that he paved the way for a new decisionism, the return of another sovereignty – at the expense of democratic sovereign power – in which sovereign was he who decides.[178] No one more effectively than Pasquino expressed the danger when he observed that "the muffled noise of war continues all around us. Which leads one to believe that there are still good reasons for following the worn-out paths of juridico-political theory – if one wishes to call it that – the paths of law, order, and peace."[179]

We must recognize, therefore, that the dystopian gestures accompanying Foucault's war/power matrix have justifiably elicited no small degree of mistrust, this despite the fact that Foucault, here as elsewhere, operated within a horizon of human freedom, working towards the advancement of universal social justice and solidarity, against which the present was to be judged. Such apprehensions about the drift of his political theory, then, were the price Foucault paid for failing to explicate how his underlying, "cryptonormative" presuppositions were to be negotiated and adjudicated concretely. Professing to advance a left-wing critique of sovereignty and statism, Foucault leapt into the brawl of the conservative text – as his readings of Boulainvilliers and Nietzsche all too well illustrated – seeking to gain redemptive political victory in the ensuing battle. It seems especially paradoxical that he immersed himself in these conservative manuals at the same time that he was trying to retrieve another, nonnaturalistic understanding of a polymorphous *struggle*, which no longer subscribed to the Hegelian-Marxist dialectic of a universal, binary history, divided along conventional class divisions. The expanded category would include not just armed struggle but a broad span of oppositional, conflictual struggles that traversed an indeterminate range of possible subject positions. For this reason, we must therefore ask again whether Foucault managed to abandon the burdensome ballast of the war matrix, as the inaugural lecture of *"Society Must Be Defended"* had set out to do. Did he successfully replace the conventional *antagonism* or dualism of bellicose political models with another, polymorphous *agonism* of strategies and tactics? In order to address these momentous issues, we must now turn to one of Foucault's late, programmatic texts, "The Subject and Power."

Agonism versus Antagonism

As other writings from around the time of the 1976 war lecture course document, Foucault was clearly preoccupied with the thorny problem of how to draw the boundaries between power and war, key concepts in the power matrix whose viability he was still testing. No doubt, his quandary about how to proceed on the matter was thrown into even starker relief through research for *Discipline and Punish*, which allowed him to examine the nature of armed struggle, military strategy, and logistics in more detail than ever before. Interested, furthermore, in real, not "ideal" war, Foucault at one point even envisaged conducting a full-length study of the technology of warfare and military institutions of domination. This much is clear from an announcement he made to his audience at the Collège de France during the lecture of January 14, noting how in the coming five years he planned to pursue the sequence war, struggle, army, as part of his teaching and research program.[180] But this large-scale project, by all accounts, never materialized. Though Foucault ended up touching on the "diplomatico-military technology" of modern political power (or "governmentality") in his 1977–78 lecture course, its prime focus really was the political management of populations, especially the arsenal of state technologies and policies that facilitated such population control.[181] Most probably, the change in plans attests to his intensified study of the dynamics of bio-power, as likely as it anticipates his radical switch to techniques of the self, or practices of self-government, in the years to come. But one must not exclude the possibility that the shift in course, at bottom, also revealed his disenchantment with the unwieldy dimensions of what threatened to become an all-enveloping power/war matrix. Lingering doubts about the homology power/war, set up in *"Society Must Be Defended,"* come to the fore, for example, in a short piece that he published in a French periodical, *Hérodote*, shortly after completing the war lecture course, which took the curious format of an intense self-interrogation. Doubling as both interviewer and addressee, Foucault confronted himself with the following questions: "The notion of strategy is essential when one wants to analyze knowledge (*savoir*) and its relations to power. Does this notion necessarily imply that one wages war across the knowledge in question? Doesn't strategy allow one to analyze the relations of power as technique of domination? Or must one rather say that domination is nothing but a continued form of war? In other words, what kind of an extension do you give to the notion of *strategy?*"[182]

Foucault's last question, asking about the scope he was willing to grant to the concept "strategy," plainly goes to the heart of the matter, as it directly concerns the elasticity the category had gained, not just in *"Society Must Be Defended."* While it seems safe to maintain that Foucault, after the 1976 lecture course, more or less gave up on the figure of war, that is, insofar as it operated as an "arche-principle of political analysis," it is equally clear that he never quite surrendered the constellation *power/strategy*, endemic to the matrix *power–domination*, not even in the period of ethics, which considered technologies of the self as counterstrategies of individual resistance. This is why his relatively late essay "The Subject and Power" offers a fascinating test case. For while it ostensibly originated in the period when Foucault already privileged the technologies of the self, it displays an undivided dedication to the constellation power/strategy. The lecture is additionally important because it indirectly reveals Foucault absorbed in a thorough scrutiny of some of his foundational premises about power and violence, indulging in a self-examination of sorts. Finally, the piece pulls together several of his thoughts regarding the nature of "polymorphous struggles," which up until then were dispersed among various of his writings.

In discussions at Berkeley, so Dreyfus and Rabinow report in the introduction to their essential Foucault monograph, he finally acknowledged that his concept of power remained "elusive but important,"[183] agreeing to "remedy" the situation by means of "The Subject and Power."[184] Under mounting pressure from friendly critics, demanding that he further explicate the category "power," Foucault turned squarely to the question as to how power was to be demarcated from violence, as if, once and for all, he wanted to legislate the categorical differences between the two terms. In agreeing to submit the essay for inclusion in the monograph that Dreyfus and Rabinow were dedicating to him, Foucault not only conceded that his definition of power was far too broad; really, what he also in part was concerned with was the critical, that is, diacritical problem of how to distinguish power from one particular type of force – violence – once the older liberal (consensual) view of power had been discarded. Implicitly, Foucault in this late stage revisited the all too elusive frontiers between mere *negative* violence/force and *enabling, positive* power, entering into covert dialogue, it would seem, with Arendt's and Habermas's theories of consensual power. For, as he set out to legislate the boundaries between force and violence, applying critical labor to the terms "power" and "subjecthood," he generated an analysis that entailed what one could conceivably call a crypto-Arendtian moment. Further amending the category of power, he now placed more emphasis on the "art or technique of government" as "conduct" and, as it turned out, on subjective freedom and individual will. That is to say, over and against the *transitive* strategic power relations that had engaged him for so many years, the essay profiled the *intransitivity* of freedom. While it is certain that all of Foucault's work all along was concerned with freedom, it must again be admitted that the category was not always fully spelled out or integrated patently into the critical model, functioning more like a distant horizon for all political action. Yet, if Foucault pitted freedom as *agonism* against the potential adversarial *antagonism* of power relations, the concluding argument of the essay unambiguously shows that, in the end, he held fast to his understanding of power as strategy, *pace* Habermas's critique of strategic action. It seems crucial, therefore, that in the final installment of this extended probe into Foucault's power/war model, we examine "The Subject and Power."

Under the influence, one conjectures, of his late work on ethics, which already fully absorbed him, Foucault declared unusually emphatically that it was "not power, but the subject, which is the general theme of my research."[185] All of his work, he asserted in the essay's opening sections, explored "the different modes by which, in our culture, human beings are made subjects," [186] much, one might add, as Althusser's theory of interpellation had charted the conversion techniques through which individuals were designated subject positions in the political arena. Three transformative mechanisms of objectification, strictly speaking, made up the core of his life-work: the truth games of scientific discourse, the dividing practices that cleaved the subject from the self and others, and, lastly, the subject's (self-)transformation into subjecthood, for example, through sexual practices, or what *The Use of Pleasure* called "sexual hermeneutics."[187] If it was up to a point correct, as Foucault reluctantly admitted, that much of his prolific work was dedicated to power,[188] then only because a radically innovative economy of power relations needed to be brought into circulation to replace the worn-out, dilapidated tools of critical analysis. What this meant, it soon became apparent, was the recruitment of a wholly different category of social struggle to match the altered configuration of power relations. To substantiate his point, Foucault once again called upon Kant's "What is Enlightenment?," whose insights were now marshaled to back up his analysis of the agonistic struggle that inflected all power relations. Placing his project in the shadow of Kant's Enlightenment philosophy and the Frankfurt School, Foucault called for a thorough rescripting of modernity's history of reason, declaring that, "rather than analyzing power from the point of view of its internal rationality, [the new economy] consists of analyzing power relations through the confrontation [*affrontement*] of strategies."[189] In order to secure a more diversified category of struggle, Foucault advised, the historian needed to renounce the transcendental laws, regulations and critical bifurcations of reason, in favor of the diverse anarchic struggles (*luttes*) that contested the rule of rationalism. Tossing, once again, the global, polarized class struggle of orthodox Marxism with the same force that characterized his 1978 interview with Yoshimoto, Foucault drew up an open-ended catalog of potential resistances, which, in spite of their variations, all shared the characteristic that they were crosscultural (*transversal*), immediate, anarchic forces; they were aimed not at gargantuan, overarching power institutions, or "statism" as such, but at specific power-*techniques*, perpetrated through regimes of knowledge as well as the ever more emphatic rule of the "government of individualization."[190] Of the three types of social struggle that thus were to be recognized – that is to say, struggles "against forms of domination (ethnic, social, and religious)," prevalent in feudal societies; those "against forms of exploitation which separate individuals from what they produce," dominant in the nineteenth century, and those against subjection, against forms of subjectivity and submission"[191] – Foucault lent special force to the latter, seeing it as the one that most fully defined the predicament of "our" present. Speaking from the culturally limited position of the Western present, he tied the rise of these identity struggles to the development of the Western state since the Renaissance, which gradually assumed "both an individualizing and a totalizing form of power."[192] If early on this statist political power had functioned by usurping the tactics of pastoral power, then over the centuries previously unknown "individualizing" tactics had surfaced, techniques of social engineering mediated through the institutions of family, science, and pedagogy. Still, Foucault's analysis ran counter to the functionalism of an automatized, self-regulating social machine. For if all constellations of power already presumed the friction of opposing points of resistance, then power automatically presupposed the possibility of freedom, the liberty of the subject to govern or conduct herself otherwise, or the choice of insubordination, refusal and revolt, so that Kant's injunction that "we" engage in a "historical ontology of ourselves" all the more rang true.

Having thus established that a Kantian-inspired critical ontology of ourselves provided the answer to the question *why* power needed to be studied, Foucault went on to analyze *how* power operated. To procure such a critique, the *what* question – what power was – needed to be shed and, with it, the fallacies of a metaphysics or ontology of power, according to which it amounted to a "mysterious substance." Adopting a materialistic vantage point, Foucault's new critique of power would proceed by asking the somewhat flat, empirical question, "Comment ça se passe" ("How does it come about/happen").[193] Without a doubt, his insistence on this post-metaphysical point of departure sounded familiar enough. Yet, less predicable, given the context of previous work, were the three relational categories he subsequently introduced – that is, objective or technical "capacities," "communication," and, finally, "power." The first field, "objective capacities," *grosso modo* designated "instrumental action," the domain of things, finalized technique, work, and other acts through which subjects transformed the real; the second comprised all communication relations, signs, and other ways of imparting meaning; finally, the third one, power relations, designated the domination of means of constraint and inequality, and, essentially, actions of humans on humans. Curious, to say the least, was that Foucault invoked the category of "communication" to replace the more familiar "discursive practices," as the term seemed uncannily similar to the much disliked paradigm of communicative action. Communicative relations, he now affirmed, involved the circulation or trans-mission of symbolic information, and could include acts that, though they might produce effects of power, were, analytically speaking, to be demarcated from power relations. However, from a practical standpoint, it would be wrong to drive a sharp wedge between these three types of relations, which, in truth, were tangled in a web of overlaps and interconnections. More germane, he concluded, would be an analysis that, in investigating, say, the educational institution of a given period, considered the interrelations among these various fields as interfacing "blocks of capacity-communication-power," or, translated back into more familiar language, disciplinary power.[194] Thus, if the use of the term "communication" for a moment seemed to indi-cate that Foucault aimed to gain closer proximity to Habermas's (formal-pragmatic) theory of communicative action, then the perhaps all too cavalier footnote that accom-panied the segment told otherwise. Certainly, Foucault acknowledged that Habermas, too, in demarcating domination (strategic action), communication, and finalized, tele-ological activities (instrumental action) from one another, refused to see them as isolated enclaves. Nonetheless, as the footnote intimated, Habermas had transfigured them into three "*transcendentaux*" – a condemning remark through which Foucault not only alluded to the indisputable Kantian horizon that overarched Habermas's thought but also inscribed the social theorist back into the Classical *epistēmē* criticized in *The Order of Things*.[195]

If it was clear that the ever-changing coordination among these interfacing fields defined "how" power was exercised, then one next needed to zero in on "what" constituted power's essence. In the discussion that followed, Foucault related his analytic of power to two poles or extremes – consent and violence – terms that, once again, hinted at Arendt's and Habermas's action theories. More important than that power relations were intersubjective, Foucault underscored, was the fact that such actions imposed modifications on the actions of others; in other words, power relations only existed *transitively*, through actions in which "power" was exercised by someone on someone else. As such, power relations always pertained to an infinite realm of the possible, opening up a virtually boundless, noncontrollable field of potentialities. Consequently, it would be erroneous to equate power with consent, Foucault added (harking back to a line of argument fleshed out in *"Society Must Be Defended"*), for this would come at the cost of renouncing one's freedom, transferring one's rights, delegating one's power to someone else. Yet, unlike he did in the lecture course, where he advocated an unrestrained critique of consensual social contracts, Foucault no longer rebuffed the politics of consent in absolute terms. Rather, his point was that power never entirely overlapped with consensual agreement, even though particular relations of power might indeed be the effect of prior, or even permanent, acts of consent. "In itself," Foucault clarified, "the exercise of power is not violence; nor is it a consent which, implicitly, is renewable. It is a total structure of actions brought to bear upon possible actions; it incites, it induces, it seduces, it makes easier or more difficult; in the extreme it constrains or forbids absolutely; it is nevertheless always a way of acting upon an acting subject or acting subjects by virtue of their acting or being capable of action. A set of actions upon other actions."[196] In other words, while consent or violence could be the instruments or effects of power, they hardly constituted "the principle or the basic nature of power." Rather than excluding "agreement" from the power equation, Foucault in fact opposed equating the "principle" or "nature" of power with either "consensus" or "violence."

Still, this revised definition of power could not allay all of Foucault's underlying doubts. Regardless of the fact that he angled his retorts at Habermas's theory of power, he remained vividly conscious of the threat that violence posed to his alternative model, all too aware that he might be reproached for advocating a contemptible philosophy of violence. Clearly playing the devil's advocate, he therefore raised the question whether it was possible that an intractable violence went hiding underneath the seemingly benign mask of power, making up its true, hidden nature. But the answer to the query, he immediately retorted, could only be negative. For violence, he specified, always involved instrumental reification, acts through which the other was reduced to abject passivity, while power relations without exception entailed the possibility of freedom in resistance. Power, he clarified, was never exercised directly upon or over others, for that would result in the objectification of one's interlocutors. Phrased differently, one *sine qua non* of power was that the other be recognized as a subject of action, who disposed over a potentially infinite (existential) freedom of possibilities.

> A relationship of violence acts upon a body or upon things; it forces, it bends, it breaks on the wheel, it destroys, or it closes the door on all possibilities. Its opposite pole can only be passivity, and if it comes up against any resistance it has no other option but to try to minimize it. On the other hand a power relationship can only be articulated on the basis of two elements which are each indispensable if it is really to be a power relationship: that "the other" (the one over whom power is exercised) be thoroughly recognized and maintained to the very end as a [subject that acts]; and that, faced with a relationship of power, a whole field of responses, reactions, results and possible inventions may open up.[197]

It is certainly interesting to note, therefore, that in order to hold his epistemic ground, Foucault needed to inject these unique qualifications into his theory of power, unlike anything previous work had stated. But a more far-reaching critical displacement followed from this liminal, delimiting exercise. If, in *"Society Must Be Defended,"* he had focused on *power/war/struggle*, now his concern was with the constellation *power/governing*. Power, Foucault stated, was less of the adversarial, combative order, involving the confrontation between two adversaries, than of the order of *conduct*, whose equivocal meaning (*conduire, se conduire*),[198] he averred, was "one of the best aids for coming to terms with the specificity of power relations." For while "conduct" captured the "mechanisms of coercion" through which one could lead others, it even more interestingly referred to "a way of behaving within a more or less open field of possibilities," meaning that one took care (*amenager*) of probability – an aspect quite clearly present in the French term *pouvoir*, at once modal verb and noun, insofar as it could signify "power," "possibility," "capacity," or "to be able to."[199] Using the etymological method espoused by Nietzsche and Heidegger, Foucault retrieved the older, sixteenth-century meaning of the word "govern" from under an encrusted, administered *governmentalization* – that hard-to-pronounce word that stood for institutionalized, rationalized power.[200] "To govern, in this sense," he explained, "is to structure the possible field of action of others."[201] Crucially, the amended definition of power as an "action upon action" and the stretched term "government" thus made it possible to attend to the issue of freedom, for power was only ever exercised over free subjects, regardless of whether they acted individually or collectively. How radical Foucault envisioned the shift in vantage point to be, comes to the fore in the following pronouncement, ostensibly also directed at his own war lecture course: "The relationship proper to power would not therefore be sought on the side of violence or of struggle, nor on the side of the contract or the voluntary relation (all of which can, at best, only be the instruments of power), but rather in the area of the singular mode of action, neither warlike nor juridical, which is government."[202] As such, this non-eristic model pulled into full view the empowering force of freedom, inhering in all power relationships, no matter what. To make the point more salient, Foucault resorted to the, at first sight, startling claim that slavery first and foremost amounted to a power relation, not violence, that is to say, as long as it entailed the existential possibility of potential escape (a point partially lost, unfortunately, in the incomplete English translation). As he remarked, "Where the determining factors saturate the whole there is no relationship of power; slavery is not a power relationship when man is in chains (in this case it is a question of a physical relationship of constraint), *but precisely at the moment in which he can move himself and at the limit escape.*"[203]

Power and freedom, Foucault continued, were never mutually exclusive, nor could "freedom's refusal to submit" be disengaged from power.[204] For freedom, as he now seemed ready to state bluntly, was the condition, even *precondition* (in the sense of enabling ground), that made power relations possible in the first place. Nor did power have anything to do with voluntary servitude (Rousseau), as he clarified, for, at core, power revealed the defiance of the will, a point rendered through the substantivized verb *vouloir* rather than the noun *volonté*, featured in his earlier quasi-Nietzschean *Volonté de savoir*. More crucially, power now exposed the intransitive nature (*l'intransitivité*) of freedom.[205] Clearly, we have come, then, a long way from the (quasi-hermeneutical) "circle of violence" that sustained Foucault's investigation of Boulainvilliers's war discourse, according to whose vertiginous logic force seemed to beget ever more force. For, by confirming freedom's intransitivity, Foucault now took issue with those theories that explained power in antagonistic terms, missing the more fundamental meaning of power-governing as "conduct" that brought into play an altogether different, oppositional dynamic. Indeed, "rather than speaking of an essential 'antagonism,'" Foucault observed, "it would be better to speak of an 'agonism' – of a relationship which is at the same time reciprocal incitation and struggle; less of a face-to-face confrontation which paralyzes both sides than a permanent provocation."[206] Importantly, the term "agonistic" did not signal real combat or "physical contest,"[207] but alluded instead to differential force fields that always already opened up onto the possibility of insubordination in freedom. Linking back to the libertarian program of his Kant work, Foucault again mustered the force of subjective resistance, which strove against the "individualizing power" of subject-ing techniques. Here, once again, an immanent mode of resistance returned, the "small will" fighting the "big Will," setting up a permanent limit of resistance against a wholesale block-out of power.

Have we, then, on the face of it, come full circle, meaning that Foucault's "The Subject and Power" ended up with an Arendtian demarcation of power from violence? Might Foucault's only seemingly dystopian explanation of power/government, which now advanced a conception of action as "conduct in freedom," approximate Arendt's definition of power as an end in itself? If only for a moment, such seemed to be the implications that issued from Foucault's delineation of freedom as fundamentally *intransitive* in nature – an intransitivity or potentiality that inhabited all finite, *transitive* power relations. For isn't an intransitive verb a verb that has no direct object and refers to a state or "attitude" (*ēthos*) that subsequently must or may be realized practically? Freedom indeed was the goal of Foucauldian politics, even though freedom took the form, here, of an inherent, insurrectionary force that operated *within* the field of power relationships and, until the very last, remained agonistic by definition.

Nothing could be more curious, therefore, than the concluding segments of Foucault's "The Subject and Power," which seemed to take back some of the hard-won ground secured in what could well be called the essay's "freedom" passage. In view of our perusal of the consecutive stages that characterized his understanding of power, from power/war to power/government, it is disappointing that Foucault's writings, in the end, remained surprisingly equivocal when it came to circumscribing the precise relation between "agonism" and "antagonism." Indeed, if one goes by the gist of the essay's final section, dedicated to "relations of strategy," one might be inclined to conclude that "agonism" described an "ungrounded ground," an infinite contestation in freedom, yet one whose practical articulations invariably took the form of adversarial antagonisms rather than, say, dialogical cohabitation. To be sure, Foucault prefaced his discussion of power/strategy with an appeal, urging the analysis of social networks and concrete institutions, in which power relations were entrenched. For the "permanent political task inherent in all social existence," he advised, consisted in "the analytics, elaboration, and [putting] into question of power relations and the 'agonism' between power relations and the intransitivity of freedom."[208] However, when it came to specifying the material fiber of these relations, the essay slowly but surely gravitated back to familiar ground: to the definition of power as strategy and forceful imposition. Nothing could be more anticlimactic in light of Foucault's earlier search, even plea, for an altogether different definition of power as the art of government – a definition whose purpose it was to depose the old "power/war" grid. In other words, rather than dwell on what possible shapes freedom-granting acts of social resignification might take, Foucault retreated to the well-traversed terrain of power–domination, to which his provocative reflections on agonistic freedom, disappointingly, were ceded.

Evoking game theory and militarism, Foucault advanced three different definitions of strategy, all of which, he declared, were potentially at stake in power relations: first, strategy as the manipulation of means to reach certain ends; second, the actions one "inflicts" upon others with an eye to gain; finally, the use of winning means to procure victory over one's adversary in a situation of direct confrontation. All three meanings, he concluded, were at play in power relations, though, inevitably, such relations proved above all galvanized by confrontation strategies. Now, what is extraordinary is not just that Foucault once again located the subject's dissenting freedom at the level of concrete strategies. Certainly more astounding is the circumstance that he made his return back to the most conventional philosophical parable of adversarial confrontation or combat to have been codified in the West: Hegel's master–slave dialectic. The passages rife with Hegelian overtones deserve to be quoted at greater length:

> If it is true that at the heart of power relations and as a permanent condition of their existence there is an insubordination and a certain essential obstinacy on the part of the principles of freedom, then there is no relationship of power without the means of escape or possible flight. Every power relationship implies, at least *in potentia*, a strategy of struggle, in which the two forces are not superimposed, do not lose their specific nature, or do not finally become confused. Each constitutes for the other a kind of permanent limit, a point of possible reversal. A relationship of confrontation reaches its term, its final moment (and the victory of one of the two adversaries) when stable mechanisms replace the free play of antagonistic reactions. Through such mechanism one can direct, in a fairly constant manner and with reasonable certainty, the conduct of others. For a relationship of confrontation, from the moment it is not a struggle to the death, the fixing of a power relationship becomes a target – at one and the same time its fulfillment and its suspension.[209]

And, further:

> At every moment the relationship of power may become a confrontation between two adversaries. Equally, the relationship between adversaries in society may, at every moment, give place to the putting into operation of mechanisms of power. The consequence of this instability is the ability to decipher the same events and the same transformations either from inside the history of struggle or from the standpoint of the power relationships.[210]

Almost step by step, Foucault's explication of power struggles thus followed the consecutive dialectical moments that punctuated Hegel's master–bondsman dialectic, from the potential struggle to death to its termination in favor of an institutionalized (momentarily stable) balance of power between dominator and dominated. Schematized in such stark, structural terms, power relations in the end again materialized into relations of domination and opposing strategies of struggle that sought to reverse the existing status quo. More than just a convenient trope or figure of speech, this proto-Hegelian narrative of an antagonistic struggle instead captured the dynamic theory of power Foucault adhered to, even if this narrative was divorced from the legitimizing logic of contradiction and historical causality that defined the idealistic paradigm and even if it was stripped of Marxism's economic functionalism.

In the end, the always reversible dynamic of power struggles remained a constant across the various manifestations of power that Foucault brought to visibility, from "power–domination," "disciplinary power," "power/war," to "bio-power" and "power/government." As he once observed in an interview: "One is everywhere locked in struggle ... and, at every moment, one moves from rebellion to domination, from domination to rebellion, and it is this entire perpetual agitation that I wanted to make visible."[211] To have stretched the category of struggle to include a wide gamut of polymorphous struggles through which a new mode of freedom could be gained constituted both the strength of Foucault's historiographic project and its potential weakness. For "The Subject and Power" stopped short of laying out an equally vast spectrum of enabling scripts across which nonforceful interactions among nonadversarial interlocutors might occur. However, what makes this essay such a fascinating document in the annals of the Foucauldian archive is that the two tendencies, the Kantian commitment to a communal redefinition of subject positions in freedom, meant to stop self-tutelage, *and* the belligerent narrative of collective, adversarial engagement, existed side by side. As such, the essay displayed the conflicting sides of Foucault's commitment to ethics and justice, wrapped, often, in an eristic or bellicose rhetoric. For, rather than keep his distance from conservative thinkers such as Nietzsche, Foucault frequently ventured too close to them, much as did Benjamin, hoping to separate critically the good side of these philosophers from their "dangerous" one – though quite often his Nietzschean rhetoric got the better of him.[212]

In an illuminating essay on Foucault's late ethics, Paul Veyne casts Foucault in the role of the Nietzschean warrior battling in the hope of inflicting his values on others as he took on the covert or open rationalizations for ethical choices made by others. However, as my alternative readings of Foucault have tried to show, it is not clear why one would want to define his politics and ethics again in terms of "violent imposition" rather than as the serious attempt to add to the string of possible subject positions, as the critical query into who is socially entitled to such ethical self-choice, and, in the end, as the earnest demand for the cohabitation of a plurality of ethical styles – despite, to be sure, his pronounced concern with the violence of social struggles. In the same way that Foucault turned to past thinkers to salvage the political core of their thought, so these Foucault interpretations have tried to winnow what is valuable, or worth retaining, from what is not. To the list of valuables, I would submit, one might want to add his notion of "provocation," but only if it is undone of its belligerent connotations. Then the term can be understood as the reciprocal, peaceful incitation among interlocutors, as the provocative invitation to leave one's conventional limits behind and to reinvent oneself as one enters into dialogue with others.

4

THE VIOLENCE OF LANGUAGE

In recent years, notably in the post-Cold War era, the phenomenon of violence has come to the fore again with a renewed force, eliciting a wealth of publications and analytical models that have sought to come to grips with its troubling geopolitical dimensions and sociopolitical ramifications. In the wake of the large-scale atrocities committed in the Yugoslavian war, the acts of genocide in Rwanda and Burundi, or the neo-Nazi violence that ignited during Germany's so-called "second autumn" of 1992, critical discourse once again confronts the challenge of political violence. It would, surely, be a truism, or even a sign of naturalism, were one to posit that these horrific acts merely attest to the fact that violence (or the use of force) is an anthropological constant, an eternal feature of human nature and the human condition, one to have puzzled generations of historians, ethnographers, philosophers, and politicians.[1] Rather, however eternal or universal violence might be, it also seems curiously historical and specific, insofar as every generation, every historical period, produces its own sociopolitically determined forms of violence as well as its own codified discourse on the phenomenon. With a regularity that is equally disconcerting, it has become commonplace to talk about "postmodern violence" in reference to such televised spectacles as the Gulf War and the ethnic conflict in the former Yugoslavia, and to call postmodernity's value-free relativism and antinormativity befitting for our era of violence.

As far as attempts to codify the new geopolitical violence are concerned, two marked trends define contemporary discursive practices. First, grand theories about the end of ideology, exemplified by the fall of communism, are matched by no less broad claims about a new random violence, which, besides testifying to the mindlessness of its perpetrators, is said to resist getting inserted into cohesive narratives of any kind – not just Hegelian or Marxist dialectical emplotments of teleological history, which used to accompany old-style manifestations of revolutionary violence (of the sort analyzed in Arendt's *On Revolution*). Often accompanied by near-apocalyptic, eschatological predictions about the end of history, this first trend surfaces in such tracts as Hans Magnus Enzensberger's *Civil Wars*, which diagnosed the post-Cold War era as ruled by a global, postrevolutionary free-floating violence, divorced from all founding political ideologies or revolutionary intent.[2] At the far side of the spectrum, however, there emerges a second critical tendency, coming mainly from theorists associated with a new post-Marxist, left-leaning political agenda, which tackles the insidious violence that inheres in political liberalism. To be sure, such attacks on the limitations of liberalism have always been part and parcel of left-wing discourse, certainly in the 1960s, when Frankfurt School theorists, such as Herbert Marcuse, Oscar Negt, or Alexander Kluge, accused political liberalism of condoning a structural, or institutional, violence, that is, a form of violence vested in and advanced by the very political institutions that were supposed to ensure a noncoercive liberal democracy. But in the present post-Marxist, postsocialist era, in which liberalism's alleged immunity to violence once again has become suspect, the balance has shifted to an altogether different sort of indictment, voiced, for example, in Slavoj Žižek's essay "The Violence of Liberal Democracy." Under attack in particular has been liberalism's commitment to an Enlightenment program of universalism, whose historical blindness to, and potentially latent intolerance towards, cultural otherness is thought to have numbed its analytical acumen when it comes to understanding contemporary global crises. To complicate political matters even more, a similar rhetoric of universalism is reported to return, in a strangely adapted, mutated form, in the electoral campaigns and political pamphlets of neoracist, populist demagogues, such as Le Pen — or so Etienne Balibar has maintained in his provocative essay "Is There a 'Neo-Racism'?"[3] Moreover, in the current, often heated confrontations between the latest mode of Frankfurt-style critical theory and a post-Marxist poststructuralism, the same suspect universalism, or at least its phantasm, has been said to impair Habermas's universal pragmatics and discourse ethics, while the latter for his part has lamented poststructuralism's relentless, unabated search for a "narrow-minded will to power," lurking behind the mask of Enlightenment universalism.[4] A glance at recent publications in the critical field seems to confirm that the age-old dialectic between universals and particulars, between *universalia* and nominalism, has left the confines of philosophy departments to inflect citizen discussions conducted in the public square: those about identity politics and multiculturalism, cultural pluralism and a universalized liberalism.[5] Equally divided are the accompanying philosophico-political proposals, with some seeking novel mediations between (liberal) universalism and (cultural) particularism, others demanding that we give up the hopelessly utopian program of a universal human history altogether. Finally, it needs no reminding that conservative circles have been all too eager to ascribe the so-called onslaught on universal norms and the resulting cultural relativism to ethnic and political minorities, feminists included, who have been rendered responsible for all societal ills.

While the next chapter will examine the thesis about the *end of ideologies* in more detail, in the present context I would like to address the second trend, the *critique of liberalism*, albeit along somewhat less of a conventional path than is commonly traversed, namely, by considering the violence of language.[6] At the crux of my argument will be the contention that current poststructuralist critiques of universalism also implicitly contest liberalism's conception of language. More specifically, poststructuralism's emphasis on what variously is called "linguistic" or "discursive" violence must remain at odds with the foundational premises that sustain liberal definitions of political speech. To talk about the insipid violence of liberalism is to take to task one of its unquestioned bastions, namely, the instrument or medium of language, more precisely, *speech*, which, according to well-established liberal convention, counts as the organ of transparency, political power, and, in the final analysis, the advancement of universal freedom. Nowhere have these expressions been codified more clearly than in the United States, whose constitution protects free speech in the form of the First Amendment, which, together with the freedom of the press, makes up one of the "cornerstones of liberal democracy."[7] If justified in consequentialist terms, free speech is considered to be the privileged route towards the discovery of truth, while nonconsequentialist justificatory scripts either emphasize that the encroachment of the state upon the private sphere must be curbed, or else that free speech – in line with, what seems to me, is the *logos* tradition – constitutes human beings' innate rationality.[8] At once classical scholar and political philosopher, it was John Stuart Mill who in *On Liberty* most concisely defined the benefits of Socratic dialogue, or the dialectic of speech and counterspeech, for deliberative democracy.[9] Only an egalitarian (and utilitarian) free marketplace of ideas, organized around free speech and discussion, he established, could foster the consensual acceptance of the best, most persuasive argument, so that speech resolutely triumphs over the use of brute force, subordination, and, in the final analysis, tyranny. But whether conceived along consequentialist or nonconsequentialist lines, both positions understand speech not merely in representational but also in performative terms. Speech doesn't just count as the transparent means, or vehicle, for the communication of ideas and principles, whereby there exists a one-to-one relationship between word and idea. Rather, speech simultaneously constitutes the privileged medium *within* which – not just through which – such freedom is executed or performed. More than just an instrumental means to freedom, free speech time and again, without fail, enacts the most basic personal liberty, yielding nothing less than a "free-speech-act."

Taking exception to what they condemn as "first amendment absolutism," some legal scholars and critical race theorists – notably those whose work has been collected in *Words That Wound*[10] – have taken on the discriminatory gestures of exclusion towards minorities, enacted in court decisions that consider heinous acts such as cross-burning to be mere expressions of (free) speech, thus lending indirect state support to violent hate groups such as the Klan. As the authors of *Words That Wound* charge, under current legislation, violence (or force) is held to constitute a "reality" outside the purview of speech, with the rare exception of such hybrid legal categories as "fighting words," which straddle the boundaries between violent action and mere speech. As a consequence, the political dilemma that demands to be thought through is how to devise legislation that will minimize the potential clash between one person's free speech and another's potential harm or injury through assaultive, subordinating hate speech.[11] Animated by similar concerns, in her *Only Words*, feminist legal scholar Catharine MacKinnon likewise has taken on the civil libertarian agenda, which protects pornography as free speech, rather than acknowledging it to be a violent act of subordination – a project through which she, too, has disputed the conventional boundaries between so-called mere speech and "real" action.[12]

The findings of these legal scholars have resulted in practical suggestions for legislative reform, challenging some of the fundamental presuppositions that uphold liberalism's implicit language theory. Comparable contestatory practices, probing the limits between speech and violence, have transpired at what, for lack of a better term, one could call the metatheoretical level.[13] Indeed, my intent in this chapter will be to bring to the surface some of the tacit, yet foundational theoretical presuppositions, premises, and assumptions that galvanize the often contentious encounters between liberal and poststructuralist critics – confrontations, I argue, that involve markedly different views of language. Rather than charting what Richard Rorty has qualified as the (Darwinian) survival of the fittest argument, my aim is to map, bring to the surface, and amplify the softly spoken, not outspoken, unidentified premises that – to some extent, at least – make up the larger current political and cultural arena of discussion. In looking at the disparate conceptions of language that inform liberal, critical theory, and poststructuralist traditions – whether represented by thinkers as diverse as Foucault, Derrida, Butler, or Habermas – I will advance the following set of theses and working hypotheses. First, if, as suggested earlier, liberalism privileges speech, Socratic reasoning, and public deliberation, then the most recognizable manner in which poststructuralist theory diverges from these insights is by shifting the burden of analysis from (public and private) speech to "discourse" and to culturally defined discursive practices, which are said to defy the speakers' claims to unfettered, sovereign self-control or to the purity of a monolithic, monolingual language community. When gauged from a philosophical perspective, it is evident that in questioning liberalism's instrumental, referential, and freedom-producing understanding of language, poststructuralism reverses one of the underpinnings of the humanist tradition, laid down in Aristotle's definition that humans are political and speaking beings (zōon logon ekhon), all the while continuing to lay claim to the free play of freedom. If for Aristotle the relationship between humans and speech was still transitive and possessive, then the linguistic turn that took over the humanities and social sciences, first through the work of de Saussure and Levi-Strauss, later through Lacan, Foucault, and Derrida, turned upside down the hierarchy of ontological priority between subject and language. Of course, one could argue that hermeneutics and existentialism prepared the grounds for such a reversal when they posited humans' "thrown-ness" into language as a revealing, revelatory "being-in-the-world." Still, poststructuralism enforced an even more radical shift when it proclaimed the subject being formed by language to be caught in a potentially ideological, privative, antihumanistic apparatus of discursive subjection. Nowhere have these forceful subject-ing techniques been better illustrated than in Althusser's theory of subject formation through social interpellation, which advanced the allegory of a subject – or, indeed, one wonders, suspect – being hailed by a police officer on the street.

While this linguistic turn has attracted most attention in the literature that has chronicled poststructuralism's historic modes of intervention, I wish to approach the matter from yet another angle, one perhaps less commonly reviewed in the field. My central thesis, as indicated earlier, will be that it is around the intricate relations between *power*, *language*, *speech*, and *violence* that critical opinions and camps diverge. To put it succinctly, at stake is what we prosaically, in common parlance, call "the power of words." Whence does this power derive and why is it that speech *acts*, while acts *speak* (to borrow this phrase from MacKinnon's *Only Words*)? The main discrepancies between the two positions under scrutiny, I will suggest, relate to whether power, language, and violence are seen to be either mutually exclusive, or, quite to the contrary, intrinsically entwined. And, second, whether language is invested with foundationalist, rationalist claims, as is clearly the case, for example, in Arendt's and Habermas's paradigms of intersubjective, communicative action, or, quite to the contrary, seen to be inhabited by an originary violence, an agonistic moment, which compromises such an innate rationalism no less than the anticipated future arrival of universal agreement, let alone consent. For if, according to certain variants of liberalism, universal consent and consensus-formation, established through free speech and ever-evolving discussion, are the "beginning" and "end/telos" of the liberal polity, then no such assumed homogeneity can structure the radical democratic polity that draws upon the insights of poststructuralism. For an agonistic, pluralistic democracy can only aspire towards a "conflictual consensus," as Chantal Mouffe has put it, always permitting "dissensus on the interpretation of its constitutive principles."[14]

Let me first clarify the two interrelated points championed by liberal political theory – the actualization of political power *in* speech, together with the "claim to rational validity immanent within speech"[15] – by means of the example of Hannah Arendt, before attending to the poststructuralist position.

Violence External to Language

That in the liberal-democratic tradition language is not inherently violent but rather politically enabling has perhaps been most persuasively argued by Arendt, for whom violence is to be located outside the arena of democratic politics and the precinct of language. Deploring the rise of instrumental technology in the postwar and postnuclear age, Arendt's main political study, *The Human Condition*, started off mourning the deficit of language in an age in which it had been reduced to scientific jargon, while political deliberation for its part had been replaced by idle talk. Drawing on the critique of instrumental reason that upheld Adorno and Horkheimer's *Dialectic of Enlightenment* (especially in her notes on the *homo faber*), she diagnosed the postnuclear world and space-age as one in which speech – "what makes man a political being"[16] – had increasingly lost its power, having been supplanted by the mathematical symbols of the sciences or drowned out by the threat of nuclear annihilation. Starting from Aristotle's conception of praxis as well as his twin definition of humans as *zōon politikon* and *zōon logon ekhon* (a political and speaking being), her model of communicative action posited that political power was an end in itself to be realized in nonmanipulative, nonstrategic speech, yielding "the formation of a common will in a community aimed at agreement."[17] Not only was consensual power sharply to be demarcated from violence, but violence for its part was to be defined by the means–end relation of instrumentality. As such, the instrumental, strategic use of force needed to be distinguished from speech (*lexis*), which was endowed with an "agent-revealing capacity," revealing the identity of a "who" or "doer" behind the speech act. Close reader and sometime admirer of Nietzsche's philosophical work, Arendt thus took issue with the philosopher's conviction that there existed no "substratum," no " 'being' behind doing, effecting, becoming," and, consequently, that the moral fiction of a doer behind the deed needed to be abandoned.[18] For Arendt, there could be no doubt that coercion-free, deliberative speech was the organ in and through which power was actualized – not, this time, as a means to an end, but as an end in itself. Because violence constituted the limit of silence or mute aggression, as she argued in numerous of her articles and books, it simultaneously spelled the end of power, which is why it resolutely needed to be situated outside the arena of political speech. Nowhere was the silencing of all political power more palpable than in the atrocities of the Holocaust, as she pointed out in *On Revolution*:

> Where violence rules absolutely, as for instance in the concentration camps of totalitarian regimes, not only the laws … but everything and everyone must fall silent. It is because of this silence that violence is a marginal phenomenon in the political realm; for man, to the extent that he is a political being, is endowed with the power of speech. The two famous definitions of Aristotle, that he is a political being and a being endowed with speech, supplement each other and both refer to the same experience in Greek *polis* life. The point here is that violence itself is incapable of speech, and not merely that speech is helpless when confronted with violence. Because of this speechlessness political theory has little to say about the phenomenon of violence and must leave its discussion to the technicians. For political thought can only follow the articulations of the political phenomena themselves, it remains bound to what appears in the domain of human affairs; and these appearances, in contradistinction to physical matters, need speech and articulation, that is, something which transcends mere physical visibility as well as sheer audibility, in order to be manifest at all. A theory of war or a theory of revolution, therefore, can only deal with the justification of violence because this justification constitutes its political limitation; if, instead, it arrives at a glorification or justification of violence as such, it is no longer political but antipolitical.[19]

Much as in Wittgenstein's *Tractatus*, one is inclined to ponder, Arendt sought to trace the critical limits, or territorial boundaries, between the speakable and that whereof one cannot speak, lest one lapse into metaphysics. But if Wittgenstein demarcated the metaphysical from the logical on the basis of what remained purely mystical, hence philosophically unspeakable, Arendt separated the political from the non- or antipolitical by drawing the barrier between politically empowering speech and silent, mute violence.

At once powerful and compelling, Arendt's programmatic definition of political speech does not entirely escape scrutiny, as it may prove to be sensitive to several lines of query. Thus, one might wonder whether violence is ever really mute? Only, perhaps, when it is a matter of considering the silence of trauma, the "gaping, vertiginous black hole" of the traumatic experience, though even then, as psychoanalysis suggests, the silenced memory may speak through the body, through symptomatic gestures (Bourdieu's *habitus*, or embodied acts), and through the "uncanny repetition of events that duplicate ... the traumatic past."[20] However, one does better justice to Arendt's position if one understands it to attest to the same horror in the face of the Holocaust that led Adorno to formulate his oft-cited, later revised, dictum that it would be barbaric to write poetry after Auschwitz.[21] In the face of so much horror, all speech must falter, lest it minimize the incommensurable suffering of the victims. How to talk of and about violence, especially genocide, without mimetically reproducing its calamitous effects or palliating its horrendous magnitude is a question that, rightly so, will not stop inflecting the debates over visual and linguistic representations of and after the Holocaust.[22]

Drawing its momentum from the power with which she reaffirmed, but also rethought, the conventional liberal opposition between violence and speech in a post-Holocaust era, Arendt's position nonetheless has elicited criticism from within her own ranks, notably from Habermas. To be sure, Habermas's critical social theory further elaborated on her action theory insofar as it advocated democratic consent or agreement among equally situated speech partners and analyzed the formal-pragmatic speech conditions that underwrite liberal democracies, attesting to "the rational basis of linguistic communication."[23] Notwithstanding such affinities, however, Habermas took issue with her restricted, Aristotelian understanding of praxis and her correlated reluctance to consider power from a systems-theoretical perspective. Thus, her exclusion of violence from the arena of the political and from her theory of consensual power led him to challenge her inability to gauge the use of strategic action in the public sphere and hence the resulting distortion of political institutions by structural violence. For, as Habermas underscored, all historical evidence corroborates that strategic action, taking the form of political domination, is routinely deployed to secure the democratic state's legitimate power, meaning that through the production of ideologies, or the communicatively engendered formation of misrecognition, citizens may be prevented from discerning their proper interests. Thinking through her analysis of consensual power, Habermas amended Arendt's model, qualifying structural violence as "not manifest as violence; instead it blocks in an unnoticed fashion those communications in which are shaped and propagated the convictions effective for legitimation."[24] Seen this way, then, ideologies amount to communicatively produced obstructions of consensual speech.[25]

As a way of providing a preliminary summary of these observations, one could say that the political tradition of liberalism is premised on an original or originary use of language, which aspires to interpersonal understanding (*Verständigung*) and postulates a rationality immanent to speech, expressed in exchanging and debating arguments, a process at the heart of liberal democracy. Violence is either seen to be external or threatening to speech,[26] or to be an obstacle that short-circuits free political speech, which, if taking an institutional form, in Habermas's social theory becomes structural violence, or ideology.

Violence in Language (Power/Force/Violence)

Rather than taking an originary bedrock of rationality for granted, most variants of poststructuralist theory start off from the potentially violent aberration that befalls all language and speech, a position perhaps most pronounced in the work of its deconstructive representatives, Jacques Derrida and Paul de Man. If one pushes their assumptions about language to their logical conclusion, then in a first moment, deconstructive poststructuralism, just as much as its liberal antipode, harbors generalizing, universalizing propositions about language. Poststructuralist theory provides a critique of occidental logocentrism, claiming the obsoleteness of foundational origins or transhistorical, universalist propositions on the basis of historical and cultural change. But it also assumes an a priori violence that inheres in language *as such* (not just in "speech" or situated, culturally, and historically defined discourse), and that, insofar as it determines the (negative) conditions of possibility governing all individual speech acts, threatens to derail the speaker's implicit claims to authority, intentionality, sovereignty, and autonomous subjecthood. In Derrida's early thought, this insight takes the form of the Saussurian contention that the relation between signifier and signified is arbitrary, and, in the later de Man, that any given act of speaking is inadvertently undermined by the disruptive aberration of language, so that the speech act does not necessarily say what it intends to convey. Informed by the radical historico-philological method Nietzsche devised in his "On Truth and Lies in an Extramoral Sense" and the *Genealogy of Morals*, deconstruction's conception of linguistic force relies on nominalism, which emphasizes the contingency of acts of naming, and on philosophical skepticism, which introduces a radical perspectivism, casting doubt on the assumed judiciousness of established universal norms. In so doing, deconstruction operates with a homology of sorts between the arbitrary nature of conventional language, or its sign system, and the contingency of power/force. While not always made explicit in so many words, this analogy underpins de Man's essays on Rousseau, author of the *Social Contract* and the discourse on inequality. When de Man invoked

Heidegger's *Die Sprache spricht* (language speaks) to transform it into *Die Sprache verspricht (sich)*, the joke was at once on multiple political traditions. *Versprechen* can mean "to promise," but in the sense of *sich versprechen* it signifies "to produce slips of the tongue." Oscillating between these two meanings, de Man's phrase stressed how language's claims to transparency and intentional capacity were ineluctably under-mined – language producing ever more, infinite "slips of the tongue." With one and the same stroke, however, de Man's phrase also took leave of the entire political tradition of contractarianism, tethered to contractual promissory notes. It is, then, perhaps, ironic that no one other than Arendt recognized in Nietzsche's well-known saying that humans were animals *"with the right to make promises"* the liberal heritage of contractari-anism, "the force of mutual promise or contract."[27] That she was brushing Nietzsche's text against its antiliberal grain indirectly is made clear by de Man's Rousseau exegesis: despite best intent, the speech act of the political promise, including that of the social compact, never manages to avert the regime of force it was meant to quell.

As it examines how contingent discursive practices are passed off as universal norms, deconstructive poststructuralism follows Nietzsche's genealogical method, which supplanted Kant's transcendental critique of knowledge, moral action, and aesthetic judgment with a historicist critique of the force that permeates all values.[28] But deconstruction also returns to Nietzsche's insights about language's insuperable figurative nature to contest the fallacious division between an authentic, felicitous use of language and its so-called aberrant deviations – a problematic bifurcation it sees expressed in Searle's speech act theory or Habermas's discourse ethics. To be sure, critical theorists often have responded with countercharges to the effect that decon-struction, despite its critique of logocentrism, simply advances yet another philosophy of the origin, when it replaces the freedom-positing, innately "poetic" power of language with a more primordial destructive or disabling force. The charges leveled at poststructuralism's mystifying, jargon-laden rhetoric, which is said to obstruct demo-cratic transparency, recall the force with which Adorno's *Jargon of Authenticity* impugned the obfuscation and irrationalism that accompanied Heidegger's philosophy of being. Such condemnations choose to ignore deconstruction's counterclaim that it aims to criticize conventional philosophies of the origin, insofar as it jettisons the temporal logic of a plenitudinous *archē* (as both beginning and foundation, whether outside or at the very start of history) for the temporality of *écriture*, *différance*, and iteration, or – in Derrida's later work – the utopian quasi-theological futurality of the "yet-to-come" (*l'avenir, l' à-venir*). In works ranging from *Of Grammatology* to the more recent *Monolingualism of the Other*, Derrida established the futility of searching for a universal metalanguage in the face of a constitutive "incommunicability" that besets all linguistic communication, as the mark of language's ingrained "ex-appropriation." Insofar as language of necessity escaped all appropriation by speaking subjects, it imposed a privative condition on us, which, however universal, eluded our calibrating grasp. Thrown into a post-Babelic plurality of languages, speaking subjects nonetheless shared a common predicament, a basic "monolingualism of the other," which forever surrendered them to an existence in translation.[29] If it is true that all singular languages, idioms, and idiolects were marked by such primordial lack or alienation, then, according to Derrida, the condition was exemplified particularly well by the Franco-Maghrebian writer, who, in speaking French, the language of the colonizer, bore witness to this primordial trauma, the scar of terror that disfigured all language. Seeking to fathom language's unsettling, antinomic structure, Derrida recognized in the predicament of its scarred witness the relation between a transcendental, ontological universality and the singularity of existence, whose very connection he sought to understand. For in exposing "the enigmatic articulation between a universal structure and its idiomatic testimony," this witness attested to an "a priori universal truth of an essential alienation in language – which is always of the other – and, by the same token, in all culture,"[30] showing all cultures to be pervaded with a primordial "colonial" cruelty (auto-heteronomy) that dispossessed them of their autonomy.

Powerful as this analysis is when it comes to interrogating the "disseminating" force that inhabits national cultures and speech communities, it, too, must face a set of challenges, just as much as did liberalism's language theory earlier. What, one might ask, for example, is the relation between cultural regimes of violation and the general condition of ex-appropriation, postulated by deconstructive poststructuralism? Is the former but the most excruciating instantiation, the phenomenological sign, of the colonizing violence that inheres in all language? But if all languages operate by dint of a "colonizing" force, might one not risk losing sight of the singular plight that befalls historically situated, subaltern subjects reduced to silence or deprived of their embattled idiolects? How to negotiate between such insights about language's a priori structure and the collusion between culturally situated manifestations of power, force, and discursive practices? Such are some of the hard questions that a deconstructive language philosophy needs to consider as it lays out and implements the practical applications of its principles. Indeed, for all the built-in precautions with which poststructuralist theory operates in the name of postmetaphysics, especially those advising against the invocation of a metalanguage, they may not suffice to circumvent the pitfalls of a quasi- or real foundationalism. This is no less the case if, in the place of an originary – be it, natural, divine, secular, or politically empowering – language, deconstructive poststructuralism posits an originary negative violence, whose force is so deleterious that it renders even the most minimal form of harmonious communication unthinkable. It is one thing to argue that the plurality and diversity that defines interlocutors in the democratic polity affects the enabling conditions of their speech community, yet another to hypostatize a primordial force that negatively determines the conditions of possibility of individual speech acts. Similarly, one might also question what the consequences are of reducing linguistic violence to the level of a universal, antihumanistic, mechanized rhetoric, so that there is no place anymore for an Aristotelian forensic rhetoric, with its belief that political power is constituted through intersubjective deliberation.[31] Then, at least two radically conflictual interpretations of rhetoric exist side by side: the de Manian one, according to which rhetoric, with its unreliable, deviant figures of speech and tropes, is the disruptive paradigm that commands all language; and, a more politically enabling script, to be found in liberalism and philosophies of argumentation – for example, Chaim Perelman's *The New Rhetoric* – according to which the ethical application of rhetoric requires the use of peaceful, nonforceful techniques of persuasion as one interacts with one's auditor. In seeming to eliminate this liberal-political component so as to privilege the reiterative contingent structure of a generalized rhetoric, the de Manian position opens itself up to a set of rigorous queries that potentially test its political viability. What remains unaccounted for, one might reason, is how this point of view escapes the danger of an "epochal nihilism," as some critics have feared, if language, let alone speech, no longer functions as a political medium, no longer provides the anchorage point for a hermeneutical or existential being-in-the-world, but is impoverished to the point of becoming the operation of an antiteleological "inhuman, dehumanized language of linguistics."[32] Doesn't such a conception of language, reified into a transhistorical device that traverses all culturally situated discourse, run the risk of promoting, if not a deterministic, then at the very minimum, a politically disabling position?

As mentioned at the outset of this analysis, in order for deconstructive poststructuralism to make such claims about the potentially privative conditions that reign over all linguistic use, it must efface the critical distinctions between power, force, and violence that provided the linchpin to the liberal paradigm, which we saw at work in Arendt's thought. If one appropriates Nietzsche's historico-philological methodology, then such an erasure of all too rigid differences seems historically warranted insofar as the terms violence, force, and power are etymologically as well as conceptually related.[33] Indeed, nowhere has this erasure of conceptual demarcations become more visible than in Foucault's writings, whose historicist poststructuralism, especially in his later phase, claimed to eschew ontological or transcendental pronouncements about language in general, committed as his analysis remained to the historical contingency of situated discursive practices, whose "normalized" status was thoroughly at odds with Habermas's conception of a normative "discourse" (*Diskurs*).[34] In the period of *The Archeology of Knowledge*, when he was not yet explicitly preoccupied with the genealogy of political power, Foucault proved mainly interested in what he alternately termed discursive, epistemological, or hermeneutical violence – a paradigm explained most fully in his 1970 "The Discourse on Language," which assumed an agonistic interplay between competing discursive practices while making these still largely subservient to a Western will to truth or knowledge.[35] At the time, the historian's task was said to consist in the recording of disciplinary violence, propagated by the human and social sciences, and predicated on procedures, dividing practices or systems of exclusion that were the descendants of a prodigious "will to truth." Digging into the groundwork that supported epistemic and discursive conventions, such as the "founding subject,"[36] Foucault's archeology already anticipated the later analysis of discursive "subject-ing" techniques through which (desiring) subjects are constituted.[37] Yet, at the same time that his historicism claimed to be antistructuralist in style and intent, it also proved anti-Hegelian in its unswerving critique of controlling master narratives that organized history's disorder.[38] Moving even further back, to the foundations of Western thought held in place by modernity's unabated loyalty to Platonism, he reverted to Sophism, whose insights into the uncontainable paradoxes and anomalies of language had been suppressed by the Platonic tradition. As his interests shifted from rescripting the history of epistemic regimes to tackling the prescriptive scripts of political theory, he further compounded the constellation *pouvoir–savoir* by *pouvoir / guerre / force*. Taking issue with the liberal tradition of contract-power, he defined power as "war-repression," questioning the legitimacy of the modern, sovereign state as the purveyor of liberal rights, no less than contractarianism, against which he pitted the force of history and political historicism. For, when it came to gauging the "genealogy of relations of force, strategic developments, and tactics," he noted emphatically, "one's point of reference should not be to the great model of language (*langue*) and signs, but to that of war and battle."[39] Contractarianism was every bit as much a discursive convention as was the army of tropes that Nietzsche had helped march in, whose forces henceforth would occupy the territory of philosophical labor. All the genealogist needed to do, so as to measure up to the exigencies of history, was to heed the caveat that "the historicity which determines us is of a bellicose nature, not a linguistic one"[40] – a move through which Foucault hoped to loosen the squelching grip of *logos* (reason, language) on history.

Speech Acts

Only against the foil of how the conventional borders between power, force, and violence have progressively been erased can one begin to gauge the extraordinary impact a particular branch of Anglo-American language philosophy – speech act theory – has exerted on variants of poststructuralism, critical theory, and liberalism alike. Despite their outspoken, irreconcilable disagreements as regards the nature of language, both traditions have paid tribute to Austin's 1955 William James Lectures, *How To Do Things With Words* – albeit, needless to say, with diverse inflections and tonalities. Differences coalesce around what precise meaning should be ascribed to the latter's rather technical use of the word "force" to qualify a speech act's effectiveness. After the decades-long dominance that Saussurian linguistics exercised on the critical field, Austin's theory, with its emphasis on linguistic enactment, on the performance of actions in the utterance of words, seemed to introduce a provocative new tool with instant practical applications, also outside the analytical academy. For, in coining a new set of linguistic utterances, whose name was derived from " 'perform,' the usual verb with the noun 'action,' " indicating "that the issuing of the utterance is the performing of an action,"[41] Austin arguably supplied a linguistically defined action theory, which was to be put to versatile, imaginative use by critical and poststructuralist theorists alike. Certain conceptual limitations notwithstanding, Austin's language philosophy provided the advantage of knotting agency and action to "effecting" speech, generating a rich heuristic model that, besides drawing many of its examples from legal or political discourse, permitted the redescription of a whole range of discursive activities in turn.

Earlier I indicated that most common liberal conceptions of free speech rest on what appears to be an intuitive understanding of speech act theory, insofar as stress is placed on the performative enactment of political power in and through speech. Such politically liberating speech is realized through illocution, or "the performance of an act *in* saying something as opposed to performance of an act *of* saying something," to quote Austin.[42] But what in the political doctrine of free speech to a large extent was still untheorized assumption has been spelled out in Habermas's theory of communicative action, which, in leaving behind the exhausted legacy of the philosophy of consciousness no less than the Marxist category of labor, opted for a paradigm switch in favor of communicative reason and reciprocal understanding. Appropriating the term "logocentrism" for his own purposes, Habermas targeted poststructuralism's totalizing critique of reason, together with its conception of language as transsubjective "logos," in which "the subject is not master in his own house." But he also took on Anglo-American analytical philosophy, at least the branch that diminished reason's capacity ontologically, epistemologically, and linguistically speaking, by conceiving of the world in object-terms, thus reducing cognition to purposive-rational ends, while limiting language to its "fact-mirroring" or representational function, watering sentences down to assertoric, fact-stating, or fact-reproducing utterances.[43] Adopting a pragmatic logic of argumentation, Habermas sought to move away from "the logos characterization of language,"[44] relying instead on the later Wittgenstein, Austin, and Searle. But to fashion a theory of communicative action, it was also necessary to retool Weber's theory of purposive action, which worked with intentional, isolated, monological individuals, neglecting the interpersonal aspect of communication. In distinguishing between instrumental, (social) strategic, and communicative action, Habermas specified that only the latter involved *acts of reaching understanding* (*Verständigung*) not guided by purely "egocentric calculations of success."[45] Over and against strategic, purposive action, in which communication was merely used as a means for manipulative, self-centered goals, he pitted a noncoercive mode of understanding and agreement, whose ends were effective, democratically enabling conversation. The advantages offered by speech act theory were that it allowed one to theorize such a "linguistically generated intersubjectivity," to analyze context-bound illocutionary speech acts, and to deduce the formal-pragmatic, generalizable rules that guided the communicatively structured life-world.[46]

As he linked his theory of communicative action to Austin's typology of speech acts, Habermas defined locution as the utterance of assertoric or constative statements, illocution as the noninstrumental, hence "ideal," performance of communicative actions, while perlocution fell under the heading of purposive, strategic action. From this it followed that the ideal speech situation that defined deliberative democracies could only be negotiated through felicitous illocutionary speech acts, which were exchanged among equally situated interlocutors engaging in "intersubjective relationships free from violence."[47] Perlocutions, in contrast, stood to illocutions as parasitic aberrations to language's authentic, illocutionary mode, inasmuch as the speech act was placed "under conditions of action oriented to success."[48] Speech act theory, furthermore, also permitted Habermas to refine his definition of ideology: ideological effects were always of a perlocutionary nature, deviations from illocutionary force, where *force* meant neither "capacity" nor "privative" violence but rather an enabling, agent-revealing power. Indeed, formally speaking, such speech conditions were realized through a "*rationally motivated binding* [or bonding: *Bindung*] *force*"[49] to which interlocutors pledged fidelity as they entered the discursive arena. In this way, democratic speech held its distance from the power politics of the (utilitarian) compromise, destined "to harmonize nongeneralizable interests on the basis of balanced positions of power."[50] Indeed, for argumentation to result in democratic agreement, it needed to adhere to a quasi-Kantian horizon of expectation, the ideal of communicative peace and harmony, which every speech situation strove to approximate. Following this anti-utilitarian model, democratically conceived arguments required the subordination of "the eristic means to the end of developing intersubjective conviction by the force of the better argument."[51] Subscribing to a regulative ideal of linguistic authenticity, guiding every single intersubjective speech situation, Habermas thus postulated a pure mode of communicative action, nothing more nor less than an *original use of language*, with regard to which ideological abuses of language or speech were merely derivative.[52] Or, as he expressed it pithily, "reaching understanding is the inherent telos of human speech,"[53] meaning that speech and understanding never merely stood to one another as means do to ends.

No less complex than the applications that speech act theory has found in Habermas's critical social theory are the uses to which it has been put by poststructuralism. On a most general level of inquiry, one might note that poststructuralist philosophers relocated their focus of analysis again from a universally mandated, authentic use of speech, or the "pure performative," to a wide spectrum of "infelicities," potentially aberrant speech acts, generated by language's innate "structural parasitism," as Derrida put it in his exchange with Searle.[54] In his nuanced survey of how language and politics interact in the thought of representative contemporary philosophers, Michael Shapiro dedicates a substantial portion of his analysis to speech act theory, opposing the Anglo-American branch of language philosophy to its continental tradition, the first privileging action contexts and the social function of language, the second the "play of difference" and the conventional, or arbitrary, nature of the signifier.[55] But Shapiro's remarks only partially capture the dispute over the nature of speech acts that unraveled between Derrida and Searle, nor could they, obviously, anticipate the transformative resignifications Butler would lend to the paradigm. In his reply to Searle, documented in "Signature Event Context," Derrida recast *différance* as the logic of iterability, thus identifying a performative force (read:

violence) that surpassed the purview of the illocutionary speech act and violated the intentionality of the speaking agent, and hence, the general "context" Austin's speech act theory presumed. The latter, Derrida continued, overlooked the *graphematic in general*," which resided in all locution as such, prior to illocution or perlocution. Reversing Austin's assertion that only quotations were parasitical, Derrida turned every speech act into a citation or iteration "within a general iterability,"[56] whose disruptive force authorized but also interfered with communication. Essentially, iterability, or the *polemical* force of *différance*, proved to be privative and enabling at the same time, as it designated "the general space of ... possibility" within which discursive events or speech acts took place.[57]

Quite a different interpretation of speech act's "force" is to be found in Bourdieu's *Language and Symbolic Power*, whose sociological account of cultural capital and symbolic power similarly set out to demolish preconceived notions about language, albeit those dominant in the social sciences, and, above all, "the *intellectualist philosophy* which treats language as an object of contemplation rather than as an instrument of action and power."[58] Taking on Austin et al., he uncovered in "illocutionary force" a magical, mystical power that speech act theory ascribed to words, arguing that such power, in reality, was generated by societal, and hence *extra*-linguistic, conditions. Seeking to overcome the orthodox Marxist opposition between culture and economy, Bourdieu understood social relations as symbolic interactions or "relations of symbolic power," that is, actualizations of the "power relations between speakers and their respective groups."[59] As his *Language and Symbolic Power* contended, the liberal paradigm was caught in a ruse, in that it turned a blind eye to the mystical, indeed, mystifying force that so clearly imbued the authority-granting rhetorics of sovereign power or legal deliberation – "a fact concretely exemplified," Bourdieu noted at one point, "by the *skeptron* that, in Homer, is passed to the orator who is about to speak."[60] Clearly invalidating the claim that the use of language primarily served communication was the conscious or unconscious "pursuit of symbolic profit"[61] that regulated speech acts – a statement that, when seen from the perspective of discourse ethics, in fact proclaimed that speech acts merely amounted to derivative, strategic, perlocutionary action. In view of such a circuit of symbolic profit it would be naive, Bourdieu indicated, to adopt a prescriptive communicative model of the kind championed by Habermas, just as much as it would be precarious to locate a "mystical foundation of authority" at the core of language or the law as such, as did deconstruction.

That Bourdieu and Derrida in turn themselves occupy two opposing sides in the language debates, the one privileging a sociological approach that favors extralinguistic symbolic capital, the other endorsing an intralinguistic operation of force, emerges from Butler's *Excitable Speech*, which, in many ways, presents an effort to overcome the chasm between the two poles. While Butler's thought is inspired by the counterforce that Derrida's philosophy wields against all forms of "metaphysical violence," her *Excitable Speech* reflected on the potential drawbacks, especially an undesirable formalism, that might issue from deconstruction. For, as she queried, what happens if iterability becomes a "structural operation of the sign, identifying the 'force' of the performative as a structural feature of any sign that must break with its prior contexts in order to sustain its iterability as a sign?"[62] Might not the theory risk turning into a restrictive, purely formal paradigm once iterability is changed into a structural feature that rules all language? Moving from a concern with "linguistic structure" and "context" to "social convention" and "custom," Butler sought to bring Derrida's formal-structural remarks about iterability into productive tension with Bourdieu's *habitus* ("embodied act") and with Althusser's understanding of discursive conventions as social rituals or modes of interpellation. Revising these theories' respective limitations, her model, on the one side, understood social agency as the articulation, appropriation, and transformation of discursive conventions, together with their social contexts, while it also explained how discursive norms are inhabited, incorporated, or bodily performed.[63] To do so, *Excitable Speech* set up a two-tiered analysis, linking a powerful study of hate speech, informed by the insights of critical race theory, to a revamped poststructuralist theory that believes in the transformative power of insurrectionary speech. On a first level, that of *speech (parole)*, her study argued that the illocutionary force that inflects concrete verbal threats or assaultive slurs was to be understood as illocutionary *violence*, since such utterances drew on an authorizing fantasy aiming to subjugate others through the power of one's speech. On a second, more generalized level, that of *language (langue)*, her analysis shifted from the phantasmatic structure that grounded hate speech to a more general force that informed language as such. Hate speech, in that sense, was the most excruciating, violent example of how speaking subjects relied on essentialist categories (self-righteous sovereignty, overconfident intentionality) that were oblivious to the "subject-forging," subjecting force of language. Alternating between these two levels of analysis, between discursive practices and language in general, *Excitable Speech* provided an affirmative answer to the question "What if language has within it its own possibilities for violence and for world-shattering?"[64] and thus ended up subscribing again to the "violence in language" thesis. To some, such a proposition, taken to its logical conclusion, might seem to result in determinism. However, Butler, quite to the contrary, aimed to reclaim the poetic, transformative force of language, which is why her book ended by defining social change as the recovery of an altogether different insurrectionary, revolutionary discursive force. Drawing, it seems, on an avant-gardist belief in the power of poetry, her book ended up calling for the transformation of language's performative violence into a political and poetic, resignifying force.

Dissent/Consent (With a Note on Ideology Critique)

Whether it is a matter of liberal theorists, poststructuralists, or critical social theorists, the foregoing analysis has made it unmistakably clear that all consider "the political" to function as an arena of discursive activity, within which there exist manifestations of violence that, while coercive, are not physical but more insidious, yet nonetheless nefarious. One must look, then, for a category of violence that, phenomenologically speaking, is not always manifest or visible the way more graphic representations of violence are in our mediatized culture of violence; a sort of violence enacted through enunciatory and discursive practices, or else in the interstices of language, in traumatic and enforced silence. But the above review equally unmistakably revealed the justificatory limits and dilemmas that these factions run up against, when it comes to negotiating their theoretical directives about speech or language with the pluriform, concrete discursive realities that define the social arena. It seems fair briefly to reconsider some of the challenges these positions face, when pared down to their essentials.

Best known, of course, are the misgivings directed at Habermas's rationalist theory of communicative action (together with its deontological presuppositions), which contest its attempt to attain universalist, philosophical justification on the charge that the theory might once again coercively impose a hegemonic mold of "consensus" on culturally diverse subjects. Perhaps no one more vigorously than Lyotard opposed Habermas's discourse ethics, on the grounds that in an age of postindustrialist societies in which "the normativity of laws" had made way for "the performativity of procedures," its Enlightenment metanarrative of legitimation had lost its credulity.[65] Precisely because the "monstrosity" of social pragmatics lacked the clarity of scientific pragmatics, the quest for an "outmoded and suspect value"[66] of consensus needed to be shunted, no less than the concomitant assumption that, in the face of the absolute heterogeneity of social pragmatic rules, a minimum, practical agreement was even conceivable. When seen in light of the intractable range of potential language games and the virtually infinite short-term contracts they brought into play (over and against the permanence of the old, forfeited social contract), Habermas's perspective simply reintroduced the "terror" of "conflict-free agreement," which imagined discourses to be isomorphic.[67] In place of consent and consensus, Lyotard defended the "agonistics" of always dissenting language games, and, rallying for a "war on totality" in all terrains, not just aesthetics, he called for a new postmodern justice, which would come to terms with value differences.[68]

As a way of counterbalancing Lyotard's partial rendition of Habermas's position, one might note that the latter does not fail to account for cultural difference and context, as indeed his interpretation of Hegel's notion of *Sittlichkeit* demonstrates;[69] nor does his pragmatic model foreclose the possibility of nonviolent dissent and difference, though it is true that these occur within the consensually attained parameters of the (ideal) communicative situation. What is more, Habermas's political model, as we saw, does acknowledge the possible obstruction of communication through ideology or strategic action. The real points of contention in critical debates around his work, rather, pertain, on the one hand, to the desirability of universalist, normative justification in the face of value pluralism, and, on the other, to the question as to whether he can account for the multiple power differentials that suffuse concrete speech situations. Indeed, Habermas's discourse ethics does not always provide clear indicators as to how power-determined modalities of inequality among speech partners, e.g., perceived gender or race differences, are to be negotiated in the debating arena. Certainly, Habermas's egalitarian universalism presumes a *formal* equality or structural symmetry among speech partners, in a gathering organized on the model of the town hall or public square, an ideal public arena, which excludes all infractions of strife, violence, in short, nonillocutionary force. But might not the regulative ideal of rational consensus and even its weaker variant, agreement about the pragmatic procedures regulating the conversation, block the sight of difference and asymmetry, insofar as it assumes a level playing field of equitably situated partners (to borrow that much-favored figure of the football field from pragmatism) in which all are cast as equally empowered players, bracketing out the potentially unequal distribution of power among them? How does such a model relate, say, to Gramsci's category of the subaltern subject, or even Levinas's ethics of asymmetry?

If such are the charges launched at a theory of communicative action, then, conversely, poststructuralism in turn ought to remain vigilant about the danger that it might transhistoricize linguistic violence, reinstating a false rift between the empirical and the transcendental. To be sure, poststructuralist theory certainly has helped to sensitize us to ulterior modes of "symbolic violence," to adopt Althusser's term, other than those that immediately meet the eye.[70] Agonistic political theory, for example, has used Derrida's understanding of the "constitutive outside," together with his polemological conception of language, as a corrective to counteract the all too facile grounding assumption of a harmonious, friction-free collectivity of like-situated speech partners.[71] Moreover, it would be wrong to suspect that deconstruction simply turns linguistic violence into a figure of speech or a trope, as it every bit as much as critical theory examines structural, institutional, or culturally situated (ideological) articulations of violence. Given the fruitful political uses to which deconstructive poststructuralism has been put in critical race theory or feminism, the criticisms that it necessarily and automatically results in a problematic depoliticization or gives rise to a Babel-like state of dissonance, discord, and disagreement, must likewise ring hollow. All the same, it bears repeating that when linguistic or discursive violence threaten to get reified into nothing but a forbidding a priori structure, then this counterdiscourse fails to escape the charges of abstract universalization it so readily levels at Habermas's paradigm. This is why poststructuralist theory must probe its formalist postulates, and consider how its structural logic can be transformed into a social one, as Butler has noted, all the while paying due attention to complex, diverse social formations of power, without having its logic turn into an incapacitating "counterlaw."

At base, the language disputes among these theorists and critics concern the articulation of power relations, and thus, directly or indirectly, the equally embattled topos of ideology no less than the so-called "crisis of ideology critique." No one better than Žižek, one of ideology critique's staunch defenders, has captured the seemingly unsolvable dilemma that riddles our critical present. Thus, in his genealogy of the concept ideology, he noted that Habermas's understanding of ideology as a "systematically distorted communication," or "what the tradition of Enlightenment dismisses as a mere disturbance of 'normal' communication," in fact constituted the "positive condition" of communication for discourse analysis.[72] In effect, the post-structuralist coinage of the term appears to be but the latest stage in the concept's versatile history, whose long trajectory led from Marx's "critique of political economy" to Adorno and Horkheimer's "critique of instrumental reason"[73]; and from the orthodox categories of class alliance or class consciousness to Gramsci's under-standing of "hegemony" as "an articulatory practice which constitutes and organizes social realities,"[74] and then on to Althusser's decoding of social rituals and habits, sustained by institutional power. However, as the tradition progressively abandoned its earlier, dogmatic representationalist realism, the category of ideology became "too strong" (Žižek) or "too stretched" (Eagleton), meaning that in enveloping "neutral, extra-ideological ground,"[75] it provoked an epistemological crisis about the diacritical principles that were meant to winnow (political) truth from falsehood. Indeed, it seems that Althusser in particular has often been made responsible for dilating the category, not just far beyond its original, proto-Marxist reach but also beyond critical capacity, as he made it more or less identical to the process of subject formation through discursive interpellation.[76] Revisiting Aristotle's original characterization of political personhood, centered in speech, Althusser described humans as "an ideolog-ical animal by nature," substituting the qualifier ideology for *logos* (reason, language).[77] By aligning psychoanalysis and (post)structuralist discourse analysis with the material inscriptions of institutional power relations, his revamped theory was able to consider the nexus between symbolic violence and normalized subject positions that individuals could assume. Yet, missing from the model, formulated thus expansively, were sign-posts and exit routes – for example, a paradigm of intersubjectivity that would allow one to get out of the specular mechanism of (ideological) misrecognition (*méconnais-sance*), modeled on Lacan's imaginary. It is remarkable, therefore, that Žižek, rather than see the co-optation of nonideological terrain as cause for epistemological skepti-cism, has gleaned in it a positive challenge that awaits a "'postmodern' critique of ideology."[78] Brought down to a formula, the crisis in fact presented the pseudo-Kantian "antinomy of critico-ideological reason." For, as he wagered, everything "hinges on our persisting in this impossible position: though *no clear line of demarcation* separates ideology from reality, though ideology is already at work in everything we experience as 'reality,' we must none the less maintain the tension that keeps the *critique* of ideology alive."[79]

If Žižek discerned in the very attempt to leave ideology behind the ideological moment *par excellence*, then others have been far more willing to toss the term alto-gether. In order to put the (specular) crisis of ideology and ideology critique in perspective, it is necessary to specify that the deficit of these terms has been pronounced on at least a double front, either on the basis of political considerations or of epistemological objections, the former tendered mostly by conservative critics, such as Daniel Bell, the latter often, though not exclusively, by left-leaning theorists.[80]

As far as objections from the left are concerned, Foucault undoubtedly set the tone when he argued that the outmoded, no longer viable category of ideology was to be supplanted by discursive "effects of truth," so as to avert ontologizing, essentialistic claims about truth and falsehood, the heirs of a suspect will to knowledge. Though Foucault discarded the proto-Marxist model, replacing ideology with discursive tactics, he still worked, obviously, with an underlying notion of ideological distortion that permitted him, for example, to pit "political historicism" against the juridico-philosophical discourse of political theory.[81] The epistemological critique of ideology, however, is particularly pronounced in Rorty's context-bound, antifoundationalist variety of pragmatism, which resists outmoded attempts at philosophical justification, grounded in innate rationality and universalism, no less than the defunct vocabulary of representationalism. Limiting his understanding of ideology to the representational, mirroring model of mind, Rorty has maintained that the term, together with ideology critique, is to be discarded in favor of a linguistically inflected pragmatism.[82] Certainly, such a way of proceeding may seem to best fit the times, given the insolvency of theoretical, transcendental proposals, whose attempts at self-justification inevitably must result in circular argumentation or in universalist proclamations, in comparison to which pragmatism may appear as an attractive solution leading out of epistemological solipsism and specularism. Yet, an overconfident pragmatism that sees itself as the "survival of the best argument" quickly becomes suspect as soon as it passes itself off as the *sensus communis*. Here, too, just as much as was the case with justificatory, foundationalist theories, the question still remains how not to bracket out the power differentials that sustain concrete speech acts, or how not to become blind to the potential inequality ingrained in power relations. Altering Spivak's remarks on the polyvalence of the term "representation," which can refer to political representation (*Vertretung*) as well as epistemological (re)presentation (*Vorstellung, Darstellung*),[83] one might ask whether such variants of antifoundationalist pragmatism, in relinquishing the second meaning of the word on epistemological grounds, do not also risk giving up reflections on the status of political representation, that is, on who exactly is the subject of the performative utterance and in whose name it is tendered.

It was again Gramsci, not incidentally a linguist by training, who most trenchantly voiced what is still at stake in these language debates when, in his reflections on Italy's Southern Question and the illiteracy rampant among the Italian working classes, he concluded that the "question of language has always been an aspect of the political struggle."[84] For what emerges from a survey of the language conceptions that circulate in our critical field is the conclusion that all are in need of a more diversified reflection on how power is deployed concretely in various registers of language politics.[85] Only a coalition of diverse theories and practices can lay the grounds for a diversified program of discursive activism that draws on the best of what sociolinguistics and legal studies have to offer, that attends to the multilinguistic reality of the Americas, and, in a more global arena, examines the hegemony of English as the new "universal medium," or Esperanto, of communication.[86] Translated into the context of the present, this means that such a new activist program will require spotting the many versions that silence or nonparticipation in democratic discourse can take, improving language learning, listening to the not just "encrypted discourse" of migrants,[87] appreciating the foreignness of languages, not only the mother tongue, and a thinking through of how to balance the democratic right to freedom of speech with the necessary resistance to the rapid spread of hate speech.[88] How to guarantee the conditions within which interlocutors can entertain egalitarian speaking positions in a plurality of cultural and political arenas, and how to recognize their necessary asymmetry or difference will require collaborative techniques of dialogue and a new discourse that go beyond the hegemony of insular language games.

5

VIOLENCE AND INTERPRETATION

Enzensberger's *CivilWars*

The events that took place in Central and Eastern Europe in 1989 to a large extent seemed to confirm Hannah Arendt's prophetic words that the twentieth century would come to be known as "a century of revolutions."[1] The nonviolent mass demonstrations in the East German cities of Leipzig and Dresden for a while at least appeared to reestablish confidence in the power of the people, as well as prove the possibility of peaceful revolutions and new beginnings. Commenting on these events in June 1990, Jürgen Habermas, however, was quick to draw attention to the "mutually exclusive interpretations" to which these revolutionary upheavals and changes had been subjected, ranging from Stalinist, Leninist, and reform-communist revisions to postmodern, anticommunist, and liberal models of explanation.[2] One of the better known interpretive models was Francis Fukuyama's "The End of History?," which gained international notoriety not only for the confidence with which it established the demise of communism as the "unabashed victory of economic and political liberalism,"[3] but also for the curious anachronism with which the events of 1989 were said to present the triumph of the "modern liberal state," whose principles of liberty and equality Hegel had hailed in the 1806 Battle of Jena.[4] Similarly, conservative historians and politicians in Germany – foremost among them Ernst Nolte – celebrated the revolutions of 1989 as the definitive overcoming of "the global civil war started by the Bolsheviks in 1917."[5] Among Germany's left-liberal intelligentsia, by contrast, the collapse of the GDR, together with the utopian potential of an alternative "middle way" democratic socialism, was to lead to a profound cultural crisis, or to what Helmut Dubiel, in a much noted article in *Merkur*, proposed to call "left-wing melancholia."[6] Habermas's position, finally, proved to be more cautionary. Already in 1990, he referred to the changes in Eastern Europe as "revolutions of recuperation," which, in spiraling back to the bourgeois revolutions of the West, did not merely abandon totalitarianism for constitutional democracy, but, on a negative note, uncritically espoused a market economy and consumerism. Rejecting both the jubilant triumph of liberalism and the left-wing melancholia of Wolf Biermann and others, he instead ascribed a critical role to socialism, which was to function as the necessary corrective to liberalism.

Today, these divisive, irreconcilable debates about collapse or regeneration, progressive democratization or the failure of a "middle way" democratic socialism, while not abated, appear to have shifted grounds as politicians and cultural critics instead seek to come to terms with the new nationalisms, ethnic violence, and xenophobia that followed the end of the Cold War bipolar world order. In a recently translated collection of essays, *Civil Wars*,[7] which garnered much critical attention in Great Britain and the United States, German author and essayist Hans Magnus Enzensberger described the wave of violence to have marked the postrevolutionary age as the explosive encounter between "the unprecedented" and the "atavistic."[8] Promising to make sense of a widespread cultural malaise, Enzensberger presented the eruptions of neonationalist and ethnic violence in postrevolutionary Europe as but part of a more global turn to violence and civil war. If in an earlier essay, "Ways of Walking" (1990), Enzensberger could still hail the East German revolution as the radical defeat of Marxist utopianism and as the decisive victory of civil society over state socialism,[9] *Civil Wars* painted a more somber picture, pronouncing the end of revolutions altogether. On this reading, the age of revolutions had been swept away by a new era of violence. Only since the end of the Cold War would it have become possible to lift the mask of these so-called revolutionary uprisings and national liberation wars to expose them for what they really were: civil wars in disguise. Thus, where Ernst Nolte established 1989 as the year that marked liberalism's victorious overcoming of the "global civil war," initiated by Bolshevism, Enzensberger instead seemed to defend a radical cultural pessimism when he *globalized* civil strife. It can hardly come as a surprise, therefore, that Fukuyama took exception to the nihilism that permeated Enzensberger's *Civil Wars*, much as his *The End of History* decried the pessimism of the twentieth century.[10]

Starting from the observation that more than "30 to 40 civil wars [were] being waged openly around the globe,"[11] Enzensberger proceeded to stretch the term beyond its customary meaning to advance it as a new conceptual grid with which to capture such culturally diverse phenomena as interethnic strife, urban unrest, or the gang warfare of inner cities. Whether it be ethnic cleansing in the former Yugoslavia, the 1992 race-related unrest following the Rodney King verdict in South Central Los Angeles, or the resurgence of xenophobia in postunification Germany – all were said to be the most palpable manifestations of a global, molecular civil war. Not only did the postrevolutionary era signal the return to the "primary form of all collective conflict," whose original account could be found in the *History of the Peloponnesian Wars*,[12] but it also introduced a *new* type of civil war, characterized by the absence of clear political goals, plans, or ideas,[13] and by an all-pervasive autism on the part of its perpetrators. Using a language that at times seemed remarkably close to Daniel Bell's pronouncements on the end of ideology, Enzensberger contended that such violence had divorced itself from all ideological foundations. As such, global violence not only announced the end of politics, but it signaled the end of all political models that in the past had either sought to interpret or change the world, from Hegel's struggle for recognition to the Marxist class struggle. What remained instead was naked, "valueless" strife, or the lapse into a Hobbesian state of permanent (civil) war. "All political thought, from Aristotle and Machiavelli to Marx and Weber, is turned upside down."[14] All that remained, Enzensberger wrote, was a negative utopia or "the Hobbesian ur-myth of the war of everyone against everyone else."[15]

Enzensberger's model of the new civil wars is a seductive one, for it not only promised to make sense of random violence, whose manifestations indeed seem to have become ever more prevalent, but it also purported to combine the soundness of what were offered as anthropological observations with claims to newness and historical periodization. It further spoke the language of return and of the encounter between barbarism, primitivism, and modernity, whose entwinement, as anthropologists such as Benedict Anderson have noted, constitutes one of the persistent paradoxes of nationalisms. Further, that violence and fratricide should belong to the ur-myths of mankind is something Hannah Arendt already observed when in *On Revolution* she suggested that the *status naturalis* counted as a "theoretically purified phrase" for the mythical insight, laid down in the tales of Cain and Abel, Romulus and Remus, that "in the beginning was a crime."[16] However, Enzensberger's popularizing discourse of a globalized violence lacked the astuteness of these theoretical models. Not only did it speak to a kind of eschatological cultural pessimism, whose manifestations seemed to become ever more pronounced towards the end of the millennium. But his account also mobilized a quasi-anthropological[17] foundationalism, essentialism, and primitivism that could no longer acknowledge structural, political, or cultural differences, linked as it was to the contention that the new civil wars portended the end of ideology. With the urge to label a new historic era came the leveling of all conceptual or political distinctions between revolutions, riots, upheavals, urban unrest, liberation wars, and uprisings – all rendered as the local outbreaks of a vast molecular civil war. To be sure, this is not to dispute the urgency of what currently is called the "war on violence" or to deny the disquieting number of civil wars in the geopolitical arena, and, even less, to condone the use of violence. Rather, what also warrants critical attention, I would submit, is the ease with which a globalizing discourse on violence, of the sort proposed in *Civil Wars*, tends to erase all structural difference, at the expense of an ability to implement political analysis. Indeed, as I hope to show by placing *Civil Wars*, first, in a German, then in a larger, comparative context, such a globalizing discourse can function as a screen for what are thought to be the flaws of increasingly multicultural or multiethnic societies.

When seen in a German cultural context, Enzensberger's essay might first of all raise questions with regard to the ease with which right-wing incidents, such as the murders of Turkish immigrants in Mölln and Solingen, were presented as symptoms of a global turn to violence. Not only does his analysis remain vulnerable to charges that it follows the conservative strategies sometimes used in the former West German republic and in postunification Germany to progressively normalize and rectify the image of Germany's so-called *Sonderweg*.[18] But his cavalier observations about German neo-Nazism are, if not reminiscent of the technique of historical analogism mobilized during the historians' debate of the 1980s,[19] then at least questionable for the haste with which they foreclose political analysis. In light of such a lack of critical acuity it should not be cause for wonder that the French philosopher André Glucksmann has seen Enzensberger's plea for a return to national and purely German concerns, together with his rejection of an ethics of "universal responsibility," bolstered by the gruesome images of global media news coverage, as the very shirking of historical accountability.[20] As a consequence, Enzensberger's intellectual biography – from his infatuation with the communist revolution in the 1960s to his current defense of a strong state – has been read as symptomatic of the turn to the right that recently, in the figures of such renowned authors as Martin Walser and Botho Strauß, profoundly shook German cultural life.[21]

Insofar as civil wars pit neighbors against neighbors, they always have counted as a significant threat to the body politic.[22] They also form the political limit that any revolution may threaten to cross. Civil wars thus put at risk legitimate violence, traditionally the monopoly of the liberal nation-state, as Benjamin – following Weber – noted in his "Critique of Violence."[23] Enzensberger seemed to imply as much when he observed: "Where the state can no longer enforce its monopoly then everyone must defend himself."[24] Thus, the inability of current governments to cope with civic feuding was said to have been caused by "the retreat of the state."[25] But if in the past terror was still "the monopoly of totalitarian regimes," then "today it returns in a de-nationalized form [in entstaatlichter Form]."[26] In fact, the global civil war in Enzensberger's account became a sort of free-floating violence that, like a "political retrovirus" of sorts,[27] at any point might threaten to spread across national borders. Enzensberger's metaphorical language here is not only problematic because it invoked a register of disease that, towards the end of the essay, would be matched by an ethics of triage, suggesting that there might exist no cure for the sick body politic, only a calculating, strategic coping with immediate social demands. Equally worrisome was the phantasm of the nineteenth-century nation-state, which formed the essay's underlying countermodel. Civil war was said to be devoid of the rationality that still typified classic warfare between nation-states, the laws and logistics of which were laid down in Clausewitz's On War. As such, the new civil wars spelled the end of an "old-style European nationalism,"[28] which, in spite of its imperialist and colonial legacy, was here primarily defended as the sponsor of human rights.

Enzensberger's skewed justification of nineteenth-century nationalism is perhaps less puzzling when seen for what it really is, namely, a covert critique of multiculturalism. To be sure, he seemed acutely aware of the pressing civic, political, and cultural difficulties that face many European nations, including Germany, as governments have proved increasingly incapable of responding adequately to global migrations and demographic changes. Thus, the essay "The Great Migration" at points convincingly argued that it would be erroneous for states to distinguish between economic and political refugees, or to propagate a "preventive migration policy." Other passages, however, appeared to suggest that the new state of civil war fundamentally was the result of a fall from "culture," from whose definition Enzensberger partially expected an answer to the many problems posed by multiculturalism. As a consequence, one might well ask to what extent the *theoretical* model of civil war served as a screen of sorts for what were perceived to be the conflictual, contentious claims of multicultural societies. In a review of potential explanations for the surge in global violence, Enzensberger lent some credence to the thought that the alleged return to the state of nature might have been brought on by claims to ethnic and cultural identity, which, with their competing demands for recognition, had proliferated beyond the frame of reasonableness. Worldwide manifestations of terrorism and religious fundamentalism that sought the enforcement of recognition through the use of violence were but the more extreme manifestations of a fundamental corrosion to have befallen the political concept of recognition, spawning the primitive struggle of all against all.[29] Enzensberger's account in this respect to some extent differed from Fukuyama's *End of History*, which optimistically hallowed political and economic liberalism as the universalization of recognition. Influenced by the Hegel scholar Kojève, who had drawn renewed attention to the "struggle for recognition" at the center of the master-slave dialectic, Fukuyama proposed to read the end of communism as the absolute validation of "universal and reciprocal recognition,"[30] guaranteed by the basic rights of liberal democracy. Enzensberger's *Civil Wars*, in contrast, established the exhaustion of the Hegelian struggle, adding that "the desire for recognition, first in cities and then across the whole world, has gathered a momentum that a certain philosopher in 1806 [i.e., Hegel] could never have dreamed of."[31] And, though he invoked Frantz Fanon, it was not to take stock of the significant modification to which the Antillean psychiatrist and activist had subjected the Hegelian dream of recognition,[32] nor was it to query the limits of what essentially remained a Western perspective. Instead, current eruptions of violence were linked to the self-destruction, aggression-turned-inward, and tribal warfare that determined the first, transitory stage of African decolonization, whose dynamics were defined in *Wretched of the Earth*. In the end, Fanon's discourse on counterviolence was merely adduced as objective proof that the claim to recognition counted as an anthropological given across cultures and societies.[33]

Significantly, the category of recognition has moved to the center of contemporary political and philosophical discussions about multiculturalism, from Charles Taylor's proposal for a more hospitable liberalism that practices a politics of equal respect without "homogenizing difference,"[34] to its thematization in the practical philosophy of Frankfurt School theorists such as Habermas, Honneth, or Benhabib.[35] But while these theorists have tried to modify the category profoundly, seeking to strip it of its apparent claims to symmetry or of its potential power dynamics, *Civil Wars* implicitly rejects such solutions on the grounds that the very demand itself never can be fully gratified. Indeed, Enzensberger thus introduced an infinity to the modality of recognition, whose needs were such that they could never be satisfied as communities produced ever more inequalities. More is at stake here than simple pessimism. By rejecting recognition for being an idealistic trope, never to be fulfilled, Enzensberger again implicitly foreclosed the kind of practical, political solutions offered by Habermas and other social scientists, who, in their interventions in the asylum and multiculturalism debates or in their comments on anti-foreigner violence, have emphasized the need for *legal* recognition. In his dialogues with Charles Taylor, for example, Habermas asserted that there could exist no fundamental contradiction between individual rights and the recognition of collective identities, once one has "a democratic understanding of the actualization of basic rights."[36] This presupposed that one think through the relation between ethics and legal recognition, that is, between "the ethical substance of a constitutional patriotism" and "the legal system's neutrality vis-à-vis communities that are ethically integrated at a sub-political level."[37] Applied to the German situation this meant that only once the Federal Republic had decided to become a genuinely political rather than an ethnic community could it take leave of the prepolitical conception of nationhood that still marred the euphoria of the unifica- tion.[38] Only if the Federal Republic would change its citizenship laws, which were still largely determined by the so-called 1913 blood laws,[39] and repealed the restrictions placed on asylum rights by the 1993 amendment to the Basic Law, would it be able to guarantee recognition through legal equality. In effect, Germany would then reach "a national self-understanding that is no longer based on ethnicity but founded on citi- zenship."[40]

Written in the early 1990s, Habermas's intervention targeted the conservative course sailed by the Kohl government, which refused to define Germany as "a country of immigration," as he called for a drastic reconsideration of older ethico-political values that still guided Germany's interpretation and actualization of basic rights. To some extent, Habermas's plea for such a radical legal and political transformation of citizenship laws was partially realized in the fall of 1998, when Gerhard Schröder's Social Democratic Party and the Greens announced a thorough reform of citizenship laws – though subsequent restrictions placed on who will qualify for dual citizenship have been much criticized.[41] Still, judging from the civic debates about the integration of immigrants currently underway or the input from emerging, progressive multi- ethnic youth cultures, all signs are there that the unified Germany is engaged in a complex but fruitful discussion of what a multicultural society in the new century might look like.

Clearly, this is not the last word on the issue of legal recognition. Though such political changes give cause for optimism, alterations in the law may prove ineffective as long as they are not actualized on the ethical level, affecting mores, customs, and daily social practices. Despite the accomplishments of civil rights and other social struggles, formal legal rights cannot automatically safeguard against exclusionary or discriminatory applications of the law. Nor does racial justice prevent day-to-day discrimination – a point driven home by the Critical Race Theory group in its reflec- tions on the 1992 upheavals that took place in South Central Los Angeles. The frame-by-frame breakdown and disaggregation of the Rodney King video in the court room, the collective suggested, could stand as an allegory for the ways in which questions of power, the law, and interpretation are still largely dissociated from one another in many liberal societies. Equally compelling was their claim that much was at stake indeed in whether the South Central Los Angeles incidents were called "riots" – following the dominant cultural narrative – or, alternatively, "insurrections" – as the counternarrative had it – that is, "as a communal response to a much larger set of issues of social power."[42]

As unquestionably as the Los Angeles events resulted in violence, they are to be read, then, not as outbreaks of a global civil war, as Enzensberger had it, but as symptomatic of "our nation," as Cornel West has suggested. West, to be sure, rejected both the labels "race riot" and "class rebellion" for the Los Angeles incidents, qualifying this "monumental upheaval" instead as "a multiracial, trans-class, and largely male display of justified social rage."[43] Yet, much like the Critical Race Theory group, West focused on the incidents' symbolic representation and narrative interpretation in the media. For despite their deep-seated ideological differences, he argued, the dominant cultural narratives mostly singled out "the problems of black people" rather than "the flaws of American society," thus failing to understand that "the presence and predicaments of black people are neither additions to nor defections from American life, but rather *constitutive elements of that life*."[44] The true challenge the Los Angeles upheavals fundamentally presented was "whether a genuine multiracial democracy can be created and sustained in an era of global economy and a moment of xenophobic frenzy."[45]

As the political complexity of these and other incidents demonstrates, then, it will not do simply to reduce such foundational rifts to irrational outbreaks of rage or violence, as *Civil Wars* inadvertently seemed to imply. If anything, Enzensberger's text still begs the question of the interpretational grid within which disparate political and social events are placed. Even if we may not yet have managed to change the world significantly, neither should we stop examining the way we interpret it.

6

ETHICS OF THE OTHER

It is a long time since the starry sky that took away Kant's breath revealed the last of
its secrets to us. And the moral law is not certain of itself.

Frantz Fanon, *Black Skin, White Masks*

Marx, misquoting Hegel, once observed that all events in world history, including
revolutions, happen at least twice, first as tragedy, then as their comic, parodic reenactment, or farce.[1] Perhaps the same can be said about philosophical models of
interpretation. For if, in our postsocialist, post-Marxist condition, the demise or
deficit of the Marxist project, as embodied in state socialism, has become apparent,
then it also seems that the specter of Hegel, hiding behind the figure of Marx, has
returned to haunt us with renewed force.[2] Hegel returns not just once, but many
times, and in many guises. Donning a conservative cloak, mediated and altered
through Kojève, Hegel has been invoked to assert the "end of history," or the coming
of eschatological posthistory, as Fukuyama did in his notoriously wrong-headed
triumphalist defense of a globalized liberalism.[3] However, as the ally of more left-
leaning liberals, Hegel's chapter on self-consciousness, especially the section on the
master–slave dialectic from the *Phenomenology of Spirit*, has been mined for its models
of recognition (*Anerkennung*), intersubjectivity, and alterity, which, it seems, never
have been more popular than at present.

Yet, if Hegel still is very much *with us*, then it is, to be sure, not so much because of
the first economic, still feudal contract of inequity that followed on the heels of the life-
and-death combat between self and other – a social contract whose measures of
economic inequality, for the longest time, formed the target of the Marxist program.
Even when Laclau and Mouffe drafted their programmatic study on hegemony, pointing
to the necessary displacement of the universalizing category of class by the multiple
subject positions of the new social movements – those that rallied around race, gender
or ecology – they still very much did so within an amended Marxist paradigm. Today, by
contrast, it is Hegel's struggle for recognition *as such* (*an sich*), uncoupled from socio-
economic inequity, or the need for redistribution,[4] that has moved to the heart of
dialogues between liberals of various persuasions, be they of the neo-Aristotelian,

communitarian mold, such as Charles Taylor, or those who have joined the cause of Jürgen Habermas's discourse ethics. These authors' positions attest to the undiminished topicality of recognition – witness their respective interventions in the multicultur- alism debates, collected in *Multiculturalism: Examining the Politics of Recognition*.[5] Conducted in the tall shadow cast by Hegel's *Phenomenology*, the exchange between Taylor, Habermas, Appiah, and others, demonstrated that "recognition" did not simply refer to an act of identification, to the gleam of pleasure the infant's face shows as it discerns itself in the mirror, nor to the glance of recognition that lights up in the eye of the other as I pass by, nor simply to the conferring of respect or prestige on an-other. In the final analysis, it signaled the demand for universal *political* recognition, or equal respect, premised on the equitable actualization of the system of rights that modern liberal democracies advocate. As Appiah phrased it, at stake was "a politics that asks us to acknowledge *socially* and *politically* the authentic identities of others."[6] To recognize in this sense didn't only mean to acknowledge an individual's or group's identity or authenticity existentially, but, crucially, to vindicate the other politically and institu- tionally, as the bearer of equal rights. But where this liberal narrative of universal, reciprocal political recognition in a fictional past of pure origins and unalloyed homogeny seemed straightforward enough, then, today – so the narrative continues – multicultural democracies struggle due to the proliferation of such demands. In Taylor's stark rendition, the multiculturalism debates appear to come to a head in the confronta- tion between two equally unbending, even adversarial positions, the one vying to assert absolute difference (identity politics), the other, "color-blind" sameness (neo-Kantian proceduralism). In this view, the model underlying these conflictual interpretations of recognition appears to be that of reflection, in which either the mirror of *sameness* is held up to the other – as when "color-blind" liberals promote a neutral liberalism – or else radical *difference* and asymmetry between self and other are asserted.

But is it quite clear what we mean when we speak of recognizing the other? Who, indeed, is the other, and what does recognition, or misrecognition, for that matter, entail? And why the need to consider, across the multiculturalism debates, as I want to claim, an ethics of the other? To be sure, much of twentieth-century philosophy and liberation politics can be seen as an attempt to undo epistemic and ontological regimes of the self that violate the alterity of the other, from Husserl's phenomenolog- ical conception of the alter ego, Buber's dialogical philosophy of I and Thou, and Levinas's asymmetric other, to Lacanian psychoanalysis and deconstruction. Of the many variants of what collectively has come to be called the "philosophy of the other," some have been founded on a theologically conceived dialogism, others on a Hegelian conception of intersubjectivity, sometimes mediated through Sartre's existentialism. But all have sought to bid farewell to the monologism of a Cartesian philosophy of consciousness no less than Kant's anti-instrumental, nonstrategic moral philosophy, whose universalizable categorical imperative – even as it mandated that the other be regarded as an end in herself, not a means – could not safeguard against the imposition of violence onto the other, as Benjamin already knew.[7] No matter how diverse these proposals for thinking the other may have been, one problem in particular invariably has plagued them. Put in simplest terms: how to combine a commitment to the universal recognition of others – whether it be a matter of ethical, cultural, or legal recognition – with a respect for the concrete particularism, difference, or asymmetry of others? How to dispel the figment of the "generalized other" that dominates substantialist versions of universalism in order to acknowledge particularized others? How to avoid the presumed ethnic, class, or gender bias that comes with imagining, let alone, recognizing the other?[8] And, additionally, how not to rarefy the otherness of the other to such a degree that she is turned into an abstract alterity (slipping from the position of other, or *autrui*, back into the reified, objectified *autre*)?[9] Lastly, and most crucially, in what way to redress the epistemic violence enacted by hegemonic Western discourses that silence or slight the subaltern other?[10]

The purpose of this inquiry cannot be to stage a grand genealogy of the other – a pursuit that quickly risks yielding yet another transhistoric metanarrative. Nor is it my aim, as the title of this chapter might misleadingly suggest, to retrace Levinas's foot-steps by arguing for an "ethics of the other" as first philosophy.[11] Instead, I wish to approach the matter more locally, across some of the multiculturalism debates, with an eye on qualifying the prominence that Hegel's struggle for recognition has gained in liberal variants of these discussions. For, first, if the goal is to design a more hospitable liberalism, one that can accommodate difference, as Taylor seems to want to do in his "The Politics of Recognition," then it might be expedient to invite interlocutors to the debating table who traditionally have been excluded from such deliberations – inter-locutors such as the Antillean psychiatrist, revolutionary, and activist philosopher, Frantz Fanon. To be sure, Taylor briefly cites Fanon approvingly to demonstrate that "misrecognition" ought to be added to the catalog of harms that can be inflicted upon others, in addition to "inequality, exploitation, and injustice." Fanon's forceful indict-ment of Western colonialism in his *Wretched of the Earth*, he agrees, rightly charged "that the major weapon of the colonizers was the imposition of their image of the colonized on the subjugated people."[12] Nonetheless, it seems to me that Fanon's work deserves a lengthier discussion and reappraisal, not in the least because he explicitly wrote a response to Hegelian philosophy in an essay titled "The Negro and Recognition"[13] – an essay that sought not so much to stand Hegel's master–slave dialectic back on its feet (to cite Marx's favorite figure of reversal) as to undo it radi-cally. Even more worthy of note, I will suggest, is that Fanon's major works merit being rediscovered as a large-scale probe into the conditions of possibility that enable ethics and the moral law in a postcolonial context, and, by extension, in our multicul-tural condition.[14] This position, admittedly, is at first less obvious if one only zeroes in on Fanon's incendiary, antiliberal embrace of revolutionary violence, which he advo-cated as he found himself in the throes of the colonial struggle in Algeria.

Second, by isolating the question of recognition as it inflects these debates, I will suggest that multiculturalism – at least, in one of its moments – ought to be reinter-preted as *multi-ethics*, if indeed that elusive noun "ethics" – should one obey the laws of the English grammar – bears being used in the plural. This is why the title of this chapter deliberately invokes at once a subjective and objective genitive, referring not only to an ethics *about* the other, but also to an ethics *belonging* to the other, or more precisely, *others*. If one extrapolates from this position, it follows that for a radical democracy multiculturalism involves not merely the cohabitation of multiple cultures, ethnic groups, or identities, with their respective claims to authenticity, equal dignity, respect, rights, or economic equity; the challenge relates also to how the coexistence of many versions of *ēthos*, ethical habits, conventions, gestures, and (substantivist) narratives about the "good life" is still possible in a rationalized modern world. As such, the question about identity and identification raised earlier – "Who is the other?" – must now be compounded by the query, "Whose ethics?" – a question that reverberates with Chantal Mouffe's similarly probing inquiry: which ethics for democracy?[15]

Third, it seems to me that, taken together and scrutinized against the letter of Hegel's text, the current multiculturalism debates in their manifold, contentious manifestations at once provide vastly diverse, often incompatible but always revealing renditions of Hegel's chapter on self-consciousness, depending on whether they call up the specter of violence or emphasize intersubjective, peaceful cohabitation instead. It can hardly be cause for wonder, naturally, that conservative accounts stress the element of violent battle in the struggle, most crassly perhaps in Fukuyama's *End of History*. Multicultural difference here signals the possible relapse into a bellicose state of nature, a battle reminiscent of Carl Schmitt's *The Concept of the Political* in which "us" and "them," rather than being engaged in dialogical encounter, divide into friend and enemy, mutually threatened by the possible existentialist experience of one's imminent death. In the margins, it might be noted that this conservative take inadvertently also resonates in the somewhat overused, seemingly benign term "culture wars," which currently, together with "Balkanization," circulates in critical circles, as if cultures were at war with one another, tribalisms, locked in mortal strife, all contending for ascendance. Deleting this implicit bellicose intent from the Hegelian allegory, liberal positions, by contrast, have focused on selves being drawn out of them-selves in peaceful encounters with others, and in some instances – if they have pondered the potential sublation, even obliteration, of alterity that might come with an unreflected liberal stance – have unmasked the possible blots of misrecognition that always threaten to impair any such acts of recognition.

Though liberal accounts have sought to remain true to the democratic principle of nonviolence, an element of strife almost unintentionally has come to define the exchange between interlocutors. Certainly, in Taylor's communitarian account identity politics and procedural, so-called color-blind liberalism are rift apart by a logic of mutual contradiction, in which the particularism of identity claims propagated in the name of group rights is at odds with a difference-leveling universalism that adheres to basic rights. Thus, in discussing neo-Kantian procedural liberalism – especially in its Rawlsian and Dworkian variants – Taylor reasserts his allegiance to a neo-Aristotelian communitarianism, which criticizes the preference of formal rights over substantive goods. Procedural formalism, according to him, is deficient because it must reject all identity politics for proffering particularistic claims that are not automatically universalizable. To craft a more hospitable liberalism that will avert the inadequacies of its leveling procedural counterpart, he therefore proposes that the politics of equal respect be complemented by the recognition of a minority culture's equal value. Paired off against one another, procedural and communitarian versions of liberalism thus can be seen to be representative of the conventional distinction made between Kant's moral theory (*Moralität*) and Hegel's *Sittlichkeit* (ethical life), or between a monological understanding of moral reasoning and an intersubjective, dialogical interpretation of community. In overcoming the deficiencies of Kant's subjective idealism, it is commonly held, Hegel showed the path away from an atomistic conception of the self – despite remedial categories, such as "empathy" or "enlarged mentality,"[16] meant to correct the Kantian subject's monadic self-enclosure – to a model that defined the self as constitutively directed towards the other. As he demonstrated in the *Phenomenology*, the state of a consciousness-in-and-for-itself (*an und für sich*) could only be reached through the double movement of two forms of consciousness, which "*recognize* themselves as mutually recognizing one another."[17] In altered guise, these two seemingly mutually exclusive renditions of subjecthood, one Kantian, the other Hegelian, still imbue the encounters between neo-Kantian liberals and civic republican communitarians, the first wedded to honoring individual rights, the second to giving priority to a collective, neo-Aristotelian *ēthos* to which such rights are bound. That the two positions need not necessarily be mutually exclusive is certainly one of the repeated points Habermas makes in his contribution to the debate, as he does elsewhere. Occupying the middle ground between the two, his procedural discourse ethics has sought to mediate between Kantian and Hegelian practical philosophy, wedding justice to solidarity, and proposing "an intersubjective interpretation of the categorical imperative by taking over Hegel's theory of recognition, but without dissolving the moral in the ethical." Insofar as for Habermas private and public autonomy are inherently and necessarily entwined, the Kantian misconception of reading basic rights morally, that is, "as the legal expression of the mutual respect that persons ought to show one another as morally autonomous agents,"[18] is thereby also overcome. In shifting the emphasis away from Taylor's still all too abstract discussion of basic or group rights to their contextualized actualization, Habermas certainly makes visible the ethical fabric that must inexorably sustain any procedural recognition of the other.

Now, in using, in what follows, the term "ethics" rather than "moral law," I assume the philosophical convention that defines these debates, of distinguishing Kant's *Moralität* from Hegel's *Sittlichkeit*, understood as an intersubjective, dialogical conception of community. Centrally, Kant and Hegel also very much define the two poles between which Fanon wrote his major works, insofar as he took his theory of "violence as imposition" from Hegel's struggle for recognition, while holding on to the

Kantian dream of universalism. What I will seek to do, then, in invoking Fanon's thought as an alternative vantage point from which to gauge the multiculturalism debates, is to ask what its conventional, mainly First World interlocutors might learn from his work, hinged as it is between Kant and Hegel. Given the need for pluralist democracies that can come to terms with multiculturalism, how might Fanon complicate the existing dialogue between speech partners? Further, how might his writings intensify attempts to grapple with the dialectic between ethnic, cultural particularism and universalism? Asking about Fanon's unabated, contemporary relevance also has the added advantage, crucially, of restoring him to his proper place as a philosopher who desired to be remembered for the intrinsic political value of his contributions, beyond the particularism of the historical condition to which he refused to be reduced. By reclaiming the theory of recognition from Hegel, Marx, but also Lacan, Fanon at once sought to take back the dream of a true universalism in which he demanded his rightful place to participate. In revisiting the corpus of his work from this less common perspective, I will argue that his thought, first of all, lends credibility to the suspicion that liberalism in many ways still works with a monolithic understanding of recognition, one that neglects the power dynamics or different modalities of recognition that Hegel articulated in the master–bondsman relationship. Going against domesticated liberal narratives of the Hegelian dialectic, Fanon asks us to reconsider the pernicious power relations, the dynamics of subordination, and the deep antagonisms that imbue pluralistic difference.[19] Against this background, I will seek to lend new currency to a psychoanalytic phrase Fanon coined, that of *ethical transit* [*glissement*] – a term that might be understood to refer to the operations of *ethical transitivism*, or the unconscious identification with uncontested hegemonic subject positions, which burden certain liberal scripts of recognition. Lastly, Fanon also urges us to revisit the overdetermined, embattled term "universalism," whose prominence in current political arguments in many ways seems to be another version of the humanism controversies of earlier decades. Certainly, Fanon's relevance for the recognition debates might be contested on the grounds that his advocacy of violence stands in stark contrast to the doctrines of nonviolence advocated by Gandhi, Nehru, or King. Yet, only if one focuses uniquely on his embrace of revolutionary violence must one fail to see the prophetic philosophy of recognition that overarched all of what he wrote.[20] In more than one way, his thought points us to the interrelations between the ethical and the political at the center of the multiculturalism debates.

Contextualizing the Struggle for Recognition

In view of the prominence Hegel's struggle for recognition recently has gained, one does well to contemplate the plurality of Hegel commentaries that for the longest time have existed side by side, in addition to political liberalism's better-known exegesis, which emphasizes intersubjectivity, normativity, and political (legal) recognition, at the expense, quite often (though by no means always) of the dynamics of

191

power. Surely one of the most provocative, no less than troubling texts to have been generated by Western philosophical modernity, Hegel's philosophical parable of self and other, encapsulated in the *Phenomenology*'s section on self-consciousness, from the start lent itself to an unusually broad spectrum of interpretations, of which the Marxist variant is undoubtedly the better-known one. Where more conventional, contractarian readings understood the section to allude to the overcoming of the state of nature, following Hobbes's *Leviathan*, Marx interpreted the ensuing social contract as typical of prepolitical, premodern feudal societies, while Kojève would offer an anthropologized account of the allegory's scene of violence. In placing unusual emphasis on how existentialist human action proceeded by means of negating violence, Kojève would prove to have an inordinate influence on generations of pre- and postwar intellectuals. Rejecting this Eurocentric account for adulating bare violence and self-fulfillment through forceful subordination, the writings of David Brion Davis, Orlando Patterson, and Paul Gilroy have established how the Hegelian narrative can be interpreted as a vindication of Western colonialism and slavery.[21] Conjecturing that "the time has come for the primal history of modernity to be recon-stituted from the slaves' point of view," Gilroy especially has called for a heightened awareness of how the Hegelian dialectic functions as the deep structure not just of Western subjecthood but also of hegemonic articulations of its history.[22]

What has occupied generations of Hegel interpreters is precisely the fact that he did not conceive of the "self coming to it-self," or self-consciousness, as a process that transpired in monadic isolation, but as one that was mediated, reflected – quite liter-ally – through the eyes and presence of another. In doing so, Hegel moved from an *ontological* dialectic between same and otherness (*das Andere*), examined early on in the chapter, to an *existential* encounter between self and other, that is, to a reflexive confrontation with a personified other (*der Andere*).[23] This encounter with the other, however, as he affirmed, was fraught from the outset by the prospect of violence. Reworking Hobbes's account of the *status naturalis*, Hegel's grand narrative about self-consciousness chronicled the first violent encounter between two only seemingly self-contained beings, their ensuing, potentially mortal combat, and their eventual decision to turn the forceful battle into a power balance that mediated two socially determined positions: mastery and servitude. In effect, several tempos punctuated the process through which the subject laid claim to the universal truth of self-consciousness, the first ruled by specular symmetry, the other – the so-called social dialectic – rift by a wrenching asymmetry. Initially projected along the mechanisms of a mirror reflec-tion, the original dialectic between self and other staged the dynamics between two participants who gained self-enhancement through an interactive mediating process of mutual recognition. Describing what he termed a process of duplication (*Verdopplung*), Hegel observed that, in this stage, "each sees the *other* do the same as it does," only to conclude that, eventually, "they *recognize* themselves as *mutually recognizing* one another."[24] Or, to reiterate Hegel's chiastic turn of phrase, "I" turns out to be "we," "we" "I." Almost immediately, however, a dramatic change upset the seeming equanimity and balance of the scene. A moment of disharmony entered the stage, a radical inequality that, on the face of it, was generated by force or violence, as self and other became antagonists, locked in mortal combat. Remarkably, the fierce battle upon life and death that ensued in truth was said to enact the self's bid for freedom through a trial by death. But for all the battle's fury, in the end ultimate death was averted as the elimination of both adversaries would result in mutual abstract negation and objectification, a dead unity that lacked the dialectical tension between extremes. Instead, what had started out as a battle of forces now transformed into a power relation of domination and subordination, establishing the socially defined (institution-alized) positions of master and bondsman. In this asymmetrical dialectic, the master, through the mediation of the serf's labor, could satiate his desire for the (manufac-tured) object, while the serf for his part, paradoxically, gained freedom through self-consciousness in servile labor, thus also overcoming his fear of death.

Though this compact, slightly narrativized rendition of the master–slave dialectic hardly does justice to the parable's philosophical complexity, it will serve the purpose of throwing some of its elements into starker relief. Ultimately, the Hegelian passage demonstrated that there existed not just one single mode of recognition – as liberal renditions of the allegory all too often fail to acknowledge – but various modalities, depending on whether one was recognized as master or bondsman. Furthermore, it is precisely in the switch from radical symmetry in *equality* to asymmetry in *inequality*, engendered through the initiation of force, that lies the potential for the highly diver-gent interpretations these few pages have received, historically speaking. Particularly pernicious have been those commentaries that have isolated the dialectic of violence, turning it into an anthropological justification of an eternal human nature, mapped, subsequently, onto an existentialist fold of subjecthood, or – more likely – onto a masculinity that masquerades as the universal mean. Indeed, as noted, in Kojève's highly anthropologized, even vitalistic reading of Hegel, the mortal combat gained immoderate precedence to the point where violence no longer merely referred to the lawlessness of the state of nature, but transformed into the most primordial human deed. Modeled on Genesis, the act of human creation transformed "the world that is hostile to a human project into a world in harmony with this project." At once "humanizing and anthropogenetic," explained Kojève, such action amounted to "the act of imposing oneself on the 'first' other man one meets," resulting in reciprocal violence.[25] To be sure, Kojève sincerely was interested in the "end of war," or the end of human negating action, believing in Hegel's diagnosis that the Napoleonic era spelled the "end of history." Yet it was precisely through his description of the negating principle that defined human action, desire, and freedom that he would impact Sartre, Lacan, but also Fanon. Divesting Kojève's Hegel reading of its existentialist aura, Fukuyama teased out its conservative program when he mapped the "end of history" onto the post-Cold War triumph of liberalism. On first impression, his philosophico-political interpretation seemed seductive enough as it postulated that "the end of history," or the end of totalitarian violence, meant universalized equality, the recognition of all on a "mutual and equal basis."[26] The French Revolution, as Hegel announced, but also the American one, had turned "slaves into masters" through the politics of citizenship and the granting of rights. Yet, such seemingly moderate, plausible pronouncements were accompanied by the disconcerting logic of a difference-obliterating liberalism and a belief in presentism, as the "now" of the present was turned into the realization, actualization of a universalized liberalism.[27] In teasing out the Nietzschean strands in Kojève, Fukuyama in fact operated with two models of recognition – a good and a bad one: one, in which the struggle for life disintegrated into a Hobbesian or Nietzschean "state of nature" – a battle waged by the last men, revolving around pure prestige and pure materialism, whose contemporary variant Fukuyama discerned in the material pursuits of inner-city youths; the other, the true liberal one, which welded economic prosperity to *thymos* (Plato's version of self-esteem) and was realized in the posthistorical world of a correctly understood liberalism. As a further sign of this framework's conservatism, cultural diversity was put on a par with a troublesome relativism, as especially came to the fore in the book's concluding chapter. Arguing against "cultural relativism," Fukuyama actively advocated the convergence or "homogenization of mankind" so that in the end "the apparent differences between peoples' 'languages of good and evil' will appear to be an artifact of their particular stage of historical development."[28] Rather, then, than finding an ethical philosophy of the other in Fukuyama's work, we encounter a conservative moralistic frame, one that not only threatened to eliminate pluralism or difference but confused ideological globalization with universalism.

In more positive Hegel commentaries, in contrast, principally in the variants designed by Frankfurt School theorists Jürgen Habermas and Axel Honneth, the emphasis has been placed on how the section fits within Hegel's broader theory of intersubjectivity.[29] Above all, Hegel was seen to pave the way for a profound reconceptualization of normativity, which was no longer justified abstractly, but realized communicatively. Indeed, in *The Philosophical Discourse of Modernity* Habermas maintained that the young Hegel, in crafting his budding new theory of intersubjectivity, proved potentially far more radical, even in his early Jena philosophy, than the mature philosopher of the *Phenomenology* and *Philosophy of Right*. In the stress that Hegel's juvenile writings, such as "The Spirit of Christianity and Its Fate," placed on "just fate," love, and life, Habermas detected the early seeds of a "communicative reason," lodged against Kant's subjective reflection and abstract practical reason. But this potentially explosive insight – so Habermas, and in his wake Honneth, argued – was quelled when later he recuperated intersubjectivity by assimilating it into the constitution of self-consciousness. Eventually, the model of intersubjectivity thus was subjected to the laws of absolute spirit, so that the *Phenomenology*, in truth, ended up advancing a "critique of subjectivity puffed up into an absolute power."[30] To do so meant not simply to sublate the alterity of the other into the selfsame, but furthermore to lapse into the entrapments of a philosophy of consciousness and reflection. By slipping into the model of self-consciousness, Hegel, not unlike Kant, eventually proved unable to escape the philosophy of reflection. Evidently, Habermas was not interested in gleaning from the passage on self-consciousness a contractarian political model, or a parable of social alienation, the way the young Marx did in his early Paris manuscripts, the older in *Capital*. Rather, his main point was that by embedding intersubjectivity in the specular formation of self-consciousness, Hegel perpetuated the metaphysical violence endemic to the idealistic philosophy of consciousness. Struggling against this tradition, Habermas for his part sought to overcome its metaphysical legacy by turning to language philosophy, pragmatism, in discourse ethics. As he elaborated further on Habermas's comments, Honneth similarly jettisoned Marx's labor paradigm and concern with economic redistribution, seeking to distill "the foundations for a social theory with normative content"[31] out of Hegel's struggle for recognition. Minimizing the importance of the social struggle, Honneth instead aimed for a theory of communicative action, anchored in a "concept of morally motivated struggle," of which there were three forms: love, law, and solidarity (or love, rights, and esteem). Marx's interest in economic competition and inequity, he declared, exposed the predominance of a utilitarian streak in his thought to the detriment of the more fundamental moral struggle. [32]

Interested in the moral struggle for recognition more so than in the social struggle for economic redistribution, Habermas and Honneth condemned Hegel's lapse back into subject philosophy. But however plausible their historicized Hegel reading might be, it should not detract from the fact that, in the move to self-consciousness, Hegel's *Phenomenology* spelled the very truth of a psychic regime of power or force,[33] as elucidated by the use to which his dialectic of recognition has been put in psychoanalytic theory. For, however erroneous it might seem, judged from Habermas's standpoint, to read the chapter on self-consciousness as a process of *psychogenesis*, Lacan nonetheless put the error to great benefit, when, along Hegelian lines, he demonstrated the specularity, or *misrecognition* (*méconnaissance*), that lies at the foundation of the first constitution of the ego in the mirror phase – the phase in which a primordial *imago* is fashioned, refracted through the other. Misrecognition can, as Taylor pointed out, manifest itself as the withholding of equal respect, or as the false projection of the self onto the other, a moment that Lacan, via his own reading of Hegelian self-consciousness, saw as constitutive of a first, so-called presocial identification, which yielded the Ideal-I, mediated through the image of the other.[34] In fact, by displacing these Hegelian and Lacanian systems in turn into the realities of the colonial struggle, the Antillean psychiatrist Fanon corrected them even further, revising them by means of a sociogenic (not just phylogenetic or ontogenetic) account that demonstrated how this primordial moment of "recognition in mis-recognition" among colonial subjects really came about through the pathogenic incorporation of the white other as Ideal-I.

Fanon's Ethics of Recognition

Fanon's multifaceted Hegel interpretation certainly can count as one of the more complex adaptations of that narrative, as it interweaves psychoanalytic, existentialist, and Marxist strands of analysis.[35] In all of his works, Fanon advocated an "ethics of recognition," though in the period of anticolonial activism his message went hiding under the very force with which he sought to set an end to colonialism's imposition of force, striving to rupture the colonizer's cycle of violence. His was a philosophy animated by the sincere, albeit utopian belief that it might be possible to recapture a new concrete, universalist humanism that would once and for all supplant its earlier, abstract parody, or farce, though this should never happen at the expense of recognizing diverse cultural identities, whether it be the literary movement of *négritude* or the culture of the *Maghreb*.

Familiar with Hegel's philosophy through Hyppolite's translation of the *Phenomenology*, Kojève's lecture courses, and Sartre's *Being and Nothingness*, Fanon radically refracted the dialectic of recognition through the colonial experience. The new understanding he furnished of the Hegelian paradigm comprised two distinct phases. First, prior to his active involvement in Algeria's anticolonial struggle, his psychoanalytic essays – collected in *Black Skin, White Masks* – used Hegel to amend Adler's inferiority complex and correct Lacan's mirror stage, all in an attempt to diagnose the defective self-image of the Antillean subject. Already here, before his revolutionary activism, he illuminated how Hegel's master–slave dialectic might be comprehended not just as a fictional parable but as a philosophical justification of real Western colonialism. Second, in the revolutionary phase of *Wretched of the Earth*, he further teased out the implications of Hegel's "violence of imposition" and the frenzied desire for substitution it awakened in the colonized native, likening the colonial experience to the Hobbesian state of nature. Additionally, he brought the model of recognition to bear on Marxism, whose view of the class struggle and the role of the *Lumpenproletariat* needed to be altered, making it fit to account not only for the inequalities in economic distribution, but also for colonial racism and the process of decolonization. Still, it would be a gross misconception to label Fanon's work on recognition, as it emerges from these writings, as simply "reactive," written out of "ressentiment" by an (elite) colonized intellectual – to invoke the odious Nietzschean rhetoric he himself frequently deployed in *Black Skin, White Masks*. To say so would mean to imply that he remained purely "fixated," traumatized, by the particularism that defined his historical position. Rather, in reclaiming the theory of recognition from Hegel, Lacan, but also Marx, Fanon at once sought to take back the dream of a true universalism, articulated through the cultural particularism of the Antillean subject.

In *Black Skin, White Masks*, Fanon demonstrated how the primordial process of "recognition in mis-recognition" among colonial but also postcolonial subjects involved the pathogenic incorporation of the white other as Ideal-I. Writing the psychopathology of everyday colonial life, Fanon historicized Lacan's phenomenological reading of Hegel, which emphasized the specular dynamics that informed the look of recognition. As he entered the phenomenal world of the white gaze, Fanon wrote, the black subject was rejected at the level of body image, stigmatized as the unidentifiable, unassimilable not-self, the *non-semblable*, who represented absolute alterity in nonhuman form. But this phenomenological experience for the Antillean, he continued, proved hardly analogous to that of the exemplary white subject, insofar as, on the imaginary level, he perceived his fellow black neighbor not in absolute but in comparative white terms. In the long corrective footnote he dedicated to Lacan's mirror stage, Fanon further compounded the fictionality that already structured the process of ego formation, adding yet another frame, which resulted in a double displacement of the imaginary, so to speak. If the process of ego formation already involved the alienating assumption of the *imago* of one's *semblable*, then in the colonized subject it additionally entailed the adoption of the white double as "Ideal-I," yielding the imaginary of the imaginary, so that the process of alienation was raised to the second degree. Beleaguered by an internalized inferiority complex and weak ego, the Antillean subject became an obsessional neurotic, engaged in constant self-reproach, nausea, and despair, provoked by the incorporated *imago* that obsessed him.[36] As his traumatic experience in metropolitan Paris indisputably revealed, Fanon's face-to-face with the little white child that named his difference from the white norm resulted in the fragmentation of his body image, lending a new meaning to the aggression inherent in the Hegelian battle for recognition.

In an effort to reverse this specular dynamic of *méconnaissance*, Fanon called his book a mirror that was meant to reflect this "unconscious" alienation back to the Antillean subject, so as to end it once and for all.[37] By advancing a Nietzschean genealogy of colonial morals, he intended to bring the "Manicheism delirium"[38] of colonialism and its neurosis of ethics into full view. To be sure, Hegel – so Fanon observed, paraphrasing the *Phenomenology* – had posited that "man is human only to the extent to which he tries to impose his existence on another man in order to be recognized by him."[39] But in imposing his existence onto the black slave – so Fanon continued, now reading Hegel through Nietzsche's *Genealogy of Morals* – the white master at once had instituted a pathological, dualistic moral system. Along lines similar to Nietzsche's transvaluation of values, Fanon posited that the result of this "imposition of culture" was the forceful impressing of contingent values onto the Antillean subject, as a result of which he, structurally speaking, could only see himself as defined by "mere comparison." Alluding, no doubt, to the psychological phenomenon of transitivism, known in child psychology as a child's inadvertent imitation, mimicry, of another child's gestures or affects, Fanon added that such cultural imposition effected what he termed an ethical transit (*glissement*)[40] in the Antillean subject. The result of an unconscious identification with a white moral agent, this phenomenon of ethical transitivism pointed to the surreptitious mechanism through which the colonial subject split off his black self, turning it into a Kleinian abject object of disgust and moral depravity. Indeed, what else, one might again ask, did Fanon relive in the well-known scene, when the white child pointed in horror at him – what else did he relive than the exemplary reenactment of this traumatic scene of moral splitting?

In *Black Skin, White Masks*, Fanon sought to remedy the internalized colonialism that persisted in the postcolonial Antillean subject, doing so via the intellectual work of *désalienation*, laboring on a revised cultural theory that, in helping to undo the Antillean subject's *misrecognition* of self, might operate as effective therapeutic ideology critique. Essentially, he sought to release the black subject from the neuroses in which he remained trapped, the captive of too much memory – for Freud the predicament of the hysteric – prisoner of a particularist past that blocked off equal access to the universal. Yet, Fanon's application of the Hegelian dialectic in *Black Skin, White Masks* was, at the very least, overdetermined. In the introduction he clearly stated, "man is not merely a possibility of recapture or of negation," adding: "If it is true that consciousness is a process of transcendence, we have to see too that this transcendence is haunted by the problems of love and understanding. Man is a *yes* that vibrates to cosmic harmonies."[41] It is, then, between the aspiration to attain such transcendence in love and understanding, on the one side, and the negativity of force, on the other, that his dis-alienating project oscillated. That for Fanon the Antillean could only attain self-consciousness by resorting to violence clearly emerged in "The Negro and Hegel," a subsection of the essay "The Negro and Recognition." Having established the psychological condition of the black Antillean subject as fraught by an Adlerian inferiority complex, Fanon explained – now applying the Hegelian model to the postcolonial present – how he had failed to traverse all the steps in the fierce struggle for freedom through recognition. For did not the quality of being human, Fanon implied, depend on one's forceful *imposition* of oneself onto another in order to be recognized? Like Kojève, Fanon chose to isolate the intense aggression in the dialectic of the encounter with the other.[42] If at the foundation of the Hegelian dialectic lay "absolute reciprocity," through mediation and recognition, then the "human reality in-itself-for-itself" was to be achieved through conflict and through the risk of life, as one sought to satiate one's desire for recognition. "This risk means that I go beyond life toward a supreme good that is the transformation of subjective certainty of my own worth into a universally valid objective truth," bringing about "a transformation of subjective certainty (*Gewissheit*) into objective truth (*Wahrheit*)."[43] Such an induction into the realm of universality, however, was not the prerogative of the Antillean subject. Living in the postcolonial condition of Martinique, this subject merely occupied a position that preceded the first step necessary for the attainment of self-consciousness. Because of Martinique's liberation from slavery by the French – unlike Haiti, where the revolution of the black Jacobins was led by Toussaint L'Ouverture – the struggle of life and death had gone missing, so that even freedom had been imposed externally, from above. And, contrary to the *Phenomenology*, the French white master did not even quest after recognition from the Antilleans. Laughing "at the consciousness of the slave," what the white master demanded from him was not recognition but simply labor.[44] Having failed to fight for their lives themselves, Antilleans had not even attained the stage of Kierkegaardian anxiety – the result of having too much freedom at one's disposal – let alone gained access to the universal right to self-consciousness and subjectivity.[45]

Seeking to undo this *pathos of distance*, enforced by the "aristocratic" white colonizer or barbaric settler, Fanon predicted – using unmistakable Nietzschean locution – that the struggle for recognition henceforth could only take one form: it would mean relinquishing the passivity of slave morality, so as to assume a position of actional agency, a new positing of values that would no longer be belated, reactive, or merely comparative. But this meant taking up a contradictory position, answering the white other with both a "yes" and a "no." Indeed, Fanon did not seek to reduce the position of the black subject to pure negativity and alterity, as in fact Sartre had done in his "Black Orpheus," that primer of the white subject's alienated consciousness.[46] Instead, he demanded that the Antillean subject occupy a double, a-logical position, which joined affirmation to negation: "*Yes* to life. *Yes* to love. *Yes* to generosity. But man is also a *no*. *No* to scorn of man. *No* to degradation of man. *No* to exploitation of man. *No* to the butchery of what is most human in man: freedom."[47]

This contradictory logic clearly punctuated all of the psychoanalytic essays, suspended as they remained between the emphatic affirmation of love and the negating force of violence. But the full span of this logic's potential applications only truly surfaced in *Wretched of the Earth*. Composed in the throes of the anticolonial struggle, Fanon's famous revolutionary manual did not just spell out the violent logic that issued from Hegel's struggle for recognition, but, in the course of doing so, also rewrote earlier advocacies of revolutionary violence. Mapping the class struggle onto the colonial one, it hailed the coming of a new humanism, for the outcome of violent decolonization was "the creation of new men," via all means possible, the only valiant one being "absolute violence."[48] Clearly, violence was not an end in itself, but a way of leaving the state of inactivity, inaction, *ressentiment*, passivity, through the rhythm of revolutionary *élan*. But the *yes* of affirmation, it appeared, now could only be realized in and through the *no* of violence. Fundamentally, Fanon asserted, the opposition between settler and native violated Aristotle's logical principle of noncontradiction: as two irreconcilable adversaries, colonizer and colonized were clasped in a pattern of "reciprocal exclusivity."[49] In view of this violation of classical logic, a rational confrontation no longer proved possible, only obliterating violence could ensue. Ruled by an Aristotelian, not Hegelian (or dialectical) logic of contradiction in which mediation was still possible, colonialism now proved governed by a ruthless antagonism, in which adversaries sustained themselves by a fierce desire for substitution, without the aspiration for reciprocal recognition.

Siding with the "starving peasant, outside the class system," not the elitist colonized intellectual, who – together with the liberals in the colonizing home country – embraced the values of the "universal abstract,"[50] Fanon described colonialism as "violence in its natural state," which "will only yield when confronted with greater violence."[51] Written from amidst the ranks of the colonized *Lumpenproletariat*, in whose revolutionary potential he, unlike Marx, believed, his tract depicted the colonial situation as a real, not just imaginary, warring "state of nature," in which settler and native were caught in a vicious cycle of violence. Fixed in the confines of this frame, the colonized subject saw no exit, remaining the hostage of the desire to radically and violently usurp the place of the settler. To shed further clarity on this state of affairs, Fanon returned to the Manichean world order, first propounded in *Black Skin, White Masks*. Colonialism, he vouched, was "not a treatise on the universal, but the untidy affirmation of an original idea propounded as an absolute. The colonial world is a Manichean world."[52] In the dualistic mindset that ruled the colonial world, the native functioned as absolute evil, as "insensible to ethics," and hence "the enemy of values."[53] But from this binary logic that the settler inflicted upon the native followed that it could only be countered by a mirroring logic, emanating from the oppressed: "On the logical plane, the Manicheism of the settler produces a Manicheism of the native. To the theory of the 'absolute evil of the native' the theory of the 'absolute evil of the settler' replies."[54] Force, it followed, was the only appropriate means to set an end to the aggressor's violence. Citing Engels's *Anti-Duehring* approvingly, Fanon hailed the instrumental force of violence, stressing the need for the colonized to reclaim not just the means of production, but in particular the instruments of violent reproduction, if they hoped to become contenders in the spiral that linked the armament race to the manufacturing of weapons. In the vicious cycle of violence and counterviolence, "the violence of the colonial regime and the counterviolence of the native balance each other and respond to each other in an extraordinary reciprocal homogeneity."[55] Influenced not just by Engels, but also Sorel's *Reflections on Violence*, Fanon proposed a typology of violence that eventually – in a cynical twist of the quest for a concrete, not just abstract universalism that he celebrated – seemed to become a new unifying, if not universalizing force. Advocating a form of "universal violence"[56] that would unite the oppressed, he contended that, "at the level of individuals, violence is a cleansing force. It frees the native from his inferiority complex and from his despair and inaction; it makes him fearless and restores his self-respect."[57] As he anatomized the different stages in the natives' uprising against colonizing forces – from traumatic, internalized revolt to the successful overthrow of the settlers – he also listed the successive transitions and changes in the channels of violence: from ritualized religious activities and cathartic manifestations of violence enacted in dance; acting out as the neurosis of aggression inflicted upon fellow sufferers; to the fully externalized unleashing of violence upon the settlers, whose fervor amounted to history-making action or agency. It was Sartre, tellingly, who, responding almost immediately to Fanon's call, recapped the various stages of this process, as he laid it out for the public in the colonizer's home country. Recognizing the mirrorings of a reflective logic that had gone awry, he summarized the three phases of violence as follows: that of the settler's, followed by the destructive violence turned inward of the colonized, and, finally, the return of violence to its point of origin. Like a boomerang,[58] the violence launched by the settler was hurled back at him, at the moment the natives' volcanic "mad fury" erupted. [59] Thus, in Fanon's advocacy of revolutionary violence, Sartre discerned the historical dialectic that lay hidden under the hypocritical veil of liberalism: "the same violence is thrown back upon us as when our reflection comes forward to meet us when we go toward a mirror."[60]

Though Fanon's endorsement of violence never assumed force as an end in itself, but as the situated, historical response to colonial violence, there is no doubt that it was infused by a theory of Sorelean spontaneism and a highly problematic creative vitalism.[61] His position was entirely at odds with the tradition of pacifism, situated at a far remove as it was from Gandhi's principle of *ahimsa*, or nonviolence, which, sheltered in the seat of the heart, was to be mustered against the fetish of force. As a consequence, it has virtually been impossible to glimpse in Fanon's unambiguous embrace of violent struggle the ethical impulse that so clearly marked the earlier work. To grant his ethics of recognition more relief, it might therefore be worthwhile to place his work briefly in line with Levinas's philosophy, despite the ostensible dissimilarities that separate the one from the other. As he aspired to reach an ethics of the other, Levinas sought to overcome the polemical realm of politics, which, as *Totality and Infinity* suggested, propagated the continuation of war by other means. In positing that ethics resolutely preceded the arena of politics, Levinas abandoned the Hegelian battle for recognition, or the struggle of life and death, demanding that the other no longer be assimilated to the self, in its pursuit of self-certainty in self-consciousness. In other words, ethics was to be situated logically, temporally, but also ontologically, before politics, war, the "state of nature" – terms that, despite obvious conceptual differences, functioned interchangeably. In so doing, Levinas jettisoned the interpsychic dynamics of the Hegelian model to posit a "nonsymmetrical,"[62] hence nonreciprocal intersubjective relation, which radically modified the figment of mutual requital.[63] Letting go of the other meant letting the other be, and seeing the other no longer entailed subjugating him to an imposing, specular gaze but respecting the other's infinity, as it emanated from his face. Levinas thus described a subject that was no longer driven by the need to command the other fully. Assuming the subject position instead meant that one acquiesced to being "subject-ed" – not in the Foucauldian disciplinary sense, but that one relinquish oneself to the other, and, crucially, to one's responsibility for the other. The main trope that structured this ethical task was that of substitution, a "substitution for another," not to usurp his place, but to place one's responsibility for his well-being before the Hegelian struggle for life and death.[64]

Fanon, too, repeatedly made use of the term "substitution," but so as to grasp all of its ramifications – especially when held against Levinasian thought – one must consider the seminal changes the term underwent, as it migrated from *Black Skin, White Masks* to *Wretched of the Earth*. Surely, Fanon's later troubling embrace of violence as a way of taking-the-other's-place is a far cry from the plea for transcendence in intersubjective love that framed the earlier work. In the poetic chapter on *négritude*, at the heart of *Black Skin, White Masks*, Fanon paid tribute to a non-Western conception of substitution – a magical way of trading places, typical of an organic, holistic mindset, devoted to the powers of animism and mana, whose harmonic sounds this lyrical philosopher heard reverberate in the poetry of *négritude*. But by the time he wrote *Wretched of the Earth*, the poetic cosmos of fulfillment had been forcefully replaced by an abject state of nature. The new logic of substitution no longer resounded with the ethical overtones this word carried in Levinas's philosophy no less than in his own early work. Though he desperately hoped to seize the lost – or never realized – universalism of ethics, Fanon could not yet occupy that safe place outside the warring arena of politics, whose undeniable realities had been forced upon the colonized. To judge Fanon from the secure position of those not immersed in that struggle seems to judge history.

One might well ask, then, whether the difference that marks *Black Skin, White Masks* and *Wretched of the Earth* can also be interpreted as the breach that separates aspiration from reality. Drawing quasi-Levinasian gestures, the very last lines of *Black Skin, White Masks* delineated a sentient ethics of touching, awakened by a longing to feel the other, letting the other reveal himself in all his mystery. Freedom was "the open dimension of all consciousness," a technique of perpetual self-interrogation – struggle proved just an intermittent phase, the passing of time. As a way of undoing the "vicious circle" of a double narcissism that riddled the relations between blacks and whites, Fanon demanded the realization of a "new humanism," a taking on of "the universality inherent in the human condition."[65] More than violent negation, humans were positive affirmation – a "yes" – while consciousness was a process of transcendence that involved love and understanding. As a psychoanalytic handbook, punctuated by paroxysms of revolutionary verve and poetic *élan*, *Black Skin, White Masks* ended with a rallying cry to *act*, *agir*, which found its response in *Wretched of the Earth*, the manual for revolutionary change Fanon realized in his Algerian phase. Thrown between a desire for activist force and a tranquil Kantian-inspired universalism, *Black Skin, White Masks*'s muted call for counterviolence still remained framed by a pacifistic poetry that yearned for the unmediated encounter with the other. In so positioning his work, Fanon resolutely rejected the choice offered between sameness and difference, also voiced in Taylor's two choices of an expanded liberalism. For the two positions, that of "color-blindness" versus the "color-conscious" embrace of the racial mark, merely amounted to two alternatives in a drama staged by white others, a neurosis out of which the black agent needed to escape, by projecting into the future the figure of a universal, human being. Such a projection, Fanon romantically hoped, might return the luster to Kant's proverbial starry sky, or, as he put it in the scansion of his characteristic poetic diction: "It is a long time since the starry sky that took away Kant's breath revealed the last of its secrets to us. And the moral law is not certain of itself."[66]

Ethical Transitivism

Though Fanon, rereading Lacan, crafted the term *ethical transit* to diagnose the psychological well-being of Antillean subjects, it might not altogether be implausible to use the mechanism as a way of understanding similar latent transfers that transpire in the broader ethical field. Viewed from this perspective, certain unreflective liberal scripts then can be seen to impose a psychological transitivism, according to which the reciprocating other is assumed to mimic the liberal subject's moral gestures at the imaginary level. To name but one of the better-known examples, one might consider, for instance, whether such an automatism still functions in Kohlberg's neo-Kantian psychological theory of cognitive moral development. Indeed, as Carol Gilligan's feminist critique of Kohlberg's universalist ethics of justice showed, his model of moral role-taking, which required the adoption of the other's point of view, was fraught with an unspoken, yet pernicious gender bias. In imagining the subject of moral deliberation to be male, Kohlbergian theory excluded an array of additional moral perspectives, especially the sense of self and ethics of care, often favored by women.[67] Applied to our focus on the Habermas-Taylor dialogue, we might ask whether such a mechanism of ethical transitivism isn't operative in Taylor's neo-Hegelian contribution and Habermas's reply. With this query in mind, it seems appropriate that we return to their exchange about multiculturalism.

In his contribution to the debate, Taylor enumerated the merits of the discourse of recognition, from Rousseau to Hegel,[68] to bolster the virtues of a communitarian liberalism that protects group rights, enabling the survival of endangered cultures – a case in point being Francophone Québec. At the same time, he remained all too conscious of the problems that stem from assimilating the authenticity of the other to the "dominant or majority identity,"[69] addressing the coercion exerted through cultural logics of imposition. Readily acknowledging the centrality of Fanon in the pluralism debates, he noted how *Wretched of the Earth* had made explicit the struggle to reverse the inculcation of identity images. Though Fanon's use of force was not adopted by all of his adherents, as Taylor stressed, "the notion that there is a struggle for a changed self-image, which takes place both within the subjugated and against the dominator, has been very widely applied."[70] Insofar as they fought for the revision of forcibly imposed identity images, feminist and multicultural identity struggles, Taylor indicated, remained indebted to Fanon's anticolonial program.[71] Yet, Taylor's main concern, in the end, lay with the campus canon debates, which bore on the need to universalize equal esteem for diverse cultures. To promote the acceptance of non-Western texts as objects worthy of study required, he advised, that all embrace the hypothesis according to which cultures intrinsically carried a "presumed worth" – a value judgment that subsequently could be put to the test through the actual study of individual cases.[72] Naturally, Taylor's proposition for such a much-needed, thorough canon reform that potentially would include all cultures indiscriminately is sound and worthy of adoption. Indeed, hesitation is not due as regards the tenets of his proposal for reform, but rather as regards the presuppositions, or foundational premises, that would guide its future implementation. For, as laudable as his position sounds, in the course of his discussion Taylor slipped comfortably into a presumably homogeneous, undifferentiated "we," a collective subject that, as it appeared, would study the "other" ethnographically and anthropologically. Such a study would yield a fusion and expansion of interpretive horizons, he surmised, adding that this position was informed by Gadamer's hermeneutical theory of understanding, without, however, noting that this perspective, in typical Hegelian fashion, relied on the figure of the self returning to itself, charted through an expansive, grand journey to the other. Following the idealistic figure of self and other, all too familiar by now, Taylor in the end risked retracing the voyage toward the (Hegelian) certainty of self-consciousness at the expense of the other, sublating, or – phrased yet differently – translating the "other" into the homogeneity of a collective "we." For in the absence of specifications about how this collective subject was to be constituted, the gesture of hermeneutical recognition threatened to absorb, and hence to transliterate, all difference in fusion.[73] The same reservation is due to Taylor's invocation of Herder. Sliding from a discussion of "equal respect" to one of "equal worth" or "value," Taylor speculated that, in the grand course of history there lay a moral duty to recognize "our" own relatively futile cultural contribution to the vast expanse of world culture, conceived along Herderian lines. But what could it mean for Taylor to adopt Herder's perspective and to presume a final, ultimate theological "horizon from which the relative worth of different cultures might be evident?"[74] In a similar vein, how is one to understand the Hegelian span of history that once again seeps into the discussion? Applying even more pressure to the Hegelian presuppositions that upheld Taylor's argument, one might go so far as to ask whether it would truly be advisable to reconcile a secular theory of multiculturalism, governed by the sober language of formal legal and political rights, with the kind of theodicy or Christian eschatology Hegel predicted at the end of his *Lectures on the Philosophy of History*.[75]

At least one other seminal point of critique with regard to Taylor's model emerges. Don't judgments about worth and value – for which individual cultures are to be tested – again presume an underlying (substantivist) consensus on values, a position that might reintroduce a foundationalist axiological system, no longer subject to communal debate and dialogue, let alone dissent? On this point, I can only agree with Habermas's rejoinder in his essay "Struggles for Recognition in the Democratic Constitutional State" that the presumed, substantivist claims of excellence about a culture should not detract from, even less eclipse, the need for more primordial, procedurally (formally) defined rights to equal respect. As Habermas convincingly argued, Taylor's analysis was rooted in a false antithesis insofar as he didn't pay due consideration to the fact that bearers of individual rights were always situated intersubjectively. Thus, the problem did not lie in the contradiction between two competing sets of rights (collective vs. individual ones), but in the very *actualization* of basic rights. Normative decisions enacted by the law were contingent insofar as they reflected the citizenry, which is why they would always prove to be permeated by the fiber of ethics. In effect, it is this very paradox between political recognition and ethical values – the lived mores, codes, customs of particular communities, Hegel's *Sittlichkeit* – that Habermas shows us must be thought through, thus returning us back to a question asked earlier: "Whose ethics for democracy?"

Writing as a dual observer of the multiple struggles that mark the American and European scenes, Habermas noted that the life-world of a nation's citizens or their contingent horizons of experience, including the *ēthos*, defined not only a nation's patriotic self-understanding but also its legal system, resulting in what he called a *juridified ethos*. Precisely this "ethical-political self-understanding on the part of [a] nation," as he added, was continuously altered and profoundly affected by migration and multiethnicity. Moreover, because multicultural societies are not simply multi-ethnic but also *multi-ethic* in constitution, as I suggested at the outset, they require that one be recognized not just as a citizen, but also as a member of a culture or, to put it in Habermas's words, an "ethical community integrated around different conceptions of the good." This can only indicate that in a postconventional multicultural, pluralist democracy, ethical integration is to be radically disengaged from political integration, meaning that even if liberal constitutional democracies are inevitably weighed down by ethical substance, they must nonetheless seek to maintain a legal neutrality "vis-à-vis communities that are ethically integrated at a subpolitical level." Or, to put the issue in different terms, so as to safeguard the pluralism of democracy, there must then exist a necessary asymmetry between the ethical and the political, an unbridgeable distance between the two, which, as signified by the dash in the phrase ethico-political, ought to prevent the one from collapsing into the other. The paradox Habermas's critical theory seeks to think, then, is the following: given the inevitable ethical permeation of any pluralistic democracy, how to maintain an ethical neutrality on the procedural legal level that can guarantee the coexistence of multiple ethical positions. Needless to say, Habermas himself thereby remains susceptible to Taylor's frank acknowledgment that liberalism itself is merely a "particularism masquerading as a universalism." Nor do Habermas's rationalist (Kantian) foundationalism and conception of rational discussion entirely escape ethical transitivism – if one considers the grounded charges of antifoundationalist critics, such as Mouffe, who have repeatedly noted that his regulative idea of consensus, though "conceived as infinite," still has a "clearly defined shape," so that it runs the danger in turn of imposing "a univocal model of democratic discussion."[76] That Habermas's social theory and discourse ethics fail to secure against the possible obliteration of multiply situated differences that constitute the democratic polity is also a point that has been made, though from within the parameters of a communicative discourse ethics, by fellow Frankfurt School theorist Seyla Benhabib. In her *Situating the Self*, she has sought to amend Habermas's model by designing a "postmetaphysical interactive universalism" that no longer subscribes to a "counterfactual" ideal of consent but draws upon a context-sensitive "reversing of perspectives."[77] Thus, her proposal for an adjusted version of communicative ethics has called for a historically and culturally self-conscious universalism that reflects on its situatedness, though without relinquishing its deontological, normative perspective. In her essay on the generalized and concrete other she argued against the Kantian legacy of the "generalized other," which might result in inadvertent "substitutionalist" versions of universalism, against which she held out another universalism that, no longer gender-blind, demonstrates "the will and the readiness to seek understanding with the other and to reach some reasonable agreement in an open-ended moral conversation."[78] From this standpoint, the pragmatic presuppositions of democratic discussion could "be challenged within the conversation itself," yet without abolishing or suspending them altogether, for to do so would mean to open the gates to "violence, coercion, and suppression,"[79] and to initiate the return to the "state of nature," that is, to the "struggles onto death among moral opponents" for moral recognition.[80]

Concrete Universalisms

How should pluralist democracies negotiate between the ethical and the political without collapsing them? How to ensure the coexistence of a potentially infinite array of diverse ethical systems, approaches, and mores – such appear to be the persisting questions at the core of the multiculturalism and pluralism debates. And, though the solutions of the interlocutors in these discussions vary, to the point of seeming irreconcilable, all appear animated by a genuine adherence to a democratic "attitude," or *democratic ethos*, as Mouffe phrased it. The outer limit of such a democratic ethos is constituted by violence, or the use of force, its inner limit by the political recognition of difference. Indeed, it is precisely this outer line of democratic liberalism that Fanon crossed when he advocated, even embraced, violence, as he found himself in the thick of anticolonial warfare against what proved to be, in essence, a nondemocratic regime. But whereas his advocacy of violence demands to be understood within its historical context, his writings have retained an urgency that goes well beyond their time-bound parameters. Over and against conventional variants of the Hegelian dialectic, Fanon relentlessly interrogated the power dynamic in the struggle for recognition no less than the ethical transitivism that bound subjects to identity images. Laying bare the epistemic violence transported by the model of recognition, he also opened up a radically other dimension as he called attention to the frail, porous border that was rifted between an unreflective liberalism and violence. Fundamentally, he exacted that the "universal" – whether in its Kantian formalist or Hegelian substantivist meaning – be made to live up to its pretensions to indiscriminate inclusion, though he, as much as Levinas, deplorably, in the end endorsed a male-identified humanism. But while to some it would be easy to rebuke the holistic phantasm of universality that regulated Fanon's overturn of a Manicheistic moral order, it might perhaps be more productive to engage directly with his reflections on concrete universalism. Then, it becomes evident that the fundamental question about universalism his work poses also informs the debates about multiculturalism and pluralism: must the demand for universal recognition, in its cultural, political, and legal meanings, imply the uncontested recognition (or acceptance) of universalism? Phrased this way, it appears not only that Hegel's model of recognition is still with us but also that the old dialectic of how to mediate (negotiate) between universalism and particularism has lost none of its relevance. It is to a brief discussion of the conflictual views of "universalism" that I would now like to turn in conclusion.

At the risk of unduly streamlining current controversies, one might say that critiques of the Enlightenment ideal of universality, proffered in the name of difference or pluralism, usually take two forms. Its "weaker" version targets the coercive, manipulative and exclusionary application of the category "universal" to exclude those thought to deviate from the normative, or normalizing mean – a skewed logic historically enacted in colonialism, racism, and all forms of discrimination on the basis of gender or sexual orientation. As we saw, it is this kind of critique that Fanon promoted as he hoped to advance a concrete, not abstract, universalism. But it is also here, I believe, that one might situate Etienne Balibar's analysis of the curious bonds that connect certain strands of neoracism to the project of universalism. Less a wholesale rejection of universalism than a contestation of its imaginary manifestations, his work has warned that it may be impossible to "effectively face racism with the abstract motto of universality," since racism "has already (always already) occupied this place."[81] While it is vital for a progressive universalism to fight the primitive particularism at work in differentialist, cultural neoracism, these contestations do little to counter the rhetoric of universalism that such a neonationalist differentialist culturalism often mimics. Given that the struggle between racism and democracy transpires within the space of universalism, the hard task awaiting pluralist democrats therefore is how to "transform universalism, not to abandon it ... for this would amount to surrendering without combat."[82] Similar exigencies apply to an abstractly formulated humanism, according to Balibar, since the theoretically infused racist theories of the last decades have demonstrated that they can easily have truck with the rhetoric of a theoretical humanism. For these reasons, a purely theoretical (strategic) humanism must likewise be replaced by a workable, concrete humanism, which in the context of post-Cold War Europe for Balibar can only mean guaranteeing an "internationalist politics of citizenship."[83]

But in the conflictual field of democratic politics, other, "stronger" antifoundationalist critiques of universalism have disputed justificatory political scripts that proscribe universalist principles. Not infrequently, Habermas's discourse ethics has been taken to task for being the chief representative of such a normative universalism, while he, for his part, has opposed the relentless search for a mendacious "will to power," concealed behind Enlightenment ideals.[84] At stake in these disputes is liberalism's unificatory, normative starting point and the coercive force with which its pluralist program might level dissenting difference, as it strives for a consensus about the principles, procedures, policies, or operations of the polity. In this reading, even the most hospitable or generous liberalism could potentially limit the playing field of those joining the democratic discussion in the polity. For in presuming a moral, rational norm on the basis of which its emancipatory program can be justified, such variants of liberalism forget their contingent point of origin, as Mouffe has argued, together with the "unrecognized violence hidden behind appeals to 'rationality'." Seeking to "establish a rational and universal consensus by means of free discussion,"[85] the proponents of deliberative democracy, she maintains, link politics to morality, thus overlooking that their decisions are not moral and universal but political and contingent. Liberal democracy in Mouffe's pragmatic, late Wittgensteinian model is but one of many language games that can only "be defended in a 'contextualist' manner."[86] Anything but the advocacy of real violence or a Schmittean decisionism, her position would rely on linguistic contestation within a multiplicity of discursive practices; and, not averse to "agonistic confrontation,"[87] it would welcome social struggle, confrontation, dissent, since only "conflictual consensus" can ever be reached.[88] In rejecting justificatory scripts based on the "identification of the universal with the particular," Mouffe nonetheless still retains a quasi-Kantian position insofar as the universal can only ever function as a regulating horizon, never as an attainable endpoint. However, when it comes to the formalist/substantivist divide in political theory, Mouffe has spoken out against privileging "neutral procedures and general principles," as this would be detrimental to the democratic project itself, always entrenched as it is in "substantial ethical commitments." Notwithstanding the existing plurality of possible political language games, the main task that confronts advocates of a radical democracy is how to guarantee the construction of a democratic ethos that will foster the recognition of a democratic plurality without resulting either in mere political decisionism or else in a disavowal of the power relations that inexorably suffuse any future democratic polity.

Obviously, it won't be possible to resolve these contentious political differences among foundationalist and antifoundationalist positions, nor can they, for that matter, easily be settled insofar as they concern fundamental disagreements over the distribution of consent or dissent, no less than over the admissibility of a universal, normative, moral foundation for the democratic project. Upon closer scrutiny, furthermore, positions also appear polarized over the exact way in which the ethical and the political relate to one another, as signaled in the hyphenated construction of the "ethico-political." Thus, in his proposal for postconventional multicultural societies that integrate immigration and asylum reforms, Habermas acknowledged the inevitable contingency and contextuality that invariably inflect the formal procedures governing democratic cohabitation. If, for him, the main dilemma appeared to be how it was possible to maintain neutrality in the exercise of democratic procedures, then Mouffe's antifoundationalism, on the contrary, contested the flawed starting point of this position, doubting the attainability, no less than advisability, of such a neutral mean. Such deeply entrenched disagreements between factions, however, can't detract from the circumstance that they converge at notable junctures. Agonistic, antifoundationalist poststructuralist accounts of pluralism and multiculturalism usually subscribe to a modicum of "universalization," that is, to the (universal) *extension* of democratic rights to willing participants of the polity, all the while remaining vigilant about the issue of *whose* rights are under discussion. Moreover, whether it is a matter of privileging moral, social, legal, or political struggles for recognition, all factions agree that such struggles cannot take the form of an enforced submission to hegemonic subject positions but that they require *nonviolent*, that is to say, discursive contestation. Finally, an extended reflection on the complex relations between the ethical and political also makes it clear that the ethical (or *ēthos*) cannot refer just to Hegel's *Sittlichkeit*, or to the situated, context-bound cultural baggage of mores that the democratic project inevitably is burdened with.[89] At a more fundamental level, the ethical also betokens the place of a radical openness, a holding open of the realm of possibilities – though not necessarily in the sense that Levinas had in mind when he thought of ethics as that which precedes politics, a term thus reduced to mere strategic action. Perhaps the difficulty, then, lies rather in how to reclaim such an ethical openness *within* the political, without falling back into metaphysics, total indecidability, decisionism, or, simply, political disaffectedness.[90]

Leaving these questions open for the time being, it seems appropriate in conclusion to address briefly another crucial point that bears upon the recent controversies over the shortcomings of universalist political projects. For the intensity with which some of these exchanges about (a Kantian) universalism have been conducted should not deflect from a more worrisome current political trend, namely, the all too ready embrace of an *unreflective* globalism.[91] Doesn't Kant's utopian universal history of peacefully coexisting atomistic moral agents, who all will that the maxims governing their actions become universal law, by comparison pale, attesting as it does to a quaint, even nostalgic, anti-Babelic longing for the overcoming of glossolalia? To me, its real and purported horrors comparatively speaking seem slight contrasted to the more disconcerting realities of a globalized strategic, manipulative, pragmatic utilitarianism, including its perhaps most seductive phantasm, that of a corporate multiculturalism. Mapped out in Fukuyama's *The End of History*, this program for a globalized liberal world order, propelled by a healthy, competitive free-market capitalism, not only transforms the other into nothing but a potential economic competitor, but also sees itself as the fulfillment of a radically misunderstood dream of "universal recognition." Equally problematic, of course, is a romanticized melancholia that remains in the thralls of an internalized or incorporated alterity, where one complacently revels in the awareness that one always already is a "stranger to oneself."[92] How to retrieve the radical alterity of otherness for a truly emancipatory pluralist politics is the challenge whose extraordinary dimensions we have perhaps only just begun to recognize.

7

LIMITS OF FEMINIST
REPRESENTATION
Elfriede Jelinek's Language of Violence

War by Other Means

Elfriede Jelinek's writings can perhaps best be read as a sustained critique of the pres-ence of violence in postwar Austria. True to her programmatic Bachmann essay, "Der Krieg mit anderen Mitteln" ("War by Other Means"), most of her novels, plays, and essays dissect the covert but insidious continuation of fascist ideology and its belligerent potential in postwar gender relations. While novels such as *Die Klavierspielerin* (*The Piano Teacher*) (1983) or *Lust* (1989) place the force of the analysis on body politics and the pornographic exploitation of women's bodies to uncover their underlying war-like economy, other recent texts have turned to the epistemolog-ical and philosophical foundations of fascism, evident in *Wolken. Heim* (1988) and *Totenauberg* (1991), or to the neo-Nazism of the Austrian Freedom Party (*FPÖ*).

That gender inequity is to be regarded as the covert perpetuation of fascism and its victim–perpetrator dialectic is, to be sure, an assumption that underlies much of first-wave German feminism and women's literature as it emerged after the Second World War. Its theoretical justification had been provided by Horkheimer and Adorno in the *Dialectic of Enlightenment*, when they established a correlation between the violence of instrumental reason, the bio-politics of fascism, anti-Semitism, and the historical objectification of women as *phusis*.[1] The legacy of this tradition can be discerned in the New German Feminism of the 1970s, no less than in the powerful critical paradigm that Elisabeth Lenk set when, alluding to Arendt, she defined women as "pariahs."[2] Not until quite recently have these received assumptions and analogies obtained a necessary qualification and lost some of their compelling force through emerging scholarship in the fields of history and sociology, which aims to demystify the role of women in Nazi Germany.[3] Seen within the climate that typified Austrian and German feminism during the 1970s and 1980s, however, perhaps no other author has confronted the intersections between fascism, gender, and sexual violence with the persistence and polemical acerbity that distinguishes Jelinek's prose. At the same time, her writings appear to be informed by seemingly conflicting intentions. While they relentlessly criticize violence perpetrated against women – particularly in the form of sexual and domestic violence – and as such continue the project of first-wave feminism to which she recently reaffirmed her commitment,[4] they deploy a language of violence to do so. Often accused of writing pornographic texts and adopting the register of sexual violence, her work has provoked reactions of outrage and indignation, fueled by the graphic representations of voyeurism, sadomasochism, anthropophagy, vampirism, and the catalog of other perversions that constitute the contested hallmark of her writings. Insofar as her work enlists one mode of violence to combat another, it may seem haunted by a double specter: the mimetic reenactment of sexual violence, which risks subjugating women a second time around, and the return of the *Ungeist* of German history in the form of the very irrationalism and violence that her writings seek to ward off. How then to understand the performative contradiction in which her work seems to be caught?

Jelinek perhaps most cogently spells out the logic of her polemical writing project in her essay "War by Other Means" ("Der Krieg mit anderen Mitteln"), whose bellicose title invokes the statement of the nineteenth-century German military strategist Carl von Clausewitz, that war is the continuation of politics by other means. Originally published in 1983, the essay begins with a Krausian attack on the role of the feuilleton, citing, in fact, the famous opening lines of the *Fackel*'s inaugural issue. In these times, so the startling opening paragraph reads, when words such as *happiness, beauty, peace* and *fulfillment* have reappeared in the Austrian feuilleton without quotation marks, it becomes imperative to speak once again of struggle and war.[5] The jolting paradox that opens the essay can well be called eristic and, quite literally, polemical in nature, targeting as it does the prevailing atmosphere of peace and harmony, transmitted by the Austrian media and propagated by the journalistic establishment, the advocates of a "new positivity." Against such a screen of spurious positivity Jelinek holds the figure of Ingeborg Bachmann, whom – in an obvious allusion to the crack (*Riss*) that engulfs the I-figure at the end of *Malina*[6] – she calls *die Rissautorin*, or the first Austrian postwar author to have exposed the rents (*Risse*) in the deceptive veil of peace, as well as the insidious continuation of fascism in everyday gender relations. Commenting on the *Todesarten-Zyklus* and, notably, *The Case of Franza* (*Der Fall Franza*), which had diagnosed postwar Austrian society as afflicted by the "virus of crime,"[7] Jelinek cites Bachmann's last televised interview, "The Four Statements," in which she voiced her belief in a principle of perpetual war at the center of heterosexual relationships.[8] So, too, Jelinek maintains – in a transposition and inversion of Clausewitz's dictum – should institutionalized love or marriage be regarded as "the continuation of war by other means:" "[On love's] battlefield takes place the bloody, sometimes bloodless annihilation of the feminine, which can never become a subject, but forever must remain an object, subjugated to employment contracts not recognized by society, called marriage."[9] Here the *topos* of the battle of the sexes merges with the bio-politics of fascism, which reduces women to "pure nature, related to blood and soil"[10] – a predicament best illustrated by Franza Jordan, whose identification with oppressed Papuans, as she sums up the colonization to which she has been subjected in marriage, alludes to the discourse of eugenics.[11] If in *Malina* the crack in the wall signals the objectification and elimination of the "feminine" and symbolizes how women historically have been forced through the fissures of a male socialization process, then Franza's sexual violation, as her "sex" is ripped out (*heraus-gerissen*), exemplifies the history of traumatic markings on the female body, as it is turned into a site of sexual violence.

Because of her loyalty to what since have come to be known as the essentialist principles of first-generation feminists, Jelinek recently has been taken to task from within the ranks of the German women's movement, most notably when her film script of *Malina* was decried for digging up "the old rag of the battle between the sexes [die alte 'Geschlechterkampfklamotte']."[12] But to reduce Jelinek's entire project to a single-minded preoccupation with the "war of the sexes" or with a biological essentialism and binarism means not to take note of the real tensions that exist between essentialist and poststructuralist positions in her work. It also means not to take stock of the peculiar alliance between her sexual politics, on the one hand, and language politics, on the other. Indeed, such a reductive reading neglects the force of what Jelinek – in a playful allusion to Freud – has called her destruction or death drive [*Destruktionstrieb*].[13] Consider, for example, the recurring term *Riss* in "War by Other Means." In the course of the essay, the word reappears in a number of guises (*Risse, abreißen, herausgerissen*), accruing ever more connotations and condensing an entire register of different meanings. Not only does the term evoke the Bachmann allusions cited earlier, but it also indicates Jelinek's praxis of *die Risse sichtbar machen,*[14] that is, her attempt to expose the fault lines of society where chronic violence turns into acute violence.[15] Crucially, the word *Riss* captures the violent force, the language of fierce ruptures and satiric interventions so typical of Jelinek's style. Brandishing the "blunt knives of our language,"[16] Jelinek depicts fictional realms in which sexual desire, aggression, and violence substitute for and permutate one another. Seen within this light, the apparently diagnostic title of the Bachmann essay, suggesting a continuity between patriarchy and war, in a second moment acquires a prescriptive sense, allowing one to read it as a call to arms, in other words, as a call to continue war *by other means* or to wield a language of violence *against* violence.

In a first moment, Jelinek's preference for such a "destruction through language"[17] must be placed in the context of the aesthetics, poetics, and politics of violence that have shaped modernity. For one, her work is indebted to what Bataille once termed Sade's "violent truth," that is, to the Sadeian legacy continued by Artaud, Barthes, Foucault, and others[18] – a legacy to which she has more than once shown allegiance. If, furthermore, she has avowed her roots in French Surrealism and called *Lust* an attempt to write a feminist version of Bataille's *History of the Eye*, then it should come as no surprise that her work bears the marks of what Bachmann in her Frankfurt lectures described as the Surrealists' "poetics of violence." But to situate Jelinek in a canonical tradition of poetic and aesthetic violence may mean to temper the outrage, to assign her work a respectable position within the perspective of a literature of violence. Such a classificatory gesture does not pay heed to the diverse, eclectic traditions that come together in her praxis of linguistic destruction (*Sprachzerstückelung*) or to the postmodern transformation she proposes of these traditions. Thus, to the Austrian legacy of language critique (*Sprachkritik*)[19] — from Hofmannsthal and Kraus to Wittgenstein and Bachmann — or the language experiments of the *Wiener Gruppe* — of which she was a member — are to be added the transgressive economies of women writers such as Pauline Réage, Angela Carter, and Kathy Acker, as well as the poetics of *écriture féminine*. And, while her work does not subscribe to the utopian dimensions of French feminism — least of all, to its conception of "femininity" or *parler femme*[20] — it remains faithful to the call for a radical and revolutionary overthrow *through* language that accompanied its poetic and philosophical renewal, whether expressed in Herrmann's attempt "to steal language," Cixous's aim "to break up, to destroy," or Irigaray's injunction to "destroy the functioning of discourse."[21]

Further, in spite of the essentialist moments that punctuate Jelinek's writings, her language politics shows marked affinities to contemporary forms of poststructuralist feminism, which, informed by discourse analysis, have focused on the inherent violence of discursive and representational registers. First, her work attests to the conceptual expansion that the notion "violence" has undergone in contemporary feminisms, evident in the shift from a unique preoccupation with "material" violence to a more pronounced consideration of epistemic and discursive constructions of violence. Just as poststructuralist feminism allows for the radical redeployment of a linguistic violence that undercuts the pitfalls of a so-called naive empiricism, so Jelinek's prose betrays a belief in the power of negation and the critical potential of language. Second, to the degree that it mobilizes a language of violence against violence, her work implicitly raises the question of instrumentality for feminism. Her Bachmann essay indirectly broaches the question insofar as it offers a feminist transposition of Clausewitz's statement that war is nothing more than the (strategic) continuation of politics *by other means*. Pushing the Clausewitzian title to its limits, one could say that the Bachmann essay — and Jelinek's work as a whole — raises the issue whether poststructuralist feminism should indeed resort to a *strategic* use of counterviolence. Put differently, is it viable to deploy such a "violence" as an instrument of criticism in the interest of a feminist *critique*? What, if any, are the possible limitations of such a praxis?

To raise these issues means to resist adopting the charges of specular or mimetic violence to which some literary and cultural courts perhaps all too readily have condemned Jelinek's writings. My purpose then will not be to disclaim her work as marred by a metaphysical or, worse still, fascist principle of violence, but to historicize it by situating it in the context of a more general feminist praxis of "critical" violence. Indeed, we need to recognize that it is around the issue of violence that many of the current polarizations that seem to stultify certain feminist debates often gravitate. For example, it is over the *empirical* effects of what some perceive to be phantasmatic, imaginary, or fictional *representations* of violence that the recently renewed pornography debates have been conducted. Similarly, reified dualisms such as history or the "real" versus play, parody, or citation continue to fuel the controversies surrounding postmodernism, including postmodern feminism. Precisely because Jelinek's work confronts an entire range of violence thematized by feminism – from its domestic, fascist, and pornographic manifestations to its subversive redeployment – it also goes to the heart of those contentious issues that continue to divide the women's movement and feminism, in the United States and in Germany or Austria.

While Jelinek's work is representative of the stakes raised by these debates, the question of "representativeness" should not elide the issue of historical specificity. By this I wish to suggest that her writings persistently reflect on what it means to adopt a discourse of violence – including so-called feminist modes of violence – in a post-Holocaust German or Austrian context. That terms such as "context," "frame,"[22] or "intentionality"[23] have returned to the critical arena can be gleaned from some of the current discussions about the merits of poststructuralist and postmodernist strategies for political ends in general and feminism in particular. Insofar as Jelinek's writings raise the question of their proper historical "context" or "frame," they also point to the possible political and ethical *limits* of what can count as a poststructuralist or postmodernist feminist strategy.[24]

In what follows, I will first subject the use of strategic violence in poststructuralist feminism to closer scrutiny, given that this issue generally has received scant critical attention. Only after this theoretical frame has been set in place will it be possible to take up Jelinek's particular mode of linguistic violence as it is operative in the two terrains so central to her work: sexual politics and fascist violence. In a final section, I return to the question of ethico-political responsibility as it applies to Jelinek's language politics by focusing on some of the fundamental differences that separate her project from Bachmann's. For if Jelinek seeks to continue the critical tradition initiated by the *Todesarten-Zyklus*, her redeployment of a language of violence nevertheless radically departs from Bachmann's poetics of nonviolence.

Strategic Violence

Traditionally, the different feminisms have rallied around a collective objective, finding a common end in the defeat of a phallogocentric violence that is held in place by the infrastructure and sociopolitical institutions of patriarchy. But as the essentialism–constructionism debates arose, so did the voices of dissent. Is there not an essentialist, metaphysical remainder in the proposition that violence is male-gendered (so the argument goes) as long as such an argumentation is divorced from historical considerations? Not only have monolithic or reified conceptions of "male violence" been queried,[25] but poststructuralist feminism – in a rethinking of some of the impulses coming from Foucault's and Derrida's thought – has sought to interrogate the discursive constructions of violence and gender.

In her appraisal of how semiotics and discourse analysis have reconfigured the study of the social, including violence against women, Teresa de Lauretis nonetheless takes issue with what she terms Foucault's "rhetoric of violence" and Derrida's "violence of rhetoric."[26] Fastening on the blind spots of Foucault's critical practice, in particular his proposal to decriminalize rape, as well as the implied notion of male sexuality that underpins *The History of Sexuality*, she argues that Foucault's "technologies of sexualities" need to be complemented by "technologies of gender," that is, by a political analysis of "the techniques and discursive strategies by which gender is constructed and hence ... violence is en-gendered."[27] Indeed, if the term "rhetoric of violence" implies "that some order of language, some kind of discursive representation is at work not only in the concept 'violence' but in the social practices of violence as well," then the "(semiotic) relation of the social to the discursive is ... posed from the start."[28] The implications of de Lauretis's argument are at least twofold: not only should social practices no longer be considered independent of their institutional or discursive inscription but, concomitantly, discourse analysis no longer can assume a gender-neutral position. At the same time that her essay welcomes the discursive analysis of violence, then, de Lauretis cautions that feminism's uncritical adoption of structuralist or poststructuralist conceptions of language may cause it to lose sight of its concrete object or referent: empirical violence. Consequently, she finds fault with Derrida's quasi-transcendental notion of "arche-violence," defined as the "rhetorical construct of a 'violence of the letter,' the originary violence which pre-empts presence, identity, and property or propriety,"[29] since it would detract from empirical manifestations of "en-gendered" violence. Moving between these two poles, de Lauretis ends up positing that, insofar as both Foucault and Derrida fail to address the "historical fact of gender,"[30] both must fall short of explaining how "violence is en-gendered in representation."[31]

While de Lauretis thus seeks to foreground the potential risks involved in discourse analysis, it should also be noted that recent feminist theory has come to terms with some of the concerns voiced in her essay. This is true especially of that school in feminist legal studies that puts to use the notion "violence of the letter" to analyze how various social discursive practices find their institutional or juridical legitimation in the violence of the law.[32] By focusing on the intersections between power, violence, and language, poststructuralist feminism has begun to interrogate "epistemic violence,"[33] that is, the exclusionary presuppositions and foundations that shore up discursive practices insofar as these foreclose the heterogeneity, gender, class or race of the subject. Directed against all naive conceptions of materialism or empiricism, including those of some first-wave feminists, poststructuralist feminism increasingly has directed our gaze to a scrutiny of how violence is discursively construed, even at the risk of being charged with abstracting from "empirical" or "material"[34] violence against women. Judith Butler's publications in particular have made a convincing case for the political viability of such scrutiny and helped to dispel the fear that a turn to theory must *of necessity* violate the materiality of history or detract from the empirical violence inflicted on women. Her *Gender Trouble* has been influential through its reevaluation of the term "parody" in the service of a deconstruction of conventional gender roles, particularly normative heterosexuality. As such, her theory of parodic redeployment offers a response to and displacement of the program Irigaray formulated in the 1970s, namely that the *dérangement* of hegemonic discourses will come about through its *mimetic* reappropriation, that is, through the retraversal of the mirror that upholds metaphysical forms of speculation.[35]

At the same time that it targets the epistemic, institutional, and legal variants of hegemonic violence, however, poststructuralist feminism itself in turn deploys yet another kind of violence. Thus, poststructuralist feminism often has recourse to what is sometimes called "linguistic" or "textual violence,"[36] which as a negative critical force is said to undermine or "pre-empt" the purported ontological status of exclusionary social practices. To the degree that such a mode of linguistic violence operates as a *negative* force that undermines the essentialist foundations and identity politics of a metaphysical tradition, it could perhaps most aptly be labeled "critical violence." If Gayatri Chakravorty Spivak in the context of the essentialism–constructionism debates, and in the interest of an empowerment of postcolonial subjects, has argued for the necessity of *strategic* essentialism, then such a strategic textual or linguistic violence is perhaps its *negative* mirror image.

To the extent that poststructuralist feminism appropriates a form of instrumentality when it uses discursive violence as a strategy in order to endow it with critical potential, it brings into play the duplicity of the term, still preserved in the German word *Gewalt*, which refers to violence (*violentia*), force (*vis*), power (*potestas*), and, crucially, possession (as in *etwas in seiner Gewalt haben:* "to have something in one's power").[37] That is, insofar as such a feminist praxis seeks to take hold of linguistic violence, it also opposes those theories that reduce language to a mere performative force, divorced from agency as well as ends and means. As a consequence, a tension arises between, on the one hand, the noninstrumental, performative force of language and discourse, which poststructuralist feminism has inherited through its Lacanian, Derridean, or Foucauldian perspectives, and, on the other hand, the effective *re*-instrumentalization of violence in the interest of feminist ends or causes. In fact, this means that the question about what allows poststructuralist feminism to separate so-called critical from uncritical forms of violence is never at a far remove. To interrogate the critical potential of (an appropriated) linguistic violence therefore amounts to asking whether such strategic violence can count as an instrument of critique, in the strong philosophical sense of *Kritik* – a term that not only asks about the conditions of possibility of the object under investigation,[38] but further presupposes the possibility of *diacritical* separation. At the same time, the suspicion arises that there remains a residual utopian moment in poststructuralist feminism, even as violence is mustered for critical purposes, namely, the hope that such a "pure" form of counterviolence might be able to escape the vicious circle of violence.[39]

Although these theoretical observations may seem to engage the all too abstract conditions of poststructuralist feminism, their very real effects are readily noticeable in one of feminism's most contentious fields: the pornography debates. Nowhere has the instability of the conceptual boundaries that define "violence" become more apparent than in the ideological differences dividing antipornography feminists from anticensorship groups such as FACT (Feminist Anticensorship Task Force). While the former have emphasized the causal link between pornographic violence and rape and rallied around Susan Brownmiller's influential phrase that "Pornography is the theory, and rape the practice,"[40] the latter have used notions such as *intent*, *consent* or *play* to claim and safeguard a *nonviolent* pornographic realm for women. Complex and culturally diverse as these debates are, they often have pushed feminists to align themselves along stark ideological divisions, based on whether pornography is considered to be a matter of representation, fantasy, (protected) speech or believed to constitute a violent act. In the United States, Andrea Dworkin and Catharine MacKinnon, authors of the contested 1983 Minneapolis ordinance, have sought to expose the liberal edifice of the old obscenity laws, which define pornography as a matter of morality rather than gender inequality, and of a flawed "First Amendment logic,"[41] which treats pornography as protected speech or ideas, rather than as harmful prosecutable action.

Notably, MacKinnon's pamphlet *Only Words* (1993) has made it clear that the pornography debates not only concern matters of legal definition but to no small degree also bear upon linguistic questions or, more precisely, philosophico-political conceptions of language and the real. Indeed, if some would qualify the pornography debates, especially when it comes to pornography's visual forms, as a "battle over images," for MacKinnon it is no longer a matter of representation but of actionable speech, as summarized by her pun "Speech acts.... Acts speak."[42] Further, while she is not entirely unamenable to the possible restrictions revised legislation might place on gay and lesbian forms of expression, her staunch realistic position when it comes to matters of speech does not allow for stylistic difference, intent, irony, or parody, once the contested material can be proven to enable gender inequity.[43] In fact, she decisively repudiates the notion that literary or artistic value should have precedence over the pornographic. As her side references to "postmodernism" and "deconstruction" imply, such practices are to be regarded as irresponsible, even pernicious instances of sexual and textual license, willing to invest, and hence to fetishize, any commodity with (aesthetic) value. Small wonder, then, that anticensorship feminists have recognized the MacKinnon–Dworkin bill and ordinances to be a new guise of the old censorship and obscenity laws that target "sexually explicit material," rather than sexual violence. Not only do the ordinances "[entrust] the patriarchal state with the task of legally distinguishing between permissible and impermissible sexual images,"[44] as the authors of *Caught Looking* maintain; but insofar as Dworkin and MacKinnon's proposal does not provide for context, intent, or the consensual use of force – defined as "nonviolent sexual play" – it gives credence to the Moral Majority, which has successfully co-opted a quasi-feminist rhetoric for its political agenda.

Irreconcilable as the positions of these two groups must remain, their exchanges not only demonstrate a radical divisiveness over where the boundaries of sexual violence are to be drawn and over what constitutes the core, what the periphery, of pornography.[45] Critically, their encounters also have brought to a head the battle over the very *legitimacy* of a strategically redeployed "violence" in the service of feminism.

Antipornography

Despite historical, cultural and legislative differences, the pornography debates in Germany and Austria show clear affinities to those waged in the United States, as well as mutual influences, evident, for example, in Andrea Dworkin's contribution to *Emma*'s 1988 special issue on pornography. Given that the question of pornography has served to divide feminists along stark ideological lines on both sides of the Atlantic, it may seem startling that Jelinek should have participated in campaigns organized by the competing parties. Not only did she publish an excerpt of *Lust*, accompanied by a short essay, in a propornography collection called *Frauen & Pornografie* (*Women and Pornography*),[46] but she also contributed to the 1988 *Emma* campaign for an antipornography law. Spearheaded by long-time activist Alice Schwarzer, the *Emma* action aimed to reverse the 1975 reform of criminal law, which liberalized paragraph 184 and effectively legalized pornography in Germany.[47] Defining pornography not as criminally prosecutable but as an infraction of women's human rights, the bill recommended by *Emma* interprets pornography – along lines similar to Dworkin's and MacKinnon's Minneapolis ordinance – as unconstitutional, thus entitling any woman to bring a civil action against its traffickers or practitioners.[48] Concerned about the potentially restrictive effects of such revised legislation, Claudia Gehrke has contested the *Emma* initiative, emphasizing that while sexual violence needs to be combated, the struggle should not come about at the expense of women's sexuality or sexual difference. Opposing the interdiction of images (*Bilderverbot*) and victim politics promulgated by the *Emma* collective, Gehrke's introduction to *Frauen & Pornografie* urges women to reclaim a position of agency in sexual matters (much as FACT does). This means that feminism needs to vindicate a "specifically feminine form of scopophilia,"[49] which would no longer be determined by the violent economy traditionally associated with the male pornographic gaze. Gehrke's comments are significant because they illustrate the importance of strategy on the side of so-called "propornography" feminists when it comes to claiming a new form of eroticism or pornography (whereby the boundaries between both are not always sharply drawn). Furthermore, they clearly spell out what form this strategy is to take, according to a well-known figure of thought that says that, in an initial stage at least, women are to risk traversing the arsenal of sedimented images, in the hopes of reaching new unclaimed, noncolonized territory.[50]

That Jelinek should have contributed to both Schwarzer's *PorNO* and Gehrke's *Frauen & Pornografie* is perhaps not so much indicative of a theoretical indecisiveness on her part as it is of an implicit *diacritical* principle or norm on the basis of which she seeks to separate a male, exploitative pornography from its feminist reinterpretation.[51] Thus, in the *Emma* issue Jelinek responds with a resounding "Yes!" to the legislative correction proposed by the collective, on the grounds that women should have the right to determine their symbolic representations. Only the social tabooing of pornography, she maintains, can break the vicious circle that inevitably leads from pornographic representations to sexual violence.[52] Her unwavering response here curiously jars with the "condition of stuttering" to which the magnitude of the issue reduces her in "The Meaning of the Obscene" ("Der Sinn des Obszönen"), published in *Frauen & Pornografie*.[53] Instead of advocating a categorical elimination of all obscenity, this short piece lays the brunt of the argument on the side of the authorial or *critical* intention that informs a given representation.[54] The decisive issue is "whether the humiliation of a woman, her availability as a whore, is intended or, by contrast, precisely being criticized."[55] Rather than renounce the censorship position she implicitly had taken up in *Emma*, Jelinek now hesitatingly admits that such a diacritical principle might logically lead to a banning of Sade or, ironically, even Rubens.[56]

While MacKinnon's realism must reject representational politics (in the sense of *Darstellung*) as well as the theory that words have "only a referential relation to reality,"[57] which she sees as at the heart of the liberal complacency towards pornography, Jelinek, I would maintain, locates what she calls the *anti*pornographic, consciousness-raising force of her work in the very gap that separates representation, or image, from intent.[58] Indeed, in this sense Jelinek's project can be said to be related to Angela Carter's *Sadeian Woman*, which projects the possibility that pornography might be used "in the service of women,"[59] that is, as "a critique of current relations between the sexes,"[60] insofar as it parodies sexual relations. To become the historiographer of a cultural genre that for generations has purported to be ahistorical[61] defines the task awaiting the *moral pornographer* – to adopt a term of Carter's.[62] Like Carter, who emphasizes the cultural constructedness of a genre that ostensibly harps on the invariance of human nature, Jelinek repudiates the deceptive ahistorical claims of pornography, choosing instead to chronicle the history of women's humiliation.[63] Dissecting pornography thus offers an instrument to analyze the discursive sedimentation and historical constructions of gendered power relations as they transpire via sexual relations. If Jelinek advocates the critical exploitation of the pornographic, it is because it provides a privileged foray, so to speak, into the trafficking of women and the "master–slave dialectic" that upholds patriarchal history. The distancing, critical function of aesthetic mediation is to replace the direct consumption of lust that typifies pulp pornography: "'Lust' should not to be consumed like commercial pornography. Through aesthetic mediation it should, as it were, be thrown back into the face of the reader. What I aim to achieve is that the reader no longer can roll around in lust, like a pig in its sty, but instead grows pale in the process of reading."[64]

With Deleuze one is tempted to use the label "porno-logical" for Jelinek's novels, but only under one condition. Deleuze uses the term to differentiate Sade's and Sacher-Masoch's writings from commercial pornography, which consists of imperatives and descriptions, aimed at the recipient's acting out of the commands issued. In

Sade's and Sacher-Masoch's pornology, by contrast, "personal, descriptive" (empirical) violence stands in an indexical relation to a transcendent function: in the case of Sade, Spinozean reason; in that of Sacher-Masoch, Platonic Idealism.[65] Jelinek's pornographic language likewise is put to the service of a higher function: ideology critique. Yet her work goes at least one step further when it exposes the metalanguage[66] that informs the sexually explicit, licentious and scandalous rhetoric it parades, to the point where philosophical and cultural traditions – whether it be the institutions of church and family, Austria's venerable music culture, or Germany's philosophy of *Geist* – turn out to be the very accomplices of pornography.

If feminist antipornography is to deal a decisive blow to its potential consumer, Jelinek also at times seems to entertain the hope that women might be able to take back the representation of the obscene.[67] In fact, it was with just such a feminist version of the obscene in mind that she set out to write *Lust*, as a highly controversial advertising campaign launched by her publisher early on announced.[68] That such a project of reinventing feminist pornography must fail – evidenced by the abject victim position and horrific infanticide to which her female protagonist Gerti is finally reduced – seems the inevitable outcome of a novel that incessantly and obsessively reproduces the "master–slave dialectic" of commercial pornography. Clearly, this is partly the result of Jelinek's refusal to entertain a positive, utopian realm of female sexuality in the place of which she favors negativity and critical force. By default, however, the text's apparent failure also points to the aporia of how women are to become the producers of a new form of pornography, one no longer the accomplice of a phallocratic distribution of power. Rejecting the view that sexuality is purely a transgressive force, Jelinek also takes exception to the possibility of a *pure* (politically) uncontaminated and playful sexuality, of the kind propagated, for example, by the authors of *Caught Looking*. Instead, her antipornography, which flaunts the representational register of pulp pornography in order to convert it into an implement of critical analysis, ends up turning sexuality into labor or hard work.

Limits of Shame

In their critique of the metaphysical subject, poststructuralist theorists over the past decades have devised a series of radical displacements of the Cartesian *cogito*, from Lacan's mirror stage to Theweleit's definition of the *Freikorps* psyche as "I feel pain, therefore I am."[69] But seen within a feminist perspective, Jelinek has offered perhaps the most flagrant transformation of Cartesian rationality, when in her play *Illness or Modern Women* (*Krankheit oder moderne Frauen*), Carmilla pronounces: "I am sick, therefore I am."[70] Seemingly an affirmation of the so-called feminine hysteric condition, the line is a telling example of how Jelinek seeks to inflate sexually exploitative language and stereotypes about women in order to invert the representational tradition. The object under analysis is doubled, so to speak, in the medium of analysis in an attempt to displace it. As such, Jelinek's writings follow a logic of inversions (whose dynamics partly go back to Nietzsche's technique of reversal), evident, for example, in her manifesto for an antipsychologistic and anti-illusionistic theater, "Ich möchte seicht sein" ("I would like to be shallow") (1983), which ends up transforming her actors into mere linguistic clichés or patterns of language (*Sprachflächen, Sprachschablonen*).[71] More important still for a feminist politics, as noted earlier, is the program Irigaray formulated in the 1970s, when she called for women to adopt a form of ironic mimesis that, by impersonating the subordinate roles ascribed to women, eventually would lead to their overcoming. Arguing from a similar position, the critic Marlies Janz has aptly described the effects of this process in Jelinek's work as "textual perversions" – textual deviations, as it were, from the writerly norm.[72]

The track of perversions is one of the mechanisms through which poststructuralist feminism has sought to cross and transgress strict gender and other territorial boundaries. But the language of inversion and transgression also invokes other questions: is a transgression in the sense of transcendence possible?[73] Does it merely reaffirm the law, in its legal, moral and ethical dimensions, or can it incur the radical displacement hoped for? Such a question is particularly appropriate when Jelinek usurps the stereotype of feminine masochism to advance the notion of a *necessary masochism*, which she sees most fully realized in Pauline Réage's *Histoire d'O*. Can a transgression enacted through the perverse reappropriation of Freud's "feminine masochism" and masochistic pain overcome women's passivity and the repressive economy of what Jelinek calls "the everyday violence of female hygiene?" How are we to understand the deployment of one kind of violence (transgression) against another (repression)? Finally, can (an active practice of) masochism plausibly function as a technique of demystification? In order to begin to answer these questions, I would like to consider an exemplary text of Jelinek's, called "Schamgrenzen? Die gewöhnliche Gewalt der weiblichen Hygiene" ("Limits of Shame? The Everyday Violence of Female Hygiene") (1983), which particularly clearly lays bare how central the mechanism of inversion is to her strategic counterviolence. The text will interest us not only because it explicitly seeks to overthrow conventional typologies and axiologies of violence, but also because it offers an exegesis of one of the most excruciating scenes of masochistic violence in *The Piano Teacher*.

Jelinek's celebrated novel has often been read as a literary case study. Most provocative perhaps is the interpretation offered by the analyst Annegret Mahler-Bungers, who examines the latent primary narcissism that typifies the mother-daughter relationship – ironically signaled by Erika's last name, turning her into the namesake of the late Chicago theorist of narcissism, Heinz Kohut. Erika's pathological attempt to come to terms with symbolic castration, or the symbolic inscription of sexual difference, is emblematized by the scene of self-mutilation with the "paternal all-purpose razor,"[74] which thus is turned into a veritable "slaughter scene": "Erika has gendered herself, by butchering herself [*Erika hat sich geschlechtet, indem sie sich schlachtet*]."[75] This sadistic scenario, Mahler-Bungers contends, is duplicated on the level of the reader as she is pushed into the position of voyeurism, thus effectively undercutting her need to libidinize the literary text.

However valid, even necessary such a reading of the novel in psychoanalytic or psychodynamic terms may be, it should not avert attention from the novel's status as an anti-*Bildungsroman* and anti-*Künstlerroman*, or from the satirical critique it offers of the literature, popular during the 1970s and 1980s, that idealized the pre-Oedipal mother–daughter relationship. To what extent *The Piano Teacher* goes beyond the level of the case history becomes evident if one reads it in conjunction with Jelinek's "Schamgrenzen," an essay that centers upon a passage from the novel in which Erika Kohut, following one of her abortive encounters with the student Walter Klemmer, subjects her body to torturous manipulations with household utensils while seated in front of a mirror. This is the gloss Jelinek provides of the scene:

> In my novel *The Piano Teacher* the protagonist Erika Kohut ... pierces herself with kitchen utensils, pins, clothes-pegs. She is her own voyeur in the mirror, no one else watches her. This is not a striptease with spectators, in which the ritual, the props that are being used, the length of the action, grant the entire act its real significance. In striptease the decor is always more important than the woman who gradually becomes naked. Roland Barthes describes the absurdity of a strip act, in which the undressing doesn't signify a process of sexualization but rather one of de-sexualization.[76]

At its most manifest level, Erika's masochistic self-inspection reverses the dynamics of the striptease as the position of the male spectator is occupied by her own gaze. As such, this passage is the logical extension of earlier scenes set in Vienna's red-light district, in which Erika had played at peeping tom, inverting the normative male–female spectator model and scopic economy. That Barthes's analysis of the striptease in *Mythologies* should be presented as a foil for Erika's transgressive self-analysis should alert us to at least an additional interpretive layer. In Barthes's account, the bourgeois ritual of striptease provides "localized subversions," small doses of a domesticated evil that serve as a preventive measure or inoculation against a more intractable evil or "generalized subversion."[77] Focusing on the artifice and ornamentation of the decor that frames the striptease, Barthes reads the ritual as nothing less than a negation of the flesh, part of the Christian tradition, which vilifies the female body. Inoculation thus functions as one of the principal figures through which bourgeois myths convert *anti-phusis* – that is, history and, by extension, the contingency of the bourgeois condition – into *pseudo-phusis* – that is, nature, including the illusion of a so-called eternal human essence.[78] The task awaiting the Barthean *mythologist*, therefore, is to become a "semioclast," who ruthlessly destroys fossilized cultural signs.

Against the backdrop of Barthes's *Mythologies*, Erika's masochism turns into an act of demystification. Adopting the position of the female ideology critic (*Ideologiekritikerin*), Erika demystifies the representational tradition of naturalized images of women (*Frauenbilder*) to expose how historical contingency and cultural convention parade as traits of femininity. Thus, she deploys household utensils not to perpetrate the "everyday violence of female hygiene," enacted in the rituals of cleaning and cleansing, but in order to reveal the cultural territorializations that have domesticated the female body. Just as the rite of the striptease serves to inoculate society against the putative dangers of femininity, so the socialization of women in terms of hygiene and shame serves to immunize their sexuality. As Jelinek maintains:

> Erika Kohut watches herself as she inflicts pain upon herself with household and kitchen tools. This image of a woman who is penetrated literally by all kinds of kitchen appliances reveals her attempt to demystify her own body. Erika Kohut conducts research, so to speak, conducts an analysis of her own body, an analysis that always also affects her body negatively: it is a necessary masochism, the attempt, that is, to transcend mere striptease and its rules, laid down by men. Of course she feels pain. But at least she engages in an attempt to discover more in her own body than simply the territory defined by men. Erika Kohut exercises a resistance against the feeling of shame [*Scham*]. She penetrates herself as if she were entering a house that is off limits, and she watches herself doing so. Shame can only be a weapon once women are no longer ashamed of themselves, once women's shame is no longer the property of men; when women no longer are disgusted [*sich ekeln*] by themselves but by men, and when men are left alone with their feelings of disgust [*Ekel*]; when the boundaries of shame do not cut up women, but destroy the territorializations set up by men. Shame is the recognition of the most real forms of male violence, though shame often degenerates into an acknowledgment of women's helplessness.[79]

Paradoxically, in this meta-analysis masochistic pain becomes the subversive instrument through which the body is stripped naked and – literally – dissected (*sezieren*) at the moment of its violation. By means of a "necessary" masochism Jelinek projects the transgression of man-made rules, interdictions, territorial delimitations, and ideological constructions that colonize the female body. Pain is held to be the instrument of analysis (*Analyse, Forschung*) – a term Jelinek again takes quite literally in the sense of *Zersetzung*,[80] that is, as the dissolution or subversion of the object under analysis. Similarly, the word *Scham* is to be understood in all its possible connotations, not only as the affect "shame" – a function of the mechanism of repression – but also as the female sexual organ, or *die weibliche Scham*. In explicating the relation between shame and hygiene, and in contesting the validity of women's disgust toward their bodies, Jelinek in fact inverts the principles of psychoanalysis, the rules, discursive delimitations, and definitions legitimized by the Freudian tradition.[81] That sensations of disgust figure prominently in Freud's emerging theory of female sexuality can already be gauged, for example, from a famous letter he sent to Wilhelm Fließ, which, proposing an early version of the repression hypothesis, advanced the thesis that "something organic play[s] a part in repression."[82] What Freud had in mind were experiences of disgust and shame at the sight of one's sexual organs and excrements, sensations that were said to appear at an earlier stage in girls than in boys.[83]

Working through the implications of the Freud text, "Schamgrenzen" rejects hygiene as the consolidation of women's violent socialization into sensations of disgust towards their bodily functions.[84] At stake, for Jelinek, is how women have historically functioned as *subjects* and *objects* of shame. If shame now is to operate as a weapon of sorts, it is because the figure of thought at work here again dictates that a retraversing or passage *through* violence is necessary in order to reach beyond the violent instatement of the limits of *shame*, or *Schamgrenzen*. More than just the expression of a language of desire or a simple transgression of the law, Jelinek's appropriation of masochism is an attempt to empty out and revise the conceptual and discursive apparatus about sexuality and gender in order to forever redefine or relocate its borders (*Grenzen*).[85] However, if Erika's self-dissection is to function as an instrument of analysis, then this operation on the dominant representations of women can only come about at a certain price. Following a decidedly antihumanistic twist, Jelinek turns the female body into a mere allegorical surface or exterior plane, whose contours are to be radically redrawn. Just as antipornography was to serve a higher function, so Jelinek's representation of masochism enacts the sublimation of bodily pain as it is lifted to the level of critical meta-analysis.

Aestheticizing Violence?

To try to venture beyond the limits of shame may mean not only to risk overstepping the boundaries of social taboos, but also to go beyond the proper or conventional limits of representation – in the multiple sense of "what," "who," and "how" to represent. Such a risk is particularly pertinent for anyone adopting a discourse of violence in postwar Austria or Germany, even if it takes the form of camp, postmodern pastiche, parody, collage, or quotation.[86] That aesthetics, image, and politics are not at odds with one another has been brought home by Walter Benjamin's epilogue to his technology essay, which countered the fascist aestheticization of politics with the politicization of art. What the consequences of Benjamin's essay for poetry and literature might be is evident from Bachmann's second Frankfurt lecture, "Über Gedichte" ("About Poetry") (1959–60), in which she offered the work of Kaschnitz, Sachs, Celan and others as a counterpoint to the principles of "art for art's sake," overshadowing postwar German and Austrian poetry. An attempt to formulate the ethico-political task of poetry after the Holocaust, Bachmann's lecture rejected the aestheticization of violence in poetry and poetics, whose legacy it traced from George via Dadaism, Surrealism and Marinetti's "aesthetics of war"[87] to Benn and Pound, showing that the step from pure aestheticism to barbarism was but a small one. For even if Surrealism eventually would be banned by National Socialism, Bachmann noted, Breton's infamous call for a "pistol shot in the crowd" illustrated how dangerously close the language of victims could come to the violence of perpetrators.[88]

It is precisely this pressing question about the complicity between aestheticized violence and fascism, at the center of Bachmann's lecture, that also has come to haunt Jelinek's writings. On one level, her work is affected by the debates about the politics of postmodernism, notably those contesting its practice of citation. Where modernism could still more or less unconditionally hail the disruptive and potentially violent force of citation, recent debates, by contrast, have called for a more restrained use of what often is considered to be a postmodern abuse of quotation. If speech act theory distinguishes between "use" and "mention" (or citation), it is also true that one never cites in a political, cultural, or historical vacuum. The potential perils of postmodernist techniques and strategies have become especially palpable through high-profile controversies about the "politics of representation," such as the one surrounding Syberberg's *Hitler*, a film whose neoconservative bent unmistakably raises the question of the interrelations between aesthetics, image, and contextual frame.[89] Already Susan Sontag's early essay on Riefenstahl, "Fascinating Fascism" (1974), pointed to the potential risks involved in postmodernist quotation, especially when it is a matter of parading Nazi materials. If her influential 1964 essay "Notes on Camp" celebrated camp sensibility for providing a critical transvaluation of mass culture, requiring a good deal of irony and detachment on the part of the artist-poseur, then the Riefenstahl essay, by contrast, addresses the limits of "camp" appropriation and quotation, not only in Riefenstahl revivalism but also in the excesses of contemporary art. Commenting on Robert Morris's eroticization of Nazi regalia and his statement that the Nazi icon is "the only image that still has any power to shock," Sontag's essay cautions that "shocking people in this context also means inuring them, as Nazi material enters the vast repertory of popular iconography usable for the ironic commentaries of Pop art."[90]

The gratuitousness of the desire to shock, however, seems at odds with the political investment that characterizes Jelinek's handling of Nazi imagery. While her plays aim to shock her fellow Austrians through the spectacular reenactment of their country's Nazi past — with a virulence equaled perhaps only by Thomas Bernhard — they do so in order to neutralize the media's anaesthetizing spectatorial effects and to promote critical self-reflection — in the best Frankfurt School tradition. Yet, anyone who even ironically pays tribute to Goebbels, as Jelinek does at the beginning of her *Illness or Modern Women*, must be willing to face the issue of representational propriety. As I suggested at the outset, Jelinek's use of counterviolence may not fully dispel the specter of *Ungeist*,[91] nor can this specter simply be laid to rest by seeing it as the simple return of the repressed, or even the "return of the undead," to cite one of her favorite figures of speech. Translated into the context of postmodernism, the question of whether such a representational mode is the most appropriate strategy when it comes to addressing National Socialism and the Holocaust — as Saul Friedlander has reminded us — must indeed remain a disquieting one.[92] At the same time, we may wish to heed Friedlander's remarks that it is also a matter of looking at tensions produced by individual works, as we – readers and critics – eschew leveling generalizations while simultaneously seeking to avoid partisanship or even downright intuitivism.

With these tensions and questions in mind, let me proceed then further to draw the contours of the "critical frame" for Jelinek's work, by proposing yet another way in which one can read her language of violence, namely, as an iconoclastic critique of visual and spectatorial culture. For at the same time that Jelinek's theatrical and fictional work flaunts the spectacle, it is permeated by a sustained condemnation of the image and by the belief that the disruptive force of language can serve as a possible corrective to the aestheticization of violence. Especially in the work of the 1980s, the image becomes the privileged site of critique, evident in the mock deferential salutes to Goebbels, Baudrillard, and the media with which *Illness or Modern Women* starts out, as if to suggest that there may exist a continuity between the propagandistic exploitation of the cinematic image and the current proliferation of visual simulation. Texts such as *Oh Wilderness, Oh Protection from Her* (*Oh Wildnis, oh Schutz vor ihr*) or *Totenauberg* thematize nature's commodification into commercial images through Austria's lucrative tourist industry, a commodification never at a far remove from *Heimat* ideology. Nowhere is her language more biting than in her 1986 *Heinrich-Böll* prize speech, which – in a sardonic reference to Austria's former president, Kurt Waldheim, and the leader of the right-wing FPÖ, Jörg Haider – is called "In den Waldheimen und auf den Haidern." Austria here is evoked as "a country, of which you certainly have made a mental image [*Bild*], for it is pretty like a picture [*Bild*], as it lies there in the middle of its landscape, which it owns."[93] If Baudrillard designates the age of simulation as one characterized by "the liquidation of all referents,"[94] then seen in an Austrian context such a production of the hyperreal, as Jelinek's work indicates, also implies the cancellation and annihilation of the historical past. Her mockery of modern-day Austrian tourists, whose camcorders seek to capture the forest, never seems more appropriate than when she calls them "images without memory."[95]

But Jelinek's critique of how the ideological transpires through the iconic targets, above all, as noted earlier, the tradition of *Frauenbilder* (images of women) – in other words, that aesthetic tradition which, as Christa Wolf suggests in her *Cassandra* project, objectifies and petrifies "woman" by elevating her to the position of its most cherished *eidolon*.[96] Representative in this respect is Jelinek's short text "Bild und Frau" ("Image and Woman"), which was published separately in the anthology *Blauer Streusand* but already appears in *Illness or Modern Women*, where it is subjected to a technological displacement, as it is pronounced by a mechanically sounding woman's voice over a loudspeaker. Fastening on three key terms, *image* (*Bild*), *woman* (*Frau*), *nature* (*Natur*), the text enacts a radical linguistic destruction or dissection of the phantasmatic image *woman* and a series of *Frauenbilder*, most centrally that of women's so-called mimetic relation to nature. Used in all its polysemy, the word *Bild* summons not only the meanings image, representation (*Darstellung*), simulacrum and *mimesis* (*Abbild*,

Nachbildung), or the theatrical tradition (*Bühnenbild*), but also the compound *bildschön* (pretty as a picture) or the prosaic *ein Bild von einem Mädchen* (a picture-perfect girl). Similarly, the words *Gehalt* (content, inner value, salary) and *Vermögen* (capability, fortune) are caught in a network of lexical chains in which the exchange of semantic "value" ironically simulates the exchange value of "woman" in various discursive circuits. Through the use of metathesis, homonyms, puns, neologisms, epigrams, lexical sliding, and parataxis, the text not only undercuts epistemic clichés and narrative cohesion, but also the false stability of an aesthetic tradition that uses the female body as the privileged vehicle to construct its metaphoric and allegorical images (in German: *in Bildern sprechen*). Rather than affirming women's alleged mimetic relation to nature, the text thus stages a destructive *fort-da* game in which the image "woman" slowly disappears. Or, as Eva Meyer puts it, "Woman reappears, occupied as she is with her disappearance (*[Die Frau] taucht wieder auf, beschäftigt wie sie ist, mit dem Verschwinden*)."[97]

Jelinek's condemnation of the image *through* language seems to partake in the same "anti-ocularcentric" tradition that Martin Jay has uncovered in French thought.[98] Indeed, passages such as the sarcastic "images without memory," used to refer to her compatriots, should be seen against the backdrop of her attempt to retrieve the memory of a time-honored Austrian language tradition, which was cut off by the Nazi seizure of power and the concomitant purge of the Austrian idiom. Often in the context of autobiographical revelations, Jelinek has sought to define her writerly project as the recuperation of a lost Judeo-Austrian literary and linguistic tradition, interrupted and virtually annihilated by National Socialism. It is the satirical tradition, "the tradition of dissecting [*die Tradition des Sezierens*]," most artfully exercised by Kraus and Canetti, whose last remnants she recognizes in the work of a few contemporary east Austrian writers: the poetry of Elfriede Gerstl, the essayistic *oeuvre* of the critic Franz Schor, and – as a lone exception in Germany – the satirical interventions of Marcel Reich-Ranicki. Hence the wealth of rhetorical techniques in her writings, particularly those commonly associated with Austrian culture: Freudian *Witze*, puns and slips of the tongue, and perhaps her favorite language game, the *Kalauer*, or dumb joke, popularized by the Austrian actor-playwright Nestroy.

There appears to exist a particularly strong affinity with Kraus, who, as the ardent critic of the *Neue freie Presse* became the self-appointed judge of Austrian journalism, and who, as the author of the *Sprachlehre*, went so far as to call for "penalties against public sexual offenses committed with the German language." Informed by Kraus's language politics, Jelinek takes up the mask of the inhuman satirist, whose interventions – as Benjamin's Kraus essay appropriately suggests – amount to nothing less than "the devouring of the adversary." The satirist "is the figure in whom the cannibal was received into civilization"[99] – a cannibalism, incidentally, that Jelinek *quite literally* put on the stage when she adapted Nestroy's *Hauptling Abendwind* as *Präsident Abendwind*, with President Waldheim now figuring as the barbaric man-eater. Jelinek's relation to the Austrian idiom does not display the self-hatred that marked Kraus's attacks on

Yiddish, or *mauscheln*.[100] Instead, it is precisely because the German language was stripped of all Jewish and Slavic elements that it needs to be pronounced as if it were an artificial language (*Kunstsprache*) – as the stage directions to her controversial play *Burgtheater* indicate – so it can never again be co-opted by any form of *Heimat* ideology.

> *Burgtheater* is a play about language, the destruction of language, the exodus of language from the stage and from people's minds; it is a play about the Nazi horror, which assailed the German language – a language that still has not been denazified. All Jewish elements, all language culture has been driven out. What remains on stage is kitsch and sentiment.[101]

As the inheritor of an impoverished language, the Austrian writer once again becomes an exterritorial subject, reliving the plight of the Austrian-Jewish novelist Joseph Roth. Its most representative figure in postwar Austria is Ingeborg Bachmann, whose self-imposed exile in Italy proved to be an attempt to undo the "cosmopolitan impoverishment" and vandalizing of the Austrian idiom. If Bachmann to the last remained opposed to a new German (*Neudeutsch*), which, "as a universal key," could unlock all doors, it was because it failed to open "the one door of central importance today"[102] – the door giving access to Austria's cultural past.

"Whereof one cannot speak, thereof one must write"

In taking up the heritage of Austrian *Sprachkritik*, Jelinek's continuation of the tradition appears to be marked by at least a double displacement, one informed by gender politics and discourse analysis, the other, by her position as a post-Holocaust writer, who uses linguistic destruction or *Sprachzertrümmerung* as a radical way to realize her ethical and poetic responsibilities. But the word "ethical" must appear like a contradiction of sorts when applied to a writer who so obviously taunts the morals of her fellow citizens and whose radical transvaluation of values at times may seem more indebted to a Nietzschean genealogy. Nor does her use of linguistic violence seem particularly in tune with the close connection between language and ethics that Bachmann recognized in Kraus's aphorism "All the merits of a language are rooted in morality,"[103] which she understood as a remedy against a poetics of violence that risks remaining ensnared in fascism. If according to Bachmann postwar German language is to acquire a different pace (*Gangart*),[104] its force is to come from a new moral impetus, one that precedes all customary moral and ethical systems and is founded each time anew by the writer. Granted then that both Bachmann and Jelinek engage in *Sprachkritik* to denounce a politics of violence, must not Jelinek's appropriation of linguistic violence by comparison still appear as the very embodiment of poetic or political irresponsibility? How, then, are these radically divergent views of responsibility to be reconciled?

At the risk of proposing all too rigid a conceptual grid, I would like to suggest in conclusion that if Bachmann's work points to the utopian realm of a language devoid of violence, Jelinek's writings instead expose the violent excesses of language and discursive practices. And if Bachmann thematizes silence, then Jelinek does not stop exhibiting erratic speech and the discursive derailments of language. Structured around the progressive silencing of its female protagonists, Bachmann's *Todesarten-Zyklus* presents the very renunciation of speech, exemplified by Franza Jordan's muteness or the failed mock psychoanalytic sessions the "I" has with Malina. To be sure, this does not mean that her writings fail to address the intersections between language, power, and violence. Through the narrative technique of "I-exchange" (*Ich-Wechsel*), for example, Malina becomes the grammatical subject of language and the agent of violence, pushing the "I" into the position of an impersonal "nobody" and eventually a dehumanized "something."[105] But for all its allusions to Wittgensteinian language games, the novel *Malina* remains committed to the utopian dimension of linguistic nonviolence, illocutionary speech, communicability, and dialogue, expressed in the tale of the princess of Kagran. Already the Frankfurt lectures and various other early essays seem to mourn the unattainability of pure language, one free of the artificial communicability of Esperanto or of the violence of the phrase (*die Phrase*),[106] whose inauthenticity is denounced with a force reminiscent of Kraus. The utopia of language Bachmann's work seeks to reach is that of *pure technique*, pure mediacy, located outside the realm of instrumental reason and mythical violence. Its radical anti-instrumental nature is best captured in the following seemingly unobtrusive line from the first Frankfurt lecture, whose ramifications are fundamentally at odds with the essentially polemical and strategic force with which Jelinek endows language: "If it were our turn to speak, if we possessed language, we would not need weapons [Hätten wir das Wort, hätten wir Sprache, wir bräuchten die Waffen nicht]."[107]

In the Frankfurt lectures the plight of the modernist poet remains defined by a deeply unsettling duplicity, on the one hand, an all too imperfect language, on the other, the improbable utopian prospect of a full language, one marked by plenitude, of which literature is but a fragmentary realization.[108] In her search for a commensurable language able to contain historical truth, the poet at times seems suspended between a defective, sometimes deviant language and the perils of silence:

> The literature that lies behind us – what does it amount to: words that have been carved from the walls of the heart [*von Herzwänden geschnittene Worte*] and tragic silence, and fallow fields of worn-out words [*zerredete Worte*] and ponds of foul-smelling, cowardly silence; always all of this has been part of it – language and silence – and in a two-fold way. And again and again both language and silence beckon and tempt us. Our share in error has been secured, but when it comes to our share in a new form of truth, where does that share start?[109]

Much as in Jelinek's work, one word here condenses a history of meanings. Thus, Bachmann's chronicle of silence implicitly refers to the language crisis of Hofmannsthal's "Chandos Letter," or, again, to the silence captured in Wittgenstein's well-known aphorism – "Whereof one cannot speak, thereof one must be silent" – which, in its delimitation of the boundaries that demarcate the sayable from the unsayable, was to guard against the frenzied language [*Sprachrausch*] typical of George's aestheticism or Heidegger's philosophy of being.[110] Centrally, within the context of the lecture, the word "silence" above all betokens the silence of literature in the face of the Holocaust – from the traumatic silence of the victims and the cowardly silence of those who went into "inner exile," to the inadvertent silence that befalls the postwar author, incapable as her language remains of capturing the incommensurable and horrendous dimensions of Germany's and Austria's war crimes – an incommensurability already voiced by Brecht when he asked: "What kind of times are these, when a conversation about trees almost amounts to a crime, because it implies a silence about so many atrocities."[111] If postwar poetry, however provisionally at first, is to reclaim its share in truth and justice, it is to start by confronting the historic *and* poetic errors of the past. Rejecting the violence of past poetic forms no less than their claims to authority, the postwar writer is to risk a new probing and experimental encounter with language, of the kind Bachmann recognized in Celan's *Death Fugue*.[112]

It is then as a radically different response to the very limits imposed on the postwar Austrian writer that one can understand the *excess* of language and speech that so drastically divides Jelinek's prose from Bachmann's concern with traumatic silence. How different Jelinek's take on language and silence really is, can be gauged from a short interview in which she lapses into a Freudian slip (*Versprechung*) of Wittgenstein's famous aphorism.[113] Offering an account of how her literary texts over the years have turned into nothing *but* language, Jelinek misstates Wittgenstein's aphorism, rendering it as "Whereof one cannot speak, thereof one must write." Her lapse, which, ironically, assumes the form of a *Kalauer*, dramatically changes the aphorism, turning it from a potential injunction to guarded silence into a call to write. More than just a simple confounding of *schreiben* (writing) and *schweigen* (to be silent), this Freudian lapse, I would submit, presents in condensed form the very principle at the heart of Jelinek's writerly project, namely, her radical commitment to break the silence of those responsible for covering up Austria's Nazi past. Indeed, as she indicates in the interview:

I don't think much of those who chatter about the "grey areas of the unsayable," or, as Musil called it, prattle poetically [*poeseln*] .... One can call things by their name. One can call the parties responsible for present conditions by their name; one can call the perpetrators and victims by their names; and once one is able to name these names, one must do so, and, indeed, one *can* do so.

Thus, while Bachmann's work remains marked by traumatic silence and an awareness that the magnitude of the Holocaust tests the very categories of representation,[114] Jelinek's polemical force above all aims to shatter the prohibitive public and political *taboos* that have shrouded Austria's Nazi past in silence. Going against the "grey areas of the unsayable," which risk being confounded with the truly unspeakable, Jelinek practices a destruction through language, driven by the desire to break the silence and to name victims and perpetrators unequivocally. To be sure, in her attempt to do so, Jelinek – like Bachmann – fails to examine the victim politics through which German feminism, sometimes too easily, has collapsed the difference between women's oppression and the historical phenomenon of fascism. In addition, her appropriation of representational violence at times may seem too confident of its critical, even redemptive power. Still, Jelinek's writing project thus also presents an important challenge to contemporary feminisms. Precisely because it is located at the limits of representational politics, her work invites feminism to reconsider the tenuous possibilities no less than the real limitations of a strategically redeployed violence.

8

WHATEVER HAPPENED TO FEMINIST THEORY?

To raise the question of whatever happened to feminist theory is to assume that it has come to pass, that it has come to an end, and that together with what some have called the period of *post*-feminism,[1] we now have entered the epoch of *post*-theory. To be sure, a survey of the current critical field indicates that pronouncements about theory's death or end are only half true or, to say the least, premature. The "practice of theory" is alive and well in a variety of contexts, from the literary field to political theory, from postcolonial to queer to psychoanalytic theory. Yet, whether practiced institutionally – in literature, women's studies, government, history departments – or invoked in the political playing field at large, "theory" has acquired a string of negative epithets. It is assumed to be elitist, male-identified, reifying, totalizing, totalitarian, specular, spectatorial, obscurantist, apolitical, universalizing, hegemonic, occidental, imperialistic, Eurocentric, antidemocratic, violent – to cite just a few of the most commonly heard invectives. Not just so-called highbrow theory – the branch of mostly French-inspired feminism that was *en vogue* in the 1970s and 1980s – has met with disfavor, but the word "theory" itself – often used as a stand-in or placeholder for poststructuralism or neo-Marxism – has reached the low level of a slur, made for name-calling. In its place have come situated terms that aim to reflect difference, pluralism, and context-dependence, such as praxis, experience, the real, narrativity, performance, body politics, new historicism, pragmatism. To be sure, it is hardly astonishing that feminist theory, not unlike theory "at large," has lately become the target of much political contestation, nor that some of its manifestations have been criticized by members from within the feminist movement. In fact, feminist theory has always elicited its share of suspicion, if not invariably for the same reasons. In the late 1970s and 1980s, French feminist theory increasingly came under attack for its intrinsic essentialism, ethnocentrism, and assumed universalist standpoint, in the name, often, of a more sophisticated social constructivism. Today, it is anti-foundationalist poststructuralist theory in turn that is taken to task for being counterproductive, intrinsically apolitical, not materialistic enough, or "merely cultural."[2] In that sense, the observation Judith Butler makes in *Feminist Contentions*, that we are presently in the throes of "theory wars,"[3] has lost none of its relevance.

Why, one might ask, is this the case and how exactly did we arrive at this historical juncture? And what, for that matter, do we precisely mean when we refer to "theory" or "feminist theory"? Literary theory, cultural theory, social theory, political theory? And why should the practice of theory have given rise to "wars," including, or perhaps especially, in the feminist playing field? Is all theory bad or only "pure" theory, to use nomenclature that Marx and Engels first brought into circulation through their *German Ideology*? Must theory be anathema to politics, especially a feminist emancipatory or progressive politics, or is it possible to engage in "theoretical activism"?[4] But an entirely different set of questions can be added to this list of queries, which only further compounds the issue at hand. Does theory merely mean the laying out of principles that rule practice? Is it always already normative, as is the case with a Frankfurt-style critical theory, or does poststructuralist theory elide and set adrift such claims to normativity, and, as is implied, normalization?[5] Should one distinguish between, on the one hand, "traditional" or "pure" theory, which is premised on a rigid subject–object rift, and, on the other hand, an altogether different branch of theory, a new style of ideology critique that is all too conscious of its own inevitable implication in power? Can only poststructuralist theory lay claim to such self-reflection, or is it really critical theory, as some of its adherents would affirm, that provides the most viable alternative?

What I want to do in this chapter is address the present status of feminist theory by taking a particular moment in contemporary feminist debates as a starting point, namely, the collection *Feminist Contentions* (1995), the Anglo-American translation of a book that first appeared in Germany as *Der Streit um Differenz* (1993) and originally centered around the question of feminism's links to postmodernism, in line with another collection entitled *Feminism/Postmodernism* (1990).[6] To be sure, as the collection's editor, Linda Nicholson, cautions, the book refuses to be an anthology about the state of feminist theory at the present.[7] Instead, it reflects an extended "conversation" between feminist theorists, punctuated sometimes by misunderstandings but also by "productive conflicts." Heeding Nicholson's cautionary remarks, I would nonetheless like to take her up on the invitation extended to the reader that she offer an assessment of "what the volume is about."[8] For it seems to me that the "disputes" assembled in *Feminist Contentions* prompt a range of questions about the status, viability, or even desirability of theory for feminism and point up the theoretical controversies that have seemingly fractured the group as to which "theory" it should embrace. The differences not only reflect on the state of critique, that is, whether feminism should embrace critical theory's normative critique or rather the antifoundationalism of poststructuralism. In addition to revealing deep-seated disagreements about fundamental, methodological assumptions, principles, and premises that infuse the shared project of feminism, *Feminist Contentions* also displays a triangulation that to some extent, it seems to me, has become defining for theoretical feminisms: the "contentious" encounter between the two poles – poststructuralist and critical theory – is mediated by feminist pragmatism or neopragmatism, which becomes an alternative, an exit route out of the deadlock. In fact, whenever attempts have been made to suture the rifts between poststructuralism and critical theory, the answer almost always has been pragmatism. In this context, theory then automatically equals a problematic universalism, pragmatism not just a corrective fallibilism but also judicious political practice. Those who abjure theory altogether have elected a pragmatic frame; others, themselves theorists, have opted for the mediating construction of a "pragmatic theory" that still remains theoretical yet, instead of being universalistic and abstract, is situated, fallibilistic, local, and therefore radically nonfoundationalist.[9] In reading *Feminist Contentions* as "representative," I would like to ask whether the volume isn't symptomatic of larger strategic shifts that have occurred in the feminist playing field but also in the critical arena at large – without, naturally, wanting to leap beyond our historically or culturally situated "now." In many ways, I will suggest, antifoundationalist postmodern and poststructuralist versions of feminist theory have had to make way for a rivaling neopragmatic antifoundationalism. Especially in the United States, the revival of pragmatism in the form of neopragmatism has presented itself as the only tenable alternative to theory, and not just, as we shall see, in the writings of Richard Rorty, though he has certainly been most vocal in exhorting feminists to leave behind so-called metaphysical, representational correspondence theories, and, above all, old-fashioned ideology critique. But could it be that a series of problems might threaten to go unnoticed if one cathects only on the ills or symptoms of theory? Might one over-look the dangers of a "strong" pragmatism, a position that, I would argue, could turn out to be equally limiting and perhaps as indefensible as *pure* theory?

Naturally, the present essay will not seek to reify or set in stone the debates assembled in *Feminist Contentions*, nor is it meant as a defense or apology of (pure) theory. Instead, it seeks to intervene deliberatively in some of the debates about feminist theory, in which I wish to take up the position of an interlocutor in a democratic discussion about part of what currently engages feminism. Clearly, this intervention does not want to posit that all of feminism is or should be theory, for that would amount to identifying the whole (of feminism) with only a part. But in response to critics who might peremptorily object that to focus on theory means to take away valuable time from political praxis, I want to stress that it is also high time that we take stock of the often covert discursive strategies performed under the aegis of antitheoretical charges. It is time that we look at some of the rhetorical and strategic arguments that are tendered in the service of the theory debates. What kind of perhaps untenable arguments or silent assumptions are being passed off under the rubric of the against-theory debates – arguments that concern politics, praxis, agency or the real? Can neopragmatism – especially of the sort propagated by Rorty – really lay claim to and make good on all of the positive items it lists on its political agenda? Or might it, just as much as theory, be susceptible to contestation?

To identify oneself as a theorist, these days, means finding oneself, even before the discussion has started, in a defensive mode, having to qualify what one says with frequent disclaimers. Whenever one invokes theory lately, certain doors more easily seem to get shut.[10] For one, the demand for democracy, democratic speech, and discussion is such that one must avoid obfuscation, deviousness, manipulation, rhetorical ploys. In the interest of direct, immediate access or transparent communication, all detours must be avoided, all difficult terminology shut out. Theory, especially poststructuralist theory, has not fared well in that context.[11] In Habermas's critique of poststructuralism, the latter's alleged antidemocratic intent is said to assume the guise of mere faddish aestheticism or other modes of excessive formalism. Formalism in this setting means at least two things: a quasi-Kantian ahistorical "transcendentalism," which, regardless of historical or cultural differentials, detects the same formal laws, structural similarities, and regularities everywhere. "Transcendental" – a term borrowed from Kant – then means the retrieval of the enabling conditions of possibility that either ground or, as the case may be, "un-ground," set adrift the object under analysis, say, subject positions, agency, or sexual identities. Or, again, the allusion to poststructuralism's excessive formalism (along the form-content divide) is meant to fault it for a superficial ornamentalism that fails to heed political content. If nothing else, this essay hopes to redirect the flow of current stymied debates by challenging some of these and other entrenched presuppositions that are frequently advanced to discount or discredit feminist theorists.

Without wanting to invalidate the distinctive, specific history of feminist theory, the present essay also maintains that its ends need to be analyzed not only *internally*, that is, from within the history of feminism or women's studies, but also *relationally*, that is, in the context of broader cultural and political developments in the critical field at large.[12] Thus, in studying the history of difference within the feminist movement, one must proceed internally to demonstrate how the call for diversity helped to variegate the assumed white middle-class consensus of the movement, including the early work of second-wave feminists. A contextualized reading additionally reveals that feminists in the social sciences and related disciplines were theorizing difference at the same time that corresponding developments in postmodern philosophy, epistemological antifoundationalism, and postcolonial theory were taking shape. Similarly, in examining the changed status of theory in the movement, one can proceed internally and isolate, for example, radical feminism's early criticisms of theory, made in the name of women's experience, diverse history, or the concrete exigencies of the real. If one steps outside the movement's internal history, it additionally becomes clear that the current antitheory moment in feminism is in step with a more general trend, away from theory to new historicism and neopragmatism. Thus, some strands in current antitheoretical feminisms must be situated in the wake of the more encompassing theory wars that rose to prominence in the 1980s: the "fall" of deconstruction and poststructuralism as a result of the Heidegger and de Man controversies, the trade embargo on the import of foreign, especially French theory, the renewal of American pragmatism, and, quite recently, the Sokal affair.

To be sure, in the past feminist voices have often been raised against an interpretive practice that looks beyond the movement's perimeters, for fear that feminism would once again be made to look secondary, subservient to a male-identified "master"-

theory or discourse. Assuming a complimentary external perspective, however, doesn't necessarily mean that one moves wholly outside of feminist theory or that one becomes dependent on a stronger discourse that a supposedly derivative feminism needs in order to be set on sound, validating footing. Such concerns have no place once we conceive of feminism as intrinsically interdisciplinary, always in dialogue with multiple interlocutors, engaged in an extensive, open-minded give-and-take. To assume such a "double take" – a double critical view, which attends to feminism's internal history *and* external relations – is to be better equipped as one assesses the full complexities of the issues at hand. For it means to take the project of dialogue seriously, not as a way of palliating difference but in the interest of coalition-building. Besides stressing the methodological necessity that exists for such a "double take," I also want to argue (in perhaps all too commonsensical terms) that we try to live multiply defined feminist roles that *can* include theory. Just as we readily acknowledge difference, multiple cultural positions, identity allegiances and alliances when we discuss subject formation across race, class, and gender, so we may need to stop casting ourselves and other feminists in single-issue either/or roles: either you're a practical activist *or* a theorist, but you can't be both. On the level of theoretical formulations, too, this means giving up dogmatic territorial delineations and delimitations, jettisoning the turf wars and factionalism that increasingly have come to define theoretical feminisms as I am writing this. Certainly, a measure of healthy *agonism* (to evoke Chantal Mouffe's conception of the term) may be warranted, but must we settle for a full-blown, crippling *antagonism* that makes all dialogue impossible? Don't we misconceive of the nature of political contestation and the struggle that are supposed to accompany progressive politics when we instate unbridgeable borders between ourselves? Don't we then internalize antagonisms under the false perception that politics amounts to polemics?[13] Contentiousness, then, surely has nothing to do anymore with the productive contestation that directs progressive political struggles. In the interest of constructive debate, dialogue, and discussion, the present essay, therefore, will shuttle back and forth from analyzing claims about theory to examining claims about feminist theory. Before concentrating on the historical juncture that produced *Feminist Contentions*, I will first trace the more notable moments that have governed the antitheory climate.

Against Theory

To consider the current antitheory positions in their full complexity, one does well to emphasize that the word "theory" has come to stand for a subfield or part that often – following the logic of synecdoche – is confounded with the whole: poststructuralist theory, including all of its offshoots, such as poststructuralist psychoanalysis.[14] Thus, poststructuralist theory is supposed to have claims and pretensions to lasting foundations, so that, if unqualified, it amounts to nothing more than a transhistorical metaphysics, quaintly archaic and out of date in an era of new historicism. Trapped in language, theoretical poststructuralism is said to cast unremitting doubt on the "phenomenal" and the "referential" from the perspective of its self-enclosed linguistic universe. Such critical arguments about poststructuralism are less concerned with the theoretical enterprise as such, expressed, say, in scientific theories that test general principles on the basis of evidence, and make adjustments to the model in order to finetune or, if necessary, discard the theory under consideration. Rather, in presuming that poststructuralist theory hovers above the real, its critics in many ways hark back to the ancient theory-praxis divide, including the scholastic distinction between *vita activa* and *vita contemplativa*. For its detractors, poststructuralism fundamentally exposes a "will to theory" (to paraphrase Nietzsche–Foucault) that hopelessly remains trapped in a pernicious power-knowledge model.[15] But in an even more restrictive use, theory simply stands for literary theory. When de Man, for example, spoke of a resistance to theory, he literally meant literary theory (though also more), swayed as he was by the euphoria of having literature and theory operate as instruments of ideology critique. The exuberance with which theory was greeted in the 1970s partially derived from the belief that the critic could use literary theory as a tool of ideology critique, much as the bygone humanist deployed literature as a lens on the eternally human.

In the mid- to late 1980s, poststructuralist theory entered into a political crisis, augmented by historical events, above all the revelations about Heidegger's and de Man's Nazi pasts, which seemed to lend credence to the suspicion that deconstruction depended on intrinsically suspect, nihilistic premises. The critique of poststructuralism's politics, however, had started well before the full-blown political crisis came about. In the early 1980s, pragmatist critics began to equate "theory" – be it mainly literary theory – with the apolitical. The signature text that sparked considerable controversy was "Against Theory" (1982) by Steven Knapp and Walter Benn Michaels. Seemingly speaking for all of pragmatism, though confining themselves to the field of literary criticism and studies, Knapp and Michaels successfully put a string of antitheory arguments into circulation that produced ripple effects well beyond the walls of literature departments.[16] In setting the tone for the post-(French) theory climate that gained prominence in those years, they took on the ontological and epistemological misconceptions that accompanied what they called the "theoretical impulse," maintaining that the Anglo-American theory tradition had been almost exclusively concerned with knowledge production: "If the ontological project of theory has been to imagine a condition of language before intention, its epistemological project has been to imagine a condition of knowledge before interpretation."[17] In Stanley Fish's *Is There a Text in this Class?*, they detected "the theoretical impulse in its purest form," a cryptofoundationalist theory of sorts that positioned itself outside of practice.[18] Idealistic epistemology *à la* Fish purported to stand outside of belief, when it erroneously postulated that it could devise a "theory" about belief, while the pragmatic position, defended by Michaels and Knapp, always already understood itself to be nothing but a "belief of a belief." In reality, theory quite simply was the antipode of praxis and good leftist activism, while pragmatism could pride itself on being wholly

saturated with unwavering practical commitment. In no uncertain terms, their manifesto clearly summed up the arguments that were to recur in ensuing debates,
especially the polarization of theory against practice:

> In our view ... the only relevant truth about belief is that you can't go
> outside it, and, far from being unlivable, this is a truth you can't help but live.
> It has no practical consequences not because it can never be *united* with prac-
> tice but because it can never be *separated* from practice. The theoretical
> impulse, as we have described it, always involves the attempt to separate
> things that should not be separated: on the ontological side, meaning from
> intention, language from speech acts; on the epistemological side, knowledge
> from true belief. Our point has been that the separated terms are in fact
> inseparable. It is tempting to end by saying that theory and practice too are
> inseparable. But this would be a mistake. Not because theory and practice
> (unlike the other terms) really are separate but because theory is nothing else
> but the attempt to escape practice.[19]

The net result of such stark, undiversified statements, which cast the two terms as
irreconcilable antipodes (not just propagated by the authors of this manifesto), was a
far-reaching factionalism that slowly but surely took hold over not a few literature
departments. At times it appeared that it would forever be impossible for students or
scholars of literature to profess to both occupations at the same time, that is, to be
simultaneously a theorist and pragmatist, or a theorist and new historicist. So ingrained
is this perception of mutual exclusiveness in the critical field that one easily forgets that
for founding philosophical pragmatists, such as William James, not all theory was
impossible, just as long as pragmatic theories attended to the antidogmatic safeguards
James favored in his day: nominalism, utilitarianism, and positivism.[20] Indeed, Cornel
West's "Theory, Pragmatics and Politics" makes the point convincingly when he maintains that pragmatism need not be against theory *per se* – be they small or grand
theories – but, rather, should eschew all forms of brazen dogmatism. Impassioned by
pragmatism's seemingly exclusive claims to epistemic antifoundationalism, the authors
of "Against Theory," he notes, mistakenly take *all* theory or "the theoretical enterprise
as a cover for new forms of epistemic foundationalism."[21] West's own vocational,
prophetic pragmatism, by contrast, largely depends on grand theories such as
Marxism, which are enlisted for heuristic not dogmatic ends.[22] If one elaborates
further on West's critique, it becomes apparent that Knapp and Michaels's inability to
conceive of "grand" metanarratives versus "small" theories or *récits*, foundationalist
versus nondogmatic metatheories, led them to ignore the kind of nonfoundationalist,
nondogmatic fallibilistic theories that, as we shall see, many feminists prefer.

While never referring to Knapp and Michaels explicitly, Homi Bhabha's "The
Commitment to Theory" still in many ways took issue with their assumptions, when he
declared that theory does not automatically and of necessity shut out the political.[23]

His defense of theory's hybridity helped to dismantle the suspect protectionist, exclusive rights to political practice to which antitheorists often lay claim. But Bhabha also did decidedly more than simply debunk dubitable claims to the prerogatives of praxis. For it seems to me that his analysis enables one to understand the problematic nationalistic (perhaps even protectionistic) phantasms that increasingly have come to determine the antitheory debates. As theory was rejected for being the vehicle of a new intellectual recolonization, prompting charges of elitism, imperialism, and Eurocentrism, postcolonial critics such as Homi Bhabha and Gayatri Spivak took issue with such wholesale denunciations and undiversified invectives, all the while acknowledging the shortcomings of "capital t Theory."[24] In his "Commitment to Theory," Bhabha plainly charged that the antitheory debates meant to polarize in order to polemicize. Criticizing the projection of the geopolitical polarity of the West and the East along a theory versus creativity axis, he warned that theory thus threatened to become identified with the Western perspective. "Are the interests of 'Western' theory necessarily collusive with the hegemonic role of the West as a power bloc? Is the language of theory merely another power ploy of the culturally privileged Western elite to produce a discourse of the Other that reinforces its own power-knowledge equation?"[25] In his view, it was mandatory to set an end to the "popular binarism between theory and politics, whose foundational basis is a view of knowledge as totalizing generality and everyday life as experience, subjectivity or false consciousness." For "[theory] does not foreclose on the political, even though battles for power-knowledge may be won or lost to great effect. The corollary is that there is no first or final act of revolutionary social (or socialist) transformation."[26] Indeed, postcolonial theorists such as Fanon demonstrated the entwinement between theory and practice, making us aware of the hybridity or cross-fertilization that exists between cross-cultural theories.

In order to cast further light on this more recent theory–praxis split, artificially held in place by antitheory critics, one might well return to some older attempts to overcome the divide. For, pursuing this genealogy of theory in descending direction, one soon remembers that before poststructuralist theory there was critical and Marxist theory. Defining for modernity's conceptual horizon, the term "pure" theory is of Marxist coinage – though the opposition to practice is, as mentioned earlier, of much older date.[27] Indeed, in its current incarnation, the division between theory and practice unmistakably leads back to Marx and Engels's early writings, to the "Theses on Feuerbach" and the contemporaneous *German Ideology*. In that tract, Marx and Engels described the origin of ideology (the first "ideologues," according to their doctrine, being priests) and the genesis of "pure theory" as the products of an originary, problematic "division of labor" that lay at the foundation of modern society, and, by extension, modernity at large.[28] "Pure theory," or ideology, was of a kind with the equally objectionable "mere criticism" – a derogatory term they reserved for the Young Hegelians, on whom they tried out their new instrument of critique. True theory as ideology critique no longer was divorced from a material base but able to overcome the alienating consciousness-matter divide.[29] In an attempt to finetune this terminological apparatus, Max Horkheimer returned to Marxist foundations when in 1938 he wrote a manifesto titled "Traditional and Critical Theory," which would become defining for what later was to be called the Frankfurt School. In it, he clearly differentiated between a (neo-Kantian) traditional theory, on the one hand, and a Marxist, immanent, critical theory, on the other, which no longer occupied an Archimedean position outside its object. Bad theory – to extrapolate from Horkheimer's essay – is, much like his conception of traditional theory, fraught with a suspect epistemological split between object and subject, while critical theory assumes the mutual enmeshment of both, all the while being painfully aware of its own implication in power.[30] Foucault mainstreamed this insight when in an explicit return to the Frankfurt School's critical theory tradition, he posited the co-implication of knowledge/power, even as he was weary of all manifestations of pure theory.

If it is wrong, therefore, to identify all theory with ideology, it is equally misguided to equate all theory with ideology critique. "Theoretical activism" only works if it is thought of as immanent critique, as an effort to overcome the theory/praxis divide. To fetishize theory, by contrast, is to ascribe magical aura to it, the energy of power, force, or simply social prestige. Theory then functions as "cultural capital" (Bourdieu), whose exchange value is such that it adds cultural status and standing, a theoretical *chic*, to its user. Seen from a Marxist perspective, fetishized theory is an alienated product, the naturalized version of a cultural construction, a social hieroglyphic or commodity that may end up showcasing its user's alienation from praxis. Instead of fetishizing it, the theorist must bravely assess the critical damage done to her theory, in order to assemble the shards and move on. Indeed, as I hope to show, this is precisely what the assemblage of feminist theory shows us to have been the case. For, when held against the template of the conditions that govern sound theory-construction, the *history* of feminist theory attests to a dynamic process in which theoretical assumptions are continuously tested or finetuned, and various categories of analysis – "woman," "sex," "gender" – adjusted. Testing itself against the real, feminist theory over the decades has changed in the process of an ever-evolving critical activism.

For Feminist Theory

Feminist theory only exists as a multicolored assemblage of threads, a web – to allude to the much cherished, somewhat threadbare yet nonetheless effective metaphor – that draws upon but also extends beyond literary, social, cultural, critical or political theory. Because there is no one unitary theory, but pluralities of theories, feminist theory's history consists of numerous strands and diverse threads, not all of which, naturally, can be disentangled in the context of this essay. That said, perhaps it might be possible to point to a few of the most representative discussions that have occupied feminists, in which the dialectic between "materialism" versus "idealism" in various manifestations seems to return. If one looks at feminist debates of the last three decades, what becomes most clear is that feminism has moved away from working with the implicit assumption that there exists a "consensus" among women to the increased recognition of difference, even "dissent." The exclusive concern with a presumed ideological, if not cultural equality among subjects came at the expense of differences across race, class, and sexual orientation, because women's particularities were subsumed under a totalizing or universalizing feminist agenda. To be sure, internal and external historical forces worked together to bring about these far-reaching transformations, yielding an increased perception and awareness of difference.[31] Second-wave feminism, for example, saw its unified platform crumble, first through radical challenges to its underlying ethnocentrism and neglect of sexual difference, later through feminism's encounter with the antifoundationalism of post-modernism and poststructuralism. To some extent, the Second Wave's shortcomings in recognizing the full spectrum of difference among women were the result of inade-quate levels of theorization. In her valuable overview anthology, *The Second Wave*, Nicholson has suggested that "differences among women were acknowledged, but minimally incorporated into the basic threads of the theory," implying that the move-ment's language failed to adequately render women's diversity.[32]

Looking back, for example, at one of the most turbulent controversies that raged in the 1980s and 1990s – the essentialism-constructionism dispute mainly angled at French feminist theory – one sees that it was played out, early on, along the idealism versus materialism axis. Operating with a monolithic, Western female subject, French feminist theory, especially the poeticizing *écriture féminine*, was taken on for unwit-tingly reproducing the fallacies of patriarchal discourse. It is ironic that Irigaray, one of the most astute genealogists of what was wrong with occidental theory, eventually would come under attack for replicating its ills. In her influential *Speculum of the Other Woman*, she traced the roots of theory back to Plato, to the idolatry of a "specular ocularcentrism," drawing on the etymological roots of the word *theoreîn*, "to see." Bad or pure theory for her was of the order of "mere speculation," as expressed, for example, in her observation that "Every theory of the 'subject' will always already have been appropriated by the 'masculin' [Toute théorie du 'sujet' aura toujours été appro-priée au 'masculin']."[33] Read carefully, her pronouncement not only connected the manufacturing of subjecthood to masculinity – as the line ordinarily is interpreted – but also to the very privilege of theory-construction, that is, who gets to tinker with theories, who not. Yet, at the same time that her work deconstructed "high theory," it also performed it under the banner of appropriating male discourse in order to displace it parodically. Thus, her own position in the 1970s came under scrutiny from materialist feminists, such as Christine Delphy and Monique Wittig, so that the theory-praxis, speculation-materialism dualism was played out between them early on. For might not the category of "Woman" in feminine writing refer to a problematic myth, rather than to a historical materialist practice, implying that "women do not belong to history, and that writing is not a material production"?[34]

Not all those who criticized Irigaray's work, however, would follow Wittig's materi-alistic bent. Some voices of dissent seemed to be informed by a disputable

theory–creativity divide, which, much as in Bhabha's analysis of geopolitical polarization, recast the dualism in terms of gender binarisms, maintaining that theory always
already was male-identified. Here, the old gendered dualism of feeling, affect, and
emotive experience versus rationalism threatened to rear its ugly head. While such
gender-biased responses largely remained essentialistic, in some cases even biologistic,
some feminist critics tendered more sophisticated critiques about the dangers of
getting recuperated by a patriarchal power politics through theory. Though her own
work has added significant contributions to the field of feminist theory, Rosi Braidotti,
for example, maintained that radical feminism could not "result in the revalorization of
the discourse of 'high theory' and especially of philosophy."[35] Taking on female theorists
and intellectuals such as de Beauvoir, Irigaray, or Spivak, her *Nomadic Subjects* warned
that feminism might be in danger of duplicating "one of the most ancient mental habits
of patriarchy: the overinvestment of the theoretical mode, as exemplified by philosophy, with the consequent glorification of the figure of the philosopher."[36] Against the
"false universalisms" of theory, one ought to hold the praxis of "nomadic questioning."
"What is needed in women's studies as a practice of sexual difference in the nomadic
mode is a critique of the implicit system of values conveyed by high theory in its
support of a conventional image of thought and of the thinker as sovereign in its text."[37]
High theory, in this argument, rightly becomes like high culture or high modernism,
the vehicle of power that suppresses the lower classes, while advancing the cultural
elitism of the white upper class. To be sure, cast in this guise one must abjure theory,
but is this necessarily the whole picture? Not all philosophy is inherently identical with
"metaphysics," especially not social or political philosophy, or, say, feminist contributions to an ethics of care.[38] We should, for sure, acknowledge the excesses of
theoretical language, as practiced in the 1970s and 1980s and, no doubt, at present, but
we must also ask whether it is true that theory is intrinsically or necessarily antidemocratic, whether it is without fail a tool of obfuscation. Must theoretical talk
automatically get one into the traps of a performative contradiction; must it always be
exclusionary? To me, it seems that the question of whether there can be a theoretical
activism, or whether "to theorize" can be a praxis, should be answered in the affirmative for Irigaray, as well as other feminist theorists, regardless of the incontestable
defects or flaws their respective models may, over the years, have exposed. When
Irigaray decried women's exclusion from the discipline of philosophy, the gist of her
theoretical gesture was not to set up a new republic of feminist philosophers that would
exclude poets, writers, performers, politicians, partisans, guerrilla troops, amazons.
Feminist theory *is* a praxis insofar as it has fundamentally and radically reshaped
conceptual categories or definitions of sex, gender, oppression, identity – always in an
ongoing dynamic process of debate and continued, never-ending discussion. In my
mind, there does not need to exist a contradiction between, first, acknowledging that
the critique of French feminist theory's localism, classism, or luxurious literariness is
justified from the standpoint of global, diversified communities, and, second, celebrating it as an extraordinarily creative, rich phase in the history of feminist theory.

It is no small feat that the critique of feminism's exclusionary practices, its denial of radical difference among women, slowly but surely brought about a sea change in its theoretical foundations. For, along with the twin attacks on American radical feminism and *écriture féminine* occurred a major shift away from the category "woman" – a mark of feminism's "gynocentrism"[39] – to "gender," culminating in Butler's *Gender Trouble*. In taking on "essentialism"[40] through "constructivism" and "antifoundationalism," feminists engaged in multiple alliances and in coalition-building with postmodernism, poststructuralism, and postcolonial theory. But it is here precisely that lies the crux of some of the current stymied confrontations that are still with us. Some fear that too much theory, especially too much deconstruction of the category "woman," will supplant the category "women" by "gender" altogether, so that the collective object as well as the common objective that all feminisms minimally share will be abandoned.[41] Such an abandoning of feminism's communal goals will then automatically precipitate the very end of feminism – despite the reassurances to the contrary of so-called postfeminist theorists. Others, mainly representatives of critical theory, instead contest poststructuralism's and postmodernism's lack of normativity, shared first principles, and regulative norms, whose absence is said to hamper its political effectiveness. Representatives of poststructuralism, by contrast, often will take on the presumed universalism and totalizing gestures that accompany normative agendas, in the name of the particularisms of identity politics. However, the difficulty the historian of feminist theory encounters in trying to map all of these differences is not only the terminological confusion that beleaguers terms such as postmodernism, poststructuralism, universalism, normativity, and antifoundationalism but also the ambivalent valence these terms have acquired. Not only have attempts been made to map these terms onto the spectrum of left- versus right-wing politics – augmented by Habermas's undiversified, negative valorization of an entire school of thought[42] – but to some degree differences also pertain as to whether one operates in the humanities or social sciences. Does antifoundationalism mean political groundlessness or merely the attempt to adopt a historical, relativistic position that is conscious of its limitations and shuns totalization? Should we shunt essentialism but retain a "strategic essentialism," lest the empirical gets elided, as Spivak has charged? Does postmodern feminist social theory risk looking uncannily similar to the value-free conservatism it was meant to correct?[43] And, how do some critical theorists seek to conjoin an antifoundationalist methodology to a normative model of social change?

Among the most cogent responses to these complicated issues are, no doubt, Jane Flax's and Sandra Harding's contributions to the postmodernism debate, included in Nicholson's *Postmodernism/Feminism* – interventions so valuable, it seems to me, because they directly consider the vexed conundrum of normativity that has split apart critical theorists and poststructuralists. Flax's commonsensical observation that to get to feminist theory we must return to its purported object – gender – still very much rings true. If the common or, if you will, shared goal of all feminist theory pertains to gender relations of some sort, then it also involves thinking about gender.

Consequently, feminist theory always entails a *metatheoretical* moment, according to Flax, that is, a reflection on how gender is thought and, therefore, a "thinking of thinking."[44] The plurality of women's social practices and experiences is reflected in the diversity of definitions feminists have given of gender relations – as Flax continues her all too logical argument, pointing to disagreements over the sex/gender split, patterns of gender socialization, gendered social differences, modes of embodiedness, and the public/private split.[45] But in addition to recognizing innovations coming from the fields of anthropology, ethnic studies, and history, which were successfully incor-porated into feminist theory, one should not underestimate the influence of postmodernist and poststructuralist antifoundationalism. Here, it seems, lies the crux of the matter of what, according to some, might be "wrong" with contemporary femi-nist theory: how to prevent an *epistemological* antifoundationalism from slipping into a skepticism and relativism that eventually results in a *political* groundlessness, and, consequently, paralyzing inactivity? Or, to put it quite simply, how can we judge, let alone alter, the everyday political arena, aspire to improve women's situation locally and globally, if we operate with a theory that lacks clear normative directives and values? Harding expresses the dilemma of contemporary debates cogently when she wonders whether too much postmodern or postmetaphysical theory might erode justificatory political strategies needed as "a justifiable guide to practical decisions."[46] In the social and natural sciences, she convincingly argues, it may well be necessary to adopt a feminist empiricism or standpoint theory to avoid hollowing out the strongholds of self, truth, and knowledge, which could lead to a relapse into a posi-tivistic, value-free science or interpretationism.[47]

Let me try to summarize the set of problems this current methodological dilemma raises in practical terms: feminist theory must seek to hold the balance between anti- or nonfoundationalist (epistemological) strategies that correct essentialism, without falling into a political indecisiveness. Though epistemic antifoundationalism was neces-sary, strategically speaking, to set an end to a problematic essentialism, it is now said to have lost its beneficial effects, to the point of producing antipolitical aftereffects. In other words, too high a dose of it may lead to skepticism and relativism – charges not dissimilar to the ones made outside the field of feminisms. However, when such points acquire the status of mantras that are simply repeated, without a detailed considera-tion of the position under attack, they also deserve to be challenged, and, if necessary, rebutted. For, as I want to claim, it means to confound epistemology with politics if one believes either that an epistemological antifoundationalism automatically trans-lates into politically legitimate agendas or, quite the opposite, that a critique of foundationalism must always end in antipolitics. Put differently, an epistemological antifoundationalism need not stand in contradiction to a politically founded program (which is not the same as "foundational," meaning "totalizing" or "universalizing," at the expense of difference). Conversely, the other side of the coin also holds true: antifoundationalism does not *eo ipso* result in a correct political praxis. To posit such cause-and-effect relations may mean to get entangled in an obsessional, systematic logic, when in fact it is the *dogmatism* that accompanies theoretical *no less than* antitheo-retical positions that needs to be avoided. It is in an attempt to avert such false dualisms that some feminist theorists have countered the charges of a dogmatic universalism, by pointing, for instance, to a situated universalism, where provisional universalist programs are tested and corrected as seen fit.

Enter neopragmatism. That some feminists have tried to replace postmodernism and poststructuralism by neopragmatism largely seems due to the unwieldiness or negatives that these labels were unable to shed. Exchanging labels in practice meant choosing a different kind of antifoundationalism that seemed less beleaguered by the flaws or charges of neoconservatism marking the earlier intellectual traditions. Presenting itself as a more viable alternative, pragmatism thus became a new strategy to retain or rescript feminist theory. Critical theorists Nancy Fraser and Iris Marion Young have been most vocal in these efforts. Coming themselves from strong theoret-ical positions associated with critical theory, they have proposed some of the most pronounced defenses for the pragmatic turn, Fraser by arguing for "postmodern theory" and "neopragmatism" respectively, Young by pointing to a "pragmatic theo-rizing."[48] Feminist theory for Young is to presuppose a subject defined by "serial collectivity," but without the universalizing and essentializing claims that come with a totalizing theory. Postfeminism, it seems to me, becomes a moot point, once the historical category of "women" is seen, following Young, as a serial collective.

But the first real signs of this new terminological shift, not surprisingly, became apparent in the context of the feminism-postmodernism debates. Indeed, in 1988 Fraser and Nicholson published a highly influential article, entitled "Social Criticism without Philosophy: An Encounter between Feminism and Postmodernism."[49] Feminism, the authors argued, had "tried to rethink the relation between philosophy and social criticism so as to develop paradigms of criticism without philosophy."[50] As is clear, they did not reject the term theory as such, for they evoked "feminist theory"[51] (if to detect its essentialism), while turning to the critique Lyotard and Rorty had proffered of "Philosophy with a capital P." These philosophers had established that "philosophy, *and, by extension, theory in general*, can no longer function to *ground* politics and social criticism. With the demise of foundationalism comes the demise of the view that casts philosophy in the role of *founding* discourse vis-à-vis social criticism."[52] But as the authors saw it, this also meant the replacement of a modernist by a postmod-ernist position, in which "criticism floats free of any universalist theoretical ground."[53] The switch away from the linguistic turn meant that criticism would become "more pragmatic, *ad hoc*, contextual, and local."[54] Thus, at the same time that they were sympathetic to the postmodern project, they also developed a staunch critique of Lyotard for advocating the "illegitimacy of several genres of social criticism," such as "large-scale historical narrative and social-theoretical analyses of pervasive relations of dominance and subordination."[55] That is, he went "too quickly from the premise that Philosophy cannot ground social criticism to the conclusion that criticism itself must be local, *ad hoc*, and nontheoretical. As a result, he throws out the baby of large historical narrative with the bathwater of philosophical metanarrative and the baby of social-theoretical analysis of large-scale inequalities with the bathwater of reductive Marxian class theory."[56] In fact, what they argued for was a "postmodern theory," but with the following *caveat*: "if postmodern-feminist critique must remain theoretical, not just any kind of theory will do. Rather, theory here would be explicitly historical, attuned to the cultural specificity of different societies and periods and to that of different groups within societies and periods."[57] The result would be a postmodern feminist theory that was historicist, nonuniversalist, comparativist, pragmatic, and fallibilistic. "It would tailor its methods and categories to the specific task at hand, using multiple categories when appropriate and forswearing the metaphysical comfort of a single feminist method or feminist epistemology. In short, this theory would look more like a tapestry composed of threads of many different hues than one woven in a single color."[58] Not simply rhetorically but clearly politically persuasive, Fraser and Nicholson's essay stipulated that feminism's claim to diversity only could be achieved through a versatile methodological apparatus that would be reconfigured or retooled as the political cause saw fit. Indeed, it is this very call for pragmatism that returned prominently – now as the mediating position – in *Feminist Contentions*.

Contentious or Debating Feminisms?

The theoretical "antagonisms" that emerged in *Feminist Contentions* were a historical product entirely missing from an earlier 1987 collection titled *Feminism as Critique*, which had already brought together many of the same contributors.[59] Its editors, Seyla Benhabib and Drucilla Cornell, did not make an attempt to separate factions but housed them all under the broader (Marxist) rubric "critique." Rather than defining the term "critique" unequivocally, they rerouted the question through the political trajectory of the women's movement, as it emerged "alongside and in some cases out of the New Left in Europe and North America," noting that feminist critique would bid farewell to feminism's first phase, defined by the *deconstruction* of the Western tradition, to focus now on theoretical *reconstruction*.[60] Similarly, in its dialogue with Marxism, feminist critique needed to scrutinize the Marxist paradigm of *production*, without simply replacing it by the gendered category *reproduction*, or losing sight of the need for distributive justice. But if in 1987 the term "critique" was left standing as a larger label under which a diverse collective of feminist theorists could be cataloged, then the elements of the debate shifted quite dramatically in the mid-1990s when *Feminist Contentions* appeared in print. By that time a firm polarization had sedimented between a Frankfurt-style normative critique (Benhabib), on the one hand, and a poststructuralist, performative theory of "resignification" (Butler), on the other, while Fraser sought to mediate between the two, arguing that feminism needed both. Clearly, the disagreements that emerged in full view were not merely formulaic but, rather, revelatory of deeper, substantive differences that divided the collective. At the center of these contentions lay an entire lexicon of key words, such as critique, power/force, consent/dissent, norm/normativity, universality/particularity, foundationalism, utopia. Yet are these differences truly as unremediably unbridgeable as some of the interlocutors intimated, or might they to a large extent be formal, perhaps even methodological, and hence subject to review? It seems worthwhile to reconsider some of the most salient differences between the participants from this new angle.

In answering her critics, Butler started off questioning the catchall nature of the label "postmodernism," whose totalizing status threatened to brush over the unwieldiness of the historical field, choosing instead for a deconstructive poststructuralism. This further meant differentiating her own position from a Frankfurt-style critical tradition. For, though Fraser had coined the label "dereifying critique" for her work, Butler in one of her interventions qualified the tradition of "critique," placing the term in distancing quotation marks, while at the same time finetuning it: "My argument is that 'critique,' to use Fraser's term, always takes place *immanent* to the regime of discourse/power whose claims it seeks to adjudicate, which is to say that the practice of 'critique' is implicated in the very power-relations it seeks to adjudicate."[61] Regardless of the fact, however, that Butler here merely cited the term "critique" – using it parodically, as it were – her version of poststructuralism nonetheless remains faithful to (Marxist) immanent critique, as defined earlier, insofar as the object of analysis from which it cannot extract itself is power. Centrally, power here does not refer to the kind of empowering force at the disposal of autonomous individuals, precious to political liberalism, but to a Foucauldian frame of reference in which power mostly equals a "subject-ing" regime of force or symbolic violence.

However, the main bones of contention, undoubtedly, were the *normative* and *universalistic* claims that infuse critical theory, which, according to Butler, risked turning it into a "metapolitical site of ultimate normativity." Taking on "normative political philosophy" for allegedly assuming a stance "beyond the play of power,"[62] she went on to note that it was not simply a matter of pitting a poststructuralist antifoundationalism against a Frankfurt-style foundationalism, for that would merely amount to privileging the other side of the same coin. "Rather, the task is to interrogate what the theoretical move that establishes foundations *authorizes*, and what precisely it excludes or forecloses."[63] Again and again, her contribution returned to querying the "authorizing power" that is performatively lent to speaking positions.[64] Her remarks thus raised the question of legitimation, suggesting in Bourdieu-like fashion that claims to legitimacy result from authoritative speech acts, which at once feed on and performatively renew authority.[65] By contrast, deconstruction allowed for the exposure of power ploys, so that, rather than being a negating act, it disclosed a new space of possibilities: "To deconstruct is not to negate or to dismiss, but to call into question and, perhaps most importantly, to open up a term, like the subject, to a reusage or redeployment that previously has not been authorized."[66] All normativity in truth shielded itself from critical dissent, driven as it was by the "ruse of authority that seeks to close itself off from contest that is, in my view, at the heart of any radical political project."[67] Furthermore, normative values such as "subjecthood" or "universality" proved to be unfounded, literally, for the historical crisis to which they had been subjected, in postcolonial or feminist discursive arenas, patently demonstrated the loss of "ground" these terms had suffered — a loss no longer to be undone by willful reflection. Her principal target, clearly, was the term "universality." Instead of being either a *procedural* or *substantive* term, "universality" in reality amounted to a "site of insistent contest and resignification,"[68] for as a foundational (Enlightenment) norm its totalizing claims had been challenged in feminist and postcolonial discourse alike. To no small degree, Butler's argument thus also remained vested in the disputes over universalism that raged in the wake of the debates sparked by Habermas's Frankfurt lectures about the legacy of the Enlightenment in the postmodern condition.

It is evident that Butler's contestations revolved unremittingly around the vexed issue of normativity. But in postulating that all normative critique incorrigibly remained oblivious to its vested interests in power, her observations were fundamentally at odds with Benhabib's. In fact, their differences illustrated the far-reaching equivocations that have accrued around terms such as norms, normative, and normalization. In a post-Nietzschean frame of reference, distinguished by the relativism of values, all norms must merely amount to the perspectival, even forceful, imposition of values. But phrased as such, this post-Nietzschean position at the same time proves highly debatable insofar as norms can of course be agreed upon democratically and deliberatively, that is, reflect the acquired consensus of principles in a democratic playing field with built-in correctives to adjust or jettison defunct, obsolete, exclusive, in other words, insufficiently inclusive norms. This is why Benhabib, for example, has in numerous publications acknowledged and addressed the power claims that imbue Habermas's model, no less than her own normative position. Most explicitly she has done so in her important essay "The Generalized and Concrete Other," which sought to amend the assumed universal moral perspective of Habermas *et al.*, by drawing on Carol Gilligan's ethics of care.[69] Rather than automatically being apodictic or imposed from above, radically democratic norms can find validation and vindication in rational, even emotive discussion or be challenged through contestation, dissent, disagreement.

Shifting the terms of the discussion considerably, Fraser sought to mediate between the interlocutors, hoping to undo the dualism or "false antitheses" by deflecting from the status of their respective theories and appealing to the negotiating work of neopragmatism. Butler's and Benhabib's positions were fundamentally "complimentary,"[70] she asserted, insofar as the former could be aligned with "the local, the discrete, and the specific," the latter with "provisional totalization."[71] In wrapping up her assessment of the factions, she suggested that "Butler's approach is good for theorizing the micro level, the intrasubjective, and the historicity of gender relations. It is not useful, in contrast, for the macro level, the intersubjective, and the normative."[72] Feminism, in that sense, needed to be informed by what she called "the eclectic spirit" of neopragmatism. "This means adopting theoretical conceptions that permit both dereifying critique and normative critique, as well as the generation of new emancipatory significations."[73] Doubting, however, that Fraser's neopragmatism was postmodern,[74] Benhabib remained unswayed in her retort, disinclined to take the step Fraser had taken, insisting on the "clash of theoretical paradigms," on "serious differences" and "genuinely different conceptual options."[75] Butler, for her part, mainly regretted the state of the debates, noting their parochialism and disputing that they were "representative," inasmuch as they excluded discussions of race as well as the dynamics of the "theory wars." Looking back on the dispute's limited scope, she observed that their interactions had failed to take full stock of the "presupposed sense that theoretical reflection matters." The debate never touched on "the rarefied status of theoretical language, the place of narrative in or as theory, the possibility of a theoretical activism, the tension between theory and empiricism, the question of whether poststructuralism is the only theory that counts as 'theory.'"[76] Indirectly, Butler thereby acknowledged that, though the contributors to the book shared a commitment to theory, they disagreed over the theoretical paradigm to be embraced as well as to the scope of its practical implications. In the end, the rigorous principles that underlay, indeed founded, these triangulated conceptual theories – whether poststructuralist, critical, or pragmatic theory – determined the disagreements that preoccupied these feminist theorists. Must we conclude, then, that the encounter merely resulted in a new impasse, or might there be ways of realigning its terms and key words in new constellations? As a way of answering this question, let me formulate another possible response to the disputes.

First of all, it seems problematic to suggest that poststructuralist feminism, as represented by Butler's position, merely proves the cordoning off of theory, reflection, or philosophy from political struggle as such.[77] Such a claim once again returns us to the false duality between theory and praxis, which arises precisely when we assume that the theoretical and the practical stand opposed to one another, according to a Kantian model of critique, rather than a (neo-)Marxist one, moored – however unsteadily – in immanent critique. It is in positivistic models that separate pristine objects from interpretation and deny the reality of the "hermeneutical circle" that theory and practice, theory and object, must be rift from one another. Once we do not subscribe to that position, however, things become less simple than some critics would have us believe. The more pressing question that needs to be raised instead is how we define politics and the political, and whether these categories are broad enough to include multiple feminist programs and agendas, all the way from identity politics that address gay and lesbian claims to equal legal and cultural recognition, to improving the socio-economic condition of so-called "welfare mothers" (to cite that highly problematic term), to exercising remedial solidarity with Third World women, and, in fact, to ensuring that all of us can be subjects of political agency, not just on the receiving end of solidarity. In that sense, it also seems invaluable to heed Fraser's injunction, made in her *Justice Interruptus*, that we keep both perspectives – (cultural) recognition *and* economic redistribution – in view.[78] This also means that we need to remain realistic about what single theories can do and that we acknowledge the need for an assemblage of different theories with partial, sometimes small-range objectives, rather than grand totalizing goals.

Second, like Fraser I believe that, up to a certain point, both positions – critical theory and poststructuralism – may be able to converge, certainly more so than their representatives seem willing to concede. Granted, these feminisms differ most funda-mentally as to whether or not they subscribe to a universalizing project – a Kantian universal horizon of expectation, if you will – and as to whether they assume "agree-ment" (deliberative agreement – Benhabib) or "disagreement" (agonistic difference and contestation – Butler) as the beginning and end-all of the political playing field. Furthermore, as noted earlier, the first position remains wedded to normativity, the other exposes the reputed violence or exclusionary gestures that emanate from what it sees as a normative foundationalism (collapsing the two terms). But once we look more closely at the conundrum of normativity, things again appear less simple, insofar as critical theory acknowledges historical and cultural contingency while poststruc-turalism, for its part, draws on a minimal "normative" program. Thus, Butler acknowledges "contingent foundations" or a "historically constrained perspective"[79] respectively, while Benhabib amends her universalist program by recognizing "situ-ated" – cultural and historical – "foundations." As noted earlier, it also seems false to assume, as Butler does, that all normativity is merely a matter of "authority" and "violent imposition," rather than possible democratic discussion that does not exclude dissent. Undeniably, she is right in seeing deconstruction as the opening of categories of exclusion, but perhaps she too readily collapses the difference between, on the one hand, normativity, the "normal," "norm," or the "mean," and, on the other, an incul-cating normalization executed through performative rituals, on the model of Foucault's *Discipline and Punish*.[80] Conversely, the argument that critical theory oper-ates with a founding normativity can also be turned back onto poststructuralism, including its feminist version. Here again it is useful to distinguish between epistemic and political levels of practice, in line with our earlier discussion in the section "Against Theory." For, despite its avowed *epistemic* antifoundationalism, deconstructive feminism adheres to a "normative," *politically* founded agenda, insofar as it seeks to attain of universal justice, even if it defines it in Derridean, perhaps even quasi-Messianic fashion, as a "justice to come," *à-venir*.[81] The tensions between the epistemic and political demands of Butler's poststructuralist feminism become palpable when she asserts that deconstruction constantly rifts the term "feminism," which, for its part, needs to be "affirmed as the ungrounded ground of feminist theory."[82] It is clear that, in order to respect the full diversity of all feminisms, Butler here has recourse to the antinomic construction of an "ungrounded ground." Arguably, this paradoxical claim fits within her epistemological framework, which ceaselessly seeks to get the better of the potentially totalizing, universalizing pretensions of her own nomencla-ture. Yet the phrase hardly captures the programmatic, less than merely contingent truth of feminist politics. The issue in the foregoing passage, it seems to me, is once again one of definition. For Butler, foundationalism becomes synonymous with normativity, which is why she has recourse to the fiction of an ungrounded ground. All ideology critique – including feminist ideology critique – however, remains normative insofar as it works with a representational theory and the truth-falsehood distinction on the basis of which it measures the real against the ideal – this despite Foucault's well-intended attempt to undo the left-wing "will to knowledge" by getting rid of the term "ideology" altogether. To my mind, there can be no doubt that both Butler's and Benhabib's positions are incontestably ideology-critical *and* "utopian" in nature, that is, guided by utopian regulative ideas whose ideals are, if perhaps never to be realized fully, then maximally to be approximated by feminism. One such ideal might be a global – if you will, "universal" – justice, in other words, cross-cultural legal and cultural equality for women across the globe, which respects their multiple differences. Indeed, to believe in a justice-yet-to-come, as Butler's poststructuralist feminism does, is not to be adverse to utopianism.

Let me propose therefore that we change the terms of the encounter from contentious to debating feminisms. In order to do so, we need to revive a notion of interlocutors, rather than foes or contenders, in discourse and discussion. Discursive exchange need not exclusively be concerned with repressive power but can draw upon enabling power, without having to relapse into the pitfalls of an *unreflective* liberalism. This means opting not just for a subversive discourse but also for inclusive dialogue, without wanting to give up the incommensurability or asymmetry of difference. My point simply is that we need to see the different feminisms as standing side by side, ready to acknowledge a minimal division of labor, with limited objectives and tasks, so that a so-called cultural feminism that demands the recognition of identity claims can cohabit with other branches, for example, those concerned more specifically with economic redistribution. It is precisely when either one of the multiple feminisms makes grander claims than it can make true that we get into dogmatic positions that must cancel each other out. Here I am thinking specifically of the latest discussions that are symptomatic of the fracturing in left-wing ranks, notably the dispute around "conservative leftism," the topic of a conference at Santa Cruz and the label used for those feminists who have criticized poststructuralism and identarian politics in the name of materialistic redistribution. In many ways, these disputes are the latest version of what I earlier called the idealism-materialism stand-off, also new transformations of the earlier essentialism-constructivism controversy. Butler rightly has taken issue with the return of this old divide in new guise in her "Merely Cultural," in which she convincingly argues that a cultural feminism interested in analyzing heterosexual marital economies, for example, does not necessarily stand opposed to materialism insofar as it harks back to Engels's analysis of the family. Most divisive in intent, no doubt, has been Martha Nussbaum's *New Republic* review article of Butler's work.[83] Though it certainly may be healthy to enter into debate with fellow feminists, as Nussbaum encourages us to do in *Cultivating Humanity*, it is quite another matter to engage in wholesale vituperations, and not only strategically speaking, as such infightings are appropriated for the agendas of non- or antifeminists. While this is not the place to engage all the issues Nussbaum's review raises,[84] suffice it to say that she mainly faults Butler for being preoccupied with a narrowly particularistic, identarian program, over and against which she holds the only tenable alternative of a universalism realized through legal and legislative transformation. Clearly, her demand for social change makes sense, less clear is why it needs to be couched in the undiversified indictment of another feminist. For, *pace* Nussbaum, we can't demand of our fellow feminists that we symmetrically recognize our own theories in their proposals. To demand of all feminists that they only formulate legal theories or legislative recommendations, social policy blueprints that lay claim to exclusive political transformation, is to exclude literary, poetic, performative critics, historians or still other voices from the discussion, some of which, on the surface, may seem more descriptive, but on which the feminist legal theorist might want to draw – as indeed Nussbaum has done in *Poetic Justice* –or by which the activist is inspired. To exclude these multiplicities of views or to assume justificatory, argumentative superiority is not only to operate with a hierarchical axiology but also to assume the universal claims of one's theory, a theory that can do everything. Thus, there is a difference between a fallible theory that works with the goal of approximating universal, global justice, as hospitable versions of feminism do, and a universalizing (totalizing) theory that suppresses difference, be it in the name of universalism *or* particularism (the universalization of a particularistic standpoint).[85]

Finally, there's yet another reason why I do not necessarily deplore the discussion that ensued between the participants of *Feminist Contentions* or why I don't find cause to agree with Butler that the resulting encounter was merely parochial, so that these disputes can be dismissed for being merely academic or simply elitist. To say so may mean to downplay the pedagogical project of feminism and feminist theory, the dialogue that takes place in the classroom or on the street, the extraordinary way in which many of us have been affected by feminist theory, even if we take issue with it. To my mind, feminist theory still can function in the service of consciousness-raising or the kind of citizen learning that accompanies progressive politics and the emancipatory struggle, in which case it hasn't lost its edge of promoting political literacy. Certainly, the importance of the discussions in *Feminist Contentions* should not be blown out of proportion, but they should also not blind us to what is happening out there in the critical field.

One other vector that defines that field, to which I would like to turn now in closing, involves a question with which we started out, namely, whether pragmatism, even neopragmatism – which, unlike the old version, takes into account the operations of power[86] – should automatically be hailed as the new savior. Does the pragmatic turn provide an answer to the current impasses of theory, including feminist theory? If so, whose pragmatism does feminism need to adopt, given that today there exist as many pluralities of pragmatisms as there are theoretical feminisms? To look ahead to the argument I will develop in this chapter's final section, it seems to me that feminism could, and indeed *does*, make use of a *weak*, methodological form of pragmatism, if only to establish a coalition between different voices across race, class, and sexual orientation. At the same time, it may also be necessary to heed the rhetoric of a more problematic, *strong* pragmatism, of the sort advocated, for example, by Rorty, despite the gestures to peaceful dialogue and discussion on which his model seemingly hinges. If it is safe to say that the relations between pragmatism and feminism are fairly new,[87] then it is Rorty who most avidly, but also most controversially, has sought to bridge the two, while Fraser has been most theoretical in crafting a feminist neopragmatism. It therefore makes sense to turn to Rorty, because he is one of the few pragmatists to have made a persistent appeal to feminism, but also because his most recent work, *Achieving Our Country*, directly takes on the "cultural left," including versions of "cultural feminism," for being spellbound by too much spectatorial theory.

The Pragmatic Turn

In an era in which the deficit of so many models, including the liberal one, has become patently apparent, a pragmatic eclecticism seems to work best, turning us all into tinkerers, handy-people, picking up tools to solve problems, discarding them as we see fit, in a grand effort to retool pluralistic, radical democracy. Pragmatism translates into concrete terms Levi-Strauss's description of the anthropologist as *bricoleur*, mainstreamed by Roland Barthes. Under duress and in crisis, we all end up in the *ER*, or emergency room, seeking to make do with whatever life-support systems are on hand, with some even resorting to the pragmatics of *triage*, if need be.

Following Lyotard's *The Postmodern Condition*, our postmodern era has become the playing field *par excellence* for pragmatism. Yet, despite his dedication to Wittgenstein *et al.*, Lyotard seemed to offer a "nonpragmatic" variant of pragmatism, at least, when set beside the American pragmatism advocated by Rorty and others. In Lyotard's variety, pragmatism not only assumed that there no longer existed a consensus that could be reached, only the falling apart of the grand narrative of legitimacy, but the result was a "paralogism" that spelled the end to liberalism's prospect of eventually reaching universal understanding. As a result, Lyotard's tract seemingly ended up pointing to the impossibility of all practical forms of politics that still embraced utopian scripts, demolishing the normative claims of theory altogether. Returning to Horkheimer's 1938 essay, cited earlier, he showed how traditional theory's totalizing claims needed to be situated in the context of a conception of society that was unitary, while its corrective – critical theory – was intrinsically dualistic and dialectical. In the course of twentieth-century history, especially high modernism, these dialectical tools in turn had been instrumentalized by totalizing systems, whether they were liberal or Marxist in slant. Eventually, however, as the new postmodern condition showed, *agonistic* pragmatics (not the Rortian variant) had superseded liberalism and the dualisms of Marxism, opening onto an agonistic field of language games, where rules were immanent to the game and legitimacy was simply gained by the repetitiveness of performativity. In asserting that the end or goal of dialogue was not consensus but "paralogy," Lyotard's agonistic pragmatism clearly could not be farther removed from Habermas's universal pragmatics or even Rorty's liberal "antifoundationalism."

Of all the brands of pragmatism currently in stock, Rorty's repeated pleas for pluralistic pragmatism have seemed especially appealing since he allows us to do away with last foundations and justifications, to discard old-model Enlightenment terms such as universalism no less than dilapidated remnants of ideology critique, even to discard the burdensome baggage of moral philosophy. No longer weighed down by the Kantian categorical imperatives of universalizable moral obligations, a community of "we's" agrees that liberalism can ensure a better good. Differences in opinion are to be settled through conversation, argumentation, dialogue, or persuasive rhetoric rather than force or violence. But in contradistinction to Habermas's universal or formal pragmatics, Rorty's pragmatism claims to be radically antifoundationalist in nature. Influenced by the language philosophy of the later Wittgenstein, author of the *Philosophical Investigations*, Rorty presents political liberalism as a contingent language game, whose truth can no longer be justified, except through circular forms of reasoning. Unlike for Habermas, for Rorty the invocation of universality or rationality as the philosophical, last, or final justification of the liberal paradigm merely describes a problem incorrectly, versed in the outmoded language of an old (philosophico-political) vocabulary that has served its time. In spite of these differences, neither thinker escapes the circularity of electing political liberalism as the preferred paradigm of choice, with Rorty harping on its contingency, Habermas seeking to found it rationally, arguing that consensus-forming conversation is structured like a democratic felicitous and illocutionary speech act. However, despite assertions to the contrary, Rorty similarly retains the model of consensus in the construction of a pluralistically constituted "we." The awareness that there only exists contingency does not lead him to relativism or cause him to give up utopian hope, for he still charts a history of "progress" – though the term itself is defunct – this time on an adaptive (Darwinian) scale in which liberalism functions as a tool for attaining the "greater" good. Both pragmatists emphasize the enactment of freedom in the speech act.

Given the seductiveness of Rorty's model, with its claim to logical and argumentative superiority, it seems all the more necessary to probe how this pragmatism retains a contingent foundationalism, but foundationalism nonetheless. The "stories" Rorty's pragmatism tells, in its switch from metatheory to narrative, are justificatory theories passed off as contingent narratives or examples that, in reality, often have the status or stature of exemplarity. In that sense, his pragmatism only confirms what he observes about the ironic theorist, whose main problem is "how to overcome authority without claiming authority,"[88] since he continually may lapse into metaphysics again. Some of these recidivist dynamics come to the fore in his controversial essays "Feminism and Pragmatism" and "Feminism, Ideology, and Deconstruction." The persuasive energy Rorty unleashes in these pieces is aimed at convincing feminists that their beliefs can be fitted into pragmatism's emancipatory politics or the pragmatic "view of moral progress with relative ease,"[89] that is, on condition that the universalist, realist, as well as Marxist ideology-critical model be shunted.[90] "We have to stop talking about the need to go from distorted to undistorted perception of moral reality, and instead talk about the need to modify our practices so as to take account of new descriptions of what has been going on."[91] In other words, behavior modifications and descriptive rescripting must drop the idea of the moral law, as well as the other Kantian notion that "competing groups will always be able to reason together on the basis of plausible and neutral premises." Since all justificatory scripts rely on universal essences or intrinsic attributes, feminists ought to reject them for a Deweyan–Davidsonian–Putnamian pragmatism (the linguistification of Dewey). Pragmatists "abandon the contrast between superficial appearance and deep reality in favor of the contrast between a painful present and a possibly less painful, dimly-seen, future."[92] However, because feminism's task is creative rather than descriptive, its only method is "courageous and imaginative experimenta-tion,"[93] which means in fact that ideology-driven radical politics must give way to utopianism and the use of the imagination. Feminism, Rorty prescribes, can only be prophetic, since prophecy is left when all argument fails. Or, prophecy becomes femi-nism's preferred game of choice, with which it is supposed to undo the myriad other, less desirable competing nominalist language games. Norms then for Rorty, too, equal normalization, except that he lapses into a nominalism that doesn't even factor in the power balance anymore: "'Truth' is not the name of a power which eventually wins through, it is just the nominalization of an approbative adjective."[94] Lacking any concep-tion of normativity that can be subjected to justificatory scripts, Rorty concluded that decisions about the usefulness of certain practices become entirely *ad hoc* linguistic games in which interlocutors seek to persuade each other of the merits of their own game. Clearly, this hardly means that Rorty's own strong pragmatist position is devoid of implied, unaccounted-for "norms" or, perhaps better, normalizing values. Surely, feminism may want to resist the Nietzschean read this cynical pragmatist gives us of the historical narrative of women's oppression, when he – unselfconsciously, without a dose of salutary irony – posits the following: "Neither pragmatists nor deconstruc-tionists can do more for feminism than help rebut attempts to ground these practices on something deeper than a contingent historical fact – the fact that the people with the slightly larger muscles have been bullying the people with the slightly smaller muscles for a very long time."[95] With this quasi-Nietzschean endorsement of a history of (physical) force, Rorty is flexing the muscles of his "strong" pragmatism, which remains mired in an essentialistic, almost biologistic dualism of weak versus strong.

The cryptonormativity Rorty's pragmatism carries along has come to the surface most recently in his *Achieving our Country*, which weds staunch invectives against the cultural left, including feminism, paralyzed by too much theory, to a new American pride that claims to be merely healthy national self-esteem without becoming patho-logically nationalistic. In his programmatic defense of the Reform Left, Rorty pleads for new alliances among the left, for social hope over and against cultural pessimism, which originally belonged to the right, and for the construction of a "vision of a country to be achieved by building a consensus on the need for specific reforms,"[96] as a way, also, of reconnecting with national pride. In his exhortations against the cultural left, he takes on those mesmerized by cultural politics rather than galvanized by real politics, marked by "stigmata" and "victim politics" rather than interested in economic redistribution. Informed perhaps by Arendt's Kant lectures, he holds the cultural left's aestheticized spectatorship, produced by excessive specular theoretization, against real political agency. Unambiguously addressed also to feminism, reduced now to what for him amounts to a suspect identity politics, Rorty's manifesto has more than one aside to feminist theory. Thus, MacKinnon and Butler are asked to unite, not to fight, since they risk missing out on the real political action that goes on elsewhere.

Just as Rorty's *Contingency, Solidarity, Irony* was covertly working with the corresponding vessels "liberalism-pragmatism-freedom," so his *Achieving Our Country* operates with the entwinement of national pride-America-pragmatism. Achieving our country, rekindling its patriotism becomes coterminous (or codynamical) with the pragmatic turn away from last foundations and from the quest for ultimate justification. Dewey surmised that America would be the *first nation-state* to do so. Antiauthoritarianism on a philosophical level, that is, Dewey's rejection of the correspondence truth of theory, comes to equal poetic creation, creation *ex nihilo*, the United States as a Romantic poem: "It is to envisage our nation-state as both self-creating poet and self-created poem."[97] Aside from invoking such political organicism, Rorty's exhortations against the so-called spectatorial cultural left are mediated via a weak critique of economic globalism, which is not decried primarily for its own sake but for the negative effects it might have on the United States, for that which might return to the shores of the States in the form of a backlash, in the disenchanted, virtually economically disenfranchised "proles." If other intellectuals have opted for a rootless cosmopolitanism, Rorty seems to have turned toward a new defensive national pride. Most ironically, his manifesto suffers from a performative contradiction insofar as it abjects the cultural left as the spectatorial, phantom other, the Gothic double, at the same time that it purports to want to create a communal platform. Not willing to embrace the reflective universalism of the rootless cosmopolitan, Rorty falls for the contingency of American pride, which taunts the seriousness of identity politics, including feminism. Under the banner of pragmatism, we end up with a displaced universalism that is no longer transcendent but located "immanently" (i.e., pragmatically) in the presumed consensus of the speaking community, and all dissent is a deviation from those immanent rules or veiled norms. The alleged violence imputed to spectatorial theory now is supplanted by an enforced pragmatism that becomes difference-obliterating.

For all these reasons it may be upon us to probe not just the consequences of "capital t Theory" but also those that follow from a "strong," unchallenged capitalized Pragmatism. True, respected attempts have been made to suture the theoretical differences that mark feminist theories via neopragmatism. As we saw, Fraser has sought to craft "a more consistent and thoroughgoing pragmatism,"[98] which, like Rorty's, rejects a "moral realism and universalism" to embrace a historicist view. Far from being a sympathetic reader of Rorty's,[99] she regards her pronounced contentions with Rorty in reality to amount to "a disagreement within pragmatism." Thus, her early work, *Unruly Practices*, criticized him for assuming a gendered split between the public and private and for promoting an aestheticized irony. Under the latter were subsumed a depoliticized theory and public politics, which became the privileged precinct of the (male) liberal reformist. Yet, despite these strong misgivings, her sympathies go out to a thoroughly revamped neopragmatism, whose mandate she defines as follows: "How can we retrieve a version of pragmatism that is compatible with radical democracy, polylogic abnormal political discourse, and socialist-feminist discourse?"[100] This requires winnowing "pragmatism from cold war liberalism"[101] to construct a "demo-cratic-socialist-feminist pragmatism" that is no longer totalizing, but proceeds by trial and error, inspiration and conjecture. But shorn of its political utilitarianism, pragma-tism ends up becoming an instrument and formalized tool, as in the playful multi-ingredient recipe she concocts, which has little to do anymore with either Rorty's narrowly liberal or West's vocational, prophetic pragmatism:

> Begin with the sort of zero-degree pragmatism that is compatible with a wide variety of substantive political views, with socialist feminism as well as bourgeois liberalism. This pragmatism is simply antiessentialism with respect to traditional philosophical concepts like truth and reason, human nature and morality. It implies an appreciation of the historical and socially constructed character of such categories and of the practices from which they get their sense, thereby suggesting at least the abstract possibility of social change. This sort of zero-degree pragmatism is a useful, though hardly all-sufficing, ingre-dient of socialist feminism.[102]

For all the persuasive force that accompanies Fraser's defense of a new socialist femi-nism, it may not entirely be clear what is meant here by pragmatic metatheories, nor is it apparent what, shorn of its substantive claims, such a formal, methodological neopragmatism offers beyond the structuralist's *bricolage* or the tools of antiessen-tialism and antifoundationalism discussed earlier – besides, perhaps, a new name, not burdened, like "theory," by years of negative valorization.

Between *pure* theory and a *strong* pragmatism lie many possibilities. We may not want to underestimate the political effects that could follow from a politicized "substantivist" pragmatism, also, and especially, for feminism, just as much as we do well to hold the grand gestures of pure theory at bay. As we reviewed some of the contentious theoretical and antitheoretical positions in feminism in the course of this essay, however, it became evident that current disputes between theoretical, antitheo-retical, and neopragmatic feminisms need not give cause for pessimism. To be sure, testing each other's theories and practices often means that positions are subjected to vehement critique, but *critique* need not automatically be *crisis*, just as long as we don't submit positions to destructive dissections with our critical scalpel – taking the word *critique* (from *krinein*, "to cut") all too literally. We should neither lose sight of dialogical negotiation nor present our theories as capable of doing more than they could ever accomplish. Further, negotiations need not lead to a watered-down "politics of compromise" that remains adverse to productive contestation, for they can generate a viable, enabling form of coexistence and cohabitation that recognizes feminist (theoretical) activism in all its diversity. Finally, by *historicizing* part of feminist theory, as I have attempted to do in this essay, it also becomes possible to peer beyond what seem to be current impasses or rut-like junctures. By looking beyond the immediacy of our historical "now," it becomes conceivable to think of feminisms, including theoretical feminisms, as engaged in an ongoing process of debate, contestation, and critical revision. Theoretical feminisms then appear as positions "with attitude," certainly not with a brazen, brash attitude but with a critical, even ethical (never a moralizing) one, in line with the original meaning of that time-honored word *ēthos*.[103]

NOTES

INTRODUCTION

1 On *agon* as defining for political speech, see especially Chantal Mouffe's "Decision, Deliberation, and Democratic Ethos," in *Philosophy Today* 41.1 (Spring 1997): 24–9. On agonistic political theory, see Seyla Benhabib's introduction to *Democracy and Difference: Contesting the Boundaries of the Political* (Princeton, N.J.: Princeton University Press, 1996). See also Barbara Herrnstein Smith, *Belief and Resistance: Dynamics of Contemporary Intellectual Controversy* (Cambridge, Mass.: Harvard University Press, 1997).

2 In the context of this introduction, it is impossible to address the many theoretical and political differences that exist between the representatives of a Frankfurt-style critical theory and poststructuralism. Such differences will be brought out in subsequent chapters.

3 In her introduction to *Deconstruction and Pragmatism*, Chantal Mouffe argues that the disagreement between antifoundationalist thinkers, such as Derrida or Rorty, and Habermas is "not political but theoretical. They share [Habermas's] engagement with democratic politics but they consider that democracy does not need philosophical foundations and that it is not through rational grounding that its institutions could be made secure." Mouffe, "Deconstruction, Pragmatism, and the Politics of Democracy," in Chantal Mouffe, ed., *Deconstruction and Pragmatism* (London and New York: Routledge, 1996), 1.

4 Nancy Fraser, "False Antitheses," in Seyla Benhabib, Judith Butler, Drucilla Cornell, and Nancy Fraser, *Feminist Contentions: A Philosophical Exchange* (New York and London: Routledge, 1995), 59–74.

5 Derrida's "Force of Law: The 'Mystical Foundation of Authority'" originally appeared in the *Cardozo Law Review*, 11.5–6 (1990): 919–1726 and was reprinted in Drucilla Cornell, Michael Rosenfeld, and David Gray Carlson, eds., *Deconstruction and the Possibility of Justice* (New York: Routledge, 1992), 3–67. On force in law/right, see also Stanley Fish, *Doing What Comes Naturally: Change, Rhetoric, and the Practice of Theory in Literary and Legal Studies* (Durham, N.C.: Duke University Press, 1989).

6 On the meaning of *krinein*, see Hannah Arendt's discussion of Socratic midwifery, in relation to Plato's *Sophist*: "Socrates' method consisted in emptying his partners of all unfounded beliefs and 'windeggs' – the mere phantasies that filled their minds [*Theaetetus*]. According to Plato, he did this by the art of *krinein*, of sorting out and separating and distinguishing (*technē diakritikē*, the art of discrimination) [*Sophist*]." Hannah Arendt, *Lectures on Kant's Political Philosophy*, ed. Ronald Beiner (Chicago: University of Chicago Press, 1982), 37.

7 On the history of the concept and practice of "critique," see Seyla Benhabib, *Critique, Norm, and Utopia: A Study of the Foundations of Critical Theory* (New York: Columbia University Press, 1986).

8 Max Horkheimer, "Traditional and Critical Theory," in Horkheimer, *Critical Theory: Selected Essays*, trans. Matthew J. O'Connell et al. (New York: Continuum, 1995), 218.

9 Immanuel Kant, "Preface to the Second Edition," *Critique of Pure Reason*, trans. Paul Guyer, ed. Allen W. Wood (Cambridge and New York: Cambridge University Press, 1998), 115.

10 The distinction between bounds and limits is foundational to Kant's establishment of the bounds of pure reason, as defined by *experience*. See especially Immanuel Kant, *Prolegomena to Any Future Metaphysics that Will Be Able to Come Forward as Science, with Selections from the Critique of Pure Reason*, trans. and ed. Gary Hatfield (Cambridge and New York: Cambridge University Press, 1977), 104–18, as well as the Kant sections in Chapter 2, below.

11 See Reinhart Koselleck, *Critique and Crisis: Enlightenment and the Pathogenesis of Modern Society* (Oxford and New York: Berg, 1988); also cited in Benhabib, *Critique, Norm, and Utopia*, 19–20.

12 See Benhabib, *Critique, Norm, and Utopia*, 33.

13 Horkheimer, "Traditional and Critical Theory," 242.

14 I take the term "theoretical activism" from one of Judith Butler's contributions to Benhabib et al., *Feminist Contentions*, 132. For a more extensive discussion of this issue, see also Chapter 8 in this book.

15 Horkheimer, "Traditional and Critical Theory," 211.

16 Michel Foucault, "Nietzsche, Genealogy, History," in Paul Rabinow, ed., *The Foucault Reader* (New York: Pantheon, 1984), 88.

17 Friedrich Nietzsche, *On the Genealogy of Morals and Ecce Homo*, trans. Walter Kaufmann and R.J. Hollingdale (New York: Vintage, 1969), 20.

18 See the chapter on values in Herbert Schnädelbach, *Philosophy in Germany 1831–1933*, trans. Eric Matthews (Cambridge: Cambridge University Press, 1984), 161–91. See also Barbara Herrnstein Smith, *Contingencies of Value: Alternative Perspectives for Critical Theory* (Cambridge, Mass.: Harvard University Press, 1988).

19 Antithetical thinking has a long tradition: it is the *either/or*, or *Entweder/Oder*, that Kierkegaard sought to leap out of in his theological response to Hegel's dialectical dualism. In the Hegelian system, it is the generative motor, the antagonism but also mutual interpenetration of the dialectic, which, as Hannah Arendt noted in her *On Violence*, also returned in Marx as the "motor" of history.

20 See Derrida on justice, especially "Force of Law," but also Judith Butler's "Universality in Culture," in Martha C. Nussbaum et al., *For Love of Country: Debating the Limits of Patriotism* (Boston, Mass.: Beacon Press, 1996).

21 Seyla Benhabib and Drucilla Cornell, eds., *Feminism as Critique: On the Politics of Gender* (Minneapolis: University of Minnesota Press, 1987).

22 Butler, in Benhabib et al., *Feminist Contentions*, 138–9.

23 Robert M. Cover, "Violence and the Word," in Martha Minow, Michael Ryan, and Austin Sarat, eds., *Narrative, Violence, and the Law: The Essays of Robert Cover* (Ann Arbor: University of Michigan Press, 1992).

24 See the critical responses collected in vol. 11 of the *Cardozo Law Review*, cited in note 5 above. See also Werner Hamacher, "Afformative, Strike: Benjamin's 'Critique of Violence'" in Andrew Benjamin and Peter Osborne, eds., *Walter Benjamin's Philosophy: Destruction and Experience* (London: Routledge, 1994); Anselm Haverkamp, ed., *Gewalt und Gerechtigkeit: Derrida–Benjamin* (Frankfurt a.M.: Suhrkamp, 1994).

25 See Ronald Gottesman and Mauricio Mazon, eds., *Encyclopedia of Violence in the United States* (New York: Charles Scribner's Sons, forthcoming).

26 I return to the question of theoretical violence and the violence of theory in the final chapter of this book.

27 See Nietzsche's preface to his *Genealogy of Morals*, 17, which recounts how, as a young boy, he wrote his "first literary childish trifle," solving the origin of evil by ascribing it to God.

28 See Judith Butler's *The Psychic Life of Power: Theories in Subjection* (Stanford, Calif.: Stanford University Press, 1997), which further elaborates on this model of interiorization in an attempt to link Foucault's genealogy of power to psychoanalysis, via the notion of "passionate attachments."

29 On the history of the concept "power," see the work of Thomas Wartenberg, especially Thomas E. Wartenberg, *The Forms of Power: From Domination to Transformation* (Philadelphia: Temple University, 1990).

30 See also Jane Flax, *Thinking Fragments: Psychoanalysis, Feminism and Postmodernism in the Contemporary West* (Berkeley: University of California Press, 1990); Seyla Benhabib, "Feminism and Postmodernism: An Uneasy Alliance," in Benhabib et al., *Feminist Contentions*, 18ff.

31 Claude Levi-Strauss, *The Savage Mind* (London: Weidenfeld & Nicolson, 1966); Jean-François Lyotard, *The Postmodern Condition: A Report on Knowledge* (Minneapolis: University of Minnesota Press, 1984). In his introduction to *The Archeology of Knowledge*, Foucault quite explicitly addresses the tools with which historians, the proverbial "workers in the historical field," have unearthed the sedimentary strata of history. Michel Foucault, *The Archeology of Knowledge and the Discourse on Language*, trans. A.M. Sheridan Smith (New York: Pantheon, 1972), 3 and 15.

32 Foucault, "Nietzsche, Genealogy, History," 93.

33 As is the case with critical theory and poststructuralism, pragmatism is a label that applies to a host of views and tendencies, whose various forms require study in their own right. For a helpful overview, see especially James T. Kloppenberg, "Pragmatism: An Old Name for Some New Ways of Thinking?," 83–127; and Morris Dickstein, "Introduction: Pragmatism Then and Now," 1–18, in Dickstein, ed., *The Revival of Pragmatism: New Essays on Social Thought, Law, and Culture* (Durham, N.C., and London: Duke University Press, 1998).

34 Nancy Fraser, "Pragmatism, Feminism, and the Linguistic Turn," in Benhabib et al., *Feminist Contentions*, 167.

35 See the discussion of Foucault's "The Subject and Power" in Chapter 3, below. For a similar analysis of the concept of freedom in Foucault, and of *ethos* as possibility, see Richard Bernstein, "Foucault: Critique as a Philosophical Ethos," in Michael Kelly, ed., *Critique and Power: Recasting the Foucault/Habermas Debate* (Cambridge, Mass., and London: MIT Press, 1994), 211–41.

1 ON THE POLITICS OF PURE MEANS: BENJAMIN, ARENDT, FOUCAULT

This chapter was first presented at the University of Amsterdam's 1994 conference on violence and published in an earlier version in H. de Vries and S. Weber, eds., *Violence, Identity, and Self-Determination* (Stanford, Calif.: Stanford University Press, 1997).

1 Gershom Scholem, *Walter Benjamin: The Story of a Friendship*, trans. Harry Zohn (New York: Schocken, 1981), 93.

2 Walter Benjamin, *The Correspondence of Walter Benjamin, 1910–1940*, ed. Gershom Scholem and Theodor W. Adorno, trans. Manfred R. Jacobson and Evelyn M. Jacobson (Chicago and London: University of Chicago Press, 1994), 174, translation slightly modified.

3 Scholem, *Walter Benjamin*, 80.

4 Its second part, entitled "Die wahre Politik" ("True Politics") was to comprise two chapters, "Abbau der Gewalt" ("Dismantling Power") and "Teleologie ohne Endzweck" ("Teleology without a Final Goal"), now widely held to be the "Theologico-Political Fragment." See Benjamin, *Correspondence*, 168–69; and Scholem, *Walter Benjamin*, 93.

5 See Oskar Negt, "Rechtsordnung, Öffentlichkeit und Gewalt," in Heinz Grossmann and Oskar Negt, *Die Auferstehung der Gewalt: Springerblockade und politische Reaktion in der Bundesrepublik* (Frankfurt a.M.: Europäische Verlagsanstalt, 1968), 168–85.

6 Jürgen Habermas, "Walter Benjamin: Consciousness-Raising or Rescuing Critique," in Gary Smith, ed., *On Walter Benjamin: Critical Essays and Recollections* (Cambridge, Mass.: MIT Press, 1988), 118–19.

7 Jürgen Habermas, "The Horrors of Autonomy: Carl Schmitt in English," in Habermas, *The New Conservatism: Cultural Criticism and the Historians' Debate* (Cambridge, Mass.: MIT Press, 1989), 137. On Schmitt, see further Stephen Holmes's *The Anatomy of Antiliberalism* (Cambridge, Mass.: Harvard University Press, 1993), which offers a genealogy of conservative antiliberalism, from de Maistre via Schmitt to Leo Strauss and Christopher Lasch, among others. I am grateful to Andreas Huyssen for emphasizing the importance of this study.

8 Walter Benjamin, "Für die Diktatur: Interview mit Georges Valois," in Walter Benjamin, *Gesammelte Schriften*, eds. Rolf Tiedemann and Hermann Schweppenhäuser (Frankfurt a.M.: Suhrkamp, 1974) vol. 4, 1/2, 487–92. See also Michael Rumpf, "Radikale Theologie: Benjamins Beziehung zu Carl

Schmitt," in Peter Gebhardt et al., *Walter Benjamin – Zeitgenosse der Moderne* (Kronberg: Scriptor, 1976), 37–50.

9 Benjamin, "Diktatur," 489.

10 Ibid., 491.

11 As Derrida has argued in "Force of Law," "Critique of Violence" participates in a Kantian tradition in that it announces itself as a "judgment, evaluation, examination that provides itself with the means to judge violence." As such, it presents "an attitude that permits us to choose (*krinein*) and so to decide and to cut decisively in history and on the subject of history." (Jacques Derrida, "Force of Law: The 'Mystical Foundation of Authority'," *Cardozo Law Review*, 11.5–6 (1990): 1031). On Benjamin's connections to Kant, see also Michael W. Jennings, *Dialectical Images: Walter Benjamin's Theory of Literary Criticism* (Ithaca, N.Y., and London: Cornell University Press, 1987); Gary Smith, "Thinking through Benjamin: An Introductory Essay," in Smith, *Benjamin: Philosophy, History, Aesthetics* (Chicago and London: University of Chicago Press, 1989), vii–xlii; as well as my *Walter Benjamin's Other History: Of Stones, Animals, Human Beings, and Angels* (Berkeley and London: University of California Press, 1998).

12 For a related discussion of this "diacritical principle," which informs many discussions of violence, including feminist and postmodern appropriations of violence, see also Chapter 7, below, "Limits of Feminist Representation: Elfriede Jelinek's Language of Violence."

13 See the entry on "Mittel" ("Means") in *Historisches Wörterbuch der Philosophie* (Darmstadt: Wissenschaftliche Buchgesellschaft, 1971–), vol. 5, 1431–39.

14 Hannah Arendt, *On Revolution* (London: Penguin, 1990), 19.

15 This issue has become topical again in the recent multiculturalism and immigration debates, insofar as nonliberal modes of socialization fundamentally question the assumed cohesiveness and uniformity of the liberal community. See especially Habermas's contribution to these debates in Amy Gutmann, ed., *Multiculturalism: Examining the Politics of Recognition* (Princeton, N.J.: Princeton University Press, 1994).

16 Legal positivism also forms the target of Schmitt's *The Crisis of Parliamentary Democracy*; see Ellen Kennedy, "Introduction: Carl Schmitt's *Parlamentarismus* in Its Historical Context," in Carl Schmitt, *The Crisis of Parliamentary Democracy* (Cambridge, Mass.: MIT Press, 1988), xxxv.

17 Walter Benjamin, "Critique of Violence," *Reflections: Essays, Aphorisms, Autobiographical Writings*, trans. Edmund Jephcott (New York: Schocken, 1986), 279. In the original, the phrase appears as *geschichtsphilosophische Rechtsbetrachtung*.

18 See the entry "Gewalt" in *Historisches Wörterbuch der Philosophie* (Darmstadt: Wissenschaftliche Buchgesellschaft, 1971–), vol. 3, 562–70.

19 Horst Folkers, "Zum Begriff der Gewalt bei Kant und Benjamin," in Günter Figal and Horst Folkers, *Zur Theorie der Gewalt und Gewaltlosigkeit bei Walter Benjamin* (Heidelberg: F.E.S.T., 1979), 25–57.

20 Benjamin, *Critique of Violence*, 300.

21 On the means–end relation, see the entry "Mittel" in *Historisches Wörterbuch der Philosophie*, vol. 5, 1431–39.

22 Benjamin, "Critique of Violence," 285.

23 See Günter Figal, "Die Ethik Walter Benjamins," in Figal and Folkers, *Zur Theorie der Gewalt und Gewaltlosigkeit bei Walter Benjamin*, 4ff.

24 Benjamin, "Critique of Violence," 287.

25 Ibid., 293.

26 Ibid., 292.

27 On Sorel, see Ernesto Laclau and Chantal Mouffe, *Hegemony and Socialist Strategy: Towards a Radical Democratic Politics* (London: Verso, 1985), 36–42.

28 Schmitt, *The Crisis of Parliamentary Democracy*, 69.

29 The passage from Schmitt's *The Concept of the Political* reads as follows: "The political entity is by its very nature the decisive entity, regardless of the sources from which it derives its last psychic motives. It exists or does not exist. If it exists, it is the supreme, that is, in the supreme case, the authoritative entity. That the state is an entity and in fact the decisive entity rests upon its political character." Carl Schmitt, *The Concept of the Political*, trans. George Schwab (Chicago: University of

Chicago Press, 1996), 43–44. Schmitt's notion of the extreme situation is analogous to his concept of the "Ausnahmezustand," developed in his *Political Theology*, for sovereign is the one who decides on the exception. In his *Concept of the Political*, Schmitt invoked the thesis first formulated in *Political Theology* that "juridic formulas of the omnipotence of the state are, in fact, only superficial secularizations of theological formulas of the omnipotence of God" (ibid., 42).

30 Ibid., 28.

31 Carl von Clausewitz, *On War*, eds. Michael Howard and Peter Paret (Princeton, N.J.: Princeton University Press, 1984), 87. As Clausewitz observed: "The political object is the goal, war is the means of reaching it, and means can never be considered in isolation from their purpose."

32 Schmitt, *The Concept of the Political*, 35.

33 For a discussion of Benjamin's theory of means in relation to the "Theologico-Political Fragment," see Werner Hamacher, "Afformative, Strike: Benjamin's 'Critique of Violence'," in Andrew Benjamin and Peter Osborne, eds., *Walter Benjamin's Philosophy: Destruction and Experience* (London and New York: Routledge, 1994), 110–38.

34 Going even further in his interpretation, Derrida posited that Benjamin's "bloodless violence" ultimately could not be conceptually demarcated from the technological extermination of the Holocaust. See Derrida, "Force of Law": 1040–45.

35 For a related discussion of Benjamin's film theory, see Samuel Weber, *Mass Mediauras: Form, Technics, Media*, ed. Alan Cholodenko (Stanford, Calif.: Stanford University Press, 1996).

36 Hannah Arendt, *On Violence* (San Diego, New York, and London: Harcourt Brace Jovanovich, 1970), 9.

37 Ibid.

38 Ibid., 5.

39 Ibid., 54.

40 Ibid., 36 and 37n.

41 Ibid., 37.

42 Ibid., 38.

43 Ibid., 56.

44 Ibid., 4.

45 Ibid., 46.

46 Ibid., 79.

47 Ibid., 51.

48 Ibid.

49 On peace as an absolute, see Arendt, *On Violence*, 51.

50 Arendt, *On Revolution*, 18 and 19.

51 Jürgen Habermas, "Hannah Arendt: On the Concept of Power," in Habermas, *Philosophical-Political Profiles* (Cambridge, Mass.: MIT Press, 1983), 174.

52 Ibid., 172.

53 Ibid., 173.

54 Ibid., 179.

55 This is corroborated by Habermas when he states that, following the Greek model, the "conduct of war is the classic model of strategic action. For the Greeks, strategic action took place outside the city's walls; for Arendt, too, it is essentially apolitical, an affair for experts."

56 Arendt, *On Revolution*, 19.

57 See Negt's comments on Marcuse in his 1968 "Rechtsordnung, Öffentlichkeit und Gewalt," *passim*.

58 Arendt, *On Violence*, 56.

59 Ibid., 30–31.

60 Arendt, *On Revolution*, 98–99.

61 See Jean-Paul Sartre, "Preface" in Frantz Fanon, *The Wretched of the Earth*, trans. Constance Farrington (New York: Grove Press, 1963), 7–31. On Fanon's critique of Hegel, see his "The Negro and Recognition," in *Black Skin, White Masks*, as well as Chapter 6 in this book.

62 See Gayatri Chakravorty Spivak's discussion of Foucault's notion of epistemic violence, in her "Can the Subaltern Speak?" in Cary Nelson and Lawrence Grossberg, eds., *Marxism and the Interpretation of Culture* (Urbana: University of Illinois Press, 1988), 280–81.

63 Michel Foucault, *The History of Sexuality, Volume I: An Introduction*, trans. Robert Hurley (New York: Vintage, 1978), 93. Foucault also refers to Clausewitz and war in "Two Lectures," in Michael Kelly, ed., *Critique and Power: Recasting the Foucault / Habermas Debate* (Cambridge, Mass.: MIT Press: 1994), 28. See Chapter 3, below.

64 Ibid., 96.

65 Ibid., 102.

66 Michel Foucault, "Politics and Ethics: An Interview," in Paul Rabinow, ed., *The Foucault Reader* (New York: Pantheon, 1984), 378–80.

2 BETWEEN KANT AND NIETZSCHE: FOUCAULT'S CRITIQUE

1 Hannah Arendt, *On Revolution* (London: Penguin, 1990), 221.

2 Hannah Arendt, *On Violence* (San Diego, New York, and London: Harcourt Brace Jovanovich, 1970), 82.

3 Jürgen Habermas, *The Philosophical Discourse of Modernity: Twelve Lectures* (Cambridge, Mass.: MIT Press, 1987), 127.

4 On the question of Foucault's alleged adherence to sociological functionalism, see David Couzens Hoy, "Introduction," in Hoy, *Foucault: A Critical Reader* (Oxford, England, and Cambridge, Mass.: Blackwell, 1986), 7–8.

5 Nancy Fraser, *Unruly Practices: Power, Discourse, and Gender in Contemporary Social Theory* (Minneapolis: University of Minnesota Press, 1989), 32. Taking on the Weberian tradition, Arendt proposes in her *On Violence* a set of rigorous definitions for keywords such as power, force, strength, etc. See her *On Violence*, 44ff. Habermas, too, refers to Weber's conflation of power and violence in his "Hannah Arendt: On the Concept of Power," in Jürgen Habermas, *Philosophical-Political Profiles*, trans. Frederick G. Lawrence (Cambridge, Mass.: MIT Press, 1983), 171–72.

6 Hubert L. Dreyfus and Paul Rabinow, *Michel Foucault: Beyond Structuralism and Hermeneutics*, 2nd edition, with an Afterword by and an Interview with Michel Foucault (Chicago: University of Chicago Press, 1983), 184.

7 Habermas, *Philosophical Discourse of Modernity*, 7. On Habermas's preference for a Weberian definition of modernity, as opposed to other alternatives, see Gérard Raulet's comments in the interview he conducted with Foucault called Michel Foucault, "Critical Theory/Intellectual History," in Michael Kelly, ed., *Critique and Power: Recasting the Foucault / Habermas Debate* (Cambridge, Mass.: MIT Press, 1994), 125. Originally published as "Structuralism and Post-Structuralism: An Interview with Michel Foucault" in *Telos*, XVI.55 (Spring 1983): 195–211, and reprinted as "Structuralisme et poststructuralisme" in Michel Foucault, *Dits et écrits, 1954–1988*, 4 vols., eds. Daniel Defert and François Ewald (Paris: Gallimard, 1994), vol. 4, 431–57.

8 See Habermas, *Philosophical Discourse of Modernity*, 1.

9 Habermas, "Modernity – An Incomplete Project," in Hal Foster, ed., *The Anti-Aesthetic: Essays on Postmodern Culture* (Port Townsend, Wash.: Bay Press, 1983), 8.

10 Habermas, *Philosophical Discourse of Modernity*, 113.

11 Ibid., 4.

12 Ibid., 86. Nietzsche's quote is from the second *Untimely Meditation*, or *On the Uses and Disadvantages of History for Life*, in Friedrich Nietzsche, *Untimely Meditations*, trans. R.J. Hollingdale, ed. Daniel Breazeale (Cambridge: Cambridge University Press, 1980), 59–123.

13 Habermas, *Philosophical Discourse of Modernity*, 95.

14 Ibid., 96.

15 Ibid., 116.

16 Ibid.

17 Ibid., 119.

18 Ibid., 283.

19 As Habermas stressed in *The Philosophical Discourse of Modernity*, Foucault invoked the term "felicitous positivism" in his "Discourse on Language" to define the operations of archeology. See

Foucault, "The Discourse on Language," in Michel Foucault, *The Archeology of Knowledge and The Discourse on Language*, trans. A.M. Sheridan Smith (New York: Pantheon, 1982), 234; and Habermas, *The Philosophical Discourse of Modernity*, 248. In fact, as Habermas communicated to Foucault biographer James Miller, in a final encounter with Foucault, he "tried to press him about his 'happy positivism.' I told him, 'look, it makes no sense to refrain from explaining normative premises if one proceeds in such a critical way as you do.' " However, as Miller reports, Habermas was highly surprised by Foucault's response. For, "he told me, 'Look, this is a question I'm thinking about just now. And you will have to decide when I finish my History of Sexuality, how I will come out'," James Miller, *The Passion of Michel Foucault* (New York, London, Toronto, Sydney, Tokyo, and Singapore: Simon & Schuster, 1993), 339.

20 Habermas, *Philosophical Discourse of Modernity*, 107.

21 See Michael Walzer, "The Politics of Michel Foucault," in Hoy, *Foucault: A Critical Reader*, 51. Foucault later responded to Walzer's invectives, though without naming him, in "Polemics, Politics, and Problematizations," noting that he liked discussions, not polemics: "If I open a book and see that the author is accusing an adversary of 'infantile leftism,' I shut it again right away. That's not my way of doing things." Foucault, "Polemics, Politics, and Problematizations," in Paul Rabinow, ed., *The Foucault Reader* (New York: Pantheon, 1984), 381.

22 See Hubert L. Dreyfus and Paul Rabinow, "What is Maturity? Habermas and Foucault on 'What is Enlightenment?' "; Ian Hacking, "Self-Improvement," in Hoy, *Foucault: A Critical Reader*, 109–21 and 235–40; David R. Hiley, "Power and Knowledge," in Hiley, *Philosophy in Question: Essays on a Pyrrhonian Theme* (Chicago and London: University of Chicago Press, 1988), 86–114. See also Richard Bernstein, "Foucault: Critique as a Philosophic Ethos"; Thomas McCarthy, "The Critique of Impure Reason: Foucault and the Frankfurt School"; and James Schmidt and Thomas E. Wartenberg, "Foucault's Enlightenment: Critique, Revolution, and the Fashioning of the Self," all in Kelly, *Critique and Power*. See also Christopher Norris, "What is Enlightenment?: Kant and Foucault," in Gary Gutting, ed., *The Cambridge Companion to Foucault* (Cambridge: Cambridge University Press, 1994), 159–96.

23 Michel Foucault, "The Subject and Power," in Dreyfus and Rabinow, *Michel Foucault: Beyond Structuralism and Hermeneutics*, 210.

24 See Jürgen Habermas's "Taking Aim at the Heart of the Present: On Foucault's Lecture on Kant's *What Is Enlightenment?*" in Kelly, *Critique and Power*, 150.

25 The notable exception is Axel Honneth's suggestive chapter "From the Analysis of Discourse to the Theory of Power: Struggle as the Paradigm of the Social" in Honneth, *The Critique of Power: Reflective Stages in a Critical Social Theory*, trans. Kenneth Baynes (Cambridge, Mass., and London: MIT Press, 1991), 149–75. I will return to Honneth's interpretation of Foucault in Chapter 3.

26 Michel Foucault, "Space, Knowledge, and Power," in Foucault, *Foucault Live (Interviews, 1961–1984)*, ed. Sylvère Lotringer (New York: Semiotext(e), 1996), 343.

27 Foucault used the locution "antidogmatic violence" to refer to the 1968 student revolts, observing that these movements "sometimes carried revolutionary Marxist discourse to the height of exaggeration," but "were often inspired at the same time by an antidogmatic violence that ran counter to this type of discourse." See Foucault, "Critical Theory/Intellectual History," in Kelly, *Critique and Power*, 111.

28 In "Critical Theory/Intellectual History," Foucault acknowledged his indebtedness to Nietzsche's work from the period beginning in 1880, but textual evidence indicates that he was also heavily influenced by the earlier writings of the 1870s, especially the second *Untimely Meditation*. See Foucault, "Critical Theory/Intellectual History," in Kelly, *Critique and Power*, 114 and 122.

29 Friedrich Nietzsche, *On the Genealogy of Morals and Ecce Homo*, trans. Walter Kaufmann (New York: Vintage, 1969), 20.

30 On this jointly edited translation, see their interview for *Le Figaro littéraire*, "Michel Foucault et Gilles Deleuze veulent rendre à Nietzsche son vrai visage," and "Introduction générale" to the *Œuvres philosophiques complètes de F. Nietzsche* (Paris: Gallimard, 1967), both of which can be found in Foucault, *Dits et écrits*, vol. 1, 549–52 and 561–4. Their intention, ostensibly, was to reclaim Nietzsche from the anti-Semitic mold imposed on his work by Nietzsche's sister, Elisabeth Förster-Nietzsche. See also Foucault's interview with Gérard Raulet, "Critical Theory/Intellectual History,"

where he recounts that he started reading Nietzsche in 1953, in Kelly, *Critique and Power*, 114. Of note, furthermore, is Foucault's *Madness and Civilization*, which celebrated Nietzsche, along with Hölderlin, Nerval, and Artaud, for pitting "unreason" against the tyranny of reason, exercised in so-called rationalist psychiatric practices. See Foucault, *Madness and Civilization* (New York: Pantheon, 1965), 278.

31 Foucault, "Critical Theory/Intellectual History," 114–15.

32 See the editorial notes to Foucault's "Notice historique," the preface to his Kant translation, *Anthropologie du point de vue pragmatique*, in Foucault, *Dits et écrits*, vol. 1, 288, as well as the helpful "Chronologie," to vol. 1 of Foucault's *Dits et écrits*, 23.

33 To be sure, the analogy with Dilthey should not be pressed too far, though in his earliest writings on the subject of psychology, Foucault acknowledged Dilthey's seminal role in disaffiliating the human from the natural sciences. See especially the section, "La découverte du sens," in his "La psychologie de 1850 à 1950," in Foucault, *Dits et écrits*, vol. 1, 126–27.

34 Michel Foucault, *The Order of Things: An Archeology of the Human Sciences* (New York: Vintage, 1994), 341.

35 Ibid., 342.

36 Ibid., 343.

37 Ibid., 305.

38 Ibid., 342. Here, Foucault already followed Heidegger's positive assessment of Nietzsche's "end of metaphysics" as new beginning, put forth in his Freiburg Nietzsche lectures.

39 Ibid., 328.

40 It should be pointed out, however, that Foucault used the term as early as 1963, in his study *The Birth of the Clinic: An Archeology of Medical Perception*.

41 Foucault, *The Archeology of Knowledge*, 204 and 219.

42 Ibid., 231.

43 Ibid., 220.

44 Discussing his plan for an "epistemological mutation of history," centered on the principle of discontinuity, Foucault rejected the assumption that his methodology was structuralistic, criticizing the then popular "structure/development" opposition. Foucault, *The Archeology of Knowledge*, 11. See also "The Discourse on Language," where, having explained the principles of archeology, he stated sarcastically: "Let those who are weak on vocabulary, let those with little comprehension of theory call all this — if its appeal is stronger than its meaning for them — structuralism" (Foucault, *The Archeology of Knowledge*, 234). For a more developed discussion of structuralism's formalism, see Foucault, "Critical Theory/Intellectual History," in Kelly, *Critique and Power*, 111.

45 On this point, see also Habermas, *Philosophical Discourse of Modernity*, 254.

46 See Nietzsche, "On Truth and Lies in an Extramoral Sense," where he uses the term "drive for truth" (*Trieb*) rather than the later "will to knowledge," and where he advances his deconstruction of truth as a "movable army of tropes." In Nietzsche, *Philosophy and Truth: Selections from Nietzsche's Notebooks of the early 1870's*, trans. Daniel Breazeale (Amherst, Mass.: Humanity Books, 1979), 80 and 84. Here and elsewhere in this study, I have translated Nietzsche's *außermoralisch* as "extramoral."

47 For a critique of "origin" as *archē*, see Foucault, "Man and His Doubles," in Foucault, *The Order of Things*, 328ff, but also the introduction to his *Archeology of Knowledge*, 14. Nietzsche uses the phrase *wirkliche Historie der Moral* in the preface to his *Genealogy of Morals*. The English translation renders the designation as "actual *history of morality*." Compare Nietzsche, *Genealogy of Morals*, 21, and the German original, in Friedrich Nietzsche, *Werke: Kritische Gesamtausgabe*, eds. Giorgio Colli and Mazzino Montinari (Berlin and New York: de Gruyter, 1967). See also Foucault, "Nietzsche, la généalogie, l'histoire," in Foucault, *Dits et écrits*, vol. 2, 147.

48 Foucault, "Nietzsche, Genealogy, History," 83.

49 Ibid.

50 Ibid., 81. Here Foucault treats paragraph 244 of *Beyond Good and Evil*, in which Nietzsche "vivisects" the so-called profundity of Germans and points to the "manifold" and "diverse origins" of the German character. Not infrequently, the paragraph is used to vindicate Nietzsche's antinationalistic, anti-German sentiment and exoneration from racist politics. Friedrich Nietzsche, *Beyond Good and*

Evil: Prelude to a Philosophy of the Future, trans. Walter Kaufmann (New York: Vintage, 1989), 177ff. For a longer discussion of Foucault's critique of racism, see Chapter 3, below.

51 Ibid., 83.

52 Ibid., 84.

53 Ibid., 85.

54 Nietzsche, *Genealogy of Morals*, 65.

55 Foucault, "Nietzsche, Genealogy, History," 84. Foucault relies here on the third essay of Nietzsche's *Genealogy of Morals*, "What Is the Meaning of Ascetic Ideals?" See Nietzsche, *Genealogy of Morals*, 97ff.

56 Indeed, in his analysis of ideological state apparatuses, Althusser asserts that human actions and practices "are governed by the *rituals* in which these practices are inscribed, within the *material existence of an ideological apparatus*, be it only a small part of that apparatus." Appropriating Pascal's "Kneel down, move your lips in prayer, and you will believe," Althusser transposed Pascal's "Jansenist defiance to a language that directly names reality" into his own Marxist vocabulary to vindicate the material existence of ideas. For, as he noted, an individual's "*ideas are his material actions inserted into material practices governed by material rituals which are themselves defined by the material ideological apparatus from which derive the ideas of that subject.*" Louis Althusser, "Ideology and Ideological State Apparatuses (Notes towards an Investigation)," in Slavoj Žižek, *Mapping Ideology* (London and New York: Verso, 1994), 127.

57 Foucault, "Nietzsche, Genealogy, History," 86.

58 Ibid., 88, translation modified; Foucault, "Nietzsche, la généalogie, l'histoire," 148. I here retranslate the last sentence of the quote to place emphasis on the term *lutte*, or "struggle," which does not simply have the meaning of "conflict" as the English translation leads one to surmise.

59 Ibid. See Gilles Deleuze, *Nietzsche and Philosophy*, trans. Hugh Tomlinson (New York: Columbia University Press, 1983), 10, where he points to the Nietzsche–Hegel links in the *Genealogy of Morals*. Honneth discusses the connections between Hobbes's and Hegel's eristic model in his *The Struggle for Recognition: The Moral Grammar of Social Conflicts*, trans. Joel Anderson (Cambridge, Mass.: MIT Press, 1996). On the topic of the Hegelian master–slave struggle, see also Chapter 6, "Ethics of the Other," below.

60 Foucault, "Nietzsche, Genealogy, History," 78.

61 Ibid., 76.

62 Ibid., 87. For Nietzsche's discussion of the "suprahistorical perspective," see Nietzsche, *Untimely Meditations*, 65ff.

63 Ibid., 88–89. One of the most famous passages in which Nietzsche introduces the figure of the web-spinning spider can be found in his "On Truth and Lies in an Extramoral Sense," which uncovers man's self-construed conceptual domes, or vaults, of truth as cobwebs. See Nietzsche, "On Truth and Lies in an Extramoral Sense," 85. The reference to the play between chance and necessity is drawn from Nietzsche's *The Dawn of Day*, paragraph 130.

64 Foucault, "Nietzsche, Genealogy, History," 89.

65 Ibid., 90.

66 Ibid., 88. In French the passage reads: "C'est que le savoir n'est pas fait pour comprendre, il est fait pour trancher." Foucault, "Nietzsche, la généalogie, l'histoire," 148. Nietzsche captures the dangerous process of such a rifting critical history most forcefully in the third section of his second *Untimely Meditation, On the Uses and Disadvantages of History for Life*. When it is acknowledged that a certain "thing" (a privilege, a caste, a dynasty) needs to be dispensed with, "then its past is regarded critically, then one takes the knife to its roots, then one cruelly tramples over every kind of piety." Nietzsche, *Untimely Meditations*, 76.

67 On numerous occasions, Nietzsche playfully puns on the German words *begreifen* and *greifen*, for example in his *Genealogy of Morals*, where, contesting that the purpose of a law is to be found in its origin, he adds that one's insight into the utility of physical organs – "the eye being made for seeing, the hand being made for grasping (*greifen*)" – explains just as little about their origin (Nietzsche, *Genealogy of Morals*, 77 and 79). See also Nietzsche, *The Will to Power*, where he defines the "entire apparatus of knowledge," including ends and means, as tools to claim possession of things: "With 'end' and 'means' one takes possession of the process (one invents a process that can be grasped)."

Nietzsche, *The Will to Power*, trans. Walter Kaufmann and R.J. Hollingdale (New York: Vintage, 1968), 274.

68 Foucault, "Nietzsche, Genealogy, History," 93; Foucault, "Nietzsche, la généalogie, l'histoire," 153. For a similar critique of idealistic historical memory, see also Foucault's introduction to *The Archeology of Knowledge*, 7.

69 Foucault, "Nietzsche, Genealogy, History," 97.

70 Ibid., 95–96.

71 See Nietzsche's discussion of medicines as "deadly poisons" in Friedrich Nietzsche, *The Birth of Tragedy and the Case of Wagner*, trans. Walter Kaufmann (New York: Vintage, 1967), 40.

72 Foucault, *The Order of Things*, 317.

73 Foucault, *The Archeology of Knowledge*, 229.

74 Consult the discussion of Foucault's "*Il faut défendre la société*" in Chapter 3, below.

75 Foucault had already introduced this figure of turning weapons against themselves in his *The Order of Things*, 333.

76 See Nietzsche, *Birth of Tragedy*, 94.

77 Foucault, "Nietzsche, Genealogy, History," 93, translation modified; Foucault, "Nietzsche, la généalogie, l'histoire," 152.

78 Ibid., 96 and 156.

79 Heidegger introduces the concept "countermovement" in his first Nietzsche lecture, "forward-looking counterposition" in the second. See Martin Heidegger, *Nietzsche. Volume I: The Will to Power as Art*, trans. David Farrell Krell (New York: HarperCollins, 1991), 28 and *Volume II: The Eternal Recurrence of the Same*, 206.

80 Michel Foucault, "Interview de Michel Foucault," in Foucault, *Dits et écrits*, vol. 4, 703.

81 Cited in Heidegger, *Nietzsche. Volume I*, 154. Commenting on the early Plato note, Heidegger conjectured that Nietzsche, in aiming to end metaphysics through its reversal, in fact secured a new commencement for metaphysics, meaning that the iconoclast, in truth, proved to be the last meta-physician. For a critique of Heidegger's own method of inversion and inability to get out of the entrapments of subject philosophy, see Habermas, *Philosophical Discourse of Modernity*, 97ff and 131–60.

82 Nietzsche, *Genealogy of Morals*, 119. In the margins, one might note here that Nietzsche operated with several meanings of the term reversal or inversion. Sometimes it could refer to the specular games of reason (e.g., Kant's) or to the masochistic diversions of the ascetic ideal as it turned against the body and against itself. At other times, reversal designated the upsetting of the *status quo* between forces, the seizure of power, by a forceful, Nietzschean will, which counteracted history's reactive forces. As the context from which the above quote from the *Genealogy of Morals* is taken makes clear, Nietzsche's perspectivism renounced the proto-Kantian philosophical position of a "pure, will-less, painless, timeless knowing subject." Such a position erroneously demanded, he explained, that we "think of an eye that is completely unthinkable, an eye turned in no particular direction, in which the active and interpreting forces, through which alone seeing becomes seeing *something*, are supposed to be lacking; these always demand of the eye an absurdity and a nonsense." Nietzsche, *Genealogy of Morals*, 119.

83 The salutary effects Nietzsche expected from tropological reversals, enacted on the plane of world history, are nowhere more tangible than in the penultimate section of the third essay of *Genealogy of Morals*, which ended with a grandiose apocalyptic vision, portending the overcoming of nihilism, that is to say, nihilism's self-overcoming through self-destruction on the stage of world history: "All great things bring about their own destruction through an act of self-overcoming," Nietzsche proclaimed. For, "as the will to truth thus gains self-consciousness ... morality will gradually perish now: this is the great spectacle in a hundred acts reserved for the next two centuries in Europe – the most terrible, questionable, and perhaps also the most hopeful of all spectacles." Nietzsche, *Genealogy of Morals*, 161.

84 In formulating these injunctions, Foucault's critique didn't only follow the drift of Nietzsche's subversive technique, but it also approximated the logic that Adorno and Horkheimer laid out in their *Dialectic of Enlightenment*. In assembling a genealogy of instrumental reason, their jointly authored tract did more than simply chart the bifurcation of reason into an original benign branch

and an aberrant, self-perpetuating instrumentality that had derailed over the course of modernity's history, culminating in capitalism and, eventually, National Socialism. Instead, the *Dialectic of Enlightenment* still operated under the assumption that reason's positive mode eventually could work as an antidote, become redemptive – on condition, however, that it adopt a nonobjectifying stance towards nature. This meant that the implements of a reflective reason needed to be wielded against its split-off, aberrant, rationalized instrumentality. Foucault did not share Adorno and Horkheimer's utopian belief in a redeemed nature, although, as we shall see, he did focus on the aesthetic – its "promesse de bonheur" – as a possible locus of redemption from the alienating effects of modernity's excessive "governmentalization." But he certainly seized on the ruined figure – the allegory – of the dialectical movement that traversed their work when, in like fashion, he assumed that the tools of historical genealogy could undo the mere instrumentalization of a rationalized, bureaucratized historiography. For Nietzsche's discussion of art's "promesse de bonheur" (promise of happiness), a figure he ascribed to Stendhal, see Nietzsche, *Genealogy of Morals*, 104. Furthermore, see the section "Baudelaire's Aestheticism" below, as well as Martin Jay's discussion of the Frankfurt School's aesthetic theory in Jay, *The Dialectical Imagination: A History of the Frankfurt School and the Institute of Social Research 1923–1950* (Boston, Toronto, and London: Little, Brown & Co., 1973), 173ff.

85 Arendt, *On Violence*, 56.

86 Alexander Nehamas, *The Art of Living: Socratic Reflection from Plato to Foucault* (Berkeley, Los Angeles, and London: University of California Press, 1998), 183.

87 An English translation, titled "What Is Critique?," which does not include the transcript of the question-and-answer period, can be found in James Schmidt, ed., *What Is Enlightenment? Eighteenth-Century Answers and Twentieth-Century Questions* (Berkeley, Los Angeles, and London: University of California Press, 1996), 382–98. The original French version, "Qu'est-ce que la critique? [Critique et *Aufklärung*]," was not published until 1990, when it appeared in *Bulletin de la Société française de Philosophie* 84 (April–June 1990): 35–63, although it was omitted from the collected *Dits et écrits* (1994), where it is mentioned briefly in the *Chronologie*, which opens the first volume. See Foucault, *Dits et écrits*, vol. 1, 54. Foucault is reported to have confided to Henri Gouhier that the actual title of the lecture should have been "What Is Enlightenment?"

88 Michel Foucault, "The Art of Telling the Truth," reprinted in Kelly, *Critique and Power*, 139–48. Published in Foucault, *Dits et écrits*, vol. 4, 679–88. An English translation, entitled "Kant on Enlightenment and Revolution," appeared in the journal *Economy and Society* 15.1 (February 1986): 88–96. The original French text was published as "Un cours inédit" in *Magazine littéraire* 207 (May 1984): 35–39. This short text is an extract of the course he conducted on January 5, 1983, "Le gouvernement de soi et des autres" ["The Government of Self and Others"]. In Michel Foucault, *Résumé des cours: 1970–1982* (Paris: Julliard, 1989), the course title is simply cited, with no accompanying text, since he was at the time too ill to submit a "résumé" for the last courses.

89 An amended translation appears in Michel Foucault, *Ethics: Subjectivity and Truth*, ed. Paul Rabinow (New York: New Press, 1997), 303–19. The French original is included in vol. 4 of *Dits et écrits*, 562–78.

90 See Habermas, "Modernity – An Incomplete Project," 14.

91 See "Chronologie," *Dits et écrits*, vol. 1, 62, and Miller, *The Passion of Michel Foucault*, 337ff.

92 Habermas, "Taking Aim at the Heart of the Present," in Kelly, *Critique and Power*, 150.

93 Foucault, *Foucault Live*, 342.

94 Michel Foucault, *Discipline and Punish: The Birth of the Prison*, trans. Alan Sheridan (New York: Vintage, 1995), 222.

95 Michel Foucault, "Georges Canguilhem: Philosopher of Error," in *Technologies of the Human Sciences* (Autumn 1980): 54.

96 Foucault, *The Order of Things*, 242–43.

97 Ibid., 242.

98 See the "Chronologie" to Foucault, *Dits et écrits*, vol. 1.

99 Hannah Arendt, *Lectures on Kant's Political Philosophy*, ed. Ronald Beiner (Chicago: University of Chicago Press, 1982), especially 43–44; see also 65.

100 Kant, "Preface to First Edition," in Immanuel Kant, *Critique of Pure Reason*, trans. Paul Guyer, ed. Allen W. Wood (Cambridge and New York: Cambridge University Press, 1965), 100–01. I have replaced the English "criticism" with the more appropriate "critique."

101 Immanuel Kant, "Taste as a Kind of *Sensus Communis*," §40 of Kant, *The Critique of Judgment*, trans. James Creed Meredith (Oxford: Clarendon Press, 1952), 152. Cited in Arendt, *Lectures on Kant's Political Philosophy*, 31.

102 In addition to the three published Kant lectures, other significant texts that treat Kant include the already mentioned "Georges Canguilhem: Philosopher of Error" and the interview "Critical Theory/Intellectual History," as well as "*Omnes et Singulatim*: Towards a Criticism of 'Political Reason'." See note 104 below and "The Subject and Power," the latter included in Dreyfus and Rabinow, *Michel Foucault*, 208–26.

103 Foucault, "What Is Critique?," in James Schmidt, *What Is Enlightenment?*, 383. See Foucault, "Qu'est-ce que la critique?," 38, where he defines this attitude as "à la fois morale et politique," or in the English translation, "at once a moral and political attitude."

104 Foucault, "*Omnes et Singulatim*: Towards a Criticism of 'Political Reason'" in *The Tanner Lectures on Human Values*, vol. 2 (Salt Lake City: University of Utah Press, 1981), 224–54. The English title erroneously translates Foucault's critique as "criticism," rather than "critique," thus missing the allusion to Kant. Foucault's related essay, "Governmentality," was published in *Ideology and Consciousness* 6 (Autumn 1979): 5–21.

105 Foucault, "What Is Critique?," 384; Foucault, "Qu'est-ce que la critique?," 38.

106 Indeed, as Kant explicitly stated in "What is Enlightenment?," "a public can only achieve enlightenment slowly. A revolution may well put an end to autocratic despotism and to rapacious or power-seeking oppression, but it will never produce a true reform in ways of thinking. Instead, new prejudices, like the ones they replaced, will serve as a leash to control the great unthinking mass." Immanuel Kant, "An Answer to the Question: 'What is Enlightenment?'" in Kant, *Political Writings*, 2nd enlarged edition, ed. Hans Reiss, trans. H.B. Nisbet (Cambridge: Cambridge University Press, 1991), 55.

107 "Unser Zeitalter ist das eigentliche Zeitalter der Kritik, der sich alles unterwerfen muss." Kant, *Kritik der reinen Vernunft, Gesammelte Schriften*, ed. Royal Prussian Academy of the Sciences (Berlin: de Gruyter, 1969–), A XIIn. See also Arendt, *Lectures on Kant's Political Philosophy*, 32.

108 Foucault, "Qu'est-ce que la critique?," 61.

109 Foucault, "What Is Critique?," 386.

110 Ibid.

111 Kant, "What Is Enlightenment?," in Kant, *Political Writings*, 55.

112 Foucault, "What Is Critique?," 387–8. See also Foucault, "Qu'est-ce que la critique?," 41.

113 Michel Foucault, *Remarks on Marx: Conversations with Duccio Trombadori* (New York: Semiotext(e), 1991). Foucault's "Georges Canguilhem: Philosopher of Error" similarly treated the dissimilar national responses to the "critique of reason," however in slightly different terms. Thus Foucault noted that in Germany this critique took the form of social theory, while in France it manifested itself as the history of science, whose main representatives were Bachelard, Koyré, Cavaillès, and Canguilhem. Of additional note, in this context, is Foucault's introduction to Georges Canguilhem, *On the Normal and the Pathological* (Dordrecht, The Netherlands: Reidel, 1978).

114 Michel Foucault, "*Omnes et Singulatim*," 225. For the same point, see also Foucault, "The Subject and Power," 210.

115 See Foucault, "The Subject and Power," 208; Foucault, "Critical Theory/Intellectual History," 118.

116 Foucault, "Critical Theory/Intellectual History," 117.

117 Gérard Raulet, "Entretien avec Jürgen Habermas," in *Allemagnes d'aujourd'hui: revue française d'information sur les deux Allemagnes*, 73 (1980).

118 Foucault, "Critical Theory/Intellectual History," 118.

119 Ibid., italics added.

120 See Raulet, "Entretien avec Jürgen Habermas," 45. See also Foucault, "Georges Canguilhem: Philosopher of Error," 54. It would be more accurate to say, however, that Foucault did not abandon the "universal" as such, but that he instead engaged in a genealogy of the various historical articulations that signifier had received. Along the same lines, he also sought to overcome the conventional

antinomy between rationalist models and the paradigm of contingency. Especially in his homage to the French historian of science, Georges Canguilhem, he declared as much, when he noted that the critical task of the historian consisted in joining the best of Kant to the most acceptable of Nietzsche, or phrased differently, that it meant thinking together rationality (Kant) and contingency (Nietzsche). Like Bachelard, Cavaillès, and Koyré, Canguilhem understood the future of post-Kantian philosophy, whose "historico-critical dimension" Kant was the first to have disclosed (Foucault, "Georges Canguilhem," 53). Furthermore, though they professed to a different style, the French historians of science resembled the critics of the Frankfurt School. Like their German neighbors, these historians pursued the paradox of "a rationality which claims universality while developing itself in the contingent," and, like Adorno and Horkheimer, they saw the shrill contrast between the unrealized potential of Enlightenment rationality and the realities of a "despotic Enlightenment." Although Canguilhem proved to be the eminent "historian of rationalities," he was not any less so a "philosopher of reason." Concentrating on the history of the sciences of life, Canguilhem did not seek to extol "life," vitalism, or "lived experience." Instead, he drew Nietzschean conclusions from his study, realizing that error was intrinsic to life and that the discontinuous history of the sciences added up to a "series of 'corrections'," or "a new distribution of the true and the false which never finally and forever frees the truth" (Foucault, "Georges Canguilhem," 61).

121 Foucault, "What Is Critique?," 393.
122 Ibid.
123 Ibid., 398.
124 Ibid.
125 See Foucault, "Qu'est-ce que la critique?," 59. This section is not included in the English translation.
126 Foucault, "The Art of Telling the Truth," in Kelly, *Critique and Power*, 140.
127 Ibid.
128 Ibid., 141.
129 Ibid.
130 Kant, "The Contest of Faculties," in Kant, *Political Writings*, 181.
131 Foucault, "The Art of Telling the Truth," 145.
132 Kant, "The Contest of Faculties," 183.
133 Ibid., 182.
134 Ibid., 184
135 Ibid., 187.
136 Foucault, "The Art of Telling the Truth," 148.
137 Ibid., 147.
138 Ibid.
139 Ibid.
140 As Arendt points out, "In practical matters, not judgment but will is decisive, and this will simply follows the maxim of Reason. … Practical means moral in Kant, and it concerns the individual *qua* individual." Arendt, *Lectures on Kant's Political Philosophy*, 61. As she notes further, "Kant's condemnation of revolutionary action rests on a misunderstanding, because he conceives of it in terms of a coup d'état" (ibid., 60).
141 Foucault, "The Art of Telling the Truth," 148.
142 Ibid., 147.
143 Foucault, "What Is Enlightenment?," in Foucault, *Ethics*, 303–04.
144 Ibid., 303.
145 Ibid., 309.
146 Ibid., 308.
147 Ibid., 309.
148 Ibid.
149 Ibid., 312.
150 Ibid.
151 Ibid., 313.
152 Ibid., 314.

153 Ibid., 315.

154 Ibid. I have replaced the English "criticism" with the word "critique" to render Foucault's *critique*.

155 Habermas, *Philosophical Discourse of Modernity*, 255. One might add that "transgression," indeed, is the word used in the original English translation of Foucault's "What Is Enlightenment?" included in the 1984 edition of Rabinow's *The Foucault Reader*, 45.

156 Immanuel Kant, *Prolegomena to Any Future Metaphysics that Will Be Able to Come Forward as a Science*, *with selections from the Critique of Pure Reason*, trans. Gary Hatfield (Cambridge and New York: Cambridge University Press, 1997), 101.

157 Foucault, "What Is Enlightenment?," 315–16.

158 Foucault, "What Is Enlightenment?," 316, modified translation; Foucault, "Qu'est-ce que les Lumières?," in Foucault, *Dits et écrits*, vol. 4, 574.

159 On Foucault's understanding of *pouvoir* in this sense, see also Chapter 3, below.

160 Foucault, "What Is Enlightenment?," 316. Again, Foucault here made use of the term *historical ontology*, welding together two seemingly incongruous terms, the stasis of ontology with the change of history. Harking back to the Dilthey–York von Wartenburg dispute, related in Heidegger's *Being and Time*, the phrase clearly was meant to signify a radically historicized structure of hermeneutical self-understanding.

161 Ibid., 317.

162 Ibid., 319.

163 Ibid.

164 Foucault, "The Subject and Power," 216.

165 Foucault, "What Is Enlightenment?," 310ff.

166 Ibid., 311. See, on this point, Benjamin's description of Baudelaire, when he notes how, eventually, "the glitter that had bedazzled the *flâneur*, had dimmed" for the poet. Walter Benjamin, "On Some Motifs in Baudelaire," in Benjamin, *Illuminations*, trans. Harry Zohn, ed. Hannah Arendt (New York: Schocken Books, 1969), 193.

167 Foucault, "What Is Enlightenment?," 312.

168 Both Benjamin and Foucault are indebted to the following passage from Baudelaire's "The Painter and Modern Life," where he states: "Beauty is made up, on the one hand, of an element that is eternal and invariable, though to determine how much of it there is is extremely difficult, and, on the other, of a relative circumstantial element, which we may like to call, successively or at one and the same time, contemporaneity, fashion, morality, passion." Charles Baudelaire, "The Painter and Modern Life," in Baudelaire, *Selected Writings on Art and Literature*, trans. P.E. Charvet (London: Penguin, 1992), 392. In the Kant lecture, Foucault furthermore draws on Baudelaire's "On the Heroism of Modern Life," reprinted in Baudelaire, *The Mirror of Art: Critical Studies by Charles Baudelaire*, trans. Jonathan Mayne (London: Phaidon, 1955). For a discussion of Benjamin's conception of allegory, see the chapter "The Aesthetics of Transience" in my *Walter Benjamin's Other History: Of Stones, Animals, Human Beings, and Angels* (Berkeley and London: University of California Press, 1998), 66ff.

169 Habermas makes the point that "the occasions for protest and discontent originate precisely when spheres of communicative action, centered on the reproduction and transmission of values and norms, are penetrated by a form of modernization guided by standards of economic and administrative rationality – in other words, by standards of rationalization quite different from those of communicative rationality on which those spheres depend." Habermas, "Modernity – An Incomplete Project," 8. Habermas further expands on and amends his views on aesthetic modernity in his "Neoconservative Criticism in the United States and West Germany: An Intellectual Movement in Two Political Cultures" and "Questions and Counterquestions," both included in Richard J. Bernstein, ed., *Habermas and Modernity* (Oxford and New York: Blackwell, 1985).

170 Habermas, *Philosophical Discourse of Modernity*, 8. While Habermas's "Modernity – An Incomplete Project," mainly dated the contemporary definition of aesthetic modernity, meaning "newness," back to Baudelaire, in his Frankfurt lectures he principally isolated Nietzsche as the initiator of aestheticism, who furthermore brought to completion the irrationalist strand of German Romanticism. See also Habermas, "Questions and Counterquestions," in Bernstein, *Habermas and Modernity*, 200–01.

171 Habermas, "Modernity – An Incomplete Project," 4 and 5.

172 Habermas, "Questions and Counterquestions," 202.

173 Ibid.

174 Habermas, "Modernity – An Incomplete Project," 9.

175 Jürgen Habermas, "Taking Aim at the Heart of the Present: On Foucault's Lecture on Kant's *What Is Enlightenment?*," in Kelly, *Critique and Power*, 149ff. Because of the subtitle of Habermas's eulogy, it should be stressed that he refers to Foucault's "The Art of Telling the Truth," also reprinted in Kelly's *Critique and Power*, not to the 1983 Kant lecture included in Rabinow's *The Foucault Reader* and Foucault's *Ethics*.

176 The matter of how Foucault related to the term "modernity" during the course of his intellectual career, as we have seen throughout this chapter, is quite complex, but his thoughts on the nature of "postmodernity" were no less intricate. In the insightful 1983 interview he conducted with Raulet, Foucault did not only dispute the need for the term "postmodernism," but he also called the label "modernity" arbitrary, thus showing that he lived up to his propensity for nominalistic analysis. As far as the question of postmodernity was concerned, he opposed Lyotard's theory of the collapse of the "narrative of reason," no less than the crypto-Hegelian moment marking philosophies that welcomed the postmodern as the "present of transformation." But, characteristically, in thinking through the challenges of the present, Foucault's main interest was directed toward Kant, whose philosophy of the present did not "consist in a simple characterization of what we are but instead – by following lines of fragility in the present – in managing to grasp why and how that-which-is might no longer be that-which-is. In this sense, any description must always be made in accordance with these kinds of virtual fracture which open up the space of freedom understood as a space of concrete freedom, that is of possible transformation." Foucault, "Critical Theory/Intellectual History," 126–27.

177 Habermas, "Taking Aim at the Heart of the Present," 152–53.

178 Habermas, *Philosophical Discourse of Modernity*, 7.

179 Ibid., 13.

180 Habermas, "Modernity – An Incomplete Project," 11.

181 See Jürgen Habermas, "Walter Benjamin: Consciousness-Raising or Rescuing Critique," in Gary Smith, ed., *On Walter Benjamin* (Cambridge, Mass.: MIT Press, 1991), 90–128.

182 Habermas, *Philosophical Discourse of Modernity*, 14.

183 Among the most representative treatments of Foucault's ethics are Alexander Nehamas, *The Art of Living: Socratic Reflections from Plato to Foucault* (Berkeley and London: University of California Press, 1998); Pierre Hadot, "Reflections on the Notion of 'The Cultivation of the Self' "; Rainer Rochlitz, "The Aesthetics of Existence: Post-Conventional Morality and the Theory of Power in Michel Foucault," in *Michel Foucault Philosopher*, ed. Timothy J. Armstrong (New York: Routledge, 1992), 225–32 and 248–59; Arnold I. Davidson, "Ethics as Ascetics: Foucault, the History of Ethics, and Ancient Thought," in Gary Gutting, ed., *The Cambridge Companion to Foucault* (Cambridge: Cambridge University Press, 1994), 115–40; Paul Veyne, "The Final Foucault and His Ethics," in *Critical Inquiry* 20.1 (Autumn 1993): 1–9; David M. Halperin, *Saint Foucault: Towards a Gay Hagiography* (Oxford and New York: Oxford University Press, 1995), 73ff; John Guillory, "The Ethical Practice of Modernity: The Example of Reading," in Marjorie Garber, Beatrice Hanssen, and Rebecca L. Walkowitz, eds., *The Turn to Ethics* (New York and London: Routledge, 2000), 29–46. Going against moralizing critiques of Foucault's late phase, Guillory in particular takes seriously his new conception of reading, using it to reflect on the moral and ethical differences between professional (academic) and lay reading practices. For a discussion of the phrase "the turn to ethics," see Marjorie Garber, Beatrice Hanssen, and Rebecca L. Walkowitz, "Introduction," in *The Turn to Ethics*, vii–xii.

184 Foucault's 1984 lecture at the Collège de France specifically focused on Socrates and the Cynics. For an account, see Thomas Flynn, "Foucault as Parrhesiast: His Last Course at the Collège de France," in James Bernauer and David Rasmussen, eds., *The Final Foucault* (Cambridge, Mass.: MIT Press, 1994), 102–18. See also Alexander Nehamas, "A Fate for Socrates' Reason: Foucault on the Care of the Self," in Nehamas, *The Art of Living*, 157–88. For Foucault's views on truth-telling, see

furthermore his 1984 interview, "The Ethics of the Concern for Self as a Practice of Freedom," in Foucault, *Foucault Live*, 444ff.

185 Michel Foucault, "On the Genealogy of Ethics: An Overview of Work in Progress," in Rabinow, *The Foucault Reader*, 340. See also Guillory, "The Ethical Practice of Modernity," 35.

186 Foucault, "On the Genealogy of Ethics," 350.

187 See Hadot, "Reflections on the Notion of the 'Cultivation of the Self'," 230 and Foucault's "On the Genealogy of Ethics," 362, where Foucault disputes that the "Californian cult of the self" as the discovery of one's true self is similar to the Greek concern with selfhood.

188 Michel Foucault, "Technologies of the Self," a lecture held at the University of Vermont in 1982, in Luther H. Martin, Huck Gutman, and Patrick H. Hutton, eds., *Technologies of the Self* (Amherst, Mass.: University of Massachusetts Press, 1988), 19.

189 Foucault's final interview, "Le retour de la morale" (May 29, 1984), is reprinted in *Foucault Live* under the title "The Return of Morality." As the editors of Foucault's *Dits et écrits* explain, however, this misleading title was given to the piece by the interviewers. See Foucault, *Dits et écrits*, vol. 4, 696. Though Foucault certainly was concerned with the "history of morality," as he observes in the interview, the phrase "turn to ethics" (as we shall see) better captures the gist of his research.

190 Foucault, "What Is Enlightenment?," 318.

191 Foucault, "On the Genealogy of Ethics," 351.

192 Foucault, "On the Genealogy of Ethics," 342 and 352; Michel Foucault, *The History of Sexuality, Volume I: An Introduction*, trans. Robert Hurley (New York: Vintage, 1980); Michel Foucault, *The Use of Pleasure, Volume 2 of The History of Sexuality*, trans. Robert Hurley (New York: Vintage, 1985); Michel Foucault, *The Care of the Self, Volume 3 of The History of Sexuality*, trans. Robert Hurley (New York: Vintage, 1986). For an account of the unfinished manuscript *Confessions of the Flesh*, which he dedicated to Cassian, Augustine, and Tertullian, see the entries for the years 1979, 1983, and 1984 in "Chronologie," in Foucault, *Dits et écrits*, vol. 1, pp. 56, 61, and 64.

193 See Foucault, "Technologies of the Self," lecture held at the University of Vermont, 1982, in Foucault, *Technologies of the Self*, 16–17.

194 For an account of Foucault's work on early Christianity, especially the thought of De Vio and Cassian, see the 1979–80 course synopsis, "On the Government of the Living," in Foucault, *Ethics*, 81–85.

195 Foucault, *The Use of Pleasure*, 4.

196 Ibid., 6.

197 Ibid., 9.

198 Ibid.

199 Ibid.

200 Ibid., 10.

201 Foucault, "On the Genealogy of Ethics," 348.

202 Foucault, *The Use of Pleasure*, 10–11.

203 Ibid., 13.

204 Foucault, "On the Genealogy of Ethics," 362 and 370.

205 Consult, also, the analysis of Baudelaire, above, in the section "Baudelaire's Aestheticism." In a footnote to the introduction to *The Use of Pleasure*, Foucault pays tribute to Burckhardt, Benjamin and Stephen Greenblatt's study, *Renaissance Self-Fashioning* (1980). See Foucault, *The Use of Pleasure*, 11n.

206 Ibid., 13.

207 Ibid., 25.

208 Ibid., 26.

209 Foucault, "On the Genealogy of Ethics," 346.

210 Ibid., 352.

211 Foucault, *The Use of Pleasure*, 37.

212 See Foucault, "Ethics of the Concern for Self," in Foucault, *Foucault Live*, 438 and Foucault, "On the Genealogy of Ethics," 345. For expert accounts of Greek conceptions of sexuality, especially homosexuality, see Kenneth Dover, *Greek Homosexuality* (Cambridge, Mass.: Harvard University Press, 1986) and David M. Halperin, *One Hundred Years of Homosexuality and Other Essays on Greek Love* (New York: Routledge, 1990), 30ff.

213 See Foucault, "On the Genealogy of Ethics," 342.

214 Nehamas, *The Art of Living*, 167.

215 Cited in Nehamas, *The Art of Living*, 169.

216 Foucault, "Technologies of the Self," 24.

217 Foucault, *The Care of the Self*, 44; Foucault, "On the Genealogy of Ethics," 348. In his lecture "Technologies of the Self," Foucault more carefully describes the Platonic model, noting that it still privileges the Delphic "Know yourself," a relationship that will be reversed in the Hellenistic and Greco-Roman periods, as it shifted from a concern with knowledge to self-caring. See Foucault, "Technologies of the Self," 26.

218 Foucault, "On the Genealogy of Ethics," 348 and 356.

219 Foucault, "Technologies of the Self," 35. On the "writing of the self," consult also Foucault "The Return of Morality," in Foucault, *Foucault Live*, 468.

220 Pierre Hadot, "Reflections on the Notion of the 'Cultivation of the Self'," 228. See also Foucault's account of writing as self-exercise in Foucault, "Technologies of the Self," 27ff, and Foucault, "On the Genealogy of Ethics," 363–5.

221 On the link with Kierkegaard, see also Thomas Flynn, "Foucault as Parrhesiast," 113. Furthermore, see Rorty, who, for quite different purposes, casts Foucault in his strident quest for autonomy in the role of Kierkegaard's knight of faith (a reference to *Fear and Trembling*). Richard Rorty, "Moral Identity and Private Autonomy," in Armstrong, *Michel Foucault Philosopher*, 329.

222 Foucault, "On the Genealogy of Ethics," 348.

223 Foucault, "Ethics of the Concern for Self," in Foucault, *Foucault Live*, 434–5.

224 Veyne, "The Final Foucault and his Ethics," 2.

225 Foucault, "Ethics of the Concern for Self," 437.

226 Foucault, "On the Genealogy of Ethics," 345–6.

227 Nietzsche, *Genealogy of Morals*, 20.

228 Ibid., 55.

229 Ibid., 118.

230 Ibid., 118–19.

231 Ibid., 56.

232 For a more extensive discussion of Foucault's nominalism, see also Chapter 3, below.

233 Habermas, "Modernity – An Incomplete Project," 14; Richard Wolin, "Foucault's Aesthetic Decisionism," in *Telos* 67 (Spring 1986): 71; Slavoj Žižek, *The Sublime Object of Ideology* (London and New York: Verso, 1989), 2; Terry Eagleton, *The Ideology of the Aesthetic* (Oxford, England, and Cambridge, Mass.: Blackwell, 1990), 395; Richard Rorty, "Moral Identity and Private Autonomy," in Armstrong, *Michel Foucault Philosopher*, 328.

234 In his final interview, Foucault partially agreed that his liking of Nietzsche was "the source of the misunderstandings which surround your work," as the interviewer phrased it. See Foucault, "The Return of Morality," 471.

235 Veyne, "The Final Foucault and His Ethics," 7.

236 Foucault, "The Return of Morality," 466. Books of especial influence were Pierre Hadot, *Philosophy as a Way of Life: Spiritual Exercises from Socrates to Foucault*, ed. Arnold I. Davidson (Oxford, England, and Cambridge, Mass.: Blackwell, 1995), and Peter Brown, *The Making of Late Antiquity* (Cambridge, Mass.: Harvard University Press, 1978).

237 For a staunch critique of Foucault's understanding of Stoicism, see Hadot, "Reflections on the Notion of the 'Cultivation of the Self'," 229–30.

238 See the exchange about Nietzsche's *The Gay Science* in Foucault, "On the Genealogy of Ethics," 351.

239 Ibid., 348.

240 Foucault, "Sexual Choice, Sexual Act," in Foucault, *Foucault Live*, 370.

241 Foucault, "Sex, Power and the Politics of Identity," in Foucault, *Foucault Live*, 384. For a discussion of Foucault's views on homosexuality and S&M, see also Leo Bersani, *Homos* (Cambridge, Mass.: Harvard University Press, 1995), 77ff. As Bersani comments, Foucault interpreted S&M as a "theatricalized imitation of history," a "playing with power" in which actors could step in and out of an eroticized master–slave configuration. See also Halperin, *Saint Foucault*, 85–93 and *passim*.

242 Nehamas, *The Art of Living*, 157–88.

243 Ibid., 164.

244 Ibid., 168.

245 Ibid., 169.

246 Ibid., 180.

247 Ibid., 169.

248 Rorty, "Moral Identity and Private Autonomy," 330 and 332. It seems crucial to add here that Rorty's own brand of pragmatism does not endorse a wholesale rejection of Nietzsche. On numerous occasions, Rorty has presented the philosopher, including his theory of perspectivism, as consonant with pragmatism's antifoundationalist slant. See, for example, Richard Rorty, *Consequences of Pragmatism (Essays: 1972–1980)* (Minneapolis: University of Minnesota Press, 1982), *passim*.

249 Ibid., 328.

250 Ibid., 331.

251 Ibid., 329.

252 Ibid., 332.

253 Within the context of the present chapter, it won't be possible to consider the possible constraints of Rorty's hospitable version of liberalism. However, see Chapter 8 of this book, where I rejoin the Rortian train of thought to question it with respect to its "representational" limits.

254 Nehamas, *The Art of Living*, 178.

255 Benjamin makes the distinction between *Erlebnis* and *Erfahrung* in his celebrated Baudelaire essay. While both terms are often translated in English as "experience," the second one, confusingly, as "lived experience," *Erlebnis* has a vitalistic ring to it (*cf.* Dilthey), whereas *Erfahrung* designates a genuine, historically consummated experience. See Walter Benjamin, "On Some Motifs in Baudelaire," in Benjamin, *Illuminations*, 156ff.

256 Habermas here responds to Albrecht Wellmer's earlier critique of the original, stark division between three demarcated fields – cognition, practical action, and aesthetic authenticity – which underwrote Habermas's *The Theory of Communicative Action*. For a lengthier discussion of the issue, see Habermas, "Modernity – An Incomplete Project," 13; see also Habermas, "Questions and Counterquestions," 199–203, and Albrecht Wellmer, "Truth, Semblance, Reconciliation: Adorno's Aesthetic Redemption of Modernity," in Wellmer, *The Persistence of Modernity: Essays on Aesthetics, Ethics, and Postmodernism* (Cambridge, Mass.: MIT Press, 1991).

257 Foucault, "On the Genealogy of Ethics," 341.

258 Compared with earlier work, Foucault's late writings focused disproportionately on the rise of "individualizing powers," such as the various modern transformations of (Christian) "pastoral herding," as well as on the subversive, remedial counterstrategies that were meant to countervail and neutralize them. It seems clear that he endorsed the image of an alienated subject, whose core of autonomous selfhood needed to be restored through self-government. In a way, he thus also returned to the category of the individual that Adorno already had activated in his analysis of modes of resistance that counteracted the totalitarian power of National Socialism. See, for example, Theodor W. Adorno, "Auf die Frage: Was ist deutsch?" in Adorno, *Stichworte: Kritische Modelle 2* (Frankfurt a.M.: Suhrkamp, 1969). For stern criticism of Foucault's reduction of Christianity to "pastoral power," see Rochlitz, "The Aesthetics of Existence," 256. For a favorable account of Foucault's call for practices of "individualization," other than those "operated" by the state, see Dreyfus and Rabinow, *Michel Foucault*, 308.

259 Rochlitz, "The Aesthetics of Existence," 256.

260 Foucault, "On the Genealogy of Ethics," 343.

261 Ibid.

262 Ibid.

263 Arnold I. Davidson, "Archeology, Genealogy, Ethics," in Hoy, *Foucault: A Critical Reader*, 221–32.

264 See Foucault's précis for the 1980–81 Collège de France course, "Subjectivity and Truth," in Foucault, *Ethics*, 88.

265 Foucault, "History and Homosexuality," in Foucault, *Foucault Live*, 364. Foucault's comments are made in relation to a book that much influenced him on the topic, namely, John Boswell, *Christianity, Social Tolerance, and Homosexuality* (Chicago: University of Chicago Press, 1980).

266 See the contributions collected in Domna C. Stanton, ed., *Discourses of Sexuality: From Aristotle to AIDS* (Ann Arbor: University of Michigan Press, 1992), especially the section dedicated to Foucault's *History of Sexuality*, with interventions by Domna C. Stanton, Lesley Dean-Jones, Lynn Hunt, Abdul R. JanMohamed, and Catharine A. MacKinnon. Furthermore, see the debates in Irene Diamond and Lee Quinby, eds., *Feminism and Foucault: Reflections on Resistance* (Boston: Northeastern Press, 1988), and Jana Sawicki, *Disciplining Foucault: Feminism, Power, and the Body* (New York and London: Routledge, 1991).

267 See the discussion in this chapter of Foucault's statement that in order to think through the legacy of the *Aufklärung* it is necessary to consider the "historicity of thinking about the universal." Foucault, "The Art of Telling the Truth," 147.

268 Foucault, "Ethics of the Concern for Self," 446.

269 Foucault discusses the convergence between different kinds of social struggles (those against ethnic, social and religious domination, against economic exploitation, and against the subjection of subjectivity) in "The Subject and Power," 212–13. For a lengthier analysis of this essay, see Chapter 3, below. Clearly, in referring to the opposition between the politics of recognition versus redistribution, I am referring to the work Nancy Fraser has done in this field, especially in her *Justice Interruptus: Critical Reflections on the "Postsocialist" Condition* (New York and London: Routledge, 1997). On the politics of recognition, see Chapter 6, below.

270 Indeed, if in the 1971 Nietzsche essay Foucault launched invectives at asceticism, adopting the tone of the *Genealogy of Morals*, which derided the nihilism and "anti-nature" advocated by ascetic ideals, then in the late work he appropriated the term "asceticism" for the subject's practice of self-formation. "Asceticism," he explained, was to be understood "in a very general sense, in other words, not in the sense of a morality of renunciation but as an exercise of the self on the self, by which one attempts to develop and transform oneself, and to attain to a certain mode of being." Foucault, "The Ethics of the Concern for Self," 433. See also Foucault, *The History of Sexuality*, 141, where he briefly takes issue with "the role of an ascetic morality in the first formation of capitalism," a clear reference to Max Weber's *The Protestant Ethic and the Spirit of Capitalism*.

271 Foucault, "Ethics of Pleasure," in Foucault, *Foucault Live*, 379.

3 POWER/FORCE/WAR (ON FOUCAULT'S "SOCIETY MUST BE DEFENDED")

1 Axel Honneth, *The Critique of Power: Reflective Stages in a Critical Social Theory*, trans. Kenneth Baynes (Cambridge, Mass.: MIT Press, 1991), 150 and 153.

2 Ibid., 151.

3 Ibid., 152. Honneth's next chapter, "Foucault's Theory of Society," further elaborates on this systems-theoretical perspective and functionalism, adding: "Foucault argues in terms of a historically guided functionalism that steadfastly regards cultural traditions, and thus historically shaped ideas and values, only from the perspective of the objective function they perform in a systemic process characterized by the increase of power" (ibid., 182).

4 Jürgen Habermas, *The Philosophical Discourse of Modernity: Twelve Lectures* (Cambridge, Mass.: MIT Press, 1993), 255.

5 Honneth, *Critique of Power*, 322 n.9.

6 Ibid.

7 Ibid., 155.

8 Ibid., 157.

9 Ibid., 164.

10 Ibid., 162.

11 Ibid., 174.

12 Thomas Hobbes, *Leviathan*, ed. Richard Tuck (Cambridge: Cambridge University Press, 1994), 90.

13 Honneth, *Critique of Power*, 172. On the mechanics of normalization, see especially the section "Normalizing Judgement," in Michel Foucault, *Discipline and Punish: The Birth of the Prison*, trans. Alan Sheridan (New York: Vintage, 1995), 177ff.

14 Honneth, *Critique of Power*, 201.

15 See, for example, Linda Nicholson, "Introduction," in Seyla Benhabib, Judith Butler, Drucilla Cornell, and Nancy Fraser, *Feminist Contentions: A Philosophical Exchange* (New York and London: Routledge, 1995), 11; as well as Chapter 8, below.

16 On the figure of Boulainvilliers, see Harold A. Ellis's helpful study, *Boulainvilliers and the French Monarchy: Aristocratic Politics in Early Eighteenth-Century France* (Ithaca, N.Y., and London: Cornell University Press, 1988).

17 In what follows, I rely on the French publication of the course: Michel Foucault, "*Il faut défendre la société*": *Cours au Collège de France (1975–1976)*, ed. Mauro Bertani and Alessandro Fontana (Paris: Seuil/Gallimard, 1997). The opening sessions of "*Il faut défendre la société*," delivered on January 7 and 14, 1976, originally appeared in English translation as "Two Lectures," in Michel Foucault, *Power/Knowledge: Selected Interviews and Other Writings, 1972–1977* (New York: Pantheon, 1980), 78–108 and were reprinted in Michael Kelly, ed., *Critique and Power: Recasting the Foucault/Habermas Debate* (Cambridge, Mass., and London: MIT Press, 1994), 17–46. I will quote from the Kelly edition, while providing my own translations for other passages drawn from the as yet untranslated lecture course. It should be noted that a few paragraphs are missing from the English translation, for example, the two concluding paragraphs of the first lecture. See Michel Foucault, "*Il faut défendre la société*," 18–19. For other readings of "*Il faut défendre la société*," see James Miller, "The Distant Roar of Battle," in Miller, *The Passion of Michel Foucault* (New York, London, Toronto, Sydney, Tokyo and Singapore: Simon & Schuster, 1993), 285–318; Pasquale Pasquino, "Political Theory of War and Peace: Foucault and the History of Modern Political Theory," *Economy and Society* 22.1 (February 1993): 76–88; and Ann Laura Stoler, *Race and the Education of Desire: Foucault's History of Sexuality and the Colonial Order of Things* (Durham, N.C., and London: Duke University Press, 1995).

18 Alessandro Fontana and Mauro Bertani, "Situation du cours," in Foucault, "*Il faut défendre la société*," 249.

19 Ibid.

20 Michel Foucault, "Society Must Be Defended," in Foucault, *Ethics: Subjectivity and Truth*, ed. Paul Rabinow (New York: The New Press, 1994), 59.

21 Ibid., 60.

22 See Etienne Balibar, "Foucault and Marx: The Question of Nominalism," in Timothy J. Armstrong, ed. *Michel Foucault Philosopher* (New York: Routledge, 1992), 38.

23 Foucault, "*Il faut défendre la société*," 96.

24 For a discussion of the British counterdiscourse, see ibid., 42–43, 51–52, 88–96, and 126–27.

25 Ibid., 51.

26 Ibid., 111–12.

27 Foucault uses the terms "translation" and recodification in the lecture of January 28 (ibid., 70).

28 Ibid., 194.

29 Foucault, "Two Lectures," in Kelly, *Critique and Power*, 26. Foucault makes a similar point in "The Subject and Power," where he states: "One of the numerous reasons why [fascism and Stalinism] are, for us, so puzzling, is that in spite of their historical uniqueness they are not quite original. They used and extended mechanisms already present in most other societies. More than that: in spite of their own internal madness, they used to a large extent the ideas and the devices of our political rationality." Michel Foucault, "The Subject and Power," in Hubert L. Dreyfus and Paul Rabinow, *Michel Foucault: Beyond Structuralism and Hermeneutics*, 2nd edition (Chicago: University of Chicago Press, 1983), 209. See also Honneth, who objects to Foucault's belief in a "coercive model of societal order," adding "[like] Adorno, Foucault seems to see the process of technical rationalization as culminating in the 'totalitarian' organizations of domination of highly developed societies." Honneth, *Critique of Power*, 199.

30 Foucault, "Two Lectures," 35.

31 Ibid., 70.

32 Ibid., 161 and 193.

33 Foucault's *The Order of Things* is dedicated to an archeology of the respective "grids" that structure or order knowledge in the Classical and modern *epistēmē*. Michel Foucault, *The Order of Things: An*

Archeology of the Human Sciences (New York, Vintage, 1994). See, for example, p. xxiii, where he discusses "language as the spontaneous *tabula*, the primary grid of things," and *passim*. In *The History of Sexuality*, he refers to the "grid of historical development" (Michel Foucault, *The History of Sexuality, Volume I: An Introduction* [New York: Vintage, 1980], 90).

34 Foucault, "Two Lectures," 19, translation slightly modified; Foucault, "*Il faut défendre la société*," 7.

35 Ibid., 21.

36 Ibid., 20–21; Foucault, "*Il faut défendre la société*," 8.

37 Foucault, *The Archeology of Knowledge*, 130–31. Cited also in Gilles Deleuze, "What is a Dispositif," in Armstrong, *Michel Foucault Philosopher*, 165.

38 Foucault, "Two Lectures," 22.

39 Ibid., 27.

40 Hannah Arendt, *The Human Condition* (Chicago and London: University of Chicago Press, 1989), 200.

41 Michel Foucault, "Politics and Ethics," in Paul Rabinow, ed., *The Foucault Reader* (New York: Pantheon, 1984), 378.

42 Foucault, "Two Lectures," 29.

43 Ibid., 28.

44 In a 1976 interview with Alessandro Fontana and Pasquale Pasquino, Foucault admits that his *Madness and Civilization* still worked with the assumption that "madness" had been suppressed by the mechanisms of power. See Michel Foucault, "Entretien avec Foucault," in Foucault, *Dits et écrits, 1954–1988*, 4 vols., eds. Daniel Defert and François Ewald (Paris: Gallimard, 1994), vol. 3, 148. For Derrida's critique of the dualistic logic that underpins *Madness and Civilization*, see his "Cogito and the History of Madness," in Jacques Derrida, *Writing and Difference*, trans. Alan Bass (Chicago: University of Chicago Press, 1978), 31–63; and Robert Young, "Foucault's Phantasms," in Young, *White Mythologies: Writing History and the West* (London and New York: Routledge, 1990), 69ff.

45 Foucault, "Two Lectures," 28.

46 Foucault, "*Il faut défendre la société*," 41.

47 Foucault, "Nietzsche, Genealogy, History," in Rabinow, *The Foucault Reader*, 85.

48 Foucault, *Discipline and Punish*, 308.

49 Foucault, "Society Must Be Defended," in Foucault, *Ethics*, 60.

50 As Foucault summed it up: " 'Discipline' may be identified neither with an institution nor with an apparatus; it is a type of power, a modality for its exercise, comprising a whole set of instruments, techniques, procedures, levels of application, targets; it is a 'physics' or an 'anatomy' of power, a technology." Foucault, *Discipline and Punish*, 215.

51 Ibid., 168.

52 Ibid., 26.

53 Ibid., 27.

54 Ibid., 183–84.

55 Ibid., 222.

56 Ibid., 169.

57 Ibid., 222.

58 Foucault, *History of Sexuality*, 81–82.

59 Ibid., 89.

60 See Arendt, *Human Condition*, 27.

61 Foucault, *History of Sexuality*, 137.

62 Ibid.

63 Ibid., 139.

64 Ibid., 141.

65 Ibid., 144.

66 Ibid., 148.

67 Ibid., 150.

68 Indeed, both *The Order of Things* and *Discipline and Punish* ascribed the errors committed under the rubric of representation to the eighteenth-century French *ideologues*, especially Destutt de Tracy.

For, to operate solely at the level of signs and ideas was to follow in their steps and to fail to absorb that the new power mechanisms targeted humans as living, concrete, malleable bodies.

69 Foucault, *History of Sexuality*, 92–93.

70 Ibid.

71 For a similar analysis, see Dreyfus and Rabinow, *Michel Foucault*, 187.

72 Foucault, *History of Sexuality*, 102.

73 Ibid.

74 Ibid., 97.

75 Balibar, "Foucault and Marx," 56.

76 Foucault, *History of Sexuality*, 93.

77 It is not improbable that Foucault's critique of political theory referred to another seminal passage from this same Nietzsche text, full of allusions to Hobbes's "war of all against all." In the passage, Nietzsche explicitly linked the social contract, brokered through the peace treaty, to the "truth drive" and to the dissimulating language games in which humans engaged, for, as he observed: "[From] boredom and necessity, man wishes to exist socially and with the herd; therefore, he needs to make peace and strives accordingly to banish from his world at least the most flagrant *bellum omnium contra omnes*. This peace treaty left in its wake something which appears to be the first step toward acquiring that puzzling truth drive: to wit, *that* which shall count as 'truth' from now on is established." Nietzsche, "On Truth and Lies in an Extramoral Sense," 81.

78 Foucault, "Two Lectures," 30; Foucault, "*Il faut défendre la société*," 17.

79 Foucault, "Two Lectures," 30. The available English translation cites a negation ("not") where there should have been a qualifier (*tout de même*, "all the same"). I cite the passage with the correction in square brackets: "It is obvious that all my work in recent years has been couched in the schema of struggle—repression, and it is this – which I have hitherto been attempting to apply. [Now, insofar as I applied this schema, I was all the same] forced to reconsider it, both because it is still insufficiently elaborated at a whole number of points, and because I believe that these two notions of repression and war must themselves be considerably modified if not ultimately abandoned. In any case, I believe that they must be submitted to closer scrutiny." Cf. Foucault, "*Il faut défendre la société*," 17–18.

80 Foucault, "*Il faut défendre la société*," 38.

81 Ibid., 40.

82 Ibid.

83 Ibid., 21.

84 Ibid., 38.

85 Ibid.

86 Ibid., 38–39.

87 Ibid., 39.

88 Foucault, "Society Must Be Defended," in Foucault, *Ethics*, 63.

89 Foucault, "*Il faut défendre la société*," 78.

90 Ibid., 78–79.

91 On the Hegelian master—slave dialectic, see also Chapter 6, below.

92 Foucault, "*Il faut défendre la société*," 85.

93 See Richard Tuck, "Introduction," to Hobbes, *Leviathan*, xix.

94 Foucault, "*Il faut défendre la société*," 85.

95 Ibid., 51.

96 Foucault, "*Il faut défendre la société*," 46.

97 Ibid., 48.

98 Friedrich Nietzsche, *The Birth of Tragedy and the Case of Wagner* (New York: Vintage, 1967), 43.

99 Foucault, "*Il faut défendre la société*," 186.

100 Ibid., 47.

101 Ibid., 50.

102 Ibid.

103 Ibid., 150.

104 Ibid., 116.

105 Ibid., 127.
106 See ibid., 146 and 149, where Foucault interprets Boulainvilliers's historiography as a "history of subjects," and hence as the actual precursor, curiously enough, of Jules Michelet's *The People*.
107 Ibid., 146.
108 Ibid., 193.
109 Ibid., 154.
110 Ibid., 203.
111 Foucault, "*Il faut défendre la société*," 211–12.
112 Hannah Arendt, *The Origins of Totalitarianism* (New York: Harcourt Brace Jovanovich, 1973), 165.
113 Ibid., 162.
114 For a useful analysis of this nationalistic "Germanist tradition in French history," see Martin Thom, "Tribes within Nations: The Ancient Germans and the History of Modern France," in Homi K. Bhabha, ed., *Nation and Narration* (London and New York: Routledge, 1990), 23–43.
115 See, for instance, "*Il faut défendre la société*," 145.
116 On the question of the etymology of "frank," see ibid., 131–32.
117 Friedrich Nietzsche, *On the Genealogy of Morals and Ecce Homo*, trans. Walter Kaufmann (New York: Vintage, 1969), 40ff.
118 Foucault, "*Il faut défendre la société*," 132.
119 Ibid.
120 Ibid., 139.
121 "L'histoire est la germanité, si vous voulez, par rapport à la nature." Foucault, "*Il faut défendre la société*," 140.
122 See Michel Foucault, "Le jeu de Michel Foucault," in Foucault, *Dits et écrits*, vol. 3, 323–24. It is furthermore interesting to observe that, in the very same interview, Foucault stripped Boulainvilliers more or less of his privileges and revised the reflections on the philosophy of difference, propounded in the Collège de France lecture course. Depriving him of his arche-genealogical position, Foucault now placed Boulainvilliers on a par with Rousseau, for, despite their mutually opposed models, one emphasizing invasion, the other mythic-juridical law, both presumed an original state in which all were equal, a state lost through the introduction of power and inequality. In the final analysis, however, it is beyond doubt that Foucault's attitude toward Boulainvilliers resembled very much his generous interpretation of Nietzsche, which similarly sidestepped the latter's troubling racist politics. As became clear in Chapter 2, above, Foucault's 1971 essay "Nietzsche, Genealogy, History" systematically abstracted from the ignoble subtext of the philosopher's pronouncements about race, in fact, often reversed them, reading them as deconstructions of myths about racial purity. However, as Hubert Cancik and other historians have demonstrated, the fact that Nietzsche opposed the "vulgar anti-Semitic propaganda" and "Aryan myth" of the time did not exculpate him from the charge of anti-Semitism. Rather, in his capacity as "anti-anti-Semite," he developed an "aristocratic anti-Semitism," whose principles were laid out in such texts as *Beyond Good and Evil*. In other words, also in race politics, Nietzsche's method of reversal and negation did not get him out of the circle of reasoning he meant to contest. See Hubert Cancik, " 'Mongols, Semites and the Pure-Bred Greeks': Nietzsche's Handling of the Racial Doctrines of his Time," in Jacob Golomb, ed., *Nietzsche and Jewish Culture* (London and New York: Routledge, 1997), 55–75.
123 "The old reproach that Boulainvilliers directed at the French monarchy – that it used the law and jurists to do away with rights and to bring down the aristocracy – was basically warranted by the facts. Through the development of the monarchy and its institutions this juridico-political dimension was established. It is by no means adequate to describe the manner in which power was and is exercised, but it is the code according to which power presents itself and prescribes that we conceive of it. The history of the monarchy went hand in hand with the covering up of the facts and procedures of power by juridico-political discourse." Foucault, *History of Sexuality*, 87–88.
124 Foucault, "*Il faut défendre la société*," 43.
125 Ibid., 49.
126 Ibid., 185.
127 Best known is Heidegger's invocation of Heraclitus in the famous letter he sent to Carl Schmitt in the 1930s. See, furthermore, Robert Young's remarks on poststructuralism's relation to this

ontology of death in Young, *White Mythologies: Writing History and the West* (London and New York: Routledge, 1990).

128 Emmanuel Levinas, *Totality and Infinity: An Essay on Exteriority*, trans. Alphonso Lingis (Pittsburgh: Duquesne University Press, 1969), 21.

129 See Nietzsche's discussion of greyness in Nietzsche, *Genealogy of Morals*, 21.

130 Foucault, "Two Lectures," 26; Foucault, "*Il faut défendre la société*," 13.

131 Foucault, "*Il faut défendre la société*," 19.

132 Foucault, "Society Must Be Defended," in Foucault, *Ethics*, 63.

133 In his 1978 interview with Foucault, the Japanese philosopher Ryumei Yoshimoto traces Foucault's rethinking of aleatory history back to Nietzsche's disengagement of history from conventional narratives of cause and effect, whose link can only be semiotic (or, phrased differently, rhetorical or nominalistic). Michel Foucault, "Méthodologie pour la connaissance du monde: comment se débarrasser du marxisme," in Foucault, *Dits et écrits*, vol. 3, 598.

134 Foucault, *Discipline and Punish*, 25–26. Again, faint echoes of Arendt's *On Violence* are to be heard, except that Arendt constantly sought to rectify and undo modernity's inversions, returning the grotesque back to acceptable proportions.

135 Foucault, "*Il faut défendre la société*," 71.

136 Ibid., 52. To bolster his point, Foucault asserted that Marx's binary class struggle did not so much elaborate on Hegel's master–slave dialectic, as conventionally accepted, but that, in reality, it was the progeny of a racial understanding of history. Leaning on a quote wrongly attributed to Marx, which presented Thierry as the "father of the class struggle," Foucault suggested that Marx had borrowed the concept of the class struggle from French historians (ibid., 74, n.6).

137 Foucault discovers the roots of this conversion in the work of A. Thiers, especially his *Histoire de la Révolution française*, Paris, 1823–1827, and *Histoire du Consulat et de l'Empire*, 1845–1862. See Foucault, "*Il faut défendre la société*," 74, n.7.

138 Ibid., 71.

139 Ibid.

140 For a discussion of Foucault's analysis of the ruptures in and recuperation of a racial grammar, see Stoler, *Race and the Education of Desire*, especially 61, 64, 68, and 72–73.

141 Balibar, "Racism and Nationalism," in Etienne Balibar and Immanuel Wallerstein, *Race, Nation, Class: Ambiguous Identities* (London and New York: Verso, 1991), 55.

142 Foucault, "*Il faut défendre la société*," 57.

143 In the opening notes to the lecture of February 4, Foucault addressed the complaints and concerns of his course auditors about the origin of racism, especially about Christian and medieval articulations of anti-Semitism that existed well in advance of the operative "race war" matrix, at the center of the course. Rather than disputing their existence, he went on to explain that such older, premodern expressions of anti-Semitism were reanimated under National Socialism. In other words, Nazism's myth-producing machinery functioned with a logic of reinscription, according to which the "racism of the state [was implanted] in the legend of the warring races." (ibid., 72 and 75).

144 Michel Foucault, "Truth and Power," in Rabinow, *The Foucault Reader*, 56.

145 Ibid., 56–57; Foucault, "Entretien avec Michel Foucault," 145.

146 Foucault, "*Il faut défendre la société*," 52–53, italics added.

147 Ibid., 67.

148 Ibid., 52–53. Italics added.

149 See, for example, ibid., 12, 112, and 120. As far as Foucault's critique of totality is concerned, one might also draw parallels with Lyotard's similar analogizing logic, according to which totalizing becomes totalitarian. See his "Answering the Question: What Is Postmodernism?," where he pleads, "Let us wage a war on totality," in Jean-François Lyotard, *The Postmodern Condition: A Report on Knowledge* (Minneapolis: University of Minnesota Press, 1997), 82.

150 Ernest Gellner, "Nationalism and Cohesion in Complex Societies," in Gellner, *Culture, Identity and Politics* (Cambridge: Cambridge University Press, 1987), 8. Cited in Thom, "Tribes Within Nations," 23. See also Benedict Anderson, who puts Renan's signature text to use to bolster his conception of modern nations as "imagined communities," in Benedict Anderson, *Imagined*

Communities: Reflections on the Origin and Spread of Nationalism, revised edition (London and New York: Verso, 1991), 6 and 199–201.

151 For an excellent account of how the complexity of colonialism fell off Foucault's conceptual map, see Stoler, *Race and the Education of Desire*, 55ff.

152 Foucault, *"Il faut défendre la société,"* 75.

153 Ibid., 67.

154 Ibid., 89. For similar criticism of Foucault's glaringly sparse account of colonialism and the concept of "return effect," see also Stoler, *Race and the Education of Desire, passim.*

155 See also Chapter 6, below, where I discuss Fanon's interpretation of Hegel.

156 See, especially, Raymond Aron, *Clausewitz; Philosopher of War*, trans. Christine Booker and Norman Stone (New York: Simon & Schuster, 1986); and Ernesto Laclau and Chantal Mouffe, *Hegemony and Socialist Strategy: Towards a Radical Democratic Politics* (London and New York: Verso, 1996), which refers to Clausewitz's impact on Marx and Lenin.

157 See Didier Eribon, *Michel Foucault* (Cambridge, Mass.: Harvard University Press, 1991).

158 Balibar, "Foucault and Marx," 53.

159 See Foucault, *Discipline and Punish*, for references to Marx's *Capital*, specifically pp. 163, 175, and 221.

160 Laclau and Mouffe, *Hegemony and Socialist Strategy*, 2.

161 Ibid., 67.

162 Ibid.

163 Balibar, "Foucault and Marx," 54.

164 Michel Foucault, "Méthodologie pour la connaissance du monde: comment se débarrasser du marxisme," in Foucault, *Dits et écrits*, vol. 3, 595ff (interview conducted on April 25, 1978).

165 Ibid., 599.

166 Ibid., 606. Although it is true that the strategic deployment of mythical counternarratives played no small role in *"Society Must Be Defended,"* it would be unjustified to assume that Foucault advocated a Bergsonian vitalism or a Sorelian "ethics of violence," according to which war constituted the indispensable element in cementing working-class identity, while violence was the only force that could keep alive the antagonism and class war described by Marx. See Georges Sorel, *Reflections on Violence*, trans. T.E. Hulme and J. Roth (New York: Collier Books, 1961), 64ff.

167 Michel Foucault, "Inutile de se soulever?" in Foucault, *Dits et écrits*, vol. 3, 790–94; translated as "Is it Useless to Revolt?," trans. James Bernauer, *Philosophy and Social Criticism* 8 (1987). On this essay, see also James Schmidt and Thomas E. Wartenberg, "Foucault's Enlightenment: Critique, Revolution, and the Fashioning of the Self," in Kelly, *Critique and Power*, 282–314.

168 Charles Taylor, "Foucault on Freedom and Truth," in David Couzens Hoy, *Foucault: A Critical Reader* (Oxford, England, and Cambridge, Mass.: Blackwell, 1994), 69–102.

169 For a discussion of these uncanny affinities between the left and the right, see Chapter 1 of this book, as well as Stephen Holmes, *The Anatomy of Antiliberalism* (Cambridge, Mass., and London: Harvard University Press, 1993). For Schmitt's views on liberal politics, see John P. McCormick, *Carl Schmitt's Critique of Liberalism: Against Politics as Technology* (Cambridge and New York: Cambridge University Press, 1997).

170 Carl Schmitt, *The Concept of the Political*, trans. George Schwab, with Leo Strauss's "Notes on Schmitt's Essay," trans. J. Harvey Lomax, Foreword by Tracy B. Strong (Chicago and London: University of Chicago Press, 1996), 69.

171 Ibid., 27–28.

172 Ibid., 28.

173 Ibid., 33.

174 Ibid., 34.

175 Ibid.

176 See Schmitt's discussion of political anthropology, ibid., 58–61, and Leo Strauss, "Notes on Carl Schmitt, The Concept of the Political" (ibid., 90 and 95–96).

177 See Carl Schmitt, *Theorie des Partisanen: Zwischenbemerkung zum Begriff des Politischen*, 4th edition (Berlin: Duncker & Humblot, 1995 (1963)), particularly 15 and 45–52.

178 Carl Schmitt, *Political Theology: Four Chapters on the Concept of Sovereignty*, trans. George Swab (Cambridge, Mass.: MIT Press, 1985).

179 Pasquino, "Political Theory of War and Peace," 84.

180 Foucault, *"Il faut défendre la société,"* 21.

181 For the proceedings of the 1977–78 course, "Security, Territory, and Population," see Foucault, *Résumé des cours, 1970–1982*, reprinted in Foucault, *Ethics*, 67–71. The ensuing courses were dedicated to "The Birth of Bio-Politics" (*Naissance de la biopolitique*, 1978–79); "On the Government of the Living" (*Du gouvernement des vivants*, 1979–80); "Subjectivity and Truth" (*Subjectivité et vérité*, 1980–1); "The Hermeneutic of the Subject" (*L'herméneutique du sujet*, 1981–82); and finally, "The Government of Self and Others" (*Le gouvernement de soi et des autres*, 1982–83) and "The Courage of Truth" (*Le Courage de la vérité*, 1983–84), for which there exist no course summaries.

182 Michel Foucault, "Des Questions de Michel Foucault à *Hérodote*," in Foucault, *Dits et écrits*, vol. 3, 94. The article appeared in the July–September 1976 issue of *Hérodote*.

183 Dreyfus and Rabinow, "Preface," in Dreyfus and Rabinow, *Michel Foucault*, xiii.

184 Michel Foucault, "The Subject and Power," 208–26. The French original is titled "Le sujet et le pouvoir," in Foucault, *Dits et écrits*, vol. 4, 222–43.

185 Ibid., 209.

186 Ibid., 208.

187 Ibid. Attesting to its broad scope, the essay comprised two very distinct parts. The first, "Why Study Power: The Question of the Subject," furnished a typology of social struggles and ended by summoning Kant's libertarian philosophy, suggesting that ethical self-fashioning could serve as an antidote to conventional techniques of subject formation. The second, "How Is Power Exercised?," was dedicated mainly to a *critique* of power as "action" and led up to one of the few explicit discussions of freedom in agonistic terms.

188 Ibid., 209.

189 Ibid., 211. The English translation at this point uses the term "antagonism" for Foucault's *affrontement*, but in view of the subsequent technical use I will make of the terms "antagonism" versus "agonism," I have opted for the more neutral "confrontation."

190 Foucault, "The Subject and Power," 212, translation modified; "Le sujet et le pouvoir," 227.

191 Ibid.

192 Ibid., 213.

193 Foucault, "Le sujet et le pouvoir," 233.

194 Foucault, "The Subject and Power," 218–19.

195 Ibid., 218n. In numerous interviews, furthermore, Foucault was often asked to comment directly on Habermas's theory of communicative action. One might think here of exchanges such as "Space, Knowledge, and Power," "How Much Does It Cost for Reason to Tell the Truth?," or "Problematics," in Foucault, *Foucault Live*, 342–43, 358, and 416ff. However, the interview "Problematics" indicates that Foucault sometimes misinterpreted Habermas's paradigm of communicative power, as comes to the fore in the following statements, which allege that the social scientist more or less identified the concept of power with domination: "What makes me uncomfortable with these analyses [of modern domination] – at least those by Habermas – is the fact that when he speaks about power, he always understands it as domination. And he translates "power" by "domination." Well, in our society there are production-relations, communications-relations and power-relations. By themselves neither production-relations, nor communications-relations, nor power-relations are bad or good." Foucault, "Problematics," 416.

196 Foucault, "The Subject and Power," 220.

197 Ibid., translation slightly modified.

198 As the anonymous translator of "The Subject and Power" points out, "Foucault is playing on the double meaning in French of the verb *conduire* – to lead or to drive, and *se conduire* – to behave or to conduct oneself, whence *la conduite*, conduct or behavior." (ibid., 221n).

199 Ibid., 220. In her critique of Foucault's theory of power, Gayatri Spivak similarly dwells on the conceptual resonances that issue from the French "pouvoir." See Gayatri Chakravorty Spivak, "More on Power/Knowledge," in Spivak, *Outside the Teaching Machine* (New York: Routledge, 1993), 25–51.

200 Foucault, "The Subject and Power," 224.

201 Ibid., 221.

202 Foucault, "The Subject and Power," 221, translation modified.

203 Ibid. The French passage reads as follows: "l'esclavage n'est pas un rapport de pouvoir lorsque l'homme est aux fers (il s'agit alors d'un rapport physique de contrainte), mais justement lorsqu'il peut se déplacer et à la limite s'échapper." Foucault, "Le sujet et le pouvoir," 237–38.

204 Foucault, "The Subject and Power," 221; "Le sujet et le pouvoir," 238.

205 Foucault, "Le sujet et le pouvoir," 238. The English translation renders intransitivity as "intransigence," failing to capture the term's opposition to the "transitive" nature of actions, or verbs requiring an accusative object.

206 Foucault, "The Subject and Power," 222, translation modified. The English translation reads "essential freedom," the French original "essential 'antagonism'." "Le sujet et le pouvoir," 238.

207 Against Foucault's interpretation of *agon* here, which is nonadversarial, the translator suggests that "Foucault's neologism is based on the Greek *agōrisma* meaning 'a combat.' The term would hence imply a physical contest in which the opponents develop a strategy of reaction and of mutual taunting, as in a wrestling match." Foucault, "The Subject and Power," 222n.

208 Foucault, "The Subject and Power," 223.

209 Ibid., 225.

210 Ibid., 226.

211 Foucault, "Pouvoir et savoir," a 1977 interview with S. Hasumi, in *Dits et écrits*, vol. 3, 407. Also cited in "Situation du cours," "*Il faut défendre la société*," 253.

212 By seizing upon a strategic model of political action, Foucault presented *récits* and discursive practices as so many tools that could be wielded for extra-discursive goals and thus for both right- and left-wing ends. Similarly, emphasizing the process-like nature of revolutions, he stressed the various strategic uses to which philosophies could be put, so that, for example, Hegel's system could operate simultaneously as "an ideology, a method and a revolutionary tool, but also as something conservative." This was even more the case with Nietzsche, who had been appropriated by the Nazis, but also used by thinkers of the left. As Foucault concluded, "We can't know, therefore, in a sure way, whether what we say is revolutionary or not." See Michel Foucault, "Dialogue sur le pouvoir." In Foucault, *Dits et écrits*, vol. 3, 476. In fact, Foucault never had qualms about admitting his undiminished admiration for Nietzsche. He was particularly impressed by a conversation he had with Habermas in 1983, a meeting during which the latter recounted to him the shock he had experienced upon learning that one of his teachers, "a great Kantian," had been a Nazi collaborator. Foucault used the episode as an allegory to explain that not the substance of a philosopher's statements mattered but his actions, for there existed "a very tenuous 'analytic' link between a philosophical conception and the concrete political attitude of someone who is appealing to it." See Foucault, "Politics and Ethics: An Interview," in Rabinow, *The Foucault Reader*, 373–74.

4 THE VIOLENCE OF LANGUAGE

This chapter was first presented as a lecture at Harvard's Bunting Institute in October 1997 and at the UCLA conference, "Talking Violence" (November 1997), organized by Joseph Bristow and Vincent Pecora.

1 For a critique of such a naturalist discourse about violence, in the field of anthropology, see especially Pierre Clastres, *The Archeology of Violence*, trans. Jeanine Herman (New York: Semiotext(e), 1994), 143ff.

2 Hans Magnus Enzensberger, *Civil Wars: From L.A. to Bosnia* (New York: The New Press, 1994). For a discussion of Enzensberger, see Chapter 5, below.

3 Etienne Balibar, "Is There a 'Neo-Racism'?" in Etienne Balibar and Immanuel Wallerstein, *Race, Nation, Class: Ambiguous Identities* (London, New York: Verso, 1991), 17–28.

4 Jürgen Habermas, "The Critique of Reason as an Unmasking of the Human Sciences: Michel Foucault," in Habermas, *The Philosophical Discourse of Modernity: Twelve Lectures* (Cambridge, Mass.: MIT Press, 1993), 414 n.26.

5 For contemporary responses to the universalism debate, see, for example, Ernesto Laclau, "Universalism, Particularism, and the Question of Identity," in John Rajchman, ed., *The Identity in Question* (New York and London: Routledge, 1995), 93–108; and Judith Butler, "Universality in Culture," in Martha C. Nussbaum et al., *For Love of Country: Debating the Limits of Patriotism* (Boston: Beacon Press, 1996), 45–52.

6 My position and angle of analysis are quite different from the linguistic approach presented in Jean-Jacques Lecercle's, *The Violence of Language* (London and New York: Routledge, 1990).

7 Kent Greenawalt, *Fighting Words: Individuals, Communities, and Liberties of Speech* (Princeton, N.J.: Princeton University Press, 1995), 3.

8 For a more extensive discussion of the difference between such consequentialist and nonconsequentialist scripts, see Kent Greenawalt, *Fighting Words*, 3ff.

9 John Stuart Mill, *On Liberty and Utilitarianism* (New York: Alfred A. Knopf, 1992).

10 Mari J. Matsuda, Charles R. Lawrence III, Richard Delgado, and Kimberlè Williams Crenshaw, *Words That Wound: Critical Race Theory, Assaultive Speech, and the First Amendment* (Boulder, San Francisco, and Oxford: Westview Press, 1993).

11 On this point, see especially Mari J. Matsuda, "Public Response to Racist Speech: Considering the Victim's Story," in Matsuda et al., *Words That Wound*, 17–51.

12 Catharine A. MacKinnon, *Only Words* (Cambridge, Mass.: Harvard University Press, 1993). For a more extensive discussion of MacKinnon's position, see Chapter 7 in this book.

13 To be sure, in turning from the politics of real speech to this metadiscursive field, I do not wish to reaffirm the suspicious division of labor between (academic) theory and practice. On the question of theory, see Chapter 8 in this book.

14 Chantal Mouffe, "Decision, Deliberation, and Democratic Ethos," in *Philosophy Today* 41.1 (Spring 1997): 27.

15 Jürgen Habermas, "Hannah Arendt: On the Concept of Power," in Habermas, *Philosophical-Political Profiles* (Cambridge, Mass.: MIT Press, 1983), 173.

16 Hannah Arendt, *The Human Condition* (Chicago and London: University of Chicago Press, 1989), 4. See also Seyla Benhabib, *The Reluctant Modernism of Hannah Arendt* (Thousand Oaks, Calif.: Sage Publications, c.1996).

17 Habermas, "Hannah Arendt," 172.

18 Friedrich Nietzsche, *On the Genealogy of Morals and Ecce Homo*, trans. Walter Kaufmann (New York: Vintage, 1969), 45. Arendt's position stands in stark contrast to the interpretation Butler has lent to the phrase "the doer behind the deed." See Judith Butler, *Gender Trouble: Feminism and the Subversion of Identity* (New York and London: Routledge, 1990), 25.

19 Hannah Arendt, *On Revolution* (London: Penguin, 1990), 18–19.

20 Dori Laub, "Bearing Witness, or the Vicissitudes of Listening," in Shoshana Felman and Dori Laub, *Testimony: Crises of Witnessing in Literature, Psychoanalysis, and History* (New York and London: Routledge, 1992), 64 and 65.

21 Adorno first formulated this negative injunction in his 1951 essay, "Cultural Criticism and Society" (in Theodor W. Adorno, *Prisms* [Cambridge, Mass.: MIT Press, 1981]) and later qualified the charge, among others, in his *Negative Dialectics* (1966), where he remarked: "Perennial suffering has as much right to expression as a tortured man has to scream; hence it may have been wrong to say that after Auschwitz you could no longer write poems." Theodor W. Adorno, *Negative Dialectics*, trans. E.B. Ashton (New York: Continuum, 1994), 362.

22 See, especially, the contributions to this debate collected in Saul Friedlander, ed., *Probing the Limits of Representation: Nazism and the Final Solution* (Cambridge, Mass.: Harvard University Press, 1992).

23 Jürgen Habermas, "An Alternative Way out of the Philosophy of the Subject: Communicative versus Subject-Centered Reason," in Habermas, *Philosophical Discourse of Modernity*, passim.

24 Habermas, "Hannah Arendt," 174.

25 Ibid., 184.

26 See, on this point, Judith Butler's *Excitable Speech: A Politics of the Performative* (New York and London: Routledge, 1997), 6, which takes issue with Elaine Scarry's *The Body in Pain* for defining violence and terror uniquely as world-shattering and language-obliterating, in other words, as exterior to language.

27 Nietzsche, *Genealogy of Morals*, 57; Arendt, *The Human Condition*, 243 and especially 245. For a fine reading of Arendt in this context, see Alan Keenan, "Promises, Promises: The Abyss of Freedom and the Loss of the Political in the Work of Hannah Arendt," in *Political Theory* 22.2 (May 1994): 297ff.

28 See Nietzsche's "Preface" to his *Genealogy of Morals*, especially 20.

29 Jacques Derrida, *Monolingualism of the Other; or, The Prosthesis of Origin* (Stanford, Calif.: Stanford University Press, 1998), 40.

30 Ibid., 59 and 58.

31 See, for example, Paul de Man, "Rhetoric of Tropes (Nietzsche)," in de Man, *Allegories of Reading: Figural Language in Rousseau, Nietzsche, Rilke, and Proust* (New Haven, Conn., and London: Yale University Press, 1979), 104. I would like to refer here to an excellent essay by Louise Shea, a graduate student in my Harvard Nietzsche seminar, which further explores the inordinate, seminal influence that Nietzsche's views on rhetoric had on de Man's work.

32 Paul de Man, "'Conclusions': Walter Benjamin's 'The Task of the Translator'," in de Man, *The Resistance to Theory* (Minneapolis: University of Minnesota Press, 1986), 96.

33 For a more extensive discussion of this point, see Chapter 1 of this book, in which it was noted that there exist pronounced connections between these various concepts, insofar as the word *Gewalt* can refer to violence (*violentia*), force (*vis*), and power (*potestas*).

34 For a discussion of the distinctions between Foucault's and Habermas's understanding of the term "discourse," see Manfred Frank, who rightly notes that Habermas's *Diskurs* "would have to be seen as the form of language in which claims to validity are founded," a foundationalist presupposition missing from Foucault's *discours*. See Manfred Frank, "On Foucault's Concept of Discourse," in Timothy J. Armstrong, ed. *Michel Foucault Philosopher* (New York: Routledge, 1992), 100.

35 Michel Foucault, "The Discourse on Language," in Foucault, *The Archeology of Knowledge and the Discourse on Language*, trans. A.M. Sheridan Smith (New York: Pantheon, 1982), 218–19; and Frank, "On Foucault's Concept of Discourse," 115–16.

36 Foucault, "The Discourse on Language," 227.

37 Michel Foucault, *The History of Sexuality, Volume I: An Introduction* (New York: Vintage, 1980), 85.

38 Foucault, "The Discourse on Language," 228.

39 Foucault, "Truth and Power," in Paul Rabinow, ed., *The Foucault Reader* (New York: Pantheon, 1984), 56.

40 Ibid., 57.

41 J.L. Austin, *How to Do Things with Words*, eds. J.O. Urmson and Marina Sbisà (Cambridge, Mass.: Harvard University Press, 1975), 6–7. Furthermore, see Stanley Cavell, *Philosophical Passages: Wittgenstein, Emerson, Austin, Derrida* (Oxford, England, and Cambridge, Mass.: Blackwell, 1995).

42 Ibid., 99–100.

43 Habermas, *Philosophical Discourse of Modernity*, 311. Already in *The Theory of Communicative Action*, Habermas took issue with analytical philosophy for misreading Aristotle and isolating formal logic at the expense of other forms of linguistic utterances and expressions; the changes also came at the expense of Aristotle's original division of disciplines, which Habermas saw mirrored in the formal characteristics of argumentative speech, to wit: rhetoric, dialectic, and logic. To rhetoric – here to be understood in the sense of forensic rhetoric – corresponded the elimination of repression and inequality as well as "the intention of convincing a *universal audience* and gaining general assent for an utterance." Habermas, *The Theory of Communicative Action*, vol. 1, 26. This required *process*, that is, certain pragmatic presuppositions or formal conditions, such as symmetry conditions among the participants as well as the presupposition that no *force* would be applied "except the force of the better argument." To dialectic corresponded the *pragmatic procedures* or formalizable rules to which argumentation was subjected. Finally, to logic corresponded the production of *cogent arguments*.

44 Habermas, *The Theory of Communicative Action*, vol. 1, 278.

45 Ibid., 286.

46 Habermas, *Philosophical Discourse of Modernity*, 299.

47 Habermas, "Hannah Arendt," 173.

48 Habermas, *The Theory of Communicative Action*, vol. 1, 293.

49 Ibid., 278.

50 Ibid., 35.

51 Ibid., 36.

52 Ibid., 288.

53 Ibid., 287. To be sure, although Habermas's definition of such a noninstrumental form of human speech might, at first sight, resemble Benjamin's critique of bourgeois, vehicular theories of language, the distinctions are far-reaching. For Habermas, Benjamin's assumption of an original mystical mode of language, corrupted by bourgeois utilitarianism, amounts to an embrace of an apolitical mysticism. Walter Benjamin, "On Language as Such and on the Language of Man," in Benjamin, *Reflections: Essays, Aphorisms, Autobiographical Writings* (New York: Schocken, 1978), 314–32.

54 Jacques Derrida, "Signature Event Context," in Derrida, *Limited Inc.* (Evanston, Ill.: Northwestern University Press, 1988), 17.

55 Michael Shapiro, "Introduction," in Shapiro, *Language and Politics* (Oxford: Blackwell, 1984), 5ff.

56 Derrida, "Signature Event Context," 18.

57 Ibid., 7. On Derrida's conception of an originary, yet nonfoundational *polemos*, or performative force, see Jacques Derrida, "Force of Law: The 'Mystical Foundation of Authority'," *Cardozo Law Review* 11.5–6 (1990): 919–1045.

58 Pierre Bourdieu, *Language and Symbolic Power*, trans. Gino Raymond and Matthew Adamson, ed. John B. Thompson (Cambridge, Mass.: Harvard University Press, 1991), 37.

59 Ibid.

60 Ibid., 109.

61 Ibid., 67.

62 Butler, *Excitable Speech*, 48.

63 In this emphasis on the speaking body, Butler is also indebted to Shoshana Felman's *Literary Speech Act: Don Juan with J.L. Austin, or Seduction in Two Languages,* trans. Catherine Porter (Ithaca, N.Y.: Cornell University Press, 1983).

64 Butler, *Excitable Speech*, 6.

65 Jean-François Lyotard, *The Postmodern Condition: A Report on Knowledge*, trans. Geoff Bennington and Brian Massumi (Minneapolis: University of Minnesota Press, 1997), 46.

66 Ibid., 65–66.

67 Ibid., 66.

68 Ibid., 66, 67, and 82. Lyotard's call to arms ("let us wage a war on totality") appears in his "Answering the Question: What Is Postmodernism?," where he links "terror" to the desire for totality and the "fantasy to seize reality," and defends a postmodern aesthetics of the sublime, in tune with the unrepresentable. See, furthermore, *Just Gaming* and *The Differend: Phrases in Dispute*, where he returns to the task of how to think a nonnormative, pragmatic conception of justice. For Lyotard's understanding of language games as a "general agonistics," see Lyotard, *The Postmodern Condition*, 10, and especially 88, where he advances a genealogy of the term, drawing especially on Nietzsche's early "Homer's Contest": "Agonistics is the basis of Heraclitus's ontology and of the Sophists' dialectic, not to mention the early tragedians. A good part of Aristotle's reflections in the *Topics* and the *Sophistici Elenchi* is devoted to it." See, furthermore, the discussion of Foucault's "conception" of agonism in Chapter 3, above.

69 See, for example, Jürgen Habermas, "Discourse Ethics: Notes on a Program of Philosophical Justification," in Seyla Benhabib and Fred Dallmayr, eds., *The Communicative Ethics Controversy* (Cambridge, Mass., and London: MIT Press, 1995), 60–110. For a similar analysis from the Habermasian perspective, see Peter Dews, "Editor's Introduction," in Jürgen Habermas, *Autonomy and Solidarity: Interviews* (London: Verso, 1986), 17ff.

70 Althusser, in fact, refers to "symbolic repression," identifying it as one of the techniques (besides ideology) through which Ideological State Apparatuses function. See Louis Althusser, "Ideology and Ideological State Apparatuses (Notes Towards an Investigation)," in Slavoj Žižek, ed., *Mapping Ideology* (London and New York: Verso, 1994), 112; and Terry Eagleton's discussion of Bourdieu's remarks on symbolic violence in the latter's *Outline of a Theory of Practice*, in Eagleton, *Ideology: An Introduction*

(London: Verso, 1991), also reprinted as "Ideology and its Vicissitudes in Western Marxism," in Žižek, *Mapping Ideology*, 224.

71 Mouffe, "Decision, Deliberation, and Democratic Ethos," 24.

72 Slavoj Žižek, "Introduction," in Žižek, *Mapping Ideology*, 10.

73 For an account of this transition, see Žižek, "Introduction," 8ff.

74 Ernesto Laclau and Chantal Mouffe, *Hegemony and Socialist Strategy: Towards a Radical Democratic Politics* (London and New York: Verso, 1985), 96 and 113. Furthermore, see Mouffe, "Hegemony and Ideology in Gramsci," in Chantal Mouffe, ed., *Gramsci and Marxist Theory* (London, Boston, and Henley: Routledge & Kegan Paul, 1979), 168–204.

75 Žižek, "Introduction," 16.

76 See also Eagleton, *Ideology*, 7ff.

77 Althusser, "Ideology and Ideological State Apparatuses," 129.

78 Žižek, "Introduction," 7.

79 Ibid., 17, emphasis added. On Žižek's critique of idealism, see also the chapter "Ethics after Idealism," in Rey Chow, *Ethics after Idealism: Theory–Culture–Ethnicity–Reading* (Bloomington and Indianapolis: Indiana University Press, 1998), 33–54.

80 On this point, see also the introduction to this book. In the 1950s, conservative critics such as Daniel Bell postulated that the all too real terror of Stalinism proved once and for all that not just the Soviet regime, but all of Marxism and (democratic) socialism, amounted to a totalitarian ideology of terror, meaning that Marxist theory proved politically irredeemable. See Daniel Bell, *The End of Ideology: On the Exhaustion of Political Ideas in the Fifties*, with a new Afterword (Cambridge, Mass., and London: Harvard University Press, 1988). Bell's "end of ideology" thesis was taken up again in the post-Cold War era by Francis Fukuyama, also discussed in Chapter 6, below.

81 In her assessment of the ideology debates, Michèle Barrett argues that though the label "ideology" is often rejected for imposing "closure" on history's play, it continues to be used clandestinely, mainly to qualify illusion as misrecognition. See Barrett, "Ideology, Politics, Hegemony: From Gramsci to Laclau and Mouffe," in Žižek, *Mapping Ideology*, 260.

82 See, for example, Richard Rorty, "Feminism, Ideology and Deconstruction: A Pragmatist View," in Žižek, *Mapping Ideology*, 229–30, where he takes on the "matter–consciousness" distinction, presentism, and representationialism of ideology critique, for still working with "objects external to discourses." For a critique of Rorty's perspective, see Chapter 8 in this book.

83 Spivak distinguishes between the two different meanings of representing, namely "proxy and portrait," in her interview, "Practical Politics of the Open End," specifying that the one refers to *Vertretung*, or "stepping in someone's place," the other to *Darstellung*, or "placing there." Gayatri Chakravorty Spivak, *The Post-Colonial Critic: Interviews, Strategies, Dialogues*, ed. Sarah Harasym (New York and London: Routledge, 1990), 108.

84 Antonio Gramsci, "The So-called 'Question of the Language'," in Gramsci, *Selections form Cultural Writings* (Cambridge, Mass.: Harvard University Press), 187.

85 Ibid., 186.

86 See Doris Sommer, *Proceed with Caution, When Engaged with Minority Writers* (Cambridge, Mass.: Harvard University Press, 1999).

87 Homi K. Bhabha, *The Location of Culture* (London and New York: Routledge, 1994), 164.

88 Matsuda, *Words That Wound*, 15.

5 VIOLENCE AND INTERPRETATION: ENZENSBERGER'S *CIVIL WARS*

An earlier version of this chapter appeared previously in M. Garber, P. Franklin, and R. Walkowitz, eds., *Field Work: Sites in Literary and Cultural Studies* (New York and London: Routledge, 1996), 67–76.

1 Hannah Arendt, *On Revolution* (London: Penguin, 1990), 18.

2 Jürgen Habermas, "Nachholende Revolution und linker Revisionsbedarf. Was heißt Sozialismus heute?" in Habermas, *Die nachholende Revolution. Kleine Politische Schriften VII* (Frankfurt a.M.:

Suhrkamp, 1990), 179–204; translated as "What Does Socialism Mean Today? The Revolutions of Recuperation and the Need for New Thinking," in Robin Blackburn, ed., *After the Fall: The Failure of Communism and the Future of Socialism* (London and New York: Verso, 1991), 25–46.

3 Francis Fukuyama, "The End of History?," in *The National Interest* 16 (Summer 1989): 3.

4 Francis Fukuyama, *The End of History and the Last Man* (New York: The Free Press, 1992), xi and 64.

5 Habermas, "What Does Socialism Mean Today?," 30. Habermas's reference is to Ernst Nolte's article, "Nach dem Weltbürgerkrieg? Erhellung der Vergangenheit durch die Gegenwart," which appeared in *Frankfurter Allgemeine Zeitung* (February 17, 1990).

6 Helmut Dubiel, "Linke Trauerarbeit," *Merkur* 496 (June 1990): 482–91.

7 Originally published in German as *Aussichten auf den Bürgerkrieg* (Frankfurt a.M.: Suhrkamp, 1993). An excerpt, entitled "Ausblicke auf den Bürgerkrieg. Hans Magnus Enzensberger über den täglichen Massenmord und die überforderte Moral," appeared in *Der Spiegel* (June 21, 1993): 170–76. In the United States, the collection appeared under the title *Civil Wars: From L.A. to Bosnia* (New York: The New Press, 1994); in Great Britain, however, it was published as *Civil War*, trans. Piers Spence and Martin Chalmers (London: Granta, 1994). All references will be to the American edition. Unless otherwise indicated, the main focus of the following analysis will be on the collection's title essay, "Civil War."

8 Enzensberger, *Civil Wars*, 12.

9 Hans Magnus Enzensberger, "Ways of Walking: A Postscript to Utopia," in Blackburn, *After the Fall*, 18–24.

10 See Fukuyama's book review of Enzensberger's *Civil Wars*, "The New World Disorder," in *The New York Times Book Review* (October 9, 1994): 12–13. As he notes: "Given that the post-cold war world presented in this book is in many respects much better than its predecessor, the question remains why its author and other Europeans like him are so pessimistic."

11 Enzensberger, *Civil Wars*, 14.

12 Ibid., 11.

13 Ibid., 18.

14 Ibid., 31.

15 Ibid. The English translation omits the term "negative utopia." See Enzensberger, *Aussichten auf den Bürgerkrieg*, 36.

16 Arendt, "On Revolution," 20.

17 Enzensberger's use of "anthropology" as a final category or the endpoint of reasoning is also evident in his "Ways of Walking," where he justifies the end of utopianism by asserting that "utopian thinking is by no means an anthropological constant" (20).

18 See Habermas's lecture, "The Asylum Debate," in which he discusses Arnulf Baring's attempt to reverse the *Sonderweg* hypothesis and specifically the latter's argument that Germany "after unification is … once again the old one." Jürgen Habermas, "The Asylum Debate," in Habermas, *The Past as Future*, trans. and ed. Max Pensky, foreword by Peter Hohendahl (Lincoln and London: University of Nebraska Press, 1994), 137. On these strategies of progressive normalization, see particularly Andreas Huyssen, "After the Wall: The Failure of German Intellectuals," and "Nation, Race, and Immigration: German Identities after Unification," in Huyssen, *Twilight Memories: Marking Time in a Culture of Amnesia* (New York and London: Routledge, 1995). For a related discussion, see also my "Christo's Wrapped Reichstag: Globalized Art in a National Context," in *Germanic Review* 73.4 (Fall 1998): 350–67.

19 On the use of historical analogy in the *Historikerstreit*, see Charles S. Maier, *The Unmasterable Past: History, Holocaust, and German National Identity* (Cambridge, Mass., and London: Harvard University Press, 1988), *passim*.

20 André Glucksmann's comments originally appeared in *Globe Hebdo* and are reprinted as "Ein neuer Vogel Strauß. Der Philosoph André Glucksmann antwortet Hans Magnus Enzensberger," in *Der Spiegel* (September 13, 1993): 247–49.

21 See Enzensberger's interview with André Müller, "Ich will nicht der Lappen sein, mit dem man die Welt putzt," *Die Zeit* (January 27, 1995): 13.

22 See Arendt, *On Revolution*, 34.

23 See also Chapter 1 in this book.

24 Enzensberger, *Civil Wars*, 46.

25 Ibid.

26 Ibid., 27.

27 Ibid., 30.

28 Ibid., 22.

29 Ibid., 38.

30 Fukuyama, *The End of History and the Last Man*, xviii.

31 Enzensberger, *Civil Wars*, 38; the parentheses are my addition. Enzensberger does not applaud liberalism in Fukuyama's sense, for whom this political model is the consecration of Hegelian recognition. Yet an argument could be made that he takes over Fukuyama's discussion of another, false version of a recognition gone awry, which structures modern societies. I will return to these two models of recognition in the next chapter, "Ethics of the Other."

32 See Frantz Fanon's "The Negro and Recognition," in Fanon, *Black Skin, White Masks*, translated from the French by Charles Lam Markmann (New York: Grove Weidenfeld), 210–22. For a more extensive discussion of Fanon's work, see also Chapter 6, below.

33 Enzensberger, *Civil Wars*, 37ff.

34 Charles Taylor, "The Politics of Recognition," in Amy Gutmann, ed., *Multiculturalism: Examining the Politics of Recognition* (Princeton, N.J.: Princeton University Press, 1994), 61.

35 See K. Anthony Appiah's response to Taylor, "Identity, Authenticity, Survival: Multicultural Societies and Social Reproduction;" Jürgen Habermas, "Struggles for Recognition in the Democratic Constitutional State," in Gutmann, *Multiculturalism: Examining the Politics of Recognition*; Axel Honneth, *The Struggle for Recognition: The Moral Grammar of Social Conflicts*, trans. Joel Anderson (Cambridge, Mass.: MIT Press, 1996); Seyla Benhabib, "In Defense of Universalism — Yet Again! A Response to Critics of *Situating the Self*," in *New German Critique* 62 (Spring/Summer 1994): 173–89.

36 Habermas, "Struggles for Recognition," 116.

37 Ibid., 134. As Habermas puts it: "The neutrality of the law vis-à-vis internal ethical differentiations stems from the fact that in complex societies the citizenry as a whole can no longer be held together by a substantive consensus on values but only by a consensus on the procedures for the legitimate enactment of laws and the legitimate exercise of power." Ibid., 135.

38 See also Jürgen Habermas's "The Asylum Debate," in Habermas, *The Past as Future*, e.g., 129.

39 See Rogers Brubaker, *Citizenship and Nationhood in France and Germany* (Cambridge, Mass., and London: Harvard University Press, 1992), 165ff.

40 Habermas, "Struggles for Recognition," 148.

41 See, for example, the report about the citizenship reforms in *The New York Times*, October 15, 1998, "Two German Parties Reach Deal to Relax Law on Citizenship."

42 Kimberlè Crenshaw and Gary Peller, "Reel Time/Real Justice," in Robert Gooding-Williams, ed., *Reading Rodney King, Reading Urban Uprising* (New York and London: Routledge, 1993).

43 Cornel West, "Introduction: Race Matters," in West, *Race Matters* (New York: Vintage, 1994), 3.

44 Ibid., 6.

45 Ibid., 13.

6 ETHICS OF THE OTHER

I wish to express my indebtedness to discussions with Isaac Julien, Ernesto Laclau, and Chantal Mouffe, which helped me further refine the argument of portions of this chapter.

1 See Karl Marx, "The Eighteenth Brumaire of Louis Bonaparte," in Karl Marx and Frederick Engels, *Collected Works*, trans. Richard Dixon et al. (New York: International Publishers, 1975–), vol. 11, 103. Marx's full quote runs as follows: "Hegel remarks somewhere that all facts and personages of great importance in world history occur, as it were, twice. He forgot to add: the first time as tragedy, the second as farce." As David Fernbach, the editor of the Penguin edition of Marx's writings, points out, the figure is in all likelihood to be attributed to Engels, who made similar comments in an 1851

letter to Marx. See Karl Marx, *Surveys from Exile: Political Writings: Volume 2* (London: Penguin, 1992), 146n.

2 See Jacques Derrida, *Specters of Marx: The State of the Debt, the Work of Mourning, and the New International*, trans. Peggy Kamuf, with an introduction by Bernd Magnus and Stephen Cullenberg (New York and London: Routledge, 1994). Derrida pursues the economy of a "hauntology" in Marx's work but also the return, or perhaps persistence, of a discourse of the modern apocalypse and of the "last human" in the postmodern present.

3 Francis Fukuyama, *The End of History and the Last Man* (New York, Oxford, Singapore, and Sydney: The Free Press, 1992). On Fukuyama, see also Derrida's *Specters of Marx*, 56–68, which takes on the Christian eschatology, the gospel-like nature of Fukuyama's world-historical project.

4 See Nancy Fraser, *Justice Interruptus: Critical Reflections on the "Postsocialist" Condition* (New York and London: Routledge, 1997), especially the chapter, "From Redistribution to Recognition? Dilemmas of Justice in a 'Postsocialist' Age."

5 Amy Gutmann, ed., *Multiculturalism: Examining the Politics of Recognition* (Princeton, N.J.: Princeton University Press, 1994). This book assembles contributions by Charles Taylor, K. Anthony Appiah, Jürgen Habermas, Steven C. Rockefeller, Michael Walzer, and Susan Wolf. In what follows, I will focus principally on Charles Taylor's essay, "The Politics of Recognition," and Jürgen Habermas's "Struggles for Recognition in the Democratic Constitutional State."

6 K. Anthony Appiah, "Race, Culture, Identity: Misunderstood Connections," in K. Anthony Appiah and Amy Gutmann, *Color Conscious: The Political Morality of Race* (Princeton, N.J.: Princeton University Press, 1996), 92, emphasis added. See also his "Identity, Authenticity, Survival: Multicultural Societies and Social Reproduction," in Amy Gutmann, *Multiculturalism*, 149–63.

7 Walter Benjamin, "Critique of Violence," in Benjamin, *Reflections: Essays, Aphorisms, Autobiographical Writings*, trans. Edmund Jephcott, edited and with an introduction by Peter Demetz (New York: Schocken, 1986), 285. Benjamin comments on the "minimal program" of Kant's categorical imperative, namely, "act in such a way that at all times you use humanity both in your person and in the person of all others as an end, and never merely as a means." As he observes in a footnote: "One might, rather, doubt whether this famous demand does not contain too little, that is, whether it is permissible to use, or allow to be used, oneself or another in any respect as means. Very good grounds for such doubt could be adduced." Benjamin, *Reflections*, 285n.

8 On the problem of imagining the other, see, for example, Elaine Scarry, "The Difficulty of Imagining Other People," in Martha C. Nussbaum et al., *For Love of Country: Debating the Limits of Patriotism* (Boston: Beacon Press, 1996), 98–110.

9 The category of "alterity" or "otherness" (*autre*) must be demarcated from the position of the personalized other (*autrui*), insofar as the former often is held to refer to a logical category (in French, *le même et l'autre,* in German, *das Selbe und das Andere*). In his early work on the history of insanity, *Madness and Civilization*, for instance, Foucault demonstrated how this ontological dialectic grounded epistemic regimes of violence, in which order was imposed to mark off and tame uncontrollable alterity. See, furthermore, Michel Foucault, *The Order of Things: An Archeology of the Human Sciences* (New York: Vintage, 1994), xxiv, and especially 326ff. For the French original, which unambiguously distinguishes *le Même* from *l'Autre*, not *autrui*, see Michel Foucault, *Les mots et les choses: Une archéologie des sciences humaines* (Paris: Gallimard, 1966), 15 and 337ff. On the philosophy of the other, see especially Michael Theunissen, *The Other: Studies in the Social Ontology of Husserl, Heidegger, Sartre, and Buber*, trans. Christopher Macann (Cambridge, Mass.: MIT Press, 1984). Paradoxically, the objectification of *autrui* into *l'autre* can be found among quite a few philosophers of otherness, certainly Levinas, whose discourse on "the feminine" elevates women to a transcendental position, stripping them of the position of actional subjecthood. The same holds for Sartre's philosophy, especially for the analysis of the existentialist subject offered in *Being and Nothingness*, which found a necessary response in de Beauvoir's *Second Sex*.

10 See Gayatri Chakravorty Spivak's "Can the Subaltern Speak?," in Cary Nelson and Lawrence Grossberg, eds., *Marxism and the Interpretation of Culture* (Urbana: University of Illinois Press, 1988).

11 See, among others, Emmanuel Levinas, *Ethics and Infinity: Conversations with Philippe Nemo*, trans. Richard A. Cohen (Pittsburgh: Duquesne University Press, 1985), 77.

12 Taylor, "The Politics of Recognition," 65.

13 Frantz Fanon, "The Negro and Recognition," in Fanon, *Black Skin, White Masks*, trans. Charles Lam Markmann (New York: Grove Weidenfeld, 1967), 210–22.

14 In many ways, this piece stands in dialogue with Homi Bhabha, who has similarly discussed the ethical impulse in Fanon's work, linking him to Levinas. See Homi K. Bhabha, "On the Irremovable Strangeness of Being Different," in *PMLA* 113.1 (January 1998): 34–39. For other important overview readings of Fanon, see Henry Louis Gates Jr., "Critical Fanonism," *Critical Inquiry* 17 (Spring 1991): 457–70, and Françoise Vergès, "Creole Skin, Black Mask: Fanon and Disavowal," *Critical Inquiry* 23.3 (Spring 1997): 578–95.

15 See the essay by Chantal Mouffe, "Which Ethics for Democracy?," in Marjorie Garber, Beatrice Hanssen, and Rebecca Walkowitz, eds., *The Turn to Ethics* (New York: Routledge, 2000).

16 See Seyla Benhabib, "Judgment and the Moral Foundations of Politics in Hannah Arendt's Thought," in Benhabib, *Situating the Self: Gender, Community, and Postmodernism in Contemporary Ethics* (New York: Routledge, 1992), 122–23.

17 G.W.F. Hegel, *Phenomenology of Spirit*, trans. A.V. Miller (Oxford and New York: Oxford University Press, 1977), 112.

18 See Jürgen Habermas, "On the Pragmatic, the Ethical, and the Moral Employments of Practical Reason," in Habermas, *Justification and Application: Remarks on Discourse Ethics* (Cambridge, Mass.: MIT Press, 1993); William Regh, "Translator's Introduction," in Jürgen Habermas, *Between Facts and Norms: Contributions to a Discourse Theory of Law and Democracy* (Cambridge, Mass.: MIT Press, 1996).

19 On the need to expose such power dynamics and relations of domination in pluralistic democracy, see Chantal Mouffe's "Democracy and Pluralism: A Critique of the Rationalist Approach," *Cardozo Law Review* 16.5 (March 1995): 1533–45.

20 On Fanon's prophetism, see Cornel West, "The New Cultural Politics of Difference," in West, *Keeping Faith: Philosophy and Race in America* (New York and London: Routledge, 1993), 13–14.

21 See David Brion Davis, *The Problem of Slavery in the Age of Revolution 1770–1823* (Ithaca, N.Y. and London: Cornell University Press, 1975), especially the epilogue "Toussaint L'Ouverture and the Phenomenology of Mind," 557–64; Orlando Patterson, "The Constituent Elements of Slavery," in Patterson, *Slavery and Social Death: A Comparative Study* (Cambridge, Mass. and London: Harvard University Press, 1982); and Paul Gilroy, "Masters, Mistresses, Slaves and the Antinomies of Modernity," in Gilroy, *The Black Atlantic: Modernity and Double Consciousness* (Cambridge, Mass.: Harvard University Press, 1993), 41–71. Gilroy, in particular, uses W.E.B. Du Bois's concept of "double consciousness," expounded in *The Souls of Black Folk* as a point of departure for his analysis of the "Black Atlantic" as a "counterculture of modernity." Referring to "the core dynamic of racial oppression as well as the fundamental antinomy of diaspora blacks," the phrase, as Gilroy goes on to show, acquires an inordinate historical complexity when seen within the context of Du Bois's work. For "double consciousness" brought into play "the unhappy symbiosis between three modes of thinking, being, and seeing," notably racial particularism, nationalism, and, finally, a "diasporic or hemispheric" strand that was "sometimes global and occasionally universalist." That complexity was only compounded by the fact that *The Souls of Black Folk* proved strongly influenced by the Hegelianism Du Bois encountered in Germany, as his adoption of a quasi-Hegelian philosophy of history demonstrated. See Gilroy, *The Black Atlantic*, 30, 27, and 134. Within the frame of the present study, focused mainly on Fanon, it will not be possible to pursue these connections further. However, anticipating the argument of my analysis, I would like to add that Du Bois's notion of double consciousness also rewrote Hegel's parable of self-consciousness, for example, when Du Bois observed: "After the Egyptian and Indian, the Greek and Roman, the Teuton and Mongolian, the Negro is a sort of seventh son, born with a veil, and gifted with second-sight in this American world, – a world which yields him no true self-consciousness, but only lets him see himself through the revelation of the other world. It is a peculiar sensation, this double-consciousness, this sense of always looking at one's self through the eyes of others, of measuring one's soul by the tape of a world that always looks on in amused contempt and pity." W.E.B. Du Bois, *The Souls of Black Folk* (New York: Vintage, 1990), 8. Indeed, the passage seems very close to Fanon's reflections on the black Antillean's alienation from the Hegelian project of freedom in his "The Negro and Recognition," in Fanon, *Black Skin, White Masks* (see the discussion below).

22 Gilroy, "Masters, Mistresses, Slaves," 55. Gilroy's critique of conventional theories of modernity specifically calls for a consideration of the historical institution of slavery, over and against the unproblematic embrace "of such central categories of the Enlightenment project as the idea of universality, the fixity of meaning, the coherence of the subject, and, of course, the foundational ethnocentrism in which these have all tended to be anchored" (ibid.).

23 On the difference between these ontological and existential moments, see Alexandre Kojève, *Introduction to the Reading of Hegel: Lectures on the Phenomenology of Spirit*, trans. James H. Nichols Jr., ed. Allan Bloom (Ithaca, N.Y., and London: Cornell University Press, 1980), 51ff.

24 Hegel, *Phenomenology of Spirit*, 112. Hegel captured this process by means of the reflexive verb "*sich gegenseitig anerkennen*," or "Sie anerkennen sich als *gegenseitig sich anerkennend*."

25 Kojève, *Introduction to the Reading of Hegel*, 11. Kojève simultaneously ascribed a biologistic predicament to the position of the serf, defining him as marked by animality, a suggestion missing from the Hegelian passage, at least in the *Phenomenology of Spirit*. See, however, Gilroy's analysis of racist motifs in Hegelian philosophy in Gilroy, *The Black Atlantic*, 50 and 134.

26 Fukuyama, *The End of History*, 152.

27 Elaborating further on the eschatological dimensions that Derrida, in particular, has discerned in Fukuyama's project, one could perhaps say that in his presentism, or adulation of the now, one encounters the strangely distorted image of Levinas's prophetic conception of the "end of history," or eschatology. The latter, for Levinas, also became an event that no longer took place at the end of time but at every instant, outside of a totalizing context or frame. See Emmanuel Levinas, *Totality and Infinity: An Essay on Exteriority*, trans. Alphonso Lingis (Pittsburgh: Duquesne University Press, 1969), 23.

28 Fukuyama, *The End of History*, 338. The pernicious slant of Fukuyama's right-leaning universalized liberalism especially surfaces in the grand image with which his tract ends, overcoming the apocalyptic danger of multicultural difference. Willfully or unselfconsciously, he clads the conquest of American liberalism in the mythical, cinematic language of the "trek to the West," evoking a fierce battle between good cowboys and bad Indians. This troubling image not only reframes the Hegelian struggle of life and death as the American myth of the conquest of the West but also offers the latest variant of the famous train metaphor that Marx had already used for the progress of history.

29 For further discussion of Habermas's Hegel interpretation in his *Philosophical Discourse of Modernity*, see also Paul Gilroy, who, in arguing for a radical, multicultural revision of modernist theory, criticizes Habermas's blindness to the imperialistic legacy in the Hegelian narrative. See the chapter "Masters, Mistresses, Slaves," in Gilroy, *The Black Atlantic*, 50ff.

30 Jürgen Habermas, *The Philosophical Discourse of Modernity: Twelve Lectures*, trans. Frederick Lawrence (Cambridge, Mass.: MIT Press, 1987), 22.

31 Axel Honneth, *The Struggle for Recognition: The Moral Grammar of Social Conflicts* (Cambridge, Mass., and London: MIT Press, 1996), 1.

32 Ibid., 59 and 63.

33 My phrase here alludes to Judith Butler's *The Psychic Life of Power: Theories in Subjection* (Stanford, Calif.: Stanford University Press, 1997). See especially the chapter "Stubborn Attachment, Bodily Subjection: Rereading Hegel on the Unhappy Consciousness," 31–62.

34 The two tempos of Hegelian self-consciousness return in Lacan's famous 1949 Zürich lecture, "The Mirror Stage as Formative of the Function of the I as Revealed in Psychoanalytic Experience." Thus, Lacan rethought the dialectic between self and alterity, cast as the process of mirror identification, while the struggle between self and other appeared as the dialectic of social ego formation, achieved through the Oedipal triangle. Lacan maintained that this first fictional, yet constitutive form of identification, mediated through a specular non-self, preceded the social dialectic of identification with the other. Linking ego psychology to a philosophico-ontological framework, he grafted his claims about the "function of the I" onto a theory of the "ontological structure of the human world," boldly setting out to undercut Cartesianism in general and Sartre's assertive existentialism in particular. Starting off from comparative psychology, namely, Köhler's *Aha-Erlebnis*, Lacan redescribed the infant's first moment of recognition, which was directed at its mirror image and followed by a sequence of gestures through which it playfully enacted (or externalized) the relation between this virtual specular complex and the reality it doubled. As he cast the mirror stage in quasi-Platonic

language, Lacan observed that the infant's "jubilant assumption" of its specular image was to be thought of, analytically speaking, as a process of identification that transformed the subject as it assumed an external *imago*. Jacques Lacan, "The Mirror Stage as Formative of the Function of the I as Revealed in Psychoanalytic Experience," in Lacan, *Écrits: A Selection*, trans. Alan Sheridan (New York and London: W.W. Norton, 1977), 2. Through primary identification with the alterity of the self-image, a primordial, symbolical form of the ego came about, pointing more particularly to the intrapsychic formation of the (narcissistic) *Ideal-Ich*. (See also the entry "*Ideal-Ich*" in Jean Laplanche and J.B. Pontalis, *The Language of Psycho-Analysis* [New York: W.W. Norton, 1973].) As emphasized before, central for Lacan was that the mirror stage, marked by the dialectic between self and mirror image, preceded the "social" stage, in which the ego objectified itself through identification with the other, no less than through its linguistic inscription into the universalism of language, accomplished in the so-called symbolic phase. Pushing the moment of alienation that structured Hegel's allegory of self and alterity to its extreme, Lacan underlined that the presocial psychogenetic process included a fictional component. That is, the ego related to itself reflexively as double, automaton, phantom, specter. Functioning as an "orthopaedic" structure, the *imago* lent the subject a primordial totality, an "armor" of an alienating identity, which it all too readily assumed. In the subject's ascent to power, the "total form of the body" was experienced as a *Gestalt*, which symbolized the "mental permanence of the I" but also prefigured its "alienating destiny." This formative specular process through which the infant set up a relation between *Innenwelt* and *Umwelt* involved a homeomorphic identification with the double, as well as a heteromorphic identification with space, the spatial ensnarement in the mirror. Eventually, the temporal dialectic of the mirror stage came to an end through a new dialectic that would "henceforth link the *I* to socially elaborated situations." Already evident in primordial jealousy, in which affect signaled a "mediatization through the desire of the other," the process of social integration would eventually culminate in the Oedipal complex. (Lacan, "The Mirror Stage," 5) One must, furthermore, consider the fact that Lacan's (if only parenthetical) reference to Charlotte Bühler's account of *infantile transitivism* showed his concern with processes in which the infant mimicked not just the self as *imago*, but also another self. As we shall see, it is precisely the mimicry of the other that will inform Fanon's analysis of the alienated Antillean subject. Finally, in rejecting Freud's original topography (perception-consciousness), Lacan relied on Anna Freud's notion of denegation (*Verneinung*), isolating it as one of the ego's major defense mechanisms, insofar as it was "*the function of méconnaissance* that [characterized] the ego in all its structures" (ibid., 6).

35 I wish to express my indebtedness to Isaac Julien's work on Fanon, above all his film *Black Skin, White Masks*, as well as to Stuart Hall's observations about the function of the Hegelian dialectic in Fanon's thought. See, further, the essays collected in Lewis R. Gordon, T. Denean Sharpley-Whiting, and Renée T. White, eds., *Fanon: A Critical Reader* (Oxford, England, and Cambridge, Mass.: Blackwell, 1996); Vergès, "Creole Skin, Black Mask."

36 Fanon, *Black Skin, White Masks*, 61.

37 The English translation reads as follows: "This book, it is hoped, will be a mirror with a progressive infrastructure, in which it will be possible to discern the Negro on the road to disalienation." However, in the original the phrase is: "in which the Negro could rediscover himself [*se retrouver*] on the road to disalienation." Fanon, *Black Skin, White Masks*, 184; *cf.* the French original in Frantz Fanon, *Peau noire, masques blancs* (Paris: Éditions du Seuil, 1995), 148. Indeed, Fanon scholar Françoise Vergès highlights the mistranslation, noting that in the English version, "the *reader* discerns the Negro in the mirror that is the book, whereas in Fanon's text the book is a mirror *to the Negro*." Vergès, "Creole Skin, Black Mask," 580n.

38 Fanon, *Black Skin, White Masks*, 183. Fanon borrows the term from Dide and Guiraud's *Psychiatrie du médecin practicien* (Paris: Masson, 1922).

39 Fanon, "The Negro and Recognition," *Black Skin, White Masks*, 216.

40 The model of ethical transit, *le glissement éthique*, is accomplished in Martinique through cultural imposition of a collective, racially marked unconscious. Though Fanon here uses a nontechnical term, *glissement*, gliding or sliding, it is perhaps not far-fetched to link the mechanism to *transitivism*, as mimetic enactment of ethical gestures, discussed also in Lacan's essay on the mirror stage. See also the French original, Fanon, *Peau noire, masques blancs*, 155–56.

41 Fanon, *Black Skin, White Masks*, 8.

42 In privileging the Kojèvian emphasis on violence, Fanon's reading concurred with Sartre's similar stress on negation in both his *Being and Nothingness* and his *Anti-Semite and Jew*, on whose insights about the "aetiology of hatred" *Black Skin, White Masks* also relied. As an interesting response to the so-called submerged violence of Sartrean existentialism, one must also read Lacan's essay on the mirror stage. In it, Lacan suggested that the death drive, the destructive instincts, and aggression resurfaced in existentialism. More so, Sartre's philosophy plainly reinscribed itself in the *constitutive misrecognitions of the ego*, as it venerated the illusions of autonomy, authenticity, freedom, and the real. Showing itself to remain mired in, or fixated on, the stage of "primary narcissism," existentialism glorified modes of action that bordered on negating aggression or destructivity, an "existential negativity," resulting in a "consciousness of the other that can be satisfied only by Hegelian murder" (Lacan, "The Mirror Stage," 6). In other words, Sartre's theory of self-consciousness bobbed on misrecognition. For a similar assessment of Lacan's forceful critique of the existentialist paradigm in its relation to Fanon's work, see Vergès, "Creole Skin, Black Mask," 589. Clearly, in advancing his theory of misrecognition, Lacan also proposed a "dialectic of knowledge," in keeping with the tradition of ideology critique, which seeks to unmask the distortions of the historical subject's flawed gaze. For analyses of the dynamics between dialectics, ideology, and *misrecognition*, see also Slavoj Žižek, "Introduction: The Specter of Ideology," and Louis Althusser, "Ideology and Ideological State Apparatuses (Notes Towards an Investigation)," especially his notes on mirror duplication, both in Žižek, *Mapping Ideology* (London and New York: Verso, 1994), 1–33, 134–35.

43 Fanon, *Black Skin, White Masks*, 218.

44 Ibid., 220n.

45 Fanon invokes Kierkegaard's concept of anguish in *Black Skin, White Masks*, 221.

46 Important, here, is Fanon's critique of Sartrean existentialism, in the chapter "L'expérience vécue du Noir" (translated in English as "The Fact of Blackness"), where he took on Sartre for turning *négritude* into a negative, transitory term, an intermediary passage on the way to the universal needs of the proletariat. Indeed, in his "Black Orpheus," Sartre defended a Marxist humanism, stating that race was merely particular, class universal. *Négritude* was a passing negative moment without value in itself, since the end goal was a universal synthesis, a society without races, to which *négritude* was not a final cause or end but simply a means, no different in status than the instrumental violence that inhered in the Hegelian dialectic. Going further, he even stripped black consciousness of affirmative power, rendering it as a lack (*manque*). Taking a resolute turn, at this point, *against* Sartre's universal (quite unlike other essays would do), Fanon condemned the philosopher's reduction of black consciousness to such a lack and, even worse, to a self-absorbed opacity or immediacy. Again and again, he took aim at Sartre's demand for a true "universal," stating that barely has the Negro's blind-fold been taken off, or he was forced to embrace the universal, when in fact he would like to savor the rewards of *négritude*. See Fanon, *Black Skin, White Masks*, 132ff; and Jean-Paul Sartre, "Black Orpheus," in Sartre, *"What is Literature?" and Other Essays* (Cambridge, Mass.: Harvard University Press, 1988), 291–330.

47 Fanon, *Black Skin, White Masks*, 222.

48 Frantz Fanon, *The Wretched of the Earth*, trans. Constance Farrington, preface by Jean-Paul Sartre (New York: Grove Press, 1963), 36–37.

49 Ibid., 39.

50 Ibid., 45.

51 Ibid., 61.

52 Ibid., 41.

53 Ibid.

54 Ibid., 93.

55 Ibid., 88.

56 Ibid., 80.

57 Ibid., 94.

58 Sartre, "Preface" to Fanon, *Wretched of the Earth*, 20.

59 Ibid., 17.

60 Ibid. In his 1961 preface, Sartre made it clear that "liberal hypocrisy" avowed its allegiance to a humanism that "claimed to be universal," while in the overseas colonies it applied a *numerus clausus* as

to who could qualify as a member of the human race, as to who could be cataloged under the rubric "human" (14–15). According to the existentialist philosopher, Fanon's tract on violence was the first since Engels (excepting the fascist Sorel) to have brought "the processes of history into the clear light of day" (14). To explicate the point, Sartre had recourse to the logic of specularity at the core of the Hegelian dialectic of consciousness, in which two warring individuals looked each other in the eye. In like manner, the dehumanizing effects of colonial violence, with its affirmation of subjugation and servitude, needed to be countered by the insurrectionary force of revolutionary socialism. Succumbing to the vicious circle of violence, Sartre avowed that the singed "marks of violence" and traumatic wounds could no longer be effaced by "gentleness," only by violence (21). Yet he tried to do away with the possible suspicion that the countercolonial rebellion would end in mere acts of savagery or "primitivism." Rather, violence was the only (creative, spontaneous) means available to thrust out colonialism, to cure the colonial neurosis, and lay claim to humanism: "[Fanon] shows clearly that this irrepressible violence is neither sound nor fury, nor the resurrection of savage instincts, nor even the effect of resentment: it is man recreating himself" (21). As he looked in the mirror held up to him as a European, Sartre saw the "striptease" of Enlightenment ideals, which were idle chatter when judged from the reality of racism (26). In racist humanism, he concluded, "the European has only been able to become a man through creating slaves and monsters. .... In the notion of the human race we found an abstract assumption of universality which served as cover for the most realistic practices" (26).

61 See Hannah Arendt's *On Violence* (San Diego, New York, and London: Harcourt Brace Jovanovich, 1970); for a critique of Arendt's Eurocentrism, however, see Chapter 1 of this book.

62 Levinas, *Ethics and Infinity*, 98.

63 As Levinas noted: "It is extremely important to know if society in the current sense of the term is the result of a limitation of the principle that men are predators of one another, or if to the contrary it results from the limitation of the principle that men are *for* one another. Does the social, with its institutions, universal forms and laws, result from limiting the consequences of the war between men, or from limiting the infinity which opens in the ethical relationship of man to man?" (ibid., 80).

64 Emmanuel Levinas, "Substitution," in Levinas, *The Levinas Reader*, ed. Seán Hand (Oxford, England, and Cambridge, Mass.: Blackwell, 1989), 115.

65 Fanon, *Black Skin,White Masks*, 8 and 10.

66 Ibid., 227. The French original reads: "Depuis longtemps, le ciel étoilé qui laissait Kant pantelant nous a livré ses secrets. Et la loi morale doute d'elle-même" (Fanon, *Peau noire*, 184), and alludes to Kant's famous stellar figure in the second *Critique*.

67 Carol Gilligan, *In a Different Voice: Psychological Theory and Women's Development* (Cambridge, Mass.: Harvard University Press, 1982). See also Seyla Benhabib, "The Generalized and the Concrete Other: The Kohlberg–Gilligan Controversy and Moral Theory," and "The Debate over Women and Moral Theory Revisited," in Benhabib, *Situating the Self*, 148–202. It should be stressed that the critical positions Fanon occupied, whether in his capacity as a psychiatrist or political activist, labored under a phallocentric model of subjecthood. That he himself, therefore, was susceptible of the very same ethical transitivism is clear from several of his writings, for example, from the chapter, "The Woman of Color and the White Man," which *Black Skin,White Masks* dedicated to Mayotte Capécia's *Je suis Martiniquaise*, and from "Algeria Unveiled" (in Frantz Fanon, *A Dying Colonialism*, trans. Haakon Chevalier [New York: Grove, 1965]). For a critique of Fanon's "construction of a Creole masculinity and femininity," see Vergès, "Creole Skin, Black Mask"; for other feminist critiques of Fanon, including "Algeria Unveiled," see also Diane Fuss, *Identification Papers* (New York: Routledge, 1995) and Madhu Dubey, "The 'True Lie' of the Nation: Fanon and Feminism," in *differences* 10.2 (Summer 1998): 1–29.

68 In fact, in "The Politics of Recognition," Taylor identifies Rousseau early on as "one of the points of origin of the modern discourse of authenticity," later on as "one of the originators of the discourse of recognition," while pointing to the obliteration of differential positions that might follow from Rousseau's general will. See Taylor, "The Politics of Recognition," 35, 44 and 48.

69 Ibid., 38 and 38n.

70 Ibid., 65.

71 Ibid., 66.

72 Ibid., 66–67.
73 It seems justified, in this context, to refer to the logic of forcible substitution that often informs conventional philosophies of translation. For an excellent account of how the idealistic trajectory of the self through the other has grounded theories and practices of translation, from Luther via Herder to Schleiermacher, and beyond, see Antoine Berman, *The Experience of the Foreign: Culture and Translation in Romantic Germany* (Albany, N.Y.: State University of New York Press, 1992). For an alternative model of multicultural translation that emphasizes how cultural difference – also, or especially, at the nonverbal corporeal level – resists being recuperated by the discursive norm, see Homi K. Bhabha, *The Location of Culture* (London and New York: Routledge, 1994).
74 Taylor, "The Politics of Recognition," 73.
75 G.W.F. Hegel, *Vorlesungen über die Philosophie der Geschichte* (Frankfurt a.M.: Suhrkamp, 1986), 540.
76 Mouffe, "Democracy and Pluralism," 1545.
77 Benhabib, *Situating the Self*, 8, 9.
78 Ibid., 9.
79 As Benhabib explains, "One thus avoids the charge of circularity: by allowing that the presuppositions of the moral conversation can be challenged within the conversation itself, they are placed within the purview of questioning. But insofar as they are pragmatic rules necessary to keep the moral conversation going, we can only bracket them in order to challenge but we cannot suspend them altogether." Benhabib's comments are made in the context of an attempt to overcome the charge of *petitio principii*, often directed at Habermas's universal pragmatics. As agonistic critics might argue, in turn, such a proposal does not solve the circularity, for it still presupposes that all participants univocally submit to the collective moral conversation, structured around universal respect and egalitarian reciprocity. Seyla Benhabib, "Afterword: Communicative Ethics and Current Controversies in Practical Philosophy," in Seyla Benhabib and Fred Dallmayr, *The Communicative Ethics Controversy* (Cambridge, Mass., and London: MIT Press, 1990), 340.
80 Ibid.
81 Using a dialectical model, Balibar contends that universalism and racism are indeed (determinate) contraries, and this is why each of them has the other one inside itself – or is bound to affect the other *from the inside*. Etienne Balibar, "Racism as Universalism," in Balibar, *Masses, Classes, Ideas: Studies on Politics and Philosophy Before and After Marx*, trans. James Swenson (New York and London: Routledge, 1994), 198.
82 Ibid., 204.
83 Etienne Balibar, "Racism and Nationalism," in Etienne Balibar and Immanuel Wallerstein, eds., *Race, Nation, Class: Ambiguous Identities* (London and New York: Verso, 1991), 64.
84 Habermas, *Philosophical Discourse of Modernity*, 414n.
85 Chantal Mouffe, "Decision, Deliberation, and Democratic Ethos," *Philosophy Today* 41.1 (Spring 1997): 26.
86 Ibid., 28.
87 Ibid., 26.
88 As Mouffe puts it: "While a pluralist democracy certainly requires a certain amount of consensus on the political principles that need to be shared by *all its members*, it is clear that those principles can only exist through competing interpretations that are bound to be in conflict. In other words, we will always be dealing with a 'conflictual consensus,' and this explains why a pluralist democracy needs to allow dissent on the interpretation of its constitutive principles." Ibid., 27.
89 In this section, I further elaborate on Ernesto Laclau's suggestive observations about the ethical in his "Identity and Hegemony: The Role of Universality in the Constitution of Political Logics," forthcoming in Judith Butler, Ernesto Laclau, and Slavoj Žižek, eds., *Universality, Hegemony, Contingency* (London: Verso, 2000). As he observes: "If the moment of the ethical is the moment of radical investment ..., two important conclusions follow. The first, that only that aspect of a decision which is not predetermined by an existing normative framework is, properly speaking, ethical. The second, that any normative order is nothing but the sedimented form of an initial ethical event. This explains why I reject two polarly opposed approaches which tend to universalize the conditions of the decision. The first are the different variants of a universalistic ethics which attempt to reintroduce some normative constant in the ethical moment and to subordinate the decision to such a constant,

however minimal it could be (Rawls, Habermas, etc.). The second is pure decisionism, the notion of the decision as an original *fiat* which, because it has no *aprioristic* limits, is conceived as having no limits at all. So what are those limits which are other than aprioristic? The answer is the ensemble of sedimented practices constituting the normative framework of a certain society. This framework can experience deep dislocations requiring drastic recompositions, but it never disappears to the point of requiring an act of *total* refoundation. There are no places for Licurguses of the social order."

90 See also Judith Butler's comments on universalism, especially when she states that there is the need for "the continuing revision and elaboration of historical standards of universality proper to the futural movement of democracy itself." Formulated in a utopian way, this means the "futural anticipa- tion of a universality that has not yet arrived." Judith Butler, "Universality in Culture," in Nussbaum, *For Love of Country*, 49.

91 Clearly, the process of globalization itself is extraordinarily intricate and polyvalent, as are the many uses to which the term has been put, whose opposite ends are defined, on the one hand, by a productive "cultural" globalization that emphasizes the increasing importance of so-called minority cultures on a global scale, and, on the other, by the suffocation of Third World economies and markets under the crushing weight of a normalized Western economy. For a lengthier discussion of these two contrasting uses of the term, see also my "Christo's Wrapped Reichstag: Globalized Art in a National Context," in *Germanic Review* 73.4 (Fall 1998): 350–67.

92 See Friedrich Nietzsche, *On the Genealogy of Morals and Ecce Homo*, trans. Walter Kaufmann (New York: Vintage, 1989), 15.

7 LIMITS OF FEMINIST REPRESENTATION: ELFRIEDE JELINEK'S LANGUAGE OF VIOLENCE

This chapter originally appeared in *New German Critique* (Spring/Summer 1996). Parts of it were first presented at the 1992 and 1993 Annual Meetings of the Modern Language Association. I am indebted to Andreas Huyssen for helpful suggestions and comments.

1 See Max Horkheimer and Theodor W. Adorno, *Dialectic of Enlightenment* (New York: Continuum, 1972), 110, where women's alleged closeness to nature is discussed in relation to colonialism and anti-Semitism.

2 Sara Lennox's essay, "The Feminist Reception of Ingeborg Bachmann," offers a historical overview of German feminism and discusses Elisabeth Lenk's impact on the movement. In *Women in German Yearbook* 8 (Lincoln and London: University of Nebraska Press, 1993): 85. A reference to Lenk appears in Elfriede Jelinek's "Der Krieg mit anderen Mitteln," in Christine Koschel and Inge von Weidenbaum, eds., *Kein objektives Urteil – nur ein lebendiges: Texte zum Werk von Ingeborg Bachmann* (München and Zürich: Piper, 1989), 312. As Lennox notes, Jelinek's essay was reprinted in a slightly altered version as "Der Krieg mit anderen Mitteln: Elfriede Jelinek über Ingeborg Bachmann," in *Emma* (February 1991): 21–24.

3 See particularly Claudia Koonz's *Mothers in the Fatherland: Women, The Family, and Nazi Politics* (New York: St. Martin's Press, 1987). See also Lennox, "The Feminist Reception of Ingeborg Bachmann," 76ff.

4 See Jelinek's interview with Gabriele Presber in *Frauenleben, Frauenpolitik: Rückschläge & Utopien* (Tübingen: konkursbuch Verlag Claudia Gehrke, 1992), 20.

5 Jelinek, "Der Krieg," 311.

6 Ingeborg Bachmann, *Werke*, eds. Christine Koschel, Inge von Weidenbaum, and Clemens Münster, vol. 3 (München and Zürich: Piper, 1978), 336.

7 Ibid., 341.

8 Ingeborg Bachmann, *Wir müssen wahre Sätze finden: Gespräche und Interviews*, eds. Christine Koschel and Inge von Weidenbaum (München and Zürich: Piper, 1983), 144.

9 Jelinek, "Der Krieg," 313.

10 Ibid., 312.

11 Bachmann, *Werke*, vol. 3, 413.

12 Jelinek, *Frauenleben, Frauenpolitik*, 20.

13 Sigmund Freud, *Gesammelte Werke*, vol. 13 (London: Imago, 1940), 376. On Jelinek's *Destruktionstrieb*, see her interview with Peter von Becker, "Wir leben auf einem Berg von Leichen und Schmerz," *Theater Heute* 9 (1992): 6.

14 Elfriede Jelinek in an interview with Anke Roeder, "Ich will kein Theater. Ich will ein anderes Theater," *Theater Heute* 8 (1988): 30–32.

15 See her video interview, *Von der mangelnden Tragfähigkeit des Bodens*, Institut für Alltagskultur, Szbg/SHB und BMUKS, Wien, 1988.

16 See her letter to Salman Rushdie in Steve MacDonogh, ed. *The Rushdie Letters: Freedom to Speak, Freedom to Write* (Lincoln: University of Nebraska Press, 1993), 76.

17 Jelinek, "Wir leben auf einem Berg," 6.

18 On Sade's significance for pornographic literature, especially in France, see Frances Ferguson, "Sade and the Pornographic Legacy," *Representations* 36 (Fall 1991): 1–21.

19 On this tradition, see Allan Janik and Stephen Toulmin, *Wittgenstein's Vienna* (New York: Simon and Schuster, 1973), which analyzes the key role this philosophical critique of language played in the cultural life of Habsburg Vienna.

20 Jelinek, "Ich will kein Theater," 144ff.

21 Claudine Herrmann, *Les Voleuses de langue* (Paris: Des Femmes, 1976); Hélène Cixous, "The Laugh of the Medusa," reprinted in *Feminisms: An Anthology of Literary Theory and Criticism*, eds. Robyn R. Warhol and Diane Price Herndl (New Brunswick, N.J.: Rutgers University Press, 1991), 334; Luce Irigaray, *Ce sexe qui n'en est pas un* (Paris: Minuit, 1977), 73.

22 On the notion of "frame," see Susan Rubin Suleiman, *Subversive Intent: Gender, Politics, and the Avant-Garde* (Cambridge, Mass., and London: Harvard University Press, 1990), 80–81. In her analysis of Bataille's *History of the Eye*, Suleiman addresses the double side of literary pornography, or its "textuality" and "reality." On the one hand, she argues, Bataille's text can be read within the context of the French theory of textuality as it came about in the 1960s. This theory enabled sexual violations to slide into textual ones by setting up "a metaphoric equivalence between the violation of *sexual* taboos and the violation of *discursive* norms" (74); on the other hand, the realities of the text's pornographic effects are to be exposed by a feminist reading that must "avoid the blindness of a textual reading," without however lapsing into an "ultra-thematic reading" (84).

23 On the need to readdress "intentionality" within the context of poststructuralism, see Barbara Johnson, *The Wake of Deconstruction* (Oxford, England, and Cambridge, Mass.: Blackwell, 1994), 48.

24 On the differences between poststructuralism and postmodernism, see Andreas Huyssen, "Mapping the Postmodern," in Huyssen, *After the Great Divide: Modernism, Mass Culture, Postmodernism* (Bloomington and Indianapolis: Indiana University Press, 1986), especially 206ff; the essays collected in Linda J. Nicholson, ed., *Feminism/Postmodernism* (New York and London: Routledge, 1990); and Seyla Benhabib, Judith Butler, Drucilla Cornell, and Nancy Fraser, *Feminist Contentions: A Philosophical Exchange* (New York and London: Routledge, 1995). In the present chapter, the term "poststructuralist feminism" will function as a denominator for that branch of feminist theory that has rethought the critiques of language and the subject, advanced by French poststructuralism (Foucault, Derrida, Lacan) as a way of focusing on the intersections between gender, power, and discourse.

25 Diana Fuss, for example, takes issue with Monique Wittig's adoption of an ahistorical form of male sexuality in *Essentially Speaking: Feminism, Nature & Difference* (New York, London: Routledge, 1989).

26 Teresa de Lauretis, "The Violence of Rhetoric: Considerations on Representation and Gender," in Nancy Armstrong and Leonard Tennenhouse, eds., *The Violence of Representation: Literature and the History of Violence* (London and New York: Routledge, 1989), 240. On the topic of violence, gender, and representation, see also Elisabeth Bronfen, *Over Her Dead Body: Death, Femininity and the Aesthetic* (Manchester, England: Manchester University Press, 1992).

27 de Lauretis, "The Violence of Rhetoric," 245.

28 Ibid., 240.

29 Ibid., 254.

30 Ibid., 245.

31 Ibid., 240.

32 Drucilla Cornell's publications are most representative of this branch of feminism. Further, in "Contingent Foundations: Feminism and the Question of 'Postmodernism'," Judith Butler reads the "violence of the letter" in terms of the violence of the Law. In Judith Butler and Joan W. Scott, eds., *Feminists Theorize the Political*, (New York and London: Routledge, 1992), 17–18.

33 This is Foucault's term in *Madness and Civilization*, cited by Gayatri Chakravorty Spivak in "Can the Subaltern Speak?" in Cary Nelson and Lawrence Grossberg, eds., *Marxism and the Interpretation of Culture* (Urbana: University of Illinois Press, 1988), 280–81.

34 Butler, "Contingent Foundations," 17.

35 Irigaray, *Ce sexe*, 129–30.

36 In *Gender Trouble,* Butler interprets the "textual violence" operative in Monique Wittig's *Les guérillères* not as the reenactment of a male-encoded violence, but as a critical force directed against the institution of compulsory heterosexuality. Since such categories are themselves social constructions, the women's wars, she argues, can be read as "textual violences, the deconstruction of constructs that are always already a kind of violence against the body's possibilities" (126).

37 See the entry "Gewalt" in *Historisches Wörterbuch der Philosophie* (Darmstadt: Wissenschaftliche Buchgesellschaft, 1971).

38 See Deborah Cameron's "Introduction: Why is Language a Feminist Issue?" in Cameron, ed., *The Feminist Critique of Language: A Reader* (London and New York: Routledge, 1990), 2.

39 Linda Nicholson and Nancy Fraser pose similar questions with respect to Butler's form of poststructuralist feminism, when they ask what kind of normativity would allow one to distinguish a subversive redeployment of existing structures from their mere repetition. Discussing Butler's contention that the performativity of language can be rethought in terms of "resignification" and agency, Nicholson observes that "this kind of appeal ... provides no means to distinguish or explain those instances of performativity which generate new kinds of significations from those which are merely repetitions of previous performative acts." Linda Nicholson, "Introduction," in Seyla Benhabib et al., *Feminist Contentions*, 11. Further, it seems premature to do away with the issue of instrumentality or to see it as the restoration of a "choosing" and hence humanist subject – as Butler does in her "Preface" to *Bodies That Matter* – given the centrality of strategy for poststructuralist feminism.

40 On Brownmiller, see Lynne Segal and Mary McIntosh, *Sex Exposed: Sexuality and the Pornography Debate* (London: Virago, 1992), 3; and *PorNO*, Emma-Sonderband, ed. Alice Schwarzer (Köln: Emma Frauenverlag GmbH, 1988). On the pornography debates, see also Varda Burstyn, ed., *Women Against Censorship* (Vancouver and Toronto: Douglas and McIntyre, 1985); Susan Gubar and Joan Hoff, *For Adult Users Only: The Dilemma of Violent Pornography* (Bloomington and Indianapolis: Indiana University Press, 1989); and Gillian Rodgerson and Linda Semple, "Who Watches the Watchwomen?: Feminists Against Censorship," *Feminist Review* 36 (Autumn 1990): 19–24.

41 Catharine A. MacKinnon, *Toward a Feminist Theory of the State* (Cambridge, Mass.: Harvard University Press, 1989), 206. See also Lynne Segal, "Introduction" in Segal and McIntosh, *Sex Exposed*, 5; and Mandy Merck, "From Minneapolis to Westminster" (ibid., 56).

42 Catharine A. MacKinnon, *Only Words* (Cambridge, Mass.: Harvard University Press, 1993), 30–31.

43 Andrea Dworkin and Catharine A. MacKinnon, "Questions and Answers," in Diane E.H. Russell, ed., *Making Violence Sexy: Feminist Views on Pornography* (New York and London: Teachers College Press, 1993), 92–93.

44 Lisa Duggan, Nan D. Hunter, and Carole S. Vance, "False Promises: Feminist Antipornography Legislation," in Duggan, Hunter, and Vance, eds., *Caught Looking: Feminism, Pornography & Censorship* (East Haven: LongRiver Books, 1986).

45 While MacKinnon sees the "indefinability of pornography" as endemic to a male-biased civil libertarian agenda, for FACT and other anticensorship groups a further narrowing of the legal definition implies the outlawing of sexual minorities. And while MacKinnon contends that, when it comes to pornography, one can clearly distinguish between its center and periphery, that is, between the "verbal imposition" of inequity as opposed to mere talk, FACT and critics such as anthropologist Gayle Rubin warn that more restrictive legislation in the hands of the right might outlaw precisely these very nonreproductive sexualities that position themselves *at the fringes*. See MacKinnon, *Toward a Feminist Theory of the State*, 202, and MacKinnon, *Only Words*, 106. See also Gayle Rubin's

discussion of a "pluralistic sexual ethics" in *Pleasure and Danger: Exploring Female Sexuality*, ed. Carole S. Vance (London, Sydney, and Wellington: Pandora, 1989), 275, 282, and 298ff.

46 Claudia Gehrke, *Frauen & Pornografie* (Tübingen: konkursbuch Verlag Claudia Gehrke, 1988).

47 Schwarzer, *PorNO*, 42–45.

48 Interestingly, Silvia Bovenschen has taken issue with Alice Schwarzer's position in an article called "Alice in Newton-Land," *Der Spiegel* 30 (1994): 94. Commenting on the recent Helmut Newton–Alice Schwarzer court case, Bovenschen accuses Schwarzer of belonging to the sentinels of political correctness. In a way, Schwarzer's and Bovenschen's opposite positions represent two extremes in the pornography controversy: on the one hand, a potential essentialism of the body, on the other hand, an equally troublesome cultural nominalism that risks falling back into the position of a depoliticized aestheticism. Bovenschen defends Newton's images, seeing them as a "rejection of the myth of the natural body" (93) and the illustration of a "model of the body, which can be constructed at will" (93). Taking the position of cultural constructionism to extremes, Bovenschen's text replaces a corporeal essentialism with a form of absolute relativism, whereby the body is a *Leerstelle*, a potential vehicle for multifarious, random significations, marked as it is by its "availability for all possible meanings" (94). As she maintains: "The body, strictly taken, is empty and does not offer any resistance to such operations; it can be invested at will with any meaning" (93). For a critical analysis of the "figure" of the body, see also Marjorie Garber, *Vested Interests: Cross-Dressing and Cultural Anxiety* (New York: HarperCollins, 1992).

49 Gehrke, *Frauen & Pornografie*, 16.

50 Ibid., 18–19.

51 In her essay " 'Echt sind nur wir!' Realismus und Satire bei Elfriede Jelinek," Konstanze Fliedl sees Jelinek's double intervention in the pornography debates as evidence that her allegiance to a (post-structuralist) theory of the autonomous sign, severed from reality, is not consistent with her critically engaged writing project. In *Elfriede Jelinek*, eds. Kurt Bartsch and Günther A. Höfler (Graz: Literaturverlag Droschl, 1991), 70–71. By thus invoking a problematic notion of linguistic "free play" and by reiterating the belief that semiotic theories must inevitably stand diametrically opposed to "realism" or the real, Fliedl's otherwise perceptive reading bypasses the fact that Jelinek's language "play" addresses the social and political *in* and *as* the discursive.

52 Jelinek, *PorNO*, 54.

53 Elfriede Jelinek, "Der Sinn des Obszönen. Vorrede" and "Der Sinn des Obszönen," *Frauen & Pornografie*, 101–103.

54 Ibid., 101.

55 Ibid.

56 On the figure of Rubens, see also Elfriede Jelinek, "Der Fall der Körper," in *Kunstpresse* 5 (November 1989): 14–16. I am indebted to Thomas Elsaesser for calling this essay to my attention.

57 MacKinnon, *Only Words*, 11.

58 Jelinek, "Der Sinn des Obszönen," 102.

59 Angela Carter, *The Sadeian Woman and the Ideology of Pornography* (New York: Harper Colophon Books, 1979), 3.

60 Ibid., 19. Proposing a preliminary account of this new brand of pornography, Carter adds that "the pornographer would not be the enemy of women, perhaps because he might begin to penetrate to the heart of the contempt for women that distorts our culture even as he entered the realms of true obscenity as he describes it." That such a reversal of the phallocratic economy of pornography might be more difficult to accomplish than Carter surmises, is perhaps already evident in the fact that her account, surprisingly, retains the personal pronoun "he" and thus fails to undo pornography's gendered binarism.

61 Jelinek, "Der Sinn des Obszönen," 102.

62 Carter, *The Sadeian Woman*, 19.

63 Jelinek, "Der Sinn des Obszönen," 102.

64 Jelinek in a conversation with Birgit Lahann, *Stern* 37 (Hamburg, 1988); also cited in Margarete Lamb-Faffelberger, *Valie Export und Elfriede Jelinek im Spiegel der Presse: Zur Rezeption der feministischen Avantgarde Österreichs* (New York: Peter Lang, 1992), 105. On Jelinek's *Lust*, see also Allyson Fiddler,

"Problems with Porn: Situating Elfriede Jelinek's *Lust*," *German Life and Letters* 44.5 (October 1991): 404–15.

65 Gilles Deleuze, *Masochism: Coldness and Cruelty* (New York: Zone Books, 1991), 18 and 22–23.

66 Jelinek about *Lust* in *Tip Magazin* (Berlin, October 1989); also cited in Lamb-Faffelberger, *Valie Export und Elfriede Jelinek im Spiegel der Presse*, 36. On the staging of metalanguage in Jelinek's *Krankheit oder moderne Frauen*, see also Marlies Janz, "Falsche Spiegel: Über die Umkehrung als Verfahren bei Elfriede Jelinek," in Christa Gürtler, ed., *Gegen den schönen Schein: Texte zu Elfriede Jelinek* (Frankfurt a.M.: Verlag Neue Kritik, 1990), 81–97.

67 Jelinek, "Der Sinn des Obszönen," 102.

68 For an account of the ramifications of this campaign, see Lamb-Faffelberger, *Valie Export und Elfriede Jelinek im Spiegel der Presse*, 104ff.

69 Klaus Theweleit, *Male Fantasies*, vol. 2 (Minneapolis: University of Minnesota Press, 1987), 164.

70 Elfriede Jelinek, *Krankheit oder moderne Frauen*, ed. Regine Friedrich (Köln: Prometh-Verlag, 1987), 44.

71 Elfriede Jelinek, "Ich möchte seicht sein," in Gürtler, *Gegen den schönen Schein*, 157–61.

72 Janz, "Falsche Spiegel," 83.

73 On the question of transgression versus transcendence, see Butler, *Gender Trouble*, 127.

74 Elfriede Jelinek, *The Piano Teacher*, trans. Joachim Neugroschel (London: Serpent's Tail, 1989), 86.

75 Annegret Mahler-Bungers, "Der Trauer auf der Spur: Zu Elfriede Jelineks 'Die Klavierspielerin'," *Freiburger literatur-psychologische Gespräche* 7 (Frankfurt a.M.: Peter Lang, 1988): 87.

76 Elfriede Jelinek, "Schamgrenzen? Die gewöhnliche Gewalt der weiblichen Hygiene," *konkursbuch* 12 (1984): 137.

77 Roland Barthes, *Mythologies*, trans. Annette Lavers (New York: Hill and Wang, 1972), 150–51.

78 Ibid., 142.

79 Jelinek, "Schamgrenzen," 137–38.

80 See the interpretation Freud offers of "analysis" in terms of *Zersetzung* in *Drei Abhandlungen zur Sexualtheorie*, *Gesammelte Werke*, ed. Anna Frend (Frankfurt a.M.: S. Fischer, 1972), vol. 5.

81 In a different context, Elizabeth Wright likewise discusses the notion of "disgust" (*Ekel*) in *The Piano Teacher*; see her "Eine Ästhetik des Ekels: Elfriede Jelineks Roman 'Die Klavierspielerin'," in *Text – Kritik* 117 (January 1993): 51–60.

82 Sigmund Freud, *The Origins of Psychoanalysis: Letters to Wilhelm Fließ, Drafts and Notes: 1887–1902*, eds. Marie Bonaparte, Anna Freud and Ernst Kris (New York: Basic Books, 1977), 233.

83 Later, in his celebrated Dora case, Freud will again propose this biological aetiology as he seeks to explain Dora's hysterical disposition as the expression of hysterical disgust.

84 Jelinek, "Schamgrenzen," 138.

85 In this sense, Jelinek's technique of dissection knows no limits, not even the limits of race. In her letter to Salman Rushdie, cited earlier, she implies as much when, in a reference to Hanif Kureishni, she defends applying "the sharp vision of irony" as well as the indiscriminate use of sarcasm, without regard for culture, race, or religion.

86 For a discussion of camp elements in Jelinek's early work, see Ingeborg Hoesterey, "Postmoderner Blick auf österreichische Literatur: Bernhard, Glaser, Handke, Jelinek, Roth," *Modern Austrian Literature* 23.3–4 (1990): 72.

87 Bachmann, *Werke*, vol. 4, 384.

88 Ibid., 205.

89 See Anton Kaes, "Holocaust and the End of History: Postmodern Historiography in Cinema," in Saul Friedlander, ed., *Probing the Limits of Representation: Nazism and the "Final Solution"* (Cambridge, Mass., and London: Harvard University Press, 1992), 206–22.

90 Susan Sontag, "Fascinating Fascism," in Karyn Kay and Gerald Peary, eds., *Women and the Cinema: A Critical Anthology* (New York: E.P. Dutton, 1977), 373.

91 On the figure of *Ungeist*, see Elfriede Jelinek, "Die Österreicher als Herren der Toten," *Literaturmagazin* (April 1992): 23–26.

92 My analysis of Jelinek's appropriative violence here owes much to Friedlander's introduction to *Probing the Limits of Representation*. Discussing Adorno's statement that no poem can be written after the Holocaust, Friedlander emphasizes that the Shoah, as an "event at the limits," fundamentally

"tests our traditional conceptual and representational categories." As he notes, the ethical and political limitations that characterize certain postmodern treatments of Nazism and the Shoah are especially evident in the films of Luchino Visconti, Lina Wertmüller, and Hans Jürgen Syberberg. See Saul Friedlander, "Introduction," in Friedlander, *Probing the Limits of Representation*, 4.

93 Elfriede Jelinek, "In den Waldheimen und auf den Haidern. Rede zur Verleihung des Heinrich-Böll-Preises in Köln am 2.12.1986," in Barbara Alms, ed., *Blauer Streusand* (Frankfurt a.M.: Suhrkamp, 1987), 42.

94 Jean Baudrillard, *Selected Writings*, ed. Mark Poster (Stanford, Calif.: Stanford University Press, 1988), 166.

95 Elfriede Jelinek, "Der Wald," in Alms, *Blauer Streusand*, 35.

96 Wolf discusses the figure of Helena in her "Vierte Frankfurter Vorlesung," *Die Dimension des Autors: Essays und Aufsätze, Reden und Gespräche*, vol. 2 (Frankfurt a.M.: Luchterhand, 1990), 626–59.

97 Eva Meyer's phrase is taken from the motto to *Krankheit oder moderne Frauen*. See also Meyer's response, "Den Vampir schreiben: Zu 'Krankheit oder moderne Frauen'," in Gürtler, *Gegen den schönen Schein*, 98–111.

98 Martin Jay, *Downcast Eyes: The Denigration of Vision in Twentieth-Century French Thought* (Berkeley, Los Angeles, and London: University of California Press, 1993); on the relation between image and writing, see also Russell A. Berman, "Written Right Across Their Faces: Ernst Jünger's Fascist Modernism," in Andreas Huyssen and David Bathrick, eds., *Modernity and The Text: Revisions of German Modernism* (New York: Columbia University Press, 1989), 60–80.

99 Walter Benjamin, *Reflections: Essays, Aphorisms, Autobiographical Writings*, trans. Edmund Jephcott, ed. Peter Demetz (New York: Schocken Books, 1986), 260.

100 See Sander L. Gilman, *Jewish Self-Hatred: Anti-Semitism and the Hidden Language of Jews* (Baltimore and London: Johns Hopkins University Press, 1986), 233–38, 240–41.

101 Modified quotation, from the report Brigitte Landes gives of an interview with Jelinek: "Kunst aus Kakanien: Über Elfriede Jelinek. Eine Lesung. Ein Gespräch. Eine Uraufführung," *Theater Heute* 1 (1986): 7.

102 Jelinek, "Der Krieg," 318.

103 Bachmann, *Werke*, vol. 4, 206. On Bachmann's conception of a *Moral der Moral*, see also her Musil radio essay, "Der Mann ohne Eigenschaften" (ibid., 96).

104 Ibid., 192.

105 Ibid., 337.

106 Ibid., 185.

107 Ibid. The first part of Bachmann's phrase is difficult to translate as it literally means, "If we had, or possessed the word," but also refers to the idiomatic expression "*das Wort haben*," "to have one's turn to speak."

108 Ibid., 268.

109 Ibid., 209.

110 Bachmann's philosophical dedication to Wittgenstein is well known and can be traced through several of her writings, particularly "Ludwig Wittgenstein – Zu einem Kapitel der jüngsten Philosophiegeschichte" (1953), and her radio essay "Sagbares und Unsagbares – Die Philosophie Ludwig Wittgensteins" (1953); see Sigrid Weigel, "'Ein Ende mit der Schrift. Ein andrer Anfang.' Zur Entwicklung von Ingeborg Bachmanns Schreibweise," in Koschel and von Weidenbaum, *Kein objektives Urteil*, 265–310. As Sara Lennox suggests in her essay "Bachmann und Wittgenstein" (*Kein objektives Urteil*, 600–21), the utopian dimensions of Bachmann's language theory seem to coincide with Wittgenstein's notion of the unsayable. It is further noteworthy that both Bachmann and Jelinek have taken to task Heidegger's language: Bachmann most explicitly in her dissertation *Die kritische Aufnahme der Existentialphilosophie Martin Heideggers*, Jelinek in *Totenauberg* and in "Wir leben auf einem Berg von Leichen und Schmerz," 6ff.

111 Brecht's poem, "An die Nachgeborenen" ("To Those Born Later"), is cited in Bachmann, *Werke*, vol. 4, 215. On the polyvalence of silence in the face of the Holocaust, see also Peter Haidu, "The Dialectics of Unspeakability: Language, Silence, and the Narratives of Desubjectification," in Friedlander, *Probing the Limits of Representation*, 277–99; and George Steiner's study, *Language and Silence: Essays on Language, Literature and the Inhuman* (New York: Atheneum, 1967).

112 Bachmann, *Werke*, vol. 4, 215–16.
113 Jelinek, *Von der mangelnden Tragfähigkeit des Bodens*.
114 Friedlander, "Introduction," *Probing the Limits of Representation*, 3.

8 WHATEVER HAPPENED TO FEMINIST THEORY?

This chapter was first presented in the "Feminist Theory" seminar at Harvard's Humanities Center. I am grateful for the stimulating discussion with the seminar's participants that followed the presentation, especially with Lynne Layton, Linda Nicholson, Naomi Schor, Kalpana Sheshadri-Crooks, Susan Suleiman, Sarolta Takács, and Andrea Walsh.

1 The term "postfeminism" ordinarily refers to a specific branch of post-second-wave, pluralistic, theoretical feminism, which, in aligning itself with postmodernism and postcolonialism, invokes the prefix *post-* as a way of overcoming the reputed essentialism of earlier feminisms. See, for example, Ann Brooks, *Postfeminisms: Feminism, Cultural Theory and Cultural Forms* (London and New York: Routledge, 1997), who tries to argue for the viability of the neologism. While *post-* is to have temporal, i.e., sequential implications, it seems hard to protect the term from getting confounded with the "end of feminism." Such an "endism" is certainly present in the terms on which the label is modeled, that is, "postmodernism" and "postcolonialism," which invoke the overcoming of modernism and colonialism, respectively.
2 Judith Butler, "Merely Cultural," *Social Text* 52/53, 15.3–4 (Fall/Winter 1997): 265–77. See also the section "Contentious or Debating Feminisms" in this chapter.
3 Seyla Benhabib, Judith Butler, Drucilla Cornell, and Nancy Fraser, *Feminist Contentions: A Philosophical Exchange* (New York and London: Routledge, 1995), 132.
4 Judith Butler, "For a Careful Reading," in ibid., 132.
5 Though the term "critical theory" is nowadays often used in a broad sense, so that it can include poststructuralism, in this chapter it will refer exclusively to the Frankfurt School tradition, which draws on Max Horkheimer's manifesto of the movement, "Traditional and Critical Theory." For a discussion of that essay, see also the section "Against Theory" in this chapter.
6 Linda J. Nicholson, ed., *Feminism/Postmodernism* (New York and London: Routledge, 1990).
7 Linda Nicholson, "Introduction," in Benhabib et al., *Feminist Contentions*, 1–2.
8 Ibid., 16.
9 This is how the term "non-" or "antifoundationalist" is used in contemporary theories of social constructivism, while its opposite, "foundationalism," refers to a- or transhistorical epistemological and political models that presume their own contingent or culturally defined standpoint to carry universal validity.
10 The present text is twice guilty, doubly so, insofar as its topic is theory – feminist theory – and insofar as it may not be able to eschew theoretical language altogether.
11 The most infamous recent incident is the so-called "Bad Writing Contest," organized by the journal *Philosophy and Literature*, which in 1999 selected Homi Bhabha and Judith Butler as the prize winners. The claim that (poststructuralist) theory produces "bad writing" also reached the mainstream media; see, for example, *The New York Times*, February 27, 1999, "When Ideas Get Lost in Bad Writing; Attacks on Scholars Include a Barbed Contest With Prizes'." Judith Butler's response appeared in *The New York Times* on March 20, 1999.
12 See Teresa de Lauretis, who distinguishes between intrinsic and extrinsic analyses of feminism in her important "Upping the anti [sic] in feminist theory," in Simon During, ed., *The Cultural Studies Reader* (London and New York: Routledge, 1993), 74–89.
13 See Michel Foucault, "Polemics, Politics, and Problematizations: An Interview with Michel Foucault," in *The Foucault Reader*, ed. Paul Rabinow (New York: Pantheon, 1984), 381ff.
14 In her capacity as one of the co-organizers of the 1998 English Institute conference, "What's Left of Theory?," Butler observed that "theory" under attack often stands as a synecdoche for poststructuralism. Importantly, she added that the resistance to theory indicated at least a double threat or risk: antitheorists fear that politics may get contaminated by theory, and, conversely, theoretical

elitists (in the vocabulary of the present essay, pure theorists) want to stave off theory getting corrupted by politics. Judith Butler, introductory remarks to "What's Left of Theory?," English Institute, Harvard University, Fall 1998.

15 Bhabha evokes this charge in "The Commitment to Theory," in Homi K. Bhaba, *The Location of Culture* (London and New York: Routledge, 1994), 20ff.

16 Knapp and Michaels defined (literary) theory as "the attempt to govern interpretations of particular texts by appealing to an account of interpretation in general." Walter Benn Michaels and Steven Knapp, "Against Theory," in W.J.T. Mitchell, ed., *Against Theory: Literary Studies and the New Pragmatism* (Chicago: University of Chicago Press, 1982), 11.

17 Ibid., 25.

18 Ibid., 26.

19 Ibid., 29–30.

20 William James, "What Pragmatism Means," in Louis Menand, ed., *Pragmatism: A Reader* (New York: Vintage, 1997), 98.

21 Cornel West, "Theory, Pragmatisms and Politics," in West, *Keeping Faith: Philosophy and Race in America* (New York and London: Routledge, 1993), 93. See also West's full-length study of pragmatism, *The American Evasion of Philosophy: A Genealogy of Pragmatism* (Madison: University of Wisconsin Press, 1989).

22 West, *Keeping Faith*, 104.

23 Bhabha, "The Commitment to Theory," 30.

24 Spivak, for example, uses the term to criticize what she calls "capital t Theory within feminism" or "high feminism" in her "The Intervention Interview," in Gayatri Chakravorty Spivak, *The Post-Colonial Critic: Interviews, Strategies, Dialogues* (New York and London: Routledge, 1990),119–20.

25 Bhabha, "The Commitment to Theory," 20–21.

26 Ibid., 30.

27 See, for example, Kant's "On the Common Saying: 'This May be True in Theory, But It Does Not Apply in Practice'," in Immanuel Kant, *Political Writings*, ed. Hans Reiss (Cambridge: Cambridge University Press, 1991).

28 Karl Marx and Frederick Engels, *The German Ideology: Critique of Modern German Philosophy According to Its Representatives Feuerbach, B. Bauer and Stirner, and of German Socialism According to Its Various Prophets*, in Marx and Engels, *Collected Works*, trans. Richard Dixon et al. (New York: International Publishers, 1975–), vol. 5, 44–45. See, furthermore, Marx's "Theses on Feuerbach," in which " 'revolutionary,' 'practical-critical' activity" overcomes the theory–practice divide still present in Feuerbach's reversed idealism (ibid., 3).

29 Put differently, the ideological divide between pure theory and mere practice was to be replaced by a new materialistic theory that overcame the alienating split. Or, the untethering of the material from the realm of consciousness is the work of metaphysical ideology. On the difference between "critique" and "criticism" in Marx's work, see especially Seyla Benhabib's comprehensive study, *Critique, Norm, and Utopia: A Study of the Foundations of Critical Theory* (New York: Columbia University Press, 1986), *passim*.

30 That theory, taken in the sense defined by Horkheimer, need not be opposed to practice/praxis is a point Habermas indirectly underscored when he qualified theory as ideology critique. See Jürgen Habermas, *The Philosophical Discourse of Modernity: Twelve Lectures* (Cambridge, Mass.: MIT Press, 1987), 116. West similarly makes the point that ideology-critical demystification is a theoretical activity: "Demystification is a *theoretical* activity that attempts to give explanations that account for the role and function of specific social practices." West, *Keeping Faith*, 89.

31 Some of the important publications in this area include bell hooks, *Feminist Theory From Margin to Center* (Boston: South End Press, 1984); Teresa de Lauretis, "Displacing Hegemonic Discourses: Reflections on Feminist Theory in the 1980s," in *Inscriptions* 3.4: 127–45; Barbara Johnson, *A World of Difference* (Baltimore: Johns Hopkins University Press, 1987). For overviews, see also Linda S. Kauffman, ed., *American Feminist Theory at Century's End: A Reader* (Cambridge, Mass.: Blackwell, 1993); and Michèle Barrett and Anne Phillips, eds., *Destabilizing Theory: Contemporary Feminist Debates* (Stanford, Calif.: Stanford University Press, 1992).

32 Linda Nicholson, ed., *The Second Wave: A Reader in Feminist Theory* (New York and London: Routledge, 1997), 261.

33 Luce Irigaray, *Speculum de l'autre femme* (Paris: Editions de Minuit, 1974), 165.

34 Monique Wittig, "The Point of View: Universal or Particular?" in Wittig, *The Straight Mind and Other Essays* (Boston: Beacon Press, 1992), 60. For a more extensive discussion of Wittig's criticism, see also Butler, *Gender Trouble*, 25ff.

35 Rosi Braidotti, *Nomadic Subjects: Embodiment and Sexual Difference in Contemporary Feminist Theory* (New York: Columbia University Press, 1994), 209.

36 Ibid., 210.

37 Ibid., 211.

38 See Carol Gilligan's influential *In A Different Voice: Psychological Theory and Women's Development* (Cambridge, Mass.: Harvard University Press, 1982).

39 Linda Nicholson, "Introduction," in Nicholson, ed., *The Second Wave*, 3.

40 On the terminologically slippery word "antiessentialism," see Spivak's observations in the interview "In a Word," reprinted in Nicholson, *The Second Wave*, 361. As Spivak there notes, "essentialism" sometimes functions as a codeword for the empirical or the real.

41 This is a concern that has been voiced, for example, by Naomi Schor. See, also, her "French Feminism is a Universalism," in Schor, *Bad Objects: Essays Popular and Unpopular* (Durham, N.C.: Duke University Press, 1995), 3–27.

42 See Habermas, *Philosophical Discourse of Modernity*, passim.

43 On this point, see Benhabib's contribution, "Feminism and Postmodernism: An Uneasy Alliance," in Benhabib et al., *Feminist Contentions*, 17–34.

44 Jane Flax, "Postmodern and Gender Relations in Feminist Theory," in Nicholson, *Feminism/Postmodernism*, 39–62.

45 Ibid., 43.

46 Sandra Harding, "Feminism, Science, and the Anti-Enlightenment Critiques," in Nicholson, *Feminism/Postmodernism*, 89.

47 Ibid., 90ff.

48 Iris Marion Young, *Intersecting Voices: Dilemmas of Gender, Political Philosophy, and Policy* (Princeton, N.J.: Princeton University Press, 1997), 17.

49 Nancy Fraser and Linda J. Nicholson, "Social Criticism without Philosophy: An Encounter between Feminism and Postmodernism," in Nicholson, *Feminism/Postmodernism*, 19–38.

50 Ibid., 19.

51 Ibid., 20.

52 Ibid., 21, first italics added.

53 Ibid.

54 Ibid.

55 Ibid., 25.

56 Ibid. In principle, I agree with the starting point of their article, when they retain what they call "large social theories" for feminist analysis. One needs to be able to analyze sexism crossculturally, which is different from adopting "pure metanarratives" or "ahistorical normative theories about the transcultural nature of rationality or justice." However, I do not agree when they say that "these social theories purport to be empirical rather than philosophical" (27) insofar as the authors disregard the viability of such movements as social or political philosophy, thus risking to reconfirm women's exclusion from philosophy.

57 Ibid., 34.

58 Ibid., 35.

59 Seyla Benhabib and Drucilla Cornell, eds., *Feminism as Critique: On the Politics of Gender* (Minneapolis: University of Minnesota Press, 1987).

60 Ibid., 1.

61 Butler, "For a Careful Reading," in Benhabib et al., *Feminist Contentions*, 138–39.

62 Butler, "Contingent Foundations," in Benhabib et al., *Feminist Contentions*, 39.

63 Ibid.

64 Ibid., 42.

65 In the margins, it might be noted that Butler's theory of performance does not just refer to theatrical performance but also to Austin's speech act theory and, indirectly, to pragmatism. That is, the performance of norms is founded in the speech community rather than imposed on it from without or grounded metaphysically, a fact that obviously doesn't prevent individual speech acts from either being violent or metaphysical. However, Butler's theory of performativity often shuttles back and forth between claims about the (transhistorical, quasi-transcendental) performativity of *all* languages and social forms of performativity – though in *Excitable Speech* she seeks to distance herself from Derrida via Bourdieu. In other words, there exists a tension between the "pragmatist" claims of Butler's analysis of performance and performativity as an enabling quasi-transcendental precondition.

66 Butler, "Contingent Foundations," 49.

67 Ibid., 41.

68 Ibid., 40.

69 Seyla Benhabib, "The Generalized and Concrete Other: The Kohlberg–Gilligan Controversy and Moral Theory," in Benhabib, *Situating the Self: Gender, Community and Postmodernism in Contemporary Ethics* (New York: Routledge, 1992).

70 Fraser, "Pragmatism, Feminism, and the Linguistic Turn," in Benhabib et al., *Feminist Contentions*, 164.

71 Ibid., 163.

72 Ibid., 164.

73 Ibid., 166.

74 Like Habermas, Benhabib limits the term "postmodernism" to its negative signification, since it is marked by excessive style and aestheticism: "what postmodernist historiography displays is an 'aesthetic' proliferation of styles which increasingly blur the distinctions between history and literature, factual narrative and imaginary creation." Benhabib, "Subjectivity, Historiography, and Politics," in Benhabib et al., *Feminist Contentions*, 112.

75 Ibid., 111.

76 Butler, "For a Careful Reading," 132.

77 This seems to be the case in Amanda Anderson's overview essay on the debates, which too readily pushes Butler into the a- or antipolitical camp. See Anderson, "Debatable Performances: Restaging Contentious Feminisms," in *Social Text* 54 (Spring 1998): 1–24.

78 Nancy Fraser, *Justice Interruptus: Critical Reflections on the "Postsocialist" Condition* (New York and London: Routledge, 1997).

79 Butler, "Contingent Foundations," 41.

80 See also Anderson, "Debatable Performances," on this point.

81 See Jacques Derrida, "Force of Law: The 'Mystical' Foundation of Authority," in Drucilla Cornell, Michael Rosenfeld, and David Gray Carlson, eds., *Deconstruction and the Possibility of Justice* (New York: Routledge, 1992) and Judith Butler, "Universality in Culture," in Martha C. Nussbaum et al., *For Love of Country: Debating the Limits of Patriotism* (Boston: Beacon Press, 1996).

82 Butler, "Contingent Foundations," 50.

83 Martha C. Nussbaum, "The Professor of Parody: The Hip Defeatism of Judith Butler," in *The New Republic*, February 22, 1999.

84 See the letters by feminists that appeared in *The New Republic* (April 19, 1999), in response to Nussbaum's review essay.

85 I here quote Charles Taylor's phrase from "The Politics of Recognition" out of context.

86 See on this point again West, *Keeping Faith*, 4 and 89–95.

87 The broadest project to craft a pragmatic feminism is that of Charlene Haddock Seigfried, who, in addition to a special issue of *Hypatia* 8.2 (Spring 1993), published *Pragmatism and Feminism: Reweaving the Social Fabric* (Chicago: University of Chicago Press, 1996). Seigfried's definition of pragmatism is interesting, in that she cautions that she will not reduce the term to mean "a narrow instrumentalism" (unlike Fraser). Instead, she will use it to refer to "a historically specific philosophical movement also sometimes called Classical American Philosophy," in other words, to "a range of positions originating in the classical period of American philosophy that challenge the traditional philosophical privileging of theory at the expense of practice" (277n). Though her

comprehensive study approaches the topic in its many facets, it seems to lack a developed concept of what politics might mean so that her valuable study fails, often, to get beyond the level of analogy as it tries to show how feminism might be regrounded in Classical American Philosophy. Democratic politics becomes coterminous with "community," a term that automatically is supposed to overcome the "individualism" of liberalism.

88 Richard Rorty, *Contingency, Irony, and Solidarity* (Cambridge: Cambridge University Press, 1989), 105.

89 Richard Rorty, "Feminism and Pragmatism," *Michigan Quarterly Review* 30 (Spring 1991): 236.

90 Rorty, however, gets the concept of ideology critique wrong, for example, when he implies that Marxism works with a "matter–consciousness distinction" when in fact the *German Ideology* sees this distinction itself as the product of ideology. See Richard Rorty, "Feminism, Ideology, and Deconstruction: A Pragmatist View," originally published in *Hypatia* 8.2 (Spring 1993); reprinted in Slavoj Žižek, ed., *Mapping Ideology* (London and New York: Verso, 1994).

91 Rorty, "Feminism and Pragmatism," 234.

92 Ibid., 240.

93 Ibid., 242.

94 Ibid., 250.

95 Rorty, "Feminism, Ideology, and Deconstruction," in Žižek, *Mapping Ideology*, 233.

96 Richard Rorty, *Achieving Our Country: Leftist Thought in Twentieth-Century America* (Cambridge, Mass.: Harvard University Press, 1998), 15. For a thorough critique of Rorty's assertion that the pragmatist should endorse "his own community" or "ethnocentrism" as a way of avoiding the charge of relativism, see Herrnstein Smith's discussion of his "Solidarity or Objectivity?" in Barbara Herrnstein Smith, *Contingencies of Value: Alternative Perspectives for Critical Theory* (Cambridge, Mass.: Harvard University Press, 1988), 166ff.

97 Rorty, *Achieving Our Country*, 29.

98 Nancy Fraser, "From Irony to Prophecy to Politics: A Response to Richard Rorty," in *Michigan Quarterly Review* 30 (Spring 1991): 263.

99 See Nancy Fraser, "Solidarity of Singularity? Richard Rorty between Romanticism and Technocracy," chapter 5 in her *Unruly Practices: Power, Discourse and Gender in Contemporary Social Theory* (Minneapolis: University of Minnesota Press, 1989), and "From Irony to Prophecy to Politics."

100 Fraser, *Unruly Practices*, 105.

101 Ibid., 106.

102 Ibid.

103 It is in this sense that Foucault, in his later writings, has adopted the term *ēthos*, originally "attitude," meaning fundamentally a *critical attitude*. See on *ēthos*, especially Chapter 2, above.

INDEX